The Economic Theory of Agrarian Institutions

DATE DUE

The Economic Theory of Agrarian Institutions

EDITED BY

Pranab Bardhan

CLARENDON PRESS · OXFORD

s, Walton Street, Oxford OX2 6DP

New York Toronto
Calcutta Madras Karachi
ngapore Hong Kong Tokyo
Nairobi Dar es Salaam Cape Town
Melbourne Auckland

and associated companies in
Berlin Ibadan

Oxford is a trade mark of Oxford University Press

Published in the United States
by Oxford University Press, New York

© Pranab Bardhan 1989

First published 1989
First issued in paperback 1991

British Library Cataloguing in Publication Data
Data available
ISBN 0–19–828619–8
ISBN 0–19–828762–3 (pbk.)

Library of Congress Cataloging in Publication Data
The Economic theory of agrarian institutions.
Bibliography: p.   Includes index.
1. Agriculture—Economic aspects—Developing
countries.   I. Bardhan, Pranab K.
HD1417.E24   1989   338.1'09172'4 88–28952
ISBN 0–19–828619–8
ISBN 0–19–828762–3 (pbk.)

Printed and bound in
Great Britain by Biddles Ltd
Guildford and King's Lynn

Contents

Preface

It is part of an institutional ritual in development economics, as in much of economic theory, to relegate all institutional matters into a 'black box.' The box is supposed to contain something vaguely important, but it does not usually receive more than a nodding, if somewhat intriguing, recognition in passing. In this book we squarely face the issue of theorizing about the rationale and consequences of some economic institutions and contractual arrangements that are particularly prominent in poor agrarian economies. Even though the authors draw upon at least the stylized versions of some existing institutions, the emphasis here is more on abstract model-building than on empirical details, more on rigorous analysis than on the kind of descriptive accounting that is common in the institutionalist literature. The models illustrate how some of the tools of advanced economic theory can be fruitfully used in understanding aspects of age-old institutions.

This is, of course, not to deny that a fuller understanding has to involve their social and cultural context and the underlying political and historical processes. The treatment is also partial in the sense that we focus on only a handful of institutional types, leaving out many other important agrarian institutions (for example, the extended family as a risk-pooling institution in agricultural production, institutions of intergenerational property transfer, or local irrigation organizations for communal water management and conflict resolution) which may be analysed with similar tools. Our attempt here is primarily to begin a line of enquiry in a hitherto largely uncharted and unexplored area, without any pretension of comprehensiveness either in understanding or in coverage of the territory.

In my editorial work I have received able assistance from my students, Michael Kevane, and Ashish Vaidya.

Berkeley, California   P.B.

Contributors

Pranab Bardhan, University of California at Berkeley
Kaushik Basu, Delhi School of Economics
Clive Bell, Vanderbilt University
Hans Binswanger, World Bank
Avishay Braverman, World Bank
Alain de Janvry, University of California at Berkeley
Bhaskar Dutta, Indian Statistical Institute, New Delhi
Mukesh Eswaran, University of British Columbia
Marcel Fafchamps, University of California at Berkeley
J. Luis Guasch, University of California at San Diego
Ashok Kotwal, University of British Columbia
John McIntire, International Livestock Centre for Africa, Addis
    Ababa
David M. Newbery, Churchill College, Cambridge
Louis Putterman, Brown University
Debraj Ray, Indian Statistical Institute, New Delhi
Elisabeth Sadoulet, University of California at Berkeley
Kunal Sengupta, Indian Statistical Institute, New Delhi
Nirvikar Singh, University of California at Santa Cruz
T. N. Srinivasan, Yale University
Joseph E. Stiglitz, Stanford University
Chris Udry, Yale University
Pinhas Zusman, Levi Eskol School of Agriculture, Israel

PART I
General Introduction

1.

Alternative Approaches to the Theory of Institutions in Economic Development

Pranab Bardhan

1. Introduction

Institutions are the social rules, conventions, and other elements of the structural framework of social interaction. This framework is taken for granted in much of mainstream economics, and often is pushed so much into the background that many of its central propositions are sometimes stated with a false air of institution-neutrality. We often apply the simple 'laws' of market supply and demand without being fully conscious of the complex of institutions on which contracts in actual markets crucially depend. Many anthropologists have also, quite rightly, questioned the economist's parochial and often ahistorical assumption that the market form of economic organization is ubiquitous. The criticisms of Marxists and other institutional economists in this respect have been valuable in raising the general awareness of institutional presumptions in economics.

Much of the old institutionalist literature, however, is largely descriptive[1] (and sometimes intellectually lazy: whatever cannot be easily explained otherwise is ascribed to institutional factors), and when analytical is often confined to tracing the effects of a given institution on economic activities and incentives. A rigorous analysis of the economic rationale of the formation of the institution itself has been very rare. There is, of course, some methodological resistance on the part of many institutionalists to endogenize institutions in economic terms.[2] It is, however, possible to point out, without subscribing to any cheap economic determinism, without denying that some exogenous irreducible rules and conventions must be presupposed in any economic analysis, or without ignoring the two-way feedback processes between economic and other historical–cultural factors, that in the long-run historical–evolutionary process economic factors do play an important role in the shaping of institutions.

Marxists have a well-known endogenous theory of institutions. The authoritative text from which this theory flows is the 1859 Preface to *A Contribution to the Critique of Political Economy*, where Marx states:

In the social production of their life men enter into definite relations that are indispensable and independent of their will, relations of production that correspond to a definite stage of development of their material productive forces. The sum total of these relations constitutes the economic structure of society, the real basis on which arises a legal and political superstructure. . . . At a certain stage of their development, the material productive forces of society enter into contradiction with the existing relations of production, or — what is but a legal expression for the same thing — with the property relations within which they have been at work hitherto. From forms of development of the productive forces these relations turn into their fetters. Then begins an epoch of social revolution.

The economic structure of society (which in this theory provides the foundation of its legal and political institutions) consists of property relations, and it corresponds to the level of development of the productive forces (which include all means of production and technology). The central driving force behind institutions is thus the forces of production.[3] (Marx's son-in-law Paul Lafargue is reported to have exclaimed one day: 'Dieu, ce sont les forces productives.') Changes in the forces of production, particularly technological change, produce over time some tension between the existing structure of property rights and the productive potential of the economy, and it is through class struggle that this tension is resolved in history, with the emergence of new institutions.

The nature of this tension, and the interaction between institutions and the utilization and development of the forces of production, have been studied with much greater rigour and micro-analytic details in two strands of recent non-Walrasian economic literature. One strand originates — paradoxically, at the opposite end in the political spectrum to the Marxists — from a famous paper by Coase (1960), which led to the flowering of a whole school of neo-classical writers on property rights and transaction costs. These writers developed a well articulated endogenous theory of institutions and traced changes in economic history to changes in the institutional ground rules. Although several writers with quite distinct patterns of thought are involved here, for our present purpose we shall lump them together and call theirs the Coase–Demsetz–Alchian–Williamson–North (CDAWN) school. The other strand grew out of the theory of imperfect information (particularly of the Akerlof–Stiglitz vintage). Even though it has some family resemblance to the transaction cost theory, it provides a more rigorous and sharply defined framework for analysing institutions as substitutes for missing markets in an environment of pervasive risks, incomplete markets, information asymmetry, and moral hazard. Since this environment in some respects is particularly acute in developing countries, the recent literature in development economics has seen a number of attempts to model institutions, especially in agriculture, on these lines.[4] Most of the subsequent chapters in this volume consolidate and extend this particular line of building a theory of institutions. All three of these approaches to the endogenous theory of institutions — of the Marxist, CDAWN, and imperfect information schools — have in my judgement some broad similarities, however uncomfortable that may be for the purists on all sides. In my fits of heretical eclecticism, I also believe that Marxists can profitably draw upon some of the ideas of the other two schools in building firmer micro foundations for their theory of historical materialism, just as at least one distinguished member of the CDAWN school, Douglass North (1981), seems to have integrated a significant part of Marxist ideas in his neoclassical property rights theory of history. In this chapter I shall point out that some of the weaknesses and problems of the other two theories are partly shared by the orthodox Marxist theory as well, but that at the same time some of the concerns expressed in the latter, although not often rigorously analysed, need to be seriously addressed in the other theories.

2. Transaction Costs and Imperfect Information

According to the CDAWN school, transaction costs, and institutions that evolve to minimize these costs, are the key to the performance of economies. These costs include those of information, negotiation, monitoring, co-ordination, and enforcement of contracts. When transaction costs are absent, the initial assignment of property rights does not matter from the point of view of efficiency, because rights can be voluntarily adjusted and exchanged to promote increased production. But when transaction costs are substantial, as is usually the case, the allocation of property rights is critical. One of the main pillars of traditional neoclassical economics — the separability of equity and efficiency — breaks down under these circumstances: the terms and conditions of contracts in various transactions, which directly affect the efficiency of resource allocation, now depend crucially on ownership structures and property relations.

In the historical growth process, there is a trade-off between economies of scale and specialization on the one hand and transaction costs on the other. In a small, closed, face-to-face peasant community, for example, transaction costs are low, but the production costs are high, because specialization and division of labour are severely limited by the extent of market defined by the personalized exchange process of the small community. In a large-scale complex economy, as the network of interdependence widens, the impersonal exchange process gives considerable scope for all kinds of opportunistic behaviour (cheating, shirking, moral hazard), and the costs of transacting can be high. In Western societies over time complex institutional structures have been devised (elaborately defined and effectively enforced property rights, formal contracts and guarantees, corporate hierarchy, vertical integration, limited liability, bankruptcy laws, and so on) to constrain the participants, to reduce the uncertainty of social interaction — in general, to prevent the transactions from being too costly and thus to allow the productivity gains of larger-scale and improved technology to be realized. North and Thomas (1973) have explained the economic growth of Western Europe between the tenth and the eighteenth centuries primarily in terms of innovations in the institutional rules that governed property rights. As in Marxist history, property relations that were socially useful at one time become 'fetters' on the further development of the forces of production, and an appropriate redefinition of property rights becomes necessary. New property rights emerge which allow an increase in gains from trade by economizing on transaction costs (including gains from new production or exchange, which were unprofitable under earlier high transaction costs and the consequent 'market failure').

North and many other neoclassical institutional economists believe that the basic source of institutional change is fundamental and persistent changes in relative prices, which lead one or both parties in a transaction to perceive that they could be better off under alternative contractual and institutional arrangements. Historically, population change is judged to have been the single most important source of relative price changes, although techno-logical change (including that in military technology) and changes in the costs of information are also deemed as major sources. Demographic, as opposed to technological, change as a primary source of growth of productive forces is usually de-emphasized by Marxists, but there is no important reason why it cannot be incorporated into a more general version of their 'materialist' interpretation of institutional change.[5]

The imperfect information theory of institutions is closely related to that of transaction costs, since information costs constitute an important part of transaction costs. But the former theory is usually cast in a more rigorous framework, clearly spelling out assumptions and equilibrium solution concepts, drawing out more fully the implications of strategic behaviour under asymmetric information, sharply differentiating the impact of different types of information problems, and yielding somewhat more con-crete and specific predictions than the usual presentations of transaction cost theory about the design of contracts, with more attention to the details of terms and conditions of varying contractual arrangements under varying circumstances.[6] The models of sharecropping and other forms of land and livestock tenancy, bonded labour and other forms of labour tying, credit rationing, interlinkage between credit and land lease, labour hiring and output sales transactions, institutions of hedging against risks in production and marketing, co-operative institutions in production and credit, and so on that readers will find in the subsequent chapters bear ample testimony to the remarkable fruitfulness of the imperfect information approach in analysing institutions in the context of agrarian development. Since agriculture is a business with slow turnover of capital and with all kinds of high risks, and since extreme poverty leaves little scope for 'internal financing' by peasants, credit and insurance needs are crucial; many of the key institutions modelled in the subsequent pages are those that emerge to substitute for missing credit, insurance, and futures markets.

Marxists often cite some of these production relations as institutional obstacles to development in a poor agrarian economy, overlooking the microeconomic rationale of the formation of these institutions. Under a set of informational constraints and missing markets, a given agrarian institution (say, sharecropping) may be serving a real economic function; and its simple abolition, as is often demanded on a radical platform, without taking care of the factors that gave rise to this institution in the first place, may not necessarily improve the conditions of the intended beneficiaries of the abolition programme. Marxists have also a tendency to equate some of the pre-existing production relations mechanically with the 'feudal' or 'semi-feudal' mode of production, ignoring how in the real world the same institution (say, sharecropping) adapts itself to the development of the forces of production (with numerous cases of capitalist share-tenant farmers — as, for example, in Punjab — or more widespread cases of cost-sharing and other forms of landlord–tenant partnership in adoption of the new technology of high-yielding varieties in agriculture). The neoclassical institutional economists, on the other hand, have the tendency to apply their logic of voluntary contracts to many pre-capitalist forms of production relations (like slavery or *corvée* labour), ignoring that the sanctions underlying these relationships are often based on extra-economic coercion, and that the standard maximizing calculus on the part of the agents is somewhat out of place.

3. The Process of Institutional Change

The Marxist, CDAWN, and imperfect information theories are all equally murky on the mechanism through which new institutions and property rights emerge. All three sets of theory, in explaining historical transition, show how new institutions will serve the interests of economic progress and old institutions are a hindrance and are 'ripe' for a change — but as if ripeness is all: as if there is no need to specify a predictable model of the *process* of change. Historical teleology, ahistorical functionalism, and vulgar Darwinism abound in the literature on this point. An institution's mere function of serving the interests of potential beneficiaries is clearly inadequate in *explaining* it, just as it is an incompetent detective who tries to explain a murder mystery only by looking for the beneficiary, and on that basis alone proceeds to arrest the heir of a rich man who has been murdered. The explanation by Demsetz (1967) that 'the emergence of new property rights takes place in response to the desires of the interacting persons for adjustments to new benefit–cost possibilities' is no more helpful than the Marxists' routine reference to the laws of motion of history. Among CDAWN theorists, North comes closest to recognizing the enormity of the collective action and free-rider problems that limit the ability of potential gainers to get their act together in bringing about institutional changes, just as among Marxists the Brenner debate on the transition from feudalism (see Ashton and Philpin 1985) has increased their awareness of the importance of specific historical processes of class capacity for resistance and struggle.

We have noted before the neoclassical economic historians' strong belief that relative price changes fuel the main motive force for institutional changes in history (primarily by inducing the development of property rights to the benefit of the owners of the more expensive factor of production). In particular, demographic changes altering the relative price of labour to land lead to the incentive for redefinition of property rights on land and a rearrangement of labour relations; North (1981) and Hayami and Ruttan (1985) give several examples from European and recent Asian history, respectively. But from Brenner's analysis (1976) of the contrasting experiences of different parts of Europe on the transition from feudalism (those between Western and Eastern Europe and those between the English and the French cases even within Western Europe), we know that changes in demography, market conditions, and relative prices are not sufficient to explain the contrasts. Changes in relative prices may at most change the costs and benefits of collective action on the part of different classes (creating new opportunities for political entrepreneurs), but they cannot predetermine the balance of class forces or the outcome of social conflicts. Hayami and Ruttan (1985) refer to the case of mid-nineteenth-century Thailand, where the expansion of international trade triggered a rise in rice prices which led to a major transformation of property rights: traditional rights in human property (*corvée* and slavery) were replaced by more precise private property rights in land. But one should not forget that the expansion of grain trade in seventeenth-century Poland had helped the *relapse* into serfdom.

A related question in that of the presumed optimality of persistent institutions. The CDAWN or the imperfect information school, like the functionalist Marxist view, often unthinkingly implies the application of the market analogy of competitive equilibrium to the social choice of institutions or the biological analogy of natural selection in the survival of the fittest institution. As we all know from experience, dysfunctional institutions often persist for a very long period. Akerlof (1984) has built models to show how economically unprofitable or socially unpleasant customs may persist as a result of a mutually sustaining network of social sanctions when each (rational) individual conforms out of fear of loss of reputation from disobedience. In such a system potential members of a break-away coalition fear that it is doomed to failure, and thus failure to challenge the system becomes a self-fulfilling prophecy. Kuran (1987) has a related model of collective conservatism which is reinforced by the influence on an individual's *private* preference formation of the justifications that others give for their *public* preferences for the status quo. A similar self-reinforcing mechanism for the persistence of socially suboptimal institutions may be in operation when *path-dependent* processes are important, as is now recognized in the literature of the history of technological innovations. (The QWERTY typewriter keyboard, the narrow gauge of British railroads, US colour television system, etc., have been given as examples of the persistence of technologies that were *ex ante* inferior.) As Arthur (1985, 1988) has emphasized, when there are increasing returns to adoption of a particular (technological or institutional) innovation — when, the more it is adopted, the more it is attractive or convenient for the others to join the bandwagon on account of infrastructural and network externalities, learning and co-ordination effects, and adaptive expectations — a path chosen by some initial adopters to suit their interests may 'lock-in' the whole system for a long time to come, denying later, more appropriate, technologies or institutions a footing. This lock-in happens dynamically as sequential decisions 'groove' out an advantage that the system finds it hard to escape from. The process is *non-ergodic*; there are multiple outcomes, and historical 'small events' early on may well decide the larger course of structural change.[7,8]

The biological analogy of survival of the fittest is particularly inappropriate as path dependence is assigned an important role in biological processes. To quote Gould (1980), 'Organisms are not billiard balls propelled by simple and measurable external forces to predictable new positions on life's pool table. . . . Organisms have a history that constrains their future in myriad, subtle ways. . . . Their complexity of form entails a host of functions incidental to whatever pressures of natural selection superintended the initial construction.' The arguments against the operation of natural selection in social institutions are obviously much stronger.

The recognition of path dependence does not necessarily lead to a completely chaotic, or 'Cleopatra's-nose', view of institutional history. There are certain regularities in the evolution of social institutions as social agents repeatedly face the same types of social problems and adapt their behaviour. Schotter (1981) and Sugden (1986) have given game-theoretic accounts of the spontaneous evolution of institutions as self-enforcing stable solutions to iterated games of strategy. Sugden analyses the evolution of three kinds of institutional rules, or what he calls conventions: (1) conventions of co-ordination, which evolve out of repeated play of games of pure co-ordination (examples from social life are road rules, use of money, weights and measures, market-places and market days, languages), where the degree of conflict of interests is minor; (2) conventions of property, which evolve out of repeated play of games where the players are in dispute over something that they all want but all cannot have (examples from social life include the 'finders keepers' rule, queues, and occupancy rights on land); and (3) conventions of reciprocity, which evolve out of repeated plays of Prisoners' Dilemma games (for example practices of mutual restraint and mutual aid, and the highly suggestive success of tit-for-tat in Axelrod's (1984) well-known computer tournament). Schotter, similarly, has a model that depicts the process of institution creation as a Markovian diffusion process whose absorbing points correspond to stable social institution; the institutional problem is phrased as a supergame. There is, of course, a certain amount of indeterminacy in such an analysis: we do not expect to isolate a unique institutional form as stable; rather, we must content ourselves with a set of forms that, when taken together, are stable.

At this point it is also important to note, as many evolutionary economists remind us, the distinction that Carl Menger (1883) made between what he called 'organic' and 'pragmatic' institutions. The contractarian approach of the CDAWN and imperfect information schools emphasizes the latter — those that are the direct outcome of conscious contractual design, as in the case of some corporate structure and practices. Organic institutions like the conventions of Sugden and Schotter, on the other hand, are comparatively undesigned, and they evolve gradually as the unintended and unforeseeable result of the pursuit of individual interests.[9] (As Furet 1978 observed, 'men make history but they do not know which one'). Menger's theory of the origin of money, in which the self-interested actions of traders led to the evolution from a barter economy to one in which a single commodity became the universal medium of exchange, is a prime example of the evolution of an organic institution. But, unlike in the case of Menger's theory of money, it is possible to have cases where an institution is created organically but preserved pragmatically. This is a case of what Elster (1983) calls 'filter explanation', as opposed to functional explanation, where the actors eventually become aware of the function an institution serves for them and then consciously maintain it even though it originally came to being unintended. Langlois (1986) gives an interesting (and ironical) example from Edelman's (1964) theory of government regulatory commissions:

Voters are plagued with vague fears about and a sense of powerlessness over certain phenomena they cannot control. The fear of monopoly is one of these. In order to gain votes, politicians make symbolic gestures to placate these fears — in this case, the formation of regulatory commissions. But, once in place, the commissions . . . are quickly captured in the familiar way by those they were supposed to regulate. Thus a quite different mechanism *maintains* them once created; they serve the function of cartelizing the industry and are kept in business by the political action of that industry.

4. Redistributive Institutional Change

The neoclassical institutional economists focus their attention on allocative efficiency-improving institutions, whereas Marxists often emphasize how institutions change or do not change depending on considerations of surplus appropriation by a dominant class.[10] In particular, progress towards a more productive institution may be blocked if it reduces the control of surplus by this class. (Even when historically valid, such a statement, of course, needs better micro foundations, showing how individuals within the class that could gain from the new institution are frustrated in their efforts by the aggregative necessity of retaining control for the whole class.) The emphasis on the effect of an institutional change on control of surplus by a particular class also suggests that the question of *efficiency-improving* institutional change cannot really be separated from that of *redistributive* institutional change, particularly when issues of collective action, class capacity, mobilization, and struggle in the historical process are important. This means that the distinction that Hayami and Ruttan (1985) make between the 'demand' for institutional innovations (on the basis of changes in technological or demographic factors) and their 'supply' (depending on political entrepreneurs undertaking the necessary collective action) may be somewhat artificial. In empirical analysis of actual institutional changes, this may lead to a kind of 'identification problem': in English agricultural history, did the (second) enclosure movement in the eighteenth century come about because enclosed farming was more efficient than open-field farming, or because the (prospective) redistributive effect of enclosures in favour of landowners made collective action on their part easier? In the example of Hayami and Kikuchi (1982) from agriculture in the Philippines in the mid-1970s, where the increase in population pressure on land brought about a new employer–employee relationship (the *gamma* system, replacing the traditional *hunusan* system), lowering the wage rate, did it come about because the disequilibrium between labour productivity and wage 'demanded' such a change, or because population pressure on land made collective action on the part of employers easier (or that on the part of labourers weaker), thus facilitating the 'supply' side?[11]

A shift in the focus of attention from the efficiency aspects of an institution to the distributive aspects inevitably confronts us with the question of somehow grappling with the elusive concept of 'power' and with political processes that much of neoclassical institutional economics would abhor. Marxists, of course, deal directly with these issues, but they are often methodologically careless. The concept of 'power' is often used in a question-begging way: differences in institutional arrangements are supposed to be explained by blanket references to differences in the power of the dominant class without an *independent* quantification of the latter. The literature — Marxist or non-Marxist — on a rigorous analysis of power is rather scanty in economics, compared with that in sociological and political theory. Game theorists have used the idea of bargaining power[12] in dividing up the surplus in bargaining games, or the idea of power exercised as the Stackelberg leader taking the weaker party's reaction function as given,[13] or as the ability to pre-commit credibly in non-cooperative games; these are indirectly reflected in some of the models of the imperfect information theory of institutions. In recent Marxist theoretical models in economics two distinct forms of power relations have emerged: Roemer (1982) traces the primary locus of capitalist power in unequal distribution of property, whereas Bowles (1985, 1987) traces it to the political structures of control and surveillance at the point of production, both referring to a competitive economy. Roemer reiterates the well-known Samuelsonian proposition that in a competitive model it does not matter whether capital hires labour or labour hires capital, with the important modification that in either case the wealthy 'exploit' (take advantage of) the poor. To Bowles, on the other hand, the locus of command in the production process is central to the functioning of the system. I find this distinction between domination in production and asset-based power somewhat overdrawn: who hires whom essentially depends on the capacity to be the residual claimant in production, and that in turn depends on the capacity to bear risks, the wealthy having obviously a larger risk-bearing capacity. But both these strands of Marxist theory serve as a reminder that in the CDAWN and imperfect information theories, demonstrating the constrained Pareto efficiency rationale of some existing institutions in terms of transaction costs and moral hazard, it is underemphasized that a more democratic organization of the work process (following Bowles) or a more egalitarian distribution of assets (following Roemer) might have significantly reduced (not eliminated) the informational constraints and Hobbesian malfeasance problems that form the staple of much of the principal–agent literature.

Bowles (1987) draws our attention to another aspect of power which Walrasian models of neoclassicals as well as of Roemer overlook. When markets do not clear, even in competitive equilibrium, those who are left out are the powerless — the involuntarily unemployed in the labour market, the borrowers rationed out in the credit market, and so on. Under conditions of imperfect information, costly monitoring, moral hazard, and adverse selection, Bowles (1985), Stiglitz and Weiss (1981), Shapiro and Stiglitz (1984), and others have constructed non-Walrasian models of involuntary unemployment and credit rationing in equilibrium. As Bowles (1987) comments, 'if agents are quantity-constrained as well as budget- and price-constrained, the power of an economic agent is not fully expressed by his or her initial holdings and the reigning prices of all goods and factors of production: one may not have access to a good or service even if one is willing and able to pay the going price.' Powerlessness here arises from being quantity-constrained, but one should note that claim enforcement costs or transaction costs may be sufficient, but not necessary, for a quantity-constrained economy. (Efficiency theory is not the only basis of involuntary unemployment; moral hazard and adverse selection are not the only basis of credit rationing.) But selective exclusion of some workers and payment of a wage greater than their opportunity cost to a co-opted group of workers (who derive a strategic rent in the process), as the efficiency theory implies, may be an important institutional device to maintain a two-tiered labour market — as Eswaran and Kotwal (1985a) suggest — and may provide the microeconomic basis of what Marxists call the social control of the labour process, as suggested in Bardhan (1984: Ch. 5), and Hart (1986b).

5. The Role of Ideology and the State

Finally, let us turn to two other key, and at the same time complex and amorphous, aspects of the theory of institutions that neoclassical institutional economists generally ignore: ideology and the state. North (1981) significantly differs from other members of the latter group of economists, and is nearer the position of Marxists, in assigning a theory of ideology and the state a central place in his theory of history and institutional change. The contractual environment of the CDAWN and imperfect information theorists would have been much too anarchic, and transaction costs prohibitively high, were it not for certain internally enforced codes of conduct which are shaped by ideology, with individuals constraining them-selves by their socially imbibed notions of legitimacy of the system, fairness of contracts, and the ethic of reciprocity. Our models of imperfect information are often full of super-strategists relentlessly pursuing their games of conspiratorial cleverness[14] without constraints of norms or moral obligations. Yet individuals sometimes decide to act contrary to their own interests, out of some sense of what Sen (1977) calls 'commitment'. Social ideology serves to reduce free-riding, shirking, and venality, inducing the individual often to behave in a way contrary to the presumptions of principal–agent games; voluntary co-operative institutions and a complex system of traditional norms and practices in management of village common property often defy Olson's (1965) 'logic' of the collective action problem. Marxists offer many useful clues (and some functionalist red herrings) about the structural roots of different ideological systems. Ullman-Margalit (1977) and Sugden (1986) give us a game-theoretic account of the evolution of norms in society. But it is easy to see that we do not yet have a good theory of the formation, maintenance, and institutionalization of ideology which can lend some regular predictive ability to a model of the role of ideology in institutional change.

In propagation of ideology and the socialization process, as in defining and enforcing property rights, the state plays an authoritative role. The state is relatively passive and is largely an arena of group conflicts, in the view of both orthodox Marxists and the neoclassical institutionalists: for the former the state, even when it has 'relative autonomy', acts maybe not at the behest of, but only on behalf of, the dominant class; for the latter, the state passively responds to rent-seeking behaviour of various interest groups and lobbies. Both sides tend to ignore the large range of choices in goal formulation, agenda setting, and policy execution that the state leadership, however constrained by the articulated interests of organized classes and pressure groups, usually has.[15] North gives the state a somewhat more active role compared with other members of the CDAWN school: a group with a 'comparative advantage in violence' captures the state and acts as a revenue-maximizing discriminating monopolist 'selling' protection and justice. (This is akin to the protection rackets of organized crime, as Tilly (1984) has noted.) North refers to the frequent fact (all his examples of suboptimal institutions are attributed to it) that the state, for reasons of maintaining its support structures, may prolong socially inefficient property rights. He, of course, shares with other liberal economists a basic distrust of the state, whose unbridled power and rapacity result in institutional atrophy and economic stagnation. (Marx himself largely shared the anti-étatist views of the nineteenth-century liberals; he found in the Asiatic state, with its monopoly of economic initiative, an explanation for the backwardness of the East.) Despite some of the similarities between England and Spain at the beginning of the sixteenth century, North (1986) traces the differential subsequent evolution of economic institutions, and consequently in economic growth, in the two countries to the differential development of power of the ruler *vis-à-vis* the constituents (represented by the English Parliament and the Castilian Cortes, respectively) in the history of the two countries. He also finds a reflection of this difference in the institutional evolution of the English North American colonies compared with that of the Spanish colonies in South America, with similar economic consequences.

I have at least three problems with this kind of anti-étatist explanation of institutional development or lack of it. First, the so-called Coase theorem (by the way, Coase's 1960 paper does not have the statement of any theorem, only suggestions and examples), which is the starting point of the CDAWN theorists, is often interpreted to imply inferiority of government intervention to private property rights: even when the market outcome is inefficient (as in the case of externalities), people will supposedly get together and negotiate their way to efficiency under private property rights. This view I find simply incredible. Farrell (1987a) has recently shown, with a mathematical example, the implausibility of the Coase theorem even in a second-best sense: he shows that under incomplete information voluntary negotiation under private property rights may be unable to perform as well as even an uninformed and bumbling bureaucrat. It may also be noted that, in the context of our earlier discussion of path-dependent processes and multiple equilibria, where a current institution is locked-into a suboptimal local equilibrium on account of, say, self-reinforcing co-ordination effects, it may sometimes be easier for the state to orchestrate a mandated collective change-over to a superior equilibrium.

Second, in many situations (in history and currently in many poor countries) of highly fragmented polity and economy, to blame the state for blocking institutional progress can sometimes be far-fetched and misleading. Where there is an oligopoly of violence (i.e. where the state does not have a monopoly in it) and territorial segmentation of economic domination by local overlords, the state may be too weak (and too remote) to influence local relations of production even if it wants to.

Third, it is sometimes important to distinguish between the top political leadership (let us call it the state élite), which takes general political decisions, and the hierarchy of agents, the bureaucracy, which is supposed to implement those decisions. The process of implementation often generates various kinds of rental income which, to a significant extent, accrues to the bureaucracy (and sometimes to the lower functionaries of the ruling party), and the latter may form a pressure group to secure this income flow, with goals that are much narrower than those set by the state élite. The impulses that shape major policies and actions by the state élite, on the other hand, are fuelled not merely by motives of self-aggrandizement but quite often also by what Miliband (1983) calls its 'conception of the national interest' in a way that the simple neoclassical theory of the *rentier* state or the simple Marxist class-driven state somehow fails to capture. In many cases of state-directed industrialization (the history of East Asia over the last hundred years or so provides some dramatic instances), this leadership genuinely considered itself as the trustee of the nation's deeply held collective aspirations and derived its political legitimacy from them. In a world of international military and economic competition, one form these aspirations often take is to strive for rapid economic growth. The state élite tries to carry out a restructuring of social and economic institutions towards that goal, not just out of pressure from the dominant class or as a revenue-maximizing strategy.

NOTES

1. For an account of the anti-theory inclinations of some institutionalists in the German historical school, see Schumpeter (1954).
2. For a forceful recent exposition of such a line, see Field (1981). For a convincing rebuttal of Field's position that some non-economic rules or factors must always be taken as parametric in economic history, see Basu, Jones, and Schlicht (1987).
3. For the most cogent modern exposition of this theory, see Cohen (1978). For a somewhat different interpretation, pointing to the ambiguities in Marx's writings as he grappled with the complexity of historical development, see Elster (1985: Ch. 5).
4. For some overview of this literature, see Bardhan (1984), Bell (1988), and Stiglitz (1986a).
5. Marx asserts in *Grundrisse* that pre-capitalist communal societies broke down because of an increase in population, and Elster (1985) suggests that in doing so Marx comes very close to saying that population is a productive force, the development of which breaks down existing production relations.

6. It should, however, be noted that the transaction cost theory, particularly in the formulation of Williamson, gives more emphasis on incomplete contracting arising out of (cognitively) bounded rationality and on the organizational ramifications of transaction-specific assets. It also pays more attention, in comparison with the *ex ante* mechanism design setup of imperfect information theory, to maladaptation costs incurred when transactions drift out of alignment and to methods of *ex post* conflict resolution. For a brief comparison of the imperfect information and transaction costs approaches, see Stiglitz (1986a) and Williamson (1987). I differ slightly from Stiglitz when he claims that the latter approach fails the test of falsifiability, unlike the former. In any case, neither approach has yet been subject to much of rigorous empirical hypothesis-testing.

7. One remembers Leontief's (1963) plea for 'writing history backwards' when the dynamic system confronting the historian is unstable.

8. To be fair to North, in a recent paper (1986) he shows some recognition of path dependence in institutional evolution. He compares this to the way common law evolves: 'It is precedent-based law; past decisions become embedded in the structure of rules, which marginally change as cases arise involving some new or, at least in the terms of past cases, unforeseen issue, which when decided becomes, in turn, a part of the legal framework. . . . It is essential to note that precedent not only define(s) and determine(s) many of the provisions but also dictate(s) the existing agenda, decision rules, and methods of resolution.'

9. Buchanan (1975), in his explanation of the rise of property and law, and Nozick (1974), in his discussion of the hypothetical emergence of minimal state from a Lockean state of nature, have used the idea of unintended outcomes of voluntary negotiations. On the other side of the political spectrum, Elster (1985) has given an insightful interpretation of Marxian dialectics in terms of unintended consequences in history.

10. Elster (1985) notes some ambivalence in Marx's writings on this question. On the one hand, it is consistent with Marx's emphasis on the class struggle as the basic force in history; on the other hand, it does not support his view that the productive forces tend to progress throughout history.

11. Taking another example from Hayami and Kikuchi (1982), the rapid expansion of labour-tying arrangements like *kedokan* in many parts of Java in the late 1960s, which are attributed to population growth by Hayami and Kikuchi, are explained from the 'supply side' by Hart (1986a) with reference to the drastic changes in the collective strength of the poor peasantry that the bloody political changes of the mid-1960s in Java brought about.

12. Harsanyi (1976; Ch. 9) measures the *strength* of A's power over B by the opportunity costs to B of refusing to do what A wants him to do: these opportunity costs measure the strength of B's incentives for yielding to A's influence.

13. Basu (1986) has shown some extra dimensions of power in triadic, as opposed to dyadic, Stackelberg relations. For example, a 'powerful' or 'influential' actor can extort from a weaker party more than his usual pound of flesh (say, profits in an all-or-nothing monopoly transaction) and can push the latter below his reservation utility level of the bilateral case, if he can threaten the latter's relation with a third party.

14. One is reminded of Prince Metternich, who reportedly said, when during a royal

ball an aide whispered into his ear that the Russian Czar was dead, 'I wonder what his motive could have been.'

15. This constraint may be somewhat less when the state itself is a dominant producer in the economy, as in some developing countries; but then again, as long as many of the state enterprises are losing concerns, the state's dependence on the surplus generated in the private economy is not greatly diminished.

2.

Rational Peasants, Efficient Institutions, and a Theory of Rural Organization: Methodological Remarks for Development Economics

Joseph E. Stiglitz

1. Introduction

The cogency of a theory must be judged largely by the extent to which it can explain the central 'facts' within its domain. A physical theory that could not account well for the motions of the planets, the earth, and the moon could not be taken seriously. Among the 'facts' that any economic theory must come to terms with are the dramatically different standards of living of those who happen to live in different countries, and within different regions within the same country: it is not that those who live in poverty work less hard, are less energetic or less intelligent, or have less capacity for entrepreneurship than those who live amidst plenty. Quite the contrary: the physical exertion of many of those who live in the less developed countries (LDCs) often seems beyond the capacity of even those engaged in manual work in the more developed countries, who have become accustomed to their life of relative ease.

Modern economic theory has not only, for the most part, failed to address this 'fact', but more, has adopted a stance that either is inconsistent with it, or explains the differences in terms of lack of some factor of production — capital or skilled labour. These explanations have a certain attractive aspect to them, for they provide an easy remedy for the problem: provide more of the missing factors. Yet, as I have argued elsewhere (Stiglitz 1987), while lack of capital may contribute to differences in standards of living, it can hardly be given credit as a central explanatory variable; for if production functions were in fact the same, the differences in marginal returns to capital would be huge beyond belief; and the pattern of usage of capital would differ markedly from the pattern that we in fact observe. By the same token, the absence of skilled labour cannot be central, given the frequently high unemployment rates they face within the LDCs and the fact that skilled wages are in fact

Financial support from the National Science Foundation is gratefully acknowledged. I have benefited greatly from conversations with A. Braverman and R. Sah.

lower than in the more developed countries.[1]

The persistence of lower wages, skilled and unskilled, in the face of a (seemingly) free flow of labour and capital has been noted not only within the LDCs. Wright (1987) has observed such differences in the three-quarters of a century following the American Civil War between the South and the North.

I find this seeming absence of concern for developing explanations of this central fact disturbing for several reasons. First, to the extent that our theories cannot explain, or are inconsistent with, this central fact, they are at best seriously incomplete. Second, I know of no area of knowledge, certainly no area of knowledge within the social sciences, more likely to prove to be of general benefit to mankind; for an understanding of why it is that some societies develop economically and some do not, why some societies enjoy high standards of living and some do not, while not necessarily leading to an immediate amelioration of the conditions of those who, through no fault of their own, have been born into a life of poverty and hardship, at least will enable us to set forth along a path leading to a redress of these problems, and will enable us to avoid some of the many mistaken and misguided paths. Third, because the currently fashionable economic theories fail to address this, the most central economic issue facing most of mankind today, they leave the door open to alternative theories, pandering to the inevitable quest of the subjected to a better life: it matters little to those who live under these conditions that the logical foundations of the theories are suspect, that there are internal inconsistencies, that the underlying empirical hypotheses are, at best, questionable.

As an aside, I would argue further that even those economists that are not fundamentally interested in, or concerned with, LDCs have much to learn from the study of such countries. From one perspective, a study of LDCs is to economics what the study of pathology is to medicine: by understanding what happens when things do not work well, we gain insight into how they work when they do function as designed. The difference is that in economics, pathology is the rule: less than a quarter of mankind lives in the developed economies.[2]

The objective of this chapter is, however, not hortatory, to encourage other researchers to devote their energies to addressing these issues, but rather to describe a research programme in which I, along with several co-authors, have been engaged over the past two decades. I view this research programme as a necessary part, perhaps a prelude, to any scientific understanding of the sources of development, or the lack of development. Elsewhere (Stiglitz 1987) I have summarized many of the findings of this research programme; here, I wish to emphasize its methodological underpinnings, to argue that it at least holds open the possibility of enhancing our understanding of the plight in which the LDCs find themselves. I argue further that some of the more popular alternative views simply cannot come to terms with the basic problems of development.

2. Central Tenets

The perspective that this research programme has taken can be characterized in terms of its views on *institutions, peasant rationality*, the nature and role of *markets*, and the role of *history*.

Development economics is concerned both with the low *level* of income within LDCs and with the process of *change*. It is concerned with understanding why the current level of income in the LDCs is as low as it is, with ascertaining the general properties of those countries that are currently less developed, with describing their institutional and economic relationships, and with explaining how those relationships affect both the level of per capita income and the processes by which per capita income is increased.

Traditional discussions of development (or lack of development) have emphasized the importance of institutions, and the impediments that they impose for the development process. The persistence of inefficient institutions is either left unexplained, or is ascribed to peasant irrationality.

By contrast, modern economic theory has stressed the rationality of peasants. This is supported not only by anecdotal evidence, suggesting how peasants and their institutions have addressed, and resolved, quite difficult economic problems, but also by econometric evidence, showing that peasants respond to market forces.

Once one has adopted the hypothesis of peasant rationality, it is but a small step to the efficient markets hypothesis and the Coase theorem,[3] holding that individuals would quickly get together to eliminate any inefficient resource allocation (or inefficient institutional arrangement). If one sees an institutional arrangement that *looks* inefficient, it looks so only because one has not fully understood the nature of the economic problem that is being faced. This theorem has powerful policy implications; countries, if left to themselves, would thus develop to the limit of their capacities and resources; lack of development can only be attributable to lack of resources or (harmful) governmental intervention. Since economic forces naturally lead to economic efficiency, the study of development becomes the study of the political barriers to development. 'Lack of development is always and everywhere a political, not an economic, problem.'

By emphasizing the fact that governments have often been an impediment to development, this line of thought may have performed an important service, in contesting the view that government intervention is the 'obvious' solution to development problems. Government may be the *problem*, rather than the solution. But by suggesting that markets by themselves would take care of matters, these theories have done a disservice; for they fail to take note of the important, seemingly positive, role of government in the case of so many of the developed countries[4] and the failure of development in the presence of seemingly benign governments (such as in the American South[5]).

In my own work, I have taken a more eclectic position: institutions should not be taken simply as given, but should be explained. In understanding why institutions are the way they are, economic theory can give us important insights into what functions they serve, or served at one time. Still, *conventional* economic theory cannot explain many of the central aspects of institutions; to understand these we need a broader view, informed by sociological, psychological, and historical perspectives. In the following paragraphs, I expand on these themes.

2.1. Functional but imperfect institutions

My views on institutions, particularly within the development context, may perhaps best be illustrated by my work on sharecropping. Earlier work, such as that of Marshall, had noted the dampening of incentives that results from sharecropping. Sharecropping thus seemed like an inefficient institution, whose consequences economists could analyse, but whose persistence and pervasiveness remained essentially unexplained.

Cheung (1969a) and I (Stiglitz 1974a), along with several others (Braverman and Stiglitz 1982, 1986a, 1986b; Newbery and Stiglitz 1979[6]) asked, Could we explain this seemingly inefficient institution? Could we identify economic functions which it served, and which it served better than alternative institutional arrangements? Could we explain not only the persistence and pervasiveness of the institution, but also the *form* that the institution took, both the systematic patterns (e.g. cost-sharing, interlinkage) and the differences across communities and over time? This quest has been partially, but only partially, successful.

Sharecropping clearly performs a role in sharing risks between landlords and tenants; in the absence of insurance markets (other markets for risk), this is clearly an important economic function. But I showed that this risk-sharing function could, as well, be performed by a combination of rental and wage contracts (see Stiglitz 1974).

Cheung argued that the advantage of sharecropping was associated with its savings in transaction costs. While not denying the possible importance of these costs,[7] I looked for the explanation elsewhere: I argued that, contrary to the standard view that criticized sharecropping as inefficient because it dampened incentives, sharecropping was desirable because it increased incentives. The earlier literature had implicitly assumed that inputs of labour were costlessly observable; I pursued the contrary assumption that there were quite high costs of monitoring labour inputs. Thus, sharecropping represented a compromise between risk and incentive effects: while rental contracts provided perfect incentives,[8] the tenant had to absorb all the risk; wage contracts, in which the landlord absorbed the risk, provided no incentives to work, unless workers were closely monitored.

In subsequent work, I argued that the contract form could be used not only as an incentive device, but also as a self-selection device, to identify the characteristics of different individuals. Individuals who believe that they are more productive, or more willing to work hard, will be more willing to sign contracts in which more of their pay is based on performance (see Newbery and Stiglitz 1979).

This theory could explain not only the pervasiveness of sharecropping, but also, possibly, the decline of sharecropping in more developed countries. Mechanized agriculture may have lowered monitoring costs, reducing the main disadvantage of the wage contract. By the same token, these technological changes may also have reduced the importance of the role of sharecropping as a screening device; increasing wealth among some farmers and the development of alternative institutions (such as futures markets) for risk-sharing may have reduced the need for risk-sharing through tenancy contracts, and hence made rental contracts more attractive. The theory also provided an explanation of such phenomena as the interlinkage of credit and tenancy contracts. Moreover, when augmented by a recognition of other asymmetries of information between the tenant and the landlord, for example concerning the marginal return to adding fertilizer, the theory provided an explanation of cost-sharing.[9]

These are the successes of the theory.[10] But I would be remiss if I did not, at the same time, point out some of its limitations.

The theory is a quite rich theory, providing detailed comparative-static propositions concerning, for instance, how the terms of the contract will change with differences in uncertainty, labour supply elasticities, and so on. (I derived several of these comparative-static propositions in my 1974 paper.) Some variability in contract form is observed, and that which is observed seems, at least casually, consistent with our theory. Still, the range of contract forms seems far more restricted than theory would suggest: most contracts have, for instance, shares of one-half, one-third, or two-thirds. Although there have been several attempts to explain this uniformity, none has gained general acceptance.[11] I suspect that it is here that a broader social/historical theory is required. Individuals are concerned that in their dealings they are treated fairly. Views of fairness are to a large extent conventionally (historically) determined. It does not pay to treat workers unfairly, for this will reduce their work effort. Hence, if in some society a sharing rule of 50 per cent comes to be accepted, it does not pay for a landlord to deviate from this social convention, even if, at that rate, there is an excess supply of tenants. Tenants who 'bid' a lower share would, in fact, reduce their labour effort so much (because of the 'unfair' treatment to which they had, admittedly voluntarily, subjected themselves) that the landlords' expected return would be lowered. This view argues that it will not then pay the landlord to adjust the terms of the contract from the standard just slightly, to take advantage of currently favourable (to him) market conditions.[12] The fact that markets do not adapt easily does not mean, however, that they do not adapt at all to market conditions. If conditions change so that, say, at the going 'conventional' contract there has been persistent excess supply of tenants, eventually conventions may change. How, how fast, and under what circumstances these conventions change is, or should be, an important subject of enquiry.

There are other unsatisfactory aspects of the theory of sharecropping. In general, nonlinear contracts will do better (i.e. achieve a Pareto-superior outcome) than linear contracts, and random contracts are superior to nonrandom contracts (see Arnott and Stiglitz 1988). Yet most contracts seem to be of remarkably simple form. Although one could ascribe this to a 'cost of complexity', this does not seem a completely satisfactory explanation, for contracts involving simple nonlinearities would seem to do better than the linear contracts generally observed.[13] The best we can say at this juncture is that perhaps the gains from nonlinearities are not very great;[14] and that, if it becomes conventional to employ linear contracts, suspicions will be raised about those who deviate from the norm.[15]

2.2. Rational peasants and incomplete information: a critique of the efficient markets hypothesis

More generally, while peasants may, in many respects, be rational, responding to market forces, they are not fully informed about the consequences either of their actions, or of the institutions through which they operate. Indeed, how could we expect them to be, when we, who have devoted our lives to studying these questions, are ourselves uncertain? This in itself could provide part of the explanation of why institutional rearrangements that increase productivity are not adopted.

But even if they were sufficiently well informed that in their economic relationships with those with whom they interact there are no obvious 'inefficiencies', resource allocations may not be Pareto-efficient. The theorem that asserts that market resource allocations are Pareto-efficient is of very restricted validity. Not only does it require perfect competition, but it is valid only if there is a complete set of markets and perfect information, conditions that are clearly not satisfied.

Indeed, one of the distinguishing features of LDCs is the absence of certain markets. This absence itself is something that the theory should explain, and in fact the information–theoretic models, focusing on the consequences of informational asymmetries, adverse selection, and moral hazard, have contributed to our understanding of why certain markets are likely either not to exist or to be 'thin'.

Greenwald and Stiglitz (1986) have shown that market allocations with incomplete markets and imperfect information are, in general, constrained Pareto-inefficient; that is, there exist government interventions, taking explicitly into account the costs of information and of establishing markets, which can make everyone better off. They show that there are, in effect, pervasive externalities in these markets; actions by one individual affect the welfare of others. These externalities can be partially internalized — and are done so, for instance, by the interlinking of markets within LDCs (see Braverman and Stiglitz 1982) — but a complete internalization of these externalities would obviously be inconsistent with decentralization.[16] To put the matter another way, the pair-wise efficiency of contractual arrangements does not suffice to ensure the *general equilibrium* efficiency of the economy, except under highly restricted conditions. Even if we believe that individuals are sufficiently well informed to ensure pair-wise efficiency, it is unreasonable to assume general equilibrium efficiency.[17]

Of course, societies adapt to the absence of a complete set of markets: institutions develop to perform the functions that otherwise would have been served by the missing markets. Thus, sharecropping can be viewed in part as an institutional adaptation to the absence of certain risk (insurance) markets. But, as we have emphasized elsewhere, the fact that institutions respond, that they perform certain economic functions, does not mean that they perform those functions 'optimally', that the resulting equilibrium is, in any meaningful sense, efficient.[18]

Still a further, and perhaps practically more important, barrier to the implementation of reforms that would seem to be Pareto-improving is the difficulty of making the necessary compensations. Technological changes almost inevitably hurt some individuals. It is perhaps here more than in other areas that governments, and collective actions of workers, have been most effective as barriers to progress. For those harmed by an innovation are often a relatively small and well identified group, and thus they frequently have seemingly irresistible incentives to act as special interest groups, to exercise what political powers they might have, to block the innovation. In contrast, the beneficiaries of the innovation or reform are diffuse, and hence free-rider problems impose an effective barrier to the beneficiaries acting cohesively within a political context.[19]

The difficulties in making the compensations that would facilitate such reforms/innovations is itself at least partly an information problem — the difficulty of identifying precisely which individuals are adversely affected, and the extent to which they are so affected (and the corresponding difficulty of raising funds in a way consistent with Pareto improvements, necessitating again identifying not only the beneficiaries, but also the extent to which they have benefited).

But beyond these concerns, there is a much more fundamental criticism of the 'efficient' markets perspective: establishing that a market is Pareto-efficient says nothing about whether, under an alternative distribution of wealth, national income might not be greatly enhanced. Recent work on economies with imperfect information has established that the classical dichotomy between efficiency and distribution issues is, at best, misguided. That is, traditional analysis focused first on establishing (characterizing) the set of Pareto-efficient allocations, and then asking which of those was 'socially desirable'. The second fundamental theorem of welfare economics argued that any Pareto-efficient allocation could be attained by the appropriate initial redistribution of endowments.

Once the importance of incentives is recognized, the link between distribution and production becomes much closer.[20] Sharecropping is a consequence of the disparity between the distribution of human resources (labour) and physical resources (land and capital). If the two were equally distributed, there would be no need for sharecropping (although there could still be some scope for risk-sharing, if outputs in different tracts were not perfectly correlated). Sharecropping *might* be Pareto-efficient. For example, a land reform that took land away from the landlords and gave it to the peasants would not be a Pareto improvement, since landlords would be worse off; but not only would such a reform reduce inequality, it might well increase national output substantially (if the elasticity of labour supply is positive and large).

2.3. Competition

I have focused my remarks on my views concerning the hypotheses of rational peasants and rational institutions. There is another dimension along which development economists differ markedly: on the extent of competition in markets. On the one side there are those who see the large number of, say, workers and landlords and infer from this that markets must be highly competitive; on the other side there are those who see the huge disparity in wealth between landlords and peasants, and conclude that in this unequal struggle, peasants must come out on the short end.

The view that I take lies between the two extremes. There is competition; inequality of wealth itself does not imply that landlords can exercise their power unbridled. On the other hand, markets in which there are a large number of participants (on both sides) need not be highly competitive;[21] transaction costs and, in particular, information costs imply that some markets are far better described by models of imperfect competition than perfect competition.[22] Not only may imperfect information result in imperfect competition, but the long-term relationships (and relatively high barriers to exit) that characterize village life in many LDCs are particularly conducive to establishing collusive outcomes.

2.4. History, institutions, and economic theory

The arguments of the preceding paragraphs suggested that *conventions* were important in determining at least the nature of the short-run market equilibrium, and that those conventions were at least partly historically determined. In this view, then, we may not be able to understand fully the nature of the current equilibrium simply by looking at current technology and preferences: it is essential to understand the history, the processes by which we arrived at where we are. Although this proposition may seem an obvious truism, it contradicts the prevailing neoclassical paradigm, which, at least in its conventional formulations, suggests that an understanding of history is irrelevant. That is, simply by knowing preferences and technology, both of which are assumed to be exogenous, one can explain the evolution of the economy; particular events, like wars and plagues, may affect the level of capital stock or labour supply that an economy inherits from the past, but the effects even of these major events eventually disappear.

On the contrary, I argue that history is important, for several reasons.

First, history itself creates an important asymmetry of information: individuals know more about the institutions and conventions with which they have lived in the recent past than they know of others by which they might live. The consequences of change are thus uncertain, and risk aversion itself provides some impetus to the preservation of current institutions.[23]

Second, I have argued elsewhere that to understand current technology we must also look to history; that with localized technological change (in which improvements in one technology have only limited spillovers to others), past history (past historical prices, which themselves are affected by particular events, like plagues and wars, which affect capital–labour ratios) determines which technologies are developed, and therefore determines the shape of the available opportunity set today.[24,25] Indeed, even current abilities to learn may themselves be learned, and therefore may be determined largely by historical experiences.

3. Concluding Remarks

For more than a century, there has been a certain tension between advocates of alternative approaches to the study of development economics. Institutionalists have emphasized the role of institutions, and the impediments that these institutions may impose on the development process. Historians have provided an array of what theorists refer to as 'anecdotes', tales of successes and failures in the development process. Theorists have provided models that all too often either cannot explain, or are inconsistent with, some of the basic facts of development and developing economies.

I have provided here a view that argues that all three — institutions, history, and theory — are important. Institutions have an impact on how these economies perform; although we should attempt to pierce the institutional veil, to see beyond the forms to the real substance of economic transactions, even after doing this the institutions have a life of their own. At the same time, institutions should not simply be taken as given; they need to be explained; economics has many insights to provide in understanding both the economic functions that an institution such as sharecropping serves and the consequences of those institutions. But the fact that some institution serves an economic function does not mean that it is, in any sense, 'optimal', and that historical forces do not play an important role in understanding why we have certain institutions, and not others, or why those institutions take on the particular form that they do.

I have argued further that models focusing on fully informed rational peasants working within 'rational' and efficient institutions are likely to be not only inadequate, but seriously misleading, just as models that simply hypothesize that peasants are rule (tradition)-bound, irrational, and non-economic are almost certainly misleading. Peasants are rational, but they are not fully informed. And imperfect information (as well as a variety of other transaction costs), besides limiting the effective degree of competition, creates institutional rigidities, allowing the persistence of seemingly inefficient institutions. It may not be possible to effect change in a decentralized manner — central co-ordination, that is governmental intervention, may be required. Market forces by themselves may not suffice to ensure the success of the development process. At the same time, political processes, rather than aiding development, have frequently served to impede it — not surprisingly, for reasons that we and others have pointed out.

Without the kind of broader perspective advocated in this paper, our theories simply cannot account for the variety of patterns of rural organization that are observed in the less developed countries. But beyond that, such a broader perspective is required if we are to make progress in understanding that most fundamental of questions with which we as development economists are concerned, the persistence of massive differences in standards of living, and the means by which those differences may be reduced.

NOTES

1. Again, the underlying hypothesis is that there is a single production function describing the relationships between inputs and outputs in developed countries and LDCs. In that case, factors that are in relative shortage should enjoy higher returns.
2. The list of models that have been borrowed from the LDCs, or at least have been inspired by the study of LDCs, is both long and impressive. It includes efficiency wage models, which currently are enjoying much popularity among macroeconomic theorists, and models focusing on the consequences of capital market imperfections.
3. What is generally called the 'Coase theorem' is, of course, not a theorem, but a conjecture, as I comment below.
4. Though Japan is the case that inevitably comes to mind, one should not forget the role of the federal government in the development of American railroads.

5. Each of the cited historical episodes is obviously the subject of intense controversy. The fact remains, however, that the case that governments always impede development and that, in the absence of governmentally imposed impediments, development occurs is far from proven.
6. For further references, see Stiglitz (1987).
7. Information costs can be viewed as a specific form of transaction costs; in this perspective, the two approaches are perfectly consistent with each other. The information-theoretic approach, however, yields much more precise predictions concerning the nature of the institutional arrangements; in this context, for instance, it yields much clearer predictions concerning the nature of the share-cropping contract. See also Bardhan's Chapter 1 above.
8. In later work I qualified this position. Since peasants had limited capital, rents were often paid at the end of the season, so that there was a risk of default; accordingly, peasants might not bear the full consequences of their actions. See Stiglitz and Weiss (1981) and Johnson (1950).
9. In the absence of these informational asymmetries, cost-sharing had no distinct advantage over the landlord's simply providing the inputs, or specifying the level of inputs that the tenant must supply. See Braverman and Stiglitz (1986a).
10. These are not the only successes, for the formulation of the contractual arrangements between the landlord and tenant became the prototype for the analysis of the general class of such relationships, called principal–agent relationships. As I noted in my 1974 paper, the relationship between the owners of firms (capitalists) and managers can be described by a model formally identical to the share-cropping model. (See also Ross 1973.)
11. Allen (1985a), in a very stimulating paper, has directly addressed this question. In Stiglitz (1987) I suggest that, if the output of each tract of land cannot be monitored, then in equilibrium there must be a single sharecropping 'rate'. But this in itself does not explain why that rate should not vary from place to place and from time to time.
12. There are, in effect, multiple Nash equilibria.
13. This particular anomaly has caused considerable methodological controversy. Some economists have taken the stance that, so long as we cannot explain why linear or non-stochastic contracts should be chosen, we should analyse only models in which nonlinear, stochastic contracts are employed, ignoring the counter-factual implications of these theories. Others have argued that, while we may not be able to explain why contracts are of a linear, non-stochastic form, our models should be designed to reflect contractual arrangements as we see them, and that it remains a worthwhile exercise to investigate the consequences of this admittedly restricted set of contracts. My sympathies are very much with the latter perspective.
14. Particularly since the optimal form of the contract is likely to change as circumstances change; linear contracts may thus have a robustness to them that is lacking in nonlinear contracts.
15. This gives rise to rigidities; see Allen (1985a).
16. See also Arnott and Stiglitz (1984, 1986) for a discussion of these issues in the context of incentive and moral hazard problems.
17. In addition to the limitations on the efficiency of market economies that have been stressed in the last few paragraphs, I should add the important caveat that

there are strong reasons to believe that, in the presence of imperfect information, even bilateral relationships may not be efficient, at least not in the conventional usage of the term. See Farrell (1987).

18. Indeed, Arnott and Stiglitz (1984) have shown that the institutional adaptations to the market's provision of incomplete insurance — to deal with the problems of moral hazard — actually may lower economic welfare.

19. These problems arise, of course, in all countries. The public pursuit of the public good is itself a public good (see Stiglitz 1988). But we have not explained why these pervasive impediments to development and growth are overcome in some countries and not in others.

20. Thus, Shapiro and Stiglitz (1984) show that, while if capitalists are distinct from workers the market allocation is Pareto-efficient, if capital is equally distributed among workers the market allocation is not (constrained) Pareto-efficient.

21. This point has been developed at length, in a quite different context, by Stiglitz (1987).

22. This point too has been stressed, in more general contexts, by Salop (1976).

23. In a rather different context, it can be shown that these considerations can give rise to price, wage, and employment rigidities.

24. See Atkinson and Stiglitz (1969) and Stiglitz (1987). These are special examples of a general class of phenomena, which are called path-dependent processes; see, for instance, Arthur (1985) or David (1987).

25. This is but one of many examples by which historical experiences affect the economy in a permanent, rather just transitory, fashion. No doubt similar arguments can be made for the development of preferences. It is important to realize that whatever the evolutionary forces are that shape technology and preferences — forces that determine, for instance, which firms survive and which do not, through a process of natural selection — there is no reason to believe that they have any strong optimality properties; see, for instance, Sah and Stiglitz (1985).

PART II
Land and Labour

Chapter 3 surveys the theoretical literature on the rationale of sharecropping, with special emphasis on the roles of risk-sharing, incentive provision, wealth constraints, and screening in an environment of pervasive uncertainty and information asymmetry. Chapter 4 compares and contrasts the solutions yielded by principal–agent (the dominant model) and bargaining formulations of a tenancy contract. In Chapter 5 the authors use a model of an infinitely repeated principal–agent relationship where they explore the conditions under which labour contracts with threats of sacking or contract termination will be equilibrium outcomes. In Chapter 6 the authors depart from the presumption of densely populated economies (which is common in many of the theoretical models of the other chapters) and start from an isolated, land-abundant, semi-arid economy; they study its special institutional features and show how they change with changes in demographic factors and opportunities of external trade.

3.

Theories of Sharecropping

Nirvikar Singh

1. Introduction

This chapter is an attempt to examine some of the different explanations for the existence of sharecropping. I discuss the roles of risk-sharing, incentive provision, wealth constraints, and screening. A common feature of the different theories is an emphasis on uncertainty and on asymmetries in information. I attempt to evaluate as well as describe some models of tenancy where share contracts are a useful resource allocation device. The emphasis is on theoretical considerations, and I do not attempt a systematic treatment of the historical[1] or empirical[2] aspects. Neither do I provide a mountain-top survey, revealing broad patterns and hitherto unseen connections. Instead, I attempt to cut through some of the thickets of individual models enough to expose their essentials. As will be seen, no sweeping conclusions emerge.

Some of my interpretations and analyses are no doubt idiosyncratic. Still, in analysing the specific models presented here, I have benefited from many other surveys and syntheses. These include works by Newbery and Stiglitz (1979), Binswanger and Rosenzweig (1984), Jaynes (1984), Quibria and Rashid (1984), Richards (1986), and Mohan Rao (1986). I have tried to avoid going over the same ground as these studies, and hope there will be enough that is new here even for someone who has read all the above.[3] Finally, for anyone who has not, this piece is meant to be fairly self-contained.

The remainder of this paper is organized as follows. In Section 2 it is argued that the Walrasian paradigm, where in all individuals behave as price-takers, has no place in explanations of sharecropping. The share in a share contract is not a price, of course. Furthermore, the Walrasian model makes sense only as an approximation to situations where someone sets prices. This approximation may not hold when asymmetries in information are the underlying rationale for sharecropping.

Discussions with, and comments on an earlier draft from, Pranab Bardhan, Kaushik Basu, David Newbery, Steve Stoft, and Shanker Subramanian were most helpful. Cheryl VanDeVeer did an excellent job of preparing the manuscript. Remaining errors and omissions are my responsibility.

In Section 3, explanations for sharecropping based on risk-sharing are examined. In some cases, wage and fixed-rent contracts appropriately combined can do as well as share contracts in spreading risk. Sharecropping comes into its own only when there are multiple risks of some kinds, or indivisibilities, or incentive problems.

Incentive-based explanations are the focus of the models considered in Section 4. For share contracts to be better than fixed-rent contracts, which are efficient in terms of incentive provision for the tenant, there must be some other factor as well. Different possibilities are the need for risk-sharing, input provision by the landlord with its own incentive problems, and constraints on the tenant's ability always to make a fixed rent payment. Several diverse models are considered in this section, although they all have incentive problems as an underlying common thread. This is the longest section in the chapter, and reflects the importance of providing incentives for a tenant to make more efficient decisions. Also, some issues in modelling landlord monitoring of tenant decisions are considered, since monitoring is widespread in practice.

Section 5 considers explanations based on screening of potential tenants with heterogeneous abilities that cannot be observed by landlords. The screening explanation alone seems to be unsatisfactory, but, combined with imperfect credit markets and default possibilities, it is more convincing. The last category of explanation, in Section 6, is based on the sharing of input costs, which in turn results from capital market imperfections.

We may see that these classifications are somewhat arbitrary. I might have dealt with the explanation based on conflicts between insurance and incentive provision under 'risk-sharing' in Section 3, rather than under 'incentives' in Section 4. I might also have created a category of explanations based on credit/capital market imperfections, which would have included models from Sections 4, 5, and 6. I could have provided a wholly different categorization based on imperfections in markets for insurance, labour, credit, and capital. The virtue of my classifications is directness — I have tried to emphasize proximate or significant causes in the various multifaceted explanations of sharecropping.[4] Having gone through the various models in Sections 3–6, I do not 'pick a winner'. This is because I do not think that there is a single explanation, no matter how ingenious or complicated, of the existence of share contracts or sharecropping. Sharecropping has existed in various times and places in various forms. It has disappeared over time and reappeared. Sometimes the tenant's share is one-half; sometimes it is not. Sometimes the output share equals the cost share; sometimes it does not. Sometimes productivity is higher on sharecropped land than on other types of tenancy or with self-cultivation; sometimes it is not. Sometimes sharecroppers are poor; sometimes they are prosperous. Sometimes sharecroppers produce risky cash crops; sometimes they produce for subsistence. I do not think a single theory can capture all of these aspects of sharecropping!

What will emerge from Sections 2–6, however, is that I think some approaches and some models are better than others. While sometimes these judgements are based on casual empiricism, mostly they rely on the internal logic and consistency of the models themselves. Hence I hope this piece will provide a basic sifting of theories of sharecropping.

2. The Nature of Share Contracts and Sharecropping Equilibrium

There are two points I wish to make in the section as a preliminary to discussing specific explanations of sharecropping. First, the output share in a share contract is not a price-like variable. Second, models of sharecropping where everyone is price-taker, especially in the market for land, do not seem to be logically satisfactory. Below, I expand on these observations and their implications for the nature of an equilibrium with sharecropping.

The first point — that the output share in a share contract is not a price-like variable, and should not therefore be treated as a given by individuals who are otherwise price-takers in a competitive model — has been made by Newbery (1974). He was commenting on Bardhan and Srinivasan's (1971) general equilibrium formalization of the misallocation arising from share-cropping, argued by Marshall in his famous footnote. Since then, numerous authors have made similar observations, and offered various solutions.[5]

The basic problem with the 'Marshallian' model is that the tenant taking the share as given will demand land up to the point where its marginal product is zero, whatever the share.[6] In general, there will not be an equilibrium share that clears the market for land, since the landlord has a supply function for land that will be to the left of the demand function, unless land is unrealistically abundant.

There are ways around this problem that maintain the assumption that all individuals take the share as given. Jaynes (1982) provides an elegant solution that illustrates the problems with the usual model. To describe this, I introduce the following notation. The production function is $Q(L, T)$, with constant returns to scale, where L is labour input and T is the quantity of land. We may write it as $Tq(\lambda)$, where $\lambda = L/T$. Jaynes assumes that individuals are contract-takers, where a contract specifies a pair (λ, α), and α is the tenant's share of output. Hence this implies that everyone takes the share in share contracts as given. However, they also take as given the labour–land ratio associated with a contract: they do not choose how much they would like of the other input given their own input. Furthermore, if there are many contracts available, each with a different labour–land ratio, the corresponding output share may differ as well. This last is the crucial assumption, as Jaynes shows: if the tenant's share decreases as he uses more land with a given labour input, he will no longer demand land till its marginal product is zero. A similar constraint will apply to the landlord's demand for labour. Formally, Jaynes allows for a continuum of contracts, (λ, α), which, if indexed by λ, define the share as a function of λ, $\alpha = a(\lambda)$. The tenant and landlord's first-order conditions with respect to λ are, respectively,

$$a'(\lambda)\, q(\lambda) \,+\, a(\lambda)\, q'(\lambda) \,=\, a(\lambda)q(\lambda)/\lambda \qquad (1)$$

and

$$\{1 \,-\, a(\lambda)\}q'(\lambda) \,=\, a'(\lambda)q(\lambda). \qquad (2)$$

Together, these determine the equilibrium contract $(\lambda^*, a^*(\lambda^*))$. Note that $a^{*'}(\lambda^*) > 0$; otherwise neither equality can be satisfied since, in general, $0 < q'(\lambda) < q(\lambda)/\lambda$. Hence if $a'(\lambda) = 0$ there is no equilibrium: the point made by Newbery and others. On the other hand, Jaynes shows that, with a share that varies with the labour–land ratio, and usual assumptions on utility functions, the equilibrium is identical to a standard competitive (i.e. Walrasian) equilibrium, with markets for labour and land, and individual price-takers in each market. Hence there is no need for the array of share contracts if there are wage and rental rates determined by supply and demand. This is a result that carries over to the case of uncertainty, discussed in the next section. In any event, Jaynes's construct is not meant to provide a realistic solution to modelling the determination of equilibrium shares. His own explanation (Jaynes 1982, 1984) relies on a form of capital market imperfection[7] and does not assume that all individuals take the output share in share contracts as a given.

Another way round non-existence of equilibrium while maintaining the assumption of share-taking behaviour is that of Alston, Datta, and Nugent (1984), but this has its own problems.[8] A better alternative is to do away with the assumption of share-taking behaviour. This is what is normally done in models of sharecropping. I shall argue that it is more logical to assume that one side, typically the landlord,[9] sets the parameters of the contract. Furthermore, it is not really logical to assume that landlords who set the parameters of share contracts take wages and rental rates as given by the market. This is not to say that landlords can do whatever they like. They must be able to attract tenants at the terms they offer. And this may also depend on what other landlords offer.

The basis of the argument is as follows. In the usual competitive model where everyone is a price-taker — i.e. the Walrasian model — prices are set to clear markets by a fictional auctioneer. Of course, this is not taken as a literal description of the resource allocation process. Instead, the usual justification is that the Walrasian outcome is close to the equilibrium where some individuals actually set prices, and there are appropriately large numbers, so that no single individual has much aggregate influence. The latter formulation is usually that of a game where the individuals in the economy are the players, so that there is no need for a *deus ex machina* such as an auctioneer. There are rigorous demonstrations of approximation results and equivalence in the limit, as numbers become infinite.[10] However, these results are generally available for models without asymmetries of information. And the explanations that I shall present subsequently, especially in Sections 4 and 5, depend critically on imperfect or incomplete information. Hence, even if it is possible sensibly to assume price-taking behaviour — and for moral hazard models it may not be — it does not seem reasonable in such models.

As I have said, it is usual in models of sharecropping to assume that the landlord sets the share. For example, in cases where the landlord cannot observe the tenant's effort — treated in detail in Section 4 - he chooses the tenant's share to provide appropriate incentives for effort. It is crucial that he recognizes the tenant's response to changes in the share: share-taking behaviour by the landlord will not give sensible results. However, such behaviour is sometimes combined with price-taking behaviour in a 'competitive' rental market, that is, where an auctioneer determines the equilibrium fixed rent to land.[11] This does not seem plausible. Roughly, the landlord is behaving very differently towards two different contracts in the same market — land. More formally, a landlord offering a share contract may plausibly incorporate a fixed payment to or from the tenant. If $\tilde{Q}$ is the (random) output, α the tenant's share, and C the fixed payment, the share contract specifies that the tenant gets $\alpha\tilde{Q} + C$. For any such contract, we assume that the landlord anticipates the tenant's response to the contract parameters (α, C) and chooses these parameters to maximize his own expected benefit. This presumably includes share contracts with α very close to 1, and C negative. But if $\alpha = 1$, we have a fixed-rent contract. To say that in this case the landlord's assumption about the tenant's behaviour and his own decision process change drastically seems implausible. Instead, it seems more realistic to assume that, if the landlord agrees to a fixed-rent contract with the tenant, he will do so under the same sort of conditions as for a share contract, anticipating the tenant's labour input decision and contract acceptance conditions. A similar argument applies to wage contracts, where $\alpha = 0$ and C is positive.

In the above, for simplicity of exposition, I suppressed the quantity of land. One might tackle its determination in the usual way that firm size is determined in conventional microeconomic theory, by assuming initially increasing and then decreasing returns to farm size. This allows the endogenous determination of the quantity of land per tenant, and the number of tenants per landlord (or perhaps the number of landlords per tenant). With only decreasing, constant, or increasing returns, however, the issue of farm size is problematical, as it usually is in a competitive equilibrium.

Let us conclude this section with a simple example of what a competitive equilibrium will look like in our framework. General questions of the nature, existence of efficiency of equilibrium and the role of exclusivity of contracts are discussed in a series of papers by Arnott and Stiglitz.[12] I describe the model of Shetty (1988), considered in more detail in Section 4. There are more potential tenants than landlords. The optimal landlord–tenant ratio is

1. Each potential tenant has the same reservation expected utility, determined by some other opportunities. Tenants are divided into several classes, according to their wealth levels; otherwise they are identical. There is moral hazard, so landlords choose contract parameters anticipating the tenants' effort responses. Wealthier tenants are more desirable, because they are less likely to default on agreed payments, and because they work harder in equilibrium. Hence landlords compete for wealthier tenants. Now the individuals with the lowest wealth who actually become tenants compete for tenancy. Hence they receive only their reservation expected utility; otherwise a landlord could undercut and still get the same tenant. Landlords with such tenants obtain a certain expected utility — endogenously determined. Landlords with other, wealthier, tenants must get the same expected utility; otherwise the landlords with poorer tenants could profitably steal away the wealthier, more productive, ones. Hence the wealthier tenants obtain a higher equilibrium expected utility: they get the full benefit of their higher productivity. This model, therefore, shows what a competitive equilibrium looks like in a simple model. Moral hazard implies that landlords choose contract parameters. There is no role for price-taking behaviour, however: in particular, landlords do not take as given the rental rate for land. However, the wealthiest tenants get fixed-rent contracts, and the rental rate, while chosen by landlords, is determined in equilibrium by the return to landlords with the poorest tenants. Competition equalizes returns across landlords (and tenants with the same wealth), since differences in returns will lead to undercutting by some landlord through variation in the contract terms. This is competitive behaviour in the sense of monopolistic competition: each landlord assumes that what he does will have no effect on what other landlords do, presumably because he is small relative to the market. The behavioural assumptions are consistent in such a model, and we do not have to worry about how prices are actually determined, since they are chosen implicitly or explicitly by landlords, subject to competitive pressures. Hence this type of formulation seems a good way to approach formal modelling of a competitive equilibrium with share contracts.

3. Sharecropping and Risk-sharing

The idea that share contracts might have risk-sharing advantages over fixed-rent and wage contracts was suggested by Cheung (1968, 1969a, 1969b). The basis for the argument is that a fixed-rent contract causes the worker as tenant to bear all the production risk, in the absence of insurance markets or other means for diversifying risk. In a similar situation, the landlord would bear all the risk if he or she hired the worker at a fixed wage. Hence if both landlord and worker are risk-averse, neither arrangement is optimal in terms of risk-bearing. A share contract, on the other hand, assigns some risk to each of the contracting parties, and might be preferable. This analysis assumes that there is no incentive problem, so that inputs such as labour are observable and can be specified in the contract. With this assumption, however, the strongest form of the risk-sharing explanation does not hold. This was demonstrated by Reid (1976), and by Newbery and Stiglitz in a sequence of articles.[13] The most general statement of the critique of the risk-sharing explanation is in Newbery and Stiglitz (1979). They demonstrate that, if there are constant returns to scale in production, and no indivisibilities, there will be a mix of wage and fixed-rent contracts on two subplots that gives the same pattern of returns in every state of the world to the landlord and to the tenant as does a share contract for the whole plot. Their formalization is as follows.

Let α be the tenant's share in a share contract, r the rental rate, and w the wage rate. Let L and T be the agreed-on amounts of land and labour, and let $\tilde{Q}(L, T, \theta)$ be the production function, where θ is a random variable denoting the state of the world. Suppose that a fraction k of the land is rented out and the remainder is cultivated at a fixed wage. The worker/tenant's income will be

$$\tilde{Q}(kL, kT, \theta) - rkT + w(1 - k)L = k\tilde{Q}(L, T, \theta) - rkT + w(1 - k)L, \tag{3}$$

by the assumption of constant returns to scale (CRS). Now, if k^* is chosen such that

$$rk^*T - w(1 - k^*)L = 0, \tag{4}$$

then the worker/tenant's income is $k^*\tilde{Q}(L, T, \theta)$, which is what a share-cropper with share k^* would receive in each state of the world. Now suppose that there are markets for labour and land with the above prices, w and r. Would a share contract improve matters for the tenant? For this to be the case, it must be that $\alpha > k^*$. Now, however, if the same steps are repeated for the landlord, he will get $(1 - k^*) \tilde{Q}(L, T, \theta)$ with the specified mix of wage and fixed-rent contracts. He will prefer a share contract if $1 - \alpha > 1 - k^*$, or $\alpha < k^*$. Hence there is no share contract that would improve matters for both landlord and tenant over the specified mix of wage and rent contracts; the best they can do is replicate the pattern of returns with a share contract with $\alpha = k^*$. In other words, sharecropping does not provide superior risk-sharing.

The above analysis sidesteps the issue of precisely how the wage rate, rental rate, and share are determined. In that sense it is very general. However, it would be useful to clarify how w, r, and α come about, and also briefly to look at the interaction between risk-sharing and input allocation. Having done this, I shall offer some further interpretation of the results, and examine its scope.

One possible assumption, of course, is that landlords and tenants/workers are price-takers with respect to the wage and rental rates. In that case,

Newbery (1977) has shown that the competitive equilibrium is constrained Pareto-efficent; that is, a central planner specifying labour and land inputs, base consumption levels, and output shares for all market participants[14] cannot achieve a Pareto improvement. Now if share contracts as also made available, whether both landlord and tenant take the share as given or the landlord offers a particular share, the previous argument still holds: the tenant will only accept a share $\alpha \geq k^*$, the landlord will only accept or offer a share $\alpha \leq k^*$. Hence only $\alpha = k^*$ can prevail in equilibrium, with no effect on resource allocation.

A similar argument may be given for the case where the landlord specifies land and labour inputs as well as the contract terms for his tenant, subject to providing the tenant with his reservation expected utility. We can generalize the result by allowing for side-payments in the share contract.[15] The contract-setting monopolist can do as well with a mix of fixed-rent and wage contracts as with a share contract — the latter is not needed.

As a final case, consider a monopolistic landlord who takes the wage rate as given, but chooses the rental rate based on the tenant's demand for land, $T_d(r)$; in other words, the tenant is a price-taker in the market for land. Now the resulting equilibrium will not even be constrained-efficient: there is the standard monopolistic misallocation.

In this case a share contract that achieves the competitive outcome, plus a side-payment, can make both sides better off. In some sense this is merely the result of a better input allocation. However, the point to be made is that here, while risk-sharing is partly the result of contractual choice given the input levels, the amount of risk depends on those inputs.[16] The two decisions are really intertwined. Thus the result on the irrelevance of sharecropping for risk-sharing must be interpreted as conditional in some contexts, where there are additional inefficiencies with wage and fixed-rent contracts alone.

Before we further consider the scope of the irrelevance result, a summary interpretation is in order. The essence of the argument is that any linear function of output will slope between 0 and 1 and constant term between $-rT$ and wL can be attained for the tenant through a mix of fixed-rent and wage contracts. Since share contracts are linear in output, in general, allowing share contracts does not expand the set of attainable returns. It may be noted that linear sharing rules are in general not optimal.[17] Hence a share contract with some nonlinearity might improve risk-sharing over a mix of wage and rent contracts. Subsistence constraints or tied provision of inputs might effectively introduce such nonlinearities, but there is no obvious evidence in this regard.

The assumption of constant returns to scale has been used in the analyses presented so far. Allen (1984) shows that in a sense this assumption is unnecessary. The point is simple. The arguments above assumed that production would be carried out separately for the two subplots given to fixed rent and wage cultivation. However, if the two plots can be cultivated together, output can be the same under the mixed wage and rent agreement as under sharecropping, even with economies of scale. Essentially, any share contract can be reinterpreted as assigning output from some fraction of land to the landlord and from the remainder to the tenant. There is a corresponding assignment of output from fractions of labour, so that there is an implicit exchange of land for labour, with an implicit relative price, the rent–wage ratio. Typically, this need not be a market price, and in the examples Allen presents[18] the worker or tenant did not usually have access to wage-earning opportunities at parametrically given rates. Still, these contracts specified an exchange of labour for land, and could be interpreted either as share contracts or as a combination of wage and rent contracts, with identical resource allocation patterns.[19]

A second, more important, limitation of the irrelevance result is that it assumes only that output is risky. If there are multiple sources of risk, share contracts can improve matters over a combination of fixed-rent and wage contracts. This is demonstrated by Newbery (1977) and Newbery and Stiglitz (1979). I outline their analysis below.

Suppose that the wage and rental rate are competitively determined; that is, everyone behaves as a price-taker with respect to the markets for labour and land. Suppose also that the wage rate is subject to some randomness.[20] This may be due partly to the same factors that affect output. However, there may be additional sources of uncertainty in the agricultural labour market, such as the demand for non-agricultural labour. Let $\tilde{w}$ be the random wage. Then the worker/tenant's income from mixing fixed rent and wage contracts in proportions $k:1 - k$, with L units of labour and T units of land, will be

$$k\tilde{Q} - rkT + \tilde{w}(1 - k)L$$

There are now two random variables, and as long as $\tilde{Q}$ and $\tilde{w}$ are not perfectly correlated, this is a linear function of $\tilde{Q}$ only if $k = 1$. On the other hand, a share contract still specifies $\alpha\tilde{Q} + C$ for the tenant. Hence there are now patterns of returns with share contracts that cannot be achieved with a combination of wage and rent contracts.

The above argument assumes that the share tenant's opportunity cost of labour is not subject to randomness, but is just the disutility of his labour. If the sharecropper can sell his labour at $\tilde{w}$, or has to hire in workers at $\tilde{w}$, then his income will also be subject to the additional randomness arising from labour market uncertainty. Newbery and Stiglitz look at this more complicated case. They show that the share tenant will optimally combine four contracts: a fixed-rent contract, a share contract, a wage contract, and a fixed-rent contract with a share sublease. The income from the last of these involves no labour market randomness, which is why it is undertaken. It is shown that if $\tilde{Q}(L, T, \theta) = \theta Q(L, T)$, that is if production risk has a multiplicative form, then the above combination will lead to production efficiency and optimal risk-sharing.[21] On the other hand, this is not the result with only wage and rent contracts. The result that share contracts increase the set of contingent consumption possibilities is true even if production risk is non-multiplicative, only full efficiency is not then attained.

Another case where share contracts may improve risk-sharing is if there are non-tradable inputs. Examples in some circumstances are managerial and supervisory labour,[22] and the services of draft animals. The reason for absence of these markets may be moral hazard. Here we focus on the situation where a potential tenant has a fixed amount of a non-tradable input, so there is no explicit incentive problem. Pant (1983) has considered such a model, but without uncertainty; and fixed-rent contracts, which would then be optimal, are arbitrarily ruled out. Bell (1986) considers a world with uncertainty, and argues that risk-sharing might be improved with share contracts in addition to wage and fixed-rent arrangements. Suppose there are competitively determined wages and rental rates. In the absence of a market for the non-tradable input, the competitive equilibrium will not be constrained-efficient in general. The reason is that marginal products and implicit risk prices are not equated across individuals with different endowments of the non-tradable input. Then it turns out that, if there are households that would work only for wages in the presence of wage and fixed-rent contracts, one can find share contracts that will induce these households to choose some degree of share tenancy and at the same time are profitable for landlords. The intuition is that these households can now use their endowments of non-tradables, without being exposed to the greater risk of fixed-rent contracts. Bell demonstrates this explicitly in the context of a bargaining model.[23] The above analysis is in the presence of parametric rental and wage rates. As Bell points out, if the landlord chooses all contract parameters, subject to providing the tenant/worker with his reservation utility, he can anyway appropriate the imputed rents attributable to the non-tradable. In this case, if a mix of wage and fixed-rent contracts is offered, and the subplots are cultivated together, sharecropping offers no risk-sharing advantage (cf. Allen 1984 above.)

A final rationale for sharecropping in the context of risk-sharing relies on a different labour market imperfection from wage uncertainty. Suppose true labour input is not observable. Then wage contracts provide no incentives for effort. The above analyses have all assumed that the amount of land and labour could be specified in the contract and enforced. If this is not the case, a share contract will be the preferred risk-sharing arrangement, as it also provides uniform incentives — albeit imperfect ones — for effort. A mix of a fixed-rent and a wage contract would provide correct incentives on the part of the land that was rented out, but no incentives on the part cultivated with wage labour.[24] The focus is now equally if not more on incentives rather than risk-sharing, and these issues are dealt with in the next section.

4. Sharecropping and Input Incentives

In this section we shall concentrate on labour, probably the most important input,[25] and the subject of the most debate — going back to Adam Smith — about the link between sharecropping and incentives. The well-known[26] argument is that sharecropping leads to inefficient labour input decisions because the sharecropper receives only a fraction of his marginal product of labour. The efficient solution, it has been argued, is fixed-rent or wage contracts. The theories we shall examine here provide explanations of why sharecropping might be preferred to fixed-rent contracts or in some cases wage contracts. The common assumption is that labour input cannot be measured, and hence cannot be controlled by the landlord.[27] While hours worked may be observable, actual effort may not be; in any case, it is more difficult to measure. By labour input I mean the effective input, taking account of effort variation. Initially, I consider a set of models where labour input is not observable at all by the landlord. Later, I discuss models where the landlord can imperfectly monitor the input, but at a cost.[28] With one exception, the models are static, in that the input decision is made just once, resulting, subject to uncertainty, in an output — there has been no modelling (that I know of) of the various stages and types of labour inputs involved in agricultural production.

Non-observability of labour does not in itself imply a rationale for share-cropping; the incentive problem can be dealt with by fixed-rent contracts, which provide efficient incentives. This assumes that there are no other market imperfections. Hence the theories presented here involve various types of such imperfections. The first set assumes that the tenant is risk-averse and there is no insurance market. The landlord therefore plays a dual role, providing land and insurance, and the optimal contract from his or her perspective involves a trade-off between incentive provision and insurance provision. This model was introduced to the sharecropping literature by Stiglitz (1974a), but it is a special case of the pure moral hazard principal–agent framework that goes back to Ross (1973) and Mirrlees (1974).[29] The second theory is a formalization by Eswaran and Kotwal (1985c) of ideas in Reid (1976, 1977) and Bliss and Stern (1982). It is based on provision of labour inputs (interpreted as supervisory and managerial) by both landlord and tenant. Hence there is a two-sided incentive problem. The third group has two very different models, that of Hurwicz and Shapiro (1978) and that of Shetty (1988), which both rely on wealth constraints to explain sharecropping.[30] Hence the focus in these models is on capital market imperfections:[31] the tenant cannot borrow to cover bad years.

We begin with the incentives–insurance trade-off model. We assume for simplicity that the landlord is risk-neutral. This is not at all necessary. Other simplifying assumptions are as follows. There is only one landlord and one tenant. The latter has a utility function $U(Y) - L$, where Y is income and L is labour input. The tenant's reservation utility is K. The amount of land given on rent is fixed, so is suppressed in the model. The production function is $\tilde{Q}(L, \theta) = \theta Q(L)$, where θ is a random variable with mean 1, representing exogenous uncertainties that are typical of agricultural production. As usual, $Q' > 0$ and $Q'' < 0$. The tenant's income, Y, is a function of output, as determined by the contract offered by the landlord. For example, for a fixed-rent contract, $Y = \theta Q(L) - R$, where R is the rental payment to the landlord. For a pure share contract, $Y = \alpha \theta Q(L)$, where α is the tenant's share. If there is a side-payment as well, $Y = \alpha \theta Q(L) + C$. The general theory of such models demonstrates that the optimal contract need not be differentiable, and in fact can be almost anything, depending on the parameters of the model.[32] While contracts that involve linear functions of output may be optimal, there are no economically obvious assumptions that ensure this in the one-shot framework. However, Holmstrom and Milgrom (1987) have provided a dynamic analysis where linear contracts are always optimal, and we consider this and the relevance for sharecropping below. Otherwise, this literature on sharecropping just assumes that the set of possible contracts is restricted to the examples above: one can appeal to bounded rationality, perhaps, for justification.

One approach has been to compare fixed rent and 'pure' share contracts (with no side-payment). While a fixed-rent contract is optimal if the tenant is risk-neutral,[33] it causes a risk-averse tenant to bear all the risk. The argument is then that a share contract provides some incentives, while at the same time reducing the tenant's risk. It is not clear, however, that the share contract *will* be better. For example, if the tenant is close to being risk-neutral, the landlord may not find it worthwhile to sacrifice incentives for labour input by using a share contract. It should be noted that the landlord cares about insuring the tenant because by doing so he can lessen the bite of the latter's reservation utility constraint. However, it may be less costly to do this by reducing the fixed rent and maintaining efficient incentive provision. This intuition suggests that sufficient risk aversion on the part of the tenant will tilt the scales in favour of a share contract. Newbery and Stiglitz (1979) analyze the resource allocation consequences of a pure share contract in this case. We shall concentrate on what seems a more appealing analysis, where the landlord choose α and C for the optimal linear contract, $\alpha \theta Q(L) + C$. This includes the fixed rent and pure share contracts as special cases. This kind of analysis was done by Stiglitz (1974a), and has been extended in several directions by (for example) Braverman and Stiglitz (1982, 1986a).

Using the notation developed above, the landlord's problem in this framework is

$$\max_{\alpha, C, L} \; \underset{\theta}{E}\{(1 - \alpha)\theta Q(L) - C\} \qquad\qquad (5)$$

$$\text{s. t.} \quad \underset{\theta}{E}[U\{\alpha\theta Q(L) + C\}] - L \geq K$$

$$\underset{\theta}{E}[U'\{\alpha\theta Q(L) + C\}\alpha\theta Q'(L)] - 1 = 0.$$

The first constraint is the tenant's acceptance condition. The second constraint is the tenant's first-order condition for labour input choice given the contract parameters, and its presence is the crux of the incentive issue: the landlord cannot directly monitor or control labour input. We shall assume throughout that first-order conditions characterize the solution uniquely.[34]

Given the side payment, C, which may be negative, the landlord can drive the tenant down to his reservation utility level, K. Hence the two constraints may be solved for $L(\alpha, K)$ and $C(\alpha, K)$, and substituting these in the landlord's objective function, one obtains his first-order condition (omitting arguments and using subscripts for partial derivatives):

$$- Q + (1 - \alpha)Q'L_\alpha - C_\alpha = 0, \tag{6}$$

or, rearranging,

$$\alpha = 1 - \frac{Q + C_\alpha}{Q'L_\alpha} \tag{7}$$

It is possible to show, from the constraints, that $C_\alpha = - QE(U'\theta)/E(U')$, which is negative and less than Q in magnitude with risk aversion.[35] Hence $Q + C_\alpha$ is positive, and whether α is less than 1, from the above formula, depends on the sign of L_α.[36] Now, intuitively, one would expect it to be the case that, since there is an incentive problem, in equilibrium increasing the share would increase effort. In that case $\alpha < 1$, and the model predicts that a share contract (usually with a side-payment) will be used. However, it is hard to establish $L_\alpha > 0$ in general, and I am not aware of a fully general result. It is possible to show that $U''' < 0$,[37] which is in turn implied by decreasing absolute risk aversion (DARA), is sufficient. DARA has been suggested by Arrow (1971) as a plausible condition.

I have given this issue some attention, because, while without side-payments α must lie between 0 and 1, it is not completely obvious in this case. Certainly $\alpha > 1$ could not be interpreted as a share contract. It may also be noted that the model gives no general prediction of the size of the share, in particular whether it is close to one-half, the most commonly observed value. In this respect its predictions are weak. The model also predicts that labour input will be lower than if it could be observed and controlled by the landlord, but this does *not* imply that there is a more efficient outcome given the lack of observability of labour input.

As noted, many of the above simplifying assumptions are unnecessary. Allowing for a risk-averse landlord, the choice of plot size by the landlord, competition among landlords, or more general utility or production functions does not change the character of the prediction that share contracts will be used. The assumption of possible side-payments deserves some comment. I have assumed it for logical theoretical reasons: an either–or choice of a fixed-rent or pure share contract by the landlord seems unduly restrictive. The empirical evidence is less clear-cut, since explicit side-payments are not often observed. However, one would expect them to be disguised if there are cost-sharing arrangements or production or consumption loans.[38]

We next turn to some more dynamic considerations in the context of this basic incentive model of sharecropping. In the sharecropping literature, there have been two points made in a multi-period context. First is the argument, going back at least to J.S. Mill (1848), that sharecropping involves inferior incentives for investment by the tenant. Second is Johnson's (1950) suggestion that the incentive problem described above in a static framework will be mitigated or dealt with entirely by offering short-term leases with renewal contingent on satisfactory overall perforamance. There is also a large general literature on repeated principal–agent relationships that is relevant for landlord–tenant contracts. Finally, there is the specific contribution of Holmstrom and Milgrom (1987) that looks at labour input and production as processes over time.

We begin with the general models of dynamic agency. The first such studies were those of Radner (1981) and Rubinstein (1979). Both show that, in an infinitely repeated version of the basic one-period model, the first-best solution (efficient insurance and incentives) can be achieved if there is no discounting of the future. There is a class of contracts that do this, by punishing the agent (tenant) for a period of time if aggregate output falls below expectations. The implication for explanations of sharecropping is that share contracts may not be inefficient in a repeated context: the incentive problem is fully dealt with. Note that fixed-rent contracts will still not be optimal. Also, the share contract in this framework must be supplemented by possible penalties based on the history of output.

It is interesting that recent work (e.g. Allen 1985b) shows that, if borrowing and lending is possible on perfect credit markets, then long-term contracts will be no better than a sequence of short-term contracts in the repeated model. In the models of Radner and others, however, borrowing and lending are not possible. In this sense, sharecropping and its durability are more explicable in agricultural contexts where credit markets are absent or imperfect, for there the incentive problem is efficiently handled, and so there is no cost to this institution.

The suggestion of Johnson that the incentive problem in sharecropping can be overcome by evicting tenants who do not perform satisfactorily over time may be looked at as an example of the above repeated models. However, there is a difference in that, if the relationship is not infinite, the conclusion of those models may not hold: there is a probability that the tenant may not be around to enjoy future good times. Also, severing the contractual relationship is a less efficient way of providing incentives than are monetary penalties, since the landlord gains nothing from the termination,[39] and it may reduce incentives for land-improving labour input.

Newbery (1975) has provided a partial formalization of Johnson's idea. He shows that, if the sharecropper has to provide an average return to the landlord comparable to the latter's opportunity cost, say, the return from a fixed-rent contract, he will choose an efficient amount of labour. The payment to the landlord still varies with output, so the tenant's risk is reduced from that in a fixed-rent contract. However, since this model does not explicitly model termination for poor performance, it is more in the spirit of the Radner-type models. An alternative formulation is that of Bardhan and Singh (see Bardhan 1984 Ch. 8). This is a two-period model with a pure share contract. Without side-payments, the landlord cannot in general drive the tenant to his reservation utility level. Hence there is a real loss to the tenant if he is evicted.[40] Furthermore, a contract that involves eviction if output is below a certain level provides increased incentives for effort. In this model, the conflict between static and dynamic incentives is also formalized. Some first-period labour is assumed to increase second-period output through land or other improvements. Setting the satisfactory performance level too high is costly in terms of reducing incentives for this kind of labour input.

I shall close the discussion of this set of models with a presentation of the work of Holmstrom and Milgrom (1987). This is based on Hart and Holmstrom's (1987) exposition, but it is couched in terms of landlord and tenant, and choice of rental contract.

Production and effort in his framework are modelled as processes over time. This seems especially descriptive of agriculture, where final output is the result of different stages and types of labour throughout the year. Furthermore, the landlord and tenant will be able to monitor the stages of growth of the crop from start to end. Specifically, the agent controls the drift rate μ of a one-dimensional Brownian motion $\{\tilde{Q}(t); \ t \in [0, 1]\}$, which is the analog for stochastic processes of the normal distribution. Formally,

$$d\tilde{Q}(t) = L(t)dt + \sigma dB(t), \quad t \in [0, 1] \tag{8}$$

where B is standard Brownian motion (zero drift and unitary variance). Hence the instantaneous variance, σdt, is assumed constant. $L(t)$ is here the rate of effort of the tenant, and $d\tilde{Q}(t)$ is the incremental output.

The tenant has a utility function with constant absolute risk aversion, that is, of the exponential form

$$U[Y(\tilde{Q}) - \int \delta\{L(t)\}] = -\exp\langle -a[Y(\tilde{Q}) - \int \delta\{L(t)\}]\rangle \tag{9}$$

where δ is the instantaneous cost of effort and a is the coefficient of absolute risk aversion. Here $Q = \tilde{Q}(1)$, the output at the end of the period, that is, the quantity harvested. The function $\delta(L)$ is assumed convex. The integral is with respect to time, to give the total cost of effort, measured in income-equivalent terms.

The key to the model is that the tenant can observe the growth of the crop, $\tilde{Q}(t)$, and adjust effort $L(t)$ appropriately, based on the entire path of this growth. It turns out that this large expansion of the tenant's choice set limits the landlord's options dramatically, and that the optimal rule is linear. Hence share contracts emerge naturally. For example, if the cost of effort is $L^2/2$, the optimal contract turns out to be $\alpha\tilde{Q} + C$, where

$$\alpha = \frac{1}{1 + a\sigma^2}. \tag{10}$$

Hence the prediction is that the tenant's share goes down as his aversion to risk increases, or as production uncertainty increases. If either of these factors is non-existent, then $\alpha = 1$: a fixed-rent contract is optimal.

This concludes discussion of the first group of models. I shall now describe a model where both landlord and tenant provide different types of labour inputs and these are not publicly observable.

The model is due to Eswaran and Kotwal (1985c). There is one landlord and one potential tenant. Each is risk-neutral, so insurance or risk-sharing do not enter. The plot size is fixed, so we may suppress the quantity of land in what follows. Eswaran and Kotwal allow for material inputs, purchased at a market price; but while these are relevant for the numerical simulations they carry out, their existence is not essential to the qualitative explanation, so we ignore them here. Hence we focus on labour inputs. Output is given by $\theta\hat{Q}(M, E)$, where M is managerial input, E is effective labour input, $\hat{Q}$ is expected output, and θ is a random variable with expected value 1. E is in turn given by

$$E = E(S, L; \epsilon) \tag{11}$$

where S is supervisory input, L is the amount of labour hired, and ϵ is a parameter ($0 \leq \epsilon \leq 1$) that captures the relative importance of supervision in a unit of effective labour. If the technology of supervision improves, it becomes less important, so ϵ decreases. Substituting in for E, we obtain the production function

$$\theta Q(M, S, L; \epsilon).$$

This is assumed concave in the inputs. It is assumed that L is easily observable, but managerial and supervisory effort are not. Furthermore, it is assumed that the landlord and tenant have differential abilities in providing these inputs. The landlord is better at management. One hour of the tenant's time devoted to management is equivalent to a fraction γ of the landlord's time so spent. Similarly, one hour of the landlord's time devoted to supervision is equivalent to a fraction δ of the tenant's time so spent. The justifications are that the landlord has better access to information, markets, and institutions, while the tenant is better able to supervise family labour, possibly a large component of L. The final assumptions about labour inputs M, S, and L are that they have constant opportunity costs v, u, and w ($w \leq u$, v) and that the landlord and tenant each have a fixed amount of labour that can be allocated to M or S.

There are three contractual options considered. First, the landlord can self-cultivate by hiring (unskilled) labour at the wage w and providing management and supervision himself. Second, he can lease out the land to a tenant for a fixed rent; the tenant then hires labour L and provides M and S himself. Finally, the landlord and tenant can enter into a share contract in which the former provides M and the latter S. The share contract provides the opportunity for specialization in tasks where each person has an absolute advantage. However, there is an incentive problem for each, since M and S are unobservable, and neither receives its full marginal product. The analysis proceeds by calculating the expected net income of the landlord for each of the three types of contracts. The landlord will pick the contractual form that gives him the highest expected payoff.

The fixed-wage contract requires the landlord to solve

$$\max_{M, S, L} \; Q(M, \delta S, L) \; - \; wL \; + \; (1 - M - S)v \qquad (12)$$

where output is the numeraire, his endowment of labour is scaled to be one unit, and M, S, and $M + S$ lie between 0 and 1.[41] Let this maximum be π^{lw}.

Under the fixed-rent contract, the tenant solves

$$\max_{M, S, L} \; Q(\gamma M, S, L) \; - \; wL \; + \; (1 - M - S)u \; - \; R \qquad (13)$$

with constraints as above, and R the fixed-rent total. Let this maximum be π^{tr}. Assuming that this is greater than the tenant's opportunity cost, u, and that there is competition among potential tenants for land, the rental amount will be

$$R \; = \; \pi^{tr} \; - \; u. \qquad (14)$$

Hence the landlord's expected payoff is

$$\pi^{lr} \; = \; R \; + \; v \; = \; \pi^{tr} \; + \; (v - u). \qquad (15)$$

The share contract is more complicated. Eswaran and Kotwal model it as follows. Expected output net of the optimal hired labour cost is

$$\pi(M, S) \; = \; \max_{L} Q(M, S, L) \; - \; wL. \qquad (16)$$

The share contract assigns on average $\alpha\pi(M, S) + C$ to the tenant and the remainder to the landlord. Given the share contract, the landlord and tenant non-cooperatively choose M and S respectively to solve

$$\max_{M} \; (1 - \alpha) \, \pi \, (M, S) \; + \; (1 - M)v \; - \; C \qquad (17)$$

and

$$\max_{S} \; \alpha\pi(M, S) \; + \; (1 - S)u \; + \; C, \qquad (18)$$

subject to the endowment constraints on M and S. The resulting Nash equilibrium[42] is $M^*(\alpha)$, $S^*(\alpha)$. The landlord, given these functions of the share, α, chooses the parameters α and C[43] to solve

$$\max_{\alpha, C} (1 - \alpha)\ \pi\{M^*(\alpha),\ S^*(\alpha)\}\ +\ \{1 - M^*(\alpha)\}v\ -\ C, \qquad (19)$$

subject to giving the tenant the latter's opportunity income, u. The landlord's resulting expected payoff is denoted π^{ls}.

Finally, the landlord compares π^{lw}, π^{lr}, and π^{ls}, and chooses the contract type that gives him the highest expected payoff. An explicit analytical solution is not possible, so Eswaran and Kotwal do numerical simulations, and see how varying the parameters affects contractual choice. For example, they find that, if both γ and δ are low, sharecropping is preferable to the landlord; if γ is high, a fixed-rent contract is best; if δ is high, a fixed-wage contract is best. This is all straightforward. The important point is that the numerical example establishes that all three contractual forms are possible for different parameter values. There are several other interesting comparative-statics exercises in the paper — readers are referred to it for details. The final point I wish to bring out is that the numerical examples suggest that, when sharecropping is the preferred mode, the share will be around one-half. This may be roughly interpreted as reflecting the 'partnership' nature of sharecropping in this model.

The chief virtue of the model is that it incorporates the observation that sharecropping is often associated with active participation by the landlord and with pooling of managerial skills or other non-marketable inputs. Since both sides supply such inputs, of which they have different effective endowments, neither a fixed-rent nor a wage contract may be optimal. Another useful prediction is that, with varying conditions, one contractual form or other may dominate. The model is also rich in other qualitative predictions, at least for the Cobb–Douglas production technology. A more detailed justification of the model is in the paper.

There are also several possible criticisms. First, the nature of the share contract is not clear. The tenant is assumed to have an absolute advantage in supervision because it is easier to supervise family labour. However, the cost of this labour is subtracted off before shares are calculated. Furthermore, this is also treated as a cost for the tenant, so presumably L is only outside labour. In any case, it is effectively assumed that there is full cost-sharing, i.e. in proportion to the output share.[44] This is perhaps not realistic. It is argued in the paper that the results would be similar with the more usual output-sharing. However, since the results are based on numerical calculations, this conclusion is not obviously justified. This problem extends to the model's prediction based on numerical calculations that the share will be around one-half. In spite of these strictures, however, Eswaran and Kotwal's approach is rich and worthy of extension.

The third set of models — those of Hurwicz and Shapiro (1978) and Shetty (1988) — are very different in other respects, but they share as their driving force the idea that there are wealth or income constraints on the tenant. This is certainly realistic. What it does is rule out fixed-rent contracts for tenants who are sufficiently constrained. Share contracts then play a role.

The Hurwicz–Shapiro framework is, in fact, very different from the other models in this section. There is no uncertainty in production, so risk is not a factor. A single landlord deals with a tenant whose disutility of effort is unobservable.[45] Hence, if Q is output, $Y(Q)$ the tenant's income as a function of output, and d the disutility of producing that output, the tenant's 'indirect' utility function is of the form

$$Y(Q) - d(Q; k)$$

where k is some real-valued parameter known to the tenant but not to the landlord. For example, d may be quadratic, of the form

$$d(Q; k) = kQ^2. \tag{20}$$

The results of the published paper are for this case, but they are derived for any positive d with d', $d'' > 0$, $d''' \geq 0$ in unpublished work (Hurwicz and Shapiro 1977). Note that the so-called indirect utility function is obtained simply by inverting the production function $Q = Q(L)$, and substituting for labour L in the utility function. The landlord's payoff is $Q - Y(Q)$, so is also linear in income. The constraint on the tenant's reward function is that his income cannot be negative, so $Y(0) = 0$, $Y(Q) \geq 0$. This is what rules out a fixed-rent contract, since then $Y(Q) = Q - R$ is negative for $Q < R$, which will occur for some k.

It should be noted at this point that Hurwicz and Shapiro do not stress this feature or interpretation of the constraint on the tenant's reward function. However, if this constraint were not there, the asymmetric information would not matter since the landlord could attain efficiency by a fixed-rent contract. This has been pointed out by Allen (1985a).

A major departure from the usual literature in Hurwicz and Shapiro is in the objective of the landlord faced with incomplete information. He does not maximize expected utility in a Bayesian manner. Instead, he is assumed to minimize 'regret'. In this formulation, this amounts to choosing $Y(Q)$ to maximize

$$\min_{k} \{\pi(Y, k)/\hat{\pi}(k)\} \tag{21}$$

where $\hat{\pi}(k)$ is the best payoff for the landlord if he has complete information (essentially, the total surplus), and $\pi(Y, k)$ is his payoff given the payment rule $Y(Q)$ and parameter k, determined by the tenant maximizing $Y(Q) - d(Q; k)$ with respect to Q. The lower the ratio $\pi/\hat{\pi}$, the greater the landlord's 'regret'. Since he does not observe k, he chooses $Y(Q)$ to minimize the regret in the worst possible case, which is given by the minimum over k.

Hurwicz and Shapiro proceed to show, without further restrictions on $Y(Q)$,[46] that the unique solution is $Y(Q) = \frac{1}{2}Q$, i.e. a share contract with a 50–50 split! The proof of this result is long and involved, and the intuition is not obvious. Clearly, it depends on the special objective function of the landlord. Also, it depends on disutility of producing higher outputs increasing fast enough. A very rough explanation of the result is that the landlord is constrained to a linear payment rule by his lack of information plus his desire to avoid the worst. The share of one-half is not general, in fact, since if the tenant's utility of income is concave the landlord's optimal share is three-fourths.

To some extent, then, this model remains a curiosity, but it suggests an interesting alternative to dealing with situations of incomplete information, and, like Holmstrom and Milgrom's work, leads to linear sharing rules in a natural manner.

Shetty's (1988) model is along more familiar lines. His main goal is to provide an explanation for the tenancy ladder hypothesis.[47] He does this by showing that, in a model where tenants vary in wealth, where this wealth can be collateral for amounts due as rent, and where default on fixed-rent commitments is possible, richer tenants will get fixed-rent contracts and earn higher profits than poorer tenants who get share contracts.

The formal model involves risk-neutral landlords and tenants, so risk-sharing and insurance do not matter. Hence, if a tenant's wealth is enough to cover fixed-rent commitments even if output is low, he will get a fixed-rent contract. This is preferable to other contracts because effort cannot be observed, and only a fixed-rent contract provides efficient incentives for labour input. Neglecting other inputs,[48] and using the notation from the first model presented in this section, the nominal payment the tenant receives or retains is $\alpha\theta Q(L) + C$. However, this cannot be less than the negative of this wealth, W. Hence the tenant's effective income is

$$\max \{\alpha\theta Q(L) + C, -W\}. \tag{22}$$

In words, if $\alpha\theta Q(L) + C$ is negative, the tenant draws on his assets to pay the landlord. He can do this until the lower bound $-W$ is reached. Similarly, the landlord's effective income is

$$\min \{(1 - \alpha)\,\theta Q(L) - C, \theta Q(L) + W\}. \tag{23}$$

It is easily seen that the total is always $\theta Q(L)$, the actual output. The effect of the possibility that the tenant cannot fully meet his obligations is that each party's income is no longer linear in output, but only piecewise linear. In fact, the tenant's return is convex and that of the landlord is concave.

As in the first model of this section, the landlord chooses α and C to maximize his expected income, given the tenant's utility-maximizing choice of labour input. (There is disutility of effort, as usual.) Shetty actually considers potential tenants with different wealth levels and identical reservation utilities. Wealth is observable, and landlords compete for wealthier tenants, whose expected return is higher. There is one plot per landlord, and plot size is fixed. Hence, while the tenant of marginal wealth level who is hired gets his reservation utility, the expected income of landlords from wealthier tenants is equated to that from poorer tenants. One may simply write this formally as maximizing the tenant's expected utility with respect to α and C subject to the constraints of the landlord's competitive expected income and the tenant's choice of labour input, the latter given the contract terms. The solution is mathematically similar. Of course, if W is high enough, then, as Shetty shows, fixed-rent contracts will be used; i.e., $\alpha = 1$, $R = -C < W$. In this case the bite of the incentive constraint is removed, and the efficient outcome is reached. If wealth is below the critical value, Shetty argues that sharecropping will emerge. The argument is that the optimal contract in this case will not simply involve reducing the fixed-rent payment, since a contract that involves no default can be improved on by a contract that involves increasing α and reducing C. (Note: C is negative if there is a fixed payment to the landlord.) Hence the optimal contracts for poorer tenants will involve default. Shetty also shows that the level of θ, say θ_1, at which the tenant cannot make the agreed-on payment, $(1 - \alpha)\theta Q - C$, to the landlord is decreasing in wealth.

While this reasoning establishes that a fixed-rent contract will not be used for tenants below a certain wealth level, it does not demonstrate that the actual contract will be a share contract, i.e. with α between 0 and 1. To show this, consider the landlord's choice of contract, subject to providing the tenant with utility K^* — which, owing to competition for tenants, will be above reservation utility K for tenants with more wealth than the marginal tenant — and the tenant's labour input decision. This problem is

$$\max_{\alpha, C, L} \; E\{[1 - \alpha)\theta Q(L) - C \,|\, \theta \geq \theta_1\} + E\{\theta Q(L) + W \,|\, \theta < \theta_1\} \qquad (24)$$
$$\text{s.t.} \quad E\{\alpha\theta Q(L) + C \,|\, \theta \geq \theta_1\} + E(-W \,|\, \theta < \theta_1) - L = K^*$$
$$E\{\alpha\theta Q'(L) \,|\, \theta \geq \theta_1\} - 1 = 0.$$

Now, as in the initial analysis of this section, the constraints may be solved for $L(\alpha)$, $C(\alpha)$, which can then be substituted in the landlord's objective function. His first-order condition is thus

$$\{-Q + (1 - \alpha)Q'L_\alpha\}E(\theta \,|\, \theta \geq \theta_1) - C_\alpha E(1 \,|\, \theta \geq \theta_1) + Q'L_\alpha E(\theta \,|\, \theta < \theta_1) = 0.^{49}$$
$$(25)$$

Now from the tenant's utility constraint, and using his first-order condition for labour input,

$$E\{\theta Q(L) + C_\alpha \,|\, \theta \geq \theta_1\} = 0. \qquad (26)$$

Substituting in (29) and using $E(\theta) = 1$, the landlord's choice of α is given by

$$Q'(L)L_\alpha\{1 - \alpha E(\theta \mid \theta \geq \theta_1)\} = 0. \qquad (27)$$

But the first two terms are non-zero. Hence

$$\alpha = 1/E(\theta \mid \theta \geq \theta_1). \qquad (28)$$

Since the denominator is greater than $E(\theta) = 1$,[50] the optimal α is less than 1. Hence we do have a share contract.

Thus Shetty's model predicts that poorer tenants who may default will receive share contracts. This is established in a model with wealth constraints and heterogeneous (in terms of wealth) tenants — both realistic assumptions — and with a characterization of the monopolistically competitive equilibrium. All of these are useful features.

I shall conclude this section with a discussion of costly monitoring of labour input. In all the models considered here, with the exception of Eswaran and Kotwal, it was assumed that the incentive problem arose from the non-observability of labour. One might interpret this as approximating the case where actually supervising the tenant's labour input is totally uneconomical. It is interesting to examine the implications of monitoring that is costly but worthwhile undertaking. This is because several analyses (e.g. Lucas 1979 and Alston, Datta, and Nugent 1984) have tried to provide explanations of sharecropping based on such costly monitoring. In essence, one might argue that the incentive problem is not fundamentally different if monitoring is imperfect, that is, if the landlord through his effort cannot tell precisely what the tenant or worker's effort is, but can only get a better estimate of that effort. This argument seems basically sound. The focus here is therefore on the proper modelling of monitoring technology and costs.

The general approach to monitoring in moral hazard situations is that the landlord observes some noisy signal of the tenant's or worker's effort. Such a signal is in general informative — in fact, output itself can be thought of in this way — and the payment rule will be based on it.[51] Of course, when the landlord has this extra information, the tenant will work harder in equilibrium. It is not obvious what might correspond to this in the real world. An example might be the landlord saying that the tenant has not worked very hard, and reducing the latter's share as punishment. I do not know if anything like this occurs in practice. The special case of perfect monitoring is perhaps easier to interpret. Then the landlord can exactly observe labour input. He specifies the efficient level in the contract, and if it is not provided he punishes the tenant somehow. Thus the contract payment depends on labour input as well as output. Here, of course, there is no incentive problem as such.[52] Note that a risk-averse worker will receive a fixed wage, provided he supplies the agreed-upon labour input — any other contract imposes risk. In the literature on sharecropping, the assumption of perfect monitoring is therefore not made, since it would either do away with the rationale for share contracts, if worthwhile, or be irrelevant if uneconomical. However, the models I am aware of do not treat imperfect monitoring as the observation of an additional noisy signal, perhaps because of the lack of evidence that contracts are written this way. Instead, it is usually assumed that the worker or tenant supplies more effort the more he is monitored. For example, the Eswaran–Kotwal formulation was $E = E(S, L)$. Lucas (1979) has a similar formulation except that labour time and effort are not distinguished, so $L = L(S)$, and only fixed-wage workers are monitored. The problem with such a treatment is as follows. Suppose that supervision of amount S leads to a noisy signal $\tilde{L}$ of true labour input L. S determines the precision of $\tilde{L}$. Then in general the worker or tenant's payment should be $Y(Q, \tilde{L}; S)$, where S will affect the choice of the function Y since it affects the value of $\tilde{L}$ as a variable for determining payment. For example, a linear payment rule might be $\alpha Q + \beta \tilde{L} + C$, where α, β, and C depend on S, for a given S. Now given α, b, C, the tenant chooses his labour input L. This depends on S, but through the contract form rather than exogenously. In summary, how supervision or monitoring affects labour input depends on the rewards and penalties attached to the results of supervision: these are endogenous, so the relationship between monitoring and effort is endogenous. Hence there is a problem with the Eswaran–Kotwal and Lucas specifications. Note that the above model is completed by the landlord choosing α, β, C, and S, taking into account the tenant or worker's optimal response. The optimal S will depend on costs of supervision, which may be low if the landlord is supplying managerial input as well.[53]

Alston, Datta, and Nugent avoid some of the above problems. They allow for probabilistic detection of 'shirking', that is, under-provision of contracted labour by the landlord, although this is well defined only for wage labour, since the sharecropper in their model does not contract the amount of labour.[54] The probability is essentially that of paying a fine or penalty. The less the labour input, the higher this probability. The penalties, however, are not optimally determined by the landlord, but are exogenously given functions. For wage contracts the penalty is assumed to increase with the extent of shirking. Similarly, for share contracts the penalty is assumed to decrease as effort increases. There is a logical problem here as well, since, even if penalties are exogenous, if the landlord knows what penalty to impose he must know how much labour input was supplied, but this contradicts the original notion of probabilistic detection.

The above model also has another difficulty, shared by that of Lucas. These analyses assume that monitoring cost functions differ for different types of contracts. However, they do not allow for any differences in production technology or inputs that might explain such differences. The example of a landlord supplying managerial inputs and therefore having lower monitoring costs was noted above. If the production technology is the same, then what differs from contract to contract are the benefits of monitoring, not the cost function. For example, a landlord who gives a tenant a fixed-rent contract could equally monitor him as well as a sharecropper. However, there is no benefit to supervising the former, while it pays to check on the share tenant. If the landlord supplies implements or bullocks to the sharecropper, he will also incur the cost of monitoring their use to prevent abuse. Again, however, this is not a difference in cost functions: the landlord could monitor the tenant's use of his own implements, but he gains nothing from doing so — it is the benefits that differ. As a modelling strategy, therefore, it seems to make better sense to specify a cost function for monitoring that does not exogenously depend on the form of contract. The equilibrium amount of monitoring, its cost, and the nature of the contract are all simultaneously determined.

This concludes the section on incentives. It seems that there are several avenues for fruitful theoretical research. First, there is the application of the dynamic model of Holmstrom and Milgrom. Second, further work should be done on the nature of equilibrium when the landlord contributes non-marketable inputs. Finally, monitoring, which is empirically important is share contracts, remains to be properly integrated into incentive models.

5. Sharecropping and Screening

The basic idea behind this explanation is that the landlord cannot directly observe some characteristic of potential tenants that affects productivity, such as entrepreneurial or other ability. Then, by offering a menu of contracts, including share contracts, the landlord can get individuals of different ability to select different contracts. Tenants are thus 'screened' according to ability. In general, someone — landlord or tenant, depending on market structure — will be better off than if only wage and fixed-rent contracts were available. Note that the lowest-ability individuals might not receive a contract at all — they might be screened out of the market.

The screening model has several attractive features in terms of the stylized facts. First, it explains the coexistence of sharecropping with fixed-rent and wage contracts. Second, it fits with the observation that share tenancy is often associated with lower productivity than fixed-rent tenancy (see e.g. Bell 1977), since the model predicts that the more able (and more productive) tenants will choose fixed-rent contracts and the less able will choose sharecropping. Third, and related to the second point, the model seems to agree with the agricultural ladder hypothesis, which is based on the observation that, as agricultural workers gain physical and human capital, they progress from wage labour to sharecropping, then to renting, and finally to owner-operation (see e.g. Spillman 1919, and Cox 1944).

Hallagan (1978) and Newbery and Stiglitz (1979) independently introduced similar models of screening or self-selection by contractual choice.[55]

Critiques were provided by Allen (1982) and Basu (1982). Based on his critique, Allen (1982) extended the basic model to allow for heterogeneous landlords. Finally, Allen (1985a) provided a rather different screening model, which was distinguished by having default possibilities and more than one time-period. I shall begin by presenting a version of Hallagan's model and shall then discuss the critiques of Basu and Allen. Next, I shall do the same with Newbery and Stiglitz's analysis. Finally, I shall present and discuss Allen's work.

Hallagan (1978) does not construct a formal model, but what follows captures the essential features of his argument. We initially assume that there is a single landlord with two identical plots of land. He chooses not to, or is constrained not to, cultivate them himself. There are several potential tenants, of whom one has higher ability than the rest. However, one person can just manage a single plot by himself, so the landlord must give his plots to two different tenants. He would like one to be the high-ability person, who has a higher productivity. To abstract from risk-sharing effects, all individuals are assumed to be risk-neutral. Hence, while there is uncertainty in production, this need not be treated explicitly, since only expected values matter. Also, incentive considerations are mostly avoided, although we appeal to them to avoid indeterminacy of the contractual form is some instances. Hence input choices need not be treated explicitly. Finally, there are no binding wealth constraints, so, for example, a tenant can always make the payment specified by a fixed-rent contract. Reviewing the above assumptions, we may note that the other major explanations of share-cropping — risk-sharing, incentives and input provision, and wealth constraints — have been ruled out so that we may concentrate on the screening explanation.

We now begin with the formal model. Each potential tenant, including the high-ability person, has a reservation expected income of $\overline{Y}$. Thus, implicitly, the high-ability person's skills are specific to tenant farming. This is not essential, as I shall point out below. The high-ability individual's expected output from farming is Q_1, while that of any of the low-ability individuals is Q_2, $Q_2 < Q_1$. The actual outputs are $\tilde{Q}_1$, $\tilde{Q}_2$ because of uncertainty: this means that ability cannot be deduced from actual output. We assume that disutility of labour is the same in tenant farming and the best alternative occupation, and that there are no other inputs. Hence a tenancy contract will be acceptable if it provides expected income $Y(Q_i) \geq \overline{Y}$. We assume that if this holds with equality, the tenancy is chosen. Also, we assume that $Q_i > \overline{Y}$, so that farming is worthwhile.

Initially, suppose that the landlord knows everyone's ability. Acting as a monopolist, he will charge a rent R_i such that $Q_i - R_i = \overline{Y}$, and his expected income will be $Q_1 + Q_2 - 2\overline{Y}$. Note that there is an indeterminacy, in that sharecropping contracts would also suffice. If α_i is the tenant's share, the landlord can set α_i such that $\alpha_i Q_i = \overline{Y}$, and achieve the same expected income. Hence we assume that there is some incentive effect, enough to ensure that the fixed rent contracts are better.

Now suppose that the landlord cannot observe anyone's ability. Also, because of the uncertainty in production, he cannot infer ability from actual output. Then he cannot discriminate as above, where he charges $R_1 > R_2$ to the more able tenant, because the latter would always claim to be of lower ability and ask for the lower rent. On the other hand, charging R_1 will attract only the more able tenant and the other plot will go unrented. Below it is demonstrated that the landlord can do better than collecting $R_1 = Q_1 - \overline{Y}$, or $2R_2 = 2Q_2 - 2\overline{Y}$, by offering a choice of a fixed-rent and a share contract: the more able individual will prefer the fixed-rent contract, and will choose it, while the less able individuals will prefer the share contract, and one of them will become a sharecropper.

Let the contract menu be (R_s, α_s), where 's' stands for screening. Then, for the above contract selection to occur, it must be true that

$$Q_1 - R_s \geq \alpha_s Q_1, \tag{29}$$

$$\alpha_s Q_2 \geq Q_2 - R_s. \tag{30}$$

These are known in the literature as the self-selection or incentive compatibility constraints. The first inequality says that the more able person prefers the fixed-rent contract, the second that the less able person prefers the share contract. The inequalities may be rearranged slightly to give

$$(1 - \alpha_s)Q_1 \geq R_s \tag{31}$$

and

$$(1 - \alpha_s)Q_2 \leq R_s. \tag{32}$$

Hence we see that the two inequalities are compatible, since $Q_1 > Q_2$. This would not be the case if they were reversed: it cannot be that the more able person prefers the share contract and the less able one the fixed-rent contract.

Now, assuming that the landlord rents both plots, he chooses (R_s, α_s) to maximize his expected income,

$$R_s + (1 - \alpha_s)Q_2,$$

subject to the self-selection constraints above, and the contract acceptance constraints

$$Q_1 - R_s \geq \overline{Y} \tag{33}$$

and

$$\alpha_s Q_2 \geq \overline{Y}. \tag{34}$$

Since both self-selection constraints cannot be simultaneously binding, we consider each possibility in turn. If that for the more able person is binding, $R_s = (1 - \alpha_s)Q_1$, and the landlord's expected income is $(1 - \alpha_s)(Q_1 + Q_2)$. This is maximized by setting α_s as small as possible, i.e. $\alpha_s = \overline{Y}/Q_2$, so that the less able person will just accept the share contract. Note that then $Q_1 - R_s = \alpha_s Q_1 > \overline{Y}$, so that the more able person is better off than with his alternative. The landlord's expected income is

$$(1 - \overline{Y}/Q_2)(Q_1 + Q_2) = Q_1 - \overline{Y}Q_1/Q_2 + Q_2 - \overline{Y}. \tag{35}$$

If, on the other hand, the less able person is indifferent between the two contracts, then $R_s = (1 - \alpha_s)Q_2$; but α_s must be the same, from the acceptance constraints, so that the landlord's expected income is $2Q_2 - 2\overline{Y}$, which is lower. Hence the first possibility is better. In fact, this is a special case of a more general result (see, e.g. Cooper 1984 for a good exposition) that the self-selection constraint will be binding on the person who has an incentive to pretend to be someone else: we noted above that the more able person would claim to be less able, faced with rental contracts (R_1, R_2). This is demonstrated here to elucidate the workings of the model.

It remains to check that the screening contract is better for the landlord than the alternatives. Clearly, it is better than charging R_2 to each tenant, since $2R_2 = 2Q_2 - 2\overline{Y}$. It is better than just collecting $R_1 = Q_1 - \overline{Y}$ from the more able tenant if

$$Q_2 - \overline{Y}Q_1/Q_2 > 0 \tag{36}$$

or

$$Q_2/\overline{Y} > Q_1/Q_2. \tag{37}$$

This condition is violated if the more able person is much more productive than the others. In that case, the equilibrium still involves screening, since individuals of different ability are distinguished *ex post*, but there is no role for sharecropping. Instead, there is adverse selection: the lower-ability individuals are shut out of the tenancy market. If the last inequality is satisfied, however, the equilibrium involves screening, with an essential role for share contracts in that process.

The above model involves one important simplification from Hallagan's argument: wage contracts are neglected. This was done for expositional convenience and does not alter the fundamental structure of the screening model, or sharecropping's role in it. I next describe what happens when wage contracts are allowed.

We may introduce wage contracts indirectly. In the above model, suppose that the share contract also has a fixed side-payment, C, so that the share tenant receives $\alpha_s \tilde{Q}_2 + C$. Then it turns out to be optimal for the landlord to set $\alpha_s = 0$ and $C = \overline{Y}$, that is, to offer a fixed-wage contract. Screening thus is achieved by offering a choice between a fixed-rent and a fixed-wage contract.

However, sharecropping in general has a role if there are three or more types of potential tenants, for then wage and rent contracts together will not suffice for complete screening. If that is optimal for the landlord, he will use share contracts as well. The formal model for three or more types is similar to the above two-ability model. If there are n ability levels, there will be $n(n - 1)$ self-selection constraints, but at most $n - 1$ will be binding in equilibrium: each ability level will be indifferent between that individual's contract and the one chosen by those in the next lowest ability level. The most able and least able individuals will choose rent and wage contracts respectively, and those in between will choose different share contracts, distinguished by different share and side-payment combinations. I shall not present the general model here, since it adds no new insights. Instead, I turn to Basu's critique of Hallagan's screening model.

Basu allows for competition among landlords, and this destroys the screening result in Hallagan's model. Note that this is not perfect competition in the sense of price-taking behaviour: instead, it is monopolistic competition. In terms of the simplified two-ability model presented above, suppose there are two landlords. Then the equilibrium cannot be the screening equilibrium, since there the landlord renting to the high-ability persons earns more on that plot of land. With more than one landlord, they will bid up the 'price' of the high-ability person so that the return on any plot of land is the same, namely, $Q_2 - \overline{Y}$, the return from renting to the less able person. Hence $R = Q_2 - \overline{Y}$ for the more able tenant. But this is exactly what the less able tenant pays in expected terms with a share contract $\alpha = \overline{Y}/Q_2$, so he might as well receive a fixed-rent contract. The same argument applies to a situation with many landlords, many potential tenants, and more than two ability levels: equilibrium will involve all tenants receiving fixed-rent contracts, and landlords getting a rent equal to the expected surplus of the tenant of marginal ability. There is no screening and no role for share contracts.

Allen (1982) makes a similar point to Basu. He introduces competition as price-taking behaviour. He allows plot size to vary, which is not strictly in Hallagan's model. He also assumes a competitive market for labour. He then argues, as a special case of the general result, that competitive equilibrium is Pareto-efficient; in the equilibrium individuals will hire land and labour in or out so that the standard marginal conditions are satisfied. Hence there is no role for share contracts since fixed-rent contracts achieve efficiency. The crux of the argument is that incomplete information about ability does not matter, since each person as producer knows his own ability and will make efficient input decisions based on that knowledge.[56] Hence there is no role for screening. While Allen's formulation is more general in allowing for variable amounts of land and labour, the assumption of price-taking behaviour by all market participants seems unrealistic. The usual justification in terms of the limit of monopolistic competition or other strategic behaviour may not hold when there is asymmetric information. In any case, it is clear that the screening explanation needs a stronger basis than is provided by Hallagan.

Newbery and Stiglitz (1979) independently suggested screening as a rationale for sharecropping. Their model is more general, in that they also allow for the landlord to vary the plot size. This turns out to be a crucial feature if sharecropping is to serve a screening function when there is some form of competition among landlords. Newbery and Stiglitz assume that ability multiplies labour effort in the production function, but this is inessential to their argument. I present a simplified version of their model, ignoring labour input, since it is fixed in their formulation, and concentrating on the case of two ability levels and a choice between fixed-rent and share contracts. Again, these simplifications are for expositional ease — the model is more general. I shall not present a full solution of the model, but instead shall focus on why the Newbery–Stiglitz formulation avoids some problems of Hallagan's model.

Let us assume that the production function form and amount of land are such that each landlord will want to have more than one tenant, and that there are more landlords than high-ability potential tenants. The typical higher-ability person's average production function is $Q_1(T)$, where T is the amount of land. The lower-ability person's average production function is $Q_2(T)$, with $Q_1(T) > Q_2(T)$ and $Q_1'(T) > Q_2'(T)$.[57] Furthermore, as usual $Q_i' > 0$ and $Q_i'' < 0$, $i = 1, 2$. Let r_i be the rental rate for a tenant of type i, and T_i be the amount of land he is given. Thus, the landlord with perfect information about potential tenants' abilities offers two different rental 'packages', (r_1, T_1) and (r_2, T_2).[58] He seeks to maximize $r_1 T_1 + r_2 T_2$ subject to the availability of his land, $T_1 + T_2 = \overline{T}$,[59] and to the contract acceptance constraints of the tenants, which are

$$Q_1(T_1) - r_1 T_1 \geq \overline{Y} \tag{38}$$

and

$$Q_2(T_2) - r_2 T_2 \geq \overline{Y}. \tag{39}$$

It is easy to see that the solution will involve the landlord equating marginal products on the two plots, and setting rental rates so that each tenant gets just $\overline{Y}$.

Now suppose that there is competition among landlords.[60] Then this will force the return per acre, that is the rental rate, on all land to be the same.[61] Hence any landlord is restricted to offering contracts (r, T_1) and (r, T_2). In this case, both acceptance constraints may or may not be binding at the equilibrium,[62] depending on the precise form of the production functions.[63] Now if the landlord does not observe potential tenants' abilities, he still may offer contracts of the above form, and it is possible that each type will prefer a different contract. However, the landlord can do better by offering a fixed-rent and a share contract, as I now demonstrate.

Suppose that the typical landlord offers contracts (r, T_1) and (α, T_2). The self-selection constraints are

$$Q_1(T_1) - rT_1 \geq \alpha Q_1(T_2) \tag{40}$$

and

$$\alpha Q_2(T_2) \geq Q_2(T_1) - rT_1. \tag{41}$$

Competitive behaviour by landlords requires that

$$r = (1 - \alpha)Q_2(T_2)/T_2,^{64} \tag{42}$$

so that the return per acre from each contract is equalized. This is equivalent to

$$rT_2 = (1 - \alpha)Q_2(T_2). \tag{43}$$

Hence $$rT_2 < (1 - \alpha)Q_1(T_2), \tag{44}$$

so that $$\alpha Q_1(T_2) < Q_1(T_2) - rT_2. \tag{45}$$

If the self-selection constraint for the higher-ability tenant is binding in equilibrium, it follows that

$$Q_1(T_1) - rT_1 < Q_1(T_2) - rT_2. \tag{46}$$

In words, the self-selection constraint would be violated by the pair of rental contracts (r, T_1), (r, T_2). What I have shown is that, while screening could be accomplished by offering a choice of two rental contracts, it can be done more effectively from the landlord's perspective by offering a choice between a fixed-rent and a share contract. And screening is possible even with competition, as long as the landlord has an additional dimension of control, namely the size of the plot to be rented.

The above formulation allows landlords to choose contract parameters subject to contract acceptance and the equalizing effect of competition among landlords for high-ability tenants. This is not competition in the sense of price-taking behaviour. Allen's (1982) critique of screening in Hallagan's model based on price-taking behaviour in all markets applies equally to the Newbery–Stiglitz model *if* price-taking behaviour is assumed in the latter as well. The equilibrium is then Pareto-efficient, and there is no role for share contracts or for screening. However, as argued in Section 2, this seems unrealistic.

Next we examine some flaws of the above models as explanations of share-cropping. One seemingly attractive feature of these screening models, as noted in the beginning of this section, is that they are consistent with the agricultural ladder hypothesis. However, as Basu points out, Spillman's version of this is quite different, being 'a rather Shakespearean account of the stages of a farmer's life. It focuses more on the development of farmer's skills over time than on inter-farmer differences in one situation.' On the other hand, there is cross-sectional evidence of a similar pattern (e.g. Cox 1944, and Brown and Atkinson 1981), which one might also call an agricultural ladder.

A more telling criticism does emerge from a consideration of what happens over time. In screening models, ability or land quality is generally revealed sooner or later, through self-selection of contract terms. In the real world, one would also expect such knowledge to be gained gradually by direct observation. Once this happens, screening is unnecessary and only wage and rent contracts are needed. Hence, the validity of such models in agricultural contexts where there is little in-migration and limited use of new techniques is questionable: one would expect abilities and land qualities to be well known. This seems to be the major problem with the above screening models.

Allen (1985a) presents an ingenious model that avoids the above strictures. His model predicts that share contracts will be used even after potential tenants are screened. Furthermore, only three types of contracts are used, although a continuum of ability levels is allowed for. While the possibility of default plays an essential role in this model, its interesting predictions depend on the initial lack of information about potential tenants' abilities, and the resulting screening. Hence we consider the model here, rather than in Section 3 or Section 6.

Allen's model assumes that there is a continuum of abilities, A, in the interval $[0, A_u]$. Everyone's labour supply is fixed. The production function for a person of ability A with land T is $AQ(T)$, where Q has the usual properties. Uncertainty is abstracted from, though we may think of AQ as expected output. Each person knows his own ability, but this cannot be known by anybody else until he has been seen to produce for one period. It will then be known to all the landlords in the locality. However, if the person moves, landlords elsewhere will again be initially unaware of his ability.

There is an infinite number of discrete production periods, and contracts are agreed on each period. However, at the end of each period, a tenant may choose to default on the agreed-upon payment to the landlord. He must then move to another place to avoid penalties. Initially, no moving costs are assumed, but this is not essential. People are risk-neutral, and their utility of consumption is

$$U = \sum_{t=1}^{\infty} \delta^{t-1} c_t \tag{47}$$

where $\delta(< 1)$ is the discount factor. There is no saving or wealth of tenants. Finally, it is necessary to assume that each period there is some exogenously determined turnover of population in any locality. This ensures that there are always people to be screened.

There are two stages of contracting. First, when ability is unobserved, the contract involves a payment R_s to the landlord for T_s units of land. Since landlords will offer a menu of such contracts for screening, we may think of

R_s and T_s as functions of A. The landlord's opportunity cost of land is r per unit; hence it must be that

$$R_s(A) \geq rT_s(A). \tag{48}$$

With competition among landlords, this will hold with equality, and the tenant's (expected) utility,

$$AQ\{T_s(A)\} - R_s(A),$$

is maximized. Since ability is unknown, the menu of contracts must satisfy the self-selection constraints,

$$AQ\{T_s(A)\} - R_s(A) \geq AQ\{T_s(A')\} - R_s(A') \text{ for all } A, A'. \tag{49}$$

There are several other constraints. Potential tenants have opportunity cost W per period. If the contract when ability is known is $\{R(A), T(A)\}$, it must be true that

$$AQ\{T_s(A)\} - R_s(A) + \frac{\delta}{1-\delta} [AQ\{T(A)\} - R(A)] \geq \frac{W}{1-\delta}. \tag{50}$$

The left-hand side is the utility of tenancy, and the right-hand side is the utility of working elsewhere: these are calculated using equation (47). If this inequality is binding, it defines a marginal level of ability A_0: it turns out the tenancy contract will be accepted if and only if $A \geq A_0$. Next, suppose a person of ability A_0 receives just enough land to cover his opportunity cost if he undertakes the tenancy for one period, then defaults. Let this amount be $T_0(A_0)$, which is defined by

$$A_0 Q(T_0) = W. \tag{51}$$

To avoid this problem and consequent losses, the landlord is restricted to

$$T_s(A) \leq T_0(A_0). \tag{52}$$

Also, obviously,

$$T_s(A) \geq 0. \tag{53}$$

Finally, for a contract to be enforceable in this model, it must be worthwhile for tenants to make the agreed-upon payment. The benefit of default, the screening period payment, must be less than the cost, the present value of the loss from being rescreened in another area. Thus we have the following constraint, which is essential to the model:

$$R_s(A) \leq \delta \langle AQ\{T(A)\} - R(A) - [AQ\{T_s(A)\} - R_s(A)]\rangle. \tag{54}$$

Note that at the first stage $R(A)$, $T(A)$ are taken as given.

The second stage of contracting is when abilities are known. The contracts then solve the following problem, which is similar to the previous one with the constraints imposed by asymmetric information omitted:

$$\max_{R(A),\, T(A)} AQ\{T(A)\} - R(A) \tag{55}$$

$$\text{s.t.} \quad R(A) \geq rT(A),$$
$$R(A) \leq \delta \langle AQ\{T(A)\} - R(A) - [AQ\{T_s(A)\} - R_s(A)] \rangle,$$
$$T(A) \geq 0,$$

with $R_s(A)$ and $T_s(A)$ being given.

I shall now outline the implications of this model. The complete solution is quite complicated (see Allen 1985a for details), but I can highlight some insights. First, in the screening period, the incentives of the marginal tenant of ability A_0 provide the binding constraint. To prevent this default, the screening contract must have $T_s(A) = T_0(A_0)$. Also, competition among landlords ensures that $R_s(A) = rT_s(A)$. Hence the equilibrium contract is

$$\left. \begin{array}{c} R_s(A) = rT_0(A_0) \\ T_s(A) = T_0(A_0), \end{array} \right\} \tag{56}$$

so every tenant gets the same contract in the screening period. Note that ability subsequently becomes known not through self-selection of contracts, since there is only one, but through direct observation.

In the subsequent periods, if the default constraint in (55) does not bind for a tenant, it must be that $R(A)$, $T(A)$ maximizes $AQ(T) - rT$, since $R(A) = rT(A)$. But this implies that the marginal product of land is equated to its opportunity cost. Hence this is a standard fixed-rent contract: the landlord could equivalently allow the tenant to select T given the rental rate r. On the other hand, if the default constraint binds, it determines the amount of land offered, which will be such that the marginal product at that value exceeds the 'rental rate' r: hence this cannot be interpreted as a fixed-rent contract. Let the equilibrium amount of land in this case the $T^*(A, A_0)$ — it depends on A_0 through the influence of the screening contract on the default constraint. Then the corresponding equilibrium payment is

$$R(A) = \frac{\delta}{1 + \delta} AQ\{T^*(A, A_0)\} - C \tag{57}$$

where

$$C = \frac{\delta}{1 + \delta} [AQ\{T_0(A_0)\} - rT_0(A_0). \tag{58}$$

Hence the contract for such tenants is a share contract with an associated side-payment to the tenant.

The question remains as to when the default constraint is binding. Allen provides an example with a quadratic production function, where the lowest-ability persons do not become tenants, those of middle ability become sharecroppers, and those of high ability get fixed-rent contracts. However, as he demonstrates, in general this need not be true, in that, while the lowest two groups are always non-tenants and sharecroppers respectively, thereafter there may be alternating groups who get share and fixed-rent contracts: hence there is no obvious 'ladder'. Furthermore, for the production function $Q = \sqrt{T}$, no fixed-rent contracts will be used.

Finally, Allen argues convincingly that the introduction of uncertainty, risk aversion, variations in technology across regions, or moving costs[65] does not substantively change the predictions of the model.

I shall now evaluate this framework. As noted, the model predicts that sharecropping will be used even after tenants are screened. This is because there is the possibility of default. On the other hand, default is constrained by the cost of being rescreened elsewhere. Hence, in Allen's model, share-cropping persists, unlike the previous self-selection models. Second, while there are potentially many ability levels, all share contracts are predicted to involve a share $\delta/(1 + \delta)$. This deals with the problem in other models of 'too many share contracts'. There are additional attractive features. First, the predicted share is close to one-half for reasonable values of the discount factor; for example, $\delta = 0.9$ implies a share of 0.47. Second, since the model relies on the absence of direct enforcement mechanisms such as saving and the use of collateral, their introduction in the course of economic development would explain a concurrent decline in share tenancy.

There remain some shortcomings, of course. The model still predicts a continuum of different side-payments. Furthermore, as noted, for plausible production functions it predicts no use of fixed-rent contracts. Finally, it does not give clear-cut predictions about the variation of contract type with ability. However, overall, it does seem that Allen's work focuses on some important features of the institutional setup in less developed agriculture, and provides extremely useful insights into the role of sharecropping.

6. Sharecropping and Cost-sharing

Input cost-sharing is a common arrangement in share contracts.[66] If share-cropping exists for reasons such as risk-sharing, incentive provision, or screening, cost-sharing might be a convenient way of ensuring that such inputs are used at efficient levels by the tenant, even if the landlord could directly specify input levels. In a simple model, if the cost share is set equal to the output share, then the use of the input will satisfy the usual condition that marginal (value) product equals price.[67] Although the tenant receives only a fraction of the product, he pays only the same fraction of the cost. An argument that runs in the other direction, from cost-sharing to sharecropping, is less obvious. This is made by Jaynes (1982, 1984) and is based on imperfections in the market for the shared input, which is interpreted as capital. I shall now discuss this model as a rationale for share contracts.

The formal model has no uncertainty in it. The production function is thus $\dot{Q}(L, T, I)$, where L and T are labour and land, as before, and I is some other input such as fertilizer or seeds. The price of I is p. The tenant's output share is α, and his cost share is β. There is a fixed payment of C, and his wealth is W. Hence his utility is

$$U(\alpha Q + W - \beta pI + C, L), \tag{59}$$

which is increasing in the first argument, income, and decreasing in the second argument, labour input. The tenant is assumed to choose I independently. Hence his input choice satisfies

$$\alpha Q_I - \beta p = 0. \tag{60}$$

Jaynes's justification for this is that the tenant cannot be forced to contribute more or less capital to the productive venture than he deems optimal. The landlord is assumed to maximize his utility, which is linear in income, subject to (60), and to providing the tenant with his reservation utility level, $K(W)$. The landlord's income is

$$(1 - \alpha)Q(L, T, I) - (1 - \beta)pI - C - rT.$$

Here r is the opportunity cost of land. The landlord's choice variables are α, β, C, L, and T (and, notionally, I as well).

Jaynes also allows for monitoring costs, but this is not essential. His main point is that the cost-sharing, captured by $\beta < 1$, potentially occurs because the landlord does not have enough capital himself, and hence seeks households with sufficient wealth. Jaynes shows that at the landlord's optimum $\alpha = \beta$, and hence there is output-sharing if there is cost-sharing. Cost-sharing emerges because the landlord is implicitly capital-considered and the tenant is explicitly so constrained as well.

Jaynes also addresses the question of why landlords do not offer fixed-rent contracts. He says that in that case the landlord would still have to provide some credit to the tenant. This would have to earn the landlord its opportunity cost, and the tenant would get only the return to his own labour, reducing him to a wage labourer. However, the last two clauses do *not* follow. If the tenant is still providing some capital of his own, he would get some return on that. In any case, if the landlord is capital-constrained and has to compete for wealthier tenants, such tenants should be able to earn the same with fixed-rent contracts as with Jaynes's sharecropping–cost-sharing solution. With fixed-rent contracts, the landlord would simply make a lump-sum loan, rather than subsidizing the input at the margin. Provided the tenant can borrow enough, B, from the landlord so that $pI \le W + B$ when $Q_I = p$, the optimum can be achieved. If B is not large enough, then the landlord will also not be able to provide enough of a subsidy through cost-sharing to ensure $Q_I = p$. To summarize, the efficient solution can be achieved in Jaynes's model with fixed-rent contracts and without cost-sharing, but with a production loan from the landlord.

Several other points are worth noting. First, if, unlike in Jaynes's model, labour input cannot be determined by the landlord, a fixed-rent contract has the advantage of providing efficient incentives for labour input. Second, fixed-rent contracts may no longer be optimal if there is uncertainty and the tenant is risk-averse, but then, it is sharecropping that leads to cost-sharing, rather than the other way around. Third, Jaynes's justification for the tenant independently choosing the level of input I seems weak. If the landlord can observe and enforce the level of input I, he might as well do so. (He has mono-polistic power in choosing all other variables, subject to attracting the tenant.) On the other hand, if he cannot observe the level of input I, then he cannot sensibly agree to provide a fraction of the cost. In fact, Bardhan and Singh (1982, 1987)[68] have shown that in this case an attempt at cost-sharing at the margin will not necessarily have the desired effect. This seeming problem with justifying cost-sharing itself — either it is unnecessary or it does not have the desired effect — is carefully dealt with by Braverman and Stiglitz (1986a). They show that, if the tenant's input decision is made after he obtains additional private information about productivity, the landlord will prefer cost-sharing to specifying the input level. This is because cost-sharing dele-gates the input decision to the person with better information. Note that in general, $\alpha \neq \beta$ in this model. Furthermore, if there is no incentive problem and no uncertainty, the optimal contract involves a fixed rent and no cost-sharing at the margin — the landlord may simply make a lump-sum production loan. This is because the tenant will then make fully efficient decisions. Hence it is incentives and uncertainty that drive the result that share contracts will be used, and cost-sharing follows from that.

I conclude this section, therefore, by stating that it seems that, while capital constraints and cost-sharing are important and can both be usefully incor-porated into models of sharecropping, they do not explain the institution itself. At best, we can say that both sharecropping and cost-sharing are the result of uncertainty and asymmetries in information.

7. Conclusion

I have already offered something of a conclusion in the introduction: share-cropping is a diverse phenomenon, and explanations of sharecropping are necessarily going to be divorce. The common theme, however, is, that share-cropping is a response to uncertainty and asymmetries in information. One may also view it as a response to different types of market failure, in labour, insurance, credit, and capital markets. Typically, however, these market failures can be traced back to imperfect or incomplete information as the cause. It does not follow, though, that institutions such as sharecropping will lead to outcomes that are efficient relative to the structure of information. While this may be the case, often there will be general equilibrium distortions that can be corrected by government tax and subsidy policies that are also constrained by available information, and hence are strictly feasible. Briefly, this is because, in a many-commodity, second-best world, taxes or subsidies on observable commodities can favourably affect choices of unobservables such as labour input — pecuniary externalities matter. This is an issue that has been treated by Arnott and Stiglitz in several papers (1984, 1985, 1986). This is aside from gains that might be made by improving the information structure (e.g. accreditation, licensing) and thereby mitigating market imperfections. Hence there are two general sorts of policies that might usefully be pursued in the context of agriculture with sharecropping. The detailed policy implications of the models considered above seem well worth pursuing — but in another place.

NOTES

1. The classical and neoclassical literature starts with Smith (1776), and includes Young (1788), Sismondi (1818), Jones (1831), Mill (1848), and Marshall (1920). Historical studies include Alston (1981), Alston and Higgs (1982), H. Higgs (1894), R. Higgs (1974), Reid (1975), Winters (1974), and Wright (1978).
2. Descriptive and empirical studies include Ahmed (1974), Bardhan (1977, 1984), Bell (1977), Bliss and Stern (1982), Hendry (1960), Huang (1971, 1975), Issawi (1957), Johnson (1971), Jodhan (1984), Pant (1983), Rao (1971), Roumasset (1984), Roumasset and James (1979), Ruttan (1966), and Shaban (1987). An interesting collection of studies is in Byres (1983), and an excellent recent work is that of Robertson (1987).
3. For example, I touch on some of the 'neglected themes' mentioned by Binswanger and Rosenzweig.
4. Binswanger's and Rosenzweig's Figure 1–2 (1984) provides a schematic representation of the kind of classification I have provided, though it is not identical.
5. See, for example, Reid (1976), Lucas (1979), Bell and Braverman (1981), Quibria (1982), Alston, Datta, and Nugent (1984), and Quibria and Rashid (1984). A good basic survey is in Bliss and Stern (1982).
6. There are parallel problems or paradoxes as well in terms of the landlord's decisions. See Lucas (1979) and Bell and Braverman (1981). Also see the discussion of Jaynes below.
7. See Section 6 on sharecropping and cost-sharing.
8. They assume that only a single share contract, specifying α, is available. In their model, the tenant faces some exogenous expected penalty that is inversely related to the labour-land ratio. This places a constraint on his demand for land. The landlord, on the other hand, is constrained in a different manner. In the Jaynes model, if faced with a given share, the landlord would wish to always increase the labour-land ratio, unless the marginal product of labour falls to zero. Here, instead, the landlord assumes that however much land he chooses to provide on share terms, the labour-land ratio will be the same, i.e. rather than taking the tenant's labour input decision as given, he assumes the tenant will always adjust his labour input to maintain the labour-land ratio on sharecropped land. This is

not a usual type of competitive assumption. There are other difficulties as well: the landlord does not benefit from penalties on the tenant, so it is not clear what these are; the landlord does not even realize that this monitoring affects the share tenant's behaviour; the exogeneity of penalties and differences in monitoring cost functions are not well motivated (see Section 4). Hence, while the model provided by Alston, Datta and Nugent is ingenious, it seems unsatisfactory in some respects.

9. An alternative is an explicit bargaining approach. See Bell's Chapter 4 below.
10. See, for example, the Symposium on the Limits of Non-co-operative Equilibrium in the *Journal of Economic Theory*, 1980. An early, non-rigorous attempt in the context of sharecropping is Koo (1973).
11. For example, Lucas (1979) does this in the last model in his paper.
12. See Arnott and Stiglitz (1984, 1985, 1986). By exclusivity, I mean that the landlord can require that his tenant does not contract with other landlords as well.
13. Stiglitz (1974a), Newbery (1975, 1977), and Newbery and Stiglitz (1979).
14. So the central planner is also unable to make state-contingent adjustments.
15. Thus, let (α, C) be the optimal contract for the landlord, with inputs (L, T), so that the sharecropper gets $\alpha \tilde{Q}(L, T, \theta) + C$. Suppose that the landlord can instead offer a rental contract at rental rate $\dot{r}$ for cultivation with inputs (kL, kT), and a wage contract at wage rate w for the remaining $\{(1 - k)L, (1 - k)T\}$. The tenant's return in state of the world θ is then

$$\tilde{Q}(kL, kT, \theta) - rkT + w(1 - k)L = k\tilde{Q}(L, T, \theta) - rkT + w(1 - k)L,$$

by the assumption of CRS. For this to duplicate the returns from the share contract, it must be that $k = \alpha$. Then, for the side payments to be equal,

$$w(1 - \alpha)L - r\alpha T = C.$$

Clearly, the landlord can always find a w and r so that this holds. In fact, even if he must offer a market-determined wage, w, he can select an appropriate rental rate. The key here is that the landlord has some monopoly power. If both w and r for this tenant are set by the market, then of course he cannot be necessarily driven to his reservation utility level, and instead the landlord must compete by adjusting the share and side-payment; we are back to the Newbery model, with the addition of side-payments.
16. The production decision is akin to investing in an asset with risky returns.
17. A linear sharing rule is optimal only if the utility functions have absolute risk aversions whose reciprocals are linear. See Wilson (1968).
18. These are thirteenth-century England, nineteenth-century Germany, Chile, and Peru.
19. Newbery (1977) and Newbery and Stiglitz (1979) also look at economies of scale and indivisibilities. They see these as limiting the scope of their result on the irrelevance of share contracts for risk-sharing. However, *if* the conditions Allen describes hold, their result is more general.
20. Alternatively or additionally, the rental rate could be random. Bell (1986) has suggested that the timing of the randomness may be such that the wage is known when cultivation decisions are made. Then the following argument does not hold. Newbery and Stiglitz also discuss this point.

21. A rigorous demonstration is in Newbery (1977), where it is also shown that the equilibrium share will be $\alpha^* = LQ_L/Q$, i.e. the imputed share of labour with no uncertainty.

22. Eswaran and Kotwal (1985c) look at these inputs, but the emphasis is on incentive problems, so their analysis is treated in the next section.

23. Such models are considered in Chapter 4 below.

24. This assumes that monitoring is prohibitively costly. This is relaxed in the next section.

25. One can treat other inputs similarly from an analytical point of view.

26. Mostly through Marshall's footnote.

27. If it can, there is no incentive problem, of course.

28. Empirically, monitoring is often important.

29. The literature is enormous. See the recent survey by Hart and Holmstrom (1987) for an excellent exposition and a partial bibliography.

30. Mazumdar (1975) and Sen (1981) make similar points, but not centrally to their analyses.

31. The Shetty and Eswaran–Kotwal models are actually also pure moral hazard models (or 'hidden action', in Arrow's terminology), but they do not rely on risk aversion. The Hurwicz–Shapiro model is a 'hidden information' model (see Arrow 1985).

32. Again we may refer to Hart and Holmstrom (1987) for details.

33. This is easily shown; see, for example, Harris and Raviv (1979).

34. For a discussion of such issues, see Hart and Holmstrom (1987).

35. Roughly, since $U'' < 0$, U' and θ are negatively correlated, so $E(U'\theta) - E(U')E(\theta) < 0$ and $E(\theta) = 1$.

36. With risk neutrality, $C_\alpha = Q$ and $\alpha = 1$, as we would expect: a fixed-rent contract is used. Otherwise, note that equation (9) does not give an explicit formula for the share, since the right-hand side also depends on α.

37. The result involves obtaining an expression for L_α, which turns out to be quite messy. Similar sorts of comparative statics with uncertainty are common in the literature; see e.g. Arrow (1971).

38. See Chapter 12 below, and Robertson (1987).

39. This point is made by Singh (1983) in a two-period model.

40. Alternative models, where agents get more than their opportunity cost and hence suffer if dismissed, are those of Stiglitz and Weiss (1983) and Shapiro and Stiglitz (1984).

41. The parameter ϵ is suppressed in what follows.

42. This is a situation where each person's choice is the best response to the other's equilibrium choice. It is easy to show that this equilibrium exists. It is assumed unique.

43. It is plausible that he can precommit these, but not his input M.

44. This applies to materials in their model as well.

45. This is hence a hidden information model in Arrow's terminology.

46. In the published proof, differentiability is imposed. In general, $Y(Q)$ may be kinked or discontinuous.

47. See Section 5 below on screening for more discussion of this hypothesis. Also see Wright (1978: 176).

48. In Shetty's model these are constant, and there is cost-sharing in the proportion of the output share.

49. Note that, while θ_1 is a function of L, C, and α, the derivatives with respect to θ_1 cancel out, from its definition.

50. This is easy to demonstrate mathematically. The intuition (for which I am grateful to Steve Stoft) is that the center of gravity of the distribution is shifted to the right by removing the left tail.

51. For general results, see Holmstrom (1979, 1982). For an application, see Singh (1985).

52. It is not clear if share contracts that specify labour inputs (e.g. as in Cheung's observations) are of this form, with penalties for non-fulfilment. Possibly, observed labour time is always supplied as contracted, and effort is still unobservable, so the incentive problem remains.

53. This is thus a different idea from Eswaran and Kotwal, where there are no such economies of scope. I am grateful to Lee Alston (private correspondence) for this idea on why supervision costs might be low.

54. Fixed-rent contracts are considered in their model, presumably because of asset or wealth limitations, since everyone is risk-neutral. However, these are not made explicit.

55. The idea can actually be traced to Reid (1976).

56. The details of the model are not presented, since it is a standard Walrasian one.

57. The assumption that marginal products are also ordered by ability is typically necessary in screening or self-selection models; see e.g. Cooper (1984). It is consistent with ability being multiplicative; i.e., $Q_i(T) = Q(A_i T)$.

58. In an analogy to conventional theory, the landlord is acting as a perfectly discriminating monopolist.

59. I assume that the endowment T is such that this constraint is always binding.

60. Again, this is a form of monopolistic competition since landlords still choose contract parameters.

61. Here I follow Newbery and Stiglitz. An alternative notion of competition could be that the total return from any contract is equalized. For fixed plot size, of course, the two are the same.

62. I omit a detailed analysis.

63. The self-selection constraints are then

$$Q_1(T_1) - rT_1 \geq Q_1(T_2) - rT_2$$
$$Q_2(T_2) - rT_2 \geq Q_2(T_1) - rT_1.$$

These can both be satisfied, e.g. if T_i maximizes $Q_i(T) - rT$.

64. Since plot size is variable, this equality does not completely determine the landlord's choice, unlike in the fixed-plot size case.

65. That is, provided these costs are not too high, they only change the side-payment, which may then be of either sign. If they are high enough, they may lead to irrelevance of the additional constraints in the screening period. Thus, Bell's (1986) criticism on this point is only partially valid.

66. See e.g. Ladejinsky (1977), Rao (1975), and Rudra (1975).

67. This argument was made by Heady (1947) and formalized by Adams and Rask (1968).

68. See also Bardhan (1984: Ch. 7).

4.

A Comparison of Principal–Agent and Bargaining Solutions: The Case of Tenancy Contracts

Clive Bell

1. Introduction

The use of agency theory has led to notable successes in understanding contractual arrangements. When insurance markets are absent or incomplete and the monitoring of actions is costly, so that the provision of incentives and the sharing of risks become intertwined, agency theory is a natural choice, as most of the papers in this volume testify so eloquently. There is, however, one aspect of the way in which agency theory has been used that warrants closer scrutiny than it often receives. In the principal–agent setting, the principal is free to choose the terms of the contract, which must relate to mutually observable actions or outcomes, subject only to the condition that the contract must be at least as attractive to the agent as the agent's alternative opportunities for employing his resources. In most cases, it turns out that the principal's optimum contract is such that it yields the agent no gain over the (reservation) utility from alternative employment. Thus, if there are gains from co-operation arising from the contract, they will accrue wholly to the principal.

The source of the principal's power to arrange matters to his liking appears to lie in the common assumption that he faces a perfectly elastic supply of agents. Then, if any of those he wishes to engage decline his offers, there are plenty more who will accept. To be precise, the crucial point is whether the withdrawal of a single agent into alternative employment will make the principal worse off. If it does, it is natural to say that each agent has some power over the principal, in the sense of being able to do him (economic) injury. According to Harsanyi's (1962) definition, the cost to the principal of such an action measures the *strength* of an agent's power over him. A perfectly elastic supply of agents is sufficient to deny agents any power in this sense; but it is not always necessary. Indeed, this chapter deals with one case in which agents are few but still powerless — provided, of course, that they cannot form a coalition. On the other hand, agents may possess such power, even when they are quite numerous. If they do, it is surely rather arbitrary to assume that the terms of the contract are decided unilaterally by the principal, especially if he captures all gains from co-operation. Instead, it is more natural and reasonable to assume that the terms are arrived at through bilateral negotiation, with the final outcome depending on the two parties' bargaining strengths.

In this connection, it is important to draw a distinction between a person's disagreement payoff and his power to do injury to another by declining to enter into a contract with that person. The former is simply the payoff the first person would obtain if no contract were signed, while the latter depends on his capacity to influence the other person's disagreement payoff. Thus, it is quite possible for one party to have a high disagreement payoff but no power over the other, and conversely. For example, workers of a certain kind may command high wages in alternative employment and yet be in highly elastic supply. Employers will grumble about the lucrative contracts they must offer in order to attract such workers; but there will be no scope for bargaining, as each worker possesses (virtually) no power. Then, again, the workers may have rather miserable alternative opportunities and yet possess some power, which will influence the terms and worth of the contract they agree to, even though it yields them meagre utility.

The object of this chapter is to compare the solutions yielded by principal–agent and bargaining formulations of an economic contract. The example chosen for this purpose is tenancy, which is important in peasant agriculture and has been the subject of numerous papers over the past two decades, two especially noteworthy contributions within the framework of agency theory being Stiglitz (1974a) and Newbery and Stiglitz (1979). The concepts and approach employed here can, of course, be employed equally well in the analysis of contracts involving tenancy, credit, or labour; but each requires a model tailored specially to the purpose. For want of space, therefore, a single exemplar must suffice.

In the interests of analytical tractability and, it is hoped, clear exposition, the model has been kept very simple. A non-cultivating, risk-neutral landlord faces a finite number of identical, risk-averse tenants. Each of the latter possesses an endowment of a resource that is essential in production but, unlike (unskilled) labour, cannot be traded in an auction market. In view of what is known about peasant agriculture in South Asia, this resource may be thought of as a composite of managerial and husbandry skills and animal draught power, since markets for their services do not exist or are very thin (see, example, Bliss and Stern 1982). Hence, if the landlord desires to have more of the non-tradable employed in the cultivation of his tenancies, the only course of action is for him to engage more tenants — if more are available. The terms of a contract include an unrestricted fixed payment and a share of output. It is assumed that contracts are linear in these two parameters. There is a perfect and riskless market for unskilled labour, so that tenants have a 'sure thing' alternative. However, production in the tenancy subeconomy is risky. Finally, no coalitions are allowed.

Section 2 is devoted to the case in which the monitoring and enforcement of labour inputs is costless. Thus, the provision of incentives can be separated from the allocation of risk-bearing, and a first-best outcome is attainable. In Section 3, monitoring and enforcement are prohibitively costly. Incentive considerations now get inextricably entangled with those of risk-sharing — except in the special but important case of constant absolute risk aversion, which serves as a valuable benchmark. In these sections, Nash's (1950) solution to the bargaining problem is used. Bell and Zusman (1976, 1977) do likewise; but their analysis is confined to the special case of riskless production and (pure) sharecropping contracts without side-payments. In Section 4, Nash's solution is compared with a more recent proposal by Kalai and Smorodinsky (1975), who would replace Nash's axiom of independence of irrelevant alternatives with an axiom of monotonicity. In Section 5, these comparisons are pursued in the context of two central qualitative questions in agrarian economic organization: whether there will be interlinking, and whether landlords will block certain innovations. Some concluding remarks follow.

2. Costless Monitoring and Enforcement

When the terms of a contract can be freely varied without affecting incentives, other than the requirement that the contract remain attractive relative to the two parties' alternatives, attention can be focused entirely on risk-bearing. I begin with a statement of the main assumptions.

There are $\bar{N}$ identical tenants in all, each of whom is endowed with one unit of (unskilled) labour and the non-tradable. Both endowments are supplied quite inelastically. The labour market is perfect, the parametric and certain wage being w. Hence, in the absence of a tenancy, a tenant can earn a sure income of w.

Output is produced under constant returns to scale by means of labour, land, and the non-tradable. There is multiplicative risk in production, the effects of variations in the state of nature on output being represented by the random variable θ. Thus, the output of a tenancy of h hectares cultivated with ℓ units of labour is

$$q = \theta f(\ell, h; 1). \tag{1}$$

It is assumed that, in addition to being linearly homogeneous, $f(\cdot)$ is neoclassically well behaved, and that $E\theta = 1$, where E is the expectations operator.

Attention will be confined to linear contracts, in which the tenant receives a share $\alpha \in [0, 1]$ of the gross output and pays a fixed rent β for each hectare leased in. It is assumed that β is unrestricted, so that the landlord also can make fixed payments to the tenant. The tenant is responsible for all labour costs, family and hired alike. Hence, the ith tenant's income from a tenancy of size h_i under the terms (α_i, β_i) is

$$y_i = \alpha_i \theta f^i - \beta_i h_i - w(\ell_i - 1). \tag{2}$$

The tenant maximizes expected utility, with preferences over realized income represented by $u(y)$.

There is only one landlord, who owns $\bar{H}$ hectares of land, but lacks the non-tradable. As the latter is essential in production, he cannot undertake cultivation himself and so must hire tenants. His income (profit) from the ith tenancy is simply $(1 - \alpha)\theta f^i + \beta_i h_i$. As he is risk-neutral, his utility is measured by expected total profits:

$$E\pi = \sum_{i=1}^{n} \{(1 - \alpha_i) f^i + \beta_i h_i\} \tag{3}$$

where n ($\leq \bar{N}$) is the number of tenants he engages and $\sum_{i=1}^{n} h_i \leq \bar{H}$.

2.1. The principal–agent solution

The landlord, as principal, chooses the terms of contracts so as to maximize $E\pi$, subject to the condition that, for tenants, they be at least as attractive as working for wages in alternative employment. As all tenants are identical, it follows by symmetry that all will have identical contracts, and the index i can be dropped. The landlord's choice variables are (α, β, h, n) and, if labour inputs are monitorable and contractually enforceable, ℓ also. Forming the Lagrangean

$$\mathcal{L} = n\{(1 - \alpha)f + \beta h\} + \lambda\{Eu(y) - u(w)\} + \mu(\bar{H} - nh) + v(\bar{N} - n), \tag{4}$$

we obtain the first-order conditions (FOC)

$$\left. \begin{array}{r} - nf + \lambda Eu'\theta f \leq 0 \\ \alpha \geq 0 \end{array} \right\} \text{ complementarily} \tag{5}$$

$$nh - \lambda Eu'h = 0 \tag{6}$$

$$n\{(1 - \alpha)f_2 + \beta\} + \lambda(Eu'\theta\alpha f_2 - Eu'\beta) - \mu n = 0 \tag{7}$$

$$(1 - \alpha)f + \beta h - \mu h - v = 0 \tag{8}$$

$$\left. \begin{array}{r} n(1 - \alpha)f_1 + \lambda(Eu'\theta\alpha f_1 - Eu'w) \leq 0 \\ \ell \geq 0 \end{array} \right\} \text{ complementarily.} \tag{9}$$

where f_j denotes the partial derivative of $f(\cdot)$ with respect to its jth argument, and the fact that n is an integer has been ignored.

In order that the problem be interesting, let there be some contract that yields strictly positive expected profits to the landlord and is attractive to tenants. It follows at once from the properties of $f(\cdot)$ that both ℓ and h must be positive. Hence, from (6), $\lambda Eu' = n$. As n must be positive if $E\pi$ is to be positive, it follows at once that λ is positive; so that tenants will obtain exactly the same level of expected utility from tenancy contracts as working for wages in alternative employment.

If tenants are risk-averse, $Eu'\theta/Eu' < 1$ if $\alpha > 0$.[1] Hence, from (5) and (6), $\alpha = 0$ at the landlord's optimum; that is, the tenant bears no risk. Thus, as $\lambda > 0$, $y = w$, which implies that $\beta h = -w\ell$. In effect, the tenant receives a fixed payment from the landlord which just covers the tenant's outlay on labour.

Substituting $\alpha = 0$ into (7), we obtain

$$\mu = f_2;$$

that is, the shadow price of land to the landlord is equal to the expected value of its marginal product, as intuition would suggest. By assumption, $f_2 > 0$, so that all land will be cultivated. From (9), we obtain the corresponding equality for labour, which is tradable:

$$f_1 = w.$$

As $\beta h = -w\ell$, (8) may be written as

$$f - \ell f_1 - h f_2 - \nu = 0. \tag{8'}$$

We are now in a position to determine n. There are two cases. First, suppose that the non-tradable is not essential in production, at least not at the margin; that is, $f_3 = 0$. Then, by Euler's theorem, $f - \ell f_1 - h f_2 = 0$; so that $\nu = 0$. In fact, n is indeterminate in this case; for with constant returns to scale in land and labour alone, $f_1 = w$ determines a unique labour–land ratio independently of n. As long as the expected marginal product of the non-tradable is zero on all tenancies, therefore, it will matter to neither the landlord nor the tenants whether he engages one tenant or a hundred. In this case, a tenant has no power over the landlord, in the sense that he cannot reduce the landlord's expected profits by withdrawing into wage employment, even though he himself will be indifferent between such employment and a tenancy contract, which is, in effect, an employment contract yielding the going wage.

Second, suppose that, on the contrary, the non-tradable is essential in production: that is, $f_3 > 0$. Then, from (8') and Euler's theorem, $\nu > 0$, which implies that $n = \bar{N}$: the landlord will engage all of the tenants available to him. Here a tenant certainly does possess the power to damage the landlord. To be precise, if all the rest accept tenancies on the above terms, the refusal of a contract by the remaining tenant will reduce the landlord's expected profits

— by ν if the landlord can reallocate land optimally among the rest in the wake of this particular disagreement, and by more than ν if he cannot do so. Yet the contract offered by the landlord is still scarcely attractive relative to wage employment, so that the landlord is able to appropriate all of the imputed rents associated with his tenants' non-tradables. As the possession of non-tradables gives tenants power over the landlord when $f_3 > 0$, this feature of the principal–agent solution seems especially unsatisfactory; for it is plausible that a tenant should be able to strike a more favourable deal when he possesses power in the above sense than when he does not.

2.2. A bargaining solution

We are led, therefore, to consider solution concepts in which the outcome is influenced by the power of *both* parties. If $\nu > 0$, there is a 'surplus' to be had when the two parties agree to co-operate by entering into a tenancy contract. How large that surplus is and how it is divided between them will depend, *inter alia*, on their respective bargaining strengths. The latter depend, in turn, on the payoff each party can get if they should fail to agree, their so-called 'disagreement payoffs'.

The tenant's disagreement payoff is well defined. It is the utility obtained from wage employment at the parametric and certain wage w, there being no use for his non-tradable outside cultivation and no cost of supplying it. Arriving at the landlord's disagreement payoff is rather complicated, however, because it depends on the scope for renegotiation of his contracts with other tenants and his bargaining strength in that eventuality. If full renegotiation of all terms, including the size of each tenancy, is possible, then his disagreement payoff will be *at most* the maximum value of $E\pi$ in the principal–agent case when there are $(\bar{N} - 1)$ tenants. Ignoring the fact that $\bar{N}$ is an integer, the damage inflicted on the landlord by the withdrawal of a single tenant is, in this case, ν. As I have just argued, however, this outcome is implausibly favourable to the landlord when $\nu > 0$. Moreover, if the tenant's power to damage the landlord which is implied by $\nu > 0$ for $n = \bar{N}$ is recognized, it must also feature in the renegotiation with the remaining $(\bar{N} - 1)$ tenants, in which context the value of ν will be arguably higher than when $n = \bar{N}$. Thus, there would appear to be a problem of regress, since the landlord's disagreement payoff when dealing with k tenants depends on that when dealing with $(k - 1)$ tenants for all $k \leq \bar{N}$.

Confronted with this difficulty, Bell and Zusman (1976, 1977) assumed that the remaining $(\bar{N} - 1)$ tenants would be happy to take on the $(\bar{H}/\bar{N})$ hectares earmarked for the recalcitrant tenant, without any changes in the other terms of their contracts (α, β). This certainly overstates the landlord's disagreement payoff, but perhaps not too seriously if $\bar{N}$ is sufficiently large. An alternative assumption is that the landlord makes no attempt at renegotiation with the rest if he is unable to reach agreement with a particular tenant, and the $(\bar{H}/\bar{N})$ hectares earmarked for the latter will simply lie fallow. This is certainly an executable threat, although it is unlikely to be the landlord's best course of action in the event of a disagreement. Nor, unfortunately, does it solve the problem of regress. Nevertheless, in the following, I shall adhere to Bell and Zusman's assumption that the other terms of the remaining $(\bar{N} - 1)$ contracts will not change in the event of a dispute with one tenant, but with the assurance that, in the absence of a reallocation of land, the landlord's disagreement payoff will be less seriously (if at all) overstated.

Having defined the parties' disagreement payoffs, I now introduce the main solution concept to be employed, which is Nash's (1950) solution to the two-person bargaining problem. Let $\underline{V}_i$ denote the landlord's expected profits in the event of a disagreement with tenant i. From (3),

$$\underline{V}_i = \sum_{j \neq i}^{\bar{N}} \{(1 - \alpha_j)f^j + \beta_j h_j\}. \tag{10}$$

Now define

$$\Gamma_i = \{Eu(y_i) - u(w)\}(E\pi - \underline{V}_i) \equiv \Delta Eu_i \Delta \dot{E}\pi, \tag{11}$$

which is simply the product of the two parties' gains from co-operation, relative to their respective disagreement payoffs. Nash's solution to the game between tenant i and the landlord is the contract that will yield the greatest value of Γ_i. Note that the assumption that the remaining contracts are not renegotiated in the event of a disagreement implies that

$$\Delta E\pi = E\pi - \underline{V}_i = (1 - \alpha_i)f^i + \beta_i h_i, \tag{12}$$

which depends only on the terms of the contract with tenant i.

The terms of the ith contract are $(\alpha_i, \beta_i, h_i, \ell_i)$. As the allocation of land to other tenants is taken as given. $h_i \leq \bar{H} - \sum_{j \neq i} h_j$. Subject to this constraint, together with $\alpha \in [0, 1]$, the outcome is the contract $(\alpha_i, \beta_i, h_i, \ell_i)$ that maximizes Γ_i. The FOC are

$$\left. \begin{array}{r} - f^i \Delta Eu_i + (Eu'\theta f^i)\Delta E\pi \leq 0 \\ \alpha_i \geq 0 \end{array} \right\} \text{ complementarily} \tag{13}$$

$$h_i \Delta Eu_i - (Eu'h_i)\Delta E\pi = 0 \tag{14}$$

$$\left. \begin{array}{r} \{(1 - \alpha_i)f^i_2 + \beta_i\}\Delta Eu_i + (Eu'\alpha\theta f^i_2 - Eu'\beta)\Delta E\pi \geq 0 \\ h_i + \sum_{j \neq i} h_j \leq \bar{H} \end{array} \right\} \text{ complementarily} \tag{15}$$

$$(1 - \alpha_i)f^i_1 \Delta Eu_i + (Eu'\theta\alpha f^i_1 - Eu'w)\Delta E\pi = 0. \tag{16}$$

It is clear that $\ell_i = h_i = 0$ will not maximize Γ_i; for, with strictly positive expected output from the tenancy, there will always be some (α, β) that will yield gains for both parties. Hence from (14) we get

$$\Delta Eu_i = (Eu')\Delta E\pi. \qquad (17)$$

Comparing this result with its counterpart in the principal–agent setting, namely equation (6), the ratio $\Delta E\pi/\Delta Eu_i$ plays the role of λ, the dual variable associated with the reservation utility constraint $Eu_i(y) \geq u(w)$ in that setting. This is as it should be; for λ/n is the reduction in the landlord's expected profits that would result from a unit increase in a single tenant's expected utility.

As before, $\alpha_i > 0$ implies $Eu'(\theta/Eu') < 1$; so that from (13), $\alpha_i = 0$. Here too, the landlord bears all risk, which is in keeping with the fact that the Nash solution is (constrained) efficient. Substituting into (15) and using (17), we get $f_2^i \Delta Eu_i > 0$; so that all of the land not 'earmarked' for other tenants goes to tenant i, as intuition would suggest. Moreover, from (16), we get $f_1^i = w$. Now, by symmetry, all tenants will receive tenancies of the same size, namely, $\bar{H}/\bar{N}$. Hence the allocation of resources in production will be identical in the principal–agent and the bargaining game settings.

Where they differ, of course, is in the distribution of the gains from co-operation; in particular, the principal–agent solution calls for $\Delta Eu = 0$. With $\alpha = 0$, $h_i = \bar{H}/\bar{N}$, and ℓ such that $f_1(\ell, \bar{H}/\bar{N}; 1) = w$, the value of β must be chosen to satisfy (17). We have

$$\Delta Eu = u'(y)(f + \beta\bar{H}/\bar{N}) \qquad (17')$$

where $y = -\beta\bar{H}/\bar{n} - w\ell + w$ and the expectations operator has been dropped, as y is non-stochastic in this case. Moreover, as the tenant's co-operative and disagreement payoffs are both riskless, the difference in the utilities they afford him is simply the difference in their monetary values. Hence, $\Delta Eu = y - w = -(\beta\bar{H}/\bar{n} + w\ell)$, and $u' \equiv 1$. Substituting into (17'), we get

$$\beta\bar{H}/\bar{N} = -(f - w\ell)/2; \qquad (18)$$

that is, the landlord pays the tenant one-half of the difference between the expected value of the output produced on the tenancy and all labour costs. In the absence of incentive problems, and given their respective disagreement strategies, 'splitting the difference' is a natural and plausible outcome, the landlord providing the land and the tenant the non-tradable.

The absence of incentive problems permits the risk-neutral party to absorb all risk, so that the contractual parameter β operates as a purely redistributive instrument, transferring utility from one party to the other without affecting output. Thus, the utility possibility frontier (UPF) is a straight line with a slope of (minus) unity. In Figure 4.1, AB is the section of the UPF along which both parties do at least as well as their respective disagreement payoffs. The disagreement point, D, is $[u(w), \underline{V}]$, and the set of all feasible outcomes is the triangle ABD. The outcome in the principal–agent setting is point A, while the bargaining outcome is point C. Clearly, if the tenant possesses no

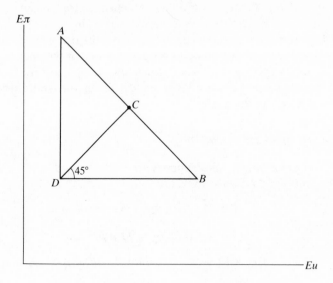

Fig. 4.1 Outcomes when monitoring is costless

power to damage the landlord in the sense discussed above, D and A will coincide and the feasible set will contract to the disagreement point. In that case, the outcomes in the principal–agent and bargaining cases will be identical in all respects; otherwise they will be identical up to a side-payment, which is the main result of this section.

3. Incentives

Now suppose that it is prohibitively costly for the landlord to monitor inputs of labour. Then the level of such inputs will no longer be specified as part of the contract, but will be chosen by the tenant in the light of the incentives he faces. Both parties will, of course, be aware of this, and the terms of the contract will be influenced by consideration of their effects on incentives.

The tenant's problem is to

$$\max_{\ell} \; Eu(y)$$

where, at the optimum, $Eu(y) \geq u(w)$ if the contract is to be attractive. The tenant's FOC is

$$\left.\begin{array}{r} EU'\theta\alpha f_1 - EU'w < 0 \\ \ell \geq 0 \end{array}\right\} \text{ complementarily,} \qquad (19)$$

from which it is immediately apparent that $\alpha > 0$; for if $\alpha = 0$, the tenant will not work the tenancy ($\ell = 0$), so that no output will be produced.

Moreover, with $\alpha = 0$, the tenant will not accept a contract specifying $\beta > 0$, as he can do better by choosing wage employment. Thus, prohibitively costly monitoring results in a displacement of risk from the risk-neutral to the risk-averse party; for without a share in output, the tenant will lack incentives. Hence the necessity of incentives has profound consequences for the terms of the contract, whether they are chosen unilaterally by the landlord or are the outcome of a bargaining game.

3.1. The principal–agent solution

Let $\ell^o = \text{argmax}\{Eu(y)\}$, and suppose that $\ell^o = \ell^o(\alpha, \beta, h; \cdot)$ is differentiable. From (4) and (19), the FOC are

$$n\{-f + (1 - \alpha)f_1\,\ell^o_\alpha\} + \lambda Eu'\theta f = 0 \tag{20}$$

$$n\{(1 - \alpha)f_1\ell^o_\beta + h\} - \lambda Eu'h = 0 \tag{21}$$

$$n\{(1 - \alpha)(f_1\ell^o_h + f_2) + \beta\} + \lambda(Eu'\theta\alpha f_2 - Eu'\beta) - \mu n = 0 \tag{22}$$

$$(1 - \alpha)f + \beta h + \mu h - \nu = 0. \tag{23}$$

We begin by proving that the landlord's optimum entails the tenant doing no better than wage employment, that is $\lambda > 0$, if the tenant's absolute risk aversion (ARA) is constant or weakly decreasing. Suppose, on the contrary, that $\lambda = 0$. Then, from (20) and (21), we have $f = (1 - \alpha)f_1\,\ell^o_\alpha$ and $(1 - \alpha)f_1\ell^o_\beta + h = 0$. Hence, $\ell^o_\alpha > 0$, $\ell^o_\beta < 0$, and $\alpha < 1$. With $\ell > 0$, total differentiation of (19) yields

$$\ell^o_\alpha = -\{Eu'\theta f_1 + Eu''(\theta\alpha f_1 - w)\theta f\}/D \tag{24}$$

and

$$\ell^o_\beta = \{Eu''(\theta\alpha f_1 - w)h\}/D \tag{25}$$

where $D = Eu'\theta f_{11} + Eu''(\theta\alpha f_1 - w)^2 < 0$, by the concavity of $f(\cdot)$ and $u(\cdot)$. On the widely accepted premiss that absolute risk aversion is non-increasing with income, it can be shown that $Eu''(\theta\alpha f_1 - w) \geq 0$, with strict equality if absolute risk aversion is constant (Srinivasan 1972). Hence, $\ell^o_\beta \leq 0$; so that, if ARA is constant, $h > 0$ implies $\lambda > 0$ in (21), which is a contradiction. It follows that $\lambda = 0$ requires decreasing absolute risk aversion (DARA), which implies $\ell^o_\beta < 0$. An increase in the level of the fixed payment by the tenant must reduce inputs of labour if the tenant is to do better than his reservation level of utility.

Where ℓ^o_α is concerned, inspection of (24) reveals that it is certainly positive if u'' is sufficiently small everywhere. Specifically, however, $\lambda = 0$ implies $\ell^o_\beta/h = -\ell^o_\alpha/f$. From (24) and (25), this implies

$$Eu'\theta f_1/f = Eu''(\theta\alpha f_1 - w)(1 - \theta).$$

From (19), this may be written as

$$Eu'(w/\alpha f) = -Eu''(\theta - \rho)(\theta - 1) \tag{26}$$

where $\rho \equiv Eu'(\theta/Eu') < 1$, by virtue of $\alpha > 0$. If $u(\cdot)$ is weakly concave and/or the dispersion of θ is sufficiently small, the right-hand side of (26) will be small. Now, without loss of generality, we may normalize u' to unity at the mean of θ; so that, under the said conditions, the left-hand side will not fall much short of $w/\alpha f$. In both cases, although absolute risk aversion is decreasing, it cannot vary a good deal over the range of outcomes. Hence, $\lambda = 0$ can be ruled out in these circumstances.

We turn, therefore, to the case in which $\lambda > 0$. Proceeding as in Section 2.1, we see from (6) and (21) that, despite prohibitively costly monitoring, β will have purely redistributive effects if $\ell_\beta^0 = 0$, that is, if ARA is constant. From (20) and (21), we get

$$\frac{Eu'\theta}{Eu'} = \frac{1 - (1 - \alpha)f_1(\ell_\alpha^0/f)}{1 + (1 - \alpha)f_1(\ell_\beta^0/h)}. \tag{27}$$

As $\alpha > 0$, $Eu'(\theta/Eu') < 1$. Hence, $\alpha < 1$; that is, the tenant will bear some but not all risk. The landlord's optimum is such that an increase in α would induce the tenant to use more labour ($\ell_\alpha^0 > 0$). Also, the value of $-(\ell_\alpha^0/\ell_\beta^0)$ is less than the expected value of the average product of land, f/h.

Where the size of each tenancy is concerned, suppose that the optimal number of tenants, from the landlord's point of view, is less than $\bar{N}$, so that $\nu = 0$. Then substituting for μ in (22) and using (19), we have

$$- n[(1 - \alpha)\{f - \ell^0 f_1(\ell_h^0 h/\ell^0) - h f_2\}] + \lambda Eu'h\{(wf_2/f_1) - \beta\} = 0. \tag{28}$$

By Euler's theorem, the first term on the left-hand side of (28) will be non-positive if $\ell_h^0(h/\ell^0) \leq 1$, even if non-tradables are not productive ($f_3 = 0$). Suppose, therefore, that an increase in h induces an equiproportional increase in ℓ^0. If $f_3 = 0$, this will induce an equiproportional increase in $(y - w)$. If, further, relative risk aversion (RRA) is non-decreasing with y, then DARA implies that $Eu'\theta/Eu'$ must have fallen as a result of the increase in h (Srinivasan 1972). But this is incompatible with $Eu'\theta/Eu' = w/\alpha f_1$; for an equiproportional increase in ℓ and h will leave f_1 unchanged if $f_3 = 0$ and will lower it if $f_3 > 0$. Hence, increasing relative risk aversion (IRRA) and DARA, which are Arrow's (1971) two postulates, imply that $\{\ell_h^0(h/\ell^0)\} < 1$.

Several interesting conclusions follow. First, $\lambda = 0$ will not satisfy (28). Thus, the conditions under which one can claim that the tenant will do no better than wage employment are considerably enlarged beyond those established above. Second, $wf_2 > \beta f_1$, or

$$\frac{w}{f_1} > \frac{\beta}{f_2}. \tag{29}$$

As $1 > Eu'(\theta/Eu') = w/\alpha f_1 > w/f_1$, the expected value of the marginal product of land is greater than β, and is greater relative to β than the expected value of the marginal product of labour is to w. Third, even if non-tradables are not productive, the (unrestricted) optimal size of tenancy, h^o, may yield a demand for tenants in excess of $\bar{N}$. In that case, the best the landlord can do is to allocate $\bar{H}/\bar{N}$ hectares to each of the $\bar{N}$ available tenants. Moreover, as $\nu > 0$, tenants will then possess the power to damage the landlord by withdrawing into wage employment, and once more a bargaining situation arises.

Before tackling the bargaining outcome, however, a comment on the finding that tenants may possess such power, even when non-tradables are not productive, is called for. As we saw earlier, when labour inputs are costlessly monitorable, it is profitable for the landlord so to arrange matters that he bears all risks. When monitoring is prohibitively costly, the absence of a complete set of insurance markets makes such an arrangement unprofitable; for unless he bears some risk, the tenant will lack incentives. As the size of his tenancy diminishes, the burden of risk on the tenant will grow lighter, for the simple reason that a progressively larger fraction of his total income will be earned from riskless wage employment. For the landlord, there will also be favourable incentive effects. Hence, even if non-tradables are not productive, so that there are constant returns to scale in land and labour alone, it may still be advantageous to the landlord to engage a large number of tenants. If there are not enough to realize the optimal size of tenancy, their limited willingness to bear risk gives each one of them some power over him.

3.2. The Nash bargaining solution

We proceed as in Section 2.2, with one difference: ℓ is no longer a contractual variable; instead, $\ell^o = \ell^o(\alpha, \beta, h; w)$ solves (19). Hence the outcome of the game is the contract (α_i, β_i, h_i) that maximizes Γ_i subject to $\ell^o = \ell^o(\cdot)$. The FOC are

$$\left.\begin{array}{r} \{-f + (1 - \alpha)f_1\ell^o_\alpha\}\Delta Eu + (Eu'\theta f)\Delta E\pi \leq 0 \\ \alpha \geq 0 \end{array}\right\} \text{ complementarily (30)}$$

$$\{h + (1 - \alpha)f_1\ell^o_\beta\}\Delta Eu + (Eu'h^o)\Delta E\pi = 0 \qquad (31)$$

where the index i has been dropped and, by symmetry, $h = \bar{H}/\bar{N}$. Clearly, $\alpha > 0$ if the tenant is to work the tenancy. Also, if $E\pi > 0$ in the principal–agent solution, then, by continuity, there will exist some contract such that ΔEu and $\Delta E\pi$ are both positive. Hence from (30) and (31) we have (27); but the value of (α, β) is not the same as that in the principal–agent case, by virtue of $\Delta Eu > 0$.

In this connection, the case of constant absolute risk aversion provides a useful benchmark; for $\ell^o_\beta = 0$ in this case, so that changes in β will affect the distribution of utilities without affecting incentives. This suggests that, as in

Section 2, the principal–agent and bargaining solutions will be identical up to a side-payment, a result that will now be proved.

As $\ell_\beta^o = 0$, we have

$$1 - \rho = (1 - \alpha)f_1\ell_\alpha^o, \tag{27'}$$

where $\rho \equiv Eu'(\theta/Eu) = w/\alpha f_1$, from (19). Now suppose that α is held constant, but Eu is increased by progressive reductions in β. As $\ell_\beta^o = 0$, it follows at once that ℓ^o will not change. This implies, in turn, that ρ will be constant as the tenant's expected utility is increased in this way. With constant absolute risk aversion, therefore, α is chosen solely with an eye on incentives, while β is used to effect a particular distribution of utilities.

Now suppose that $\nu > 0$, so that the landlord, as principal, chooses $h = \bar{H}/\bar{N}$. Let his optimum choice of the share parameter be α^o. If $\ell_\beta^o = 0$, the tenant's choice of labour input, given $h = \bar{H}/\bar{N}$, will depend on α alone. As $\rho = w/\alpha f_1$, the value of ρ will also depend on α alone. It follows at once that α^o and some value of β will satisfy (30) and (31). Moreover, as the UPF is concave and the iso-Γ contours are convex to the origin, then $(\alpha^o, \bar{H}/\bar{N})$, coupled with that choice of β, is also Nash's solution to the bargaining game.

The parallel with Section 2 can be pursued a little further in this case. From (31), $\Delta Eu = (Eu')\Delta E\pi$. As the utility indicators are invariant with respect to affine transformations, we may, without loss of generality, set Eu' equal to unity at the co-operative solution. With this normalization, $\Delta Eu = \Delta E\pi$, and the bargaining outcome also maximizes the sum of utilities ($\Delta Eu + \Delta E\pi$); for the slope of the UPF at the solution point is then -1 by construction, while that of ($\Delta Eu \cdot \Delta E\pi$) is -1 at all points along the ray $\Delta Eu = \Delta E\pi$.

The solutions to the two games are depicted in Figure 4.2. With β constrained to be zero, the UPF is *DEF*, which is generated by parametric changes in α over the interval $[0, 1]$.[2] Point *E* corresponds to the solution value, α^o, and *F* to $\alpha = 1$, in which case the landlord gets nothing from the contract in question. At *D*, $\alpha = 0$: nothing is produced, so both parties get just their disagreement payoffs. It has been proved above that the solution value of α is strictly less than unity if the tenant is risk-averse. Thus, *E* and *F* will coincide only if the tenant is risk-neutral, in which case the UPF will be linear, moral hazard will disappear, and pure fixed-rent contracts will be chosen. With no restrictions on β, the UPF becomes *AEB*, where *B* lies to the right of *F* by virtue of the fact that, holding the landlord at his disagreement payoff, it is possible to make the tenant strictly better off than he would be under the contract (1, 0) if β can be freely varied. As $\Delta Eu = \Delta E\pi$ by virtue of the normalization $Eu' = 1$, the Nash solution, *C*, is the point at which a 45° ray from *D* intersects *AEB*. The landlord's gain from this contract is the vertical distance from *C* to *DB*. By symmetry, his disagreement payoff is $(\bar{N} - 1)$ times that amount. Finally, note that *AEB* is wholly interior to the first-best UPF, which is attainable when labour inputs are costlessly monitorable, as depicted in Figure 4.1.

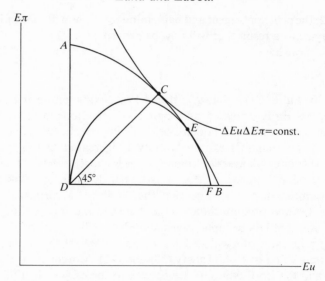

FIG. 4.2   Outcomes with prohibitively costly monitoring and constant absolute risk aversion

I have discussed the case of constant absolute risk aversion at some length because it is a valuable benchmark. If, more generally, there is DARA, then $\partial \rho / \partial \beta < 0$. Hence, if β is decreased to induce a rise in Eu with α held constant, ℓ will also rise: a purely redistributive instrument is no longer available. An important consequence is that the landlord cannot, as the principal, impose a stiff fixed payment on the tenant without blunting incentives and so, for any given value of α, diminishing the expected value of his income from the sharecropping element in the contract. This suggests that the fixed payment will account for a smaller proportion of the landlord's total expected income in the principal–agent game when there is DARA as opposed to constant ARA. In any event, it is most unlikely that with DARA the bargaining and principal–agent solutions are identical up to a side-payment. As both α and β will be employed to shift utility to the landlord in the principal–agent setting, and when thus used both entail disincentive effects, it is plausible that α will be lower and β greater than their counterparts in the bargaining solution.

4. Alternative Solution Concepts

It is well known that the outcome of a game can be rather sensitive to the solution concept employed. Indeed, the foregoing comparison of the principal–agent and Nash bargaining solutions exemplifies this point quite sharply. It is also pertinent, however, to compare Nash's with other solutions to the bargaining problem.

One of Nash's axioms, namely, independence of irrelevant alternatives, has come in for some criticism (see e.g. Luce and Raiffa 1957). Kalai and Smorodinsky (1975) have suggested replacing this axiom with an axiom of monotonicity. The latter states that if, for a given level of utility obtained by one player, the maximum feasible level attainable by the other is increased, then the solution should be such that the second player's utility will also be greater. They proved that only one solution satisfies this axiom, which has the following representation in the space of utilities. Among all points on the UPF, let Eu^* and $E\pi^*$ be the respective maximal levels of the players' utilities subject to the other getting at least his disagreement payoff. Then the solution point is the intersection of the line joining the disagreement point to $(Eu^*, E\pi^*)$ with the UPF. Kalai and Smorodinsky note that this solution was arrived at experimentally by Crott (1971).

The solutions are compared in Figure 4.3, which is simply Figure 4.2 with *DEF* deleted to reduce clutter. Now, for any co-operative outcome, the two parties' gains from co-operation relative to their respective disagreement payoffs are independent of all other contracts. Hence all co-operative outcomes can be depicted relative to a common disagreement point for the purposes of finding and comparing solutions. Note that $E\pi^*$ is associated with point A, the principal–agent solution, while Eu^* is associated with point B. The point S is the pair $(Eu^*, E\pi^*)$, and point K on the UPF is the bargaining solution of Kalai and Smorodinsky. By virtue of the normalization

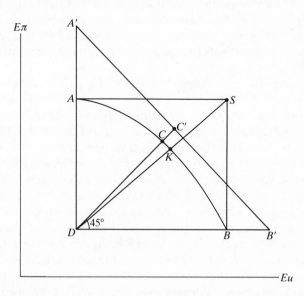

FIG. 4.3   Nash and Kalai–Smorodinsky bargaining solutions when there is constant absolute risk aversion

$Eu' = 1$, the Nash solution is such that $\Delta Eu = \Delta E\pi$, as represented by point C. However, if incentives matter and the players are not equally risk-averse, there is no reason for supposing that $AD = BD$, even in the case of constant absolute risk aversion. Hence, in general, K and C will not coincide.

In the case of constant absolute risk aversion, which is depicted in Figure 4.3, the argument establishing that A and C are identical up to a side-payment also establishes that C and K are likewise; for all points on ACB have this property in the case in question. In the absence of incentive problems, the UPF will be linear with slope (minus) one. Thus, the two bargaining solutions coincide as point C on the first-best UPF, as depicted in Figure 4.1. This frontier is drawn as $A'B'$ in Figure 4.3, and it is lies wholly to the north-east of the second-best UPF, ACB. The axiom of monotonicity implies that, were monitoring to become costless, thereby making a first-best allocation feasible at C', both parties would gain. In the case of the Nash solution, this would not always be true, although it is evidently so if there is constant absolute risk aversion. In this connection, Kalai and Smorodinsky provide a numerical example of a potential Pareto improvement in which one of the players is worse off under Nash's solution to buttress their argument that, as an axiom, monotonicity is superior to independence of irrelevant alternatives.

5. Interlinking and Innovation

An interesting and important question that arises naturally from these comparisons is whether certain qualitative outcomes are sensitive to the solution concept. In the present context, the interlinking of transactions and the adoption of innovations are two qualitative features of the agrarian economy that merit particular attention.

In the principal–agent setting, the choice of whether to interlink transactions is the principal's. Since he is always free to 'unbundle' an interlinked contract into separate deals, he cannot do worse by interlinking them. Indeed, it will usually be profitable for him to insist on interlinking. The intuition for this claim is apparent from the analysis of incentives in Section 3. If monitoring is prohibitively costly, then for any given level of the tenant's expected utility, the landlord will be strictly better off with two instruments (α, β) than with either alone, provided each has an influence on the tenant's actions which is not completely collinear with the other's. Interlinking enlarges the set of instruments at the principal's disposal and will, therefore, usually enable him to sharpen incentives without adverse effects on the sharing of risks. In that case the feasible set of utilities will be enlarged too, in such a way that the UPF with interlinking will lie wholly to the north-east of that in its absence. An exception to this result is the case in which the agent's actions are costlessly monitorable and enforceable, when a first-best outcome is attainable. But in this case there would be no rationale for interlinking.

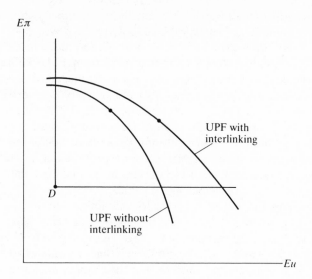

FIG. 4.4 Interlinked contracts are chosen in both principal–agent and (Nash) bargaining settings

In a bargaining situation, the qualitative choice of whether to have an interlinked contract will be the object of bargaining just like the values of the continuous contractual parameters. For as the Nash solution is (constrained) efficient, the outcome must be sought over all feasible arrangements. It follows at once that an interlinked contract will emerge from a bargaining game if, and only if, an interlinked contract is chosen by the principal in a principal–agent setting. For it is always possible to find a higher value of the product $\Delta Eu \cdot \Delta E\pi$ on a UPF that lies farther from the disagreement point than on one that lies closer. This result is depicted in Figure 4.4.

It should be noted that, if the introduction of interlinking induces a sufficiently non-neutral shift in the UPF, the disadvantaged party could wind up worse off under Nash's solution. By definition, this cannot happen under the axiom of monotonicity, which illustrates an importance difference between the solution concepts of Nash and Kalai–Smorodinsky.

Turning to the adoption of innovations, the possibilities are somewhat richer. Some innovations, coupled with feasible contractual arrangements, may induce a Pareto-improving shift of the UPF, like that depicted in Figure 4.4. In that case they will be enthusiastically adopted, whether the decision is the principal's or the outcome of a (Nash) bargaining game. In the light of the previous discussion, it is clear that the shift thus induced in the UPF depends not only on the character of the innovation, but also on the degree to which the available contractual instruments can separate incentive considerations from those of risk-sharing. For example, if a purely redistributive instrument is available, any innovation that yields an increase in expected output net of costs will be adopted.

In the absence of such redistributive possibilities, many mean-increasing innovations may induce strongly non-neutral shifts in the UPF. Suppose, for example, that an innovation also increases risk. If the tenant's absolute risk aversion is decreasing with income, his willingness to adopt the innovation will diminish if a large fixed payment is imposed. If, further, the character of the innovation is such that the tenant needs a large share of output for adequate incentives, it may turn out that the landlord cannot impose a fixed payment sufficiently large to make adoption profitable to himself without making the contract unattractive to the tenant. In that case, the innovation would be rejected in a principal–agent game.

In the neighbourhood of the (Nash) bargaining solution on the UPF without the innovation, however, the innovation may shift the UPF outwards, so that, locally at least, both parties stand to gain from adopting it. The reason why the shift may take this form is that, not only will the tenant be better off in the bargaining outcome, but the changes in contractual terms that make him so will also plausibly make him more willing to bear risk. In this connection, the discussion of DARA in Section 3 is certainly relevant. Thus, an innovation that is shunned by the principal may nevertheless be adopted as the outcome of a bargaining game. This possibility is depicted in Figure 4.5. By switching the labels on the axes, it is also clear that the converse can be true, too.

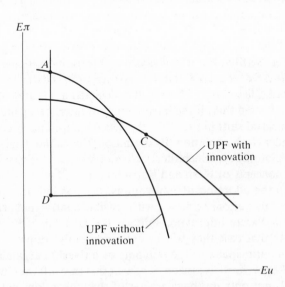

FIG. 4.5 An innovation whose acceptance depends on the solution concept

6. Concluding Remarks

In pursuing this comparison of the principal–agent and bargaining solutions to a tenancy contract, the tenant's power, if any, over the landlord has played a central role. It is important at the very outset, therefore, to establish whether the situation being analysed is one in which the agent may possess power over the principal. Even in an agrarian economy, the setting of their dealings may differ considerably: landlord–tenant, employer–worker, trader–cultivator, borrower–lender, and interlinked variations thereof are all relationships that need separate scrutiny.

As for the detailed results themselves, it has been shown that, when the tenant's actions are costlessly monitorable, the solutions are identical up to a side-payment. The risk-neutral landlord bears all risk, and resource allocation is fully efficient. In this case utility is also completely transferable. When monitoring is prohibitively costly, the solutions diverge, except in the special case of constant absolute risk aversion, when they are also identical up to a side-payment. With decreasing absolute risk aversion, it appears that the bargaining solution(s) will involve both a higher output share for, and a lower fixed payment by, the tenant, a result that stems from the fact that incentives and risk-sharing cannot then be separated. Moreover, the bargaining solutions of Nash and Kalai–Smorodinsky no longer fully coincide, even if absolute risk aversion is constant.

Another interesting result is that, if a principal chooses an interlinked contract, interlinking will also emerge from a (Nash) bargaining game. However, some innovations that would be blocked by a principal may be adopted in a bargaining outcome, and conversely. This finding exemplifies the point that certain qualitative outcomes are also sensitive to the choice of solution concept.

Finally, a practical point: although the solution of Kalai and Smorodinsky is simple to represent in the space of utilities, it is not easy to calculate in the space of contractual parameters; for, unlike Nash's solution, it requires that the utility possibility frontier be derived in explicit form, which is usually very hard to do. Thus, while the axiom of independence of irrelevant alternatives may remain controversial, Nash's solution has a significant advantage where analytical tractability is concerned.

NOTES

1. If $u(\cdot)$ is strictly concave, u' will be negatively correlated with θ, since y is increasing in θ if $\alpha > 0$.
2. *DEF* has been depicted as continuous, smooth, and strictly concave. Both parties'

payoffs are continuous in α. Smoothness seems reasonable in view of the assumptions on $f(\cdot)$ and $u(\cdot)$. Strict concavity is more open to question: but if E is suitably defined, nothing of importance hinges on it. That both parties are strictly better off than at D for all $\alpha \in (0, 1)$ with $\beta = 0$ is proved as follows. For any $\alpha > 0$, the concavity of $f(\cdot)$ ensures that there exists an $\ell > 0$ such that

$$y - w = \alpha\theta f - w\ell > 0, \quad \forall\theta > 0.$$

For the landlord, any $\alpha < 1$ and $\ell > 0$ ensure that

$$\Delta\pi = (1 - \alpha)\theta f > 0, \quad \forall\theta > 0,$$

which establishes the claim.

5.

Contracts with Eviction in Infinitely Repeated Principal–Agent Relationships

Bhaskar Dutta, Debraj Ray, and Kunal Sengupta

1. Introduction

There is by now considerable evidence to suggest that labour markets do not conform to the usual textbook paradigm of a uniform wage for a pool of homogeneous workers. Involuntary unemployment is an instance of such non-uniformity. The unemployed would like to work at the going wage rate, and in fact possess the abilities to do so, but the labour market does not absorb them. Evidence from a variety of sources also indicates that labour markets are often divided into submarkets for 'permanent' labour and 'casual' or 'spot' labour.[1] Moreover, it is usually the case that permanent workers earn wages (or utility levels) that are higher than those of their casual counterparts, although there may be no intrinsic differences in abilities between the two groups.[2]

In a situation of involuntary unemployment, why do wages not fall to clear labour markets? In the case of permanent labour, why does the employer not lower the wages of permanent workers to a level even below that of casual workers? After all, risk-averse workers would presumably be willing to insure against the vagaries of the spot market, such as the possibility of unemployment or, more generally, an uncertain wage. The task of this chapter is to explore one avenue of research that bears on these questions, namely, *the use of endogenously created utility differentials as an incentive device for workers who can be only imperfectly monitored*. We are also going to restrict ourselves to models that have a strong bearing on rural labour markets in developing economies.[3]

It should be mentioned that the particular direction that we take deliberately excludes a sizeable literature that deals with involuntary unemployment or even with permanent labour contracts in rural economies. One paper is simply not sufficient to handle all the issues. There is, for example, a literature on unemployment based on costly labour turnover, and more generally on 'efficiency wage' considerations.[4] In the specific context of developing

We are grateful to Shubhashis Gangopadhyay for helpful comments on an earlier draft.

economies, nutrition-based theories of the labour market have played a
significant role in our understanding of unemployment and of permanent
labour in rural markets.[5] We mention these to place the present paper in
proper perspective.

Our concern is, then, with a branch of the literature that explains 'equilibrium' wages higher than the market-clearing wage as an incentive device.
Specifically, we are concerned with papers that study principal–agent
relationships where the principal cannot directly monitor the agent's effort.
The principal must therefore offer 'reward' or incentive schemes that will
attempt to induce the agent to supply the 'right' quantity of effort. This
would be a standard principal–agent model,[6] were it not for the fact that
among the various rewards and threats that the principal can offer is also the
possibility of termination of the contract, or, briefly, *eviction*. Of course, for
such a threat to be credible in a dynamic context, the agent must be
replaceable.

Our basic setting is, therefore, a situation of 'surplus labour', where a principal has access to a ready supply of agents at a given level of reservation
utility.[7] The threat of eviction is then one of the instruments that the principal
might choose to use.

The questions that arise in this chapter concern the use of eviction threats
in equilibrium. Is contract termination with positive probability part of an
equilibrium incentive scheme? Or can the principal devise better schemes that
do not involve eviction? To this end, in Section 2 we briefly review some of
the literature in this area and evaluate their merits and inadequacies. We find
that for answering these basic questions in a satisfactory way the existing
literature is not adequate, for reasons that are spelled out below. In Section 3
and in the rest of the paper, we set out a model that attempts to remedy some
of these deficiencies.

Readers uninitiated into this branch of the literature might well be wonder-
ing what contracts with eviction have to do with the phenomena of involuntary unemployment or permanent labour. This connection is so important
that, at the risk of belabouring the obvious (to some), we make it explicit. The
crucial point is this: *if contracts involving eviction threats exist in an
economy, then there will be utility differentials between workers of similar
abilities but engaged in different occupations.* Consider a simple example
where there is only one type of job (and unemployment) and all workers are
homogeneous. If worker effort on the job is to be partly maintained by
eviction threats, then there *must* be a cost to being unemployed. However,
this cost is positive only if the utility of being unemployed is less than the
utility of being employed. In a more complicated scenario, with many different jobs (but nevertheless a homogeneous working population), the endogenous presence of contracts with eviction would suggest that: (1) there are
utility differences between jobs performed by otherwise identical workers;
(2) jobs where monitoring of effort is *more* difficult will generate *higher*

utilities to those workers that get them; (3) jobs with perfect monitoring will entail workers being paid their reservation utility (in a labour-surplus economy), and will therefore best qualify for the title of 'casual labour jobs'; and (4) 'permanent' labour, or labour whose remunerative contracts are renewed with some probability, will exist in jobs that are difficult to supervise or monitor.[8]

None of these implications, attractive though they may seem, can be drawn unless we have a satisfactory theory of contracts in a model that allows for strategic interaction between the principal and the agent. To throw some light on such a theory is the task of the subsequent sections.

2. A Brief Survey of the Literature

There is a large literature[9] which suggests that the threat of eviction, that is, the possibility of non-renewal of a contract, may act as an incentive device in principal–agent relationships where the principal cannot directly monitor the agent's effort. In this section we briefly discuss a part of this literature, restricting attention to those papers that have a direct bearing on rural labour markets where the principal (landlord) has access to a ready supply of labour at a fixed reservation utility. We emphasize at this stage that our main concern is with the structural features of the various models, and not so much with the specific results or comparative-static exercises reported in these papers.

The basic structure underlying principal–agent relationships and the attendant moral hazard problem is too well known to deserve any detailed explication. Output is a function of the agent's effort and a random variable representing exogenous uncertainty. The agent can increase expected output by increasing effort, but at some cost to himself since effort involves disutility. Moreover, the principal can observe only output and not the amount of effort put in by the agent. Hence, the reward schedule to the agent can be conditioned only on output, and not on effort.

The risk-neutral principal's aim is to devise a contract that maximizes his expected payoff net of payments to the agent. Since agents are assumed to be *risk-averse*, the 'obvious' solution of a fixed rental contract (which would enable the agent to reap all incremental benefits from increased output) is a non-starter. At the other extreme, one-period pure wage contracts provide absolutely no incentive to the agent to put in effort. Not surprisingly, the institution of sharecropping, which enables some sharing of risk and also provides partial effort incentives, has been interpreted as an appropriate contract in this setting.[10]

Of course, if the principal and agent enter into a *repeated* relationship, then several other possibilities emerge. In particular, the principal can extract greater effort today by promising higher rewards in the future if the agent's performance as measured by realized output in the current period is deemed satisfactory. Two caveats are necessary. First, a 'better' tomorrow must mean a reward higher than what the agent can get from other sources of employment. Second, such incentives must be accompanied by a threat to terminate the contract if the agent's performance is below the 'minimum' performance standard stipulated by the principal.

This intuition has been used by Eswaran and Kotwal (1985c) to provide a rationale for the institution of permanent workers. These exist 'to elicit loyalty and trustworthiness from hired workers, so that they can be entrusted with important tasks that are inherently difficult to monitor', and are accomplished by offering contracts that provide them with utility levels higher than their opportunity levels. We briefly look at their model.

Assume that a single crop is produced each year, with agricultural operations involving two distinct periods during the year. Type 1 tasks are performed during the first period, and these *cannot be monitored*. The second period involves routine type 2 tasks that are relatively easy to supervise. An employed worker in each period is required to supply $\bar{e}$ units of effort. However, unless he is monitored, a worker will put in zero effort since effort gives rise to disutility. Although type 1 tasks cannot be monitored, the landlord can accurately infer a worker's effort in period 1 at the end of period 2.[11] In order to provide incentives, the landlord offers type 1 workers a *permanent* contract over the infinite horizon in which the worker receives a wage w_p per period provided he has not shirked in type 1 tasks. If the worker does shirk, then he is fired or evicted at the end of the crop year. Assume also that casual workers are hired only in period 2 at a wage of w_c.

It is sufficient to look at the supply side of the labour market in order to understand the nature of incentive contracts in this setting. Let $V(w,e)$ be the indirect utility function of a typical worker who works for one period at a wage rate of w and an effort level e. V must be a decreasing function of e since effort gives rise to disutility. Suppose β is the *per period* discount factor.

The present value utility of a permanent worker who never shirks is given by

$$V_p^N = V(w_p, \bar{e})/(1 - \beta). \tag{1}$$

The corresponding value for a casual worker is

$$V_c = \beta V(w_c, \bar{e})/(1 - \beta^2). \tag{2}$$

What will guarantee that a permanent worker never shirks? Since any shirking is bound to end in termination of the contract at the end of the second period, the decision to shirk implies that effort level in period 1 will be put to zero. Hence a shirker's discounted lifetime utility will be

$$V_p^S = V(w_p, 0) + \beta V(w_p, \bar{e}) + \beta^2 V_c. \tag{3}$$

In order to ensure that permanent workers never shirk, the landlord will have to guarantee that

$$V_p^N \geq V_p^S. \tag{4}$$

But, then (4) is equivalent to

$$V(w_p,\bar{e})/(1 - \beta) \geq V(w_p,0) + \beta V(w_p,\bar{e}) + \beta^3 V(w_c, \bar{e})/(1 - \beta^2)$$

So

$$(1 - \beta + \beta^2)V(w_p,\bar{e}) \geq (1 - \beta)V(w_p,0) + \beta^3 V(w_c,\bar{e})/(1 + \beta)$$
$$> (1 - \beta)V(w_p,\bar{e}) + \beta^3 V(w_c,\bar{e})/(1 + \beta)$$

Hence

$$V_p^N > V_c \tag{5}$$

Hence, at any w_p that provides permanent workers with an incentive to put in the required amount of work, the permanent worker receives a strictly higher utility in a permanent contract than in a series of spot contracts.

The utility differential in the contracts between permanent and casual workers is necessitated by the need to provide incentives to workers who cannot be monitored. The threat of being caught shirking and hence being thrown into the casual labour market at a lower utility earning is an effective monitoring device as far as the permanent worker is concerned. Notice that this also implies that there is *involuntary unemployment* in the permanent labour market, since casual workers will voluntarily work for less than w_p in the first period, but are unable to land such jobs.

In an earlier paper, Shapiro and Stiglitz (1984) had essentially put forward the same explanation for involuntary unemployment in a general equilibrium setting. In this model, landlords cannot monitor workers perfectly, but can detect shirking with a probability q. Now, suppose w_c is the market-clearing wage. If a worker receives w_c, then eviction represents an empty threat since he can shirk, be fired, and get employment on the same terms with another landlord. So in order to induce his workers not to shirk, a landlord will try to pay more than the 'going wage' because eviction must imply a penalty. But, then all landlords will attempt to follow this, thereby raising wages and cutting down the demand for labour. With unemployment, even if all *employed* workers get the same wage, every one has an incentive not to shirk. Given all other things, the equilibrium unemployment rate must be higher, the smaller the probability q of being detected shirking.

The justification for considering *pure wage contracts* rather than contracts in which rewards are contingent on output has been usually couched in terms of a double moral hazard problem, arguing that the principal will, *ex post*, claim that an output necessitating a large payment has simply not occurred! In the rural contact, this 'justification' has little to commend it. For instance, sharecropping and fixed rental contracts are not unknown, and these are clearly contracts where 'wages' are state-contingent. Another reason for not restricting attention to wage contracts is that the *assumption* of such contracts simply begs the question of whether eviction can be part of an equilibrium strategy. If wages are fixed, then the *only* way in which the worker can be induced to work is by fixing wages at levels higher than that obtaining in alternative opportunities, *together* with a threat of eviction. Hence, the results of Eswaran and Kotwal (1985c) or Shapiro and Stiglitz (1984) are not surprising at all.

Bardhan (1984), Singh (1983), and Stiglitz and Weiss (1983) have permitted the landlord greater flexibility in the design of incentive contracts by allowing for contingent contracts. A common feature of these models is that the landlord offers the worker a *two-period* contract. The restriction to two periods is presumably for analytical convenience, since their results can easily be extended to contracts of longer but *finite* duration. We will, however, comment later on the significance of contracts to be of finite duration.

Bardhan's landlord offers a two-period pure sharecropping contract with α being the tenant's crop-share. Suppose $F(x;e)$ is the distribution function for output x given e. F is induced by the distribution of a random variable and the production function. The agent's utility function in terms of income and effort is of the form $u(\alpha x) - Q(e)$, with u being strictly concave and Q strictly convex. Let the agent's opportunity cost be v, the reservation utility level.

In the second period, the landlord's maximization problem is essentially a one-shot problem:

$$\max_{\alpha,e} E\{(1 - \alpha)x\} \tag{6}$$

s. t.

$$e \in \text{argmax } E[u(\alpha x) - Q(e)] \text{ and} \tag{7}$$

$$E\{u(\alpha x)\} - Q(e) \geq v. \tag{8}$$

Bardhan (1984) shows that the expected utility frontier of the landlord and tenant will be of the shape illustrated in Figure 5.1. Hence, if $v < v^*$, it is optimal for the landlord to ensure that the tenant's second-period expected utility, say ϕ^A, exceeds his reservation utility v.

The landlord also stipulates that the tenant will be evicted if the first-period output falls below a critical level $\underline{x}$. Notice that the landlord loses nothing by firing the worker since there are no learning-by-doing effects *and* there is a pool of readily available and identical agents.

The tenant's expected utility from the contract is then given by

$$\max_e \int_0^\infty u(\alpha x)f(x;e)dx - Q(e) + \beta\{\phi^A - (\phi^A - v)F(\underline{x};e)\} \tag{9}$$

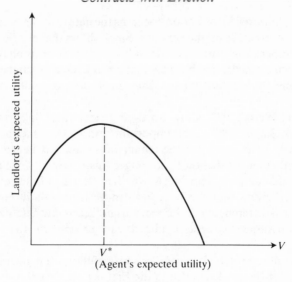

FIG. 5.1

where β is the tenant's discount factor and f is the density of x induced by F. The first-order condition for the tenant is therefore

$$\int_0^\infty u(\alpha x)f_e(x;e)\mathrm{d}x - Q'(e) - \beta(\phi^A - v)F_e(\underline{x},e) = 0. \qquad (10)$$

Since increased effort reduces the probability of output falling below $\underline{x}$, $F_e <$ 0. Since $\phi^A > v$, the sum of the first two terms of (10) is negative. Hence, the threat of eviction does increase the tenant's effort in the first period.

Singh (1983) allows for more general reward schemes, the only restriction being that $r(x)$, the reward to the tenant if realized output is x, must belong to the class of functions of bounded variation which satisfy $c \leq r(x) \leq d + x$, where c and d are real numbers. (The landlord is not constrained to specify the same $r(\cdot)$ in each period.) Thus, the landlord is unable to penalize the tenant to any arbitrary extent, either because there are institutional constraints or because resources available to the tenant are limited. Similarly, the landlord is also constrained in the maximum he can pay the tenant because of 'resource constraints'.

Singh goes on to explore the efforts of asymmetric prior information on the nature of the equilibrium contract. Various kinds of prior information are modelled. In one version, the tenant receives additional information about his reservation utility after signing the contract with the landlord, and he is allowed to alter his action on the basis of such information. In another version, the additional information concerns the nature of the outcome functions for the contract. In all the versions, Singh shows that eviction contracts can serve as superior incentive devices only if the restrictions on $r(x)$ become binding. In other words, if arbitrarily high or low rewards can be offered to the tenant, then the landlord will not find it profitable to employ the threat of dismissal.

Stiglitz and Weiss (1983) allow for even greater flexibility in the reward schedule than Singh (1983) in an important respect. Assume that there are only two levels of output: 0 if the tenant fails, and 1 if he succeeds. The second-period reward function is no longer 'history-free' since the *success wage* in period 2 can vary according to whether the tenant failed or succeeded in period 1. (Failure wages will be zero in both periods in equilibrium.) Another crucial difference with the previous models is that Stiglitz and Weiss (1983) also assume that the landlord can *precommit* the two-period contract.[12]

The landlord's contract also specifies a probability p of being retired in the second period if the worker failed in the first period. It is shown that p can take only the extreme values 0 and 1. Hence, for certain values of the parameters, contracts with eviction again turn out to be effective incentive devices.

As we have remarked earlier, a common feature of these models is that contracts are of finite duration. If contracts cannot be precommitted, then in the last period, both the principal and the agent must be using one-shot equilibrium strategies. Moreover, if there are no constraints on reward functions in Singh's model, or if the reservation utility is high enough in Bardhan's case, the principal will always force the agent down to his reservation utility. Hence, eviction in the second-last period cannot serve as a punitive threat. By the familiar backwards induction argument, there cannot be any eviction in equilibrium in *any* period. Conversely, if the one-shot Nash equilibrium involves agents getting rewards higher than their reservation levels, then the emergence of eviction contracts as incentive devices becomes easily explicable.

We believe that the real test of whether contracts with eviction can be sustained as equilibrium contracts must be sought in formulations where the principal and agent contract over an infinite time-horizon. It is by now well known that infinitely repeated games can sustain many more equilibria than their finite counterparts. Thus, in principle, it is possible that the conditions that guarantee that the principal will use the threat of dismissal as an incentive device in finite-horizon models may no longer turn out to be sufficient for this phenomenon in infinitely repeated games, since some other equilibrium contract may now turn out to be better from the principal's point of view. Against this setting, our result (see Proposition 3 below) that the threat of eviction will be an 'effective' deterrent to shirking, even in cases when the one-shot Nash equilibrium involves the agent getting just his reservation utility, turns out to be a far more powerful rationale for the use of this threat.

Of course, if the principal can precommit contracts, then it no longer follows that the last-period contract (in finite-horizon models) must be a Nash equilibrium. The reason for the emergence of eviction contracts is no longer so transparent. However, the problems of precommitment lie elsewhere. For suppose that the principal solves an infinite-horizon maximization problem at date 0 by choosing a *sequence* of contracts: is there any reason for the agent to believe that future contracts will be honoured by the principal?

In this context, the answer is generally no, and it is easy to see why. Consider, for example, the case where there is no lower bound on contingent wages, with a reservation utility of *M* for the worker. Now, the principal's optimum sequence of contracts will, in general, reward the agent with a 'better' contract sequence if the agent's past performance has been good, and will punish the agent with a 'worse' contract, or with eviction, if past performance has been bad. *However, the value to the agent of the contract sequence, viewed from date 0, must be equal to M.*

Now suppose that the agent is successful in the first period. The optimum contract sequence now dictates a sequence with expected infinite-horizon utility to the agent *strictly greater* than *M*. *But this 'residual' sequence cannot be an optimum for the principal from the new date onwards.* This is the problem of dynamic inconsistency.

In this context, it is very difficult to imagine that the principal will be able effectively to precommit the entire sequence of contracts. In the absence of an adequate legal system designed to enforce such contracts, there is no reason why the agent will believe the pre-announced sequence and act accordingly.

For this reason, it is necessary to model the repeated principal–agent relationship as a game, where the principal 'plays' not only the agents, but also future 'incarnations' of himself.[13]

In view of the remarks made above, we model principal–agent relationships in which the principal uses contingent contracts but cannot precommit contracts beyond the 'current' period.

3. Labour Contracts Involving Threats of Eviction: The Model

In this section we set out the basic model that will be used subsequently.

Our stylized model consists of two types of individuals, the *principal* (or 'employer') and the *agent* (or 'worker'). There is only one principal, but a countable infinity of identical agents. The principal deals with only one agent at any point of time. A switch of agents occurs when the former agent is evicted (or 'fired').

An active agent, that is, an agent currently dealing with the principal, chooses a level of effort *e* between zero and unity. The level of his effort is assumed to be equal to the probability that the job will be *successful* (1 unit of output). *Failure* means that output equals 0. The effort expended by the agent is not observed by the principal. Both observe the realized output.[14]

At each date, the principal offers a one-period contract to the active agent, and lays down conditions under which a new contract will be offered in the next period. *Apart from these, the principal can precommit nothing.*[15]

At the end of each period, the agent is retained or evicted, according to the terms laid down in that contract. The cost of eviction to the principal is taken to be zero. In the next period, the active agent is offered a new contract and the entire process repeats itself.[16]

We end our informal description by describing the two main situations that will concern us. In the first situation, which we call *unlimited liability*, the worker may be paid arbitrarily low wages at any date. That is, there is no restriction on the type of contracts that may be offered to the worker. (Of course, there is always the restriction that the worker must be willing to participate in the offered contract.) The second, more realistic, situation, one of *limited liability*, is of greater interest to us. Here we stipulate that the wages offered in any contract must be uniformly bounded below. In other words, there are limits on what the principal can extract from the agent at any date. Without loss of generality, we take it that in this case wages paid must be non-negative.[17]

We now turn to a more formal description. We assume that the agent has a one-period von-Neumann–Morgenstern utility, which is separable in income and effort, and so is of the form

$$u(w) - Q(e) \tag{11}$$

where $u(w)$ is utility from income w and $Q(e)$ is disutility from effort e. The function u is defined on all of $\mathbb{R}$,[18] and is assumed to be increasing, twice differentiable, and concave. The function Q is increasing, twice differentiable, and convex. In addition, we make the following assumption on Q, for technical ease in the proofs:[19]

$$Q''(e)(1 - e) \text{ is non-decreasing in } e. \tag{12}$$

The assumption in (12) requires, broadly, that disutility be rising at a 'fast enough' rate as effort goes to its maximum level. An example of a disutility function satisfying (12) is $Q(e) = e/(1 - e)$, but the quadratic function $Q(e) = e^2$ does not satisfy (12).

A *contract c* is a pair $(\overline{w}, \overline{p}) = \{(w_0, w_1), (p_0, p_1)\}$ where w_i is the wage paid and p_i is the probability of eviction if output equals i, $i = 0, 1$. Denote by C the set of all possible contracts. Of course, C varies with the context, depending on whether we are considering limited liability situations or not.

Given a contract c, and effort level e, we can write the *one-period* expected utility of the agent as

$$k(c,e) \equiv eu(w_1) + (1 - e)u(w_0) - Q(e). \tag{13}$$

The agent has a discount factor δ, $0 < \delta < 1$, and seeks to maximize the expectation of the infinite-horizon sum of utilities.

We assume that the agent has alternative opportunities that can earn him $m \in \mathbb{R}$ in every period if he does not accept the contract. This number is his *one-period reservation utility*. His (infinite-horizon) *reservation utility* is given by $M \equiv m(1 - \delta)^{-1}$.

The principal is assumed to be risk-neutral. So for a contract $c = (\bar{w},\bar{p})$ and effort level e, his one-period return is given by

$$e(1 - w_1) - (1 - e)w_0. \tag{14}$$

Using a discount factor ρ, $0 < \rho < 1$, the principal seeks to maximize the expectation of the infinite-horizon discounted sum of one-period returns.

4. Strategies and Equilibrium

We conceive of the principal as employing a *strategy* which assigns a contract at each date to every possible history[20] of the repeated relationship up to that date. Similarly, an agent's strategy is a rule that, at each date, when confronted with a history up to that date and a current contract at that date, decides whether or not to accept the current contract. Moreover, if the current contract is accepted, then the rule also assigns the choice of a particular effort level. However, we shall always be concerned with contract sequences that yield the agent at least his infinite-horizon reservation utility, so we shall really be focusing on the effort choice, rather than whether or not to accept the contract.

A combination of strategies, one for each individual, is an *equilibrium* if for each date, and for every history up to that date, no individual can profitably deviate from the action prescribed by his strategy, assuming that all other strategies are given. Hence, the concept of equilibrium being used here is related to Selten's (1975) *subgame perfect Nash equilibrium*, and, to be precise, is that of *sequential equilibrium* (Kreps and Wilson 1982). We will call a strategy $\{S_t\}_{t=0}^{\infty}$ for the principal *stationary* if it prescribes the same contract irrespective of history; that is, for all t and every history h_t, $S_t(h_t) = c \in C$. A *stationary contract* refers to the contract prescribed by a stationary strategy for the principal.

Our model will be concerned with stationary contracts and the structure of such contracts. Readers should note that stationary contracts have received the greatest attention in the literature on eviction. Apart from Eswaran and Kotwal (1985c) and Shapiro and Stiglitz (1984), the list includes Eaton and White (1982), Calvo (1977), and the references in Calvo (1985). In particular, the literature has focused on *stationary wage contracts* with threats of eviction. These are stationary contracts with $w_1 = w_0$, that is, paying a fixed wage regardless of output. As mentioned before, if attention is restricted to stationary wage contracts, then the principal cannot but use eviction as an incentive device.

The real test of whether eviction contracts can be sustained in equilibrium is to see whether 'current incentives' (captured in $w_1 \neq w_0$) can fully substitute for incentives created by the threat to evict. It is for this reason that we restrict ourselves to stationary contracts, so that this trade-off may be explored and understood in detail.

An *equilibrium stationary contract* is a contract that is stipulated by an equilibrium using a stationary strategy for the principal.

Observe that equilibrium stationary contracts are full-blown equilibria in the larger class of strategies. We are allowing the stationary strategy to be 'tested' against *all* other strategies for the principal, whether stationary or not.

Now we define a *maximizing equilibrium stationary contract* (MESC). This is an equilibrium stationary contract which provides the highest return to the principal in the class of all equilibrium stationary contracts. Such contracts are of special interest. In general, there may be many stationary equilibrium contracts, but, as Myerson (1986) suggests, the principal is often in the position to stipulate which equilibrium will be played. So it is reasonable to study an MESC.

Next, we define the *one-shot arrangement*. This is obtained by solving the one-period principal–agent problem, that is, to choose (w_1, w_0) to

$$\max(1 - w_1)\tilde{e} - (1 - \tilde{e})w_0 \tag{15}$$

s. t.

$$\tilde{e} \in \text{argmax } eu(w_1) + (1 - e)u(w_0) - Q(e) \tag{16}$$

and

$$\max_e eu(w_1) + (1 - e)u(w_0) - Q(e) \geq m. \tag{17}$$

This describes the unlimited liability situation. In the limited liability situation, the principal faces the further constraint

$$w_1, w_0 \geq 0. \tag{18}$$

Throughout, we shall assume that there exists *some* choice (w_1, w_0) and e such that (16) and (17) are satisfied (and (18), too, in the limited liability case), *and* the expression in (15) is positive. This is a harmless assumption, but ensures the existence of a contract that is both 'incentive-compatible' for the agent and profitable for the principal.

5. The Results

We first start with a result that is not of interest in itself, but sets the stage for later developments.

PROPOSITION 1. In both the limited and the unlimited liability models, there is a unique solution to the one-shot principal–agent problem.

(a) In the unlimited liability problem, the agent's utility from the contract is exactly m.

(b) In the limited liability problem, there exists $m^* > 0$ such that the agent's utility from the contract is strictly greater than m if $m < m^*$, and is equal to m if $m \geq m^*$.

Denote by $q(m)$ and $v(m)$ the one-period payoff to the principal and agent respectively under the one-shot problem when the reservation utility of the agent equals m. We shall use the same notation for both the limited liability and the unlimited problems, but the particular context will be made clear.

Finally, we define *stationary contracts with eviction*. Consider a stationary contract $c \equiv \{(w_1, w_0), (p_1, p_0)\}$. It is easy to check that, given the reservation utility M, there is a unique number V that solves the equation

$$V \equiv \max_e [eu(w_1) + (1 - e)u(w_0) - Q(e) +$$
$$\delta\{e(1 - p_1) + (1 - e)(1 - p_0)\}V + \delta\{ep_1 + (1 - e)p_0\}M]. \quad (19)$$

Equation (19) has a standard interpretation. The total infinite-horizon expected utility to the agent from a contract c is today's expected utility (the first three terms on the RHS) plus the discounted infinite-horizon expected utilities from next period on, conditional on retention or eviction (the fourth and fifth terms on the RHS).

We say that c is a *stationary contract with eviction* if $V > M$. That is, conditional on retention, the expected utility to the agent strictly exceeds the reservation utility. If for some reason such a contract were offered to a *subset* of identical agents, the following implications may be drawn.

1. The 'unemployment' suffered by those agents who do not receive the contract is strictly involuntary; for there is non-identical treatment of identical agents (as in Dasgupta and Ray 1986, and Shapiro and Stiglitz 1984).
2. The threat of eviction will act as an incentive to work; for there is a divergence between the utilities of 'employment' and 'unemployment'.

These are important implications. But what are their behavioural foundations? This is what we discuss below.

Consider, first, the unlimited liability case.

PROPOSITION 2. Under unlimited liability, there exists no stationary equilibrium contract with eviction. The MESC is given by any contract composed of the one-shot arrangement and arbitrary probabilities of eviction conditional on success and failure.

Several remarks are in order to understand this result. First, to restate the proposition, we are arguing that, with unlimited liability, there can be no stationary contract that extracts some effort via the threat to fire *and* is simultaneously an equilibrium. This result holds irrespective of the discount factor of the agent, that is, irrespective of how much he values the future relative to the present.[21]

Observe that this result is *not* the same as the 'bond-posting observation' made by Carmichael (1985) in response to the Shapiro–Stiglitz paper. There, the argument is that the employer can extract the entire difference in infinite-horizon utility $(V - M)$ demanding a lump-sum payment from the agent in the very first period. But such an arrangement is *not* a stationary contract, and in no way proves that a stationary contract *cannot* be an equilibrium. (See also the analysis in the limited-liability case below.)

What, then, is the intuition underlying this result? To see this, we need a simple but important preliminary observation: *the one-shot arrangement is always an equilibrium, and is in fact the equilibrium with the lowest infinite-horizon payoff to the principal.*[22]

To see this, note that, *given* the belief that the one-shot contract will be offered from tomorrow onwards, and since the agent's utility from the one-shot contract is exactly m, the agent will use the current contract only to determine current effort levels. Given this, the principal can do no better than offer the one-shot arrangement today. Likewise, given the stationary strategy of the principal that offers the one-shot arrangement, the agent's best response is to choose effort as he would under the one-shot contract. Finally, readers can easily check that, *given* the principal's ability to precommit one-period contracts, he cannot be pushed to any equilibrium that gives him a lower payoff than that arising from a stationary sequence of one-shot arrangements.

This preliminary statement yields our second observation and the basic starting point: *a stationary contract is an equilibrium if and only if its infinite-horizon payoff to the principal is at least as great as the infinite-horizon payoff arising from the stationary sequence of one-shot arrangements.*

To understand why, consider a stationary contract sequence. The agent is responding to this by choosing effort levels as described in the problem (19) and so has no incentive to deviate. The principal, however, always has an incentive to deviate from the ongoing sequence, and the reason for this arises from the dynamic inconsistency problem discussed earlier.

To show, then, that the stationary contract sequence is an equilibrium, it is *necessary and sufficient* to show that a principal's deviation at date t, followed by an imposition of the worst equilibrium (from the principal's viewpoint) at date $t + 1$, leads to a *total* payoff for him that does not exceed the total payoff under the stationary contract sequence.[23] But the worst equilibrium from $t + 1$ onwards is the sequence of one-shot arrangements, as discussed earlier. With this anticipated by both principal and agent, the principal can do no better in his deviation today (at date t) than deviate to the one-shot arrangement today, too! Consequently, the total payoff from deviation today plus imposition of the 'worst' equilibrium thereafter is *exactly* the pay-off from the stationary one-shot arrangement, and this establishes the truth of our second main observation.

The intuition behind Proposition 2 therefore rests on understanding why stationary contracts with eviction yield a return to the principal that is strictly less than the sequence of one-shot arrangements.

The key to this lies in analysing the choice of the 'failure wage' w_0. Suppose that we have a stationary contract with $V > M$. It is easy to see that, if this contract is replaced by another stationary contract with $p_1 = 0, p_0 = 1$, but with the same wage structure as before, the return to the principal cannot fall and it is still true that $V > M$. So let us restrict ourselves, without loss of generality, to such contracts. Now, let us reduce the failure wage w_0 by a small amount to get a new stationary contract. Two things happen. First, there is a tendency to expend more effort on the part of the agent, because there is a greater discrepancy between 'success' and 'failure' wages. Second, there is a disincentive effort, because the eviction threat is less potent ($V - M$ comes down). However, the former effect outweighs the latter because disincentive effects are all 'lagged' one period into the future, and are therefore discounted (relative to the present) by the agent. Therefore the new contract elicits greater effort and the principal pays out less when failure occurs. One can continue this process until $V = M$. But in this case eviction carries no threat. So the return to the principal from such a stationary contract cannot exceed his return from a stationary sequence of one-shot contracts. This completes the argument.[24]

Note that this argument relies on unlimited liability in two important ways. First, we argued that the sequence of one-shot arrangements (with arbitrary probabilities of eviction) is an equilibrium. This assertion relies heavily on the fact that, for all m, $v(m) = m$ under unlimited liability. Second, the main argument proceeds by lowering w_0. This may not be possible, *ceteris paribus*, in a situation of limited liability.

Indeed, for the particular applications that we have in mind, limited liability is likely to be far more relevant. We have nevertheless discussed the unlimited liability case in some detail because it usefully isolates some of the essential mechanisms of the model. Let us now turn to its limited liability counterpart.

In a situation of limited liability, wage payments in each period must be non-negative. In such a case, the following proposition, in somewhat sharp contrast to Proposition 2, can be established.

PROPOSITION 3. Under limited liability, there exists a one-period reservation utility $m(\delta)$ (depending on δ) with the following properties:

(a) stationary equilibrium contracts with eviction exist if and only if $m < m(\delta)$, and the MESC involves eviction under exactly the same conditions;

(b) $m(\delta) > m^*$ for all $\delta \in (0,1)$;

(c) $m(\delta)$ is strictly increasing in δ.

The kernel of Proposition 3 is part (b), but let us start our discussion more broadly. This proposition states that there is a threshold one-period reservation utility $m(\delta)$, such that, if $m < m(\delta)$, there are stationary equilibrium contracts involving eviction. In particular, the MESC (which we show to be unique) is an eviction contract under these circumstances. But this is not surprising. Recall that, by Proposition 1, if $m < m^*$, then the one-shot arrangements involve $v(m) > m$. Under such conditions, it is hardly interesting that infinite-horizon stationary contracts will also involve $V > M$. What *is* of interest is the case $m \geq m^*$. In this situation, the one-shot arrangement yields $v(m) = m$, so that, in a sense, the limited liability condition is not binding because the reservation utility is 'high'.

Nevertheless, there is a region $[m^*, m(\delta)]$ where the MESC will continue to involve eviction, even though it is possible to drive down the agent to his reservation utility (and in fact is *optimal* to do so in the one-shot arrangement). In fact, the higher is δ, the larger will be this region (part (c) of the proposition).[25]

For a full understanding of this result, readers are invited to study the proof in the Appendix. But some intuition can be provided. It will help to return to the one-shot arrangement described earlier. Note that, for $m < m^*$, it *must* be the case that $w_0 = 0$. (Otherwise it is easy to contradict the optimality of the one-shot arrangement from the principal's viewpoint.) Using a continuity argument,[26] $w_0 = 0$ when $m = m^*$. Now, inspect the 'success' wage w_1 at m^*. It is positive, so small changes in w_1 should create no 'first-order' changes in the principal's payoff (this is the 'first-order condition'!) in the one-shot arrangement.

Now suppose that exactly the same pair (w_1, w_0) is considered as a candidate for an infinite-horizon stationary contract. By using the same arguments as in the unlimited liability contract, readers may verify that this arrangement, with arbitrary probabilities of eviction, forms a stationary equilibrium contract. But is it the MESC? The answer is no.

To see this, we start by putting $p_1 = 0$ and $p_0 = 1$ (no eviction if success and sure eviction if failure). Now consider a small increase in w_1. By the earlier one-shot optimality calculations, there is no first-order effect on the principal's payoff from any 'current' incentive changes. However, there is now, *in addition*, an extra positive effect on effort — that arising from the fact that an increase in w_1 induces a spread between V and M — and this does have a first-order positive effect on the principal's infinite-horizon payoff. We have constructed a new stationary contract with $V > M$ that yields greater payoff than the one-shot arrangement at m^*. By carefully using arguments similar to those in the unlimited liability case, we can now see that the new contract is a stationary equilibrium contract with eviction.

Note that $w_0 = 0$, and so we *cannot* lower the failure wage, as we did in the case of unlimited liability. This shows why, at m^*, the one-shot arrangement involves no eviction, yet the infinite-horizon MESC does.[27]

In fact, it is important to observe that, if the MESC involves eviction, then the failure wage *must* be zero. If this were not true, then arguments similar to the unlimited liability case can be used to arrive at a contradiction. But the success wage at an MESC must be strictly positive! We have therefore informally established the final proposition.

PROPOSITION 4. An MESC can never be a stationary wage contract.

This proposition tells us that, irrespective of the utility function of the agent, there must be *some* effort incentives from *current* reward structure, whether further incentives (via eviction threats) are being provided or not.

One implication of all this is that, in situations where direct supervision of effort is difficult but outputs are observable, we will have some combination of current incentives and eviction threats, but never the latter without the former. A perfect example of such a situation is the market for land-leasing in rural economies. Our simple model predicts that, if this market is characterized by an excess supply of potential tenants, the tenancy clauses that will be provided will typically have *short leases*, coupled with a promise to renew the lease if output is satisfactory. This will be combined with a contract that allows the tenant some share in incremental produced output. The land-lease market will also exhibit an excess demand for land (provided that the reservation utility of potential tenants is below the critical value in Proposition 3).

6. A Summary

In Section 3 we described a model of an infinitely repeated principal–agent relationship. There is an excess supply of potential agents, so that the principal can use two devices for extracting effort from the agent: (1) the usual reward scheme that links the agent's payment to his output, and (2) the threat of contract termination. We focused on stationary (perfect) equilibria. Our main question was whether the threat of contract termination would be used in equilibrium. Throughout, we have not permitted the principal to precommit beyond the current contract.

We first examined a situation of unlimited liability, where the agent could be paid arbitrarily low rewards at any particular date (subject, of course, to his overall participation constraint). Here the result was that there exists *no* stationary equilibrium contract involving eviction (Proposition 2).

We emphasize that this result is fundamentally different from similar observations that have been made in the context of *finitely* repeated principal–agent relationships. There, a familiar argument reveals that, because the agent will be driven down to his reservation utility in the very last period, so (working 'backwards') eviction threats can never be real. But in situations where a relationship *might* carry on indefinitely, a finite-horizon model is inappropriate. What is needed is an infinite-horizon repeated relationship, discounted, of course, to incorporate both time preference and the possibility that the principal–agent relationship itself might be terminated.

In such a model, it is far from clear that unlimited liability will yield the impotence of eviction as a threat. However, we did obtain this result as Proposition 2. The intuition underlying this is discussed in some detail in the text.

Our main result, however, concerns a situation of limited liability. Here, the agent must receive some minimal amount at *each* date. In the particular context of the rural economy, this scenario is far more appropriate. Imperfections in the credit market, basic subsistence needs, and moral–economic considerations on the part of the principal combine to make limited liability the appropriate postulate.

Here, Proposition 3 states that stationary equilibrium contracts will involve eviction, *even when the reservation utility of the agent is high enough for it to be binding in the one-shot arrangement*. Observe the basic difference between this result and its analogue in a model of a (commonly known) finite relationship. There, eviction is possible (as a threat to elicit effort) *only* when the reservation utility of the agent is so low that the optimal one-shot contract cannot drive the agent's return to this level. We have tried to explain these differences clearly in the main text.

We inferred that in many rural situations where output is observable but effort is not, the employer (or landlord) will offer contracts that combine both current incentives and the threat to evict. In fact, Proposition 4 suggests that the latter is likely to coexist with the former. For instance, land-lease markets should display a mix of 'sharecropping-type' arrangements and short leases. In addition, it is predicted that there should be an excess *demand* for land leases at the going contractual rates, but that this excess demand will be chronic and not a 'disequilibrium' state.

It should be emphasized that these points are not new. Our main thesis is that the *models* employed to make these points are not adequate. They are often models where a fixed wage payment is *assumed*, in which case the fact that eviction threats must be used is a foregone conclusion. Or they are models with a finite horizon, which can yield eviction only if the one-shot arrangements do not yield a binding reservation utility for the agent. Or they are models that presume that the principal has the ability to precommit over the *entire* duration of the relationship. We feel that such models are inappropriate in rural situations because (1) precommitment outcomes are always dynamically inconsistent in this context, and (2) there is no effective legal mechanism to honour such levels of prior commitment. In the absence of (2), precommitment is extremely difficult to justify, given (1). (We reviewed examples of such models in Section 2.)

We have therefore constructed a framework which assumes neither precommitment nor a finite-horizon relationship, and does not presume a fixed wage contract. In this model, we characterized exactly the conditions under which contracts with eviction threats will be equilibrium outcomes.

APPENDIX

Proof of Proposition 1:

Given one-shot arrangements w, w', etc., we denote the corresponding effort levels by e, e', etc. The principal's payoff under w is $\tilde{q}(w)$, and that of the agent is $\tilde{v}(w)$. Observe that, if we have two arrangements w, w' with $\tilde{v}(w) \geq m$, $\tilde{v}(w') \geq m$, $w_0 \leq w'_0$, and $w_1 \geq w'_1$, with at least one strict inequality in the last two inequalities, then $e > e'$. We now proceed by steps. Denote by UL the case of unlimited liability and by LL the case of limited liability.

Step 1. Under an optimal arrangement w, we have $w_1 > w_0$.
   Proof. Obvious, using the fact that there exists some $\hat{w}$ with $\tilde{q}(\hat{w}) > 0$.

Step 2. (i) Under UL, the optimal arrangement satisfies

$$\frac{1 - w_1 + w_0}{Q''(e)e(1 - e)} - \frac{1}{u'(w_1)} + \frac{1}{u'(w_0)} = 0. \tag{A1}$$

(ii) Under LL, the optimal arrangement satisfies

$$\frac{1 - w_1 + w_0}{Q''(e)e(1 - e)} - \frac{1}{u'(w_1)} + \frac{1}{u'(w_0)} \geq 0 \tag{A2}$$

with (A1) holding if $w_0 > 0$.
   Proof. We establish (i), the proof of (ii) being very similar. Let $d\alpha$ be a parameter that captures simultaneous infinitesimal changes in w_1 and w_0 which keep the agent's payoff constant. By the envelope theorem, it can be checked that

$$d\alpha = e\,u'(w_1)dw_1 = -(1 - e)\,u'(w_0)dw_0. \tag{A3}$$

In the unlimited liability case, we must have $dq/d\alpha = 0$, where q is the principal's payoff. Performing the appropriate calculations yields (A1).

Step 3. Under an optimal arrangement, $1 - w_1 + w_0 \geq 0$.
   Proof. Use Step 1 and inspect (A1) and (A2), applying the concavity of $u(\cdot)$.

Step 4. Let w be an optimal arrangement. Then
(i) under UL, $\tilde{v}(w) = m$;
(ii) under LL, if $\tilde{v}(w) > m$, then $w_0 = 0$.

Proof. (i) Suppose that $\tilde{v}(w) > m$. Now observe that, for any w and corresponding e, the principal's return is given by

$$\tilde{q}(w) = (1 - w_1 + w_0)e - w_0. \tag{A4}$$

Differentiating with respect to w_0 (for fixed w_1), we have the derivative

$$(1 - w_1 + w_0)\frac{de}{dw_0} - (1 - e) \tag{A5}$$

and using step 3 and the end-point conditions on $Q(e)$, this derivative is strictly negative. So there exists an arrangement w' with $w_0' < w_0$, $w_1' = w_1$, $\tilde{v}(w') \geq m$ with $\tilde{q}(w') > \tilde{q}(w)$, a contradiction.

(ii) Argue by contradiction as in (i). We now choose the 'competing' contract, w' with $w_0' \geq 0$ (in addition to its other characteristics).

Step 5. There exists precisely one optimal arrangement in both the UL and LL cases.

Proof. Existence can be verified by standard methods. Now start with the case of UL. Suppose, on the contrary, that there are two optimal one-shot arrangements w, w'. *WLOG* $w_0 \leq w_0'$. Now, in fact, $w_0 < w_0'$. (For if $w_0 = w_0'$, we have $w_1 \neq w_1'$ contradicting $\tilde{v}(w) = \tilde{v}(w') = m$, by Step 4.) Therefore $w_1 > w_1'$ (otherwise Step 4 is again contradicted), and so it must be that $e > e'$.

Now, using (A1), we have

$$\begin{aligned}
0 &= \frac{1 - w_1' + w_0'}{Q''(e')e'(1 - e')} - \frac{1}{u'(w_1')} + \frac{1}{u'(w_0')} \\
&> \frac{1 - w_1 + w_0}{Q''(e)e(1 - e)} - \frac{1}{u'(w_1)} + \frac{1}{u'(w_0)}.
\end{aligned} \tag{A6}$$

(Here we use the technical assumption (12).) But w is an optimal arrangement, so (A6) contradicts step 2.

Now we turn to the case of LL. Again, if $w_0 < w_0'$, we note that $w_1 > w_1'$. For if not, then $\tilde{v}(w_1') > v(w_1) \geq m$ and $w_0' > w_0 \geq 0$, contradicting step 4. Now we can follow exactly the same argument as in the UL case.

It remains to consider the case $w_0 = w_0'$. In this case, *WLOG* $w_1 > w_1'$. But then $\tilde{v}(w) > \tilde{v}(w') \geq m$, so $w_0 = w_0' = 0$ by step 4. Also note that $e > e'$.

Readers can easily check that at w_1 we must have (as a necessary condition for the optimality of w)

$$\frac{(1 - w_1)u'(w_1)}{Q''(e)} - e = 0, \tag{A7}$$

while at w_1'

$$\frac{(1 - w_1')u'(w_1')}{Q''(e')} - e' \leq 0. \tag{A8}$$

However, using $w_1 > w_1'$, $e > e'$, the concavity of u, the observation that $(1 - w_1) \geq 0$ (step 3), and the fact that $Q''(e)$ is non-decreasing in e (following from (12)), we have

$$\frac{(1 - w_1')u'(w_1')}{Q''(e')} - e' > \frac{(1 - w_1)u'(w_1)}{Q''(e)} - e \qquad (A9)$$

and (A9) contradicts (A7) and (A8).

So steps 5 and 4(i) together establish the proposition, save for one remaining point.

Step 6. Under LL, there exists $m^* > 0$ such that if $m < m^*$, then $v(m) = m^*$, while if $m > m^*$, $v(m) = m$. (Here $v(m)$ is the agent's return (now uniquely defined) under the optimal one-shot arrangement, when his reservation utility is m.)

Proof. Consider the problem

$$\begin{aligned} &\max (1 - w_1)\, e \\ &\text{s. t. } Q'(e) = u(w_1). \end{aligned} \qquad (A10)$$

It is easy to see (using methods similar to those above) that an optimum exists and is unique. Denoting the values by $(\hat{e}, \hat{w}_1)$, one can check that $\hat{w}_1 > 0$, $(1 - \hat{w}_1) > 0$, and that (A7) holds for $(\hat{e}, \hat{w}_1)$. Define $m^* \equiv \hat{e}\, u(\hat{w}_1) - Q(\hat{e})$.

Now suppose $m < m^*$. Let w be the optimal one-shot arrangement. If $w_0 = 0$, it is easy to see that $v(m) = m^*$. Now suppose $w_0 > 0$. Then it must be the case that $v(m) = m$. So $w_1 < \hat{w}_1$, and therefore $e < \hat{e}$. Moreover, the reader can check that

$$\frac{(1 - w_1 + w_0)u'(w_1)}{Q''(e)} - e \leq 0. \qquad (A11)$$

However, given the observations above, we have

$$\frac{(1 - w_1 + w_0)u'(w_1)}{Q''(e)} - e > \frac{(1 - \hat{w}_1)u'(\hat{w}_1)}{Q''(\hat{e})} - \hat{e} \qquad (A12)$$

and (A12) contradicts (A7), evaluated at $(\hat{e}, \hat{w}_1)$.

Finally, let $m \geq m^*$. Suppose, contrary to our claim, that $v(m) > m$; then for the optimal one-shot arrangement w, we have $w_0 = 0$ and $w_1 > \hat{w}_1$. This means that $e > \hat{e}$. Moreover, readers can check that (A7) holds. But, by arguments as above, it is easily seen that (A7) cannot then also hold for $(\hat{e}, \hat{w}_1)$, which is a contradiction.

The proposition is now proved. Q.E.D.

Proof of Proposition 2

Again, we proceed by means of steps. All arguments are for the UL case.

Step 1.   Consider a contract $c = (w, p_1, p_0)$ where w is the optimal one-shot arrangement, and $0 \le p_0, p_1 \le 1$. Such a contract is a stationary equilibrium contract.

Proof.   Tedious but straightforward, and so is omitted.

Let $\tilde{q}$ be the principal's return under the optimal one-shot arrangement.

Step 2.   A contract c is a stationary equilibrium contract if and only if the infinite-horizon expected return (given e is chosen optimally) to the principal is at least as great as $\tilde{q}/(1 - \rho)$.

Proof.   It uses step 1 and the line of argument is indicated in the text. Omitted here.

By step 2, we are done if we can prove that the MESC yields a payoff of exactly $\tilde{q}/(1 - \rho)$ to the principal, and is a sequence of optimal one-shot arrangements with arbitrary eviction probabilities.

Define $M \equiv m(1 - \delta)$. Readers can now easily verify (again using step 2) that, in solving for an MESC, it is equivalent to solving

$$\max(1 - w_1)e - (1 - e)w_0 \tag{A13}$$

$$\text{s.t.} \ V \ge M \tag{A14}$$

where V solves

$$V = eu(w_1) + (1 - e)u(w_0) - Q(e) + \delta eV + \delta(1 - e)M \tag{A15}$$

and subject to

$$Q'(e) = u(w_1) - u(w_0) + \delta(V - M). \tag{A16}$$

(The verification of the equivalence between this problem and the MESC is aided by the observation that, in looking for an MESC, it suffices to study contracts with $p_1 = 0$ and $p_0 = 1$. The proof is omitted.)

One can easily check that a solution exists to (A13)–(A16). We now establish step 3.

Step 3.   The solution to the problem above involves $V = M$.

Proof.   Suppose not: then $V > M$. We now claim that in the solution, $1 - w_1 + w_0 \ge 0$. For suppose not: observe that the principal's return is given by

$$(1 - w_1)e - (1 - e)w_0 = (1 - w_1 + w_0)e - w_0. \tag{A17}$$

Note that the derivative of the RHS (A17) with respect to w_1 (keeping w_0 constant but incorporating the effect on e via (A15) and (A16)) is strictly negative. But this means that there exists a contract $(w', 1, 0)$ with $w'_0 = w_0$, $w'_1 < w_1$, and $V' \ge M$ such that

$$(1 - w'_1 + w'_0)e' - w'_0 > (1 - w_1 + w_0)e - w_0. \tag{A18}$$

But this contradicts the optimality of (w_1, w_0, e).

Next, we observe that the derivative of the right-hand side (A17) with respect to w_0 (keeping w_1 constant but incorporating the effect on e via (A15) and (A16)) is strictly negative. This derivative is

$$(1 - w_1 + w_0) \frac{de}{dw_0} - (1 - e), \tag{A19}$$

and, given the observation that $(1 - w_1 + w_0) \geq 0$ and $1 - e > 0$, it suffices to show that $de/dw_0 < 0$. We now do just that, to complete the proof. Note that from (A16)

$$Q''(e) \frac{de}{dw_0} = -u'(w_0) + \delta \frac{dV}{dw_0}, \tag{A20}$$

and, using the envelope theorem on (A15) (noting (A16)), we can evaluate dV/dw_0 simply as

$$\frac{dV}{dw_0} = \frac{(1 - e)u'(w_0)}{1 - \delta e}. \tag{A21}$$

Using (A21) in (A20),

$$Q''(e) \frac{de}{dw_0} = -\frac{(1 - \delta)u'(w_0)}{1 - \delta e}, \tag{A22}$$

and, noting that $Q''(e) > 0$, we are done.

Step 3, taken together with our earlier remarks, establishes the proposition. For (w_1, w_0) must now be the optimal one-shot arrangement.

Let $q(m)$ be the principal's optimal payoff from the one-shot arrangement when the agent's reservation utility is m.

Proof of Proposition 3:
Here too, we proceed in a number of steps. All arguments apply to the case of LL.

Step 1. Suppose $m < m^*$. Then every equilibrium involves a payoff to the principal that, evaluated from each date onwards, is at least as great as $q(m)/(1 - \rho)$.

Proof. It suffices to show that the principal can always *guarantee* himself $q(m)/(1 - \rho)$ from any date onwards. The result then follows from standard arguments.

Consider any date t. Let the principal offer a contract $c \equiv (w_1, w_0, 1, 1)$ at that date, where $w = (w_1, w_0)$ is the optimal one-shot arrangement. (In such a contract, the principal is also evicting the agent with probability 1.) Clearly, by offering such a contract at date t, the principal can *guarantee* himself $q(m)$ at that date. And this can be done for each date. So we are done.

Step 2. Suppose $m < m^*$. Then all stationary equilibrium contracts involve eviction.

Proof. Let $c \equiv (w_1, w_0, p_1, p_0)$ be a stationary equilibrium contract. Let V denote the infinite horizon return to the agent from this contract. If $V = M = m/(1 - \delta)$, then it is clear that the contract involves a one-period utility to the agent that is *equal* to m at every date. But then (w_1, w_0) is a feasible one-shot arrangement. By Proposition 1, the one-shot return to the principal from c must be strictly less than $q(m)$ at each date. But then this stationary equilibrium contract contradicts step 1.

Now consider the following problem:

$$\max(1 - w_1)e - (1 - e)w_0 \qquad (A23)$$

$$\text{s.t. } V \geq M \qquad (A24)$$

where V solves

$$V = eu(w_1) + (1 - e)u(w_0) - Q(e) + \delta e V + \delta(1 - e)M \qquad (A25)$$

and subject to

$$Q'(e) = u(w_1) - u(w_0) + \delta(V - M) \qquad (A26)$$

$$w_1, w_0 \geq 0. \qquad (A27)$$

Step 3. For each m, a solution to (A23)–(A27) exists and is a MESC when (w_1, w_0) is offered as a contract together with $p_1 = 0, p_0 = 1$.

Proof. Easy but tedious and so omitted.

Note that step 3 guarantees that stationary equilibrium contracts with eviction exist when $m < m^*$. We are now going to study the case $m \geq m^*$.

Given the way in which Proposition 3 is stated, it will be useful to first establish step 4.

Step 4. There exists a unique solution to (A23)–(A27).

Proof. Existence follows standard methods. Here we prove uniqueness. Suppose, on the contrary, that there exist two distinct arrangements, w, w', that solve (A23)–(A27). Denote by V, V' the corresponding utilities to the agent.

Case A. $V = V' = M$. In this case, it is easy to see that both w and w' must also solve the *one-shot* problem given by (15)–(18). But then $w = w'$, by Proposition 1, and we have a contradiction.

Case B. $V > M, V' > M$. In this case, we argue first that $w_0 = w_0' = 0$. To do so, suppose, on the contrary, that w_0(or w_0') > 0, and follow exactly the same argument as in step 3 of the proof of Proposition 2 to arrive at a contradiction.

WLOG, $w_1 > w_1'$. Then it is easy to see that $e > e'$. Moreover, a little calculation will reveal that the following equations must hold for w_1 and w_1',

$$\frac{(1 - w_1)u'(w_1)}{Q''(e)(1 - \delta e)} - e = 0. \tag{A28}$$

$$\frac{(1 - w_1')u'(w_1')}{Q''(e')(1 - \delta e')} - e' = 0. \tag{A29}$$

Recall that $w_1 > w_1'$, $e > e'$. Moreover, it is easy to check that, given (12), $Q''(e)(1 - \delta e)$ is non-decreasing in e. But then (A28) and (A29) both cannot hold, a contradiction.

Case C. $V > M$, $V' = M$. Consider the arrangement w for which $V > M$. Again, just as in case B, we have $w_0 = 0$ and (A28) holding. Now take w', with $V' = M$. Readers can check that

$$\frac{(1 - w_1' + w_0')u'(w_1')}{Q''(e')(1 - \delta e')} - e' \le 0 \tag{A30}$$

But now observe that $w_0' \ge 0$, and so $w_1' < w_1$ (for $V > V'$). Therefore $e > e'$. Putting all this together,

$$0 \ge \frac{(1 - w_1' + w_0')u'(w_1')}{Q''(e')(1 - \delta e')} - e' > \frac{(1 - w_1)u'(w_1)}{Q''(e)(1 - \delta e)} - e \tag{A31}$$

and (A31) contradicts (A28).

This completes the proof.

By the uniqueness result, we can write not only the return of the principal as a unique solution (and therefore function) of (m,δ), $q(m,\delta)$, but also the arrangement w as a function $w(m,\delta)$ and the agent's return as a function $V(m,\delta)$.

Step 5. $q(m,\delta)$ and $w(m,\delta)$ are continuous functions of m and δ.

Proof. Inspect (A23)–(A27). It is clear that all the conditions of the maximum theorem are satisfied, so $q(m,\delta)$ is a continuous function and the set of optimal arrangements is an upper-hemi-continuous correspondence in m. But by step 4, there is a *unique optimal arrangement for each m*. Therefore $w(m,\delta)$ is a continuous function.

Step 6. $V(m,\delta)$ is a continuous function of m and δ.

Proof. Use step 5 to observe that $w(m,\delta)$ is continuous. Now inspect (A25) and (A27) as m changes to obtain the result.

Step 7. Suppose $V(\hat{m},\delta) > \hat{M} = \hat{m}/(1 - \delta)$ for some $\hat{m}$. Then $V(m',\delta) > M' = m'/(1 - \delta)$ for all $m' < \hat{m}$.

Proof. Suppose not: then there exists $m < \hat{m}$ such that $V(m,\delta) = M$. Let $w = w(m,\delta)$, $\hat{w} = w(\hat{m},\delta)$. Then it is clear that (i) $\hat{w}_0 = 0$ (see case B of step 4); (ii) $w_0 \ge 0$; (iii) $w_1 < \hat{w}_1$; and (iv) $e < \hat{e}$.

Furthermore, it is clear that (A28) holds for $w_1 = \hat{w}_1$ and $e = \hat{e}$, and that (A30) holds for $w_1' = w_1$ and $e' = e$. Now proceed just as in case C of step 4 to obtain a contradiction.

Recall that in the one-shot problem we are assuming that there exists an arrangement where the principal's return is positive. Define $\bar{m}$ as the supremum of all one-shot reservation utilities such that this assumption is valid. Clearly, $\bar{m} < \infty$ and it is easy to see that $\bar{m} > m^*$.

Now define, for each δ,

$$m(\delta) \equiv \sup\{m \in (-\infty, \bar{m})/V(m,\delta) > M\}.$$

By step 7 we have $m(\delta)$ *uniquely* defined, and by step 6 we have $V(m(\delta),\delta) = m(\delta)/(1 - \delta)$ if $m(\delta) < \bar{m}$. Also, $m(\delta) > m^*$ for all $\delta > 0$.

Step 8. If $m(\hat{\delta}) = \bar{m}$ for some $\hat{\delta}$, then $m(\delta) = \bar{m}$ for all $\delta \geq \hat{\delta}$. If $m(\delta) < \bar{m}$, it is strictly increasing in δ.

Proof. Let $m(\hat{\delta}) = \bar{m}$ for some $\hat{\delta}$, and suppose that $m(\delta) < \bar{m}$ for some $\delta > \hat{\delta}$. Using the continuity of $V(m,\delta)$ in m and δ, there exists some $\delta' < \delta$ such that $\bar{m} > m(\delta') > m(\delta)$. Define $m \equiv m(\delta')$. Suppose that the discount factor is δ'. Then, by our construction and step 7, we have

$$V(m,\delta') > \frac{m}{1 - \delta'}, \tag{A32}$$

and using (A32) for the optimal one-shot arrangement that prevails here (call it w'), we have $w_0' = 0$ (just as in case B of step 4). We also have, at w',

$$\frac{(1 - w_1')u'(w_1')}{Q''(e')(1 - \delta'e')} - e' = 0. \tag{A33}$$

Now, if the discount factor is δ, we have $V(m,\delta) = m/(1 - \delta)$ for the optimal one-shot arrangement prevailing in this case (call it w) and

$$\frac{(1 - w_1 + w_0)u'(w_1)}{Q''(e)(1 - \delta e)} - e \leq 0. \tag{A34}$$

Now observe that $\delta > \delta'$ (by construction), and that $w_0 \geq w_0' = 0$, while $w_1' > w_1 > 0$. Moreover, it must be that $e' > e$ (simply inspect (A26)). Therefore

$$0 \geq \frac{(1 - w_1 + w_0)u'(w_1)}{Q''(e)(1 - \delta e)} - e > \frac{(1 - w_1')u'(w_1')}{Q''(e')(1 - \delta'e')} - e' \tag{A35}$$

and (A35) stands in contradiction to (A33).

If $m(\delta)$ is less than $\bar{m}$, the argument proceeds exactly as above, with the initial adjustments for $m(\delta) = \bar{m}$ unnecessary.

Observe, too, by step 8 and the fact that $m^* < \bar{m}$, we have $m(\delta) > m^*$ for all $\delta > 0$.

This completes the proof of the proposition.

NOTES

1. For example, see Bardhan and Rudra (1978) for evidence in the context of a rural developing economy.
2. See, e.g., Calvo and Wellisz (1978) for a theoretical treatment and Sundari (1981) for an interesting description of some permanent contracts in Indian agriculture.
3. The exact sense in which our model is relevant for developing agrarian economies will, we hope, become clear below.
4. Readers are referred to the recent collection edited by Akerlof and Yellen (1986) and to papers by Yellen (1984) or Mookherjee (1986) for some recent approaches to modelling involuntary unemployment in this way. The incentive role of high wages is also usually brought under the general umbrella of efficiency wage theories. However, we feel that a careful analysis of the incentive model necessitates a structure that is really quite different from the usual efficiency-wage models.
5. See, for example, Leibenstein (1957), Bliss and Stern (1978) and Dasgupta and Ray (1986, 1987) for unemployment theories, and Dasgupta and Ray (1987) and Guha (1987) for theories of permanent labour based on nutrition-efficiency relationships.
6. For readers unfamiliar with the 'standard' model, Mirrlees (1975) and Holmstrom (1979) are good starting points.
7. Our setting, therefore, like most other models in this literature, is unabashedly partial-equilibrium. The focus is on the principal–agent relationship, and the objective is to derive equilibrium contracts with eviction endogenously. For an approach that simply postulates contracts with eviction but then goes on to study the general equilibrium implications, see Shapiro and Stiglitz (1984).
8. It should be plain that there are many applications of this theoretical structure. For example, one can draw the conclusion that large firms (e.g. multinational corporations (MNCs) in developing countries) are more likely to pay high wages for the same kind of jobs than small firms (e.g. domestic competitors of MNCs). The more complex organizational structure of a large firm makes supervision of an individual employee that much more difficult. (We are talking here of jobs that require some individual decision-making, not mechanical production-line jobs.) Consequently, the large firm might offer a reward package that includes a threat of eviction. For this threat to be operative, the employee must be offered a higher utility than his next-best alternative, which is to work in the small-scale sector.
9. See Calvo (1977), Akerlof and Yellen (1986), the papers discussed below, and references therein.

10. See, in this context, work by Stiglitz (1974a) and Newbery and Stiglitz (1979a).
11. The assumption that enables the landlord to do so is explained in Eswaran and Kotwal (1985c).
12. Singh (1983) also allows for precommitment in one version of his model.
13. This is precisely the way in which the literature on 'consistent plans' addresses a similar problem. See Strotz (1956) or Phelps and Pollack (1968), for example.
14. The model here resembles that of Radner (1985).
15. The crucial thrust of the assumption is that the principal cannot precommit for the entire (infinite-horizon) duration of the game. Finite-horizon precommitments greater than one period are not allowed here, but they lead to similar results. For finite-horizon (typically two-period) principal–agent models with precommitment throughout, see also Rogerson (1985) or Stiglitz and Weiss (1983).
16. Of course, the agent may choose not to take up an offered contract, given his expectations of how the principal will behave in the future. But then (given identical agents) no agent will take up the contract. Therefore, the principal must respect certain participation constraints on the part of the agent.
17. Radner (1985) analyses this limited liability case in his single-principal, single-agent model; see also Singh (1982).
18. This is to handle the UL case. In the LL case, we need only define u on $\mathbb{R}_+$.
19. This assumption cannot be dropped free of charge, but can be replaced by far weaker assumptions, which, however, necessitate undue technicalities.
20. A *history* up to some date is a complete listing of all that has transpired and been commonly observed until that date, but not the choice of effort levels, which the principal cannot see and therefore cannot condition upon. The agent can in principle condition his current actions on his past effort choices.
21. Of course, the discount factor must be less than unity. Also, note that this result is true only for stationary contracts; with non-stationary contracts, things are much more complicated.
22. We are being informal here. In the UL case, the one-shot arrangement always involves $v(m) = m$, and so what we are saying is that any stationary contract $((w_1,w_0), (p_1,p_0))$ with (w_1,w_0) equal to the one-shot arrangement and (p_1,p_0) arbitrary can be realized as an equilibrium.
23. We are using strongly the insights of Abreu (1984b), developed for discounted repeated games.
24. There are other intuitive arguments which appear equally compelling, but are in fact not correct. For example, note that the result is true irrespective of the degree of risk aversion of the agent. Now consider, for instance, a stationary wage contract. No current risk is borne by the worker, but for any effort to be forthcoming there must be a threat of eviction, so the worker does bear a risk of a different kind (in terms of the uncertainty in future utilities). The one-shot contract offers no such risk in future utilities, but 'current' risk ($w_0 \neq w_1$) is in fact borne by the worker. The following argument is then tempting. The principal replaces the stationary wage contract by a one-shot contract, and this effectively changes the nature of risk borne by the worker, but not its quantitative magnitude. However, the principal gains because the worker is driven to his reservation utility. But this argument, as we shall see, does not work in the limited liability model.

25. This also indicates why the intuitive arrangement described in n. 24 is not strictly correct.
26. By standard arguments, the one-shot arrangement changes upper-hemi-continuously with respect to m. By Proposition 1, the one-shot arrangement is unique for each m. Upper-hemicontinuity plus uniqueness yields continuity.
27. The argument is therefore completely different from, say, Bardhan (1984: Ch. 8), where the eviction threat arises from the fact that one-shot contracts fail to drive agents to their reservation utility levels. See also Singh (1982).

6.

Production Relations in Semi-arid African Agriculture

Hans Binswanger, John McIntire, and Chris Udry

1. Introduction

This chapter is designed to extend the economic analysis of production relations in agriculture to semi-arid environments, with special reference to semi-arid Africa. We place particular emphasis on describing how the diverse institutions that organize the exchange (or lack thereof) of outputs and factors of production in an initially land-abundant, isolated area are affected by population growth, migration, and the introduction of external trading relations. We follow Binswanger and Rosenzweig (1986) in defining production relations to be the relations of people to factors of production in terms of their rights of ownership and use in production, and the corresponding relations of people to each other as factor owners and renters, as landlords, tenants, workers, employers, creditors, and debtors.

Along with considerations of risk, risk aversion, and information problems, we incorporate into our analysis the technical features of agricultural production and the material attributes of its factors of production. In addition, we pay particular attention to the constraints that arise when information is costly and market mechanisms for risk diffusion and other intertemporal exchanges are incomplete.

In Section 2 we briefly summarize some basic results from Binswanger and Rosenzweig (1986) that will be of use in our analysis.

The study of production relations in a particular region requires specific knowledge of the agro-climatic conditions and endowments of the region. In Section 3 we describe the 'base case' of an isolated, land-abundant, semi-arid economy with simple technology and where slavery is banned. We describe, in that context, land, labour, and credit markets, the determination of the degree and type of household extension, and the relationship between the output market and the operational scale of farming. We show that agricultural production will be characterized by specialization in herding or farming, and we discuss the economic interactions between specialized herders and farmers, and the role of livestock in capital accumulation and as an insurance substitute.[1]

In Section 4, while maintaining the assumption that the area has a poorly developed transport and communications network, we consider the consequences of population growth. We discuss the distribution of operational and ownership holdings of land, the development of tenancy and factor rental and sales markets, the decline of transhumance and specialized herding activities, the importance of land as collateral, the interlinking of contracts, the dominance of distress sales in the land sales market, landlessness, and the rental out of land by smallholders.

It should perhaps be noted at this point that we consider only generalized population growth resulting in an increasing scarcity of land over a fairly broad area. We do not discuss the case of agriculture centred on an urban concentration based on mining, or the production and long-distance trading of manufactures or luxuries.[2]

In Sections 5 and 6 we examine the consequences of opportunities for external migration and trade, again assuming a low population density. Some of the direct effects of emigration on the agricultural system are simply the inverse of those resulting from population growth. However, remittances from migrants play an important role in restructuring the risks faced by households, and thus induce a variety of changes in institutional arrangements. Opening up the region to trade in bulk agricultural produce has more complex consequences. We discuss the different effects of exports of former staples and of new crops, and the results of the intensified use of agricultural inputs. The effects of these changes on factor markets, household extension, herder–cultivator relations, and various insurance substitutes are analysed.

Many of the individual phenomena discussed in this chapter have received explanations before. However, our goal is to achieve not a novel explanation of each individual phenomenon, but an integrated explanation of them in different environments. Because of this integrative approach, we do not use mathematical derivations within formalized models.

2. Foundations

We make the following six general assumptions:

ASSUMPTION 1.   *Risk*: Individuals face risks from the production process, from the market, and from health factors.

ASSUMPTION 2.   *Costly information*: The acquisition and transmission of information involves costs.

ASSUMPTION 3.   *Behaviour*: Individuals are interested in their own well-being.

ASSUMPTION 4.   *Behaviour*: Individuals value consumption.

ASSUMPTION 5. *Behaviour*: For all individuals, there is a point beyond which they begin to dislike additional effort.

ASSUMPTION 6. *Behaviour*: Individuals are risk-averse whenever gains and losses exceed trivial levels of income.[3] The degree of risk aversion may vary between individuals and for the same individual between different levels of wealth.

These six assumptions have the following general consequences (which are explored more thoroughly in Binswanger and Rosenzweig 1986).

C1. *Asymmetric information.* Information has value and is costly to acquire. Since individuals are selfish (Assumption 3), they will not part with information unless it is to their advantage.

C2. *Incentive problems.* When information is costly and asymmetrically distributed, incentive problems arise in all transactions that involve payments or deliveries of goods or services at a future time (i.e. credit, insurance, labour, or rentals of assets). The incentive problems include adverse selection or screening effects and moral hazard.

C3. *Imperfect enforcement of property rights.* Where information is costly and asymmetrically distributed, property rights cannot be perfectly enforced.

C4. *Insurance contracts and insurance substitutes.* Risk aversion implies that individuals would be willing to pay some positive amount to insure against the risks that they face. Where insurance is unavailable they would be willing — at some cost to themselves — to alter their behaviour in other ways to reduce their exposure to risk. Insurance substitution may include the holding of reserves, the diversification of prospects, conservative input levels, credit and investment in 'creditworthiness', and the extension of social ties.

C5. *Collateral.* At a given interest rate, collateral has four effects: (1) it increases the expected return of the lender and reduces that of the borrower; (2) it partly or fully shifts the risk of loss of the principal from the lender to the borrower; (3) it provides additional incentives for the borrower to repay the loan; and (4) it has a screening effect on the applicant pool. One would in general expect positive selection as borrowers with lower expected returns and higher risks drop out of the pool. Stiglitz and Weiss (1981), however, show that adverse selection will also occur as poorer debtors, who have no collateral but would undertake less risky projects, drop out of the pool.

C6. *Forms of collateral.* Not all assets are equally suitable as collateral. In order to serve as collateral, an asset must be appropriable by the lender in case of default, and must not be subject to collateral specific risk; in addition, the returns from the asset must accrue to the borrower. Lenders must be confident that the collateral cannot easily be stolen (or hidden and claimed to be stolen), or damaged by fire, accident, misuse, or (in the case of animals) disease.

C7. *Collateral substitutes.* People living in economies that have few collateral options, or borrowers who own few assets usable as collateral, either will not borrow much or will resort to a variety of collateral substitutes. These include pawnbroking, third-party guarantees (co-signer requirements), the threat of loss of future borrowing opportunities, and tied contracts.

3. Production Relations in Semi-arid, Land-abundant Agriculture

In addition to the general assumptions above, it is necessary to specify some of the particular environmental, technological, and historical conditions of this application.

S1. *Dispersed, low-density population.* The immobility of land leads to the geographic dispersion of agricultural production. The population density is low.

S2. *Transport costs.* Transport and communication costs are high, both within a local region (because of the dispersed population) and interregionally. Only low-weight, low-volume items of high value can be transported over long distances.

S3. *Semi-arid climate.* (a) In the absence of irrigation there is one short growing season, so the seasonality of crop production is pronounced. Farming operations are highly synchronic. (b) Weather risk is high. (c) Within small areas, crop yields have high positive covariance.

S4. *Simple technology.* The available technology is simple, confined to hand tools and possibly draught animals. Technical economies of scale in farming are unimportant. Gathering and hunting provide supplemental income to agriculture.

S5. *Land and labour rights.* External powers have not created property or land use rights for expatriates. Coerced labour is illegal and the ban is enforced.

3.1. Land market

PROPOSITION 1. Simple technology and a low population density imply that land is abundant and has no sales price. In the absence of coercion, residents have access to land use rights at no cost or in exchange for token payments.

3.2. Labour market

PROPOSITION 2. There is no locally resident agricultural labour class.

PROPOSITION 3. There is almost no hiring or exchange of labour among resident farmers during the peak labour season, which in this case is the sowing and weeding season.

Incentive problems (C2) imply that hired labour is more costly than family labour[4] because it either requires supervisory inputs by family members or leads to smaller effort in the absence of supervision.[5] Easy access to land (Proposition 1) and simple technology (S4) imply that a worker's output is at least as large on his own plot as on an employer's plot. Therefore, given supervision cost (Assumption 2), the employer cannot compensate a worker for the latter's forgone output on his own plot, resulting in Proposition 2,[6] the absence of a labour pool. Note that Proposition 2 does not rule out temporary hiring or exchange of labour: certain tasks may be easier or more enjoyable to perform in a group.

The absence of hired or exchange labour during sowing or weeding (Proposition 3) occurs because these operations are highly time-bound and synchronic (S3). Sowing is possible only for a few days after infrequent and unreliable showers whose timing, amount, and frequency cannot be known in advance. Postponing one's own sowing to work for someone else tends to result in a reduced yield because it shortens the length of the aready short growing season. It also implies higher risks. The optimal timing of the first weeding follows from the time of sowing; weeding delays reduce yield and increase weeding effort.[7]

The principle exception to Proposition 3 occurs when individuals cannot borrow enough for subsistence needs. Their only available collateral substitute (C7) may be a tied contract in which they pledge their labour services in exchange for subsistence needs. This tied contract may involve a patron–client relationship.[8]

Widespread use of hired labour occurs primarily in two circumstances. Temporary migrants can be hired from a nearby agro-climatic region with a different sowing period; annual migrants can be hired from a poorer agro-climatic region. In the latter case, labour productivity at the destination must be sufficiently high to allow employers there to compensate migrants for their forgone cultivation at home. Only if the migrants are prevented from acquiring cultivation rights will they remain in the labour pool.[9]

A consequence of Propositions 2 and 3 is:

PROPOSITION 4. Cultivated area per working household member is largely invariant with household size or wealth.

The assumptions needed for this proposition are that households have access to different land qualities in roughly the same proportions, or (less likely) that land quality be uniform.

3.3. *Specialization of herding and farming activities*

PROPOSITION 5. Livestock production will occur through transhumance (the seasonal migration of livestock with herders across different agro-climatic regions).

In an arid or semi-arid climate (S3) with simple technology (S4), a low population density (S1), and limited access to external markets for farm output (S2), transhumance dominates other methods of livestock production. That is, for a given level of mean output and risk, transhumance minimizes labour input over all alternative methods of cattle production. This results from the fact that both water and pasture vary in availability across both time and space. Any attempt to keep cattle in one place throughout the year rather than allowing the herd to move with the changing availability of resources would require additional labour inputs, including the digging of wells and drawing of water, the gathering and cutting of fodder, and the production of specialized fodder crops. For given labour cost, the risk of reduced water or fodder availability (leading directly to reduced livestock output) is increased by an attempt to remain in a fixed location year-round.

Livestock output includes milk, meat, live animals, in some cases transportation services, manure, and draught services, and in a few instances blood. Manure has a low value, as fallow periods are sufficient to rejuvenate the soil. Shifting cultivation implies that farming is carried out with hand tools; that is, there is no demand for animal draught.[10] As pature is abundant, crop residue will have little fodder value. Thus the gains to keeping livestock stationary are limited, and are dominated by the additional risks and labour costs of such a production process.

This result does not apply to small flocks of ruminants (i.e. goats) or to poultry, which are produced with virtually no labour input, are based on browse, and need very limited pasture and water.

PROPOSITION 6.   Operational units will be completely specialized in herding or farming.

While there are few fixed costs associated with farming *per se*, a herder faces high costs of starting crop cultivation. To begin to farm, he would have to adjust away from that transhumance pattern most closely synchronized with seasonal water and pasture availability. He may need to return early from dry season pasturage in order to plant, or leave late to the dry season pasturage in order to harvest. The costs of this adjustment are higher risks and an increase in the necessary labour input in order to draw water or cut fodder.

Conversely, it is clostly for cultivators to enter herding. Given abundant pasture, herding exhibits approximately constant returns to scale in *labourers* as the number of herds multiplies. For a fixed number of herders, however, transhumance is characterized by strongly increasing returns to labour input, up to an optimal herd size per herder. Thus, the herding of a single animal implies the loss to farming of the same amount of labour power as the herding of an optimal herd size.

From the cost side, therefore, complete specialization in one agricultural system dominates partial specialization. If opportunities for the exchange of crop and livestock products exist or can be created, and if consumer preferences do not bar this specialization (that is, if the grain requirements of herders can be met by farmers, and the meat demand from farmers can be met by herders), operational units will specialize in herding or farming.[11]

3.4. The output market and the determination of cultivated area

Specialization in herding and farming implies that:

PROPOSITION 7.   There will be a regular exchange of agricultural output between herders and farmers.

Owing to high transport costs (S2), crop output will not be exported from the region; thus the expansion of the market for food crops is limited by the demand of herders, and that for animal products by farmers. Because of this limit on the demand for crop output, the terms of trade between crop and animal products will decline rapidly with an expansion of cultivation. In general, one might expect farming households' in such isolated areas to work fewer hours than farmers in technologically similar peasant societies where export markets exist.[12]

3.5. Insurance and credit markets

Binswanger and Rosenzweig (1986) show that crop insurance is infeasible as a consequence of moral hazard, covariant yield risks, and geographical isolation.

Collateral options are extremely limited; because land has no sales value (Proposition 1), it cannot serve as collateral. Animals are a poor form or collateral as they are subject to a high degree of collateral-specific risk. And with simple technology, no important stock of machines exists to serve as collateral. The tropical climate and transhumance imply a limited quantity of housing investment. The major collateral is therefore gold or other precious commodities which do not have a positive expected return.

Collateral substitutes in the form of marketing credit and labour credit linkages, while feasible, are of restricted usefulness. The limited nature of the output market implies that only a small amount of credit can be supported by forward sales of crops. Forward sales of labour imply a reduction in self-cultivation opportunities and are thus an expensive means of guaranteeing loans in a land-abundant economy. It is inefficient as a collateral substitute and is used only under extreme duress.[13]

PROPOSITION 8.   Restricted options for collateral and collateral substitutes imply that the credit market is sharply limited from the supply side.

PROPOSITION 9.   The credit market is also limited from the demand side. This follows from simple technology (S5) and the unimportance of hired labour (Propositions 2 and 3), and implies that the demand for working capital is composed primarily of the need for a wages fund for the household. The only important component of credit demand is as an insurance substitute.

3.6. *Insurance substitutes and capital accumulation*

In an environment where no crop insurance exists, and where credit markets are very thin, households must find other means of self-insurance. Two kinds of risks arise. Covariant risks are variations in crop or livestock output which all farmers in a small geographic subregion experience at the same time. Specific risk if defined as uncorrelated variation in outcomes for a specific unit of production and includes individual-specific health risks and plot-specific production risks.

Social institutions such as extended families cannot perform well as insurance substitutes for covariant risks unless they cover extensive geographic areas. The supply-side limitations discussed above prevent the credit market from performing well as an insurance substitute for any type of risk.

PROPOSITION 11.   Capital accumulation is the major insurance substitute.

Binswanger and Rosenzweig (1986) show that households must hold their own food stocks. Common granaries across households would help pool specific risks. However, moral hazard imposes costs which — given covariate yields — are not offset by the risk-pooling benefits. The pooling benefits could be increased only if lower transportation costs allowed the pooling to be spread over a larger area.

Some wealthier households could specialize in accumulating stocks for selling at high prices during years of crop failure. This option is, however, limited by several factors. Holding stocks is costly because of storage losses and the limited durability of food grains. Because of the uncertainty surrounding weather, accumulation of grain stocks is a risky speculative venture: stocks might have to be held through a succession of favourable years in which there is limited food demand. Substantial wealth will therefore not be accumulated as food stocks. Gold and jewellry have little storage cost but also do not have a positive expected return. Land has no value (Proposition 1). Livestock, however, has a positive expected return. In addition, livestock production (under transhumance) is less risky than crop production, and the covariance between crop and livestock output is less than the covariance between the yields of different crops in the same area. Therefore accumulation of cattle provides an important means of risk diversification. Rate-of-return calculations to livestock ownership usually take into account only the expected stream of output. By ignoring the insurance benefit, they underestimate the overall value of livestock ownership. We may conclude that:

PROPOSITION 13. Livestock is the major form of wealth and insurance substitute.[14]

In some semi-arid environments, the vegetation in forests and in grass and bush fallows contains useful plants providing roots, tubers, or nuts which do not deteriorate rapidly. Gathering and hunting on these common-property resources therefore not only is an income source but also may be especially valuable in bad years.

PROPOSITION 14. Common-property resources may provide an insurance substitute.

3.7. Livestock tenancy

Livestock constitute the primary store of value, but, given the dominant advantages of specialization, farmers will not care for cattle themselves. The cattle will be entrusted to herders. This pattern of livestock tenancy obviously entails a high level of moral hazard: animals may be stolen or poorly treated and returned in underfed condition. These sources of moral hazard are overcome partly by the design of the farmer–herder relationship, which usually extends over many years. In order to encourage proper care, the herder's payment includes milk and a share of the offspring. An underfed cow in poor health does not produce offspring. A cow without regular offspring does not produce milk, and once a calf is born, the amount of milk depends directly on the quantity and quality of fodder.[15]

Given the incentives for crop cultivators to own cattle and the moral hazard inherent in livestock tenancy, why do we not see the integration of crop and livestock production within one ownership unit which runs specialized operational units for crop and livestock production? Should we not see kinship links across the cultivator–herder divide to capitalize on the possibility of risk diffusion between the enterprises?

The skills needed to become a herder can be learned only over a period of years spent with herders. This results from the need to know not only the techniques of animal husbandry, but the pattern in time and space of fodder and water availability. This pattern will change from year to year as a result of fluctuations in weather, hence the need for several years spent in the company of herders. This long-term separation of a herding kin member from his cultivating family eliminates the potential reducton in moral hazard from such an arrangement.

There is a tendency for the division between specialized herders and cultivators to correspond to an ethnic and cultural division. The exchange of livestock and short-term information about resource availability facilitates and is facilitated by the development of social ties within the herding group. The management of potential conflicts over access to grazing land and water resources leads to spatially extended social interactions among herders that require a common cultural context. The different production relations required by transhumance and shifting cultivation contribute to the development of different cultural forms.[16]

Complete ethnic specialization will not hold continuously. The most important exception will occur after a prolonged period of drought or an epidemic that drastically reduces livestock populations. Those pastoralists who are left with herds too small to continue specialized transhumance will become farmers until they are able to rebuild their herds.[17]

3.8. Household size

Following Meillassoux (1981), we define a household as a group of individuals who produce in common on at least one field and who receive food out of a common food store. We will consider the determinants of the extension of the family beyond the nuclear unit. We define two forms of extension. A vertically extended household is composed of nuclear units of succeeding generations. A horizontally extended household is composed of nuclear units of siblings. Of course, a household can be both vertically and horizontally extended.

We hypothesize that extended households provide an insurance substitute. There are two types of insurance benefits associated with household extension. The first, proposed by Meillassoux, arises when older individuals in vertically extended households have accumulated assets to which they have exclusive claim; these provide insurance substitutes to younger household members against covariant risks such as area-wide crop failure. The second type, contribution to a common granary, can insure members against specific risks. These risks are uncorrelated and risk-pooling benefits are substantial. Both horizontally and vertically extended households can provide insurance for non-covariate risks.

Individual ownership of wealth and control over common food stocks provides older individuals with powerful means of extracting labour services from younger family members, a central point in Meillassoux's explanation of production relations in this environment. If the insurance benefit provided by the household head is not counted, the expected contribution of children to output and household wealth would exceed the payment they receive, that is, their consumption out of the common store. The household head provides insurance in exchange for cheap labour, which might enable the household to accumulate faster than it otherwise would. An added incentive for vertical extension arises from the fact that older people have a greater knowledge of the highly variable production conditions in the semi-arid tropics.[18] This also provides an incentive for production on common fields. The break-up of a vertically extended household entails a loss of cheap labour to the household head. Young adults will be able to break away from their vertically extended household only when they have accumulated sufficient capital for (1) a wages fund, that is, seed and subsistence until harvest time, and (2) an insurance fund, in the form of animals or grain sufficient to survive a crop failure.

3.9. Long-distance trade and coercive relations

In land-abundant settings herders have often been involved in long-distance trade. They have often exerted dominance over cultivator groups.[19] This involved the extraction of tribute through a variety of mechanisms, and in certain cases outright slavery until bans on slavery were enforced.

The nature of transhumance is such that the seasonal pattern of movement crosses into different ecological subzones. These different areas are characterized by different climates, soil types, and mineral endowments. Thus, the relative values of different commodities are different in the different regions. There are therefore potential gains (and profits) from trade between the different regions, provided transportation costs are sufficiently low.

The ownership of a stock of animals and an established pattern of movement into different ecological zones implies that the costs of entrance into the long-distance trade are small for transhumants. Therefore, there are strong incentives for herders to enter into the long-distance trade. A product of entrance into trade along transhumance routes will be the development of trading skills and organizations among herders that will be transferable to other trade routes where the complementarity with herding is not as pronounced. A further product is access to military technology from outside the region.

Cultivators are subject to significantly higher opportunity costs to engaging in long-distance trade, even if such trade occurs in the slack labour demand season. Pack animals would need to be kept year-round despite the seasonality of trading activity. Furthermore, home production normally undertaken during the slack season would be forgone. Cultivators may however engage in long-distance trade, particularly in areas inaccessible to animals.

Cultivators have substantial immovable investments in cleared plots, wells, storage facilities, and housing. In contrast, the transhumance pattern of herders is flexible as long as pasturage is abundant and alternative water sources are available. Thus herders are more mobile. The ability of herders to change transhumance routes inhibits retaliation by cultivators in response to raiding activity by herders. This advantage is weakened if water, pasture, or another resource needed by herders is scarce in the regions inhabited by cultivators. It is offset by the presence of a state controlled by the cultivators.

Both trading and raiding activities involve potential profits which are dissipated if competition prevails in these activities. Herders thus have an incentive to organize politically to exercise monopoly control over these activities in order to extract these benefits. The strong interdependencies between herders that result from the transhumance method of livestock production facilitates this development.

4. The Effects of Population Growth

In a closed region, population growth changes many of the characteristics of the low-population density farming system. In Boserup's (1965) analysis, population growth has eight principal effects: (1) it reduces the fallow period; (2) it increases investment in land; (3) it encourages the shift from hand hoe cultivation to animal traction;[20] (4) it encourages soil fertility maintenance via manuring; (5) it reduces the average cost of infrastructure; (6) it permits more specialization in production; (7) it induces a change from general to specific land rights; (8) it reduces the per capita availability of common-property resources (forest, bush and/or grass fallow, communal pastures).[21]

The first four effects result from the necessity to raise land productivity and to offset the increase in labour requirements associated with more intensive cultivation. The fifth and sixth effects follow from economies of scale in the provision of infrastructure in more densely populated areas and the concomitant increase in intra-regional trade.

The transition to specific land rights, while subject to enormous regional variation, is a common tendency. With general land rights, cultivators typically own only the right to *use* a specific plot and to do so only as long as they actually cultivate it; when the cultivator departs — usually to leave the plot fallow — the use right reverts to the lineage. With the development of specific land rights, the cultivator can begin to assert certain rights in plots, starting with the right to resume cultivation of a specific plot after a period of fallow. At a later stage he asserts, and will receive, the right to assign the plot to an heir or to a tenant; the use right in the plot does not revert to the lineage anymore. With increasing population density and farming intensity, the rights assignable by the individual cultivator become more extensive and eventually include the right to refuse stubble grazing and, most importantly, complete alienability: he can lease and sell plots to individuals of his own choosing. This transition to secure specific land rights provides incentives to undertake investments in specific plots, investments that are required for the intensification of production and the preservation of fertility.[22]

4.1. Population growth and risk

Population growth has little effect on person-specific or covariate risk, but it has important effects on the means to diffuse them. Population growth mitigates the effects of person-specific risk in two ways. (1) It leads to markets for specialized crops (e.g. fruits and vegetables) and non-farm products, and allows greater diversification into them. (2) It reduces the average cost of infrastructure, thus allowing further market expansion for some goods, and further diversification.

Population growth diffuses covariant risk by reducing the average cost of infrastructure. Since it costs less to trade with other nearby areas in bad years, there will be a reduction in intra-regional risk even if the region is not open to external trade. The reduction in covariant risk, imputed to a reduction in costs of access to nearby regions, would occur even if the area produced everything it did in the same proportion before the transport cost reduction.

4.2. Population growth, money-lending, and landlessness

With induced innovation and investment (i.e. 'Boserupian effects' 2, 3, and 4), the demand for both working and investment capital rise, as does the demand for trading capital to accommodate increased intra-regional specialization. To the extent that the labour market develops (see below), the demand for credit to finance wages will rise. As population pressure increases and specific land rights develop, a market for land sales develops and land acquires a sales value. Land therefore becomes useful as collateral. This new availability of a major collateral asset increases the supply of credit. Landowners can now use the credit market as a partial insurance substitute if they have not mortgaged all of their land. However, as shown in Rosenzweig and Binswanger (1986), credit will not be available for the purchase of land.[23] Land purchases will therefore be financed out of self-generated funds, from savings. This would tend to make any given distribution of landholdings more unequal, despite the greater utility of land to smaller owners (because of its insurance and collateral value, and lower labour costs).

The emergence of the credit market based on the collateral value of land leads to the emergence of a class of money-lenders and a class of non-owners of land. Increased collateral options make money-lending more profitable in the short run. Moreover, money-lending becomes a means of acquiring land pledged as collateral. A class of non-owners arises because land pledged as collateral is surrendered on default. A positive frequency of default arises because for each individual it is not optimal to pursue a borrowing strategy that implies a zero probability of involuntary default. Once land is lost, it cannot be bought again with borrowed funds. All of the above tendencies are stronger with more induced investment.

4.3. Land tenancy and the distribution of land[24]

In a land-scarce environment, the value of land as collateral implies that owners of large amounts of land will be able to acquire credit more cheaply than smaller landowners. Does this production cost advantage of large landowners imply that the distribution of landownership will importantly affect operational scale?

Binswanger and Rosenzweig (1986) show that a landless person with a family who owns animals and/or machines, possesses some managerial skill, and has a wage fund will find it more profitable to rent in land than to hire out his endowments separately. Their argument follows from the higher costs of hired labour compared with family labour discussed above (C2; Propositions 2 and 3). Similarly, a large landowner will find it more profitable to rent out land than to manage a large operation because of the scale diseconomies arising from the use of hired labourers.[25] There is thus a potential market for the rental of land, which would tend to make the distribution of operational holdings more equal than that of ownership, and to move the former closer to optimal operational scale.

The existence of a land rental contract between a large landowner and a tenant is likely to entail the provision of credit by the owner to the tenant. This is because of economies of scale in monitoring, because the owner is likely to have superior information about his tenant compared with other potential lenders, and because the cheaper credit can be embodied and even disguised in owner-provided inputs which can encourage their proper use. The linkage of contracts is thus likely to be common.

To the extent that tenancy arrangements are feasible, there is an indefiniteness to the distribution of ownership holdings. While transactions and supervision costs rise with the number of tenancy agreements and thus with the size of land holdings, this rise in costs is likely to be small. For very large holdings, specialization in rent collection is likely and the use of family members as supervisors of tenants reduces principal–agent problems. As noted above, the need to purchase land out of equity leads to a tendency for land to accumulate in the hands of persons with greater production endowments — bullocks, family labour, managerial skills — but this also means that land will tend to accumulate faster among persons with already large landownership. Thus, while both the land rental and sales markets promote the efficient allocation of factor endowments, land sales are likely to exacerbate landholding inequality, necessitating greater use of tenancy contracts. Land sales and land rentals thus evolve as complementary transactions.

4.4. Labour market

Despite the apparent attractiveness of tenancy arrangements, there will be labour available for hire in a land-scarce setting. Severe moral hazard problems imply limitations on the development of draught animal rental markets (see Binswanger and Rosenzweig 1986). Therefore, small landowners who do not own such animals will rent out their land and supply their labour to the market if bullock-ploughing is used in cultivation. *A fortiori*, landless families who do not own bullocks will also supply labour.

Even before the transition to the use of draught power is complete, individuals who lack sufficient capital or management skills will supply labour to the market rather than lease land. As noted above, tenancy agreements will often provide access to credit, but this credit is based on a rather poor collateral substitute, the interlinked contract, and may not be sufficient to cover subsistence and working capital requirements over the course of the growing season. These limitations on the ability to lease in land become stronger as more induced investment occurs.

Despite the lower cost of family labour, the optimal permanent labour force is smaller than the peak season requirement because of the high committed cost of family or permanent labour. On the other hand, the optimal permanent labour force is larger than the slack season requirement because of the risk of not finding casual labourers during the peak season. Therefore most farmers will both hire in labour in the peak season and attempt to hire out labour during the slack season. Where there are no slack season jobs, there will be seasonal underemployment.[26]

Given the availability of labour for hire in a land-scarce environment, the optimal farm scale may exceed that based on the family labour force, as workers can be hired on long-term contracts. But long-term hired workers do not share in profits and therefore have a lower incentive to work than family members. Farms based on long-term workers would therefore not be competitive with farms based exclusively on family workers. Only if there are other economies of scale can this disadvantage be overcome. Such economies of scale can arise from the lumpiness of the management of draught power inputs. Households owning large quantities of these inputs (relative to their family size) will find it to their advantage to hire long-term workers. Economies of scale can also be transmitted to the farm from a processing plant, provided that farm output cannot be stored and the operation of the plant must be co-ordinated closely with farm operations, as in the case of sugar cane. This co-ordination can be achieved by placing the processing plant and the farm under the same management, as in a plantation. For a detailed discussion, see Binswanger and Rosenzweig (1986).

4.5. Household structure and the land market

Improvements in land, credit, and output markets associated with population growth will lead to a decline in the prevalence of horizontally extended families, as such markets provide superior opportunities to diffuse person-specific and even covariant risks. No prediction can be made, however, as to the prevalence of vertically extended families.

4.6. Transhumance and herder–farmer exchanges

As population density rises, high-quality pasture is converted to crop production and fallow periods decline. Grazing opportunities become scarcer and therefore crop residues emerge as the dominant source of fodder. As fallow periods decline, soil fertility must be maintained by applying some form of organic matter (or chemical fertilizer). Farmers exchange fodder for manure, with side-payments depending upon changing conditions of supply and demand. The return from keeping livestock in one area for longer periods becomes greater. As transhumance patterns adjust in response to these changes, the costs to herders of entrance to farming fall, and settled transhumance (seasonal migrations from a settled base at which cultivation occurs) becomes the system of livestock production. The transition from specialized herding and farming to a mixed farming system has begun.

As landownership becomes a major form of investment, the role of animals as stores of wealth declines. They remain important insurance substitutes because of the low covariance between crop and livestock output. However, as renting out land involves fewer incentive problems than does renting out animals, livestock tenancy will decline. Farmers and settled transhumants may begin producing fodder crops, and formerly specialized cultivators will begin to keep cattle year-round as their draught power and manure become more valuable.[27]

4.7. Coercive relations

Apart from the impact of the ban on slavery and the imposition of colonial rule, population growth undermines the material basis of coercive relations of herders over cultivators.[28] As common-property resources become scarce, herders' freedom to choose transhumance routes is constrained. The fodder basis shifts from grazing on commons and fallows to the grazing of crop residue and stubble which cultivators control (and can burn if they want to deprive the herders of it). Herders must start engaging in more co-operative relationships where the right to graze crop residues is exchanged for manure.

A comparative advantage in livestock production shifts to integrated crop livestock systems, herders become sedentary pastoralists, eliminating the advantages of mobility altogether.

5. The Effects of Migration

In a formerly closed, land-abundant region, new opportunities for emigration or seasonal migration during the farming season reverse many of the Boserupian effects discussed above. The labour force available for agriculture drops or grows less than it otherwise would have done, reducing the years of use of land between fallows and increasing the marginal product of labour (at the original level of hours per capita). Land investment is inhibited (as a proportion of investment; there are however offsetting wealth effects); animal traction and soil fertility maintainance through manuring are discouraged; the average cost of infrastructure rises; the availability of common-property resources per capita increases; and the transition to specific land rights is slowed or halted.

Remittances from migrants (or their savings when they return) can substantially reduce both specific and covariant risk. If struck by a plot-specific crop failure, for example, one or more household members can migrate temporarily to offset the income loss. Covariance of incomes across households is substantially reduced where remittances add a major new income source not dependent upon local weather.

Because land is abundant and has no sales price, it continues to have no collateral value. The limitations on the supply of credit discussed above therefore remain. The demand for credit is lower as the risk diversification associated with the additional income reduces the need for credit as an insurance substitute.[29] The credit market remains poorly developed.

Both forms of household extension are likely to decline in the face of improved possibilities for risk diffusion and the lower covariance of income. Other features of the base case remain unaltered.

6. The Effects of External Trade

The availability of external markets in crops for which the region has a comparative advantage eliminates the limitations on the demand for agricultural output described previously. This immediately raises the marginal value products of all factors at their former levels of utilization, leading to an intensification of cultivation that closely parallels many of the effects described by Boserup (Section 5). In particular, fallow periods are reduced, investment in land is promoted, the shift towards animal traction is encouraged, and the movement away from general land rights is speeded up. The transition to specific land rights occurs near roads and other transport facilities while land in less accessible areas remains uncleared. The development of specific land rights is thus not tied exclusively to population density.

6.1. Trade and risk

The consequences for risk of the new opportunity to engage in external trade depends upon the nature of that trade.

1. If one of the old staple crops is exported, the covariance between farmers' incomes will rise. In addition to correlated output shocks, they now face correlated external price shocks. However, savings and credit are now more effective insurance substitutes because deficit households will be able to buy staple crops at prices that do not rise sharply when crops fail locally. In such years exports can be reduced or the export channels can be used to import from climatically unrelated regions. Similarly, livestock can be traded more easily towards the outside of the region, so its price will not decline as

sharply during drought. (See Jodha 1978 on this effect.) The effect of external trade in this case is thus to improve the capacity of wealth stored in forms other than foodstuffs to act as insurance substitutes for the region as a whole.

2. If the export crop is a new or previously minor crop, there is a decline rather than an increase in covariant risk. The new crop is a source of portfolio diversification, reducing the impact of local weather on the variance of total output. Furthermore, its price is uncorrelated with that of the local staple. Finally, the export channels can still be used to import food in bad years.

In the first case, there is likely to be an increase in the incentive for vertical extension of the household. Covariant risks have increased, and the effectiveness of savings by the lineage head as an insurance substitute has also increased. In the second case, covariant risks have declined, so there is less need for the vertical extension of households.

6.2. Trade and money-lending

The use of intermediate inputs such as fertilizer and pesticides increases as these inputs can be supplied through the external trade channels. The demand for credit to finance working capital increases. If the export is a new crop, the demand for credit as an insurance substitute declines as covariant risks are reduced and a given amount of credit protects against a larger production shock. If the export crop is a former staple, we cannot predict the effect on the insurance demand for credit.

The new exports support the extension of additional credit based on marketing–credit links. Inputs or working capital can be provided by a trader in exchange for a commitment that he obtain the crop output under preferential conditions.

This process is encouraged by the ability of traders to overcome a fundamental problem of local credit markets: since the traders can obtain capital from a different agro-climatic zone, an urban area, or abroad, the high positive correlation between deposit withdrawal and loan demand can be circumvented (see Binswanger and Rosenzweig 1986; Sect. 2). These traders are now able to lend out of externally borrowed funds as well as out of their own equity. Landlessness may develop, but its spread will be slow as long as uncleared land remains available. Along with the development of a land sales market, tenancy contracts emerge.

6.3. Labour

The increased productivity of labour may make it possible to attract migrants from the outside. However, as long as land remains abundant in less accessible areas, some long-term migrants will obtain temporary or permanent cultivation rights, especially where different subregions or lineages compete for the migrant labour.

6.4. Transhumance

As long as common-property resources remain abundant, transhumance is likely to remain the primary method of livestock production. However, the growing value of manure, draught power, and crop by-products in the zone where the intensity of cropping has risen implies that more cattle will remain for longer periods around the farms of settled cultivators.

As covariant risks decline or are more easily diffused by alternative means, the use of livestock to diversify risks diminishes and the proportion of wealth held in livestock declines. Once again, however, there is an offsetting wealth effect that will tend to increase the demand for livestock. The net effect on cattle tenancy is ambiguous.

7. Conclusion

The survival and growth of societies depends upon the generation of a set of relationships governing production, exchange, and ownership which allow individuals and households to achieve their specific and collective goals effectively in the presence of risk. Production relations therefore should be expected to adapt, however imperfectly, to the current and intertemporal problems that arise as a result of changes in material conditions. In this chapter we have attempted to delineate the principle behavioural and technological factors that act as important determinants of production relations in semi-arid agriculture. Our analysis has departed from many of those existing in the literature in its applications of general risk and information problems, which have been the focus of much recent work in microeconomic theory, to the unique technological characteristics of agriculture in a semi-arid environment in order to provide an internally consistent explanation of many well documented institutional features of that environment.

We shall not summarize our results by section. Instead, we contrast the propositions established for the land-abundant base case with those derived for the land-scarce case.

Boserup's (1965) work focused on the technological changes and investments induced by population growth. She also summarized the impact of population growth on the transition from general to specific land rights. In discussing the transition from land-abundant to land-scarce conditions, we have incorporated these known endogenous effects but have, in addition, analysed other endogenous changes which typically occur in production relations.

The absence of a sales value for land under low population density has several profound implications.

1. As no major productive asset exists with high collateral value, credit supply is sharply limited. Therefore, money-lending is not a major avenue for wealth accumulation and no class of professional money-lenders exists.

2. As no crop insurance exists, storage and asset accumulation are necessary to guard against covariant risks regardless of population density. But apart from storage, low population density implies that the only vehicle for productive investment is livestock, and wealth inequality is expressed in unequal livestock holdings, not unequal landownership.

3. In semi-arid, low-population-density areas, the cost advantage and risk diversification associated with extensive grazing encourages specialized transhumance as the most efficient form of livestock management. Transhumance, however, creates an incentive problem by making it expensive for the animal owner to monitor herder performance. The incentive problem is mitigated by long-term entrustment relationships in which the herder's payment depends closely on the health and nutritional status of the animal. For wealthy individuals, long-term livestock tenancy performs the same function as does long- or short-term land tenancy in land-scarce environments.

4. Land abundance, associated with the weak credit market, prevents the emergence of a class of landless labourers. The labour market is constrained to various forms of labour exchange among self-cultivators outside the peak season. The very limited availability of hired labour implies that ambitious farmers cannot raise output by adding extra labourers, but only by adding extra household members. Again, wealth differences are not reflected in sharp differences in operated area per household member, as they are in a land-scarce environment.

5. Regardless of population density, vertical extension of households and patron–client links are similarly useful as insurance against covariant risks. Horizontal extension of households, on the other hand, is less desirable in land-scarce than in land-abundant environments.

NOTES

1. This base case was first analysed by Binswanger and McIntyre (1987), who also deal with other agro-climatic regions. Here the issue of herder–farmer interactions as analysed by Udry (1986) has been fully integrated into the argument.
2. Such development was not uncommon in the areas of Africa considered in this study (see Curtin 1984).
3. For empirical evidence, see Binswanger (1980).
4. See Binswanger and Rosenzweig (1986).
5. For implications under land scarcity, see Feder (1983).

6. See for example Norman (1972), Spencer and Byerlee (1976), and Longhurst (1985) on the limited use of hired labour during the peak season. Longhurst includes a discussion of the impact of an intensive agricultural development project on the labour market. See Eicher and Baker (1982; 99–105) for further references.

7. Most importantly, see Ruthenberg (1971). See also Swanson (1981), Cleave (1974), and Etuk (1986).

8. See Feeny (1982) for an extreme case in Thailand. Hill (1972) observes this phenomenon in northern Nigeria.

9. See Eicher and Baker (1982; 227–8) on seasonal migration. 'Stranger farmers' are seasonally found in many societies in semi-arid Africa, from the Gambia (Swindell 1978) through Nigeria (Hill 1972) to the Sudan.

10. Pingali *et al.* (1987) show that, under shifting cultivation, the average cost of production with hand tools is lower than with draught animals. This is because the use of the plough requires the de-stumping of plots, i.e. a system of permanent cultivation. Such a system, however, requires much higher energy inputs for land preparation, weeding, and soil fertility maintenance than the shifting cultivation system. It also requires overhead labour inputs into the maintenance of draught animals. Only when the option of shifting cultivation does not exist because of high population density (see Section 4) will the unit cost of production using the plough be lower than that using the hand hoe.

11. This set of hypotheses on the advantages of transhumance and specialization is supported in a wide range of cases across Africa. In Dar Fur the Baggara were transhumant herders while the Fur cultivated (O'Fahey 1973, 1985). In Kenya, Pokomo farmers trade output with Somali herders (Townsend 1978). Bahima herders and Bairu cultivators in western Uganda also trade output (Karugire 1971; Doornbos 1977). The most commonly cited case is that of Fulani transhumants, who trade with a variety of settled cultivators across the Western Sudan: with the Mossi (Skinner 1964; McCown *et al.* 1979), with the Bambara (Johnson 1976), with the Hausa (Stenning 1959; Baier 1980; Frantz 1975), with the Mbum and Tikar in the northern Cameroons (Abubakar 1977), and with the Jalonke (Derman 1973; Balde 1975).

12. See Cleave (1974) for a review of empirical studies that support the hypothesis that farmers will generally work fewer hours in more isolated areas.

13. Interlinked credit and the labour market transactions may be used for other purposes (see e.g. Basu 1983). However, in such situations the role of the linkage is not to discourage or prevent default. It may instead serve to circumvent restrictions on some subset of the contractual terms. For instance, if there are customary or legal restrictions on the interest rate, the wage rate can be used to adjust the total cost of an interlinked credit–labour contract. The joint contract may also provide an extra instrument in a principal–agent game. For example, because a worker's demand for credit depends upon his wage (and his supply of labour depends upon the credit contract he is offered), a lender/demander of labour may increase his profits by taking into account these intedependencies and setting the terms of both contracts simultaneously. (A phenomenon analogous to this is analysed by Braverman and Srinivasan 1984.)

14. The importance of livestock as a store of wealth to non-herding farmers has been

emphasized in a number of case studies; see McCown *et al.* (1979) for a review. Also see Dahl and Hjort (1976).

15. Livestock tenancy has been a topic of interest to anthropologists for many years, and recently economists have begun to consider the phenomenon. The references in n. 12 above document the importance of livestock tenancy, with the exception of the readings on the Bahima and the Bairu, where it did not occur.

16. A powerful example of this process was observed in the west of Sudan by Haaland (1969). As Fur cultivators accumulated more cattle, which were herded by the Baggara, the advantages of eliminating the risk of loss of their cattle through theft or maltreatment by herding themselves became so large that they abandoned cultivation. This transformation of specialized cultivators into specialized herders occurred at the rate of about 1% of the Fur population per year in the 1950s.

17. See Baier (1980) and Lovejoy (1979, 1983).

18. See Rosenzweig and Wolpin (1983).

19. The existence of herder involvement in long-distance trade, and of herder dominance over cultivators, has been documented in numerous cases: in Futa Jallon (Lovejoy 1983; Derman 1973; Balde 1975), the Sokoto Caliphate (Lovejoy 1978, 1979; Hogendorn 1977), and the interior delta of the Niger (Johnson 1976; Roberts 1981) this involved Fulani herders, see O'Faney (1973, 1985) on Dar Fur, Townsend (1978) on the Tana River in Kenya, and Baier (1980) and Olivier de Sardan (1983) for the Tuareg.

20. See n. 10.

21. The effects considered by Boserup are well documented in a variety of cases across Africa. See Eicher and Baker (1982; 110–12) for a brief review. For empirical tests of several of these effects see Chs. 2 and 3 and Part II of Pingali *et al.* (1987).

22. See Nonrohna (1985) for a comprehensive review.

23. Ownership of unmortgaged land provides access to credit at a lower interest rate. Even assuming that this yields no higher net profit from the land in any given year, the discounted value of unmortgaged land is higher than that of equally productive mortgaged land (which is discounted at the higher interest rate). The price of land will therefore be higher than its discounted value to those who would have purchased it through a mortgage.

24. This section summarizes Section B4 of Binswanger and Rosenzweig (1986).

25. Exceptions to this general rule occur in the cases of a few plantation crops, rarely found in semi-arid climates. These crops are either long-term crops with high maintenance intensity (i.e. some tree crops), or crops with important scale economies in processing combined with co-ordination problems between harvesting and processing (i.e. sugar cane). See Binswanger and Rosenzweig (1986).

26. For a fuller exposition, see Binswanger and Rosenzweig (1986; Sect. I.C).

27. The effects of an increasing population density on herder–cultivator exchanges and the growth of settled transhumance have been documented by Balde (1975) in Futa Jalon, by Toulmin (1983) in central Mali, and (somewhat less clearly) by Frantz (1975) in Niger.

28. Historically, this factor has also been compounded with the growth of state

power in the hands of cultivators (e.g. in the ninteenth-century rise of the forest kingdoms in West Africa) and increased long-distance trade through the hands of cultivators, giving them equal access to foreign weapons. See the references in n. 19. See also Skinner (1964) and Kottak (1972) for examples of the importance of dense populations and cultivator-controlled states in the determination of the character of farmer–herder relations.

29. There is a (generally small) offsetting income effect if the demand for credit is income-elastic.

PART III
Credit and Interlinked Transactions

In Chapter 7 the author models alternative structures in the informal credit market as devices for extracting surplus from the borrowers, and show how extremely exploitative money-lenders may have some superficial resemblance to markets with perfectly competitive money-lenders. In Chapter 8 the authors trace the key role of unequal access to both production and consumption credit in shaping the agrarian class structure. Chapter 9 shows that when there is credit rationing some technological innovations may increase inequality, and that latter in turn may have adverse effects on long-run productivity. In Chapter 10 the author looks into the conditions under which borrowing under a voluntary 'bonded labour' contract (whereby one may repay loans by providing labour services at less than one's opportunity cost) will be chosen by a sharecropper if another source of credit besides the landlord is available. In Chapter 11 the authors explore, in a principal–agent model of interlinking of production credit and crop marketing, the terms of equilibrium contracts under risk neutrality; in particular, they examine the situation where one of the two relevant instruments — the rate of commission on crop sale and the rate of interest on credit — is redundant. In Chapter 12 the author, in a brief overview of the theoretical literature on interlinked transactions, tries to balance the efficiency advantages with the possible adverse distributional consequences. In Chapter 13 the authors make explicit the assumptions required for the frequent presumption of an 'interlocker's edge'; and, given one or more of these assumptions, they try to find out if the theory of interlinking predicts certain patterns of competition between lenders.

7.

Rural Credit Markets: The Structure of Interest Rates, Exploitation, and Efficiency

Kaushik Basu

1. Introduction

Suppose a field worker finds that peasant A in his survey area borrowed Rs.100 from a money-lender on condition that he would return Rs.120 in a month's time. A standard way in which an economist would present this *finding* to other economists is this:

> A peasant borrowed money at an interest rate of 790 per cent per annum.[1]

I shall argue that presenting credit data in this manner can be misleading and, in the context of backward agrarian economies, often is. Notice that the economist's *statement* entails normalizing the *finding* over two dimensions: loan size and duration. The per *cent* refers to the former and per *annum* refers to the latter. In fact, it is so common to do such normalizations that the qualifying terms 'per cent' and 'per annum' are often not even stated: we all know what it means to say, for instance, that 'interest rate is 10'.

While the normalizations may be reasonable in organized credit markets, where interest rates are relatively invariant with respect to loan size and duration, they should be used with much greater caution in presenting the findings of backward markets. Such normalizations can be misleading because different findings can be made to look deceptively similar. Suppose a certain peasant (call him B) is found borrowing Rs.100 for a year on condition that he pays back Rs.890 at the year's end. The economist's statement of this finding will be exactly the same as the statement used to describe peasant A's predicament. Yet it is very likely that A and B face very different credit situations. From empirical findings (see e.g. Sarap 1986: Ch. 6) and theoretical models (as we shall soon see), we know that interest rates (per annum) on shorter-duration loans are usually higher than those on long loans. Hence if B

I have benefited from seminars at the Indian Institute of Technology, Kanpur, the Centre for Development Studies, Trivandrum, and the Madras Institute for Development Studies. I am grateful to the Indian Council for Social Science Research for financial support.

tried to borrow Rs.100 from his money-lender for just a month, he would probably have to pay a higher interest rate than 790 per cent. So it is likely that B faces a more extortionate credit environment, though this fact gets lost in a normalized statement.

Problems can arise the other way around as well. Two persons confronting the same options could be made to appear as if they face different situations. This could happen with respect to what, in the South Kanara district of Karnataka, India, is known as *holi* loans (Nagaraj 1981, 1985). For these loans, repayment has to occur at a fixed point of time, namely, after the harvest. This is irrespective of when the loan is taken in the previous year. In practice, people have been recorded as borrowing anywhere between six months and a week before the repayment date. Further, the amount that has to be repaid is independent of when the loan is taken. Consequently, normalized over time, the interest rate would be enormous for a person who borrows a week before the repayment date and relatively small for one who borrows six months in advance. Hence two individuals who face the same options would show up very differently in a simple normalized description of credit market transactions.

It sounds hackneyed but is true that many concepts and methods developed in the context of industrialized-economy credit markets turn out to be inadequate for analysing markets in less developed economies. Nagaraj (1985: 271) may well be right when, referring to the rural Indian credit market, he observes, 'The whole notion of a *rate* of interest appears simply to be absent' (my italics). In a similar vein, Rudra (1982: 69) notes that 'the usual concept of a "rate of interest" is not valid' in the context of the Indian countryside. Of course, we could always compute the implicit rate of interest in any credit transaction, but we ought to remember that this is an analyst's construct. Moreover, there are situations where, in talking about interest *rates*, we would be advised also to state the size and duration of the loans involved. These are the two variables that I shall discuss in this chapter, but the analysis should warn us that there may be others.

In this chapter I try to derive some simple testable propositions regarding the relation between interest rates, size of loan, and duration. This is done in Sections 3 and 4. Section 2 analyses the polar case where the lender is able to extract *all* surplus from the borrower. This is useful in removing some misunderstandings; it also establishes a theoretically easy (but nevertheless widely misunderstood) result: that, if in an economy one person is 'perfectly' exploitative, then efficiency is guaranteed.

Before venturing further, it is useful to provide a brief account of some of the more popular theories of credit in backward economies, especially since I refer to these in the next sections. The existing theories can be partitioned into competitive and monopolistic models. The former visualizes a rural market with many lenders in competition with one another and many atomistic borrowers. Such a theory gives rise to the familiar demand–supply cross. If, in addition, it is assumed that the lenders have free access to the organized, urban-sector credit but are unable to affect its interest rate, then the supply curve of credit in the rural sector becomes horizontal. In equilibrium, the rural interest rate is equal to the urban interest.

Such a pure case of competition is easily rejected by the evidence and has very few adherents among economists. Those who have maintained the competitive line of argument have done so by building special features into the above pure case. The most popular model in this class is the *lender's risk hypothesis*. Proposed by Tun Wai (1958) and Bottomley (1975), it has received a large amount of critical attention (Bhaduri 1977; Raj 1979; Basu 1984a). The lender's risk hypothesis utilizes a competitive framework but allows for the possibility of credit default. According to this hypothesis, when a rural money-lender gives credit, he undertakes the risk that the lender will abscond with the principle. If we deduct this expected cost from the *nominal* interest rate, that is, the interest rate that the borrower is supposed to pay, then we get the *effective* interest rate. In some sense this is the real interest rate — the one that affects the supply of and demand for credit. In equilibrium the effective interest rate in the rural market is equal to the urban interest rate. But for this to happen in the presence of a high default rate, nominal interest has to be much higher than the effective interest rate. Since the interest rate *observed* by field workers is the nominal one, the lender's risk hypothesis provides an explanation of the exorbitantly high interest rates that have been observed in the unorganized credit markets of less developed economies (see Griffin 1974).

The lender's risk hypothesis came under criticism for several reasons; in particular, it was felt that rural markets were too fragmented to be modelled, even as an approximation, as a case of competition. Further, it was empirically confirmed in the case of India (see Raj 1979) that the actual default rate is not sufficiently high to be able to explain the high rural interest rates.

This dissatisfaction led to heightened research activity at the other polar end: credit markets were now being modelled as *monopolies* (Bhaduri 1977; Mukherji 1982; Rudra 1982; Basu 1984b). However, what has been poorly understood is that monopolists can have different amounts of exploitative powers. The all-or-nothing monopolist is a very exploitative individual; the traditional monopolist is less so. What is more confounding is that the more exploitative monopolist, on the surface, looks less exploitative. This has been the source of much misunderstanding and some ideological embarrassment, and the next section is devoted to this problem.

2. Exploitation and Efficiency

A curious feature of rural credit markets is that, when the money-lender is perfectly exploitative,[2] the market outcome resembles a competitive one in which a money-lender has no power of exploitation. For instance, when markets are interlinked and the money-lender also happens to be the landlord of the borrowers, he may be able to extract all consumer's surplus from his borrowers through the labour market contract, and it may be in his interest to charge in the credit market an interest rate equal to the organized sector interest rate. This gives the impression of a benign money-lender in perfect competition with many other practitioners of the same trade. This has led to a mistaken charge that, in models of interlinkage where the lender charges a 'low' interest rate (e.g. Braverman and Stiglitz 1982; Basu 1984a), the lender is not as exploitative as he is in reality. The truth is different. In these models the landlord is *more* extortionate than he is in models where he charges high interest rates (e.g. Bhaduri 1977). This realization presents us with a theoretical problem. How do we reconcile the well-known fact that rural interest rates are often exorbitant with the equally well-known fact about the exploitative character of rural money-lending? I have argued (in Basu 1987) that this may have something to do with wage rigidities and the heterogeneity of borrowers. This will be taken up briefly in a later section.

Another more obvious, though equally widely misunderstood, property of a market with a perfectly exploitative money-lender is that its outcome is usually efficient.[3] The reason is simple enough. If one agent can ensure, under all circumstances, that the other will get no more than his fixed reservation utility, then it is in his interest to maximize output because that would maximize his own share. A corollary of this proposition is that if the credit market is inefficient then the money-lender must be less than fully exploitative.[4] Thus, ironically, most of the writers on agrarian structure who harp on the inefficiencies of the market are assuming a less extortionate money-lender. In contrast, some so-called neoclassical writers who are also careful theorists (which is a small subset of all economists who are labelled 'neoclassical') have modelled credit markets where the lender is perfectly exploitative.

The connection between exploitation and efficiency may be elucidated with a simple example. Suppose a poor peasant, who has no paddy of his own, has a technology open to him whereby he can convert L units of paddy loan into $X(L)$ units of paddy.[5] Thus,

$$X = X(L), X' > 0, X'' < 0. \tag{1}$$

On the other hand, there is a money-lender (or a paddy-lender) who has M units of paddy. He has a technology whereby he can convert each unit of paddy into $1 + r$ units. This mimics the idea of an exogenous organized sector interest rate. If he wants access to technology (1), he has to lend the paddy to the poor peasant; that is, he does not have direct access to the machine that can convert L into $X(L)$. In order to ensure the existence of an interior solution, I assume

$$X'(M) < 1 + r \quad \text{and} \quad X'(0) > 1 + r.$$

If the money-lender gives a loan of L to the peasant, he has $M - L$ left for himself. Hence the maximum that can be produced in the economy is given by

$$\max_{L} X(L) + (1 + r)(M - L) \equiv X^*.$$

By the first-order condition, we know this happens where $L = L^*$, which is defined as follows:

$$X'(L^*) = 1 + r. \qquad (2)$$

Hence, the technologically feasible production possibility frontier is as shown in Figure 7.1.

Figure 7.2 shows the output-maximizing loan size. This outcome is the efficient or Pareto-optimal outcome. Since there is only one good, all points on the frontier X^*X^* in Figure 7.1 are efficient. (That is, from the point of view of efficiency, it does not matter who gets how much, as long as their shares add up to X^*.)

Now let us see what the market outcome will be if the lender is perfectly exploitative. Let x be the borrower's 'reservation consumption'; that is, if he cannot earn at least x from borrowing, he will quit this credit market. I shall here take x to be his subsistence consumption; that is, if he gets less than x he will not survive. A *perfectly exploitative money-lender* is someone who can always ensure that the borrower gets x and he gets the rest.

Thus, if he lends L to the peasant, his income, $\pi(L)$, is $(1 + r)(M - L) + X(L) - x$. He chooses L to maximize this. The first-order condition is

$$X'(L) = 1 + r.$$

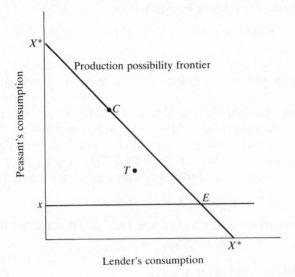

FIG. 7.1

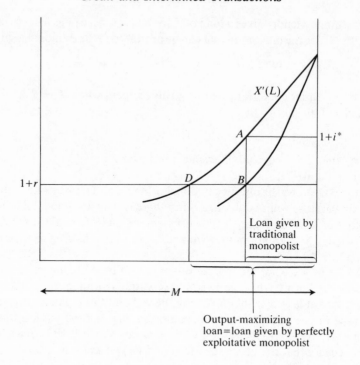

FIG. 7.2

This is the same as (2). Hence total output is X^* and efficiency is guaranteed. At equilibrium, the lender's income equals

$$\max_{L} (1 + r)(M - L) + X(L) - x = X^* - x,$$

by the definition of X^*. Hence the peasant's consumption is x. Thus, with a perfectly exploitative money-lender the equilibrium occurs at point E in Figure 7.1.

Let us now describe the equilibrium where the money-lender acts like a traditional monopolist. Let us first work out the credit demand function that the monopolist confronts. Given an interest rate i, the peasant's aim is to choose L so as to maximize $X(L) - (1 + i)L$.[6] The demand for credit is implicit in the first-order condition of this maximization exercise:

$$X'(L) = 1 + i. \tag{3}$$

The money-lender's aim is to choose i and L and maximize his profit,

$$(1 + r)(M - L) + (1 + i)L,$$

subject to the demand constraint (3).

Writing the Lagrangean for this maximization problem as

$$Z = (1 + r)(M - L) + (1 + i)L + \lambda\{X'(L) - (1 + i)\},$$

we have the following first-order conditions:

$$L - \lambda = 0$$
$$(1 + i) - (1 + r) + \lambda X''(L) = 0$$
$$X(L) - (1 + i) = 0.$$

Together, these imply that

$$1 + r = X'(L) + LX''(L).$$

Since the right-hand side is $\partial\{LX'(L)\}/\partial L$, this is the familiar 'marginal revenue equals marginal cost' condition.

Thus, in Figure 7.2, if we treat $X'(L)$ as an 'average' curve and draw its corresponding 'marginal' curve, the loan given by the traditional monopolist is shown by the point of intersection between this 'marginal' curve and the $(1 + r)$ line. The interest charged is shown by $1 + i^*$. Hence the output loss caused by traditional monopoly is given by the area ABD.

Hence in Figure 7.1 point E depicts the perfectly exploitative monopolist's equilibrium[7] and a point like T represents the traditional monopolist's equilibrium. Note that T entails inefficiency. It is well known that competitive markets are efficient. Hence what we have demonstrated is this: if, beginning from competitive behaviour, a money-lender becomes a traditional monopolist, equilibrium would shift from efficient to inefficient, from a point like C to T. If then the money-lender's exploitative power increases further and he becomes a perfectly exploitative lender, equilibrium would once again be efficient, this time at E. It is further possible, especially when the credit market is interlinked with other markets,[8] that the perfectly exploitative lender will charge the interest r (which is the same interest that a competitive lender would charge) because he will do the surplus extraction through the other market. This superficial resemblance between competition and perfect exploitation has led some observers mistakenly to charge the latter models as being models that do not endow the money-lender with the exploitative powers that he possesses in reality. They have been happier with the traditional monopoly characterization (as in Bhaduri 1977, Mukherji 1982, or Basu 1984b), which has high interest rates and inefficiency. In other words, what I am arguing is that someone like Rudra (1982: Ch. 4) is right in criticizing the myth that rural money-lending is competitive, but that he is wrong in jumping from this to the conclusion that rural credit markets are inefficient.[9]

3. Interest Rates and the Duration of Loan

If a money-lender is able to bargain separately for the terms and conditions of each unit of loan with each borrower, he may succeed in extracting all the surplus accruing to the borrowers. Such perfect exploitation, as described in the previous section, may not be possible, for two reasons. First, he may have inadequate *a priori* information about the borrowers, and the transaction cost of such elaborate bargaining (which may help elicit some information) may be too high. Second, such a procedure may violate the social and political norms of an economy and may, for this reason, be impossible to implement. One of the most major sources of dissent when a group of similarly placed individuals (e.g. borrowers) interacts with someone who is in a position of advantage (e.g. a monopolist money-lender) is the feeling of intragroup discrimination. If, among a group of labourers, one person's wage is increased, this causes dissension among other labourers unless the wage increase is explained according to some universalizable principle. Of course, what is viewed as discrimination may differ widely from one society to another. In the United States, if two professors in the same university department get different salaries this will generally not cause dissension (I know of exceptions!); but in India (and also many European countries), if professors in *different* departments get salaries that do not match, there may be a charge of discrimination, and, in fact, such salary differentials may not be feasible at all for this reason. And indeed, one can think of reverse examples, where a particular kind of differential treatment would be considered acceptable in India but would be the basis of discontent in the United States. These variations in the norms (and consequent differences in what is politically feasible) in different societies could arise for many reasons, including a people's history, experience, and genetic structure. I do not go into that here but simply consider alternative definitions of 'discrimination'.

I shall assume that there is a monopolist money-lender who wants to maximize profit, but who cannot 'discriminate' between potential borrowers (as this will cause dissension and inflict other kinds of cost on the lender). If a lender wants to charge two borrowers different interest rates, he will have to couch it in some *universalizable* principle.

In this section we look at the case where people's need for credit varies over time. And while the lender cannot charge Mr A less for being Mr A, he can make the interest rate depend on the length of time for which a loan is taken. Thus, he can indirectly impose a lower charge on A. For example, if he announces that *whoever* takes a long loan from him will pay a lower interest rate, and A happens to be a person with a need for a long loan, A will get credit at a lower charge.

By using this indirect method of making the interest rate depend on the length of the loan, a lender would be able to extract more surplus than he could by charging the same interest rate always. Also, this gives us a way of constructing a theory of interest rate variation in relation to the duration of loan. It is possible to construct theories of interest rate formation with more arguments, like the size of loan (Basu 1986), purpose of loan, wealth of the borrower (Sarap 1986), and so on. Some of these are discussed later.

Suppose there are $n + 1$ time-periods denoted by $0, 1, \ldots, n$. The borrowers are poor and save nothing. Using C_t to denote a borrower's consumption in period t, we write his utility function as

$$u = u(C_0, \ldots, C_n) \equiv u(\{C_t\}_t) \tag{4}$$

and assume $\partial u / \partial C_k > 0$ for all k. Let us denote the borrower's endowment by $w \equiv (w_0, \ldots, w_n)$.

Let L_{kt} denote the amount of loan taken in period k by the borrower for t periods; that is, it has to be paid back with interest in period $k + t$. Every vector $[L_{kt}] \equiv (L_{01}, \ldots, L_{0n}; L_{11}, \ldots, L_{1(n-1)}; \ldots; L_{(n-1)1})$, where $L_{kt} > 0$ for all k, t (i.e., a borrower cannot lend), will be referred to as a *credit plan*. A credit plan refers to a full plan of the borrower as to when he will take how much loan and for how long.

An *interest structure* is a vector

$$[i_t] \equiv (i_1, \ldots, i_n)$$

in which i_1 denotes the (per-period) interest rate payable on a loan taken for one period, i_2 denotes the (per-period) interest rate payable on a two-period loan, and similarly for all integers up to n. The interest rate structure is a choice variable of the lender. He chooses it, taking into account the fact that borrowers are free to respond with their optimal credit plan, and tries to maximize his profit (to be defined in a moment). By a *uniform* interest structure I shall mean a $[i_t]$ such that $i_1 = i_2 = \ldots = i_n$.

Let us now examine the borrower's problem. His initial endowment w denotes his consumption (and also income) stream over time if he is unable to get any credit. We could use this (although we could also conceivably use the utility function) to explain the need for credit, and also to capture the idea of credit need varying over time, being acute in one period, non-existent in another, and so on. Thus, for instance, if the utility function is symmetric in the $(n + 1)$ variables, and if w_t is very small compared with the endowments in other periods, the borrower's credit need will be 'acute' in period t. And he would ideally like to pay back the loan in a period in which his endowment is high.

To capture these ideas formally, note that the consumption of a borrower with endowment w, interest structure $[i_t]$, and credit plan $[L_{kt}]$ in period 0 is

$$w_0 + \sum_{t=1}^{n} L_{0t}.$$

His consumption in period 1 is

$$w_1 + \sum_{t=1}^{n-1} L_{1t} - (1 + i_1)L_{01}.$$

Similarly for consumption in periods 2, 3, . . ., n. Hence, we could define a person's utility, $\bar{u}$, as a function of w, $[i_t]$, and $[L_{kt}]$ as follows:

$$\bar{u}([L_{kt}], [i_u], w) \equiv u\left(\left\{ w_k + \sum_{t=1}^{n-k} L_{kt} - \sum_{t=0}^{k-1} (1 - i_{k-t})^{k-t} L_{t(k-t)} \right\}_t\right).$$

(5)

Since the endowment will generally be treated as unchanging, I shall be brevity drop the w from the $\bar{u}$-function in (5). That is, I shall write $\bar{u}([L_{kt}], [i_t])$.

The borrower's problem is to maximize $\bar{u}$ by choosing a credit plan, taking the interest structure offered by the producer as a given:

$$\max_{[L_{kt}]} \bar{u}([L_{kt}], [i_t]).$$

I shall use the function $f([i_t])$ to denote the credit plan $[L_{kt}]$ which solves the above maximization problem. In case there is more than one credit plan that maximizes $\bar{u}$, I follow the convention of taking $f([i_t])$ as the one (among these best credit plans) that maximizes the lender's profit (defined below.)[10] From the definition of profit below, it will be clear that this convention implies the assumption that, if a borrower is indifferent between two credit plans, the lender can persuade him to choose the one commensurate with his own interest.[11]

As in most of the literature on credit markets in backward agrarian economies, it will be assumed here that the money-lender has access to organized markets. In particular, he has access to the organized credit market, and he can borrow from it or lend to it at an exogenously fixed interest rate r. Strictly speaking, we do not need this assumption. It suffices to treat r as simply the exogenously given opportunity cost to the lender of giving loans in the rural sector. Its basis can be the organized credit or the return on investment in the rural sector or anything else.

The lender confronting $[i_t]$ and $[L_{kt}]$ will have the following net incomes from his rural sector lending activity:

In period 0: zero
In period 1: $(1 + i_1)L_{01} - (1 + r)L_{01} = (i_1 - r)L_{01}$
In period 2: $(i_1 - r)L_{11} + \{(1 + i_2)^2 - (1 + r)^2\}L_{02}$
and so on.

The lender's total profit, $\bar{\pi}$ (from rural lending), is defined as the present value of the above stream of per-period profit, discounted at the organized sector interest rate, r:

$$\bar{\pi}([L_{kt}], [i_t]) = \sum_{k=1}^{n} \left[\frac{\sum_{t=1}^{k} \{(1 + i_t)^t - (1 + r)^t\}L_{(k-t)t}}{(1 + r)^k} \right].$$

(6)

Define

$$\pi([i_t]) = \bar{\pi}\{f([i_t]), [i_t]\}. \tag{7}$$

The monopolist money-lender is a profit-maximizer who knows that, for every interest structure $[i_t]$ that he chooses, the borrower will respond by choosing the credit plan $f([i_t])$. Hence his aim is to maximize $\pi([i_t])$ by choosing an interest structure. I shall denote a profit-maximizing interest structure by $[i_t^*]$. This will also be referred to as the *equilibrium* interest structure.

The above definition of profit has been given assuming only one borrower. This is only for simplicity. It is easy to extend the same idea when there are H borrowers. If all the H borrowers have the same utility function and same endowment vectors, they will be described as *homogeneous*. Otherwise they are *heterogeneous*.

Actually, the class of homogeneous borrowers can be extended a little further. Suppose there are two borrowers 1 and 2 and their utility functions and endowment vectors are denoted by $u^i(\cdot)$ and w^i. Suppose that these are such that

$$\bar{u}^1([L_{kt}], [i_t], w^1) = \bar{u}^2([L_{kt}], [i_t], w^2) \tag{8}$$

for all $[L_{kt}]$ and $[i_t]$. Clearly, these two consumers will respond identically to the rural credit market. This is a case where, although $\bar{u}^1 \neq \bar{u}^2$ and $w^1 \neq w^2$, the two differences 'cancel out' when it comes to the rural credit market. Hence in our analysis borrowers 1 and 2 may be treated as homogeneous; that is, the theorems that are derived for the case where borrowers are homogeneous would allow for differences in utility functions and endowments as long as they satisfy (8).

If the borrowers are homogeneous, then the lenders' profit will simply be H times the profit shown in (7). If borrowers are heterogeneous, every borrower will have his own response function $f^s([i_t])$. Hence the lender's total profit when he offers the interest structure $[i_t]$ will be

$$\sum_{s=1}^{H} \bar{\pi}(f^s([i_t]), [i_t])$$

in (7). When stating and proving the theorems, I shall not each time state this modification, but instead shall treat it as obvious.

The results that emerge from this model are essentially formalizations of the observation that short-term loans entail higher interest rates. These results are stated and proved in the remainder of this section. But before that, I need to mention two simple conventions that I follow. These make the statements of the results simpler. First, it will be assumed that, whenever the money-lender earns the same profit from uniform and non-uniform interest structures, he chooses the former. Second, if the money-lender's profit-maximizing profit is zero, he will not lend in the rural sector at all.

THEOREM 1.   In a three-period model (i.e., $n = 2$) with homogeneous borrowers, (i) the short-term interest rate (i.e. i_1) is never less than the long-term interest rate (i.e. i_2) in equilibrium; and (ii) there are parametric configurations such that in equilibrium the short-term interest rate exceeds the long-term rate.

The theorem assets that the short-term interest rate is always greater than or equal to the long-term rate and that there are situations where it is actually greater. From the proof it will be clear that i_1 will in fact generally, exceed i_2. Remember that interest rates (whether i_1 or i_2) are always stated in per-period terms; in other words, the unit of time does not matter.

Part (i) of the theorem is quite obvious. If the short-term interest was less than the long-term interest, no borrower would take a two-period loan: he would take a one-period loan, repay it, and immediately take another one-period loan. Therefore the lender gains nothing by setting i_2 above i_1.

Part (ii) can be proved by constructing an example. Instead of constructing such an example, I sketch the *method* of constructing such examples. This has the advantage of highlighting the fact that there is a *class* of situations where this will hold.

Proof of Theorem 1.   (i) It is first shown that if $i_2 > i_1$ then no borrower will take a long loan. Since borrowers are assumed to be homogeneous, there is no harm in speaking as if there is one borrower.

Suppose $[i_t]$ and $[L_{kt}]$ are such that $L_{02} > 0$ and $i_2 > i_1$. Consider now the alternative credit plan, $[L_{kt}^*]$, defined as follows:

$$L_{01}^* = L_{01} + L_{02}$$
$$L_{02}^* = 0$$
$$L_{11}^* = L_{11} + (1 + i_1)L_{02}.$$

It is easy to check that this alternative credit plan leaves consumption in periods 0 and 1 unchanged but raises consumption in period 2 by $\{(1 + i_2)^2 - (1 + i_1)^2\}L_{02}$. Hence $L_{02} > 0$ cannot occur in a borrower's optimum. Thus, long loans are never taken if $i_2 > i_1$.

Now if $i_2 = i_1$, whether the borrower takes one long loan at i_2 or an equivalent amount of short loan at i_1 is behaviourally indistinguishable. Hence we could assume that if $i_2 = i_1$ the borrower will not take a long loan. Hence whatever profit the lender earns from (i_1, i_2) with $i_2 > i_1$, he earns by choosing the interest structure $(\bar{i}_1, \bar{i}_2)$ such that $\bar{i}_2 = \bar{i}_1 = i_1$. Hence he will not charge a higher interest on long loans.

(ii) The proof consists of constructing a suitable example. I construct here an outline of an example. Suppose $u(\cdot)$ and w are such that, if the interest rate is uniform and less than or equal to $\bar{i}$, the borrower would borrow in period 0 and repay in period 1 and will not take any other kind of loan. If the interest rates are non-uniform, then there is a small and positive number e such that, if $i_1 \geq i_2 + e$, the borrower would borrow the same amount of loan as he would when confronted with a uniform interest of i_2 but now he would be taking this loan for two periods.

With borrower preference as above, interest rates can easily be shown to be non-uniform. This may be proved by contradiction. Suppose that the equilibrium interest rate is uniform and equal to i^*. Clearly, this must be less than $\bar{i}$ (otherwise there would be no borrowing) and greater than r (otherwise the lender's profit would be less than or equal to zero and he would close shop).

From the borrower's preference, we know that a loan of some size, say L, will be taken in period 0 for one period. If somehow the borrower could be persuaded to take the same loan for two periods, the lender's profit would rise by

$$\frac{\{(1 + i^*)^2 - (1 + r)^2\}L}{(1 + r)^2} - \frac{\{(1 + i^*) - (1 + r)\}L}{1 + r} = \frac{(1 + i^*)(i^* - r)L}{(1 + r)^2}.$$

If, now, instead of offering the uniform interest of i^*, the lender offers $[i_t]$ where $i_1 \geq i^* + e$ and $i_2 = i^*$, then the borrower will take a loan of the same size as before (i.e. L), but for two periods. As just shown, this would enhance the lender's profit. Hence a uniform interest structure cannot be an equilibrium. And from part (i) of the theorem, we know that the interest rate for short loans must exceed the interest rate for long loans. Q.E.D.

It is worth noting that, in the example sketched in the above proof, the short-term interest rate (in equilibrium) turns out to be a notional one, because no one takes short loans. Of course, notional does not mean unimportant. It is *because* i_1 is set high that people take long loans. So, although in equilibrium no one is found borrowing at the interest rate i_1, it plays the important role of dissuading borrowers from taking short loans. It is worth noting that examples can easily be constructed, with heterogeneous borrowers, where *some* people would be taking short loans in equilibrium. The idea is simple. In the above example we could append another borrower who always takes short loans (or nothing), and his borrowing is so small that the lender's main source of profit is the borrower already depicted. Thus the equilibrium interest structure will look the same as above, but there will be borrowers (those of the second kind) who will be taking short loans in equilibrium.

The restrictions on Theorem 1 — that the borrowers be homogeneous and there be only three periods — were imposed to make the proof more transparent. Once the logic of the proof is followed, it will be clear that these restrictions are not essential. However, since with more than three periods there will be a whole range of interest rates, we cannot speak about *the* short-term interest or *the* long-term interest. The general idea that short borrowing will entail higher interest rates than long borrowing is still true, but one has to be careful in formalizing this. I first state the theorem and then explain.

THEOREM 2.   The equilibrium interest structure in an $(n + 1)$-period model in which borrowers may be heterogeneous has the following property: for all $k = 2, 3, \ldots, n$, for all positive integers h, and for all non-negative integers $t_1, \ldots, t_h$ such that $t_1 + \ldots + t_h = k$,

$$(1 + i_{t_1})^{t_1}(1 + i_{t_2})^{t_2} \ldots (1 + i_{t_h})^{t_h} \geq (1 + i_k)^k. \tag{9}$$

There are parametric configurations where the strict inequality holds.

The proof of Theorem 2 is similar to that of Theorem 1 and is not given here. The similarity becomes obvious as soon as inequality (9) in Theorem 2 is understood. The inequality asserts the following. Suppose a person takes a k-period loan. Now consider all ways of achieving the same consumption stream by breaking up the k-period loan into shorter-duration loans, for example one loan for d periods (where $0 < d < k$) and another one for $k - d$ periods. What (9) asserts is that the borrowers must not be able to do better by this process of choosing a sequence of shorter loans. The last sentence of the theorem is important. It asserts that non-uniformities in interest rates with respect to the duration of loan can be used by the lender to extract more consumers' surplus from the borrower. Non-uniformities can arise *vis-à-vis* other variables as well, and this is the subject matter of the next section.

The broad approach developed in this section can be used to analyse many particular credit institutions observed in reality. Let us, for instance, consider South Kanara's *holi* loans, which I mentioned in the introduction.[12] In the case where the loan is taken as rice and repaid as paddy, the interest works out to approximately 50 per cent, irrespective of the duration of loan.[13] Recall that each year's *holi* loans are repaid with interest after the harvest, irrespective of when the loan was taken. This means that the (implicit) interest rate per annum increases sharply as the date of taking the loan approaches the repayment date. The interest rate for a loan taken six months before the repayment date is 125 per cent; for that taken one month before repayment, the interest rate works out to 12,975 per cent! How does one explain this? There are two broad approaches. One is to argue that chronological time is unimportant in a primitive rural setup. As far as effective time is concerned, what matters most in a rural economy is whether a transaction is pre-harvest or post-harvest. Apart from this, the exact timings are (relatively) unimportant from the point of view of *both* the lender[14] and the borrower. Consequently, contracts are struck where the amount of interest is insensitive to the exact timings as long as the harvest occurs in between the points of time when borrowing takes place and when the loan is repaid. I have not pursued this line in this paper but believe it is important.

The argument that would follow from the model of this section is that borrowers are heterogeneous; and it is quite likely that a borrower who takes a loan closer to the repayment date has a more inelastic demand for credit. Consequently the *holi* loan system is a method of subjecting such individuals to a higher (implicit) interest charge. Thus, it is a system for price-discriminating between borrowers without being openly discriminatory. While I do not go in for formal modelling along these lines here, it certainly does seem to be a direction worth pursuing in the future.

4. Interest Rates and the Size of Loan

What we have analysed thus far is the case where the (per-period) interest rates vary with the number of periods for which a loan is taken. However, interest rates are known to vary with several other parameters of the loan. It could, for instance, depend on the size of the loan, or the purpose of the loan.[15] In the light of the discussion in the above two sections, we have a way of interpreting these interest rate variations. This could be done by viewing the variations as modes of extracting surplus from heterogeneous borrowers, where outright discrimination between borrowers is not feasible.

The interest rates vary with loan size has been widely noted empirically (Sarap 1986; Swain 1986); and I have analysed these variations (in Basu 1987). In that paper I assumed that there are two periods and that labourer j's utility, u^j, depends on his consumption in the two periods. That is,

$$u^j = u^j(L,C),\ u^j_L,\ u^j_C > 0,$$

where L and C represent consumptions in periods 1 and 2. There is a large number of potential borrowers with heterogeneous preferences confronting a monopolist money-lender. All of them have the option of rejecting the lender's offer and settling for a reservation consumption stream $(\bar{L},\bar{C})$. Thus person j would not accept an offer (L,C) if $u^j(L,C) < u^j(\bar{L},\bar{C})$. It is assumed that the money-lender cannot discriminate between the borrowers in the sense of picking out each one separately and offering him a suitable package (L,C). He can however offer a sequence of packages,

$$\{(L_1,C_1),\ .\ .\ .,\ (L_n,C_n)\} \equiv [(L_j,C_j)],$$

leaving it to each borrower to pick any package he likes. There is no open discrimination in this case, because any person can choose any package from the list that is offered, but, as is well known from the literature on optimal income tax and nonlinear pricing (see e.g. Spence 1977), the landlord will generally be able to enhance his profit by offering a *sequence* of packages instead of a *unique* one. In Basu (1987) I establish some results for a case like this where the lender chooses a sequence $[(L_j,C_j)]$ in order to maximize profit. For instance, it can be shown that, if individual utility functions are quasi-concave, if $\bar{L}$ (i.e. the reservation consumption in period 1) is zero, and if interpersonally individual preferences satisfy a property known as 'agent monotonicity', then those who take the largest loan (i.e. the package where L is largest) face the lowest (marginal) interest rate.

I want to raise a different but related question here. Suppose that the lender is restricted to offering wage–interest packages instead of actual consumption packages. That is, the lender can offer any sequence

$$\{(w_1,i_1),\ .\ .\ .,\ (w_n,i_n)\} \equiv [(w_j,i_j)].$$

If a labourer chooses (w_j,i_j), then he can have any consumption stream (L,C) that has the property that $C = w_j - (1 + i_j)L$. In other words, (w_j,i_j) represents a package whereby a labourer can take as much loan as he wants in period 1 at an interest rate i_j and in period 2 he gets a wage of w_j and has to repay his debts. An everyday example of a *package* of offers is a transport company that charges a price $\bar{p}$ for every ride and also gives commuters the option of buying a monthly ticket for T rupees and then travelling free as much as they wish. If we use the ordered pair (T,p) to denote the monthly charge, T, and per-ride price, p, then the transport company's offer could be thought as a sequence of pairs, namely, $(0,\bar{p})$ and $(T,0)$.

Let $[(w_j^*,i_j^*)]$ be the sequence of packages that maximizes the lender's profit. This implies a certain relation between loan size and interest rates. What is interesting is that, unlike in the case where the landlord offers consumption streams, in this case the inverse relation between loan size and interest is established without using assumptions like agent monotonicity or even the convexity of individual preferences. In fact, all we need is the assumption that, if consumption rises in any period, *ceteris paribus*, then the consumer's utility rises. A revealed preference type argument then immediately establishes the next result.

THEOREM 3.   If the size of the loan taken by person i is greater than the one taken by person j, then the interest rate paid by i is less than or equal to the interest paid by j.

Proof.   Consider the first two elements of the sequence of offers made by a lender: (w_1,i_1) and (w_2,i_2). The budget constraints generated by each of these is shown in Figure 7.3. Package 1 gives the constraint AD and 2 gives EC. If a borrower faces these two packages and is free to choose either, he would invariably settle somewhere on ABC. This is because if, for instance, he chooses package 2 and settles at a point like F, he could do better by choosing package 1 and settling somewhere north-east of F (at a point like G). Thus, with two packages being offered, the workers' constraint is effectively ABC — the north-east region of which is a convex set. It is obvious that, as we bring in more packages, the constraint will be a line with shorter straight-line segments, but the north-east region of this will continue to be a convex set. Hence if, among two workers, one takes a larger loan, that is if his consumption in period 1 is larger, then it follows that he is on the budget constraint where it is flatter (or, more correctly, not-steeper). In other words, he pays a lower (or, more correctly, not-higher) interest rate. Q.E.D.

Sarap's (1986) study has shown that interest rates vary not only with the duration and size of loans but also with the purpose of borrowing. In partic-

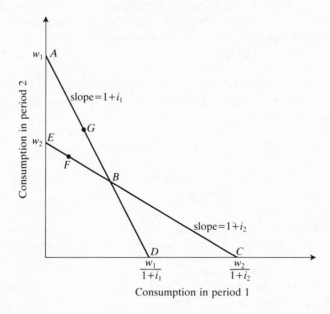

FIG. 7.3

ular, he found that interest rates for loans taken for medical purposes (from the open credit market) are higher than those taken for other purposes.[16] In the light of the above discussions, it should be clear that this could be given a rationale as a method of extracting a greater amount of surplus from the borrowers, since the demand for medical loan would generally be more inelastic.

5. Conclusion

Informal credit markets continue to be very important in developing countries. In India this seems paradoxical because, in terms of volume and even the share of the total credit market, institutional credit has grown sharply. This is evident from the latest of the ten-yearly surveys conducted by the Reserve Bank of India (1986; see also Panikar 1987). However, there is overwhelming evidence that institutional credit continues to cater to the better-off farmers, whereas poorer farmers are forced to turn to the informal credit market (Janakarajan 1986; Sarap 1986; Swain 1986). This is the reason for the importance of informal credit.

This chapter has presented an approach for explaining different structures and institutions in the informal credit market by viewing these as mechanisms for extracting surplus from peasants who have heterogeneous preferences. It also tried to show that markets with perfectly exploitative lenders resemble those with perfectly competitive (and thereby non-exploitative) lenders. Therefore to label models by their superficial features can be risky.

It was suggested that in primitive economies time enters calculations very differently from the way it does in organized industrial markets. This was illustrated with an example from the rural economy of Karnataka in India. The distinct nature of 'time' in backward economies is, however, a very large subject, and the remarks in this paper were meant to be suggestive and to provoke future enquiry.

NOTES

1. The figure 790 is derived by a usual compound interest rate calculation.
2. The term 'exploitation' has different connotations in different branches of economics. I use it here in its ordinary English sense. The meaning of '*perfectly* exploitative behaviour' is made precise later.
3. This is true for allocative efficiency or even 'class efficiency' (Bhaduri, 1986).
4. One suspects that Guha's (1986) tendency to associate models that have efficient outcomes with ideological conservatism is based on a failure to appreciate this proposition.
5. 'Paddy' is the name of the only good available in this economy.
6. I shall assume, in order to avoid corner solutions, that $\max\{X(L) - (1 + i)L\} \geq x$, where i is the traditional monopolist's equilibrium interest rate.
7. It is possible to conceive of a more equitable outcome, but that would entail the exercise of 'triadic' power by the money-lender (Basu 1986). For this, of course, x would have to be interpreted as a reservation consumption which is above the subsistence level.
8. There are many natural reasons for interlinkage to occur in backward economies: see Bardhan and Rudra (1978); Braverman and Srinivasan (1981); Braverman and Stiglitz (1982); Bardhan (1984); Basu (1984a); Bharadwaj (1985); Gupta (1987).
9. Indeed there may be *other* reasons for inefficiency, prominent among which would be moral hazard (see Eswaran and Kotwal 1986).
10. There may be more than one credit plan satisfying this (even after this further qualification). In such an event we would follow any arbitrary selection rule. The results that follow are insensitive to this.
11. While this seems to be a reasonable assumption, and indeed a popular one in the related literature on optimal income tax and nonlinear pricing (e.g. Guesnerie and Seade 1982), the results derived may be quite sensitive to it, as demonstrated in Deb and Ramachandran (1986).
12. For a detailed discussion of *holi* loans, see Nagaraj (1981). Similar institutions have been observed elsewhere in India; see, e.g., Sarap's (1986: 34) study of Sambalpur district of Orissa. Rudra (1982: 69, 76) reports similar findings from West Bengal and Bihar.

13. In Sarap's (1986: 34) study the interest for such loans is also exactly the same.

14. In such an explanation we would need to assume that the lender's opportunity cost of money also does not depend on the duration of lending in the usual chronological fashion, but has a once-for-all character as long as the money is lent out before the harvest and collected after it.

15. It is also possible for interest rates to be contingent on borrower behaviour. Platteau, Murickan, and Delbar (1985) note how, in Poovar (Kerala), employers give interest-free loans to fishermen on condition that they will not desert their employers during peak season. A penalty is charged if they do desert. In a very different context, namely, agricultural loans in Tamil Nadu, Janakarajan (1986) notes how *mandis* gives interest-free loans to farmers on condition that they will sell their product to the same *mandis*. If a farmer fails, he is charged an interest rate of 24 per cent per annum.

16. It should be pointed out that this empirical finding is by no means representative of rural economies. Where landlord–labourer relations are longstanding, it is often found that medical loans command a relatively low interest. This may well be for reasons of normal human compassion or selfishness with very long-run calculations.

8.

Credit and Agrarian Class Structure

Mukesh Eswaran and Ashok Kotwal

1. Introduction

In Marxist analysis, understanding the class structure of a society is fundamental to understanding the society. The analysis indicates the flows of
exploited surplus and enables predictions on the rate of capital accumulation
in that society. Moreover, to Marxists the issue of 'control' is quite important. Who makes the decisions in the production process? Who are the
bosses? It is customary in mainstream economics to treat social inequities as
synonymous with income disparities. But social status matters to people
because individuals may find it unpleasant to take orders. Moreover,
whoever the bosses are today get to make decisions that may determine the
income distribution tomorrow. The questions raised in the mainstream
development literature are much narrower. Are small farms more intensively
cultivated than large farms and, if so, why? Are self-cultivated farms better
managed than capitalist farms and, if so, why? Why do small farmers seem to
be more risk-averse in adopting new technology? All these questions indicate
an implicit belief that the configuration of class structure impinges on the
static and dynamic efficiency of the agrarian sector.

In this chapter we wish to investigate the causes and implications of
agrarian class structure in a way that would allow us to answer the above
questions pertaining to efficiency, raised in the mainstream literature. In
addition, we wish to tackle the issue of 'control' or 'power' (Sen 1981). We
will, however, refrain from tackling some of the grander questions associated
with the Marxist analysis of agrarian class structure. The main theme of this
easay is that unequal access to credit — in both production and consumption
— plays an important role in the determination of the agrarian class structure
as it exists in many parts of the less developed world today. The theme will get
clearer as the discussion proceeds.

What precisely do we mean by agrarian class structure? We will follow
Roemer's (1982) scheme, where the labour market transaction (hired in,
hired out, or neither) is chosen as a criterion for defining class. At the highest
rung of the ladder are the large capitalist farmers who operate large holdings

entirely with hired labour whom they supervise. At the lowest rung of the ladder are the landless labourers who derive all their income by selling their labour on the market. In the middle there are other categories: small capitalists who, in addition to hiring labour, contribute some labour them- selves; self-cultivators; and cultivator–labourers who, in addition to working on their own land, hire themselves out for additional incomes. Such a criterion to define classes is compatible with that used in the Marxist litera- ture on labour exploitation. Of course, any single narrow criterion like this fails to accommodate commonly observed features such as simultaneity of hiring in and hiring out, share tenancy, and interlinked market relationships. Yet this criterion, more than any other, is useful in illuminating the issues of efficiency as well as control. Bardhan (1982) has demonstrated that such a class structure as depicted by Roemer can be made operational in the context of Indian agriculture.

The conventional Marxist approach to the analysis of agrarian class struc- ture proceeds by defining classes and characterizing their distinct behavioural patterns, based on empirical surveys and historical background. Taking these behavioural patterns as immutable aggregate behaviour pertaining to growth, technology adoption, the directions of flow, and the avenues of surplus expropriation are then predicted. The work of Patnaik (1976) on peasant differentiation in the Indian countryside is a good example of such an approach.

It is somewhat unsatisfactory, however, to take class behaviour as exogenously given. Roemer (1982) was the first to endogenize the class struc- ture in an economy in which ownership of the means of production is dis- tributed unequally across the population. All agents are identical except in their wealth endowments. They maximize their leisure after ensuring a certain minimum consumption. The richest class does not have to work at all; its members can generate income by hiring on the market the labour to be used with the capital they own. These are the large capitalists. The next richest class does not have quite enough capital to be able to avoid working altogether. Its members use a part of their capital with hired labour in a capitalist production arrangement and use the rest of the capital with their own labour. These are the small capitalists. The next class consists of self- cultivators who own an even smaller amount of capital than the small capitalists. If self-cultivators hired any labour at all, their income net of the wage payments to the hired workers would not meet their consump- tion needs. Hence, they themselves provide all the labour that works their capital. The class next to that of the self-cultivators comprises labourer– cultivators who, after toiling on their own capital, find the resultant income still inadequate to satisfy their consumption needs and must hire themselves out on the labour market. The poorest class is, of course, that of the pure labourers, who have no capital. Thus, we have five classes, and their members' behaviour with respect to how they spend their time differs according to how much capital they own.

It should be pointed out that Roemer's motivation in deriving such a class structure was quite different from the motivations of this essay. Roemer wanted to persuade orthodox Marxists that their focus on the labour market for analysing either exploitation or class structure was too narrow and misguided. His derivation of the five-fold class structure discussed above is only one step in his argument. He demonstrates that a similar five-fold class structure would emerge in an economy that has no labour market but has a credit market instead. Roemer's work, therefore, is very helpful in showing us how class structure can be endogenized, but it has not been motivated to help development economists answer any of the questions raised earlier. Productivity and efficiency are uniform across different classes. The different behaviour of classes pertaining to how their members allocate their time have few social implications except for the trivial one that the rich get to consume more leisure. In Roemer's framework, the hierarchy in production matters little; it does not matter whether capital hires labour or labour hires capital. It is necessary, therefore, to extend Roemer's model of class structure for our purpose. Note that, since our focus is on an agrarian economy, capital in Roemer's model will be replaced here by land.

The first important realistic feature we would like to add is the fact that hired labour is only an imperfect substitute for a farmer's own labour. This follows from the moral hazard of the hired workers; they must, therefore, be supervised.[1] The existence of supervision has two important implications.

1. The expense associated with supervision makes labour more expensive to capitalist farmers than it is to self-cultivators. As a result, self-operators cultivate their farms more intensively; land productivity is higher on self-cultivated farms. Productivity and efficiency considerations are no longer independent of class composition.
2. Supervision implies hierarchy. There are bosses and there are workers. Bosses make decisions and workers comply with them. This corresponds to the common perceptions we have about the relationship between classes.

So far we have assumed, as in Roemer's story, that there is no market for the means of production (i.e. land in our story), but there is a market for labour. Suppose there is also a land market. The (Pareto-optimal) outcome would be that everyone becomes a self-operator; a well functioning land-leasing market would get rid of all class structure. Of course, income differences would correspond to differences in landownership, but there would be neither any bosses nor any workers.

But in present-day economies there are reasonably well functioning land-lease and labour markets, and yet we observe class structure somewhat along the lines that Roemer has derived. This means that we do not quite have an explanation yet for the heterogeneity in the activities of agents (from large capitalist farmers to landless labourers) that we observe in some LDCs today. Here, we bring in our second important realistic feature, namely, access to credit, where credit is used as working capital.

Seasonality is an inevitable feature of agricultural production; you sow today and reap after four months. Every season a farmer and his family toil for months, sustaining themselves with consumption derived either from their own savings or by borrowing until the crops are harvested and sold. It is inconceivable that a landless worker would have enough savings to sustain his family for a whole crop season. He cannot lease in land and set up self-cultivation even if the landowner agrees to accept the rent after the season is over; he will need credit to sustain himself and his family until the returns accrue. This is true for farmers in traditional agriculture. The problem is compounded in modern agriculture, which requires a significant expenditure on intermediate inputs like fertilizers, seeds, pesticides, bullock rental, and so on. Without access to sufficient working capital, poor agents cannot lease in land from wealthier agents. The movement towards a Pareto-optimal configuration in which they are only self-cultivated farms would be thwarted unless the poor agents had access to sufficient credit to cover the working capital needs. But, as a matter of fact, the poor have only a limited access to credit. Even in countries like India, where a great deal of effort has been expended to build rural credit institutions, it is highly improbable that an agent with marginal or zero land-holdings could approach such an institution and expect to secure a loan. It is evident that credit in much of the developing world is rationed; large farmers, perhaps because of their ability to offer greater amounts of collateral, have access to large amounts of credit. A number of studies on the state of credit markets in the developing countries corroborative this view. Good recent sources on this are von Pischke *et al.* (1983) and Rudra (1982; Ch. 4). Jaffe and Russell (1976) and Stiglitz and Weiss (1981) have offered different explanations of how the moral hazard of, and adverse selection among, borrowers can lead to credit rationing and differential interest rates. Carter (1988) has adapted the latter model to the LDC agrarian environment. Binswanger and Sillers (1983) offer an insightful analysis of how differential ownership of collateral (mainly land) determines differential access to credit and gives rise to credit rationing in an agrarian setting.

Whatever the reason for credit rationing, we can incorporate into our analysis the fact that the credit ceiling, to a large extent, is correlated with the wealth (land) endowment of the borrower. The restricted access to credit of the landless and marginal farmers prevents them from leasing in land from large farmers and thus blocks what would be a move towards a Pareto-optimal configuration of total self-cultivation. Unequal access to credit is thus an important determinant of agrarian class structure. It causes diversion of labour time into supervision — an activity that would be unnecessary under a system with only self-cultivation. Thus, the incorporation of two realistic features, namely, the moral hazard of hired workers and the unequal access to working capital (credit), allows us to examine, in an agrarian structure displaying heterogeneous classes, questions relating to efficiency and to the incidence of hierarchy. This is the task we set ourselves in the second section of this chapter.

Our discussion so far has brought in considerations of the deadweight loss of resources used up in supervision, thereby relating static efficiency to class configuration. But we have not discussed any dynamic processes that restrict the upward mobility of those at the bottom of the agrarian class structure. It has been argued in the literature that new technologies are perceived to be riskier, and therefore small and marginal farmers are reluctant to take risks. But why should risk preferences vary systematically across farm sizes? In fact, Binswanger and Sillers (1983) report that they found very little systematic variation in the extent of risk aversion across a sample of farmers owning different amounts of land, and yet the larger farmers had shown better adoption behaviour than the smaller ones.

What we argue in Section 3 below is that it is the superior access to consumption credit that the large farmers possess which allows them to undertake risks in production and reap the rewards. If a farmer has access to credit, so that he can borrow in bad years and pay it back in good years, he can be assumed of putting a floor below his consumption even in bad years. Credit can thus work as a device that stabilizes consumption intertemporally; a farmer who has access to it is not afraid to adopt new technology even if it means that his income may plummet in some periods. The differential rates of adoption of new technology between small and large farmers during the Green Revolution can thus be explained in terms of differential access to consumption credit.

Unequal access to credit also has an implication relevant for the question of control (and power) or hierarchy in production. Suppose two individuals want to engage in a production activity jointly such that only one makes decisions and the other provides an input that is easy to monitor. Clearly, then, the one who makes the decisions will also have to be the residual claimant so that he bears the consequences of his decisions; the other will be his fixed-wage employee. Thus, being a boss will entail becoming a residual claimant, which in turn will entail having to bear the risk in an uncertain environment. But according to our discussion above, a superior access to credit also imparts an ability to bear risk. This would be a partial explanation for why the bosses tend to come from the wealthier class. Section 3 also deals with this issue.

Lastly, there are the interlinked aspects of agrarian structure in which an employment relationship may be accompanied by a credit arrangement. Typically, a landlord may advance loans to his tenant (or worker) especially in the event of a consumption contingency. The importance of such smoothly functioning implicit arrangements in peasant societies is brought out by social anthropologists such as Scott (1976) and Breman (1974). The recent spate of articles on this issue has been sparked by the provocative speculation by some Indian economists like Bhaduri (1973) and Prasad (1974), who argue that rich landlords in some eastern states of India (characterized by them as semi-feudal) choose not to undertake the productive investment necessary for introducing new technology because they find money-lending a more lucrative alternative. The empirical as well as the theoretical support for this case has been weak (see Rudra 1982; Bardhan and Rudra 1978). Yet, the very existence of this interlinkage within the employment relationship has continued to intrigue theorists, and the search for a convincing economic explanation continues. Such an explanation, it is hoped, would shed some light on the patron–client relationships that prevail in parts of the countryside in the Third World. The crucial point to understand here is what function credit serves in such a relationship. At the end of Section 3 we have a hypothesis on this kind of employment relationship based on the 'Credit as Insurance' theme.

In short, in this chapter we propose to examine the various ways in which unequal access to credit shapes agrarian structure.

2. Production Credit and Class Structure

In this section, we will show that unequal access to credit used as working capital will lead to a five-fold agrarian class structure. The model and discussion is borrowed from Section I of our paper published in *Economic Journal* (Eswaran and Kotwal 1986).

We assume that the factor prices are exogenously given and then consider the optimization problem facing an agent who is constrained by the credit available to him and by his time endowment. The optimal time allocation made by each agent determines the mode of cultivation he will adopt.

We asume that the production process entails the use of two inputs, land (h) and labour (n), both of which are essential. The production function, $f(h,n)$, is assumed to be linearly homogeneous, increasing, strictly quasi-concave, and twice continuously differentiable in its arguments. We can write the output, q, of a farm as

$$q = \epsilon f(h,n) \tag{1}$$

where ϵ is a positive random variable with expected value unity, embodying the effect of such stochastic factors as the weather. Land and labour can be hired in competitive markets at (exogenously given) prices v and w, respectively. The price, P, of output is also exogenously given — determined, say, in the world market.

We assume that production entails the incurrence of fixed setup costs, K. While we are abstracting from all inputs other than land and labour, we introduce K as a proxy to represent the fixed component of the costs associated with other inputs. An example might be the fixed costs associated with the sinking of tube-wells for irrigation. K is a setup cost associated with each farm. While the production function itself is linearly homogeneous, these costs, required to initiate production, will render unprofitable the cultivation of extremely small plot sizes. We shall see later on that these costs are also partly responsible for the existence of a class of pure agricultural workers in the economy. The amount of working capital, B, to which a farmer has access is typically determined by the assets he possesses — mainly the amount of land, $\bar{h}$, he owns.[2] Note that, since land can be leased in or leased out, h can be greater than or less than $\bar{h}$. Thus the scale of operation of a farmer is bounded by the working capital constraint:

$$vh + w(n - \ell) \leq B - K + v\bar{h} + wt \qquad (2)$$

where n is the total amount of labour applied, ℓ is the amount of labour he himself supplies, h is the amount of land he cultivates, and t is the amount of time he sells on the labour market. The use of owned land and own labour in cultivation are valued at the going prices. In writing down (2), we have implicitly assumed that all capital outlays are incurred at the beginning of the production period. Requiring this to be so in our two-factor model provides a way of simulating the working capital necessitated by the existence, in reality, of numerous intermediate inputs. The interest rate per crop season (which does not play a substantive role in our model), is assumed to be exogenously fixed at some level $r \geq 0$.

It is well recognized that the potential for moral hazard on the part of hired workers makes their supervision imperative. Implicit in (1) is the assumption that n is the number of efficiency units of labour applied. The presence of the stochastic variable ϵ in (1) renders it impossible to infer from the knowledge of any two of q, h, and n the value of the third. Thus, even a supervisor will have the incentive to shirk and will need to be monitored — unless he is a residual claimant (Alchian and Demsetz 1972). It follows that the entrepreneur must himself undertake the task of supervision — the only substantive implication of uncertainty in our model, since we shall be abstracting from risk preferences in this section.

We assume that each agent is endowed with one unit of time. Let R denote the amount of leisure ('rest') he consumes (to be endogenized below). The agent can then allocate the remaining amount of time $(1 - R)$ across three activities:

1. selling his services (for an amount of time t) in the labour market;
2. working on his own farm (for an amount of time ℓ);
3. supervising hired labour on his farm (for an amount of time S, say).

We assume that the amount of time required of the entrepreneur to supervise L hired workers is an increasing and strictly convex function of L:

$$S = s(L) \quad (s' > 0, s'' > 0) \qquad (3)$$

with $s(0) = 0$ and, to ensure that the supervision of hired labour is not pro-hibitively costly for all L, $s'(0) < 1$. Strict convexity of the supervision function is rationalized on the traditional grounds that it renders finite the size of the enterprise despite linear homogeneity of the production function. We discuss later the consequences of relaxing the assumption of strict con-vexity of $s(L)$.

The time endowment constraint facing an entrepreneur may now be written:

$$1 - R - t - s(L) \geq 0. \tag{4}$$

The left-hand side of (4) is the amount of time, ℓ, the entrepreneur works on his own farm as a labourer.

To complete the specification of the model, we posit that all agents have identical preferences defined over the present value earnings, Y, of the period and leisure. For tractability, the utility function is posited to have the additive structure:

$$U(Y,R) = Y + u(R) \tag{5}$$

with $u' > 0$, $u'' < 0$. Further, we shall take it that the marginal utility of leisure is infinite at $R = 0$. Note that the linearity of the utility function in income implies that the agent is risk-neutral.

We now turn to the optimization problem facing an agent. For the moment we shall examine the agent's choices assuming that he opts to cultivate. We shall subsequently analyse his choice between being a cultivator and an agri-cultural worker. First, note that according to (3) the supervision time required of the entrepreneur depends only on the aggregate amount of labour he hires. Thus, the time spent on supervision cannot be lowered by operating two separate plots of land rather than one. The existence of positive setup costs associated with each operation then renders it suboptimal for an agent to operate two or more separate farming establishments. We first consider the problem confronting an agent who has sufficient capital to cultivate. (Later, we will address the question as to whether he will, in fact, opt to do so.) An entrepreneur seeking to maximize his expected utility by cultivation will thus solve

$$\max_{R,h,t,L} P\beta f(h,\ell + L) + wt - v(h - \bar{h}) - wL - K + u(R) \tag{6}$$

$$\text{s.t. } B + wt \geq vh + wL, \tag{7}$$

$$\ell \equiv 1 - R - t - s(L) \geq 0 \quad (L \geq 0, t \geq 0) \tag{8}$$

where $\beta \equiv 1/(1 + r)$ is the discount factor per crop period, and $B \equiv B - K + v\bar{h}$.

Given our assumptions on $u(\cdot)$ and $f(\cdot,\cdot)$, the problem stated in (6) has the classic Kuhn–Tucker form and admits of only one solution. Thus for given v,

w, and B there exists a unique solution to the optimization problem in (6). This solution can be parameterized by the working capital, B, available to the entrepreneur and the various exogenous prices.

The following proposition demonstrates that there are four potential modes of cultivation that can arise.[3]

PROPOSITION 1. The solution to (6) accommodates four distinct modes of cultivation, separated by three critical values, B_1, B_2, B_3 (with $0 < B_1 < B_2 < B_3$) of B, such that the entrepreneur is a

(I) labourer–cultivator ($t > 0, \ell > 0, L = 0$) for $0 \le B < B_1$;
(II) self-cultivator ($t = 0, \ell > 0, L = 0$) for $B_1 \le B < B_2$;
(III) small capitalist ($t = 0, \ell > 0, L > 0$) for $B_2 \le B < B_3$;
(IV) large capitalist ($t = 0, \ell = 0, L > 0$) for $B \ge B_3$.

The intuition for Proposition 1 becomes clear if we reason through, as we do below, how different activities become optimal at different levels of capital.

An agent with severely restricted access to capital can lease in only a small amount of land; the marginal revenue product of his labour on this piece of land would be correspondingly small. He thus finds it optimal to sell his services on the labour market for part of the time, thereby augmenting his working capital. He then earns a return on this capital by expanding his operation. Such agents are the labourer–cultivators, who are wage-earners cum entrepreneurs. The amount of leisure they consume is determined by the condition that the utility derived from the marginal unit of leisure equals the income from cultivation that is forgone as a result. Since the latter is constant for a linearly homogeneous production function, it follows that all labourer–cultivators consume the same amount of leisure.

The greater the working capital a labourer–cultivator has access to, the greater is the amount of land he can rent and, therefore, the larger is the marginal product of his own labour. Since all labourer–cultivators consume the same amount of leisure, it follows that those with larger budgets will sell less of their labour services and devote more of their time to cultivation. The agent with a budget $B = B_1$ altogether ceases to transact in the labour market: he devotes all of his non-leisure time to cultivation. If hired and own labour had the same price, an agent with a budget marginally greater than B_1 would hire outside help. This, however, is not so. While the wage rate earned by the agent in the labour market would be w, the cost to him of hiring the first worker on his own farm is $w + s'(0)u'(R)$, which is strictly greater than w since $s'(0) > 0$. Thus, this agent will not hire outside help; he will expend his entire budget on hiring land and opt to be a self-cultivator. Agents with greater access to working capital will (self-)cultivate larger farms by consuming less leisure.

Since each agent has a limited amount of time endowment, the price of own-labour (i.e. the marginal utility of leisure forgone) becomes increasingly higher at higher levels of working capital. The ratio of the effective price of hired to own-labour, namely $\{(w + s'(0)u'(R)\}/u'(R)$, declines. An agent with some sufficiently high budget $B_2(> B_1)$ will thus find it optimal to hire and supervise outside help, apart from applying some of his own labour on the farm. This agent marks the transistion from the class of self-cultivators to the class of small capitalists. We thus see that the capitalist mode of cultivation emerges as a natural response to the need of entrepreneurs to circumvent their time-endowment constraints. Agents with budgets greater than B_2 will hire greater amounts of labour and spend more time in supervision. At some level of working capital B_3 ($> B_2$), it pays the agent to specialize in supervision; all labour is hired labour, and the agent maximizes the returns to his access to working capital by only supervising hired hands. Agents with $B \geq B_3$ comprise the class of large capitalists.

In Proposition 1 we have merely derived all the modes of cultivation that are potentially observable. We have presumed that the agent in question in fact opts to cultivate. Whether or not he will do so will depend on whether or not his maximized utility, $U^*(B,v,w,K)$, in cultivation exceeds his maximized utility in the next best alternative: being a pure agricultural worker. As an agricultural worker, the maximized utility, $U_0^*(v,w,\bar{h})$, of an agent who owns (and leases out) an amount of land $\bar{h}$ is given by

$$U_0^*(v,w,h) = \max_R w(1 - R) + u(R) + v\bar{h}. \tag{9}$$

The agent will opt to cultivate if and only if

$$U^*(B,v,w,K) > U_0^*(v,w,\bar{h}). \tag{10}$$

If setup costs, K, were zero, all agents (including those with $B = 0$) would opt to cultivate if the technology were at all viable at prices (P,v,w). However, if setup costs were positive and sufficiently large, agents with meagre working capital would find it more attractive to join the labour force on a full-time basis than to cultivate on a scale so small as to be unprofitable. Those agents for whom (10) is violated will form the class of pure agricultural workers. There thus emerges a five-fold class structure in our model of an agrarian economy. In reality, cultivation may not be feasible for the poorest agents because they have to assure themselves of a minimum subsistence before they can expend resources to engage in cultivation. Thus, a pure labourer class could obtain even in the absence of scale economies. However, for expediency in modelling we shall continue with our assumption of positive setup costs in cultivation.

For the rest of this section we shall assume that all the modes of cultivation we have discussed are manifest. In other words, if B_{max} denotes the largest amount of capital that a single entrepreneur can profitably utilize in agriculture, then $B_{max} > B_3$. The quantity B_{max} is determined as the smallest value of

B for which the capital constraint ceases to bind in (6), and will depend on P, v, and w in general.

We now turn our attention to the land–labour ratio of farms as a function of the entrepreneurs' access to working capital. The following proposition records our results comparing the land–labour ratio and the average productivity per acre across farms spanning the four modes of cultivation.

PROPOSITION 2.   As a function of B,
  (a) the land–labour ratio is constant over the labourer–cultivator class and is strictly increasing over all other classes;
  (b) the (expected) output per acre of farms is constant over the labourer–cultivator class and is strictly decreasing over all other classes.

Intuition for the above proposition can be readily had. By equating the marginal utility per dollar spent on the two factors, the agents are, in effect, setting the ratio of the marginal products of land and labour equal to the ratio of their perceived prices. The perceived price of land is the same for all agents, and equals its market price. We have seen that all labourer–cultivators consume the same amount of leisure, so that the perceived price of (own) labour is constant for all $B \leq B_1$. Since the price ratio of the factors (land and own-labour) is constant for $B \leq B_1$, production from a linearly homogeneous technology will use the factors in a fixed ratio. We have also seen that, beyond B_1, increases in B induce the entrepreneurs to consume less leisure, resulting in a rising perceived price of own-labour. Since the price of land is constant, we shall observe a bias towards land in the use of factors under self-cultivation: the land–labour ratio will increase with B. In the capitalistic mode of production, this effect is further reinforced by the fact that the cost of supervising hired labour increases at an increasing rate with the amount of labour hired. Part (b) of the above proposition follows directly from part (a) and the linear homogeneity of the production function. To the extent that our thinking is conditioned by the implicit assumption that markets are perfect, these results would appear counter-intuitive. If agents were not constrained in their borrowing, for example, it would be Pareto-efficient for those agents currently operating inefficiently large farms to lease out some of their land to agents with smaller (and hence more efficient) farms. In equilibrium, we would then expect all agents to operate farms of identical sizes.

We now briefly discuss how the results of these propositions would be affected by relaxing our assumptions regarding the nature of the supervision function $s(L)$. Our results are driven by the assumption of increasing marginal disutility of effort. Even if the supervision function $s(L)$ were not strictly convex in L but the cost of supervision in terms of the entrepreneur's utility were so, these results would still obtain. Thus, if the supervision function is linear, the results of Propositions 1 and 2 would be quite unaffected except for one minor qualification: the land–labour ratio is constant for the small capitalist class. On the other hand, if the supervision function is strictly concave, the labour costs in terms of the entrepreneur's utility may not be convex. The results of Proposition 2 may then not obtain.

The above results are consistent with the hypothesis of the inverse farm size–productivity relationship suggested by the empirical findings of Ahmed (1981), Bharadwaj (1974), Cline (1970), Ghose (1979), and Kutcher and Scandizzo (1982), among others. An important paper surveying the evidence on the inverse size–productivity relationship in India is Sen (1981). This paper also discusses the validity of the longstanding hypothesis that the self-cultivators perceive a lower cost of labour than do capitalist farmers.

It should be noted, however, that our model presumes a linearly homogeneous production function; if the production function itself exhibits increasing returns, the inverse farm size–productivity relationship will be counteracted. Indeed, in highly capital-intensive agriculture as in North America, the large machinery used has created substantial economics of scale. In Asian countries with high labour–land ratios, there are many areas where such machinery is not introduced and it becomes meaningful to talk of the small self-cultivated farms as being the most efficient mode of cultivation. In these countries, land reform that would distribute land in an egalitarian way would also improve efficiency. It is interesting to note that the inefficiency of an agrarian economy in which land ownership is skewed stems from the unequal access to credit. If a marginal farmer or a landless labourer could borrow enough working capital, the size of each operated holding and the land productivity on it would be identical; there would be no resources wasted in supervision. The inefficiency of a polarized class structure is thus intimately related to the way in which credit markets operate. Put differently, in agrarian economies equity and efficiency considerations cannot be divorced from each other (as they are in standard neoclassical theory), a point repeatedly noted by Stiglitz (1985a, 1985b).

3. Role of Consumption Credit in Risk-bearing

Access to credit has important implications for the risk-bearing abilities of individuals — implications that have serious consequences for agrarian structure. The conventional view on risk behaviour attributes observed differences in the behaviour of individuals under uncertainty of differences in their (unobservable) risk preferences. There is no reason to believe, however, that the distribution of risk preferences among the rich would be systematically different from that among the poor. How, then, is one to explain the stylized fact that the rich systematically behave in a less risk-averse fashion than do the poor? Conventional theory has no answer to this question.[4] An explanation can be found, however, once we take cognizance of the facts that (1) the effects of risk-bearing impinge on many periods, and (2) capital markets are imperfect (Eswaran and Kotwal 1987a).

The role of access to credit in facilitating risk-bearing can be seen quite simply. Consider an economic agent confronted with a risky income in each of several periods. An obvious example in the agricultural context is a farmer's weather-dependent income in the absence of irrigation facilities. We shall take it that individuals prefer an even time-profile of consumption to an uneven one. If the realization of the random income is poor in any period, the agent would like to borrow for present consumption against future expected income. If, however, the realized income is high, the agent would prefer to save part of it to prevent possible downswings in consumption in the future. Thus, by saving in the good states and borrowing in the bad ones, the agent will smooth out his consumption profile. Essentially, by pooling the risk across many periods, an agent will achieve a relatively stable consumption stream. The scope for this consumption-smoothing, however, is clearly restricted by the agent's ability to borrow. Rich agents (or those with considerable access to credit) are better equipped to prevent fluctuating incomes from translating into fluctuating consumption levels. Those with only meagre access to credit will behave in a fashion that would appear to be more risk-averse, but this merely stems from their inability to cope with downswings in their consumption levels. All this can be seen a little more formally.

To illustrate the point, let us restrict ourselves to a two-period world. Let $U(c_1,c_2)$ denote an agent's von Neumann–Morgenstern utility function over the two periods, where c_1 and c_2 are, respectively, the consumption levels in periods 1 and 2. This utility function will be strictly concave in c_1 and c_2 for risk-averse agents.[5] Further, let us assume that $U(c_1,c_2)$ is separable in the two consumption levels:

$$U(c_1,c_2) = u(c_1) + u(c_2) \tag{11}$$

where $u(\cdot)$ is strictly concave in its argument. For ease of exposition, let us assume that the second-period income is certain and is y. The first-period income is assumed to have the same expected value but can take either of the two values $y \pm a (0 < a < y)$ with equal probability. Finally, we assume that the individual can borrow, for consumption purposes, up to a ceiling C. Since the interest rate plays no essential role here, we shall assume it to be zero.

From the concavity of the utility function, it follows that the agent would seek to equalize the consumption levels in the two periods — if that is feasible. If it is not, he will bring the two consumption levels as close as possible. Suppose he realizes the good state in period 1. Then he clearly will save $a/2$ in the first period and consume $y + a/2$ in each of the two periods. The two-period utility of the agent will be $2u(y + a/2)$. If, however, the bad state is realized in period 1, he would like to borrow $a/2$ in that period, pay it back in the next period, and thus consume $y - a/2$ in each of the two periods. But if the credit ceiling is binding, that is, if $C < a/2$ — as we will assume to be the case — the best the agent can do is consume $y - a + C$ in the first period and $y - C$ in the second. His two-period utility is then $u(y - a + C) + u(y - C)$.

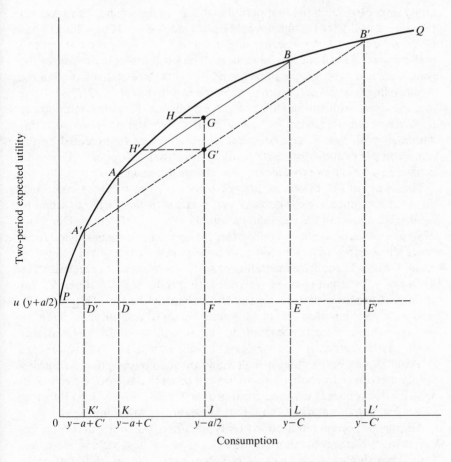

FIG. 8.1 How consumption credit impinges on risk-bearing ability

The two-period expected utility is an equally weighted average of the two-period utilities for the good and bad realizations, respectively. We can see this diagrammatically from Figure 8.1. The intercept OP represents the contribution of the good state to the expected utility. The contribution of the poor realization can be inferred from the curve PQ, which represents the function $u(\cdot)$.

If the bad state is realized, the agent achieves an utility level of AD in the first period and BE in the second, with an average of GF. The expected two-period utility is then GJ. The agent would be willing to pay an amount GH for the privilege of being able to consume $y - a/2$ in each of the two periods in the event of a poor realization. Consider another agent who has a lower credit ceiling, $C'(< C)$. If the bad state is realized, this agent would achieve an utility level of $A'D'$ in the first period and $B'E'$ in the second. The expected two-period utility for the agent would be $G'J$, and he would be willing to pay $G'H'$ to be assured of a consumption level of $y - a/2$ in each of the two periods were the bad state to be realized. The worth, in utility terms, of the good state is, of course, the same for both agents since in that situation the credit ceiling is irrelevant. From this and the fact that $G'H' > GH$, it follows that the agent with the smaller access to credit will find uncertainty more unpleasant and, therefore, will put a greater premium on its elimination. Although both agents have identical risk preferences (represented by the same von Neumann–Morgenstern utility function), the poorer agent will behave *as if* he is more risk-averse than the wealthier agent.

The theory of risk behaviour presented above differs from the traditional theory in its emphasis on the role of endowments (which facilitate access to credit); the conventional view emphasizes the role of preferences. Our fiew, while general, is particularly appropriate for agrarian economies. The dependence on weather makes production uncertainty an important reality of economic life. The subsistence nature of such economies also exacerbates the importance of contingencies unrelated to production — illnesses, for example. Coupled with this is the fact that capital markets in LDCs generally tend to be very imperfect and institutional sources of consumption credit, in particular, are almost non-existent; consumption credit is invariably obtained from informal money markets on stiff terms. All these factors lead to economic agents putting a high value on the consumption-smoothing service performed by credit. One outcome of this is that some of the capital in agrarian economies is diverted from productive investments into informal consumption loans markets, and, to that extent, growth is inhibited.

Another important implication of this pertains to the choice of technology by farmers. New production technologies (like the high-yielding varieties, HYVs) have higher yields, in expected value terms, than the traditional technologies. The former, however, also exhibit more variation in the output than the latter because they typically require greater care and are more sensitive to deviations from required procedure. This makes the HYVs more attractive than traditional technologies in expected value terms but less attractive in terms of riskiness — at least initially, until the know-how required for use of the HYVs is mastered. Our view of risk behaviour presented above would imply that farmers with greater access to consumption credit will more readily adopt the new technology than those with little or no consumption credit. This result is formally demonstrated in Eswaran and Kotwal (1987b).

The above conclusion is consistent with evidence drawn from India on the effects of the Green Revolution. It is now acknowledged that farmers with large landholdings benefited disproportionately from the new technology as compared with those with small holdings, thereby increasing the income disparity between them. Binswanger and Sillers (1983), in their experimental work on Indian farmers, found that, although the farmers in their sample were seen to have fairly homogeneous risk preferences, large farmers adopted the new HYV technology more readily than did the small farmers. The authors attributed this to the greater access to production credit enjoyed by the large farms; our explanation, with its emphasis on consumption credit, is complementary to theirs.

It must be noted that access to credit derives its important role in risk-bearing essentially from the concavity of the von Neumann–Morgenstern utility function of risk-averse agents. It is this concavity that makes consumption-smoothing desirable. Even in the absence of any uncertainty, however, consumption-smoothing would be desirable if the agent exhibit diminishing marginal rate of substitution between today's and tomorrow's consumption. Then even contingencies that are probabilistically certain events — like daughters' wedding expenses, — would generate a demand for the consumption-smoothing service of credit. The fact that in many LDCs peasants become bonded labourers in exchange for trivial sums of money provided at the appropriate time bears testimony to the astronomical shadow-price of this service to these peasants.

Our view of risk behaviour also sheds some light on the *raison d'être* for interlinked markets, an issue that has drawn considerable attention from researchers. Why is it the case that the employers and the creditors of peasants in agrarian economies are often the same agents, namely, their land-lords? Since landlords are considerably richer than labourers, it follows that they are more capable of absorbing risk. There is thus scope for Pareto-improving insurance contracts in which the landlords insure the landless and assetless agents from consumption contingencies. This, however, would entail verification of the contingencies by the landlords in order to prevent false claims. To get around the need for such verifications, landlords would prefer to give credit instead. To ensure that the borrowers do not default, landlords will be inclined to lend to their own employees since they can withold the workers' incomes in the event of default. Thus, interlinked contracts emerge as transaction-cost-minimizing means of implementing what are essentially insurance contracts.

In Section 2 we saw the unequal access to production credit generates a five-fold class structure in general. It is easy to see that unequal access to consumption credit could independently generate a similar class structure. Agents with considerable access to consumption credit could insure, against production uncertainies, those with little or no credit. This they can do by hiring the latter as workers on fixed wages, and absorbing the production risks themselves by becoming residual claimants. Agents with intermediate amounts of consumption credit may not be able either to insure the would-be workers, or profitably to seek to be insured by the richest agents; these agents would opt to be self-cultivators. Thus we immediately see that three classes would arise: workers, self-cultivators, and large capitalists. If agents can adjust the amount of production risk they expose themselves to by choosing the scale of operation appropriately, we see that the remaining two classes also would come into existence, namely, worker–cultivators and small capitalists. This observation underlines the fact that capital determines class structure even when it is used neither to purchase other inputs nor as a factor of production. It appears that one might be able to provide the theoretical underpinnings of class structure along lines somewhat more general than those of Roemer (1982).

4. Conclusions

This essay has taken as its premise the empirically sound stylized fact that access to credit is unequally distributed across economic agents. The incorporation of this empirical fact as an axiom into the theoretical framework enables us to understand some institutions that are prevalent in agrarian economies. Unequal access to capital provides a rationale for hierarchies in agrarian production organizations and, more generally, explains the emergency of agrarian class structure; it explains why the rich behave in a less risk-averse fashion than do the poor and, as a corollary, why they adopt new technologies more rapidly; it provides an explanation for the existence of interlinked contracts that are ubiquitous in agrarian economies. Thus, to understand agrarian structure, it is essential not to abstract from the manner in which capital markets actually operate. Adoption of the conventional neo-classical assumption that all agents are able to obtain unlimited amounts of credit at the going rate of interest would force us into providing either *ad hoc* or contrived explanations for the myriad institutions that are prevalent in agrarian economies.

Why is access to credit so inegalitarian across agents in agrarian economies? Any reasonable answer to this question must incorporate, as an essential ingredient, the limited liability of borrowers. By this we do not necessarily mean limited liability in the legal sense of the term, for peasants in the rural countryside are often unaware of their legal rights. More generally, *de facto* limited liability would arise if the costs of collecting debt are high in terms of time, effort, and money — implying low penalties to borrowers for default. The limited liability of borrowers gives scope for moral hazard on their part and gives them the incentive to misuse production credit by, for example, diverting some of it to comsumption (Carter 1988) or utilizing the credit with a suboptimal amount of their own effort (Eswaran and Kotwal 1985b). To achieve greater alignment of borrowers' objectives with their own, lenders would insist on collateral. Because rich agents can offer assets of greater value as collateral than can the poor, they will have access not only to larger amounts of loans but also at lower interest rates, since these loans would be viewed as being less risky. Unequal distribution of endowments thus translates into unequal access to credit. If the expected return on credit given to agents without collateral does not cover the opportunity cost of capital, it is conceivable that these agents get completely cut off from the credit market. To the extent that different agents have different abilities (for farming, entrepreneurship, etc.) which are known only to themselves, it follows that able but poor agents may never get to utilize their skills.

Can government intervention improve the efficiency of the outcome in the credit market by redistributing the available credit? This question warrants more investigation because of its important policy implications. On the face of it, the answer seems to be in the negative. Unless the government has available to it more information on borrowers than do the private bankers, or has more effective means of preventing default — both of which are unlikely possibilities — there is little reason to believe that market efficiency can be improved upon by government intervention in the credit market. We saw in Section 2 that unequal access to production credit is responsible for the institutions of small and large capitalism — institutions that necessitate the deadweight loss of supervision, which can be avoided by self-cultivation. It might thus appear that redistributing credit from rich farmers to labourers so as to render capitalistic farming infeasible would improve social welfare by eliminating the need for supervision. Unfortunately, this is not true. Private bankers, in their computations of the effective rates of return on lending to various agents, will recognize the reduction in their return from lending to large capitalists arising from the supervision requirement of hired labour. If, in spite of this, they choose to lend to large farmers rather than to small ones, it is because their perceived return is nevertheless still higher for the former than the latter. A redistribution of credit from large to small farmers, then, would reduce the return on capital; the gain from the elimination of supervision will be more than overwhelmed by the loss arising from increased default. While such a redistribution would be desirable from the point of view of equity, we have no efficiency argument for it.

Stiglitz (1985a) has noted that, when markets suffer from moral hazard (and adverse selection) problems — or, more generally, from informational asymmetries — the government can use taxes and subsidies to improve market efficiency. To see how this might work in principle, consider the case in which the default probability increases if a borrower consumes more leisure and applies less effort in his production activity than would be deemed optimal by the lender. The argument by Stiglitz would suggest that the credit market can be made more efficient by levying a tax either on leisure or on a good complementary to leisure. But leisure cannot be taxed in this instance; its unobservability is what gave rise to the moral hazard in the first place. It is also difficult to come up with examples, in the context of poor agrarian economies, of goods complementary to leisure which could be taxed.

Government intervention in credit markets can have, on the other hand, rather serious perverse effects in LDCs because of political forces ignored in the discussion above. In India, for example, where agricultural credit is administered through nationalized banks or credit co-operatives at the explicit dictates of government policy, the default rates, paradoxically, are much higher for large farmers than for small ones. This is because large farmers use their political clout to achieve what is essentially immunity against default. Since the average size of the loans to these defaulters is quite large, the ultimate effect of such intervention would clearly be unviability of the financial institutions. Thus, there does not seem to be an easy counter-measure to the process by which credit markets tend to accentuate inequalities in the countryside.

NOTES

1. Disutility of working for others could serve the same function.
2. In most agrarian economies, the total wealth of an agent is strongly correlated with landownership. The use of other assets besides land for collateral would not change our results qualitatively. Note that we take the distribution of landownership as exogenously given.
3. The proof of this and the following proposition is given in Eswaran and Kotwal (1984).
4. This stylized fact is incorporated into conventional theory by the assumption of declining absolute risk aversion.
5. See Eswaran and Kotwal (1987a) for a proof of this.

9.

Credit Rationing, Tenancy, Productivity, and the Dynamics of Inequality

Avishay Braverman and Joseph E. Stiglitz

1. Introduction

In earlier work, we argued that it was mistaken for economists to treat institutions as given: many institutions frequently found in market economies arise endogenously as a response to informational considerations and inequality in the distribution of wealth. In particular, these considerations can explain the persistence and pervasiveness of sharecropping in LDCs (Stiglitz 1974; Braverman and Stiglitz 1986a) and credit rationing in capital markets in both developed and less developed countries (Stiglitz and Weiss 1981).

This chapter has three objectives: to show how sharecropping and capital market imperfections affect rural productivity; to sketch a general equilibrium theory of land tenancy; and, finally, to show how changes in technology and in publicly provided infrastructure may affect the equilibrium distribution of land and, hence, the prevalent tenancy relationships. These relationships are important because they influence the long-run increase in national income made possible by changes in technology or infrastructure.

Recent literature has considered the effect of inequality on technological change. Concern has been expressed, for instance, that the inequality within LDCs has impeded the adoption of certain innovations.[1] In an earlier paper (Braverman and Stiglitz 1986b) we examined the validity of that contention and showed that, although the standard exploitation arguments may not be valid, there were indeed innovations that might increase output, for each level of input, that would not be adopted; these innovations, however, exacerbated the incentive problems (e.g. associated with sharecropping).

This paper is concerned with the other side of the relationship between technological change and inequality: the effect of technical change on inequality, and the effect of inequality, in turn, on productivity. We shall show that an increase in inequality may have a deleterious effect on productivity. The effect of changes in technology and infrastructure is ambiguous. For some changes long-run inequality is reduced, and for these changes the long-run productivity gains are accordingly likely to be greater than those in the short run. On the other hand, for some changes long-run inequality is

increased. These innovations, while increasing output in the short run, may
— in the absence of countervailing actions by the government — in the long
run have a deleterious effect on the economy. It is important to recognize this
possibility, so that attention can be drawn to institutional reforms designed
to ameliorate these inequality-related long-run productivity effects.

The fact that technological change can have an adverse effect on inequality
has long been recognized. Indeed, it is known that it is possible that a technological change would so reduce the demand for, say, unskilled labour that
not only its share, but also the absolute value of the real wage of unskilled
workers might fall. This might be the case, for instance, if the innovation is
'labour-augmenting' (so that one worker can do what ten workers previously
could) and the elasticity of substitution between unskilled labour and other
factors is very low (so that, given the increase in the effective supply of
labour, the wage per efficiency unit falls more than proportionately to the
increase in the productivity of the workers).

The mechanism by which technological change can have an adverse effect
on workers in our analysis is, however, quite different. It is based on two
hypotheses:

1. Many forms of technological change are capital-using; that is, they
   require as complementary inputs additional capital. (Equivalently, at the
   original levels of the inputs of capital, the value of the marginal product of
   capital is increased.)
2. Capital markets are imperfect, so that poor farmers cannot easily borrow
   the additional required capital. Even if they could, of course, the technological change could have an adverse effect on the distribution of
   wealth (income); for it will increase the scarcity value of capital, and thus
   the return to capital. But our concern is not with this static or short-run
   effect, but rather with a long-run effect that is a consequence of credit
   rationing.

The lack of access to capital means that, after a technological change, land
will be more valuable to someone who has the capital to use with it than to
someone who does not. This, in turn, will induce some of the poorer farmers
to sell their land to richer landlords. In the short run, this simply represents a
change in the form in which wealth is held. But because the wealth distribution in one period depends not only on the distribution of wealth in the previous period, but also on the form in which different wealth-groups hold their
wealth, this sale of land may have adverse long-run effects on the wealth
distribution.

Finally, an adverse effect on wealth distribution has an adverse effect on
productivity. The reason for this is that, as inequality increases, it is more
likely that sharecropping arrangements will be employed;[2] and, although
sharecropping arrangements may be 'Pareto-efficient' (that is, given the constraints on monitoring the worker and the risk aversion of workers, there may

not be an alternative contractual arrangement between workers and land-lords that makes both of them better off), still, output may be significantly lower with sharecropping than it would be with owner-operated farms.[3]

Our contention then that certain changes in technology (certain govern-mental projects, such as irrigation projects) may have long-run adverse effects on the economy that partly offset the short-run effects requires a number of steps to establish, each of which is of some interest in its own right. In the subsequent sections, we provide simple models establishing conditions under which each of the contentions we have put forward is valid.

2. Productivity and Sharecropping

The standard formulation of the sharecropping contractual arrangement (where the contract is chosen to maximize the expected utility of the worker, subject to a constraint on the expected return per acre of the landlord) makes it clear that such contracts are (at least pairwise-)efficient. But that does not mean that national income might not be higher — significantly higher — in the absence of sharecropping.

Here we ask the question, What would happen if the land that a share-cropper currently works were redistributed to the worker, so that he now received the rents? The classical argument against sharecropping was that, because the worker received only a fraction of his marginal return, he would work less than he would if he received his marginal product, and accordingly such contracts were inefficient. We have already argued that sharecropping contracts are at least pairwise-efficient. The former contention, that indi-viduals would work less, is not obvious, either, since as we transfer resources to the worker he becomes better off, and because he is better off he may work less hard.

The question of whether output would be higher or lower under a land reform is thus close to the question of whether an increase in wages increases or decreases the labour supply (measured in terms of hours or effort). While an increase in the wage has a positive incentive (substitution) effect, it has a negative income effect, and the net effect is ambiguous. The question is close to, but not the same as, the question concerning whether the standard labour supply curve is backward-bending, because the marginal return to labour in the circumstances under examination here is a stochastic variable (see Braver-man and Srinivasan 1981). We can however show that, so long as workers are not too risk-averse (that is, so long as there is not a too strongly diminishing marginal utility of income), the substitution effect will outweigh the income effect, and a land reform will increase output.

To see this, we postulate that workers are risk-averse, with a utility func-tion of the form[4]

$$U(Y,L) = u(Y) - v(L) \qquad (1)$$

where

$$u' > 0, u'' < 0, v' > 0, v'' > 0,$$

and where Y is income and L is the worker's labour supply, measured in terms of effort.

We assume that the agricultural production function takes on the simple form of

$$Q = ag(\theta)f(L/a) \qquad (2)$$

where f is output per acre, θ is a random variable, and a is the representative worker's plot size. For simplicity, we shall normalize a at unity.

We assume a simple sharecropping system, where the tenant worker gets a fraction α of the return. For simplicity, we assume that this is his entire income, so that

$$Y = \alpha g f. \qquad (3)$$

Then the first-order condition for the level of effort is[5]

$$Eu'\alpha g f' = v' \qquad (4)$$

We can depict the consequences of a land reform as turning over control of the land to the worker, that is,. as an increase in α to 1. Thus, differentiating (4), we immediately obtain

$$\text{sign } dL/d\alpha = \text{sign } Egf'u'(1 - R) \qquad (5)$$

where $R = -u''Y/u'$, the elasticity of the marginal utility of income, or the Arrow–Pratt measure of relative risk aversion. Thus, provided

$$R < 1, \qquad (6)$$

that is, provided workers are not too risk-averse, a land reform will increase effort, and hence will increase mean national output. (The analogous condition for the deterministic case is in Braverman and Srinivasan (1981).

The magnitude of the response may be quite large: crop shares typically are in the order of magnitude of 50 per cent; thus, a land reform has the same effect as the elimination of a 50 per cent income tax.

2.1. Land reform and land taxes

This analysis provides some suggestions concerning the longstanding issue of the desirability of land taxes, as opposed to output taxes. Land taxes provide fixed payments to the government, just as rental payments provide fixed payments to the landlord. Output taxes are equivalent to sharecropping agreements; the government shares in production risks (as well as price risks). Land taxes have preferable incentive properties, just as rental payments do. But, just as earlier analyses (e.g. Stiglitz 1974a) argued that sharecropping contracts were preferable to fixed rents when tenants are risk-averse, so too are output taxes preferable to land taxes when landlords are risk-averse. Indeed, the case for the desirable risk-sharing properties of output taxes is even greater, for the government is able to diversify the risks that it faces better than the typical landlord.[6] To put it another way, the assumption made in the literature that landlords are risk-neutral is a much closer approxima-tion to describing the government than it is to describing the representative landlord, particularly in Asia and Africa. And, by switching from output taxes to land taxes, the feasible set of, say, mean and standard deviation of income of landlords and workers is made worse.

Moreover, in the more general case of linear sharecropping contracts, with

$$Y = \alpha g f + \beta,$$

the shift from an output tax to an equal-expected-revenue land tax may result in a rise in α, the crop share, and an offsetting change in β, the fixed rent or wage, as the landlord shifts some of his increased risk to the worker. Note that welfare may be reduced, even though average rural income may be increased (as a result of the greater effort exerted by workers because of the greater share provided by the equilibrium contract under the land tax). In the case where the landlord is risk-averse, expected utility of workers and/or landlords will be reduced. Only in the case where the landlord is risk-neutral will the switch from an output tax to an equal-expected revenue land tax leave the equilibrium unchanged.[7]

3. A Model of Land Valuation

To ascertain the effect of technical change on the distribution of land, we first need to construct a model of land valuation.

We will find it useful to distinguish between the value of land to a landlord who lets out his land, and the value of land to a farmer who works his own land. Moreover, we will need to extend the production model described in the previous section in order to incorporate the effects of technical change and capital availability. We thus postulate that the average output per acre of a plot of land is represented by a production function of the form

$$q = \bar{f}(k, \ell, t) \tag{7}$$

where k is capital per acre, ℓ is the amount of effort that each sharecropper supplies per acre of the sharecropping land (hence, $\ell \equiv L/a$), t is the state of technology, and $Eg(\theta) = 1$ (and so is suppressed). Changes in t can be thought of as reflecting not only technological changes, but also changes in the level of certain publicly provided services, such as irrigation and extension services.

Under a sharecropping contract with a fixed share α, the present discounted value of the returns to the landlord of an acre worked at intensity ℓ with capital k is just[8]

$$V^s = (1 - \alpha)\bar{f}(k,\ell,t)/r \tag{8}$$

where k and ℓ are both endogenously determined, and r is the rate of interest at which future income flows are discounted.[9] In principle, we should also make α an endogenous variable,[10] but in practice α seems to vary little, even over quite extended periods, and even in the presence of some significant changes in technology. Here we take α and the number of workers on each plot of land as fixed, leaving for a later occasion the extension to the more general case where both are endogenous.

From the first-order condition for effort (equation (4) above), we can immediately derive the equilibrium level of effort of a worker as a function of the amount of capital per acre provided by the landlord, the state of technology, and the size of the plot of land that the worker works:[11]

$$\ell = \phi(k,a,t) \tag{9}$$

where, as before, a is the number of acres per worker engaged in sharecropping. (In the previous section, it will be recalled, we took a to be unity.) k is then chosen to maximize

$$(1 - \alpha)\bar{f}\{k,\ell(k,a,t),t\} - rk; \tag{10}$$

that is,

$$(1 - \alpha)\{\bar{f}_k + \bar{f}_\ell(d\ell/dk)\} = r. \tag{11}$$

Note that in this formulation all the capital costs are borne by the landlord; this follows naturally from the assumption, which will play a central role in the subsequent analysis, that landlords have access to capital but workers do not.[12]

Equation (11) has some interesting implications: while the fact that the landlord can appropriate only a fraction of the marginal returns from his application of additional capital discourages the use of capital, the fact that additional capital may elicit greater effort on the part of workers may encourage the use of capital. $d\ell/dk$ will be positive if capital and labour are complements, that is, if an increase in the supply of capital increases the marginal return to labour[13] by enough to offset the reduction in effort supply resulting from the higher income provided by the increased input of capital.

We now derive the effect of a change in technology on the value of sharecropping land. Assuming that the landlords optimally adjust the level of k, we obtain (here, as in the remainder of this section, we drop the bar over f)

$$dV^s/dt = (1 - \alpha)\{f_t + f_\ell(d\ell/dt)\}/r. \tag{12}$$

In words, the change in technology has a direct effect (at fixed levels of inputs of effort and capital) and an indirect effect (through the effect on the supply

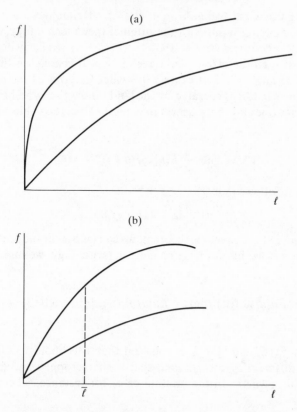

Fig. 9.1 (a) At all levels of input, technical change increases the marginal productivity of labour. (b) At all levels of input above $\bar{\ell}$, technical change reduces the marginal productivity of labour.

of effort). If the technological improvement increases the marginal productivity of effort, as in Figure 9.1a, then again there is a presumption that the supply of effort will be increased.[14] But if the technological improvement reduces the marginal productivity of effort in the relevant range ($\ell(t) > \bar{\ell}$, i.e. at the old equilibrium level of inputs, in Figure 9.1b), then the supply of effort will fall. Indeed, if the technological improvement reduces the marginal productivity at the old level of output by enough, then the indirect effect of reduced effort will outweigh the direct productivity effect, and equilibrium output will be lower. The indirect effect of a small change in technology on the input of capital can be ignored, by the envelope theorem. But the indirect effect on k of a large change in technology cannot be ignored:[15]

$$\Delta V_s = \frac{1 - \alpha}{r} \left[f\{k(t'),\ell(t'),t'\} - f\{k(t),\ell(t),t\} \right] - \{k(t') - k(t)\}$$

$$(13)$$

where t is the original technology, t' the new technology, and $k(t)(k(t'))$ represents the capital input with the original (new) technology, and where $\ell(t) \equiv \phi\{k(t), a(t), t\}$ and $\ell(t') \equiv \phi\{k(t'), a(t'), t'\}$ are similarly defined.

We now turn to the effect of the technological change on the value of owner-worked land. We first express this value in terms of the present discounted value of utility generated by the land, under the hypothesis that the worker–owner does not have access to capital. Then the value of an a-acre farm is

$$V^0 = \max_{\{\ell\}} \frac{1}{r} E[u\{agf(0,\ell,t)\} - v(\ell)], \tag{14}$$

from which it follows that

$$dV^0/dt = (aEu'gf_t)/r. \tag{15}$$

Again, because of the envelope theorem, we can ignore the induced change in the supply of effort; but for large changes in technology, we cannot, and we obtain

$$\Delta V^0 = \frac{1}{r} \langle Eu[af\{0,\ell(t'),t'\}g] - Eu[af\{0,\ell(t),t\}g] - v\{\ell(t')\} + v\{\ell(t)\}\rangle. \tag{16}$$

Comparing (16) and (13), it is apparent that a technological change can have quite different effects on land that is sharecropped and land that is worked by its owners. In the limiting case, for instance, where capital is

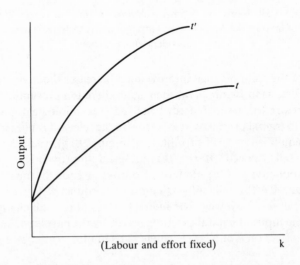

(Labour and effort fixed) k

FIG. 9.2 Technological change leaves values of capital-constrained owner-run farms unchanged, but increases values of sharecropped land.

required to take advantage of the new technology, there is no change in V^0. More generally, the technological improvement will have a larger effect on sharecropped land relative to owner-worked land,

1. the more the improvement depends on the level of capital (Figure 9.2);
2. the less the improvement depends on the level of labour effort (Figure 9.3); that is, the new technology may not increase output at very labour-intensive technologies as much as at less labour-intensive technologies;[16] and
3. the greater the effect of the technological change on the marginal productivity of effort (at least, at the levels of labour and capital employed in sharecropping).

3.1. A slight generalization

The model presented above assumed that poor farmers who worked their own land had no access to capital. A better assumption might be that they can obtain capital only by selling their land. Assume that with the initial technology the owner–farmer uses no capital, and that in fact capital is not productive. The technological change alters this. Assume that he can now sell his land to a rich landowner for a price V^s per acre, and assume that his initial endowment of land is a^*. If he retains any land to farm himself, assume that it will be optimal for him to use the proceeds of the sale to buy capital equipment. Then he will choose a, the number of acres he retains, to maximize his expected utility:

$$\max_{[\ell,a]} Eu[gaf\{V^s(a^* - a),\ell,t\}] - v(\ell); \tag{17}$$

that is,

$$Eu'g(f - af_k V^s) = 0 \quad (\text{if } a < a^*) \tag{18}$$

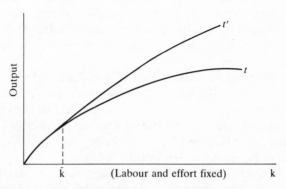

FIG. 9.3 Technological change leaves output unchanged at levels of capital input below $\bar{k}$.

or

$$f = af_k V^s \qquad (19)$$

or

$$(a^* - a)/a = f_k k/f = b(k,\ell), \qquad (20)$$

the 'share' of capital in output.

We can again consider the effects of technical change on the welfare of the owner–worker. Since, by assumption, with the original technology the owner employs no capital, by the envelope theorem, the effect of a small technological improvement is again described by equation (15). But the effect of a larger technological improvement is now given by

$$\Delta V^0 = \frac{1}{r} \, \langle Eu\{ga(t')f\}[V^s\{a^* - a(t')\},\ell(t'),t'] - Eu[ga^*f\{0,\ell(t),t\}]$$

$$- [v\{\ell(t')\} - v\{\ell(t)\}]\rangle,$$

(21)

where it should be noted that the labour supply is now different from what is was earlier, because of the change in k and a.

4. Technical Change and the Redistribution of Land

In the preceding section, we showed that a change in technology or infrastructure could have a markedly different effect on the value of sharecropped land (the welfare of landlords) and on the welfare of farmers working their own land. We now consider the effect of technical change on the distribution of land, and the effects that this in turn has.

Figure 9.4 shows the equilibrium in the land market under the assumption that the owner–workers can sell land to obtain capital. The curve *SS* is derived from equation (19). It shows the amount of land that the owner–workers are willing to sell as a function of the market price, V^s. In the figure, we have depicted the case where, as V^s increases, they sell more, although this is not necessarily the case.[17]

The curve *DD* represents the 'demand' for sharecropping land. If we assume that the number of available sharecroppers is fixed, then an increase in land under sharecropping tenancy will tend to decrease the value of each acre; V^s will normally fall. (Even if the substitution effect leads each worker to work harder, the effective labour supply per acre will fall.) Thus, the demand curve in Figure 9.4 is downward-sloping.

Now consider the effect of a technical change which increases the return to capital. This shifts the supply curve to the right, and may well shift the 'demand curve' up. Thus, as depicted in Figure 9.4 land will be transferred from owner-operators to landlords as a result of the technical change:

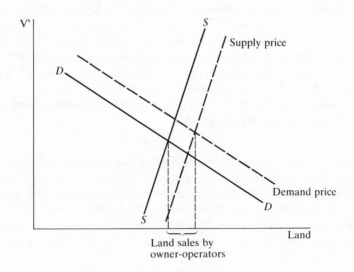

Fɪɢ. 9.4   Technical change results in a shift in landownership

the technical change has resulted in an increase in the inequality of landownership.

In this static model, the change in the distribution of landownership is welfare (and productivity)-enhancing: it enables the poor farmers, who otherwise would not have access to capital, to take advantage of the new capital-using technology. But the productivity effects are more ambiguous in a dynamic context.

5. A Dynamic Model

In spite of the enhanced productivity that might result from selling their land and using the proceeds to purchase capital, poor landowners may be reluctant to do so. They may feel that they are holding the land, which they inherited from their parents, in trust for their children. In any case, decisions to sell land may not be based solely on a rational calculation.

Land sales may occur in the event of certain stringencies, such as a crop failure or the need for funds for an emergency. Although it is only under these circumstances that land sales might occur, this does not mean that economic factors do not affect the decision. How serious the crisis must be before land is sold may depend on how much could be obtained for the land, particularly relative to what is being obtained from it at present, and what one would obtain if one became a sharecropper.

In this section, we develop a simple, stylized model to bring out the central issues. We assume that land sales do *not* occur simply on the basis of the kinds of considerations presented in the previous section. Changes in technology or infrastructure do not cause any instantaneous reorganization of land tenure arrangements. These occur only slowly. Individuals sell their land *only* in crises. For simplicity, we assume that all farms are of a fixed size, and that a farm is either tilled by its owner or under a sharecropping contract. The question then is, What fraction of land is tilled under sharecropping contracts?

We postulate that the probability that a farm that is owner-tilled will be sold, and thus become sharecropped, is

$$F = \tilde{F}(V^s, V^0, t).$$

The frequency of an owner–farmer selling his land depends on V^s and V^0, as well as on the technology itself, which may determine, for instance, the likelihood of a crop failure. What is perhaps more crucial than the absolute level of either the expected returns while owner-tilled (reflected in V^0) or the price one can obtain for selling one's land (reflected in V^s) is the ratio of the two; and for subsequent discussion we postulate that F takes on the simpler form of

$$F = F(V^0/V^s, t).$$

The changes in technology or infrastructure with which we are concerned here decrease V^0/V^s, the value of owner-tilled land with binding capital constraints (the farmers who must sell their land in the event of a crisis), relative to sharecropped land. This effect by itself increases F.

The direct effect on F of technological or infrastructural changes is ambiguous. It is often argued that the Green Revolution, while increasing mean returns, has increased the variance of the returns; the seeds are more sensitive to lack of rainfall, and thus the probability of a crisis is increased. If that is the case, then $F_t > 0$; the direct effect of the technological change is to increase the probability of a land sale. There are, of course, other changes in technology which reduce the likelihood of a crisis; irrigation projects, by making farmers less sensitive to the vagaries of weather, are likely to do this. It is even possible that this direct effect outweighs the indirect 'market value' effect, so that the overall probability of an owner–tiller selling his land is decreased.

To derive an equilibrium distribution of landownership, we have to have a theory of how some land becomes converted back to owner-worked land; otherwise, the model would predict that eventually all land would be owned by large landowners. Any model in which there are some stochastic events that impinge on landowners, eventually converting a small fraction of tenancy land into owner-tilled land, will do. Since this is not the focus of our concern here, we simply postulate that there is a probability $\tau(t)$ of an acre of sharecropped land being converted into owner-worked land.[18]

The equilibrium pattern of landownership with a given technology is thus described by

$$S\tau = (1 - S)F$$

or

$$S = F/(F + \tau)$$

where S is the share of land that is sharecropped. Thus, if a change in technology increases F/τ, it will increase the proportion of land under sharecropping.

It is thus apparent that a technological change (or change in infrastructure) that induced more owner–farmers to sell their land (increased F) could, in the long run, lead to more inequality in land ownership and an increased proportion of land under sharecropping. This is true even though the productivity on both owner-run farms and sharecropped farms has increased, so long as the productivity on sharecropped farms has increased *relatively*, say because of the increased productivity of capital.[19] This change in the distribution of tenancy may have a deleterious effect on national productivity.[20]

By the same taken, a technological change or change in infrastructure which reduces F/τ, that is, which induces fewer owner–farmers to sell their land, or which enables more sharecroppers to acquire the capital to make it possible (desirable) for them to be owner–tillers, has a long-run productivity effect that may be far in excess of the immediate, short-run, impact.

Similar results can be obtained in a more general model. The wealth distribution at time $v + 1$ depends on the wealth distribution at time v and the nature of the stochastic technology. Let $\Omega_i(v)$ be the fraction of the population with wealth i at time v. Let M_{ij} be the transition matrix, a function of t (both directly and indirectly, through the choices, say, of effort that it induces). Then in a steady state, in the obvious notation,

$$\Omega^* M(t) = \Omega^*.$$

Changes in technology will affect the distribution of outcomes at any given pattern of tenancy, and will affect the fraction of land under tenancy — see Figure 9.5. Hence changes in technology will affect the steady-state wealth distribution, and this in turn will have real productivity effects. Virtually all changes in technology that change the transition matrix M will lead to a change long-run distribution of wealth, landholdings, and tenancy arrangements.

Three tasks now lie before us. First, we need to be able to show how particular changes in technology lead to particular changes in the transition matrix $M(t)$. We need to ascertain the precise conditions under which changes in technology are likely to change significantly the long-run equilibrium distributions, both positively and negatively. (Our discussion has suggested that adverse distribution effects are more likely to arise from changes in technology which increase the variance of output — or, more precisely, the likelihood of a serious crop failure, sufficiently serious that the farmer has to sell

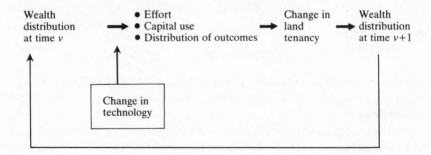

FIG. 9.5   Changes in technology lead to changes in the long-run distribution of
wealth and tenancy arrangements

his land —, and which increase the return to capital.)

Second, if there is an adverse distribution effect, we need to know the magnitude of the effect on productivity.

Third, the fact that the distribution of landholdings (tenancy arrangements) may have a significant impact on productivity suggests that institutional and other reforms which increase equality may have an important side-effect of increasing output. Economists have long focused on the trade-off between inequality and output. This analysis suggests either that there may not be a trade-off in the long run, or that the amount of output that need be sacrificed for an improvement in equality may be less than previously thought.

Our analysis suggests particular institutional reforms that *might* either ameliorate any negative distribution effects or accentuate any positive distribution effects. We have emphasized the role of capital constraints. Credit rationing, we have argued, is the natural result of informational imperfections. Informational problems are no less important for the government than for private lenders. This is not a market failure for which there is an obvious public remedy. On the other hand, our analysis points to the potential role of credit co-operatives in promoting rural development. Examples of successful co-operatives are found in Korea, Taiwan, and Kenya. Unfortunately, credit co-operatives in many other countries have failed. The reasons for the predominance of failures over successes and the analysis of effective enforcement mechanisms in credit co-operatives are the focus of Chapter 17 below.

6. Concluding Remarks

We have argued here that even if share tenancy is Pareto-efficient, productivity with share tenancy may be lower than with owner-operated farms. The prevalence of share tenancy is directly related to the inequality in the distribution of wealth, and of land-holding in particular. But the degree of inequality should itself be viewed as an endogenous variable, affected by decisions by both large landholders and small peasants concerning the choice of technique and the forms in which to hold their wealth. Both these decisions and their consequences, in turn, are affected by changes in technology and in the rural infrastructure. In the presence of credit rationing, changes in technology or infrastructure may increase inequality in land-holdings, with a long-run increase in the prevalence of share tenancy. This in turn *may* have long-run deleterious effects on productivity at least partially offsetting the initial improvements. We have suggested that the development of small rural lending institutions would reduce the likelihood of these negative effects on equality and productivity.

Here, we have only sketched the outlines of a general theory. We have, however, provided a framework which should enable one to determine whether, in any particular case, changes in technology or infrastructure have the possible adverse effects we have noted.

NOTES

1. See, e.g., Bhaduri (1973, 1979), who contends that landlords will resist innovations that reduce their power to exploit the workers.
2. There are, of course, other reasons why wealth inequality may give rise to a reduction in productivity. Dasgupta and Rey (1986), for instance, discuss the consequences of inequality in the context of an economy in which productivity depends on nutrition.
3. Although sharecropping contracts are 'pairwise efficient', in the sense that they maximize the welfare of the worker, given the expected rents of the landlord, they may not be 'globally efficient'; that is, there may exist governmental interventions (say, taxes or subsidies) which make all individuals better off. This is a general result in the theory of imperfect information and incomplete markets; see Greenwald and Stiglitz (1986).
4. Implicitly, in this formulation we are assuming that the individual's utility depends on his current income; i.e., there are not capital markets in which he can borrow or lend. This is obviously an extreme assumption, but it is far better than the opposite extreme, in which it is postulated that workers can borrow and lend at a fixed (low) real market rate of interest. Thus, the assumption of capital constraints appears as an implicit assumption even in the traditional models of sharecropping. This analysis could be extended to the case where borrowing and lending are feasible, in which case U becomes the lifetime utility function, and Y is interpreted as lifetime wealth.
5. This formulation assumes that effort is exerted before the random variable θ is known.

6. This discussion has, of course, ignored what may be the central criticism against land taxes, the administrative problems associated with levying such taxes in an equitable manner, and the abuse to which such taxes are subject. Moreover, in practice, such taxes are usually based not on the intrinsic value of the land, but on the 'improved' value of land. Thus, they are, in effect, a tax on (the present discounted value of) land rents plus a tax on capital. Because they are a tax on the present discounted value of land rents, they serve to increase the risk borne by landlords, since the present discounted value of land rents is likely to be much less variable than the annual value of land rents (and besides, tax authorities usually revise the appraised value of land only periodically). Moreover, the fact that capital is taxed, while labour is not, introduces an important distortion. As is usually the case in the theory of the second-best, it is not obvious whether a uniform distortion (taxing labour, land, and capital) is better or worse than a selective distortion (taxing land and capital). This is a question we hope to investigate on another occasion.

7. This follows from the fact that total expected payments to landlords and the government are fixed, and hence the solution to the problem of maximizing the worker's expected utility subject to that constraint is unaffected.

8. For simplicity, we assume that the rate of interest is constant (or that the market values assets as if the rate of interest were constant). (This might be true, for instance, if the rate of interest were described by a random walk, so that the expected value of future rates of interest would be equal to the current value of the rate of interest.) We also assume, somewhat less plausibly, that the market ignores all future possibilities of technological change (or changes in government-provided facilities which affect productivity). This may not be a bad approximation if such changes occur only sporadically, and real interest rates used for discounting are relatively high.

9. Clearly, if there were a perfect capital market, r would be the rate of interest at which landlords could borrow and lend. In an imperfect capital market, it is a more subtle matter to determine r. Although in principle r itself may be affected by changes in technology, t, for the purposes of this analysis, we treat r as fixed.

10. And indeed, we should introduce more complicated sharecropping contracts, e.g. with a fixed (rental or wage) component, or with cost-sharing. Each of these terms should, in principle, also be endogenously determined, and thus vary with t. Introducing these extensions would, we suspect, considerably complicate the analysis without changing the basic qualitative results.

11. For the moment, we assume that the worker engaged in sharecropping can work only on the sharecropping land. If the sharecropper has alternative opportunites, e.g. if he can work as a wage labourer, or if he owns or rents a plot of land, then this will obviously affect the amount of labour that he supplies on the sharecropping land. The landlord, in such situations, would attempt to restrict the sharecropper's access to these opportunities.

12. At the same time, Braverman and Stiglitz (1986a) show that, in the absence of an asymmetry of information concerning θ, it makes no difference whether the contract specifies that the landlord or the tenant supply capital, so long as the capital input is observable.

13. From the first-order condition for ℓ (taking α as given), we obtain

$$\text{sign } d\ell/dk = \text{sign } Eu'g(f_{\ell k} - Rf_k f_\ell/f).$$

The income effect (the increased capital increases income at a fixed effort level) discourages effort; but the substitution effect encourages it, provided $f_{k\ell} > 0$. The substitution effect will exceed the income effect, provided only that

$$R < ff_{k\ell}/f_k f_\ell \equiv 1/\sigma,$$

i.e., provided that the product of the elasticity of marginal utility (the Arrow–Pratt measure of risk aversion) and the elasticity of substitution is less than unity.

Note that, if there were a fixed fee element to the sharecropping contract, which the landlord could adjust to offset the increased income resulting from the increased capital (making, in effect, the tenant pay for the capital), or if the land-lord could adjust the share downward, to compensate for the increased capital, then there would not be an income effect. The presumption then that an increase in capital will result in greater effort will be stronger; see Braverman and Stiglitz (1986a).

14. Again, there is an income effect and a substitution effect. As in n. 13, we can show that

$$\text{sign } d\ell/dt = \text{sign } Eu'g(f_{\ell t} - Rf_t f_\ell/f).$$

There is, of course, no presumption that a technological change will, at a fixed level of labour and capital input, increase the marginal productivity of labour. Figures 9.1(a) and (b) illustrate two possibilities. For a more extended discussion of these issues, see Braverman and Stiglitz (1986b).

15. This analysis assumes that sharecropping land is purchased with its workers, i.e. that one cannot change the number of workers per acre. More generally, of course, the value of land is a function of the number of workers per acre, which itself is an endogenous variable. Obviously, if the landlord does not need to change the terms of the contract to offset a decrease in the acreage per worker, he would increase the number of workers per acre without bound, or at least until certain efficiency wage effects became significant.

16. Recall from the earlier discussion of sharecroppng that labour input will be lower with sharecropping, provided the income effects are not too large.

17. We need to differentiate the first-order conditions with respect to V^s. From equation (20) it is clear that, if we have a Cobb–Douglas production function, a is independent of V^s.

18. Clearly, we could make τ depend on the value of land under the alternative institutional arrangements. Moreover, the changes in the probability distribution of returns that affect the likelihood of owner-tilled land being converted to tenancy are also likely to affect the likelihood of tenancy land being converted to owner-tilled. For instance, if the variance of returns is large, then some sharecroppers will have large returns, enabling them to become owner–tillers. As we show below, what is crucial is the effect of technology on the ratio F/τ.

19. Assuming that credit is rationed, and that credit constraints are more binding upon poor farmers than upon wealthier ones.

20. The change in tenancy arrangements will have a more deleterious effect on productivity, the greater the difference in productivity on tenancy farms and on owner-run farms; this difference is likely to be larger the greater the elasticity of the supply of effort, and the smaller the extent to which an increase in capital increases the marginal product of effort.

10.

On Choice among Creditors and Bonded Labour Contracts

T. N. Srinivasan

1. Introduction

In Srinivasan (1980) I showed that the fact that a landlord has an opportunity to enter into a 'bonded' labour contract with his sharecropper need not blunt his incentives to introduce yield-raising innovations, owing to the possibility that improvements in yield, and hence the expected income of the share-cropper, may induce the latter to reduce his borrowing from the landlord under such a contract. A 'bonded' labour contract was defined as one in which the landlord provides consumption credit to the sharecropper in return for the latter agreeing to provide labour services (at less than his opportunity cost) to the landlord in the event that the (random) output is inadequate to repay the amount borrowed with accumulated interest. It was assumed that the only source of credit to the sharecropper is his landlord. The focus of analytical attention was the effect on amount borrowed of changes in yield, interest rate, crop share, and the pure rate of the sharecropper's time preference.

This chapter has a different objective, namely, that of characterizing the circumstances under which borrowing under a bonded labour contract will be chosen by a sharecropper if another source of credit besides the landlord is available. In particular, it will be postulated that a local institution will provide credit (up to a ceiling) at the same interest rate as the landlord. As long as the sharecropper repays the debt with interest in full, the debt is renewed in the next period. If at any time he is unable to pay in full, that is, if his total income (agricultural and non-agricultural) falls short of principal and interest due, not only does the creditor-institution appropriate his income, but he is denied credit from then on into the future.[1] On the other hand, under the same circumstances, had he taken the loan from his landlord under a bonded labour contract, he would lose his income, but by making up

I thank Pranab Bardhan and Christopher Udry for their comments on an earlier version. Udry was kind enough to check the algebra as well. Discussions with him on the problem of credit ceiling were particularly helpful. Although I am sorely tempted to place the responsibility for any errors on him, I will resist doing so.

for the short-fall in amortization and interest payments through labour services, he would be assured of a renewal of credit. Thus, while institutional credit involves the risk of denial of access to future credit because of inability to repay debt with interest, loans from the landlord assure continued access to credit at the risk of having to render labour services at below opportunity cost. The creditor, be it the lending institution or the landlord, insists on and enforces exclusivity, thereby precluding the borrower from borrowing positive amounts from both sources in a crop cycle. Further, once denied credit by one of the creditors, the borrower is denied credit by the other as well.[2] Thus, the choice problem for the sharecropper is whether to enter the credit market at all, and, if he decides to enter, from which of the two sources to borrow and how much.

Heterogeneity among sharecroppers will be introduced through differences in their non-agricultural incomes. As is to be expected, a sharecropper's decision regarding credit will be affected by his non-agricultural income. If sharecroppers are otherwise identical, then the extent of the incidence of bonded labour contracts will be determined by the distribution of non-agricultural income.

In Section 2 the model is laid out. Section 3 is devoted to a discussion of incentive compatibility, that is, the design of a loan contract by the lending institution that avoids incentives for the borrower to default wilfully. It is shown that a simple credit ceiling, appropriately set, provides the right incentives. Section 4 characterizes the solution of the sharecropper's decision problem. In Section 5 some comparative-static propositions are derived. Section 6 concludes the paper by drawing some policy implications.

2. The Model

Each crop cycle will consist of two periods, in the first of which the crop is sown and grown and in the second of which it matures and is harvested. In order to concentrate attention on credit market issues, I will drastically simplify all other aspects of crop cultivation by assuming that: (1) the borrower has taken on a given plot of land for sharecropping (with his crop share being α); (2) labour input for cultivation of this plot is the same during each of the periods in the crop cycle, and it is fixed and not subject to choice; (3) the output from this plot harvested in the second period, denoted by x, is random, so that his share αx is also a random variable. The borrower knows the probability distribution of x. Furthermore, x is assumed to be independently and identically distributed from harvest period to harvest period.

The sharecropper is assumed to have an additively time-separable welfare function, with utility in each period being a function of his consumption in that period and the labour services he delivers. The pure rate of utility discount will be denoted by β. The origin for measurement of consumption is the subsistence consumption, and that for labour, the fixed labour input for cultivation. Thus, the utility function is $u(c,\ell)$, where c is excess consumption over subsistence and ℓ is excess labour services over cultivation labour. Since the only occasion in which he exerts any labour beyond cultivation is when he has to provide bonded labour services on any loan contract he may have with his landlord, clearly, ℓ represents the extent of bonded labour. The function u is normalized so that $u(0,0) = 0$. Marginal utility of consumption $u_1(c,\ell)$ will be assumed to be positive and that of labour $u_2(c,\ell)$ negative, and $u(c,\ell)$ will be assumed to be concave in (c,ℓ).

The sharecropper will be assumed to receive non-agricultural income $y \geq 0$ in excess of his subsistence consumption in each period. He can borrow, if he chooses to, to augment his consumption in the first period of each crop cycle, with the amount borrowed to be returned with interest in the harvest period; but he cannot lend. The interest rate on debt from any source will be assumed to be the same and is fixed at i.

Let V_0 denote the expected lifetime welfare that he can achieve if he did not borrow at all in any period. Clearly, his excess consumption over subsistence in the first period will be y and that in the second period will be $y + \alpha x$, which is a random variable. Since he has not borrowed, ℓ is zero in both periods. Since, by assumption, x is independently and identically distributed over harvest periods, at the beginning of the next crop cycle the sharecropper is in exactly the same position as he was at the beginning of the first cycle, so that

$$\left.\begin{array}{l} V_0 = u(y,0) + \beta Eu(y + \alpha x, 0) + \beta^2 V_0 \\ V_0 = \{u(y,0) + \beta Eu(y + \alpha x, 0)\}/(1 - \beta^2). \end{array}\right\} \tag{1}$$

or

Suppose he decides to borrow an amount B from the local lending institution. Then once again, $\ell = 0$ in both periods. His consumption in the first period is $y + B$. In the second period, the situation is radically different compared with the no-borrowing case. One possibility is that he decides not to repay the loan with interest and not borrow thereafter; that is, he defaults regardless of his ability to repay. We discuss below the assumptions needed and the credit ceiling imposed by the institution that will ensure that it is not in the interests of the sharecropper to default. Assuming no wilful default, if the sum of his output share αx and non-agricultural income, $y + \alpha x$, is at least as large as $B(1 + i)$, he repays the debt with interest and consumes the excess $y + \alpha x - B(1 + i)$. The institution, for its part, renews his credit B for the next crop cycle. If on the other hand $y + \alpha x < B(1 + i)$, the institution appropriates $y + \alpha x$, thereby reducing his excess consumption to zero, and denies him credit for all subsequent crop cycles. Thus, if we denote by $V(B)$ the expected lifetime welfare associated with borrowing B, then, at the beginning of the next crop cycle, either his credit has been renewed and he achieves $V(B)$ as welfare for the indefinite future from then on, or he has been denied credit so that his welfare for the subsequent future is reduced to V_0. It follows that

$$V(B) = u(y + B, 0) + \beta \int_{x(B,y)} [u\{y + \alpha x - B(1 + i), 0\} + \beta V(B)]g(x)dx$$
$$+ \beta \int_0^{x(B,y)} \{u(0,0) + \beta V_0\} g(x)dx$$

where $g(x)$ is the probability density of x and $x(B,y) = \max$ $[\{B(1 + i)\} - y/\alpha, 0]$. Defining αx as z and denoting by $f(z)$ the density of z, by $F(z)$ the distribution function of z, and by $z(B,y) \equiv \max\{B(1 + i) - y, 0\}$, we get

$$V(B) = [u(y + B, 0) + \beta\int_{z(B,y)} u\{y + z - B(1 + i), 0\}f(z)dz$$
$$+ \beta^2 V_0 F\{z(B,y)\}]/\langle 1 - \beta^2[1 - F\{z(B,y)\}]\rangle. \tag{2}$$

Suppose that, instead of borrowing from the lending institution, he borrows the same amount B from his landlord. In the first period, $c = y + B$, $\ell = 0$. In the second period, if $y + \alpha x \geq B(1 + i)$, debt is repaid with interest so that consumption is $y + \alpha x - B(1 + i)$ and $\ell = 0$. If $y + \alpha x < B(1 + i)$, then the landlord appropriates $y + \alpha x$ and in addition extracts bonded labour services to the tune of $\{B(1 + i) - y - \alpha x\}/\gamma$, where γ is the (implicit) wage rate he pays for bonded labour. Thus, in this case $c = 0$ and $\ell = B(1 + i) - y - \alpha x/\gamma$. But, unlike the case of borrowing from the lending institution, since the debt is repaid in full one way or the other, the landlord renews the sharecropper's credit for the next crop cycle. Denoting by $\tilde{V}(B)$ the lifetime expected welfare the sharecropper obtains under such a contract, we get

$$\tilde{V}(B) = u(y + B,0) + \beta[\int_{z(B,y)} \{y + z - B(1 + i),0\}f(z)dz$$
$$+ \int^{z(B,y)} u(0,\tilde{\ell})f(z)dz] + \beta^2\tilde{V}(B) \tag{3}$$

where $\tilde{\ell} = \{B(1 + i) - y - z\}/\gamma$
or

$$\tilde{V}(B) = [u(y + B,0) + \beta\int_{z(B,y)} u\{y + z - B(1 + i),0\}f(z)dz$$
$$+ \beta\int^{z(B,y)} u(0,\tilde{\ell})f(z)dz]/(1 - \beta^2).$$

It is seen from (1)–(3) that, as is to be expected, $V_0 = V(0) = \tilde{V}(0)$. Now from the definition of $z(B,y)$, it follows that $z(B,y) = 0$ if $B(1 + i) \leq y$. What this means is that, if the amount borrowed is sufficiently small that it can be repaid with interest out of non-agricultural income itself, the possibility of not having enough resources to repay the debt does not arise, whatever may be the realized value of the random crop share. Since the difference between institutional and landlord-provided credit arises only under circumstances where the sharecropper cannot repay the debt in full, it follows (as can be seen from (2) and (3)) that

$$V(B) = \tilde{V}(B) \quad \text{for } 0 \leq B \leq y/(1 + i). \tag{4}$$

Of course, if $B > y/(1 + i)$, then $V(B)$ and $\tilde{V}(B)$ can differ.

In the open interval $\{0, y/(1 + i)\}$,

$$\frac{\partial V}{\partial B} = \frac{\partial \tilde{V}}{\partial B} = [u_1(y + B,0) + \beta(1 + i)Eu_1\{y + z - B(1 + i),0\}]/(1 - \beta^2) \quad (5)$$

$$\frac{\partial^2 V}{\partial B} = \frac{\partial^2 \tilde{V}}{\partial B^2} = [u_{11}(y + B,0) + \beta(1 + i)^2 Eu_{11}\{y + z - B(1 + i),0\}]/(1 - \beta^2)$$

$$(6)$$

where E denotes the expectation operator with respect to the distribution of z. Given the concavity of $u(\cdot)$, it follows that $V(B)$ ($= V(\tilde{B})$) is concave in $\{0, y/(1 + i)\}$. For $B > y/(1 + i)$, we get (using $u(0,0) = 0$ and $z(B,y) = B(1 + i) - y$)

$$\frac{\partial V}{\partial B} = [u_1(y + B,0) - \beta(1 + i) \int_{z(B,y)} u_1\{y + z - B(1 + i),0\}f(z)dz$$

$$+ \beta^2(1 + i)V_0 f\{z(B,y)\}]/\langle 1 - \beta^2[1 - F\{z(B,y)\}]\rangle$$

$$- [\beta^2(1 + i)f\{z(B,y)\}V(B)]/\langle 1 - \beta^2[1 - F\{z(B,y)\}]\rangle \quad (7)$$

$$\frac{\partial \tilde{V}}{\partial B} = [u_1(y + B,0) - \beta(1 + i) \int_{z(B,y)} u_1\{y + z - B(1 + i),0\}f(z)dz$$

$$+ \beta \left(\frac{1 + i}{\gamma}\right) \int^{z(B,y)} u_2(0,\ell)f(z)dz]/(1 - \beta^2). \quad (8)$$

By comparing (5) with (7) and (8), and using the definition of V_0 and $V(B)$, it can be shown that

$$\lim_{B \to (y/1 + i) + 0} \left(\frac{\partial V}{\partial B}\right) = \lim_{B \to (y/1 + i) - 0} \left(\frac{\partial V}{\partial B}\right), \quad \text{if } f(0) = 0 \quad (9)$$

$$\lim_{B \to (y/1 + i) + 0} \left(\frac{\partial \tilde{V}}{\partial B}\right) = \lim_{B \to (y/1 + i) - 0} \left(\frac{\partial \tilde{V}}{\partial B}\right). \quad (10)$$

It can be shown that, for $B(1 + i) > y$,

$$\frac{\partial^2 V}{\partial B^2} = \frac{1}{1 - \beta^2[1 - F\{z(B,y)\}]}$$

$$[u_{11}(y + B,0) + \beta(1 + i)^2 \int_{z(B,y)} u_{11}\{y + z - B(1 + i),0\}f(z)dz$$

$$+ \beta^2(1 + i)^2 V_0 f_1\{z(B,y)\} + \beta(1 + i)^2 u_1(0,0)f\{z(B,y)\}]$$

$$+ \frac{V(B)}{\langle 1 - \beta^2[1 - F\{z(B,y)\}]\rangle^2} \beta^2 f\{z(B,y)\}(1 + i))^2$$

$$- \frac{\beta^2(1 + i)f(z(B,y))}{\langle 1 - \beta^2[1 - F\{z(B,y)\}]\rangle} \frac{\partial V(B)}{\partial B}$$

$$- \frac{\beta^2(1 + i)f\{z(B,y)\}}{\langle 1 - \beta^2[1 - F\{z(B,y)\}]\rangle^2}$$

$$\times \quad [u_1(y + B,0) - \beta(1 + i)\int_{z(B,y)} u_1\{y + z - B(1 + i),0\}f(z)dz$$
$$+ \beta^2(1 + i)V_0 f\{z(B,y)\}]$$
$$- \frac{\beta^2(1 + i)f_1\{Z(B,y)\}V(B)}{\langle 1 - \beta^2[1 - F\{Z(B,y)\}]\rangle} . \tag{11}$$

$$\frac{\partial^2 \tilde{V}}{\partial B^2} = \frac{1}{1 - \beta^2} [u_{11}(y + B,0) + \beta(1 + i)^2 \int_{z(B,y)} u_{11}\{y + z - B(1 + i),0\}f(z)dz$$

$$+ B\left(\frac{1 + i}{\gamma}\right)^2 \int^{z(B,y)} u_{22}(0,\tilde{\ell}) f(z)dz$$

$$+ \beta f\{z(B,y)\}(1 + i)^2 \{u_1(0,0) + u_2(0,0)/\gamma\}]. \tag{12}$$

Since (11) involves derivatives of the probability distribution function of z, in general we cannot determine the sign of $\partial^2 V/\partial B^2$. Now from the concavity of $u(\cdot)$, the concavity of $\tilde{V}(B)$ follows, *provided $u_1(0,0) + u_2(0,0)/\gamma < 0$*, that is, if the implicit wage γ paid by the landlord is less than the sharecropper's opportunity cost of labour. The latter equals the opportunity cost of leisure when the sharecropper is pushed to subsistence consumption; that is, it is the ratio of the marginal utility of leisure ($-u_2(0,0)$) divided by the marginal utility of consumption ($u_1(0,0)$). Indeed, this condition is the essence of bondedness: having to provide labour services at below opportunity cost to pay off past debt.

3. Incentive Compatibility and the Credit Ceiling

It is clear that no lender will enter into a loan contract that makes it attractive to the borrower to default wilfully, whether or not he is in a position to repay. Obviously, if the maximum welfare achievable by a borrower if he does not default exceeds the maximal welfare he can attain by defaulting, then the borrower will not default. By closely monitoring the sharecropper's activities and enforcing a bonded labour contract, the landlord avoids default by the sharecropper. By assumption, the lending institution does not have this option and has to design an incentive-compatible contract.

Let us define $\tilde{\tilde{V}}(B)$ as the lifetime expected welfare of the sharecopper if he chooses to borrow from the institution and default in the second period. Of course, he will not be given any credit subsequently. Hence

$$\tilde{\tilde{V}}(B) = u(y + B,0) + \beta E u(y + z,0) + \beta^2 V_0. \tag{13}$$

It is clear that $\partial\tilde{\tilde{V}}(B)/\partial B = u_1(y + B,0) > 0$ for all B and $\tilde{\tilde{V}}(B)$ is concave. If the lending institution imposes no credit ceiling, the borrower will borrow as much as he can get and then default. However, even if there is a ceiling $\bar{B}$, if the expected lifetime welfare from borrowing and not defaulting, i.e. $V(B)$, is less than $\tilde{\tilde{V}}(B)$ for $0 \le B \le \bar{B}$, then he will borrow $\bar{B}$ *and* default. To induce the borrower not to default, the ceiling $\bar{B}$ has to be such that the maximum of $V(B)$ in $0 \le B \le \bar{B}$ is at least as large as $\tilde{\tilde{V}}(\bar{B})$.

Let the support of the distribution of z be $(0,z^M)$. Let $B^M = (z^M + y)/(1 + i)$. From the definition of $z(B,y)$, it is clear that as $B \to B^M$, $z(B,y) \to z^M$ and $F\{z(B,y)\} \to 1$, so that from (2) we get

$$\lim_{B \to B^M} V(B) = u(y + B^M,0) + \beta^2 V_0$$
$$< \lim_{B \to B^M} \tilde{\tilde{V}}(B). \tag{14}$$

This means that if, for some $\hat{B}$ in $(0,B^M)$, $V(\hat{B}) > \tilde{\tilde{V}}(\hat{B})$, then the two curves $V(B)$ and $\tilde{\tilde{V}}(B)$ have to cross at least once between $\hat{B}$ and B^M. Since $V(0) = \tilde{\tilde{V}}(0) = V_0$, a *sufficient* condition for the existence of such a $\hat{B}$ is that

$$\left(\frac{\partial V}{\partial B}\right)_{B=0} > \left(\frac{\partial \tilde{\tilde{V}}}{\partial B}\right)_{B=0}$$

or

$$\{u_1(y,0) - \beta(1 + i)Eu_1(y + z,0)\}/(1 - \beta^2) > u_1(y,0)$$

or

$$\beta u_1(y,0) > (1 + i) Eu_1(y + z,0). \tag{15}$$

If we make the *stronger* assumption that $V(B)$ is increasing in $\{0,y/(1 + i)\}$ and that

$$V\{y + y/(1 + i)\} > \tilde{\tilde{V}}\{y + y/(1 + i)\}, \text{ i.e. } \beta[u\{y + y/(1 + i),0\} - u(y,0)]$$
$$> [Eu(y + z,0) - Eu(z,0)], \tag{16}$$

then $V(B)$ will cross $\tilde{\tilde{V}}(B)$ *from above* somewhere in $\{y/(1 + i), B^M\}$. Thus, given either (15) or (16), by setting a credit ceiling at the amount $\overline{B}$ where $\overline{B}$ is the smallest B for which $V(B) = \tilde{\tilde{V}}(B)$, the lending institution can assure itself that the borrower will have the incentive to repay the loan with interest except in situations when his agricultural and non-agricultural incomes together fall short of the loan with interest. The possibility that the borrower is denied future credit can arise only if he borrows a sufficiently large B that the probability $y + z$ falls short of $B(1 + i)$ is positive. Clearly, if the ceiling $\overline{B}$ is such that $\overline{B}(1 + i) < y$, this will not arise. By assuming the stronger (16) instead of (15), one can ensure that $\overline{B}(1 + i) > y$.

It is to be noted both (15) (and (16)) are *sufficient conditions* for the $V(B)$ curve to cross $\tilde{\tilde{V}}(B)$ from above at a positive $\overline{B}$ (at a $\overline{B}$ exceeding $y/(1 + i)$). Neither is necessary — indeed, it is conceivable, though not very plausible, that $V(B)$ could cross $\tilde{\tilde{V}}(B)$ several times. We will, however, assume away such a possibility. Specifically, we assume that either $V(B)$ is always below $\tilde{\tilde{V}}(B)$, in which case $\overline{B} = 0$ (i.e., the institution will not extend any credit), or it crosses $\tilde{\tilde{V}}(B)$ only *once* and from above. Of course, a credit ceiling of zero effectively removes the lending institution as a source of credit. As such, only the second alternative is of interest. This implies (a) that (15) holds, (b) that

$[0,\overline{B}]$ the difference $V(B) - \tilde{\tilde{V}}(B)$ is positive except at zero and $\overline{B}$ where it is zero, and (c) that $\partial V/\partial B - \partial \tilde{\tilde{V}}/\partial B < 0$ at $\overline{B}$. Since $\tilde{V}(B)$ does not depend on i while $V(B)$ decreases as i increases, it follows that the credit ceiling $\overline{B}$ decreases as i increases. Both $V(B)$ and $\tilde{\tilde{V}}(B)$ increase as y increases, and as such, in general, $\overline{B}$ can increase or decrease as y increases. However, if we assume that $\partial V(B)/\partial y > \partial \tilde{\tilde{V}}(B)/\partial y$ at $\overline{B}$, that is, that an increase in income increases welfare under no wilful default more than it does under wilful default, when $\overline{B}$ will increase as y increases. We will assume this to be the case.

4. Sharecropper's Optimal Choice of Credit and Creditor

The sharecropper obviously will choose the creditor and the amount of credit so as to maximize his lifetime expected welfare. This means that he will borrow from the lending institution (landlord) if the maximum of $V(B)$ in $[0,\overline{B}]$ exceeds (is less than) the maximum of $\tilde{V}(B)$ for $B \geq 0$. Let us explore this choice in some detail.

It was shown in Section 2 that $V(B)$ and $\tilde{V}(B)$ are the same functions in $0 \leq B \leq y/(1 + i)$ and concave in $0 < B < y/(1 + i)$. If we assume that $u_1(0,0) + u_2(0,0)/\gamma < 0$, then $\tilde{V}(B)$ is concave in $B > y/(1 + i)$ as well. Thus, $\tilde{V}(B)$ is concave for all $B > 0$. With the innocuous assumption that the probability density of z vanishes at 0, the lower end of the support of its distribution, we showed that $V(B)$ has a continuous derivative at $y/(1 + i)$. The relevant range for B in the case of $V(B)$ is $(0,\overline{B})$. If $\overline{B} \leq y/(1 + i)$, $V(B)$ has been shown to be concave in $(0,\overline{B})$. If $\overline{B} > y/(1 + i)$, then concavity of $V(B)$ in $\{y/(1 + i), \overline{B}\}$ cannot be derived from plausible assumptions about the utility and probability functions and will be *assumed* where needed.

From (15), it follows that, as long as $u_1(y,0) > 0$, $\partial V/\partial B$ ($= \partial \tilde{V}/\partial B$) is positive at $B = 0$. This means that the sharecropper will be interested in borrowing a positive amount from one of the two sources. Suppose $\partial V/\partial B$ ($= \partial \tilde{V}/\partial B$) is non-positive at $B = y/(1 + i)$; i.e.,

$$u_1\{y + y/(1 + i), 0\} \leq \beta(1 + i) Eu_1(z,0). \tag{17}$$

Then, given concavity of $V(B)$ ($= \tilde{V}(B)$) in $\{0,y/(1 + i)\}$, we can assert the following.

PROPOSITION 1. Given (15) and (17).

   (i) there exists a unique B^* in $\{0,y/(1 + i)\}$ at which $\partial V/\partial B = \partial \tilde{V}/\partial B = 0$;
   (ii) if $\overline{B}$, the credit ceiling, is at least as large as B^*, then sharecropper will borrow B^* and will be indifferent as to the creditor from whom he borrows;
   (iii) if $\overline{B} < B^*$, then the sharecropper will borrow B^* from his landlord; and

(iv) since $B^* \leq y/(1 + i)$, the sharecropper can repay the debt with interest from out of his non-agricultural income itself and, as such, will never render bonded labour to his landlord in case he borrows from him. Nor will he run the risk of being denied future credit by the lending institution if he chooses to borrow from it.

Suppose (17) does not hold. Then clearly, the sharecropper would like to borrow at least $y/(1 + i)$. Thus,

PROPOSITION 2. Given $u_1(y,0) > \beta(1 + i)Eu_1(z,0)$,

(i) if $\bar{B} \leq y/(1 + i)$, then the maximum of $V(B)$ in $[0,\bar{B}]$ occurs at $\bar{B}$;

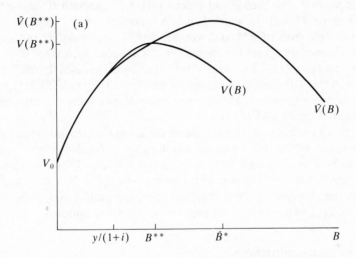

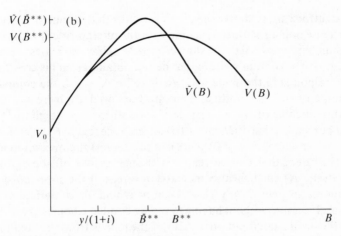

FIG. 10.1

(ii) if $\overline{B} > y/(1 + i)$ and $\partial V/\partial B$ vanishes at some B^{**} in $[y/(1 + i), \overline{B}]$, then (given concavity of $V(B)$ in $[0,\overline{B}]$) the maximum of $V(B)$ in $[0,\overline{B}]$ occurs at B^{**};

(iii) if $\partial V/\partial B$ is non-negative for all B in $[0,\overline{B}]$, the maximum of $V(B)$ in $[0,\overline{B}]$ occurs at $\overline{B}$;

(iv) the maximum $\tilde{V}(B)$ occurs at a unique $\tilde{B}^{**} > y/(1 + i)$ where $\partial \tilde{V}(B)/\partial B$ vanishes;

(v) denoting by B^{P} the value of B that maximizes $V(B)$ in $[0,\overline{B}]$, it is clear that the sharecropper will borrow $B^{\mathrm{P}}(\tilde{B}^{**})$ from the institution (landlord) according as $V(B^{\mathrm{P}}) > (<) \tilde{V}(\tilde{B}^{**})$.

If we assume (16), then $\overline{B}$ will exceed $y/(1 + i)$ and both B^{P} and $\tilde{B}^{**}$ will also exceed $y/(1 + i)$. In general, it is not possible to say whether B^{P} will exceed or fall short of $\tilde{B}^{**}$ and whether $V(B^{\mathrm{P}})$ will exceed or fall short of $V(\tilde{B}^{**})$. By assuming that the credit ceiling is not binding, so that $B^{\mathrm{P}} = B^{**}$, Figure 10.1(a) (10.1(b)) illustrates the case in which $B^{**} > \tilde{B}^{**}$ $(\tilde{B}^{**} > B^{**})$. Although in both parts of the figure $\tilde{V}(\tilde{B}^{**}) > V(B^{**})$, simply by relabelling $V(B)$ as $\tilde{V}(B)$ and vice-versa in the two parts, we can illustrate the case of $V(B^{**}) > \tilde{V}(\tilde{B}^{**})$.

We conclude this section with the observation that the *possibility* of the sharecropper borrowing from his landlord on a bonded labour contract arises only if his non-agricultural income is sufficiently low as to violate inequality (17). Even then, it is by no means certain that he will do so; it can happen that borrowing from the local institution and running the risk of losing access to all future credit may be his preferred option.

5. Some Comparative Statics

It is straightforward to derive the obvious results that, as noted in Section 3, if we increase non-agricultural income y (or the interest rate i) while keeping the amount borrowed fixed, the sharecropper's welfare increases (decreases). *A fortiori*, the maximum welfare that he can obtain, given his credit market options, responds in the same way. As is to be expected, the comparative-static response of the optimal amount borrowed to increases in non-agricultural income or the interest rate is not always unambiguous.

It will be recalled that $V(B)$ and $\tilde{V}(B)$ differ in the region $B > y/(1 + i)$. In this region, an increase in y (i) increases (decreases) the maximum amount $y/(1 + i)$ of debt that can be repaid with interest out of non-agricultural income itself. As such, it also increases (decreases) the *probability* that a given amount of debt $B > y/(1 + i)$ can be repaid out of agricultural non-agricultural income (without having to render bonded labour) in case the loan is from the institution (landlord). Also, if the loan is from the landlord on a bonded labour contract, obviously, the amount of labour services to be rendered if unable to repay the debt in full also *decreases* (increases) as y (i) increases. Of course, an increase in y in the first period, by reducing the marginal utility of consumption, blunts the incentive to borrow more to augment first-period consumption. The effect of an increase in the interest rate is reflected only in the second period of the crop cycle when the loan is to be repaid. The total effect is the algebraic sum of all these.

It turns out, given the bondedness condition $u_1(0,0) + u_2(0,0)/\gamma < 0$, that

$$\frac{\partial^2 \bar{V}(B)}{\partial i \partial B} < 0 \text{ and } \frac{\partial^2 \bar{V}(B)}{\partial y \partial B} =$$

$$\left(1 + \frac{1}{1 + i}\right) \frac{u_{11}(y + B,0)}{(1 - \beta^2)} - \left(\frac{1}{1 + i}\right) \frac{\partial^2 \bar{V}(B)}{\partial B^2}.$$

It follows therefore from the concavity of $\bar{V}(B)$ that the (unique) solution of $\partial \bar{V}/\partial B = 0$ decreases as i increases, and is of ambiguous sign as y increases. Thus, if the sharecropper finds it optimal to borrow from the landlord, the optimal amount be borrows is a *decreasing* function of i and will be an *increasing* function of y if the negative first-period income effect, $\{1 + 1/(1 + i)\} u_{11}(y + B,0)$, does not dominate the positive term, $\{1/(1 + i)\}$ $\{\partial^2 \bar{V}(B)/\partial B^2\}$, both being evaluated at the optimal amount borrowed.

It will be recalled that $z(B,y) = B(1 + i) - y$ is the excess of debt amortization and interest over non-agricultural income. In the case of a loan from the landlord, an increase in y, for instance, by reducing $z(B,y)$, reduces the range of realized crop shares z associated with zero consumption and positive bonded labour services and increases the range associated with positive consumption and zero bonded labour services. Thus, in this case the shift in the *marginal utility curve* of a loan of size $B > y/(1 + i)$ arising from changes in $z(B,y)$ at the margin is simply $\{u_1(0,0) + u_2(0,0)\gamma\} f\{z(B,y)\}$, and this is negative by assumption. On the other hand, in the case of a loan from an institution, if $B^P = \bar{B}$, the credit ceiling, then B^P decreases (increases) as i (y) increases. However, if $B^P = B^{**}$, the shift in $\partial V/\partial B$ as i changes becomes relevant. Now the sharecropper is denied future credit and is forced to a lifetime expected welfare of V_0 if he is unable to repay the existing loan in full, the probability of which event is $F\{z(B,y)\}$. As such, $\partial V/\partial B$, the *marginal utility* curve of a loan of size B, is also affected by changes in the *density* $f\{z(B,y)\}$ arising from changes in $z(B,y)$. Thus, it is not possible in general to sign the change in the optimal amount B^{**} that a sharecropper will borrow from the institution if he chooses to do so, with respect to changes in y or i. However, by inspection of $\partial^2 V/\partial i \partial B$ and $\partial^2 V/\partial y \partial B$, it can be seen that, given the assumption that $V(B)$ is concave in $(0,\bar{B})$, the presumption is that B^{**} *decreases* as i increases and *increases* as y increases, unless the effects (mainly) on the first period of the crop cycle pulling in the opposite direction dominate. To conclude, *regardless of the source of credit*, the optimal amount borrowed can be presumed to have a 'normal' response, that is, *decreasing* when the interest rate goes up and *increasing* when income (or wealth) goes up.

6. Incidence of Bonded Labour

In Section 4 it was shown that a sharecropper will consider borrowing under a bonded labour contract only if

$$u_1\left\{y\left(1 + \frac{1}{1+i}\right),0\right\} > \beta(1 + i)Eu_1(z,0). \qquad (18)$$

Given concavity of u, provided $u_1(0,0) > \beta(1 + i)Eu_1(z,0)$, there is a unique $\hat{y} > 0$ such that

$$u_1\left\{\hat{y}\left(1 + \frac{1}{1+i}\right),0\right\} = \beta(1 + i)Eu_1(z,0). \qquad (19)$$

Since $u_1(z,0)$ is a decreasing function of z, it follows that, if we consider two distributions $F(z)$ and $\hat{F}(z)$ of z where F stochastically dominates $\hat{F}$ to a first order (i.e. where $F(z) - \hat{F}(z) \geq 0$ for all z), then $Eu_1(z,0) < \hat{E}u_1(z,0)$ where E and $\hat{E}$ denote the expectation operators with respect to the distributions F and $\hat{F}$. If we view F and $\hat{F}$ as distributions associated with the post- and pre-technical change situations, then the first-order stochastic dominance of F means that the technical change, loosely speaking, raises crop yield in each state of nature. From (19), we can infer that the post-technical change $\hat{y}$ will be larger than the pre-technical change.

Consider now the case where F stochastically dominates $\hat{F}$ only to the second order (i.e. where $\int^z\{F(z) - \hat{F}(z)\}dz \geq 0$ for all $\hat{z}$). Then, if can assume that $u_1(z,0)$ is *convex* in z (a sufficient condition for which is that the Arrow–Pratt measure of absolute risk aversion, $-u_{11}(z,0)/u_1(z,0)$, is non-increasing in z), then, again, $Eu_1(z,0) < \hat{E}u_1(z,0)$. In essence, this means that a technical change leading to a less risky distribution of yields (which includes, in particular, a technical change that leaves the *mean yield unchanged while reducing risk*) will reduce the expectation of $u_1(z,0)$ and thus raise $\hat{y}$.

Finally, from (19), it is clear that

$$\frac{(1 + i)}{\hat{y}} \frac{d\hat{y}}{di} = \left(\frac{1}{2 + i} - \frac{1}{R\left\{\hat{y}\left(1 + \frac{1}{1+i}\right)\right\}}\right) \qquad (20)$$

where $R(z)$ is the Arrow–Pratt relative risk aversion measure $-u_{11}(z,0)z/u_1(z,0)$. Thus, $\hat{y}$ increases, remains unchanged, or decreases locally as i increases according as

$$R\left\{\hat{y}\left(1 + \frac{1}{1+i}\right)\right\} \gtreqless (2 + i). \qquad (21)$$

Suppose the function $H(y)$ characterizes the cumulative distribution of otherwise identical sharecroppers according to their non-agricultural income. Then $1 - H(\hat{y})$ represents the proportion of sharecroppers who will *never* borrow under a bonded labour contract. Thus, assuming non-increasing absolute risk aversion, this proportion will be *smaller* in a region with a stochastically dominant (first- or second-order) distribution of yields compared with another. If we identify stochastic dominance of a region with its being more advanced agriculturally, and also rule out the option of borrowing from the institution, then the incidence of bonded labour will be *higher* in the more advanced region! Further, if $\tilde{B}^{**}$ increases as y increases, then not only will the incidence be higher, but the aggregate amount borrowed under bonded labour contracts will be higher as well. By identifying a more advanced region as the one with a lower interest rate i, we can conclude from (20) that, if the sharecroppers are not "too risk-averse' in the relative sense, the proportion never borrowing under bonded labour will be *lower* in such regions! Once again, if the landlord is the only source of credit, the incidence of bonded labour and the aggregate amount borrowed under such contracts will be higher in the advanced region.

7. Policy Implication

Two policy implications follow from the above analysis. Policies promoting technical change, if they succeed in making the post-change distribution of yields dominate stochastically the pre-change distribution, may succeed in raising the incidence of bonded labour or at best not lowering it. Interest rate subsidization may have a similar effect. Since, in the above model, the choice of a bonded labour contract is voluntary, it will be chosen by the sharecropper only if it yields him a higher lifetime welfare compared with borrowing from the lending institution. Under such circumstances, the policy of banning bonded labour will be unenforceable or, if forcibly implemented, will *reduce* the welfare of the sharecropper.

APPENDIX

A1. *For $0 < B < y/(1 + i)$*

$$V(B) = \tilde{V}(B) = [u(y + B,0] + \beta Eu\{y + z - B(1 + i),0\}]/(1 - \beta^2).$$

$$\frac{\partial V}{\partial B} = \frac{\partial \tilde{V}}{\partial B} = [u_1(y + B,0) - \beta(1 + i) Eu_1\{y + z - B(1 + i),0\}]/(1 - \beta^2).$$

$$\frac{\partial^2 V}{\partial B^2} = \frac{\partial^2 \tilde{V}}{\partial B^2} = [u_{11}(y + B,0) + \beta(1 + i)^2$$
$$Eu_{11}\{y + z - B(1 + i),0\}](1 - \beta^2)$$
$$< 0.$$

$$\frac{\partial^2 V}{\partial i \partial B} = \frac{\partial^2 \tilde{V}}{\partial i \partial B} = [-\beta E u_1\{y + z - B(1 + i),0\} +$$

$$\beta B(1 + i)E u_{11}\{y + z - B(1 + i),1\}]/(1 - \beta^2)$$

$$< 0.$$

$$\frac{\partial^2 V}{\partial y \partial B} = \frac{\partial^2 \tilde{V}}{\partial y \partial B}$$

$$= [u_{11}(y + B,0) - \beta(1 + i)E u_{11}\{y + z - B(1 + i),0\}]/(1 - \beta^2).$$

$$\frac{\partial V(B)}{\partial y} = u_1(y + B) + E u_1\{y + z - B(1 + i),0\} > 0,$$

$$\frac{\partial V(B)}{\partial i} = -B E u_1\{y + z - B(1 + i),0\} < 0.$$

A2. *For $B > y/(1 + i)$*

$$z(B,y) = B(1 + i) - y, \tilde{\ell} = \frac{z(B,y) - z}{\gamma}.$$

$$\tilde{V}(B) = \left[u(y + B,0) + \beta \int_{z(B,y)} u\{y + z - B(1 + i),0\}f(z)dz + \beta \int^{z(B,y)} u(0,\tilde{\ell})f(z)dz \right] / (1 - \beta^2).$$

$$\frac{\partial \tilde{V}}{\partial B} = \left[u_1(y + B,0) - \beta(1 + i)\int_{z(B,y)} u_1\{y + z - B(1 + i),0\}f(z)dz + \{\beta(1 + i)/\gamma\} \int_0^{z(B,y)} u_2(0,\tilde{\ell})f(z)dz \right] / (1 - \beta^2).$$

$$\frac{\partial^2 \tilde{V}}{\partial B^2} = \left[u_{11}(y + B,0) + \beta(1 + i)^2 \int_{z(B,y)} u_{11}\{y + z - B(1 + i),0\}f(z)dz + \beta(1 + i)^2 u_1(0,0)f\{z(B,y)\} \right.$$

$$+ \beta \left(\frac{1 + i}{\gamma} \right)^2 \int^{z(B,y)} u_{22}(0,\tilde{\ell}) \cdot f(z)dz +$$

$$\left. \beta\{(1 + i)^2/\gamma\} u_2(0,0)f\{z(B,y)\} \right] / (1 - \beta^2)$$

$$< 0 \quad (\text{given } u_1(0,0) + u_2(0,0)/\gamma < 0).$$

$$\frac{\partial^2 \tilde{V}}{\partial i \partial B} = \left[-\beta \int_{z(B,y)} u_1\{y + z - B(1 + i),0\}f(z)dz \right.$$

$$+ \beta(1 + i)B \int_{z(B,y)} u_{11}\{y + z - B(1 + i),0\}f(z)dz$$

$$+ \beta(1 + i)u_1(0,0)f\{z(B,y)B\}$$

$$+ \beta \frac{(1 + i)B}{\gamma^2} \int^{z(B,y)} u_{22}(0,\tilde{\ell})f(z)dz$$

$$+ \frac{\beta}{\gamma} \int_0^{z(B,y)} u_2(0,\tilde{\ell})f(z)dz$$

$$\left. + \frac{\beta(1 + i)B}{\gamma} u_2(0,0)f\{z(B,y)\} \right] / (1 - \beta^2)$$

$$< 0 \quad (\text{given } u_1(0,0) + u_2(0,0)/\gamma < 0).$$

$$\frac{\partial^2 \tilde{V}}{\partial y \partial B} = \Big[u_{11}(y + B,0) - \beta(1 + i)\int_{z(B,y)} u_{11}\{y + z - B(1 + i),0\}f(z)dz$$

$$- \beta(1 + i)u_1(0,0)f\{z(B,y)\}$$

$$- \frac{\beta(1 + i)}{\gamma^2} \int_0^{z(B,y)} u_{22}(0,\tilde{\ell})f(z)dz$$

$$- \frac{\beta(1 + i)}{\gamma} u_2(0,0)f\{z(B,y)\}\Big]\Big/1 - \beta^2.$$

(All terms except the first are positive, given $u_1(0,0) + u_2(0,0)/\gamma < 0$.)

$$V(B) = [u(y + B,0) + \beta\int_{z(B,y)} u\{y + z - B(1 + i),0\}f(z)dz$$

$$+ \beta^2 V_0 F\{z(B,y)\}/\langle 1 - \beta^2[1 - F\{z(B,y)\}]\rangle.$$

$$\frac{\partial V(B)}{\partial B} = \Big[u_1(y + B,0) - \beta(1 + i)\int_{z(B,y)} u_1\{y + z - B(1 + i),0\}f(z)dz$$

$$+ \beta^2 V_0 f\{z(B,y)(1 + i)\}]\Big]\Big/\langle 1 - \beta^2[1 - F\{z(B,y)\}]\rangle$$

$$- \frac{V(B)\beta^2 f\{z(B,y)\}(1 + i)}{1 - \beta^2[1 - F\{z(B,y)\}]}$$

$$= \Big[u_1(y + B,0) - \beta(1 + i)\int_{z(B,y)} u_1\{y + z - B(1 + i),0\}f(z)dz$$

$$- \beta^2(1 + i)f\{z(B,y)\}\{V(B) - V_0\}\Big]\Big/\langle 1 - \beta^2[1 - F\{z(B,y)\}]\rangle.$$

$$\frac{\partial^2 V(B)}{\partial B^2} = \Big[u_{11}(y + B,0) + \beta(1 + i)^2\int_{z(B,y)} u_{11}\{y + z - B(1 + i),0\}f(z)dz$$

$$+ \beta(1 + i)^2 u_1(0,0)f\{z(B,y)\}$$

$$- \beta^2(1 + i)^2 f_1\{z(B,y)\}\{V(B) - V_0\}$$

$$- \beta^2(1 + i)f\{z(B,y)\} \frac{\partial V(B)}{\partial B}\Big]\Big/\langle(1 - \beta^2[1 - F\{z(B,y)\}]\rangle$$

$$- \frac{\dfrac{\partial V(B)}{\partial B} \beta^2 f\{z(B,y)\}(1 + i)}{1 - \beta^2[1 - F\{z(B,y)\}]}$$

$$= \Big[u_{11}(y + B,0) + \beta(1 + i)^2\int_{z(B,y)} u_{11}\{y + z - B(1 + i),0\}f(z)dz$$

$$+ \beta(1 + i)^2 u_1(0,0)f\{z(B,y)\} - \beta^2(1 + i)^2 f_1\{z(B,y)\}\{V(B) - V_0\}$$

$$- 2\beta^2(1 + i)f\{z(B,y)\}\{\partial z(B,y)/\partial B\}\Big]\Big/\langle 1 - \beta^2[1 - F\{z(B,y)\}]\rangle.$$

$$\frac{\partial \tilde{V}(B)}{\partial y} = \Big[u_1(y + B,0) + \beta \int_{z(B,y)} u_1\{y + z - B(1 + i),0\}f(z)dz$$

$$- \beta/\gamma \int^{z(B,y)} u_2(0,\tilde{\ell})f(z)dz\Big]\Big/(1 - \beta^2)$$

$$> 0.$$

$$\frac{\partial \tilde{V}(B)}{\partial i} = \left[-\beta B \int u_1\{y + z - B(1 + i), 0\} f(z) dz \right.$$

$$\left. + \beta B \int^{z(B,y)} u_2(0, \tilde{\ell}) f(z) dz \right] \bigg/ (1 - \beta^2)$$

$$< 0.$$

$$\frac{\partial V(B)}{\partial y} = \left[u_1(y + B, 0) + \beta \int_{z(B,y)} u_1\{y + z - B(1 + i), 0\} f(z) dz \right.$$

$$+ \left. \beta^2(\partial V_0/\partial y) F\{z(B,y)\} - \beta^2 V_0 f\{z(B,y)\} \right] \bigg/$$

$$\langle 1 - \beta^2[1 - F\{z(B,y)\}] \rangle + \frac{V(B) \beta^2 f\{z(B,y)\}}{1 - \beta^2[1 - F\{z(B,y)\}]}$$

$$= \left[u_1(y + B, 0) + \beta \int_{z(B,y)} u_1\{y + z - B(1 + i), 0\} f(z) dz \right.$$

$$+ \left. \beta^2(\partial V_0/\partial y) F\{z(B,y)\} + \beta^2\{V(B) - V_0\} f\{z(B,y)\} \right] \bigg/$$

$$\langle 1 - \beta^2[1 - F\{z(B,y)\}] \rangle$$

$$> 0 \text{ as long as } V(B) > V_0 \text{ since } \partial V_0/\partial y \doteq u_1(y,0)$$
$$+ Eu_1(y + z, 0) > 0$$

$$= \frac{u_1(y + B, 0) + \beta^2(\partial V_0/\partial y) F\{z(B,y)\}}{1 - \beta^2[1 - F\{z(B,y)\}]}$$

$$- \frac{1}{1 + i} \left(\frac{\partial V}{\partial B} - \frac{u_1(y + B, 0)}{1 - \beta^2[1 - F\{z(B,y)\}]} \right).$$

$$\frac{\partial V(B)}{\partial i} = \left[-\beta B \int_{z(B,y)} u_1\{y + z - B(1 + i), 0\} f(z) dz + \beta^2 V_0 f\{z(B,y)\} B \right] \bigg/$$

$$\langle 1 - \beta^2[1 - F\{z(B,y)\}] \rangle - \frac{V(B)\beta^2 f\{z(B,y)\} B}{1 - \beta^2[1 - F\{z(B,y)\}]}$$

$$= \left[-\beta B \int_{z(B,y)} u_1\{y + z - B(1 + i), 0\} - \beta^2 f\{z(B,y)\} B\{V(B) - V_0\} \right] \bigg/$$

$$\langle 1 - \beta^2[1 - F\{z(B,y)\}] \rangle$$

$$< 0 \text{ as long as } V(B) > V_0$$

$$= \left(\frac{\partial V(B)}{\partial B} - \frac{u_1(y + B, 0)}{1 - \beta^2[1 - F\{z(B,y)\}]} \right) \frac{B}{1 + i}$$

$$\frac{\partial^2 V(B)}{\partial i \partial B} = \left[-\beta \int_{z(B,y)} u_1\{y + z - B(1 + i), 0\} f(z) dz \right.$$

$$+ \beta(1 + i)B \int_{z(B,y)} u_{11}\{y + z - B(1 + i), 0\} f(z) dz$$

$$+ \beta(1 + i)u_1(0,0) f\{z(B,y)\} B$$

$$- \beta^2(1 + i) f_1\{z(B,y)\} \{V(B) - V_0\} B$$

$$- \beta^2 f\{z(B,y)\} (V(B) - V_0)$$

$$- \beta^2(1 + i)f\{z(B,y)\}(\partial V/\partial i)\Big] \Big/ \langle 1 - \beta^2(1 - F\{z(B,y)\}]\rangle$$

$$- \frac{\partial V}{\partial B} \frac{\beta^2 f\{z(B,y)\}B}{1 - \beta^2[1 - F\{z(B,y)\}]} \cdot$$

$$\frac{\partial^2 V(B)}{\partial i \partial B} = \Big[-\beta \int_{z(B,y)} u_1\{y + z - B(1 + i),0\}f(z)dz$$

$$+ \beta(1 + i)B \int_{z(B,y)} u_{11}\{y + z - B(1 + i),0\}f(z)dz$$

$$+ \beta(1 + i)u_1(0,0)f\{z(B,y)\}B$$

$$- \beta^2(1 + i)f_1\{z(B,y)\}\{V(B) - V_0\}B$$

$$- \beta^2 f\{z(B,y)\}\{V(B) - V_0\}$$

$$- 2\beta^2 f\{z(B,y)\}B \frac{\partial V}{\partial B} + \beta^2 B u_1(y + B,0)f\{z(B,y)\}\Big] \Big/$$

$$\langle 1 - \beta^2[1 - F\{z(B,y)\}]\rangle / \langle 1 - \beta^2[1 - F\{z(B,y)\}]\rangle$$

$$= \frac{B}{1 + i} \left(\frac{\partial^2 V}{\partial B^2} - \frac{u_{11}(y + B,0)}{1 - \beta^2[1 - F\{z(B,y)\}]} \right)$$

$$- \Big[\beta \int_{z(B,y)} u_1\{y + z - B(1 + i),0\}f(z)dz$$

$$- \beta^2 B u_1(y + B,0)f\{z(B,y)\}\Big] \Big/$$

$$\langle 1 - \beta^2[1 - F\{z(B,y)\}]\rangle / \langle 1 - \beta^2[1 - F\{z(B,y)\}]\rangle.$$

(Given concavity of $V(B)$, all but one term is negative when $\partial V/\partial B = 0$.)

$$\frac{\partial^2 V(B)}{\partial y \partial B} = \Big[u_{11}(y + B,0) - \beta(1 + i)\int_{z(B,y)} u_{11}\{y + z - B(1 + i),0\}f(z)dz$$

$$- \beta(1 + i)u_1(0,0)f\{z(B,y)\} + \beta^2(1 + i)f_1\{z(B,y)\}\{V(B) - V_0\}$$

$$- \beta^2(1 + i)f\{z(B,y)\} \left\{ \frac{\partial V(B)}{\partial y} - \frac{\partial V_0}{\partial y} \right\}\Big] \Big/$$

$$\langle 1 - \beta^2[1 - F\{z(B,y)\}]\rangle$$

$$+ \frac{\{\partial V(B)/\partial B\}\beta^2 f\{z(B,y)\}}{1 - \beta^2[1 - F\{z(B,y)\}]}$$

$$= \Big[u_{11}(y + B,0) - \beta(1 + i) \int_{z(B,y)} u_{11}\{y + z - B(1 + i),0\}f(z)dz$$

$$- \beta(1 + i)u_{11}(0,0)f\{z(B,y)\} + \beta^2(1 + i)f_1\{z(B,y)\}\{V(B) - V_0\}$$

$$- \beta^2[f\{z(B,y)\}] \left\{ (1 + i)\left(\frac{\partial V}{\partial y} - \frac{\partial V_0}{\partial y} \right) - \frac{\partial V(B)}{\partial B} \right\}\Big] \Big/$$

$$\langle 1 - \beta^2[1 - F\{z(B,y)\}]\rangle$$

$$= -\frac{1}{1 + i} \left(\frac{\partial^2 V}{\partial B^2} - \frac{u_{11}(y + B)}{1 - \beta^2(1 - F)} + \frac{\beta^2 f\{z(B,y)\}\partial V/\partial B}{1 - \beta^2[1 - F]} \right)$$

$$+ \{u_{11}(y + B,0) - \beta^2 f\{z(B,y)\}(1 + i)$$

$$\left(\frac{\partial V}{\partial y} - \frac{\partial V_0}{\partial y}\right)\Big\} \Big/ \langle 1 - \beta^2[1 - F\{z(B,y)\}]\rangle$$

$$= -\frac{1}{1 + i}\frac{\partial^2 V}{\partial B^2} + \left\{\left(1 + \frac{1}{1 + i}\right)u_{11}(y + B,0)\right.$$

$$- \beta^2(1 + i)f\{z(B,y)\} \left.\left(\frac{\partial V}{\partial B} + \frac{\partial V}{\partial y} - \frac{\partial V_0}{\partial y}\right)\right\}\Big/$$

$$\langle 1 - \beta^2[1 - F\{z(B,y)\}]\rangle.$$

$$\frac{\partial V}{\partial B} + \frac{\partial V}{\partial y} - \frac{\partial V_0}{\partial y} = 2u_1(y + B,0)$$

$$- \beta i \int_{z(B,y)} u_1\{y + z - B(1 + i),0\}f(z)dz$$

$$- \frac{\beta^2 i\{V(B) - V_0\}f\{z(B,y)\}}{1 - \beta^2[(1 - F)\{z(B,y)\}]} - \frac{\partial V_0}{\partial y}$$

$$= \left[2u_1(y + B,0)\right.$$

$$- \beta i \int_{z(B,y)} u_1\{y + z - B(1 + i),0\}f(z)dz$$

$$- \beta^2 i\{V(B) - V_0\}f\{z(B,y)\}$$

$$\left. - (1 - \beta^2)\frac{\partial V_0}{\partial y}\right]\Big/ \langle 1 - \beta^2[1 - F\{z(B,y)\}]\rangle$$

= all terms except one are negative.

Hence with $\partial^2 V/\partial B^2 < 0$, all but two terms of $\partial^2 V(B)/\partial y \partial B$ are positive.

NOTES

1. This rather unrealistic assumption is made for analytical convenience. If overdues are permitted by the institution, the dynamic programming problem gets much too complicated.
2. Without this assumption, the possibility of the sharecropper switching between creditors cannot be ruled out. Analysing such a switch does not appear to be tractable.

11.

Some Aspects of Linked Product and Credit Market Contracts among Risk-neutral Agents

Clive Bell and T. N. Srinivasan

1. Introduction

It is now well recognized that in the real world, in which a complete set of markets for contingent commodities in the Arrow–Debreu sense does not exist, the markets that do function and the non-market institutions exert a very important influence on the character of resource allocation. An implication that has attracted analytical attention is that a competitive equilibrium need not be Pareto-optimal, as it would be had the set of markets been complete. Greenwald and Stiglitz (1986) argue that the Pareto non-optimally of competitive equilibrium in a context of incomplete markets and asymmetric information remains even after taking into account costs of transactions and information. They point out that, if a particular risk market is absent because transaction costs are prohibitive, it does not follow that the allocation of resources through other, existing, markets is efficient. Furthermore, while a set of public interventions in the form of taxes and subsidies using only publicly available information can effect a Pareto improvement, equally, government interventions ostensibly designed to effect such an improvement (and which would have succeeded in doing so in an economy with distortions but in which a complete set of markets existed) need not succeed in doing so in the absence of a complete set of markets.

In less developed countries, where agriculture is the dominant source of employment and income for a majority of households, market and non-market (various forms of contractual arrangements) transactions relating to land, labour, production, and credit allocate resources. These determine the productive efficiency and distributional equity of the resulting allocation as well as the impact of public policies designed to influence the allocation. A salient hypothesis in this context is that, in the absence of a complete set of smoothly functioning markets for factors and commodities and above all for credit and risk, households will find it advantageous to enter into simultaneous transactions with one another in more than one market. These

We are indebted to Christopher Udry for valuable comments on an earlier version of this chapter. All surviving errors are our responsibility.

so-called 'interlocked' transactions have traditionally been viewed as an attempt by one party to extract more of the surplus from the other, compared with a situation in which the latter engages in separate transactions with other parties. Since implicit in this view is that the first party has sufficient market power over the other, it is not obvious how interlinkage adds to this power, except in so far as it permits an advantageous co-ordination of the instruments of exploitation. Recent work on incomplete markets suggests that, far from being invariably exploitative, interlinkage may actually increase economic efficiency, and its incidence has little to do with the existence or otherwise of market power for some agents.

One of the more pervasive interlocked arrangements is between the marketing of a crop and the provision of credit for financing the working capital needs of its cultivation. Typically, a trader (or commission agent, as he is called in some parts of India) enters into a contract with a farmer under which the farmer agrees to sell his harvest to (or through) the trader (often, though not always, at a price stipulated in the contract), in return for which the trader provides credit for cultivation at terms specified in the contract. The relationship between a farmer and a commission agent is often of long duration, which both parties have nurtured, since both have a stake in it.

The objective of this chapter is to develop a framework for the determination of the terms of such contracts. Clearly, these will depend on the alternative opportunities available to each party for the use of its resources other than through the contract, and on the extent to which each party can observe and monitor the actions of the other in so far as these affect contractual compliance. A natural framework for this analysis is that of agency theory.

The extant theoretical literature on this particular sort of contract is rather limited, although mention should be made of a recent contribution by Gangopadhyay and Sengupta (1987). They, too, use agency theory, but in certain key respects their assumptions differ from ours. Notably, theirs is a riskless world in which the trader/money-lender has access to funds at a lower cost than do farmers. In contrast, uncertainty has a central place in our analysis and there is free entry for traders/money-lenders. Naturally, the results obtained are rather different.

In Section 2 we present a model in which the trader is viewed as the principal who provides credit to the farmer (his agent) at an agreed rate of interest, in return for the promise of the latter to sell his harvest through the trader at an agreed commission per unit of crop sold and to repay the credit plus accrued interest at the time of harvest. The only collateral is the crop itself, but if the farmer is unable or unwilling to repay, he incurs a penalty depending on the extent of default. However, as the penalty stems from a damaged reputation, its imposition does not yield any direct returns to the trader. The size of the harvest depends on the labour committed by the farmer to cultivation and the effects of (random) weather. Labour is committed prior to the resolution of weather uncertainty, and credit can be used by the farmer either to augment his consumption in the pre-harvest period or to finance labour costs, or both. The trader can observe only the output (and not weather and labour input), so that the problem of moral hazard arises. An important feature of the model is that price and output uncertainty are resolved simultaneously at harvest time. Some consequences of this restriction are discussed in Section 5. Section 3 abstracts from the moral hazard problem by assuming that labour input into cultivation is exogenously fixed and focuses attention on the sharing of output risk between the farmer and the trader. Section 4 introduces moral hazard. In both Sections 3 and 4 there is free entry into trading, so that the contracts offered by any trader to a farmer cannot yield any above-normal profits to him; that is, the farmer chooses among a menu of contracts offered by the trader, each contract in the menu yielding zero (normal) profit to the trader. The variables of interest are: the rate of commission on crop sale, the amount of and rate of interest on credit, and labour input into cultivation (in Section 4). In particular, we examine whether one of the two instruments, the commission rate and the interest rate, is redundant. Section 5 offers some concluding remarks.

2. The Model

Output is produced by means of labour and land under constant returns to scale. There is no market for tenancies, so that land is a fixed factor for each farming household. There is a perfect labour market, with a ruling wage rate of w. Inputs of labour, ℓ, must be committed before the state of nature is revealed, and there is multiplicative risk in production:

$$q = \theta f(\ell) \tag{1}$$

where θ is a random variable summarizing the effects of the state of nature in determining realized output, q.

The household is endowed with $\bar{\ell}$ units of labour, which it supplies inelastically. Possessing no liquid assets, it can finance consumption and outlays on labour in the first, or 'lean', period, when inputs must be committed, by borrowing. Hence

$$C_1 = w(\bar{\ell} - \ell) + B \tag{2}$$

where C_1 and B denote the levels of consumption and borrowing, respectively, in the first period. Since C_1 is necessarily non-negative, $w\bar{\ell} + B \geq w\ell$.

In the second period, output is produced and then sold at price p, the value of which may not be known in the first period. Under the terms of the credit contract, the household is to pay interest at the rate r on its borrowings and possibly a commission at the rate α on the value of output (equals sales) if the lender is also a commission agent. In the event that the value of output is insufficient to meet these obligations, the lender will keep the entire proceeds from the sale of the crop, but has no other form of redress. For its part, not only does the household get no income when defaulting, but its standing in the credit market is also damaged. Let the monetary present value of this penalty depend on the size of the default:

$$\phi = \phi\{(1 + r)B - (1 - \alpha)pq\} \tag{3}$$

where $\phi(\cdot) = 0$ if $(1 + r)B < (1 - \alpha)pq$. Let $\phi(\cdot)$ be monotonically increasing in the size of the default and differentiable everywhere except at zero. Hence, the value of the household's payoff in the second period is

$$Y_2 = \begin{cases} (1 - \alpha)pq - (1 + r)B & \text{if } (1 - \alpha)pq \geq (1 + r)B \\ - \phi(\cdot) & \text{otherwise.} \end{cases} \tag{4}$$

We assume that the household is risk-neutral and has a subjective discount rate of δ. Hence its utility index is

$$W = C_1 + (EY_2)/(1 + \delta) \tag{5}$$

where E is the expectations operator.

For any ℓ and B, the household is interested only in the random variable $p\theta$. Denoting this variable by x, let x be continuously distributed with density $h(x)$ on the support $[0, \infty)$ and with mean $\bar{x}$. Let $H(x)$ denote its cumulative distribution function. As default occurs whenever $(1 + r)B > (1 + \alpha)xf(\ell)$, define $\hat{x}$ as $(1 + r)B/(1 + \alpha)f(\ell)$. Then, from (2), (4), and (5), we obtain

$$(1 + \delta)W = (\delta - r)B + w(\bar{\ell} - \ell)(1 + \delta) + (1 - \alpha)\bar{x}f(\ell)$$
$$- (1 - \alpha)f(\ell)\int_0^{\hat{x}}(x - \hat{x})h(x)dx - \int_0^{\hat{x}}\phi h(x)dx. \tag{6}$$

As $\phi(\cdot) = 0 \; \forall x \geq \hat{x}$, W is everywhere continuous and differentiable in (α, r, B, ℓ) over the domain $\alpha \in [0,1]$, $r \geq 0$, $B \geq 0$, $\ell \geq 0$, and $w\bar{\ell} + B \geq w\ell$.

Turning to the lender, we assume that he has access to a perfectly safe placement for his funds yielding a rate of interest r_0. In that case, his payoff (profit) from a loan is

$$Z = \begin{cases} (r - r_0)B + \alpha pq & \text{if } (1 + \alpha)pq \geq (1 + r)B \\ pq - (1 + r_0)B & \text{otherwise.} \end{cases} \tag{7}$$

We also assume that he is risk-neutral and that his prior distribution over (x) is the same as the borrower's. Hence his utility index is

$$EZ = (r - r_0)B + \alpha\bar{x}f(\ell) + (1 - \alpha)f(\ell)\int_0^{\hat{x}}(x - \hat{x})h(x)dx. \tag{8}$$

EZ is also everywhere continuous and differentiable over the above domain for W. Clearly,

$$(1 + \delta)W + EZ = (\delta - r_0)B + w(\bar{\ell} - \ell)(1 + \delta) + \bar{x}f(\ell) - \int_0^{\hat{x}}\phi h(x)dx. \tag{9}$$

Next, something must be said about market structure. We assume that there is free entry into money-lending. As the crop itself is the only collateral offered, lenders will insist on exclusive contracts to protect their interests; that is, each lender will insist that the borrower take loans from no other source as a condition of the loan. Thus, there will be a system of contestable monopolies, in which the set of all contracts acceptable to a lender is

$$S = \{(\alpha, B, r) | EZ(\cdot) \geq 0; \alpha \in [0,1]; (B, r) \in \Omega^2\} \tag{10}$$

where the restriction that $\alpha \in [0,1]$ and (B, r) belong to the non-negative orthant, Ω^2, is a natural one. (For a more extensive discussion, see Bell 1988.)

3. Pure Risk-sharing

To start with, suppose the household's inputs of labour depend only on the wage rate, so that changes in the terms of the contract with the lender do not affect the level of output.[1] Thus, there is no moral hazard, and the contract boils down to a risk-sharing arrangement in the context of an intertemporal transaction. This greatly simplifies matters and makes for clearer insight.

The household's problem is to

$$\max W$$

by choice of $(\alpha, B, r) \in S$.

We begin by showing that its optimum is always such that the lender's expected profit is zero. From (6) and (8), it is readily checked that, whereas W is decreasing in both α and r, EZ is increasing in the same. Hence, as at least one of α and r must be positive for $EZ > 0$, it follows at once that if $EZ > 0$, there exists some contract in S that is more attractive to the household.

Next, we establish necessary and sufficient conditions for the household to borrow. Consider first the case $\delta \leq r_0$. Suppose it is optimal for the household to borrow; i.e., $B > 0$. Then $(\delta - r_0)B \leq 0$ and $\int_0^{\hat{x}}\phi h(x)dx > 0$. As $EZ = 0$ at the household's optimum, it follows from (6) and (9) that

$$(1 + \delta)W < w(\bar{\ell} - \ell)(1 + \delta) + \bar{x}f(\ell) = (1 + \delta)W|_{B=0},$$

which contradicts the optimality of $B > 0$.

Now consider the case $\delta > r_0$. From (9), we have

$$\frac{\partial\{(1 + \delta)W + EZ\}}{\partial B} = (\delta - r_0) - \int_0^{\hat{x}}(1 + r)\phi' h(x)dx. \tag{11}$$

The integral on the right-hand side can be made as small as we please by making B arbitrarily small, provided ϕ' is bounded. Hence, the *sum* of the agents' utilities is increasing in B in the neighbourhood of $B = 0$, if $\delta > r_0$. As there exist contracts in this neighbourhood yielding $EZ = 0$, it follows at once that the household's optimal policy is to borrow.

It should be noted that, when the support of $h(x)$ includes zero, a positive level of borrowing implies a strictly positive probability of default, since $\hat{x}$ is then positive. This prompts an examination of the case in which the support is $[x_0, \infty)$, with $x_0 > 0$.

For (α, B, r) such that $\hat{x} < x_0$, (6) and (8) specialize to

$$(1 + \delta)W = (\delta - r)B + w(\bar{\ell} - \ell)(1 + \delta) + (1 - \alpha)\bar{x}f(\ell) \qquad (6')$$

and

$$EZ = (r - r_0)B + \alpha\bar{x}f(\ell). \qquad (8')$$

Proceeding as before, the household will borrow if, and only if, $\delta > r_0$.[2] It is also clear that, given any value of B, the slopes of the agents' iso-utility contours are the same in the space of (α, r). Hence, one of the two instruments (α, r) is redundant, as intuition would suggest; for both parties are risk-neutral, and if $\hat{x} \le x_0$, there is no risk of default to be shared. In view of this redundancy, we may set $r = r_0$ and $\alpha = 0$, to yield $EZ = 0$. Hence, from (6'), if $\delta > r_0$, W increases with B until the limit $B = x_0 f(\ell)/(1 + r_0)$ is reached, at which point some risk of default is about to reappear. We conclude that, if the household's optimum is such that $\hat{x} < x_0$, then $\delta < r_0$; so that there is no borrowing.

Turning to the case where (α, B, r) is such that $\hat{x} \ge x_0$, (6)–(9) and (11) hold with x_0 replacing 0 as the lower limit in the integrals. It follows at once that the household's optimum is always characterized by $\hat{x} > x_0$, so that there is a strictly positive probability of default.

The results obtained thus far may be summarized as follows.

PROPOSITION 1. If there is free entry into money-lending, lenders' expected profits will be zero; and households will borrow if, and only if, $\delta > r_0$. If borrowing occurs, the contract will always be such that the probability of default will be positive.

Proposition 1 prompts the natural question, What changes in assumptions are needed for the household to desire to borrow on terms that entail no risk of default? As we have just shown, if the household borrows, its choice of contract will be such that $\hat{x} \ge x_0$. Hence, if the risk of default is to be (barely) absent, the household's optimum must satisfy $\hat{x} = x_0$. This implies that decisions must be 'sticky' at $\hat{x} = x_0$. By Proposition 1, this will not happen if x is continuously distributed on $[x_0, \infty)$, even if $h(x_0) > 0$. However, a promising line of approach is to introduce a probability mass at x_0. There will then be a measurable chance that the worst outcome will occur.

Let the support of $H(x)$ be $[x_0, \infty)$, with $H(x_0) = \pi_0$; and let $h(x)$ be defined on (x_0, ∞), with

$$\int_{x_0}^{\infty} h\,dx = 1 - \pi_0.$$

In this case, (6) and (8) become, respectively,

$$(1 + \delta)W = (\delta - r)B + w(\bar{\ell} - \ell)(1 + \delta) + (1 - \alpha)\bar{x}f(\ell)$$
$$- (1 - \alpha)f(\ell)\int_{x_0}^{\hat{x}}(x - \hat{x})h(x)dx - \int_{x_0}^{\hat{x}}\phi h(x)dx$$
$$- \pi_0\{(1 - \alpha)f(\ell)(x_0 - \hat{x}) + \phi(x_0)\}, \quad \hat{x} \geq x_0 \tag{12}$$

and

$$EZ = (r - r_0)B + \alpha\bar{x}f(\ell) + (1 - \alpha)f(\ell)\{\int_{x_0}^{\hat{x}}(x - \hat{x})h(x)dx +$$
$$\pi_0(x_0 - \hat{x})\}, \quad \hat{x} \geq x_0. \tag{13}$$

If the choice of contract is such that $\hat{x} < x_0$, then (6') and (8') apply. It is clear that both utility indices are continuous at $\hat{x} = x_0$, but W is not, in general, differentiable there. By inspection of (11)–(13), the relevant left- and right-hand derivatives are, respectively,

$$\left.\frac{\partial\{(1 + \delta)W + EZ\}}{\partial B}\right|_{\hat{x} = x_0}^{-} = (\delta - r_0)$$

and

$$\left.\frac{\partial\{(1 + \delta)W + EZ\}}{\partial B}\right|_{\hat{x} = x_0}^{+} = (\delta - r_0) - \pi_0(1 + r)\phi'(0)_+.$$

where $\phi'(0)_+$ is the right-hand derivative of $\phi(0)$.

Now to the left of x_0 there is no default; so the derivative of $\{(1 + \delta)W + EZ\}$, that is, the sum of the agents' utilities, is simply the difference between the discount rate, δ, of the household and the opportunity cost of funds, r_0, to the trader. To the right of x_0 there is a positive probability of default, and as such the penalty incurred by the household when it defaults matters. Thus, as $\hat{x} = x_0$ implies $(1 - \alpha)x_0f(\ell) = (1 + r)B$, and as such the amount defaulted tends to zero as $\hat{x}$ approaches x_0 from the right, everything hinges on whether the right-hand derivative of the penalty function at zero default is positive. This seems entirely natural; for even defaulting to the tune of one dollar should measurably hurt one's reputation in future dealings. We conclude that, if

$$\pi_0(1 + r)\phi'(0)_+ \geq (\delta - r_0) \geq 0, \tag{14}$$

the optimum choice of contract will satisfy $(1 - \alpha)x_0f(\ell) = (1 + r)B$, with $B > 0$ by virtue of $x_0 > 0$.

Suppose, therefore, that the optimum lies at $\hat{x} = x_0$. Substituting into (12) and (13), some manipulation yields

$$(1 + \delta)W = w(\bar{\ell} - \ell)(1 + \delta) + (1 - \alpha)f(\ell)\{\delta x_0 + \bar{x} + r(\bar{x} - x_0)\}/(1 + r) \tag{15}$$

and

$$EZ = \{(r - r_0)(1 - \alpha)x_0 + (1 + r)\alpha\bar{x}\}f(\ell)/(1 + r). \qquad (16)$$

Now at the household's optimum, $EZ = 0$, which implies that

$$\alpha = \frac{(r_0 - r)x_0}{(r_0 - r)x_0 + (1 + r)\bar{x}}.$$

As $(r_0 - r)x_0 + (1 + r)\bar{x} = r_0 x_0 + \bar{x} + r(\bar{x} - x_0) > 0$, it follows that $0 \le \alpha \le 1$ implies $r \le r_0$. Substituting for α in (15), we get

$$(1 + \delta)W = w(\bar{\ell} - \ell)(1 + \delta) + \frac{\{\delta x_0 + \bar{x} + r(\bar{x} - x_0)\}\bar{x}f(\ell)}{(r_0 - r)x_0 + (1 + r)\bar{x}}. \qquad (15')$$

It is readily checked that W is maximized ar $r = 0$, since $\delta > r_0$. Hence the associated values of α and B are $r_0 x_0/(r_0 x_0 + \bar{x})$ and $x_0\bar{x}f(\ell)/(r_0 x_0 + \bar{x})$, respectively.

The above results may be summaried as follows.

PROPOSITION 2. If the support of the cumulative distribution function (CDF) is $[x_0, \infty)$, with a probability mass π_0 at x_0, and $\pi_0\phi'(0)_+ \ge \delta - r_0 \ge 0$, the household will choose the contract $\alpha = r_0 x_0/(r_0 x_0 + \bar{x})$, $B = x_0\bar{x}f(\ell)/(r_0 x_0 + \bar{x})$, and $r = 0$; so that, while the lender's return is risky, default will never occur.

The intuition for the 'stickiness' at x_0 is straightforward. If $\delta > r_0$, the household will wish to borrow and its utility will increase with the amount borrowed so long as the chance of default is zero. At the point at which that chance is about to become positive, consider what happens if the household borrows another dollar. By doing so, it gains $\delta - r_0$; for the lender must break even. At the same time, there is now a probability π_0 that it will be unable to repay the dollar in question, and so will incur the penalty $\phi'(0)_+$. Hence, if $\pi_0\phi'(0)_+ \ge \delta - r_0$, the household will choose a contract such that $\hat{x} = x_0$. It should be noted, moreover, that the condition for such a choice is independent of the terms of the contract.

How close are the values of α and B yielded by Proposition 2 to those observed in real life? Plausible ranges for r_0 and $(\bar{x}/x_0)$ are 0.05–0.15 and 2–5, respectively. These imply a range for α of 0.01–0.07 and for B of about 20–50 per cent of the expected value of output, both of which cover what is commonly found in practice. Perhaps not too much should be made of this consistency; for it is by no means clear that actual contracts are free of default risk. Nevertheless, these results are suggestive.

Another important feature of the optimum is that no interest is charged. If the loan were such that default never occurred, a contract that called for payment of interest but no commission would eliminate the lender's risk entirely. Why is this not chosen? As the lender must break even, $r = r_0$, implying a value of B equal to $x_0 f(\ell)/(1 + r_0)$. As $x_0 < \bar{x}$, this amount is less than that borrowed in Proposition 2, where the contract calls for payment of a commission on sales, but no interest. For if the lender is prepared to forgo interest, the loan can be made somewhat larger without default occurring. Of course, the lender must make normal profits — zero expected profits, to be precise — and this is accomplished by levying a commission on total sales (output-sharing). As we have seen, the household's utility increases with the amount borrowed if there is no chance of default. Thus, although both parties to the contract are risk-neutral, it turns out that it is optimal for both of them to bear some risk.

To complete our examination of pure risk-sharing, we now turn to the case in which the optimum entails a strictly positive probability of default. For this purpose, we can eliminate the probability mass at $x = x_0$, so that

$$\int_{x_0}^{\infty} h(x)dx = 1,$$

as before.[3] Recalling that $(1 + r)B = (1 - \alpha)\hat{x}f(\ell)$ and $\phi(0) = 0$, and forming the Lagrangean $\mathcal{L} = (1 + \delta)W + \lambda EZ$, the first-order conditions are

$$f(\ell)\left\{\int_{x_0}^{\hat{x}} (1 - \phi')xhdx - \bar{x} + \lambda\left(\bar{x} - \int_{x_0}^{\hat{x}} xhdx\right)\right\} + \mu_1 = 0 \qquad (17)$$

$$(\delta - r) + (1 + r)\int_{x_0}^{\hat{x}} (1 - \phi')hdx + \lambda\left\{(r - r_0) - (1 + r)\int_{x_0}^{\hat{x}} hdx\right\} = 0 \tag{18}$$

$$B\left\{\int_{x_0}^{\hat{x}} (1 - \phi')hdx - 1 + \lambda\left(1 - \int_{x_0}^{\hat{x}} hdx\right)\right\} + \mu_2 = 0 \qquad (19)$$

where μ_1 and μ_2 are the dual variables associated with the non-negativity constraints $\alpha \geq 0$ and $r \geq 0$, respectively.

From Proposition 1, we know that $B > 0$ iff $\delta > r_0$, and that if $B > 0$, then the optimum is such that $\hat{x} > x_0$. We will now show that $\mu_1 = \mu_2 = 0$ does not hold at the optimum. Suppose, on the contrary, that it does. Then, as $\lambda > 0$ by Proposition 1, (17) and (19) imply

$$\frac{\bar{x} - \int_{x_0}^{\hat{x}} xhdx}{1 - \int_{x_0}^{\hat{x}} hdx} = \frac{\bar{x} - \int_{x_0}^{\hat{x}} (1 - \phi')xhdx}{1 - \int_{x_0}^{\hat{x}} (1 - \phi')hdx}. \tag{20}$$

Now,

$$1 - \int_{x_0}^{\hat{x}} hdx = \int_{\hat{x}}^{\infty} hdx, \text{ and } \bar{x} - \int_{x_0}^{\hat{x}} xhdx = \int_{\hat{x}}^{\infty} xhdx.$$

Hence, (20) may be rewritten as

$$\frac{\int_{\hat{x}}^{\infty} xhdx}{\int_{\hat{x}}^{\infty} hdx} = \frac{\int_{x_0}^{\hat{x}} \phi'xhdx}{\int_{x_0}^{\hat{x}} \phi'hdx}. \tag{20'}$$

Clearly, the left-hand side of (20') exceeds $\hat{x}$, while the right-hand side is less than $\hat{x}$, which is a contradiction. Hence $\mu_1 = \mu_2 = 0$ does not hold at the optimum, and we have proved the following proposition.

PROPOSITION 3. *In the absence of a probability mass point at* $x = x_0$, *the* household's optimum contract, if it borrows, will take the form of either a pure commission on sales, or interest charges, but not both.

In the light of Proposition 2, it seems plausible that, if the optimum involves only a modest risk of default, no interest will be charged. Suppose, therefore, that there are interest, but no commission, charges. (By virtue of Proposition 3, there cannot be both.) Hence, $\mu_1 > 0$ and $\mu_2 = 0$. Multiplying (19) by $\bar{x}f(\ell)/B$ and subtracting from (17), we get

$$f(\ell)\left\{\int_{x_0}^{\hat{x}}(1 - \phi')(x - \bar{x})hdx - \lambda\int_{x_0}^{\hat{x}}(x - \bar{x})hdx\right\} + \mu_1 = 0.$$

If $\phi' \geq 1 \forall x < \hat{x}$ and $\hat{x} \leq \bar{x}$, this equality cannot hold, thereby contradicting the hypothesis that interest, but no commission, is charged. Indeed, as $\lambda > 0$, these are strongly sufficient conditions. Thus, we conclude that, even if the probability of default is quite high, the household's choice of contract will involve only commission charges, which further sharpens the characterization of the optimum.

The possibility that the optimum may entail a high risk of default leads to the question, Will the contract be such that the household makes over the entire crop in exchange for a loan, so that all risks fall on the lender?

To answer this, we need to consider the case in which the support of $h(x)$ is the compact interval $[x_0, x_1]$. The question can be precisely formulated as follows: Is the optimum such that $(1 + r)B \geq (1 - \alpha)x_1 f(\ell)$? We have, from (7),

$$EZ = \bar{x}f(\ell) - (1 + r_0)B.$$

Although the lender's expected payoff is independent of r, both α and B are well defined; that is, $\alpha = 1$ and $B = \bar{x}f(\ell)/(1 + r_0)$, as $EZ = 0$.

Turning to the household, if $\alpha = 1$, the penalty of defaulting will be $\phi\{(1 + r)B\}$, whatever be the outcome where x is concerned. As $B = \bar{x}f(\ell)/(1 + r_0)$, which is independent of r, the household will insist on $r = 0$, to which the lender will readily agree; for default is certain and $r = 0$ minimizes ϕ for given B. In this case,

$$(1 + \delta)W = \{w(\bar{\ell} - \ell) + B\}(1 + \delta) - \phi(B).$$

Hence, at $B = \bar{x}f(\ell)/(1 + r_0)$,

$$(1 + \delta)\frac{\partial W}{\partial B} = (1 + \delta) - \phi'\{\bar{x}f(\ell)/(1 + r_0)\}.$$

The size of the default is the expected value of output, discounted at the lender's opportunity cost of funds. If the marginal penalty suffered by the household when it borrows this amount exceeds one plus its discount rate, that is, if $\phi'\{\bar{x}f(\ell)/(1 + r_0)\} > 1 + \delta$, the contract $(1, \bar{x}f(\ell)/(1 + r_0), 0)$ is not an optimum.

Suppose, on the contrary, that $\phi'\{\bar{x}f(\ell)/(1 + r_0)\} < (1 + \delta)$. The household will desire to borrow up to the limit. It should now seek to reformulate the credit-cum-marketing contract as a tenancy contract. In that case, the lender will make a payment of $(B - w\ell)$, which will be interpreted not as a loan, but as a rental payment in exchange for exclusive rights to the crop. This reinterpretation will be of no consequence to the lender. For the household, however, there is the decisive advantage that the contract makes no mention of default, so that $\phi \equiv 0$. As a final check, it is evident that borrowing (renting out) on such terms is desirable if $\delta > r_0$.

4. Moral Hazard and Incentives

Thus far, we have confined the discussion to risk-sharing by taking the cultivator's input of labour, ℓ, as determined independently of the credit contract. The next step is to permit him to choose ℓ in the light of the incentives it provides. To keep matters as simple as possible, we shall allow him only the discrete choice of using one unit of labour or doing nothing, in which case no crop will be produced. Likewise, we assume that there are just two states of nature: if $\ell = 1$, let the value of output be either zero or ρ, with probabilities $(1 - \pi)$ and π, respectively. Hence, if nothing is produced and monitoring is prohibitively costly, the lender will not be able to tell whether this outcome is the result of indolence or bad luck.

The cultivator's expected utility is given by

$$(1 + \delta)W = \begin{cases} (1 + \delta)(w\bar{\ell} + B) - \phi(\cdot) & \text{if } \ell = 0 \\ (1 + \delta)\{w(\bar{\ell} - 1) + B\} + \pi\{(1 - \alpha)\rho - \\ (1 + r)B\} - (1 - \pi)\phi(\cdot) & \text{if } \ell = 1, \end{cases} \tag{21}$$

where in both cases the argument of $\phi(\cdot)$ is $(1 + r)B$. The lender's expected utility is

$$EZ = \begin{cases} -(1 + r_0)B & \text{if } \ell = 0 \\ \pi\{(1 + r)B + \alpha\rho\} - (1 + r_0)B & \text{if } \ell = 1. \end{cases} \tag{22}$$

If $\ell = 1$, the expected value of output is $\pi\rho$. As the crop is the only collateral, $\pi\rho$ is the most to which the lender can lay claim, averaging good years with bad. Hence, $EZ|_{\ell=1} \geq 0$ implies $\pi\rho \geq (1 + r_0)B$. Obviously, the lender will not offer a contract that will induce the cultivator to choose $\ell = 0$. In view of this restriction, the set of feasible contracts is defined as follows. Let

$$S^1 = \{(\alpha, B, r)|\ W|_{\ell=1} \geq W|_{\ell=0}; \alpha \in [0, 1]; (B, r) \in \Omega^2\} \tag{23}$$

and

$$S^2 = \{(\alpha, B, r)|\ EZ|_{\ell=1} \geq 0; \alpha \in [0, 1]; (B, r) \in \Omega^2\}. \tag{24}$$

Then the set of contracts that lenders will be willing to offer borrowers is simply $S^1 \cap S^2$.

The borrower's choice of contract is the solution to

$$\max_{(\alpha,\, B,\, r)} \; W|_{\ell\,=\,1}$$

$$\text{s.t. } (\alpha, B, r) \in S^1 \cap S^2.$$

Omitting, for the moment, the requirement that $\alpha \in [0, 1]$ and $(B, r) \in \Omega^2$, (23) and (24) may be written in explicit form:

$$\pi\{(1 - \alpha)\rho - (1 + r)B\} + \pi\phi - (1 + \delta)w \geq 0 \tag{25}$$

$$\pi\{\alpha\rho + (1 + r)B\} - (1 + r_0)B \geq 0. \tag{26}$$

The first-order conditions for maximizing $W|_{\ell\,=\,1}$ subject to (25) and (26) are as follows:

$$\frac{\partial \Phi}{\partial \alpha} = \pi\rho(\lambda_2 - \lambda_1 - 1) \leq 0, \text{ with equality holding if } \alpha > 0; \tag{27}$$

$$\frac{\partial \Phi}{\partial B} = (1 + \delta) - \pi(1 + r) - (1 - \pi)(1 + r)\phi' + \lambda_1\pi(1 + r)(\phi' - 1)$$

$$+ \lambda_2\{\pi(1 + r) - (1 + r_0)\} \leq 0, \text{ with equality holding if } B > 0; \tag{28}$$

$$\frac{\partial \Phi}{\partial r} = B\{(\lambda_2 - \lambda_1 - 1) + (1 + \lambda_1 - 1/\pi)\phi'\} \leq 0,$$

$$\text{with equality holding if } r > 0; \tag{29}$$

where the Lagrangean is

$$\Phi = W|_{\ell\,=\,1} + \lambda_1[\pi\{(1 - \alpha)\rho - (1 + r)B\} + \pi\phi - (1 + \delta)w]$$

$$+ \lambda_2[\pi\{\alpha\rho + (1 + r)B\} - (1 + r_0)B].$$

We shall deal with all possible cases.

Case (a). The lender's expected utility is strictly positive ($\lambda_2 = 0$). From (27), $\lambda_2 = 0$ implies $\alpha = 0$; and as $EZ \geq 0$, $\alpha = 0$ implies $r > 0$. Suppose the contract $(0, B^0, r^0) \in S^1 \cap S^2$ maximizes $W|_{\ell\,=\,1}$ with $EZ > 0$. Consider $(0, B', r') \in S^1 \cap S^2$ such that $B' > B^0$ and $(1 + r')B' = (1 + r^0)B^0$. Inspection of (25) and (26) reveals that such a contract exists. Moreover, inspection of (21) reveals that $W|_{\ell\,=\,1}$ is greater with the contract $(0, B', r')$; for $B' > B^0$. Thus, $(0, B^0, r^0)$ is not the optimum contract, and $EZ = 0$.

Case (b). The incentive condition is not binding ($\lambda_1 = 0$). Suppose $\alpha > 0$. Then either $B = 0$, which is an uninteresting case, or $\lambda_2 = 1$, which implies $r = 0$, as $\pi < 1$. In this case, (28) reduces to

$$(\delta - r_0) - (1 - \pi)\phi'(B) \leq 0, \text{ with equality holding if } B > 0. \tag{30}$$

Hence, $B > 0$ iff $\phi'(0)_+ > (\delta - r_0)/(1 - \pi)$. If $\phi(\cdot)$ is strictly convex, then any positive B satisfying (30) will be unique. It must also satisfy $(1 + r_0)B \leq \pi\rho$;

for otherwise, the condition $EZ|_{\ell=1} \geq 0$ will be violated, and the case $\lambda_1 = 0$, $\alpha > 0$, $r = 0$ will not be an optimum. To complete the solution, note that $EZ = 0$ and $r = 0$ imply $\alpha = (1 + r_0 - \pi)B/\pi\rho$.

Alternatively, suppose $\alpha = 0$. Then either $B = 0$, or $\lambda_2 \leq 1$, which implies $r = 0$. But $\alpha = r = 0$ and $B > 0$ implies $EZ < 0$. Hence, we have the following proposition, which is the counterpart of Propositions 1 and 2 in Section 3.

PROPOSITION 4. When there is moral hazard, the lender's expected profits are exactly zero in a free-entry equilibrium. If the incentive condition for labour input is not binding, the household will borrow iff $\phi'(0)_+ >$ $(\delta - r_0)/(1 - \pi)$. If it does borrow, the rate of interest will be zero and the lender's income will accrue only in the form of a commission on sales. The choice of B will satisfy (30), with $B \leq \pi\rho/(1 + r_0)$, and $\alpha = (1 + r_0 - \pi)B/\pi\rho$.

Case (c). The incentive and non-negative expected profit conditions both bind ($\lambda_1 > 0, \lambda_2 > 0$). Suppose $\alpha > 0$, so that $\lambda_2 = 1 + \lambda_1$. Substituting into (29), we have $\lambda_1 \leq (1 - \pi)/\pi$, with equality holding if $r > 0$.

We begin with the case $r > 0$, which implies $\lambda_1 = (1 - \pi)/\pi$ and $\lambda_2 = 1/\pi$. Substituting into (28), we get

$$(1 + \delta) - (1 + r_0)/\pi \leq 0, \text{ with equality holding if } B > 0. \tag{31}$$

Thus, the household will choose to borrow and pay both interest and commission on sales only if $(1 + \delta) = (1 + r_0)/\pi$. As δ, r_0, and π are all parameters, this condition will hold only by a fluke.

Alternatively, suppose the contract is such that the lender has exclusive claim to the entire crop, so that $(1 - \alpha)\rho < (1 + r)B$. Following the analysis of this case in Section 3, $B = \pi\rho/(1 + r_0)$ and $r = 0$, as above. Now, however, the household has no incentive to work; for $W|_{\ell=0} > W|_{\ell=1}$, and the incentive condition is not satisfied. We have therefore excluded the possibility that both r and α are positive at the optimum.

Continuing with the case $\alpha > 0$, we are left with $r = 0$ and $(1 - \alpha)\rho > (1 + r)B$. Here, α and B will satisfy (25) and (26) as strict equalities. Hence B is a solution to

$$\pi\phi(B) - (1 + r_0)B = (1 + \delta)w - \pi\rho. \tag{32}$$

Now $\phi(0) = 0$. Hence, if $\phi(\cdot)$ is strictly convex, there may be two solutions if $\pi\phi'(0) < (1 + r_0)$ and $(1 + \delta)w \leq \pi\rho$, and there will be one otherwise. From (26), $\alpha = (1 + r_0 - \pi)B/\pi\rho$. Once again, the solution must also satisfy $(1 - \alpha)\rho \geq B$; that is, $B \leq \pi\rho/(1 + r_0)$, as in case (b).

Conversely, suppose $\lambda_1 < (1 - \pi)/\pi$. As $\lambda_2 - \lambda_1 - 1 \leq 0$, it follows from (29) that $r = 0$. Moreover, as $EZ \geq 0$, we must have $\alpha > 0$. Hence, if both the incentive and non-negative expected profit conditions bind, the equilibrium contract will call for commission charges alone if, and only if, $\lambda_1 < (1 - \pi)/\pi$. Intuitively, the incentive condition must not bind too tightly if such contracts are to be chosen.

Finally, consider the case $\alpha = 0$. $EZ = 0$ implies that $\pi(1 + r) = (1 + r_0)$, which yields r at once. As $r > 0$, (29) implies that

$$(1 + \lambda_1 - 1/\pi)\phi' = (1 + \lambda_1 - \lambda_2);$$

and $\alpha = 0$ implies $1 + \lambda_1 - \lambda_2 > 0$. Hence, $\phi' > 0$, which implies $B > 0$, and $1 + \lambda_1 > 1/\pi$; that is, $\lambda_1 > (1 - \pi)/\pi$. Conversely, if $\lambda_1 > (1 - \pi)/\pi$, then from (29), $\lambda_2 - \lambda_1 - 1 < 0$, which implies $\alpha = 0$. Thus, $EZ = 0$ implies $\pi(1 + r) = (1 + r_0)$, as before. The incentive condition must bind rather tightly if the equilibrium contract calls for interest but no commission charges.

While it is obviously desirable to derive both necessary and sufficient conditions for the equilibrium contract to call for pure interest or, conversely, pure commission charges, the form obtained here involved the (endogenous) dual variable associated with the incentive condition. It would be useful, therefore, to arrive at such conditions in a form involving only the exogenous parameters of the system, even if the statement thereof is incomplete.

If $\alpha = 0$, $r = (1 + r_0 - \pi)/\pi$. Substituting for r in (28), we get

$$(\delta - r_0) - \phi'(1 + r_0)(1 - \pi)/\pi + \lambda_1(1 + r_0)(\phi' - 1) = 0$$

or

$$\{\lambda_1 - (1 - \pi)/\pi\}(1 + r_0)\phi' + (\delta - r_0) = \lambda_1(1 + r_0).$$

As $B > 0$ and $\lambda_1 > (1 - \pi)/\pi$, it follows that

$$\lambda_1 = \frac{\phi'(1 + r_0)(1 - \pi)/\pi - (\delta - r_0)}{(1 + r_0)(\phi' - 1)} > \frac{1 - \pi}{\pi} \tag{33}$$

or

$$(\delta - r_0) < (1 + r_0)(1 - \pi)/\pi.$$

Hence, we conclude that $(\delta - r_0) < (1 + r_0)(1 - \pi)/\pi$ is also a necessary condition for a solution with $\alpha = 0$ and $r > 0$. To complete the solution, we note that B must satisfy the incentive condition

$$\pi\{\rho - (1 + r_0)B/\pi\} + \pi\phi\{(1 + r_0)B/\pi\} = (1 + \delta)w, \tag{34}$$

with $\pi\rho > (1 + r_0)B$.

These findings may be summarized in the following proposition.

PROPOSITION 5. If both the incentive and zero-expected profit conditions are binding, the household will pay either a pure commission on sales ($r = 0$), or interest but no commission ($\alpha = 0$) according as $\lambda_1 \lessgtr (1 - \pi)/\pi$: A necessary condition for the former to be optimal is the existence of a

$B \in (0, \pi\rho/(1 + r_0))$ satisfying (32), in which case $\alpha = (1 + r_0 - \pi)B/\pi\rho$. A necessary condition for the latter is $0 < (\delta - r_0) < (1 + r_0)(1 - \pi)/\pi$. The value of B in this case must satisfy (34) and $r = (1 + r_0 - \pi)/\pi$.

5. Conclusions

Our principal findings are, first, that equilibrium contracts will not specify both interest and commission charges; and, second, that interest will be charged only if incentive considerations are pressing and the probability of default is sufficiently great. Taken together, they are consistent with the observation that interlinked marketing and credit contracts frequently call for commission charges alone. In a recent and valuable study of fishing communities in Kerala, Platteau and Abraham (1987) assert that this particular arrangement stems from the desirability of risk-sharing when agents are risk-averse.[4] For a wide range of circumstances, we have proved that this indeed will be the equilibrium contract, but using the weaker assumption of risk neutrality. Thus, while aversion to risk is an important fact of life in poor communities, it is not a wholly satisfactory explanation for the absence of explicit interest charges.

The second finding calls for some discussion. If the sum sought by the household is large relative to the expected value of output, and if the value of output is significantly variable, the commission rate needed for the lender to break even through commission charges alone may be quite high, with adverse disincentive effects. Hence, if incentive considerations are important, the relative incentive effects of commission and interest charges will enter into the reckoning. In this connection, a comparison of (27) and (29) reveals that, if the incentive condition binds sufficiently tightly, so that λ_1 is quite large, then the household will prefer extra interest to extra commission charges. The reason for this is that, for a loan of given size, interest charges increase the magnitude of the sum defaulted, should a default occur, whereas commission charges do not. Thus, the penalty of defaulting will be greater if interest is charged, which provides an incentive for the household to cultivate diligently in order to avoid incurring it.

There remains the awkward fact that contracts specifying both interest and commission charges are quite prevalent in practice. Two particular features of our model are, in our view, the most likely sources of our failure to account for them. First, although there are two periods, all uncertainties surrounding both the quantity and the price of output are resolved simultaneously. In reality, of course, the size of the crop is known before its price — unless the crop is sold forward. Thus, there is greater scope for the commission agent/trader to play a real role beyond that of a (passive) financial intermediary. For example, it is not uncommon for standing crops to be sold in advance of the harvest, in which case all subsequent risks are borne by the trader. More frequently, farmers wait until after the harvest before deciding on when to sell. In this case, the commission agent will often provide temporary storage facilities to those of his clients who are dissatisfied with the offers they have received and expect to do better by waiting a bit longer. This service spares them the costs of several hauls from their villages to the marketing centres in search of higher prices. The incorporation of these possibilities calls for a more complicated and subtle intertemporal structure than the one examined here.

Second, there is the pervasiveness of risk aversion. Coupled with independent resolution of uncertainties surrounding price and quantity, this seems to be the most natural and promising path along which to pursue extensions of the results obtained above.

To conclude, a brief remark on public policy is called for. The absence of interest charges in equilibrium contracts does not warrant the conclusion that interest subsidies to lenders will have no effect on resource allocation. For the lender's opportunity cost of funds features in all of the propositions proved in this chapter, and changes in its level will affect the amount borrowed and the rate at which commission is charged. Moreover, if there is free entry into money-lending-cum-trading, all the benefits of such subsidies will accrue to borrowers. Naturally, if no interest is charged, a policy of subsidizing the borrower's rate of interest will have no allocation effects. On the other hand, intervention in the form of either (binding) regulation of the commission rates charged by traders or the introduction of state trading will usually affect not only the terms of equilibrium contracts, but also borrowers' welfare. Unless state trading offers improvements in efficiency, intervention in the product markets may make borrowers worse off, while leaving traders with normal profits.

NOTES

1. As $C_1 \geq 0$, this implies that the household's choice of labour input, $\ell(w)$, must satisfy $w\bar{\ell} + B > w\ell(w)$. Moreover, as w is assumed to be exogenous, this is equivalent to assuming that inputs of labour are fixed.
2. In this case, it will be indifferent between borrowing and not borrowing if $\delta = r_0$.
3. If there were probability masses in (x_0, ∞), these, too, could be handled in the above manner, albeit with a considerable increase in complexity.
4. Platteau and Abraham (1987) also includes an extensive bibliography, especially of applied work on fisheries.

12.

A Note on Interlinked Rural Economic Arrangements

Pranab Bardhan

Over the last decade or so, a growing part of the theoretical literature on rural development has emphasized the role of interlinked, often personalized, transactions between economic agents in providing its key institutional framework. In this, the economic literature has only caught up with the relevant literature in economic anthropology. Anthropologists have often emphasized the multi-stranded nature of relationships in small face-to-face communities. Gluckman, in his studies of tribal Africa, has called such societies 'multiplex', with each individual playing not one but a variety of roles in interacting with fellow-members of his community. Generalizing from his experience with the hill peasants of Orissa, Bailey (1971) notes: 'the watershed between traditional and modern society is exactly this distinction between single-interest and multiplex relationships.' He goes on to comment that, in the cognitive map of the peasant, single-interest, functionally specialized, relationships are to be made — with due caution — only with outsiders, those who are outside his moral community.

These interlinked transactions qualitatively differ from the anonymous and systemic interdependence of economic action in competitive general equilibrium theory, and are more in the form of package deals, with the terms of one transaction contingent upon the terms in another. The usual examples take the form of landlord–tenant relations intertwined with creditor–borrower relations between the same parties, or employers hiring workers on terms that are interlocked with those on which the former provide credit (or land) to the latter, or simultaneous deals in the commodity and credit markets between a trader and a farmer where the latter gets credit on the precommitment of future crop delivery to the former. A clear understanding of the nature of these relations is obviously important in any policy agenda of institutional reforms.

Much too often in the past, these relations have been described as remnants of feudalism, and any policy to undermine them has been chalked up as a victory for the oppressed peasants and workers. First of all, however, feaudalism as a historical category is highly inappropriate to cover such relations even in most pre-capitalist cases. (There are many historians — for example Anderson (1974) — who regard feudalism as a non-universal socio-economic organization specific to the experience of Europe and, at most, Japan.) Besides, there are some qualitative aspects of these relations which are common in both capitalist and pre-capitalist economies: *personalized* transactions often characterize enduring relationships in 'customer' markets — as opposed to what Okun (1981) called 'auction' markets — even in industrially advanced countries; *interlinked* transactions are not unknown in the package deals and tie-in sales in sophisticated markets. But more important than the problem of careless labelling of the relations is the policy question. If, in our reformist zeal, we do not pay enough attention to the underlying economic rationale of pre-existing institutions and their inter-connections, and hack away parts of them, we may not always improve (and may even worsen) the lot of the poor tenant–labourer–borrower, the intended beneficiaries of our programme. There are some important political lessons here from what may be called the economics of second-best reformism. There are many examples in recent history of well intentioned land redistribution programmes rendered counter-productive by the absence of a simultaneous programme of credit reform; even in credit reform, nationalized banks spreading to reach out to the peasants have sometimes met with very limited success in the face of the potential borrower interlocked in his credit-cum-land or labour relationship with the local lender–land-lord–employer; piecemeal laws trying to put a ceiling on rents or interest rates or a floor to minimum wages have often been rendered ineffective by suitable readjustments of prices or selective rationing in interlinked transactions.

Much of the recent theoretical literature spelling out the underlying rationale of interlinked contractual arrangements[1] has served as a welcome corrective to the murky institutionalism of the past and has provided some much needed micro foundations to our study of agrarian institutions. But while I have been an active participant in this literature, I am not sure if I fully share in its main focus or in the interpretation of its main message. Not merely is the thin line between *understanding* an institution and *justifying* it often blurred (particularly by careless interpreters of the theory), but the pre-occupation with showing the allocational (constrained) Pareto efficiency of a given relation sometimes succeeds in diverting attention from the old institutionalists' main focus on processes of distribution. If the reformist zealot erred in ignoring the micro foundations of institutions, we in our turn should be careful that our theories of principal–agent games and moral hazard do not cover up the basic, often ugly, power relations involved in the phenomena we are studying. In the following paragraphs I shall attempt a slightly more balanced, if brief and schematic, account of some of the main economic features of interlinked transactions that characterize some agrarian institutions.

What are the benefits of interlinked transactions which contribute to their *raison d'être*?

1. Interlinking saves transaction costs. For example, take a frequent case of credit–labour linkage as obtains in eastern India and as analysed in Bardhan (1984: Ch. 6). In order to survive the slack season, the poor labourer (deficient in assets usable as collaterals) looks for a source of consumption credit where he can repay the loan in the form of future labour services; but this will not be acceptable to many creditors, except to the employer–creditor who is in great need of a quick supply of labour in the peak season. Such intertemporal interlinked barter transactions save on transaction costs and ensure the double coincidence of wants without which imperfectly monetized economies tend to be inefficient.
2. Interlinked transactions save on contract enforcement costs (another form of transaction costs) by making the possible discovery of dishonesty or default or shirking by an agent in one transaction too costly for him in terms of its spillover effects threatening other transactions (and the general loss of goodwill in the small closed world of a peasant community).
3. In situations of moral hazard with respect to unobserved work effort (or risk-taking), interlinked transactions can internalize some externalities. Braverman and Stiglitz (1982) analyse a tenancy-cum-credit contract from this point of view. The landlord, by altering the terms and amount of the loan that he makes available to the tenant, can induce him to work harder or to undertake projects that are more to the liking of the landlord (for example, projects with yields of higher mean as well as greater variance). Thus, if there is a positive externality of credit, there will be an incentive for the landlord to encourage the tenant to become indebted to him.
4. Interlinked transactions provide a way of partially circumventing incomplete or non-existent markets (particularly of credit and insurance). For the assetless tenant without access to an organized credit market, the tenancy contract itself can become a kind of collateral for credit transactions with the landlord–creditor; for the poor farmer it is possible to hypothecate the standing crop for raising credit from the trader–creditor. Kotwal (1985) shows how, in the absence of an insurance market, credit as a weather-dependent side-payment in tenancy (in bad years the landlord gives credit to the tenant who pays back in a better year) may solve the well-known trade-off problem between risk-sharing and incentives that is central to the tenancy literature. Bardhan (1984: Ch. 5) shows how the employer arranges various forms of seasonal labour-tying relationships with the worker (through wage advances, credit, or land allotment), essentially substituting for a futures market in seasonal labour services.

While the above-mentioned potential benefits of interlinked transactions are undeniable, it is important to look at the other side of the ledger as well. The isolated rural economic community and its dense social network often dictate a kind of captive interlinking of transactions among the same small number of economic agents, with virtually all-or-nothing choices for the weaker partners. The very nature of the rationale for personalized interlinking that we have discussed above may at the same time act as a formidable barrier to entry for third parties and is thus a source of additional monopoly power for the dominant partner in such transactions[2] (just as, in the industrial organization literature, vertical integration of firms rationalized on the basis of internalizing externalities of information and economies of transaction costs may, by the same token, lead to larger industrial concentration). An interlinked tenancy and credit contract, while having the potential of benefiting both the landlord and the tenant, may thus imply that the landlord can now brandish the stronger stick of withholding both land and credit rather than land alone, whereas the professional money-lender can no more than deny the tenant the credit he seeks.[3] Similarly, the labour-cum-credit contract may be a way for the landlord to segment the labour market. Just as in the 'commodity bundling' literature — see particularly Adams and Yellen (1976) — tie-in sales used as a price discrimination device have ambiguous welfare effects, here also the landlord may 'bundle' credit and labour transactions in order to discriminate between (and squeeze the 'consumer surplus' from) different types of labour, say, between workers with differential credit needs. Economists applying models of imperfect information usually also fail to emphasize that personalized interlocking of labour commitments and credit transactions (involving selective exclusion of others) often divide the workers and effectively emasculate their collective bargaining strength *vis-à-vis* employers, who use this as an instrument of control over the labour process[4] (as well as to command social and political loyalties). In the Bardhan–Rudra (1981) survey in rural West Bengal, we found that, in villages where some form of group bargaining or labour agitation for agricultural wage increase took place, most of our 'tied' (usually with credit) labour respondents reported non-participation in the movements, and the majority of them cited their ties with the landlord as the primary reason for their non-participation.

Many of the models of principal–agent games that abound in the theoretical literature ignore all this by confining their attention to 'utility-equivalent contracts'. In those models the peasant is already pressed down to a given reservation utility level and so he cannot by assumption be worse off as a result of contract interlinkage. But as Bell (1988) notes, in a bargaining framework the peasant may be worse off with an interlinked set of transactions than with a set of separate bilateral bargains (even when the utility possibility frontier itself shifts outward with interlinking). To illustrate this simple idea, take Figure 12.1, where the lower curve represents the landlord–tenant utility possibility frontier *without* credit interlinkage, and the outer curve represents the frontier *with* interlinkage. *D* is the disagreement payoff point (where the tenant gets his minimum reservation utility),

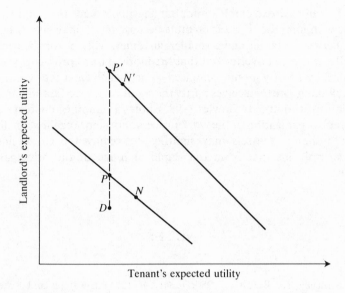

FIG. 12.1

and *P* is the standard equilibrium in a principal–agent situation, which shifts to *P'* with interlinkage (with the tenant pressed to his reservation utility level). At *P'*, compared with *P*, the tenant is no worse off, and the landlord is better off. But in a bargaining framework, let us suppose that *N* represents the Nash bargaining solution without interlinkage. Now with interlinkage it is possible (on account of factors spelled out in the previous paragraph) to end up at *N'*, where the tenant is worse off, even though interlinkage has shifted the utility possibility frontier outward (as implied by the usual rationale for interlinking discussed earlier).

So far, I have generally considered only cases of two-party interlinking. There are, however, many cases of more complicated three-cornered inter-linked exchange. Take, for example, the case that Bhalla (1976) cites from her study of Haryana villages in northern India: the worker gets supplies of essential consumer goods on credit from the village shopkeeper or grain dealer, which are repaid with his labour services to the landlord–employer (in the form of underpaid wages), who in turn repays the original creditor by adjusting his account with the latter for grain deliveries or purchases. In three-way relations it may be possible for the strong party (say, the landlord) to extract more surplus from the worker than if they were involved in only a dyadic relation. Basu (1986) has constructed a model where the landlord can even press the worker *below* the latter's reservation utility in the dyadic case, by credibly threatening that, if the worker does not accept his terms, not merely he will refuse to employ him, but he will persuade the shopkeeper not to trade with him; the threat is credible because the shopkeeper, if he has to choose between a larger and a smaller customer, will opt for the former.

Finally, it is often overlooked that the moral hazard problems leading to work-shirking, costly monitoring, and so on, which enter into the rationale for interlinking, are themselves partly the results of a specific and mutable set of social institutions; as Bowles (1985) notes in another context, a more democratic organization of the work process and a more egalitarian distribution of output and assets may significantly reduce the Hobbesian malfeasance problems that form the staple of much of the principal–agent literature.

NOTES

1. For a survey, see Bardhan (1980; 1984: Ch. 12); Binswanger and Rosenzweig (1984), and Bell (1988).
2. This increase in the exploitative powers of the stronger elements in the village through inter-penetration of markets has been pointed out by Thorner and Thorner (1962) and Bharadwaj (1974) in Indian agriculture, by Wharton (1962) for the marketing–money-lending–merchandizing combine in Malayan agriculture, and by Ransom and Sutch (1977) for the territorial monopoly of rural merchants-cum-money-lenders-cum-landlords over sharecroppers in the US South.
3. In the next chapter Ray and Sengupta spell out possible conditions (e.g. suitable nonlinear loan contracts) under which the professional money-lender could extract as much surplus as the interlocker.
4. This has also been emphasized by Hart (1986b).

13.

Interlinkages and the Pattern of Competition
Debraj Ray and Kunal Sengupta

1. Introduction

There is now a large literature on interlinkages in rural credit markets, where both theoretical and empirical issues have been studied.[1] If the various strands are carefully pulled together, we have a fairly complete analysis of the *form* assumed by an interlinked contract in different situations. However, the vast majority of these studies proceed on the assumption that there is a single monopolistic lender.

The issue of central interest in this chapter is different. We ask if the theory of interlinkage can throw any light on the nature of *competition* between lenders. Specifically, are there certain *patterns* of competition that are predicted by the theory of interlinkages?

To illustrate what we mean, consider an example. Suppose that there are two dominant money-lenders in a village. One of them is a trader in the major crop of that village; the other is a landlord. There are a number of borrowers in the village. Some are landless labourers; others own land of varying plot sizes. The question is, Is there a predictable manner in which borrowers will be divided among the two lenders? For instance, who will lend to the landless borrowers? Where will farmers with sizeable land holdings get their loans from? Such a division will be called a *pattern of competition*. Similar questions may be asked when we 'index' borrowers differently (such as by the relative importance of consumption-loan demand, as opposed to production loans), and indeed for other types of lenders.

Intuitively, we do expect that certain patterns of competition will be predicted by a properly formulated theory of interlinkage. The reason is that one kind of interlocker (say, a trader-lender) will possess certain advantages relative to another (say, a landlord-lender) for some groups of borrowers,

We are grateful to Bhaskar Dutta and Subhashis Gangopadhyay for helpful comments. Ray wishes to record special thanks to Sergy Floro, whose forthcoming Ph.D. dissertation (Floro, 1987) independently explores (theoretically and empirically) some of these issues as well as many others. Numerous conversations with her during 1984 and 1985 have led to a better appreciation of this particular topic.

and will be at a relative disadvantage for other groups.

However, we must first retreat to a basic starting point: the precise nature of the advantage that an interlocked contract yields. In particular, consider a lender who is capable of offering interlinked contracts, and compare this lender with a pure money-lender who cannot offer interlinked contracts. It is commonly accepted (see most of the references in n. 1) that the former is capable of extracting a greater return for each level of the borrower's reservation utility.

Our first task is to examine carefully this supposed advantage (Section 2 and the Appendix). In Section 2 we argue that certain assumptions are necessary for the interlocker to have a clear edge over the pure money-lender. The assumptions cannot be immediately justified *a priori*, though they may certainly be valid in particular empirical situations. Briefly, the following alternative assumptions are needed to generate an interlocker's advantage.

1. The lenders are restricted to offer only linear contracts, that is, where prices are independent of quantities transacted.
2. The interlocker–lender has advantages in the market(s) that he is active in, *over and above* his ability to be active in such markets. For example, a trader must not only be capable of trading in the output market: his trading activities must fetch him an additional pure profit that the pure money-lender or the borrower cannot obtain.
3. The pure money-lender, by virtue of his specialized occupation, can observe the realization of a *smaller* number of variables than the interlocker, and consequently cannot condition loan repayment on the unobserved variables.

These conditions are discussed in Section 2. If *none* of these assumptions holds, then we show that an interlocker actually possesses *no* advantages over a pure money-lender. In the context of our original question, it follows that no clear pattern of competition emerges when interlockers compete. This result, that under some conditions the pure money-lender and the interlocker are equally powerful, is proved in Section A1 of the Appendix.

The purpose of this exercise is to isolate and make explicit the assumptions required for an 'interlocker's edge' to emerge. Given one or more of these assumptions, an approach to the theory of competition and interlinkage can then be outlined. In Section 3, we analyse in some detail a two-stage model of Bertrand competition between a landlord-lender and a trader-lender. The landlord-lender places a higher valuation on land than does the trader; the trader-lender can sell output for a higher price than can the landlord. (We are therefore invoking the second assumption stated above.) We show that the landlord-lender will deal with 'small' farmers who possess a high loan demand relative to their assets, while the trader-lender will offer credit contracts to 'larger' farmers. The ability to interlock yields differential advantages to the two lenders, depending on the characteristics of the borrower.

Consequently, for a group of heterogeneous borrowers, there emerges a predictable division of these borrowers among the various lenders.

Interlinkages are seen, then, as complementary to the usual arguments for the existence of monopolistic lenders. There may simply be a dominant lender in a village; or, if there is more than one, a limited availability of loanable funds may prevent each from competing with the others. The lack of personal ties, developed over time, may prevent a borrower from seeking credit from another lender. Lenders may collude in a repeated, dynamic relationship which is nevertheless fundamentally non-cooperative.

None of these arguments indicates the pattern in which borrowers in a region are likely to be 'allocated' among the lenders in that region. Such a pattern *is* predicted by the theory of interlinkage. This pattern may harden into 'personal ties', strengthening the lender's advantage. It might be reinforced by dynamic collusion, or be further insulated by the limited availability of loanable funds for each lender. It is in this sense that the theory of interlinkage is complementary to theories of monopolistic advantage.

2. When It Pays To Be an Interlocker

If the theory of interlinkage is to provide a basis for the competitive theory discussed in the introduction, a basic requirement must be fulfilled. As a first step, one should be able to demonstrate that an interlocker has a clear advantage over a pure money-lender in his dealings with the borrower. In fact, this point is often regarded as self-evident in much of the literature. But a careful inquiry into the basis of the 'interlocker's edge' will reveal the assumptions on which such a statement is based. In the present section, we do precisely this. In the process, we also mention some of the recent literature on interlocked markets, and hope that this will serve as a partial introduction for those unfamiliar with the literature.[2]

Briefly, the theory of credit interlinkage highlights the additional advantages to be gained by a money-lender who is capable of intervening in some other market that the borrower is active in.[3] The *total* advantage, in a sense, should exceed the sum of the advantages in acting independently in each market. For example, consider a trader who lends money. In his dealings with a farmer, it will generally be optimal for him to lend money at a low rate of interest but buy up the farmer's output at a low price. (A precise statement of this will be made below.) This activity in the credit market cannot be fully understood without reference to his dealings in the product market, and vice versa.[4]

Our first step is to explore when such an interlocked contract yields advantages over and above that obtainable from a pure money-lending contract. We focus on interlockers versus pure money-lenders, although the arguments apply more generally to any pair of interlockers. We start with an example.

Example 1: Landlord–labourer interlocking

The model that we discuss is drawn from Bardhan (1984).[5] A labourer must see himself through a *lean season* and a *peak season*. In the peak season he can find employment for a given wage $w > 0$. He possesses one unit of labour power which he supplies inelastically. In the lean season he is unemployed, so that he must borrow to finance 'lean consumption', paying back the loan with his peak-season income of w. He has a strictly quasi-concave utility function $u(c_1,c_2)$, where c_1 is lean consumption and c_2 is peak consumption. In the *absence* of any credit, he receives a utility $u(0,w)$. This is his reservation utility.

Now introduce a landlord. He can provide loans to the labourer at an opportunity interest rate of r. He is also in need of labour in the peak season, which is available at the same wage rate w facing the labourer. The landlord can offer any combination of interest rate i and wage rate w' to the labourer. The loan is then chosen by the latter. Which contract should he offer? It is easy to establish the following proposition.

PROPOSITION 1. There is a maximizing contract involving (a) an interest rate i^* equal to the landlord's opportunity interest rate r, and (b) a wage rate w^* less than w, the 'market' wage rate.

We omit the proof (see e.g. Bardhan 1984), although a brief statement of the underlying intuition might help. The landlord wishes the tenant to choose an efficient (Pareto-optimal) level of the loan, *provided* that he can remove from the tenant the entire surplus above reservation utility by a suitable 'tax'. So the landlord offers loans at his own opportunity cost r. And, given that labour is inelastically supplied, the reduction of the wage rate serves as a perfect lump-sum tax to remove the surplus.[6] Readers unfamiliar with inter-locking models should observe that the *credit activity alone* (with $i^* = r$) provides no clue regarding the totality of the contract, or the 'implicit interest rate' involved in the transaction.

Now replace the landlord with a *pure money-lender*. This is an individual who is active *only* in the credit market. He hires no labour and so cannot demand repayment in terms of (underpaid) labour power. Suppose that he has the same opportunity cost of r for loanable funds. Can he earn the same return as the landlord?

Of course, he cannot offer the same contract: he is incapable of hiring labour. He can choose an interest rate. But in this case he *cannot* do as well as the landlord, for he must charge a rate greater than r in order to make any profit at all. However, this rate will not lead to a Pareto-optimal choice of loan on the part of the borrower, and readers can see that this observation is enough to clinch the issue in favour of the landlord.

But an implicit assumption has been made to obtain the result. This is that the money-lender *cannot* condition the interest rate on the amount of loan borrowed. If he can, it is equally easy to see that he can replicate the return of the interlocker! Observe, first, that the optimal w^* chosen by the landlord can be readily calculated given the parameters of the system. Now define a schedule $i(L)$ by

$$i(L) \equiv r + \frac{w - w^*}{L}, \text{ for } L > 0. \tag{1}$$

Readers can easily check that this indeed yields the pure money-lender the same return as the landlord.

This result is simple; yet in an important sense it runs counter to the usual statements made regarding interlocking. If a money-lender can charge a suitable nonlinear contract, it is not possible for an interlocker to earn an extra surplus in this model. We shall presently examine the generality of this observation.

Two remarks must be made concerning the money-lender's optimal contract. First, it involves an interest rate that decreases in loan size. This is certainly not at variance with empirical observation. Second, we could have obtained the same result if we had allowed the money-lender to 'force' the Pareto-efficient loan size by offering an all-or-nothing contract. However, this second route does not lead to general results in models with *incomplete* information, whereas nonlinear contracts survive this extension (as we shall see).

Now, how general is this observation of equivalence? It certainly applies to the interlocking model that we have just described, as well as to its extensions. It applies to trader-interlocking models, such as Gangopadhyay and Sengupta (1987a), to models of land–credit-interlocking, such as Braverman and Stiglitz (1982) and Braverman and Srinivasan (1981), and even to models of incomplete information, where some of the borrower's characteristics are private information and unknown to the lender.

In the Appendix to this chapter we sketch a general model, which has all the above-mentioned models as special cases, and which yields the equivalence of interlocker and pure money-lender. However, our purpose is setting up the model is *not* to argue that interlocking confers no advantages. It is to make explicit the assumptions that are used in making the claim that interlockers are at an advantage *vis-à-vis* their pure money-lending counterparts. In the rest of this section we discuss the assumptions with the aid of further examples.

ASSUMPTION 1. *Nonlinear contracts are disallowed.* This is a straight-forward restriction that immediately yields advantages to an interlocker relative to a pure money-lender. Indeed, this is the case in all the models we have mentioned. We should state, though, that we find it extremely difficult to understand the basis of such an assumption. It is certainly hard to defend it *a priori* except possibly on the grounds of complexity of nonlinear contracts. And as we have already mentioned, it is not hard to quote empirical instances where the interest rate varies with loan size.

ASSUMPTION 2. *Interlockers face better terms in the market in which they are active.* To see the implications of this, consider the following example.

Example 2: Trader–farmer interlocking

This example is based on Gangopadhyay and Sengupta (1987a). A farmer produces output using working capital and labour. The latter is inelastically supplied, so we write his (concave) production function as $f(L)$, where L is the quantity of working capital. It must be borrowed. Loans may be obtained at an interest rate of $R > 0$. The price that the farmer obtains for his output is unity. The farmer seeks to maximize his sales net of production costs (repayment of loan plus interest).

Now introduce a middleman or trader, who has access to loanable funds at an opportunity interest rate of $r < R$. The trader can also obtain a price $\tilde{p}$ for every unit of output that he sells, with $\tilde{p} \geq 1$. A contract to the borrower involves an interest rate i at which loans are offered, and a price p at which he will buy the farmer's output.[7] What contract should the middleman offer the farmer in order to maximize his own return? Here, one can establish a second proposition.

PROPOSITION 2. There is a maximizing contract which involves (a) an interest rate i^* strictly less than the opportunity cost of funds r, and (b) a price p^* that is strictly less than $\tilde{p}$, the price that the trader can obtain.

Readers might find it of interest to examine the intuition underlying Proposition 2. It is only a little more complicated than Proposition 1. Our purpose, however, is to examine what a pure money-lender can achieve under these circumstances.

Denote by L^* the level of the loan taken under the optimal trader contract.[8] We can then write the interlocker's total profit as the sum of the *implicit pure trading profits* involved $((\tilde{p} - 1)f(L^*))$ plus a residual term which captures credit market activities and the effect of interlinkage. Denote this latter term by D. Readers can now verify that, by offering a nonlinear interest schedule $i(L)$ of the form

$$i(L) = \frac{D}{L} + \tilde{r}, \text{ for } L > 0, \tag{2}$$

where $\tilde{r}$ solves

$$1/(1 + \tilde{r}) = \tilde{p}(1 + r), \tag{3}$$

the pure money-lender can earn precisely a profit of D; that is, he can pick up the *entire* surplus of the interlocker except for pure trading profits. In particular, if $\bar{p} = 1$, so that the interlocker has no extra advantages in the output market (except his ability to be active in it), the money-lender can obtain the same profit as the interlocker.

Return to the case $\bar{p} > 1$. This is precisely what we mean by our statement that 'interlockers face better terms in the market in which they are active'. For the farmer can obtain only a price of 1. In this case, there is no way for the pure money-lender to internalize the higher price $\bar{p}$ into the contract that he is offering. Nevertheless, he can capture *all* the surplus barring 'pure trading profits'. So even here, the statement that an interlocker can achieve more than the sum of his separate trading and money-lending activities does not hold water.

But it is true that an 'interlocker's edge' appears. And, despite the fact that the edge may be small (especially if $\bar{p}$ is near 1), it is capable of being translated into much larger advantages in a competitive model. On this, see Section 3 below.

There are, of course, other ways in which interlockers can command better terms in the market in which they are active. To see this, let us extend Example 1 to capture the possibility of involuntary unemployment. Specifically, suppose that in that example, there is unemployment even during the peak season. Put another way, suppose that there is a positive probability p that the labourer will receive a wage of 0 (unemployment), while with probability $(1 - p)$ he will be employed at the wage w. The landlord, on the other hand, is on the 'short side' of the market, and his opportunity cost of hiring labour is always w. In this case, it can be shown that, whenever $p > 0$, the landlord can achieve a higher surplus than a pure money-lender. *Involuntary unemployment in the labour market leads to the interlocker's edge in this example.*

ASSUMPTION 3. *Differential observability*. The equivalence result in the Appendix also leans on the assumption that both interlocker and pure money-lender observe (and therefore can condition contracts upon) exactly the same set of variables. Often, such an assumption is unwarranted. In such situations, the role of differential observability becomes critically important if the lender's return under the optimal interlocked contract is *necessarily* conditioned on more variables than just the loan itself. Observe that this is *not* the case in situations such as those described by Examples 1 and 2.[9] Once uncertainty is introduced, however, matters are entirely different.

Example 3: Farmer-lenders

Consider a farmer, or landlord, granting a fixed consumption loan L to a small farmer in the lean season preceding the harvest.[10] The farmer produces output using labour; output is uncertain owing to exogenous considerations such as weather. The production function is $f(e,\theta)$, where e is labour and θ is a random variable. In what form should the 'repayment contract' be drawn up?

Assume that the farmer has a utility function $u(y,e)$ where y is his income (net of loan repayment). Assume further that the borrower must give at least a reservation expected utility $\hat{u}$, to avoid defaulting on the loan.

The 'repayment scheme' is, then, a function $R(Y)$, where Y is the output produced. A risk-neutral lender will choose $R(\cdot)$ to solve

$$\max ER(Y) \tag{4}$$

$$\text{s.t. } Eu\{Y - R(Y),\hat{e}\} \geq \hat{u} \tag{5}$$

$$Y = f(\hat{e},\theta) \tag{6}$$

where $\hat{e}$ solves

$$\max_e Eu[f(e,\theta) - R\{f(e,\theta)\},e]. \tag{7}$$

Now observe that the problem (4)–(7) describes a standard principal–agent problem. It is well known (see e.g. Mirrlees 1975 and Holmstrom 1979) that *the optimal solution $R(\cdot)$ involves a function that is not the constant function.* This observation leads to an immediate conclusion: that interlinkage between output and credit markets will be observed in the form of output 'shares' being released in repayment for loans taken.

The important exception to this rule is when the utility function of the borrower is *linear* in income (risk neutrality), in which case a fixed rate of interest *is* optimal.

Now consider a pure money-lender who is not in a position to observe the output of the borrower. In this case, he cannot replicate the surplus of the interlocker, for exactly the same reason that fixed-rent tenancy is not generally optimal. The assumption of differential observability does matter here, unless the borrower is risk-neutral.

Examples of this sort can be multiplied. We only mention a variant that relies on an important but little studied feature: incomplete information regarding the borrower's characteristics (such as the productivity of his land or his labour).[11] Such lack of information (even without uncertainty, in the sense of Example 3 above) will lead to the necessary conditioning of an optimal interlinked contract on variables other than the loan itself. If a pure money-lender cannot observe these variables (such as the borrower's output), the interlocker who can is at an advantage.

ASSUMPTION 4. *Price uncertainty and imperfect observability.* Suppose that the interlocker operates in a market with price uncertainty. For instance, consider Example 1, and suppose that the wage rate ruling in a peak season is a random variable. In other words, there is a set of possible wages from which one will prevail: this is both the wage that would be paid to the labourer in the peak season, and the wage that must be paid by the landlord if he hires labour in the market.[12] All agents have a common prior regarding the distribution of wages.

Now, it can be easily checked that there is still an optimal contract just as in Proposition 1, where the landlord offers an interest rate on loans and a *fixed wage* (less than the expected value of the wage distribution). In this contract, *the landlord does not require to condition any payments (or receipts) on the actual realization of the market wage.* So it does not matter whether he gets to observe the realization of the market wage or not.

Suppose that he does not observe the realization of the market wage. Assuming no differential observability (that was discussed in Assumption 3), nor does the pure money-lender. But then, it can be easily seen that the pure money-lender *cannot* offer an equivalent contract to the labourer. Note that neither Assumption 1 nor 2 nor 3 holds, so that this is an additional case of non-equivalence. It is driven by imperfect (or incomplete) observability of all the variables in the system, including a price that is uncertain.

This completes our discussion of the assumptions needed to get around the equivalence problem. In the Appendix, we demonstrate in a general model that, when *none* of these assumptions can be made, the interlocker's edge does not exist.

Of Assumptions 1–4, which are the most plausible? Assumption 1 is generally made on the grounds of analytical or expository convenience. But in this case it is clear that the assumption plays more than an expository role. When some *other* condition for non-equivalence is satisfied, one might additionally invoke Assumption 1 to simplify the analysis.[13] Taken by itself, we see no justification on either *a priori* or empirical grounds. At best, a case might be made to rule out nonlinear contracts on the grounds of complexity.

Assumption 4, while certainly valid at a logical level, is probably of little significance. In the example, for instance, we have *both* landlord and pure money-lender not observing the realization of the market wage. It is very likely that the former will indeed observe its realization. If the latter does not, we still have non-equivalence, but this is really due to *differential* observability (Assumption 3). In short, one would expect the interlocker to observe the realizations of all prices in the markets in which he is active. If the pure money-lender does not observe them too, we really have a case of differential observability.

We feel on the other hand, that Assumptions 2 and 3 are important and relevant. Consider Assumption 2. It says that an interlocker faces better terms in the markets in which they are active. In the context of the trader-lender example (Example 2), this simply says that the trader can fetch a higher price for output than the farmer. He can make pure trading profits. And this, as we have shown, gives him an edge over the pure money-lender or, indeed, over a different kind of interlocker. In fact, the extent of his advantage is precisely his pure trading profits.

This does not mean, of course, that in a competitive scenario *both* trader and the pure money-lender can coexist, with the trader acting simply as a pure trader *vis-à-vis* the farmer. *The trader will have to offer interlocking contracts to retain his advantage.* See Section 3 for a detailed example.

Another instance of an interlocker facing better terms in his active market is that of a landlord who takes land as collateral for loans. With an imperfect land market, the landlord will clearly possess an edge over a pure money-lender (or a trader) who does not value land as highly. We develop this idea, too, in Section 3.

Assumption 3, dealing with differential observability, is also of great relevance. It is natural to imagine that different interlockers will possess different sets of observable variables when dealing with a particular borrower. A trader who specializes in the buying and selling of a particular crop is far more likely to be better informed about the price of that crop and the amount of it produced by the farmer he is dealing with, compared with a trader who specializes in a different crop. In turn, both can be expected to have more information than a pure money-lender. Consequently, the *domain* of variables on which an interlocker can condition is likely to vary across interlockers, and in all probability will be larger than the domain available to a pure money-lender. As we have already seen, these differences are likely to lead to advantages for the interlocker, especially in models of incomplete information.

3. Interlinkage and the Pattern of Competition

In the previous section, we discussed conditions under which an interlocker may gain an advantage over a pure money-lender, or another interlocker active in a different market. Specifically, the discussion was conducted by studying the monopoly return to an interlocker, and comparing that with the monopoly return available to a pure money-lender. We now permit the agents to compete with each other.

In this section, we briefly indicate how the theory of interlinkage might be used to construct a theory of competitive patterns. By the term 'competitive pattern', we mean a description of the *division* of various types of borrowers among the different money-lenders/interlockers who are actively interacting with them. For instance, suppose that we have, in a region, farmers growing either of two kinds of crops, A and B. Suppose that there are two trader-lenders, each specializing in one of the two crops. Each offers credit-cum-trade contracts to the farmers, and competes with each other for the farmers. It is to be expected that a 'reasonable' non-cooperative equilibrium in this scenario would involve the trader who specializes in crop A offering interlinked contracts with farmers who grow crop A, and similarly for the trader who deals in crop B. This is a particular pattern of competition.

Perhaps of greater analytical interest are the patterns of competition that might emerge when a trader-lender and a farmer-lender (or landlord-lender) compete. For instance, if potential borrowers can be indexed in terms of the *ratio* of consumption loan requirement to production loan requirement, which types are likely to gravitate to the trader-lender, and which to the farmer-lender?

Here, we provide a simple example that illustrates a pattern of competition between a trader-lender and a farmer-lender. Specifically, we try to highlight the monopolistic powers that might accrue to each as a result of their ability to interlock.

At the very outset, it should be pointed out that we are not claiming that interlocking is the basic source of monopolistic advantage. In a rural context, there might be many others. First, there could simply be a 'natural monopoly' in many villages.[14] Indeed, this is perhaps the major assumption underlying most models of interlinkage, which proceed on the premise that there is one lender. Second, there might be more than one lender (in a village or region), but each might command a segregated chunk of the market owing to historically developed 'personal ties'.[15] No doubt such ties may be strong, and they might preclude a borrower from seeking a better deal elsewhere. Lenders with little knowledge of a new borrower could be unwilling to lend to him.[16] Third, lenders might have access to a *limited* stock of loanable funds. This immediately confers on each lender a certain degree of monopoly power, for his rivals may not possess the extra wherewithal to undercut him.

Finally, what about two lenders who interlock in exactly the same way? The theory of interlinkage has little to say regarding the competitive behaviour of such agents. Far more relevant here is the theory of repeated games, which attempts to explain collusive behaviour in a backdrop of dynamic competition.[17]

It is for this reason that we emphasize the *patterns* of competition that may emerge from interlocked behaviour. These patterns might, in turn, harden into 'historical ties' and strengthen the surplus-acquiring capacity of the lender. They might be reinforced by dynamic collusion, permitting each lender a greater profit margin in his sphere of activity. They might be further insulated by limited availability of credit. We submit that in all these cases the original pattern that emerges from a study of competing interlockers will stay the same.

Now to the specifics of an example. We consider two borrowers (farmers) who are characterized by (1) the amount of *land* (collateral) they possess, K_j $(j = 1,2)$, with $K_1 < K_2$, and (2) a *production function*[18] $\theta f(K,E)$, where K is land input, E is labour input, and θ is a random variable with a distribution function G on $[a,\infty)$ where $a > 0$.

The farmers can sell their output on the market for a price of p. We take it that each places on his land collateral a valuation of z per unit.[19] Each farmer has a *fixed* demand for loan, L_j.[20]

There are two potential lenders, with the same opportunity interest rate of loanable funds, r. Lender 1 is also a landlord. Lender 2 is also a trader. Two features distinguish them from each other.

First, the landlord values land more than the trader. Specifically, we assume that the farmer-lender places the same unit value z on land as the other farmers. The trader's valuation is $z^* < z$. This reflects (a) the imperfection of the land market, and (b) the fact that the landlord has a direct use for land.

Second, the trader can obtain a higher price for output. Specifically, we assume that the landlord can obtain the same price p as the borrowers, while the trader can get $p^* > p$.

Lenders offer *contracts* to the borrowers, who are assumed to have no other source of loanable funds. The triplet $c \equiv (q,\alpha,i)$ describes a contract, where q is the price at which the lender offers to buy output from the borrower, α is the *maximum* fraction of collateral to be seized in case of a 'large enough' default (see below), and i is the rate of interest on the loan.

Implicit in a contract is what happens in the case of a default. For a borrower with inputs (K,E), loan L, and a contract (q,α,i), a default takes place if $q\theta F(K,E) < L(1 + i)$. In this case, we assume that the lender will take away only that much of the collateral that is required to settle the debt *at the valuation of the borrower*, up to a maximum of αK.[21]

The borrowers are assumed to have a utility function

$$W - v(E) \tag{8}$$

where W is wealth (collateral plus output net of loan repayment) and v is a 'disutility function' of labour effort with $v'(\cdot) > 0$ and $v''(\cdot) \geq 0$. Borrowers maximize the expected value of utilities.

Given a contract $c = (q,\alpha,i)$, borrower j chooses E_j to find

$$U_j(c) \equiv \max_E \int_a^\theta (1 - \alpha)K_j z dG(\theta) + \int_\theta^\infty [K_j + z\{qF(K_j,E) \\ - L_j(1 + i)\}]dG(\theta) - v(E) \tag{9}$$

where $\underline{\theta}$ is defined by

$$\underline{\theta} \equiv \max \theta \geq \left\{ \frac{L_j(1 + i) - \alpha K_j}{qF(K_j,E)} \right\}. \tag{10}$$

The expected income of the landlord-lender from the contract c is then given by

$$Y_1(c) \equiv \int_a^\theta \{\alpha z K_j + p\theta F(K_j,E_j)\}dG(\theta) \\ + \int_\theta^{\hat{\theta}} [p\theta F(K_j,E_j) + z\{L_j(1 + i) - q\theta F(K_j,E_j)\}]dG(\theta) \\ + \int_{\hat{\theta}}^\infty \{(p - q)\theta F(K_j,E_j) + L_j(1 + i)\}dG(\theta) - L_j(1 + r) \tag{11}$$

where $\hat{\theta}$ solves

$$q\hat{\theta}F(K_j,E_j) \equiv L_j(1 + i) \tag{12}$$

and E_j solves (5), given the contract c.[22]

The expected return of a trader-lender, $Y_2(c)$, is just the same as the expression above, with (z^*,p^*) substituted for (z,p).

We model *competition* between the two lenders as taking place in two stages. In Stage 1, each lender chooses the borrower he will deal with. There is a small (but positive) cost of dealing with each borrower. In stage 2, if a borrower has been chosen by both lenders, the latter compete in contracts, and if the borrower has been chosen by one lender, that lender behaves monopolistically with him. Or he may be chosen by neither, in which case he is excluded from all credit sources. We look at the subgame perfect equilibrium of this two-stage game.[23]

At this stage, a further assumption will be made, purely for expository purposes. Consider the farmer with more land, farmer 2. We assume that, *if* he were offered a contract at the *lender's* opportunity rate r,q set equal to the market price of the borrower p and $\alpha = 1$, then he would (using his optimal effort $\hat{E}_2$) repay the loan even in the worst state *without* using collateral. Formally, we assume that

$$aF(K_2,\hat{E}_2) \geq (1 + r)L_2 \tag{13}$$

where $\hat{E}_2$ is the optimal effort choice for borrower 2 under the contract $(p,1,r)$.

Put another way, this assumption states that the loan needs of the larger borrower are 'small enough' relative to his land holdings. We note, though, that this assumption is much stronger than necessary for our results. All we need is a statement that the loan of the smaller borrower relative to his land ownership is larger; that is,

$$L_1/K_1 > L_2/K_2. \tag{14}$$

However, we use (13) for simplicity.

We may now state the third proposition.

PROPOSITION 3. In equilibrium,

(a) no borrower faces more than one lender in the second stage;
(b) if both lenders are active, then the landlord deals with the 'small' farmer (borrower 1) and the trader deals with the 'large' farmer (borrower 2);
(c) the trader is always active. Sufficient conditions on the parameters of the system can be given so that the landlord is also active.
(For proof, see the Appendix.)

The main thrust of the proposition is that landlord-lenders are more likely to deal with small farmers, while trader-lenders are more likely to interact with middle and large farmers. Small farmers are more likely to default on loans, so that lenders who place a higher valuation on the collateral these farmers can offer are in a better position to offer them loans. Similarly, larger farmers have a smaller default probability and also produce a higher output, so that trader-lenders with an advantage in the commodity market clinch credit deals with these farmers. This is the pattern of competition that is predicted by the theory of interlinkage. As a by-product, it also provides 'spheres of influence' for each lender in which he has potential monopoly power. In our formulation, this comes out starkly in the form of part (a) of the proposition.[24]

The example described here can be used to obtain additional insights regarding the interlinkage mechanism. For instance, it can be shown that the trader will demand collateral from the borrower even if the former has no use for the collateral ($z^* = 0$). The reason is that the threat of removing the borrower's assets forces him to put in more labour in order to repay the loan. This enables the trader to charge a higher interest rate while keeping the borrower's effort level high.[25] Collateral is not asked for because the lender values the collateral: it is because the *borrower* values it, and will work harder to repay the loan. A 'tougher' loan can then be charged. Similarly, it is perfectly possible that the landlord might pay a price q that *exceeds* the price he can obtain on the market, p. Again, the idea is to elicit effort by providing a more suitable incentive structure. This surplus can then be removed by a higher interest rate.

The approach that we have outlined to describe patterns of competition can be extended to different contexts. In the particular context of landlord–trader competition, similar models can be constructed to obtain other patterns. Two examples are: (1) trader-lenders will be more likely to lend to borrowers demanding *production* loans, while landlord-lenders will deal with borrowers demanding *consumption* loans; and (2) landlord-lenders will lend to landless labourers (using their labour as collateral), while traders will interact relatively more with borrowers who own land and therefore engage in production.

Our purpose in this paper has been to indicate a way of modelling these differential relationships.

APPENDIX

A1. *An Equivalence Result for Models of Interlinkage*
In this appendix, we demonstrate that, when (a) nonlinear contracts are allowed, (b) interlockers do not face different terms (relative to other interlockers or pure money-lenders) in the markets in which they are active,

(c) there is no differential information, and (d) there is no market price uncertainty: all interlockers are equivalent in terms of the surplus they can extract. In particular, a pure money-lender can do just as well as an interlocker.

The proof of this result is intuitive, once the basic concepts are formally presented. To do this, we need some unavoidably cumbersome notation, which we now develop.

Consider an agent whom we shall call the *borrower*. Denote by $N = \{1, \ldots, n\}$ the set of all commodities. $I \subseteq N$ is the set of *non-marketed commodities* (e.g. family labour in a model with no wage labour); J is the (remaining) set of *marketed commodities*. Each commodity is an input and/or output and/or consumption good. Each commodity in J has a price. Denote by p a typical price vector.[26]

The borrower is endowed with a non-negative vector w of non-marketed commodities, and a *production technology* represented by f, where $f: R_+^n \times \Omega \to R_+^n$. That is, for each input vector $x \in R_+^n$ and the realization of a random shock $z \in \Omega, f(x,z) = y \in R_+^n$ is the output vector.[27] Let F be the class of all conceivable production functions that the borrower might have.

The borrower has a von Neumann–Morgenstern utility function $u: R^n \to R$, defined on consumption. So in this situation, the borrower chooses inputs $x \in R_+^n$ and a 'consumption function' $c(y)$ to solve:

$$\max_z E\, u(c) \tag{A1}$$

$$\text{s.t. } pc(y)^J \leq p(y - x)^J \tag{A2}$$

$$\text{for all } i \in I,\ c_i(y) + x_i \leq w_i + y_i, \tag{A3}$$

$$y = f(x,z), \text{ and } z \in \Omega \tag{A4}$$

where the notation x^J for some vector $x \in R^n$ denotes the projection of x on the coordinate subsystem J. For ease of exposition, we permit consumption to be negative, although readers can easily check that this makes no difference, for all the examples in the paper continue to be special cases.

Now for some remarks on the constraints of the maximization problem. First, we allow consumption choices to be functions of realized output. This clearly must be true of *some* consumption goods, but it applies only to those bought *after* the realization of output. Consumption items that precede the 'harvest' cannot be conditioned. This particular specification is allowable in our model. Second, (A2) refers to a standard budget constraint for *marketed* commodities, while (A3) writes down commodity-by-commodity constraints on each non-marketed commodity. Finally, (A4) refers to the connection between inputs and output for every state of nature.

Now we focus on *loans*, which we define to be a marketable commodity — say commodity 1 — described by the following characteristics. It is an 'input' and/or a 'consumption good' (but never an 'output' produced by the borrower). If it is an input (a consumption good), we take it that a positive amount of it is used in production (in consumption) at the market prices.[28]

Next, we introduce the *lender*. He is defined by three characteristics.

1. He can supply loans (commodity 1) at a price $\hat{p}_1 < p_1$. But the prices faced by him in all other markets are the same as those faced by the borrower.
2. He can be active in a certain subset $M \subseteq J$ of the set of marketable commodities. Of course, $1 \in M$. This means that he can offer the borrower price schedules *different* from market prices for these commodities. This, of course, necessitates some conditions on what he can observe in these markets.
3. Let $A = \{(x,y,c)$ triplets that can conceivably be chosen by the borrower$\}$, and Q a space of observables. What the lender can observe is given by a *mapping* $\theta: A \rightarrow Q$.[29] In particular, some function $g(x,y,c)$ is *observable* if, whenever $g(x^1,y^1,c^1) \neq g(x^2,y^2,c^2)$, $\theta(x^1,y^1,c^1) \neq \theta(x^2,y^2,c^2)$.

We now impose a condition on θ derived from M, the markets in which the lender can be active. For each $i \in M$, we assume *either* that $(c_i + x_i, y_i)$ is observable *or* that $(x_i, y_i - c_i)$ is observable. (Formally, for each i, either the function $g_i(x,y,c) \equiv (c_i + x_i, y_i)$ is observable or $g_i'(x,y,c) \equiv (x_i, y_i - c_i)$ is observable.) In other words, total purchases and sales of commodities in M are observable. We then say that M is *consistent* with θ.

Our interest lies in keeping all the characteristics of the lender fixed (including the observability function θ), *but varying M, the markets that he can interlock in.*[30] In particular, a *pure money-lender* is a lender with $M = \{1\}$.

We allow price contracts (possibly nonlinear) that are conditioned on the observables of the system. For a lender who is active in the set of markets M (an M-lender), we can define a *M-contract* as a mapping $P:Q \rightarrow R^M$. Its interpretation: for every observed $\theta \in Q$, $P(\theta)$ is the price-vector charged for the commodities in M.[31]

What is the borrower's maximization problem if he abides by an M-contract? It is: find x and $c(y)$ to

$$\max_z E\, u(c) \tag{A5}$$

$$\text{st.} \sum_{i \in M} p_i\{\theta(x,y,c)\}(y_i - c_i - x_i) + \sum_{i \in J/M} p_i(y_i - c_i - x_i) \geq 0, \tag{A6}$$

$$w_i + y_i \geq c_i + x_i, \text{ for } i \in I \tag{A7}$$

and

$$y = f(x,z), z \in \Omega. \tag{A8}$$

Denote by $R(f)$ the maximized value in problem (A1)–(A4). The borrower of type f will *accept* the M-contract if the maximized value in (A5)–(A8) is at least as great as $R(f)$.

Our main definition is: an M-contract and an M'-contract are *equivalent* if *each* borrower of type f, $f \in F$, faces exactly the same constraints (A6)–(A8) under the M-contract and the M'-contract.

Note that this is a strong definition of equivalence. In particular, it does not require us to specify the lender's maximization problem or the nature of his incomplete information about f. If equivalence in the sense of our definition holds, an M-lender and M'-lender can accomplish exactly the same outcomes.[32]

THEOREM. Fix the observability map θ. Then, for any M, M' consistent with θ, and any M-contract P, there exists an M'-contract P' such that P and P' are equivalent.

Proof. A contract that alters *only* the price of the loan as a function of θ is clearly an M'-contract, because $1 \in M'$. So we now proceed in the following way.

Define P': $Q \to R^{M'}$ as follows: for each $i \in M'$, $i \neq 1$, $P_i'(\theta) = p_i$ for all $\theta \in Q$. For $i = 1$, define first, for each (x,y,c), given the M-contract P,

$$p(x,y,c) \equiv P_1\{\theta(x,y,c)\} + \sum_{\substack{i \in M \\ i \neq 1}} \frac{[p_i - P_i\{\theta(x,y,c)\}](y_i - c_i - x_i)}{x_1 + c_1} \quad \text{if } x_1 + c_1 > 0 \Bigg\rbrace$$

$$p(x,y,c) \equiv p_1 \qquad\qquad\qquad\qquad\qquad\qquad\qquad\qquad \text{if } x_1 + c_1 = 0$$

$$\text{(A9)}$$

Note that $y_1 = 0$, so because $1 \in M$, $x_1 + c_1$ is observable. Also, for each $i \in M$, $i \neq 1$, *given* that either $(x_i + c_i, y_i)$ is observable or $(x_i, y_i - c_i)$ is observable, clearly $(y_i - c_i - x_i)$ is observable. So $p(x,y,c)$ varies *only* when θ varies.

We may therefore define $P_1'(\theta)$ by

$$P_1'\{\theta(x,y,c)\} \equiv p(x,y,c). \qquad\qquad\qquad\qquad \text{(A10)}$$

This completes our definition of the M'-contract. Readers should now check that, given our assumptions,

1. the borrower of type f will accept the M'-contract if and only if he accepts the M-contract;
2. under both the contracts, $x_1 + c_1 > 0$; and
3. the feasible sets of the type (A6)–(A8) are identical under the given M-contract and M'-contract we have constructed. Q.E.D.

Remark. In particular, when $M' = \{1\}$, we have shown that an interlocker and a pure money-lender can achieve exactly the same outcomes under the model described.

A2. *Proof of Proposition 4 (outline)*

(i) Suppose that more than one lender elect to deal with the same borrower. One can then prove that there is a unique Bertrand equilibrium *payoff vector* for each firm in stage 2, and by standard arguments it can be seen that at least one lender earns an equilibrium payoff of zero. Knowing this, and given an additional positive cost of choosing to deal with a borrower, it is not a best response (in the Nash equilibrium sense) for that lender to choose to deal with the borrower, given that the other lender is doing so.

(ii) It suffices to show that the trader deals with borrower 2. For then, by the presumption that both lenders are active and (i) above, the landlord must deal with borrower 1.

Recall the definitions of $U_j(c)$ and $Y_i(c), j,i = 1,2$, given in the body of the paper. Now consider borrower 2. Fix a number U, and define

$$\tilde{Y}(U) = \max_c\{Y_i(c)/U_2(c) \geq U\}, i = 1,2 \qquad (A11)$$

Define $U^* = \max \{U/\tilde{Y}_1(U) \geq 0\}$. Then, by the continuity of $\tilde{Y}_1(U)$ (details omitted), $\tilde{Y}_1(U^*) = 0$. For the rest of the proof, it suffices to show that $\tilde{Y}_2(U^*) > 0$. (One can verify that this suffices by using the properties of Bertrand competition, the notion of a two-stage equilibrium, and the fact that the cost of dealing with each borrower is positive, though infinitesimally small.)

Now, given the assumption (13), it is easily checked that the optimal contract to borrower 2, given a 'reservation utility' U^*, is given by $(q,\alpha,i) = (p,1,r) = \hat{c}$, say. But, again using (13), and the fact that $p^* > p$, it is easy to see that $Y_2(\hat{c}) > 0$. So $\tilde{Y}_2(u^*) \geq Y_2(\hat{c}) > 0$.

(iii) Clearly, by (13) and the argument in (ii) above, the trader is always active. We now provide sufficient conditions for the landlord to be dealing with farmer 1 in equilibrium.

To do so, consider the monopoly problem for the landlord: to maximize $Y_1(c)$, subject to the relations (9)–(12) (in Section 3). Let $\hat{Y}_1$ denote this maximum value. Now consider an artificial problem, which is to perform this maximization exercise, with the *additional* constraint on contracts that $\alpha = 0$. Let Y_1^* denote this maximum value. Our condition is:

$$Y_1^* < 0 < \hat{Y}_1. \qquad (A12)$$

Readers can easily check that (A12) can be translated into a condition that L_1/K_1 must be 'high' (so that collateral is necessary for a monopoly lender to deal with the borrower) but not 'too high' (so that, *even* with collateral, it is not worth dealing with him).

We can now establish the following lemma.

LEMMA. There exists $B > p$ such that, if $p^* \in (p,B]$, the landlord lends to the small farmer in equilibrium.

To show this, fix a number U and define, for $p^* \in [p,B]$,

$$\hat{Y}_1(U) \equiv \max \{Y_1(c)/U_1(c) \geq U\},$$
$$\hat{Y}_2(U,p^*) \equiv \max \{Y_2(c)/U_1(c) \geq U\}.$$

These are the maximum returns of lenders 1 and 2 when dealing with borrower 1 with 'reservation utility' U.

Start with $p* = p$. Look at the monopolistic solution of the trader-lender (with no reservation utility constraint for the borrower). If the lender's return is strictly negative, there is $B > p$ such that it continues to be negative for all $p* \in (p,B]$, by continuity of the trader's return. So we are done, because, by (A12), the landlord can certainly deal with the borrower.

If the trader-lender's return is *non-negative*, then by (A12), $\alpha > 0$. In this case, define U by the condition

$$\hat{Y}_2(\hat{U},p) = 0. \tag{A13}$$

Let $\hat{c}$ be the contract offered by the trader when $U = \hat{U}$. As we have observed, $\hat{c} = (q,\alpha,i)$ with $\alpha > 0$. Now let the landlord offer exactly the same contract $\hat{c}$ to borrower 1. Then, because $p = p*$ but $z* < z$ (and $\alpha > 0$), it must be the case that $Y_1(\hat{c}) > 0$. So

$$\hat{Y}_1(\hat{U}) \geq Y_1(\hat{c}) > 0. \tag{A14}$$

That is, when $p = p*$, the landlord-lender is active with the borrower 1 (by using the same reasoning as in part (ii) above). Now use continuity to define $B > p$ such that, for all $p* \in (p,B]$, conditions of the form (A13) and (A14) hold, with $\hat{U}$ suitably defined. This completes the argument. Q.E.D.

NOTES

1. For surveys of the literature, see Bardhan (1980). Theoretical studies include Bharadwaj (1974), Bardhan (1984), Gangopadhyay and Sengupta (1987a, 1987b), Basu (1983), Braverman and Stiglitz (1982), Braverman and Srinivasan (1981), Mitra (1983), and many others. Among the empirical studies are Kurup (1976), Bandyopadhyay (1984), and Floro (1987). Floro (1987) and Das and Gangopadhyay (1987) also explicitly consider the competition between different interlocking money-lenders, in independent work.
2. For an excellent survey of the literature during the 1970s and earlier, see Bardhan (1980).
3. We are focusing on credit markets and interlinkage, but the arguments apply more generally.
4. There is plenty of empirical evidence supporting such an observation, which is derivable on theoretical grounds. See references in n. 1.
5. See also Basu (1983).
6. Bardhan (1984: 91) notes — quite correctly — that the optimal contract takes the form of a two-part tariff.
7. Of course, more general contracts can be considered. But it can be shown that the optimal contract derived in the text is optimal in the class of *all* contracts.

8. Readers should check that $L^* = \text{argmax}\ \{\tilde{P}f(L) - (1 + r)L\}$.
9. The optimal contract described in Proposition 2 (for Example 2) does involve a return that is conditional on output, but it can easily be translated into a contract that depends only on the loan.
10. There are many models of interlinked contracts between landlord and tenant, although the simple version here is somewhat different. See Braverman and Srinivasan (1981), Braverman and Stiglitz (1982), and Mitra (1983), for example.
11. Newbery and Stiglitz (1979), as well as Braverman and Guasch (1984), deal with incomplete information in the somewhat different context of screening models.
12. We mention this in detail to distinguish a random wage from the randomness of the wage induced by unemployment. (See above, discussion following Assumption 2: there, the wage is random for the employee but not for the employer.)
13. Indeed, this is what we do below in Section 3.
14. For example, Bardhan (1984: 86) notes that 'many village economies are characterized by a dominant landlord who, because of the size of his assets and urban connections, is able to obtain credit more cheaply than other local agents'.
15. For a discussion of this point, see Basu (1984).
16. However, we have reservations regarding the use of this observation as a *long-run* explanation of monopoly power. Large and persistent profit opportunities open to a rival lender would eventually induce him to acquire information about the borrower and to lend to him.
17. For developments in this theory, see e.g. Friedman (1981), Green and Porter (1984), and Abreu (1984a).
18. We take it that the production function satisfies standard Inada-type condition. This eases the exposition.
19. There is no market for land in this example. Accordingly, all valuations of land are to be interpreted as *personal* valuations (see e.g. Bhaduri 1977). We are also assuming for simplicity that unit valuations are insensitive to the amount of land owned.
20. The assumption that loan demands are fixed simplifies the exposition. Dropping it requires an analysis along the lines of the examples studied in Section 2.
21. We are deliberately ruling out collateral underpricing to ease the exposition. However, the example here can be extended to yield a model of collateral underpricing in a one-lender, one-borrower context. This might be of independent interest, as existing models of collateral underpricing (see Bhaduri 1977 and Basu 1983) are not very robust (see Gangopadhyay and Sengupta 1987b).
22. If there is more than one solution of (9), we choose the one most favourable to the lender.
23. Alternatively, a 'one-stage game' could be studied, where *both* lenders simultaneously offer contracts to *both* borrowers. The equilibrium pattern of competition is unchanged, although the equilibrium profits of the lenders *are* affected. Our approach embodies (to some extent) a notion of 'personalized ties' in the second stage, should only one lender choose a borrower.
24. This part is a consequence of the two-stage modelling, the positive cost associated with dealing with each borrower, and the Bertrand-type competition that has been postulated.

25. Note that this line of reasoning is absolutely the opposite of that in Bhaduri (1977). There, a lender induces default to get at the collateral. Here, a lender asks for collateral to *prevent* default and obtain a higher interest rate.

26. The model may be easily generalized to allow for prices that depend on the quantities of purchases and sales. However, we do not permit uncertain prices.

27. We could easily allow consumption to influence production, to capture nutrition–efficiency relationships, for example. We do not do this here for ease of notation. Also note that the endowment of *marketed* commodities can be subsumed in the production function.

28. One can easily make assumptions on the primitives of the model (technology utility function) to ensure that this is the case for all production functions $f \in F$.

29. Equivalently, it is given by a partition of A, but our formulation is a bit more explicit.

30. Of course, throughout, M must be observable (relative to θ) in the sense described above.

31. The notation R^M stands for Euclidean space with dimensionality equal to the number of elements in M. Note that the lender does not price-discriminate between inputs, consumption, and output. Introducing this additional feature makes no difference to the analysis.

32. That is, if for every conceivable M-contract, there is an equivalent M'-contract, and, vice versa, the M-lenders and M'-lenders may be regarded as equivalent.

PART IV
Marketing and Insurance

Chapter 14 gives an overview of the institutional implications of the economic theory of risk and associated market failures. Chapter 15 looks upon the nexus of contracts in the village marketing system as a bilateral bargaining game and explores the properties of the equilibrium set of contracts.

14.

Agricultural Institutions for Insurance and Stabilization

David M. Newbery

1. Introduction

Elementary economics argues that free exchange between informed ind-
viduals is mutually beneficial — there are gains from trade. Organized
markets emerge to facilitate exchange, and it is a basic proposition that if
agents are individually insignificant, the market structure is complete, and its
operation is costless, then the resulting competitive equilibrium is one in
which there are no remaining unexploited gains from trade. The equilibrium
will be Pareto-efficient, meaning that there is no alternative allocation in
which some agents are better off and none worse off. An organized market is
a particular type of institution for facilitating the exchange of goods and
services via a medium of exchange (money), with the distinguishing features
that the terms of exchange (prices) are public knowledge, and access is open
to anyone wishing to trade. In reality, markets are not costless to organize
and operate, and the potential gains from trade on a particular market may
not be large enough to justify the emergence of an organized market. Even
when the gains are sufficient, it may not be possible for the marketing agent
to capture a sufficient fraction to cover his operating costs, and again the
market will fail to emerge. In such cases, alternative institutional arrangements may be able to provide similar services at lower cost. A restaurant is a
market for meals, but a family may be able to provide similar services with
lower transactions costs. (Though apparently in some West African societies
meals are provided within families in return for cash.) Perhaps the most
obvious example of an institutional alternative to the market is the firm,
whose 'distinguishing mark . . . is the suppression of the price mechanism'
(Coase 1937).

The simplest organizing principle for the study of economic institutions is
that they emerge in response to the potential for advantageous exchange, and
they have cost advantages over the market alternative. The study of a
particular set of institutions might usefully start by asking which transactions

I am grateful to Hans Binswanger and Paul Seabright for helpful comments.

they facilitate, that is, which markets they replace, and then asking what costs inhibit the market solution, and how they might be reduced by alternative arrangements. The success of this approach may be judged by its ability to predict (or, less ambitiously, to explain) those circumstances in which particular institutions will emerge and prosper, and those in which they will be at a disadvantage, and hence absent.

Insurance markets exist for the exchange of risks. An insurance company may offer farmers in a particular area insurance against hail damage. The farmer pays a premium, in exchange for which the company will pay an agreed amount in the event of a hailstorm in his locality (perhaps related to the degree of maturity of the crop). In the absence of such insurance, the farmer might suffer infrequent but significant crop losses from hail damage, which would cause his income to fail. If he has insurance, the crop losses still occur, but his income, including the payment from the insurance company, now does not fall, and hence has been stabilized. The risk of fluctuations in income resulting from hail damage has been transferred from the farmer to the insurance company in exchange for the premium, to the mutual advantage of both parties.

2. The Cost of Risk

In order to understand the demand for trade in insurance or risk, we need to understand why risk is costly, and why it might be mutually advantageous for agents to exchange risks. This should lead to a theory of the demand for trade in risk, and we can then examine the difficulties involved in organizing this trade through markets and other institutions. I shall concentrate on the case of risky agricultural production, where the nature of risk is reasonably straightforward. The exposition is intentionally informal, since the aim is to develop an intuitive feeling for the determinants of the costs of risk and the benefits of trade in risks. The formal study of the theory risk is set out in papers by Arrow (1965); Pratt (1964); Rothschild and Stiglitz (1970, 1971). The standard approach is static: the agent takes various actions at the beginning of the period (such as planting a certain fraction of his land with rice), whose outcomes will depend on the *state of the world*. At the end of period, the uncertainty will have been resolved, the outcomes will be known, and the agent then consumes the resulting income. The agent is assumed to be able to order the actions, and, under apparently reasonable rationality assumptions, this is equivalent to his having a well defined utility function over the resulting outcomes, and a set of subjective probabilities for the occurrence of any particular state of the world. His best choice or most preferred action is then the once that maximizes *expected* utility. In a one-period model there is no distinction between income and wealth, but since this distinction is important in a multi-period context, I shall suppose that the farmer's (terminal) wealth is risky. The specific question I wish to answer is how to measure the cost of this risk.

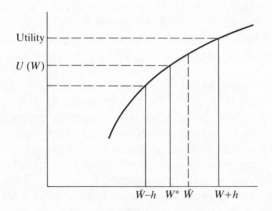

FIG. 14.1   The value of risky wealth

The standard method of measuring the cost of risk is to offer the farmer a choice between the risky wealth from farming, and a perfectly certain wealth whose value is somewhat less than the average or expected value of the risky wealth. The difference between this average value and the level of certain wealth which the farmer considers exactly as valuable is the *risk premium* associated with the risky choice, and the ratio of this premium to the certainty equivalent wealth is the *proportional risk premium* — a useful dimensionless measure of the relative cost of bearing the risk. Figure 14.1 shows the risk premium ρ associated with an equal chance of receiving an amount $\overline{W} + h$ or $\overline{W} - h$. If W^* is the certainty equivalent wealth, then $\rho = \overline{W} - W^*$. If $U(W)$ is the utility produced by receiving W, and $EU(W)$ is the expected utility, then ρ is equivalently defined by the equation

$$U(EW - \rho) = EU(W) = U(W^*). \tag{1}$$

An approximate value for ρ can be found by expanding $U(W)$ as a Taylor expansion about its mean value $\overline{W}$:

$$EU(W) \approx U(\overline{W}) + E(W - \overline{W})U'(\overline{W}) + E(W - \overline{W})^2 U''(\overline{W})/2. \tag{2}$$

(Primes refer to derivatives, and again E is the expectations operator.) The left-hand side of (1) can also be expressed as a Taylor expansion about $\overline{W}$:

$$U(\overline{W} - \rho) \approx U(\overline{W}) - \rho U'(\overline{W}). \tag{3}$$

Equate the right-hand sides of (2) and (3) to obtain

$$\rho \approx A \, \text{var}(W)/2, \tag{4}$$

where $\text{var}(W)$ is the variance of W, A is the coefficient of absolute risk aversion,

$$A \equiv -U''(W)/U'(W), \tag{5}$$

and A in (4) is evaluated at $\overline{W}$. The proportional risk premium $\rho/\overline{W}$ can be expressed in terms of the coefficient of relative risk aversion, R, and the coefficient of variation of W, σ:

$$\rho/\overline{W} \approx R\sigma^2/2, R \equiv - WU''(W)/U'(W) = AW, \tag{6}$$

where again R is evaluated at $\overline{W}$. As shown, these expressions for the risk premium are approximate, with the accuracy of the approximation depending on the shape of the utility function and the nature of the risk. In certain cases these formulas are completely accurate, for example if W is normally distributed and the utility function exhibits constant absolute risk aversion (see Newbery and Stiglitz 1981: Ch. 6.) Equation (6) is useful for practical measurements as it is dimensionless, and hence easily interpreted. One must, however, be careful to take account of all sources of wealth in defining R. For example, if the farmer has access to perfectly certain wealth W_0 to which is added a risky component y, whose variance is v^2 and expected value is $\bar{y}$, then the cost of the risk is approximately $Av^2/2$, and the proportional cost of the risk $\rho/(W_0 + \bar{y})$ is, as before, approximately $R\sigma^2/2$, but the coefficient of variation is of total wealth, i.e. $\sigma \equiv v/(W_0 + \bar{y})$, and the relevant value of W in the definition of R in equation (6) is expected total wealth, $W_0 + \bar{y}$. Equation (4) is arguably the more useful formula for gaining insights into the ways in which the costs of risk may be reduced. It should be remembered that this mean-variance approach, while simple to manipulate, is an approximation, and more satisfactory proofs can be constructed to prove the following claims.

2.1. Risk-sharing and risk-pooling

If the farmer faces a risky outcome W, then equation (4) gives an estimate of the cost of the risk. Suppose he now shares the risky outcome with a second farmer, whose remaining wealth is perfectly certain. If each farmer has the same coefficient of absolute risk aversion, A, and if each receives $W/2$, then the variance of wealth of each will be $\text{var}(W/2) = \text{var}(W)/4$, and the total cost of the risk will be $A \text{var}(W)/4$, or one-half the cost when borne by just one farmer. The argument generalizes, and if n identical agents share a risky outcome W, so that each now receives W/n in addition to their otherwise certain income, then the total cost of risk will be reduced to $1/n$ of its amount when borne by one agent. Risk-sharing, or spreading a risk over a number of agents who otherwise face no risk, is thus a potent way of reducing the cost of risk, and is a motive for advantageous trade in risk.

We can relax the assumption of perfectly identical agents, and still demonstrate the advantages of risk-sharing, as follows. Suppose there are two agents, $i = 1,2$, and that agent i has certain wealth W_i, and coefficient of absolute risk aversion A_i (which will in general depend on the level of terminal wealth). Suppose that agent 1 has access to the risky prospect y, mean $\bar{y}$, variance v^2; then he will be willing to sell a half-share in this prospect at any sum greater than $\bar{y}/2 - 3A_1v^2/4$, while agent 2 will be willing to pay up to $\bar{y}/2 - A_2v^2/4$. Provided that $3A_1 < A_2$, (or, equivalently, $3R_1/(W_1 + \bar{y}/2) < R_2/(W_2 + \bar{y}/2)$, where R_i is the coefficient of relative risk aversion of agent i), profitable trade is possible.

The next step is to consider the cost of accepting an additional risky prospect, y, when the original wealth, W, is itself risky. The certainty equivalent wealth corresponding to W is W^*, where

$$W^* = \overline{W} - A\mathrm{var}(W)/2, \tag{7}$$

while the certainty equivalent to $W + y$ is Z^*, say, where

$$Z^* = \overline{W} + \bar{y} - A\mathrm{var}(W + y)/2. \tag{8}$$

But

$$\mathrm{var}(W + y) = \mathrm{var}(W) + 2\,\mathrm{cov}(W,y) + \mathrm{var}(y), \tag{9}$$

so the net certainty equivalent value of the additional risky prospect is

$$Z^* - W^* = \bar{y} - A\{2\mathrm{cov}(W,y) + \mathrm{var}(y)\}/2. \tag{10}$$

Thus, the cost of an additional risk will depend on its covariance with existing risks. Consider the case of two farmers $i = 1,2$, each with certain wealth W_i, and the opportunity to grow a risky crop on their one acre of farmland, whose output per acre is y_i. Suppose that the mean, $\bar{y}$, and variance, v^2, of output per acre are the same, and the correlation coefficient of the two outputs is r. Consider the certainty equivalent wealth of farmer i when each exchanges a fraction λ of his crop for that of the other:

$$Z_i^* = W_i + \bar{y} - A_iv^2\{(1 - \lambda)^2 + 2\lambda(1 - \lambda)r^2 + \lambda^2\}/2. \tag{11}$$

This can be differentiated with respect to λ to give

$$\partial Z_i^*/\partial\lambda = A_iv^2(1 - 2\lambda)(1 - r^2). \tag{12}$$

Equation (12) shows that, if the two crops are not perfectly correlated (i.e., provide $r \neq 1$), then each farmer can increase his welfare (increase the value of his certainty equivalent wealth) by exchanging half the output of his crop with the other farmer. If, on the other hand, the two crops are perfectly correlated ($r = 1$), then there are no gains from trading the risky outputs. Thus, if the two farmers *pool* their risks, the total cost of the risk is again reduced (provided the two crops are not perfectly correlated). If the two crops are uncorrelated ($r = 0$), then the cost of risk will be halved.

Exactly the same argument applies to a single farmer choosing how to allocate his land among a variety of crops. By choosing a portfolio of crops, the total risk is reduced. (In the case in which there are two equally risky crops, as above, equation (11) gives the certainty equivalent wealth of allocating λ acres to the first crop and $(1 - \lambda)$ acres to the second. Again, the farmer does best by allocating half his land to each crop. If one crop has a higher average output per acre than the other, more than half, but typically less than all of the land will be devoted to the higher-yielding crop.)

Insurance companies operate by pooling risks, and then sharing the risk among the large number of shareholders. Suppose there are n individuals, each of which faces a single risky prospect with the same mean and with variance v^2. If all the risks are independent (e.g. the probability of a car accident), then the variance of the total sum of the risks is the sum of the variances, nv^2, and if this is then shared equally among the n agents, they will experience a variance $n(v/n)^2 = v^2/n$. In the limit, as n increases to infinity, the individual risk will tend to zero, and the total cost of the risk will also tend to zero.

2.2. Empirical evidence for behaviour under risk

The previous section discussed the measurement of the cost of risk and the gains from risk-sharing and risk-pooling on the assumption that individual's preferences over prospects are described by the *expected utility model*; that is, the preferences may be represented by a function of the form $\Sigma_i p_i U(W_i)$, where p_i is the probability that the outcome will be W_i and the W_i is the corresponding final wealth level. If this theory is to be empirically relevant, then it must be extended to the case in which the individual makes a series of choices over time. The natural approach is to argue that the theory should continue to apply for the case of perfect certainty, in which case the normal assumption is that the individual is ultimately concerned with levels of consumption at different moments of time, that is, with his or her lifetime consumption plan. If there is a well functioning credit market, then a particular lifetime plan will be feasible if its present discounted value is no greater than the present discounted value of future income, which can be thought of as the sum of human and non-human wealth (the former being the wage-earning capacity of the individual). The utility of wealth is thus to be thought of as a measure of the present value of the utility of consumption afforded by the wealth:

$$U(W) = \underset{\{C_t\}}{\text{Max}} \sum_t^T \delta^t u(c_t), \ W \geq \sum_t^T c_t(1 + r)^{-t} \tag{13}$$

where r is the rate of a interest on lending and borrowing, δ is the rate of pure time preference, or the rate at which the future utility of consumption, $u(c_t)$, is discounted, and the sum is taken from the present date $t = 0$, until the date of death, T.

The practical implication of this interpretation is that the individual is assumed to consider the combined effect of all his choices on the riskiness of wealth. In particular, in making a single risky choice (e.g. whether to sell grain today rather than hold it for sale tomorrow), he does not just react to the risk of that choice in isolation, but considers its effect on the total riskiness of his wealth. In particular, if the risk of this single decision is less than perfectly correlated with other risks, then there will be some risk-pooling benefits.

In an interesting experiment, Binswanger (1981) attempted to test the expected utility model of attitudes towards risk by offering Indian peasants choices in a series of games with real and high payoffs (relative to the peasants' income). He found that the peasants exhibited consistent choices (for the most part) which correlated with some of their actual farming choices, in the sense that peasants choosing the less risky game choices also adopted a more conservative farming strategy while the less risk-averse game-players were more likely to adopt new varieties sooner. These choices could best be described as exhibiting remarkable constancy of *partial relative risk aversion*, *S*, where *S* is defined in terms of the certainty equivalent, *M*, of the game. If W_0 is initial wealth, and $W = W_0 + M$, then

$$S = -MU''(W)/U'(W) = R - AW_0, \qquad (14)$$

where A and R are the coefficients of absolute and relative risk aversion defined in (5) and (6). Binswanger claimed to reject the hypothesis that agents integrated the various sources of risk into their overall effect on the riskiness of wealth, and instead postulated that they appeared to consider each game on its own, and to exhibit stable partial risk aversion to that game. The values of S ranged from 0.5 to 2.0, with a modal value of about 1, for games with outcomes ranging from Rs.0.5 to Rs.50 (the latter equal to about a week's wage.) Quizon, Binswanger, and Machina (1984) later corrected this inter-pretation, and pointed out that the tests had rejected the joint hypotheses of expected utility theory, namely those of *asset integration* and *linearity* in the way probabilities entered the determination of expected utility.

How is one to interpret these findings? One possibility that I find attractive is that agents find it conceptually difficult to make the necessary calculations to determine the impact of an additional prospect of their total asset position, and they therefore adopt simpler rules of thumb. If the prospect is a one-off event of no life-threatening significance (such as a game with positive expected value and no down-side risk), then the errors involved in ignoring correlations with total wealth will be minor. On the other hand, if the prospect is repeated from year to year, then the agents may learn how the various risks compound, how best to reduce their cost, and what that cost 'feels' like. For such choices expected utility theory has the great appeal of rationality, and consistency with the remainder of consumer demand theory.

On the question of whether agents think in terms of a lifetime consumption plan, much hinges on the availability of well functioning credit markets, and of the nature of future risks. Again, in developing countries, especially in peasant agriculture, credit may be expensive and even unavailable in adverse states, making *current* income a better determinant of current consumption (and hence utility) than the present value of future income. In such cases it may be more reasonable to define the utility function over current income, rather than wealth, and to redefine the coefficients of risk aversion over income. It is also plausible that agents have so little idea of the nature of future risks that these are better described as uncertain, rather than risky, meaning that the agent does not have a well defined subjective probability measure over the outcomes. Again, the natural reaction may be to focus attention on those decisions whose outcomes lie within the range of experience. For present purposes I shall summarize by supposing that agents behave as though they have reasonably stable preferences over current outcomes, and for choices whose outcomes are not life-threatening these preferences may be described by a utility function with constant relative risk aversion to *income* risk: $U(y) = y^{1-R}/(1 - R) (= \log y$ for $R = 1)$.

One important source of information about behaviour under risk which can illuminate some of these difficult issues of asset integration is the response of agents to disasters such as droughts, which are infrequent but nevertheless are 'expected' to occur periodically. Walker and Jodha (1982: Table 1) report the range of responses of drought-hit farms in different areas of India, compared with normal behaviour. In these areas the drought was so severe that crop and livestock income contributed only between 5 and 16 per cent of total sustenance in the four areas studied, with public relief contributing between 22 and 56 per cent of sustenance. Total consumption expenditure per household fell between 8 and 12 per cent (compared with normal), but expenditures on socio-religious ceremonies fell by up to 64 per cent, 42 per cent of households withdraw children from school, while assets were depeleted by up to 60 per cent, and debts increased by up to 192 per cent. Both family members and livestock migrated out of the area in over half the households, and although this reduced deaths to livestock to some extent, it did not eliminate it — between 28 and 53 per cent of out-migrating livestock were lost, while between 59 and 87 per cent of non-migrating livestock were lost.

The picture that emerges is one in which a great deal of consumption smoothing takes place, and a wide variety of responses to risk are evident. The depletion of assets, increases in debts, and loss of livestock all imply that the future income earning power of the household is severely reduced — particularly as debts are at high interest rates, while forced sales of assets and livestock at distress prices would have to be replaced by repurchases at market prices (or even at above-normal prices if others are similarly attempting to rebuild their assets at the same time). The fall in concept consumption, which appears quite modest compared with the fall in current income, may be associated with comparably below-average consumption levels for quite some time,[1] and hence decreases in current income may be quite a good proxy for variations in wealth.

If we assume that Binswanger's measures of partial risk aversion are a good indication of the magnitude of the coefficient of relative risk aversion of income risk, then we can calculate rough measures of the cost of various types of risk. Newbery and Stiglitz (1981: 108–10) cite various estimates of the coefficient of variation of income for farmers in different countries, and a modal value might be about 30 per cent. (The range is from 17 per cent for unirrigated Indian farms to as high as 50 per cent for rice farmers using modern techniques in the Philippines.) If we take a value for R of 2, then the relative cost of risky income might be 18 per cent of income for the modal farmer, though substantially less in the more diversified agriculture. To the extent that losses in successive years are independent and that farmers do think of evening out their consumption stream over time by lending and borrowing (or running down their accumulated assets), then this estimate will overstate the cost of income risk, as of course it will if R is lower than 2. If, on the other hand, borrowing is difficult or very expensive and asset depletion is hard to reverse, then current income falls will lead to significant falls in current and future consumption levels and will be substantially more costly, so the relevant value for R will be higher, possibly substantially so. The same applies if the measured attitudes to risk really do refer to the actual utility loss of small gambles.

We can summarize as follows. The economic theory of risk offers several important insights. First, the cost of the risk increases as the *square* of the amplitude of the fluctuation. Small fluctuations are not very costly, and it is entirely plausible that the costs of creating and operating markets or institutions to reduce these risks will not be justified, and they will not be observed. Large fluctuations are, however, potentially far more costly, and these are the risks most likely to create a demand for risk-sharing or risk-pooling. Second, all agents face some risk, and the relevant question to risk is, What determines the cost of an additional risk? The answer is that it depends on its *covariance* with existing risks — the cost will be higher the stronger is the degree of positive covariance, while negatively correlated risks will actually reduce the total cost of risk-bearing.

3. Sources and Types of Risk in Agriculture

The most obvious type of risk in agriculture is variations in output or yield, caused by variations in the weather, and in the incidence of pests and disease. For a self-sufficient subsistence farmer who does not trade significantly with anyone else, these fluctuations in output will translate into fluctuations in consumption unless they are absorbed by offsetting variations in storage (which, for livestock, may occur naturally as a consequence of consumption decisions). It is, however, unusual for the typical agent to be entire self-sufficient, and the practical question to ask is what gives rise to fluctuations in consumption in such economies, since consumption is the most plausible argument of the utility function to which the theory applies.

Consider as an example a farmer who grows a cash crop such as jute which his family cannot consume. Family consumption will depend on the income from selling the crop, and on the prices of the purchased consumer goods. The farmer's income will in turn depend on his output and on the ruling price for jute (as well as the cost of purchased inputs). The price of jute will in turn depend on the aggregate production of jute in the relevant market area (which may be the whole world), and probably on other demand factors such as aggregate income, the prices of sisal, polypropylene, and so on. Consider two extremes. On the one hand, the farmer's output may fluctuate significantly from year to year, but if all farmers experience correlated output risk, and if the price elasticity of demand for jute is unity, and the demand schedule remains stable from year to year, then total revenue from jute will be stable, and so will the income of each farmer. At the other extreme, the farmer's output may be perfectly constant, but if the price fluctuates (either in response to supply fluctuations elsewhere or because income in the consuming countries varies), then his income will vary with the price.

The risk facing consumers will similarly depend on fluctuations in their income and on the prices of the goods they buy. Famines, as Sen (1981) has reminded us, may be caused by a dramatic fall in the income of the consumer with no rise in the price of food, just as effectively as if incomes remained constant and the price of food rose excessively in response to shortage. In a well integrated economy the prices of goods are likely to be fairly uniform over wide areas, but different agents may experience very different movements in their incomes. For present purposes, it is probably useful to distinguish the following types of agents, whose incomes may move in different directions: farmers, agricultural labourers, processers of agricultural goods (including stockholders who perform storage functions), and urban workers. Once it is appreciated that the risk facing any agent depends on both his income and the prices he faces, it becomes clear that the cost of risk and demand for risk-sharing depends on the general equilibrium properties of the economy, which determine these prices and incomes, and in particular determine how fluctuations in agricultural output (or world prices) impact on the agents in the economy.

4. Avoidable and Non-diversifiable Risk

A simple example may help to demonstrate how the underlying risks are transmitted through the market structure of the economy and hence fall on various agents. The following example has been used elsewhere to demonstrate the *constrained inefficiency* of competitive but incomplete markets, but will also serve to illustrate the present point.[2]

A perfectly symmetrical island is divided into two identical halves by a mountain range running north–south. Farmers on each side of the island can grow two crops — one risky, the other safe. The risky crop does well if there is rain, poorly if not, while the safe crop always produces the same yield. If the wind blows from the west it rains in the west and is dry in the east, and conversely. With equal probability, the wind blows either from the east or the west, but the sum of the output per acre of the risky crop in the west and the east is always the same. Consumers have unit (price)-elastic demands for the two crops, and constant incomes.

Now compare two market configurations. In the first, there is no trade in the two crops between the two halves of the island, so that for agricultural purposes they are autarkic. The farmers face a unit-elastic demand for each crop, so total consumer expenditure on each crop is always the same, and hence so is revenue and farmers' incomes, regardless of the state of the world (rain or dry). Farmers therefore face no income risk, for, although their output varies, so does the price in an exactly offsetting number. Consumers bear all the risk, for their consumption of the risky crop varies with the weather.

In the alternative market equilibrium, there is free trade in agricultural goods. (Perhaps a pass through the mountains is opened up.) As both halves are identical, there is a symmetrical equilibrium in which farmers on each side plant the same area of risky crops, and the total production is constant. Consequently the price of both crops is now constant, and consumers bear no risk. The output of farmers continues to vary, but since the price is constant, their incomes now fluctuate with the weather and all the risk is borne by the farmers.

In the economy as a whole, all the risk is avoidable (at least in principle) because aggregate production is constant. If each farmer could buy a half share of a farm on the other side of the mountain, then farmers' incomes would be constant, all prices would be constant, and neither consumers nor farmers would bear any real consumption risk. If, however, farmers cannot pool their risks, then the burden of risk-sharing will depend on the market structure. With no trade between the two halves of the island, consumers bear all the risk, while with free trade farmers bear all the risk, although the consequences will also fall on the consumers, for the following reason. In response to the risk borne under free trade, the farmers will shift production out of the risky crop into the safe crop, thus driving up the price of the risky crop, and lowering that of the safe crop. It can be demonstrated that this is adverse for consumers, and it is even possible that both consumers and farmers will be made worse off by opening up trade between the two halves of the island.

On the other hand, if the mountain range formed a truly impenetrable barrier so that the two halves of the island were economically disjoint, and if there were no trade in risky assets (shares in farm output) between them, then each part would face unavoidable risk, and the only issue would be how best to share it between the consumers and farmers.

5. Costs of Risk-sharing

The obvious answer to the question of how best to share risk is to set up a market in the risk (i.e. an insurance market). Any market requires some resources to operate, though for many markets these costs may be essentially negligible. Working (1962), discussing the operation of futures markets (which are of particular interest for risky agricultural products), noted that the *gross* profit of traders transacting in futures sales of cotton amounted to about 0.023 of 1 per cent of the value of the trade, and was evidently sufficient to keep the market in being. Insurance markets, however, face two additional types of cost over and above the cost of just running the market, caused by the presence of *moral hazard* and *adverse selection*. Moral hazard arises when an agent who obtains insurance has an incentive to take less care to avoid the contingencies that give rise to claims (e.g. accidents), while adverse selection occurs when the insurance company cannot distinguish between agents who have differing probabilities of claims, and hence must offer all the same contract. The contract will be less attractive to those facing a small probability of making a claim, and they may not wish to take out such insurance, with the result that the contract only appeals to (and adversely selects) those of above-average probability of making a claim. Both problems arise because of *asymmetric information*; specifically, the insurance company cannot tell whether the agent has taken due care or whether he belongs to a high-risk category, while the agent seeking insurance is better informed about both possibilities. The costs of avoiding or reducing these two problems take several forms. The insurance agency may attempt to collect information to reduce the informational asymmetries, or it may offer incomplete insurance, which provides some incentive to take more care, or which will be unattractive to the higher-risk clients. In the first case the costs are borne by the insurance agency and will presumably be reflected in higher premiums, while in the second the costs are borne by the client, who is now unable to insure completely, and hence is left with some of the costs of the risk. In some cases there may be no contract that breaks even in competition with other insurance companies, given the unavoidable asymmetries in information (Rothschild and Stiglitz, 1976).

We can now return to the island example and ask how far these costs of risk-sharing are likely to impede the transfer of risks between agents. Consider first the case in which risks are avoidable if pooled. Ideally, farmers on each side of the mountain will match themselves up with an equally large farm on the other side and arrange to exchange half shares of total output with each other. Both problems (of adverse selection and moral hazard) present real difficulties. Any farmer from the east advertising for a suitable western farmer must worry that those presenting themselves will be less good farmers than the average, for whom the exchange is particularly advantageous, for the good western farmers, suspecting the eastern farmer to be below average in quality, will not present themselves. Even if the farmer's past faming record were available for inspection, and he were guaranteed to be of satisfactory *ability*, his *incentive* to work hard under the half-share contract would be reduced, since he would be keeping one-half of the proceeds. (The same incentive problem has long been recognized for share-rent contracts.) The problem might be overcome if area-wide yield figures were collected and published, for then each farmer might contract to pay the other one-half of the stated yield per acre times the number of acres farmed.

As an example of a privately supplied income insurance scheme similar to that proposed, consider the so-called flexible cash rent contract which is beginning to appear in areas of predominant sharecropping in the United States. In these contracts the rent payable is determined by average yields in the local agro-climatic zone (DeBraal and Wunderlich, 1983: 138 and refs.). If the weather is bad and yields are low, then rent is low and the tenant keeps a larger amount than under a fixed rent tenancy; conversely if conditions are good. If on the other hand the tenant is idle or incompetent, then his rent is not thereby reduced, as it would be under standard share tenancy contracts. One reason why such schemes are not more prevalent is that they require accurate, timely, public, and credible information on yields for well defined zones, and this information is likely to be obtained only by public agencies.

Although this contract would avoid both the adverse selection and the moral hazard problem, it runs into another obvious difficulty. It amplifies the cost of individually specific risks — those risks that affect only a single farm or a small locality — and these risks are peculiarly difficult to insure as any insurance would immediately encounter the twin problems. The problem of individually specific risk appears to be particularly serious in arid and semi-arid areas where farming is in any case very risky. Walker and Jodha (1982) gave several telling examples of this. They found that the correlation between monthly July rainfall figures collected at opposite ends of the 1400 ha research station at ICRISAT in India was only 0.61.[3] They also studied the correlation between an individual farmer's yields and the average village yield. Although for most crops the two are positively and significantly correlated, for local cotton 40 per cent of the farmers had yields that were *negatively* correlated with the average over the period 1975/6–1980/1 (though for most farmers the correlation was not significant).

6. Specialization and the Increased Demand for Risk-sharing

As economies develop, and particularly as population pressure on land increases, so agents specialize into a narrower range of activities (Boserup, 1965). In a proto-economy each family may be almost self-sufficient, and will thus have to undertake a wide range of economic activities. Its productivity in any single activity may be quite low, but if natural resources are sufficiently abundant, living standards may be quite high. More to the present point, the need to diversify to meet the variety of subsistence requirements implies that total risk is likely to be low, at least in areas of reasonable ecological diversity. As population pressure on natural resources increases, so the intensity of production increases, and transport costs between groups of families (villages) of similar size will tend to fall. Both factors encourage specialization and a consequent reduction in diversification, and may lead to an increase in individual risk-bearing, unless means are found explicitly to share the risk.

David Hirshleifer (1986) gives a particularly neat example of the way in which the process of economic specialization, in this case the dismembering of a previously vertically integrated production enterprise, creates risk previously absent, and generates a demand for risk-sharing via a futures market. Again, consider an economy in which farmers grow a single risky cash crop as well as various food crops whose output is stable. The demand for the cash crop is unit-elastic and stable, so that the revenue received is stable despite the fluctuations in output. Now suppose that the crop can be stored at modest cost from year to year, and that farmers undertake the storage. If they all have rational expectations in the sense of Muth (1961), and if they all face the same cost of storage, then they will all store the same fraction of their cash crop in years of above-average supply. The amount will be such as to arbitrage the current and future (present discounted net) prices for the cash crop. (See Newbery and Stiglitz 1982 for details.) Once again, no agent will face any risk, for the amount sold (output *less* increase in stocks) will again face a price that generates constant revenue. Of course, if any farmer stored either less or more than the average, then his sales would differ from average sales, and his revenue would fluctuate from year to year and be risky — which is why he will try and sell the same amount as other farmers.

Now suppose that specialist storage operators have a comparative advantage in storing the cash crop, and the farmers store none. If the previous equilibrium is to be maintained, the farmers will have to sell their entire crop each year, and the stockholders will buy the amout previously held in storage on the farms. In a year of above-average supply, the farmers will now receive an above-average income, and conversely in poor years they will receive below-average income (as the market price is lowered by sales from stock). The farmers' income is now risky, and so is the stockholders', for they buy at a known price in the expectation of selling at a higher price next year, but the future price is risky, and hence so is their profit. However, the *sum* of the profits of the stockholders and the revenue of the farmers is perfectly certain — their risks are perfectly negatively correlated, and if pooled would cancel, just as in the island example. This time, however, there is a cost-effective insurance contract which allows this risk pooling to take place.

6.1. Futures markets as storage insurance

A futures market allows agents (farmers, stockholders, speculators) to buy or sell promises to deliver a specified amount of the cash crop (of a specified minimum quality) at a specified future time and place. The contract is thus precisely defined, agents are symmetrically and perfectly well informed as to its nature, and it can be therefore be traded as extraordinarily low cost (as mentioned above). Futures markets provide price insurance, and as such are extremely well suited to providing insurance against the risks facing stockholders. The stockholder can buy the crop now, sell futures at a known price (in which case he is a *short hedger*[4], and either deliver the crop in due course to liquidate the contract or, more usually, sell the crop in the spot or cash market and buy back the expiring futures contract for essentially the same cash price in the maturity month. Assuming that nothing untoward happens to the crop in store, he is then perfectly insured against price and profit fluctuations. Normally the other side of the market to the hedgers would consist of *speculators*, who stand ready to assume the price risks in return for some expected gain. A futures market is thus a market in price risks, whose cost is reduced by transferring them to those for whom the cost is less, and by sharing them over a larger number of agents. It is not surprising that the demand for such contracts emerged as middlemen became increasingly specialized in the storage of crops, and that quite sophisticated futures markets appear to have pre-dated the emergence of comparably sophisticated financial contracts (Williams 1982). Nor is it surprising that most futures markets depend primarily on hedging for their existence, and that the size of the open interest follows the demand for seasonal storage closely (Working 1962).

In the present example, however, the futures sales by the stockholders will be bought by the farmers, and the effect will be just as if the farmers had bought back the amount they would have stored themselves, had there been no stockholders. More precisely, the effect is as if the farmers had sub-contracted the storage to stockholders whose storage costs are lower than those of the farmers, and in so doing they will once more cancel out the risks created by the separation of production and storage.

6.2. Tenancy, wage labour, and sharecropping

Once population pressure increases to the point at which land becomes scarce, and hence commands a market price, economic differentiation is likely to accelerate, for now more successful farmers can accumulate wealth in the form of land — typically a more durable and productive asset than such alternatives as livestock, wives, or ornaments. Land-holdings will no longer be matched to endowments of labour. One way in which availabilities of land

and labour can be better matched is for households with an above-average land–labour ratio to hire labour from those with a below-average land–labour ratio, thereby creating a need for a labour market.[5] Once more, the previously vertically integrated production enterprise of the family farm owning all the necessary resources for self-sufficient production will give way to a differentiated set of households — landowners and labourers. Once more, the separation of activities may create new risks, or amplify existing risks.

Consider first the case in which landowners hire in labour to augment their own household labour supply. Agricultural production requires a sequence of activities over the crop year (land preparation, planting, weeding, watering, etc.) almost all of which are subject to some degree of risk, in the sense that the contribution of the particular activity to increases in final harvest cannot be known with certainty. As the crop year advances, though, this uncertainty is gradually resolved. The labour market may be organized in a variety of ways — it may consist of a casual market in which workers are hired by the day (or for the task), or it may include a market for permanent or seasonal labour, in which the farmer hires a worker for agreed terms for a whole season (or longer). The casual labour market may have a market-clearing wage which responds to demand and supply, or it may be that the daily wage is fixed for a season at a non-market-clearing level.[6]

If farmers and workers have to rely on a casual labour market, then, regardless of whether the market wage is rigid or market-clearing, workers will not know their future income at the start of the crop year, and hence will face income risk. Farmers will similarly not know whether the future wage will be high (if the market wage is flexible) or whether labour will be unavailable (if the wage is rigid), and hence will also face income risk over and above the risks arising from fluctuations in the value of the crop. Once again, the risks on each side of the market are offsetting — if the wage is high, workers benefit and farmers lose, and vice versa. Again, there is the potential for beneficial trade in risks, and a need for something analogous to a futures market in labour. Labour services are quite unsuitable for a formal futures market, as they are not homogeneous and well defined, and require high transaction costs for their delivery, but a seasonal labour contract can be thought of as a surrogate futures contract.[7] Seasonal labour contracts will be drawn up at or before the start of the season, and if they are denominated in money, they will not vary with output or prices, and hence may fall short of the full potential for risk-sharing. If, for example, food prices are high, and the landowner is a net food seller, then the worker's real income or consumption will be low while that of the landowner may be high.[8] Further or better risk-sharing can be achieved by providing some fraction of the wage in the form of food, thus effectively indexing the wage.[9] On the other hand, if prices are not negatively correlated with output, then the landowner, by paying a fixed money wage, will increase the riskiness of his income, and in extreme cases may bear all of the agricultural risk. Again, advantageous risk-sharing opportunities will remain. One natural solution is for the landowner and worker to share the risk, and to do so via a share-rent contract in which the worker (tenant) rents the land and pays the landlord an agreed share of the total amount.

On the face of it, this risk-sharing argument for sharecropping looks plausible, but it encounters two obvious objections. The first is the standard moral hazard problem, better described in the present context as a *principal–agent* problem. The tenant (agent) has an incentive to undersupply labour, or to shirk, as he receives only a fraction of the additional output thereby produced. Cheung (1969a), in his influential study of sharecropping, argued that the landowner (principal) could ensure the efficiency of share-cropping by specifying the level of labour input required of the tenant, and refusing to renew the tenancy if the tenant failed to meet the terms of the con-tract. There was thus no reason why sharecropping should be any less efficient than fixed-rent tenancies, in which the tenant received the entire value of the marginal product of his labour. Cheung argued that the extra costs of negotiating the share-tenancy agreement would be offset by the superior risk-sharing advantages of sharecropping, and hence sharecropping would be a viable institutional solution to the mismatch in endowments of land and labour. As it stands, this argument is not completely convincing, for it may be difficult or costly for the landowner to specify and monitor inputs of tenant labour and to detect shirking, as output is risky. Output may be low because the tenant was shirking or because circumstances were unfavourable. Later writers (Stiglitz 1974; Newbery 1975, 1977; Newbery and Stiglitz 1979) pointed out that the principal–agent problem was not peculiar to share-cropping and applied with even greater force to hired labour — at least, with sharecropping the tenant had an incentive to work harder as he received some fraction of the extra output, whereas a worker would have no such incentive. The relative attractions of sharecropping and labour hiring would then hinge on the relative costs of monitoring hired labour, sharecroppers, and fixed-rent tenants (whose incentive is to over-exploit the land). Evidence cited in Newbery (1977) suggested that labour hiring was most profitable for the landowner, but was feasible only on nearby land, the extent limited by the supervisory capacity of the landowner. Sharecropping economized on this supervision, and was cost-effective for additional areas of land, while fixed-rent tenancies allowed essentially absentee landlord status, but yielded lower average income, and thus would be chosen for land only in excess of that which could be monitored under more profitable contracts.

The second objection to this risk-sharing explanation for sharecropping is in some ways more fundamental (Newbery 1977). If outputs are risky but prices stable, then wage contracts place all the risk on the landowner, while fixed-rent tenancies place all the risk on the tenant. Share tenancies divide the risk, but so would an appropriately chosen mixture of fixed-rent and share-rent tenancies. Indeed, such a combination would exactly replicate the levels of income and risk for the two parties, and if negotiation costs for the share tenancies were higher than for the alternative contracts, as Cheung (1969a) had argued, then share tenancies would be dominated by mixtures of pure wage and fixed-rent contracts.

Thus, although sharecropping may be an effective method of risk-sharing, it is by no means the only possible contract or set of contracts with this property, and its benefits arguably lie more in its great flexibility than in its specific risk-sharing attributes. Some support from this comes from various studies in the drought-prone district of Sholapur in India reported in Walker and Jodha (1982: 22). In 1972–3 a severe drought led to large-scale deaths and sales of the bullocks that are used to cultivate the land. The effect of the drought was to upset the balance between landownership and bullock ownership, and as a result there was a substantial increase in tenancy transactions which tended to equalize land–bullock ratios.[10] Share tenancies, being short-term and very flexible in their details, are well suited to adjusting quickly to such mismatches.

This is not the place for an extensive discussion of the determinants of the choice of agricultural contract (which is in any case discussed in Chapter 3 by Singh). For our present purpose, the point is that the process of agricultural differentiation leads to a mismatch between the pattern of endowments and the pattern of factors needed for production, which generates a demand for trade in factors. Particular forms of contract for the sale or rent of factors give rise to particular distributions of risk and of incentives, and these may conflict. Contracts that have desirable risk-sharing properties may be prone to moral hazard, and contracts that provide adequate incentives for diligent performance may (and typically do) have undesirable risk-sharing properties. It follows that some risks may be hard to exchange or insure against, and individuals may be forced to search for alternative methods of self-insurance. These are discussed in the next section.

7. Self-insurance

Rural inhabitants face two distinct types of risk: individual or specific risks, which are uncorrelated with the risks facing their neighbours, and area-wide risks common to all. Specific risks are well suited to cost reduction by risk-pooling and risk-sharing, as argued above, while common risks, or *covariant* risks, do not benefit from being pooled and shared, since the risk remains essentially the same. Specific risks may be reduced by diversification, but this may be difficult in some ecological environments, or costly where there are returns to specialization. Nevertheless, there is an extremely wide variety of such techniques available, though they may be used only in more risky environments. As noted above, in semi-arid areas rainfall may be extremely variable in quite localized areas, making *geographical diversification* highly desirable. Walker and Jodha (1982: Table 5) report a doubling of the number of scattered land fragments per farm (from 2.8 to 5.8) when comparing two semi-arid areas, the second of which had only half the probability of favourable soil moisture conditions for rainy season cropping. The plots also had a higher number of mixed crops, and the degree of crop diversification was substantially larger (34 sole crops as opposed to 20 for the less risky village). Risk-pooling may be achieved through informal agreements within extended families or wider social groupings, and one would expect these to be relatively more prevalent the more specialized and individually risky are production activities.

Covariant risks cannot be pooled within a time period, and each family must deal with them as best it may. The expected utility theory of risk argues that the cost of risk depends on the variability of consumption. If agents can borrow or lend to even out their flow of consumption, then the cost of the risky income is thereby reduced. For this to be possible, several conditions need to be satisfied. First, and most obvious, there must be some durable store of value which either can be consumed directly, or can be converted into predictable purchasing power reasonably easily; that is, the asset must be *liquid*.

Consider, for example, an isolated community of subsistence farmers under semi-arid land surplus conditions in which the main food crop cannot easily be stored from year to year. Suppose that gold ornaments are prized, and that families decide to accumulate these ornaments as a store of value. If one family has an isolated crop failure (elephants trample the plot), then it can sell its gold ornaments and buy food, and even out its consumption flow. Gold ornaments are thus an effective method of insuring against specific risks (though costly, in that their return consists solely in aesthetic pleasure). But if all farms experience a bad year in which output falls, then gold ornaments do not eliminate the risk, but at best share the shortfall more uniformly across farms. Farmers who have a larger surplus of production to subsistence may be willing to sell for gold to those in deficit. The more uniform is labour productivity, and the more homogeneous the ratio of labour power to consumption needs (which will depend on how extended the family is and on its demographic stability), the smaller will be the potential for risk-sharing. In such circumstances the price of food for gold would have to rise very significantly to persuade farmers to sell food. Gold would not be a good means of evening out variations in production, and the cost in terms of forgone current consumption (to acquire the gold) would be very high in terms of the availability of extra consumption after adverse harvests. On the other hand, if there were a greater variation in harvest across farms, then inequalities in gold holdings would translate into inequalities in access to food, with the end result that the risks of harvest failure might be concentrated on to a subset of the population — those with particularly unfavourable harvests and small gold holdings. Thus, the availability of a store of value may reduce risks for some agents but at the expense of concentrating it on others.

Once again, there is a potential conflict between institutions that spread risk satisfactorily and those that encourage efficiency. If land were communally held and the harvest were divided among all those eligible, risks would be evenly shared but there would be little individual incentive to increase output and accumulate wealth. Advanced countries faced with a similar shortage of food in wartime solved it by issuing ration coupons to everyone; the alternative of rationing by the price mechanism either would have required an unacceptably high rate of redistributive taxation, or would have resulted in an unacceptable distribution of food. Food rations that are introduced in times of extreme food scarcity may be a way of reconciling the conflicting aims of encouraging the accumulation of wealth while ensuring an equitable distribution of food in unfavourable states of the world — and food rations might be thought of as contingent contracts which pay off in adverse states. Patron–client relations, and feudal and semi-feudal obligations of the wealthy to support the destitute, are less formal substitutes.

If farmers could store food from season to season, then the problem of aggregate food variability could be reduced. Livestock has the considerable advantage that it serves not only as a potential store of food, but may do so at a positive rate of return, unlike gold. The combination of livestock with crop production is also risk-reducing; for if the harvest fails, it may still have salvage value as fodder for livestock, perhaps to the extent that returns to livestock and crops will be negatively correlated. On the other hand, in severe droughts both crops and livestock will be adversely affected, as described in Section 2.2 above, so that it may not be possible to self-insure against these most severe risks. Certain root crops, notably cassava, serve as a famine reserve, as they can be stored in the ground until needed. Such strategies are likely to be important in areas that are geographically isolated. Cereal crops pre-eminently allow food to be stored for longer than one agricultural season, and the shift to cereal cultivation represents a decisive change in the possibility of consumption-smoothing over time.

On the other hand, if the region has good transport connections with other, climatically differently affected, regions, then the ability to store purchasing power in gold ornaments or the equivalent may be quite effective at dealing with locally covariant risk. A poor harvest and a low income would lead to sales of gold in neighbouring towns and the import of food, which would permit more stable consumption than production. One useful measure of the extent to which financial assets can buffer fluctuations in income is the degree of correlation between local production and the cost of living: if they are strongly negatively correlated then the local risk is unavoidable, while if they are uncorrelated, then financial assets will be a good means of insuring against low output states.[11] Credit markets would in principle be even better at evening out fluctuations in income, since there would be no need to accumulate unproductive but liquid assets — instead, productive but illiquid assets could be held and used as collateral for consumption loans. Once again, however, credit markets suffer from the same problems are insurance markets — moral hazard and adverse selection. Borrowers have an incentive not to repay their debt unless the cost of not doing so is higher than the benefit of consuming the loan and not repaying, while the type of borrower attracted by the terms offered by a credit agency or money-lender may be those least likely to repay. Collateral makes repayment desirable, but limits loans to those who have already accumulated assets. Unsecured debt from local money-lenders is, however, quite common in village communities, but it requires the lender to be sure that the borrower will wish to continue to borrow in the future. The lender therefore has to collect information about the future income prospects, reliability, and reputation of the borrower, and he has to ensure that the borrower will not go elsewhere and borrow from an alternative money-lender, at least, not without discharging his outstanding debts. The relationship between money-lender and borrower is thus likely to be a longstanding one, and may appear (and actually be) exploitative. The money-lender will favour arrangements that tighten the ties between the two participants, and increase the degree of dependency of the borrower on the lender, for these ties will reduce the incentive to renege on the debt, and increase the market power of the money-lender. It is therefore not uncommon to find that the borrower buys his inputs from and sells his output to the money-lender, who may also be a middleman or merchant.

Another solution to the problem of moral hazard in credit markets is the *vertically extended household*, which is composed of nuclear units of successive generations. Older members of the household have had time to accumulate assets which either are directly available for consumption-smoothing, or can be used as collateral. Members will leave the extended household once they have accumulated enough to ensure adequate self-insurance. Given the tensions of such arrangements, they are more likely in areas where credit markets are poorly developed or moral hazard is potentially serious, for example where farmers can easily move elsewhere. The optimal household size will also tend to diminish as the demand for self-insurance falls, for example in more diverse ecologies such as the wet humid tropics compared with arid and semi-arid areas (Binswanger and McIntire 1987, who attribute this explanation of the vertically extended household to Meillassoux 1981).

The net effect is that the costs of risk reduction are likely to be higher for the poor, who have to borrow on probably very unfavourable terms, than for the rich, who can borrow against collateral or reduce their own liquid assets at small cost. The poor may thus be forced into occupations that face less risk (seasonal labouring), but which again yield lower returns, while the rich, who have access to a variety of risk-reducing activities, can afford to take on riskier and more productive activities (introducing new varieties, or new methods of farming, such as mechanisation, fertilizers, tube wells, etc.). This process, operating over time, is likely to increase the degree of differentiation and inequality of wealth. Eswaran and Kotwal (1986), developing an idea of Roemer (1982), have shown how principal–agent problems and the costs of enforcing contracts for credit and labour hire lead from a non-uniform distribution of the means of production to a class structure — that is, a classification of agents according to their activities. In the simple neoclassical model of production, landless labourers could as readily hire in land as hire out labour, and all agents would combine factors in efficient proportions, so that there would be no class structure as such. Transaction costs and principal–agent problems mean that hired labour is less productive than own labour, while the inability of the poor to borrow to finance working capital means that they cannot rent in land. Agents will thus be either pure labourers, tenant farmers, labour-hiring landowners, or landlords, depending on their endowments of land. The process described above will introduce a dynamic element into this structure. Land reform, involving the redistribution of the ownership of land, is likely to increase output by reducing principal–agent problems, and also to improve the degree of risk-sharing in the society. The threat of land reform may, of course, have exactly the opposite effect.

8. Government Interventions to Reduce Risk

Economic development, which leads to economic specialization of agents within communities and greater interdependence between communities, changes the nature of total risk in the community and its distribution between agents. In some cases agents can share or transfer risks at relatively low cost because the informational problems at the root of moral hazard and adverse selection can be overcome at modest cost — futures markets providing perhaps the leading example — but in other cases these costs are so high as to prevent the emergence of markets or their substitutes. In such cases the government may be able to offset some of the market failures, though it is important to check that the transaction costs that are the cause of private market failures do not also undermine the government solution.

8.1. Crop and livestock insurance schemes

Crop insurance schemes are peculiarly prone to moral hazard and adverse selection, for reasons that should now be clear. As an example, consider the observations of K.M. Choudhary, reported by Walker and Jodha (1982) of the Gujarat Crop Insurance Scheme for Hybrid-4 Cotton: 'It was further alleged by villagers that some of the participants had avoided interculturing, weeding, application of the last dose of fertilizers, etc., when they realized that they would not obtain the expected yield.' Although general crop insurance appears to be very unsuccessful, cattle insurance in some circumstances appears to work quite well. Seabright (1987) reports that the General

Insurance Corporation of India has increased the number of cattle insured from just under 30,000 in 1974 to over 10 million in 1983, and the number continues to grow rapidly. Cattle insurance is compulsory for cattle purchased under IRDP (Integrated Rural Development Programme) loans (thus avoiding problems of adverse selection to some extent), and mortality rates of insured cattle appear no higher than those of uninsured cattle. Cattle have to be inspected before insurance, and the availability of widespread vetinerary services makes it possible to monitor moral hazard at low cost — death is, after all, a more specific and infrequent event to check than neglect of a crop.

8.2. Price stabilization via marketing boards

Commodity prices are notoriously unstable, and primary producers have been vocal proponents of price stabilization or price support, especially when prices are low. The governments of primary producing countries are in turn tempted by commodity price booms to increase the export taxes on these commodities, arguing that they are both stabilizing the price and obtaining extra government revenue at very low cost. (If the price is above the supply cost, then the tax is almost like a rent tax.) The combination of these two pressures has been to encourage the emergence of marketing boards which set the price to the farmer, and whose apparent justification is to stabilize the domestic price. The classic study of such marketing boards is Helleiner (1964), which suggests that, whatever the initial motives behind such boards, their attraction as mechanisms for extracting rent from the producers, either in the form of a fiscal surplus transferred to the government, or dissipated in the form of excessive employment and/or corruption, outweighs their advantages as risk-reducing institutions for the producers. Some countries, notably Papua New Guinea, may have been more successful in avoiding this tax element (at least, for agricultural commodities), and it remains an interesting question to ask whether such marketing boards have a useful role to play in reducing the risks facing producers.

The short answer is that the case for domestic price stabilization on risk-reducing grounds looks rather weak, for the following reason (set out more fully in Newbery 1983a). Unbiased futures markets offer unambiguously better *income* insurance than perfect price stability unless the correlation coefficient of output with the price is less than a critical level, r^*, where

$$r^{*2} = \sigma_p^2/(1 - \sigma_p^2) \qquad (15)$$

where σ_p is the coefficient of variation of price. The intuitive explanation for this is that futures markets offer a guaranteed price, just like price stabilization, but leave the farmer free to choose the amount of price insurance he would like to purchase. In general, he will not wish to purchase full price insurance, because he is interested in income insurance rather than price insurance, and can take advantage of the correlation between price and output, and hence between price and income to choose a more satisfactory combination of price and output risk. If he could purchase price insurance for his entire crop, then a revealed preference argument would demonstrate that futures markets were unambiguously better than being forced to buy full price insurance from a marketing board, and it is only when the correlation coefficient is low that this argument breaks down, for in such cases he would like to hedge his entire actual output on the futures market, but all he can do is hedge his *expected* output.

If the correlation coefficient is below r^*, then in principle a (costless) marketing board is better than an unbiased futures market, and Newbery (1983a) shows that the advantage of the marketing board over the futures market when the correlation coefficient is zero amounts of about $R\sigma^2\sigma_p^2/2$, where, again, R is the coefficient of relative risk aversion, and σ is the coefficient of variation of output. For plausible values of $\sigma_p(0.1-0.3)$, $\sigma(0.1-0.4)$, and $R(1-2)$, this will amount to less than 1 per cent of the value of output. The benefit of the marketing board has, however, been calculated on the assumption that during the course of the crop year, as the uncertainty about output is gradually resolved, there is nothing that the farmer can do to vary output. In general this is an unreasonable assumption, and one would expect the farmer to vary his effort (on weeding, fertilizing, spraying, etc.) in response to the latest information about predicted future prices (available from the price of futures contracts). If the farmer has sold his crop forward on a futures market he still has every incentive to produce efficiently, since he receives the full value of his production at the going price (the futures contract just providing offsetting insurance payments or receipts). If the world price is high, then he will attempt to increase output, while if the price is low, he will economize on inputs or, in extreme cases, avoid the cost of harvesting. If, on the other hand, he is committed to sell to the marketing board, then he has no incentive to adjust inputs efficiently. It is hard to believe that the cost of the inflexibility introduced by the marketing board will be less than the rather small benefit of risk reduction.

There are various minor qualifications to make to this argument. First, when one examines crops and countries to measure the actual correlation coefficients relative to the critical value, r^*, it rapidly becomes clear that the main distinction is between countries that are small producers of the commodity, and hence have little influence on the world price and a low correlation with the price, and countries that are relatively large, and therefore have potential market power (Newbery 1983b). Dominant producers of primary products who face linear demand schedules have an incentive to store an above-average fraction of the world total (Newbery 1984), and may, like Brazil for coffee, organize this storage through marketing boards. But the main purpose of such marketing boards is not so much to reduce risks facing domestic producers as to exercise intertemporal market power on the world market.

Second, it may be argued that small farmers make little use of futures markets, so the comparison is academic. This, however, misses the point. It is true that the minimum contract size on a futures market may be inconveniently large for a small farmer, and the inconvenience of trading on a distant, possible foreign futures market, meeting margin calls, etc., may make it relatively unattractive; but if he were keen to sell his crop forward, then the existence of the futures market means that merchants or middlemen can offer forward contracts (as opposed to futures contracts; see n. 7). The merchants can then hedge these risks themselves on futures markets, while the futures markets give the farmers the information about the appropriate terms on which to conclude the forward contract.[12] Indeed, if such middlemen were in short supply, the government might be better advised to offer forward contracts rather than a guaranteed price compulsory for all. The same applies if there are reasons to believe that the futures market is systematically biased (though empirically the evidence for bias is rather weak). The government could speculate profitably on the futures market and offer unbiased forward contracts to the local farmers.

8.3. International price stabilization

Similar arguments apply to international buffer stock schemes, though there are also important differences. A domestic marketing board can indeed perfectly stabilize the price, since it does not have to store the commodity and can export the surplus of production over domestic consumption (or input the shortfall). Neither export nor import is feasible for the world as a whole, and the only way prices may be stabilized is by storage. At the international level, therefore, futures markets and buffer stocks are complementary, not competitive. Nor is it possible to perfectly stabilize the price at a level that equates expected supply and demand, for this would require an infinitely large (and hence infinitely costly) buffer stock. One useful benchmark to examine is the case in which the international buffer stock replicates the activities of risk-neutral private storage operators, and hence arbitrages the price. One can then ask whether it would be desirable on risk-reducing grounds to undertake more storage, and if so whether there is a case for claiming that the private market would tend to undersupply storage (Newbery and Stiglitz 1981: Ch. 30; 1982). The reason why a competitive market may fail to supply an efficient level of storage and risk reduction is straightforward. The theme of this chapter is that the distribution and magnitude of risk-bearing in an economy depends on the interaction of a large number of individually rational decisions, and can be thought of as a public good. Each agent takes the distribution of risk as given in making decisions, but collectively these decisions influence the amount and cost of the risk. Just as competitive markets fail to supply an efficient level of public goods, so competitive markets will in general fail to supply an efficient level and distribution of risk (Newbery 1988). If, on the other hand, too much storage is already being supplied privately, there is not much that the international agency can do, since it is unlikely to have the necessary tax powers to discourage national storage. At best, then, it may be able to increase the amount of storage, and this is likely to be most effectively done by subsidizing private storage activities, rather than assuming the entire amount of storage into public hands.

8.4. Income stabilization

Price stabilization is an indirect way of reducing the risks for producers, who are more concerned with fluctuations in their income, though price stabilization may be of direct value to consumers, at least to the extent that their money incomes are not positively correlated with the price of food. Why not, therefore, attempt to stabilize incomes directly? By now the answer should be fairly obvious — problems of moral hazard and adverse selection make individual insurance impractical. However, a marketing board could offer at least partial income insurance for covariant risks by offering a price inversely proportional to *aggregate* supply. Specifically, if the normal or trend level of revenue is $\bar{R}$, and if actual production in a given year is Q, then the marketing board could set the price at $p = \bar{R}/Q$. Provided each farmer's output were reasonably well correlated with total output, this would offer income insurance. Moreover, this system of insurance appears to avoid the problem of moral hazard, as it is still in the interest of each farmer to produce the efficient level of output, because his own production would not affect the price he received. (Some systems of crop insurance guarantee a minimum return per acre, regardless of the farmer's effort. In such cases the farmer often has no incentive to care for the crop.) This proposal raises two obvious questions: if it is so attractive, why don't private insurance companies offer such contracts and second, if they don't, why don't governments offer them instead? The answers are that we do observe contracts offered by the private sector which have some similarity to that suggested, and there are government schemes of this kind.

An example of a privately supplied (partial) income insurance with similarities to that proposed is the flexible cash rent contract discussed earlier. Share contracts have already been cited as a risk-sharing and hence cost-reducing response to risk, but they appear to have the disadvantage that, by not rewarding the tenant with the full value of his marginal product, he will be encouraged to shirk unless carefully monitored. Sharecropping is very prevalent in the mid-West of the United States, and recently contracts have emerged in which the rent payable is determined by average yields in the local agro-climatic zone (DeBraal and Wunderlich 1983: 138 and refs.). If the weather is bad and yields are low, then rent is low and the tenant keeps a larger amount than under a fixed-rent tenancy; conversely if conditions are good. If on the other hand the tenant is idle or incompetent, then his rent is not thereby reduced, as it would under standard share tenancy contracts. (Although a landlord suspecting such behaviour would be unlikely to renew the contract, so there are incentives for efficiency even under traditional sharecropping.) In principle it would be possible for a private insurance agency to offer to pay the difference (positive or negative) between expected revenue per acre (futures price times forecast average yield) and the area's average revenue per acre (actual price times actual average yield), provided there was accurate, timely, public, and credible information on yields for the zone. This information, however, is likely to be obtained only by public agencies.

As examples of a government response with almost exactly this form, both the European Community's STABEX and the Compensatory Financing Facility of the IMF operate by lending the shortfall on export earnings on favourable terms to commodity exporters. The main difference is that, for the scheme to provide the relevant agents with insurance, the funds have to be transmitted on to the farmers via a marketing board, and this aspect of the scheme has not yet been implemented to my knowledge. There are two difficulties with the government scheme which might account for their absence. The first is that it runs into the same efficiency problem that any price stabilization scheme faces — by confronting the producer with a price that differs from the efficiency or shadow price, it encourages him to apply the wrong level of inputs. This is a greater problem the more discretion he has over inputs during the period when the uncertainty about the future world market price is being resolved. The second is that the schemes may be vulnerable to arbitrage, either between producers and consumers, between neighbouring countries,[13] or over time via storage.[14]

9. Conclusions

The economic theory of risk offers several important insights. First, the cost of the risk increases as the *square* of the amplitude of the fluctuation. Small fluctuations are not very costly, and it is entirely plausible that the costs of creating and operating markets or institutions to reduce these risks will not be justified, and they will not be observed. Large fluctuations are, however, potentially far more costly, and these are the risks most likely to create a demand for risk-sharing or risk-pooling. Second, all agents face some risk, and the relevant question to ask is, What determines the cost of an additional risk? The answer is that it depends on its *covariance* with existing risks — the cost will be higher the stronger is the degree of positive covariance, while negatively correlated risks will actually reduce the total cost of risk-bearing.

This in turn means that, if all agents face similar risks (as they might if each were a semi-subsistence farmer in an ecologically uniform but isolated area), then this risk cannot be reduced much by trading the risk between the participants. On the other hand, if the process of economic differentiation leads to activities that are complementary from a risk point of view, being performed by different agents (for example, production and storage, hiring and supplying wage labour), then there are potential gains from trade in risk which may lead to such institutions as futures or forward markets, share tenancy, and the like. Third, the natural market for the exchange of risk is an insurance market, but insurance markets are prone to the twin market failures of moral hazard and adverse selection. A major determinant of the nature of contracts and of the institutional setting in which risk-sharing and risk-pooling takes place will be the costs of monitoring the actions of insured agents, and the solution will be the one with the lowest cost relative to the insurance benefit. In many cases the cost will exceed the benefits and the risks will have to be borne by the individual or household (and the size of the household may be partially influenced by the need for self-insurance). Fourth, the cost of risk depends on the variability in consumption over time, so that lending and borrowing (if feasible), or asset accumulation (where credit markets fail for the same reasons as insurance markets) may be the most cost-effective ways of reducing risk. Fifth, the amount and distribution of risk in an economy will depend on its level of development and its agro-climatic conditions. Increased specialization will tend to increase and concentrate individual risk, though it may facilitate the emergency of markets and institutions to shift, share, and reduce those risks. Improved communications will tend to reduce price risk and potentially reduce aggregate risk, though, by removing the negative correlation between price and output facing producers, it may increase the income risk facing farmers. It will also increase the effectiveness of financial assets for consumption-smoothing.

Finally, the major scope for public intervention to improve risk-sharing lies in its potential to take account of the public good nature of risks — the fact that the amount and distribution of risk in an economy is the general equilibrium outcome of a large number of uncoordinated individual decisions. Subsidized storage *may* in some cases improve risk-sharing between producers and consumers, while transport infrastructure may greatly reduce the risks of famine within a previously isolated area, especially if associated with food rations to avoid famines caused by income shortfalls. The state also has the potential to collect and use information that might allow the creation of new risk-sharing institutions, or that might alleviate problems of asymmetric information — the income insurance scheme, and the collection of area-wide yield figures which facilitate new share contracts are good examples. Again, it is the public good nature of the information that is the cause of the failure of the private market. Having said this, the evidence from the past operation of marketing boards in developing countries and the current operation of farm support schemes in developed countries does not give much cause for optimism on this front.

NOTES

1. This can be established only by studying household consumption levels over time, and Walker and Jodha (1982) bemoan the paucity of panel data that would allow the risk adjustment of small farmers to be adequately studied.
2. See Newbery and Stiglitz (1981: Ch. 23; 1984). The market structure is incomplete if it lacks risk markets which would permit agents to insure against all risks, and it is constrained-inefficient if the government could intervene on the *existing* set of markets and make everyone better off.
3. Seabright (1987) reports that the squared correlation coefficient between the two closest rainfall stations 25 miles apart in an area in southern India was 0.15 over a 30-year period, though the average levels differed by only 22 per cent.
4. He is long in actuals, and short in futures, hence a 'short hedger'. Had be bought futures to meet some future processing requirement, he would have been a 'long hedger'.
5. The alternative, in which labour hires (or rents in) land, will be discussed below.
6. Jean Drèze reports that in the Indian village of Palanpur the *daily* wage is remarkably uniform over workers of differing ability and rigid over substantial periods of time, though it does adjust periodically. As a result, the market does not clear, and the more able workers are more likely to be hired than the less able. On the other hand, the wage for specific tasks is determined by bilateral bargaining between the landowner and the worker, and fluctuates according to supply and demand (Drèze and Mukherjee 1987).
7. Bardhan (1984: Ch. 5). A more accurate description would be a surrogate *forward* contract. A forward contract differs from a futures contract in that it need not be homogeneous since it is a contract between two agents for a future delivery, and is unlikely to be transferred to other agents during its lifetime. Futures contracts typically change hands 10–30 times over their life.
8. If the reason for the high food prices is a shortage of local supply, then whether the landowner's real income is high or low will depend on the correlation between his marketed suplus and price, which in turn will depend on the elasticity of demand, the fraction of production sold, and the level of aggregate local income.
9. This motive for paying wages partly in kind rather than entirely in cash should be distinguished from the efficiency wage argument, in which the landowner attempts to increase the productivity of the worker by ensuring that he has an adequate food ration, and does not go hungry in favour of his family. See Bliss and Stern (1978).
10. The alternative in which bullock services are traded appears to involve more serious problems of moral hazard or much higher monitoring costs.
11. If the cost of living were positively correlated with output, fewer financial assets would be needed to buffer consumption.

12. This may be one of the most valuable functions of the futures market, for it removes the fear of assymetric information which might otherwise discourage the farmer from entering into forward contracts with middlemen.

13. Producers in a country with a large harvest, and hence a low marketing board price, will be tempted to smuggle the crop to a neighbour paying the world price, and conversely in poor years.

14. The marketing board effectively confronts producers with a unit-elastic demand schedule, as in the example of David Hirshleifer (1986), discussed above. In that model storage was socially profitable, and, if undertaken by farmers holding objectively rational expectations, also stabilized their income. Here the price announced by the marketing board is not the social value, but a price designed to provide insurance. If output is high and the world price is not far below next year's expected level, then storage is inefficient, but the low marketing board price might make it appear attractive. This will place a constraint on the extent to which the marketing board price can fall below the world price, but will not invalidate the scheme.

15.

Peasants' Risk Aversion and the Choice of Marketing Intermediaries and Contracts: A Bargaining Theory of Equilibrium Marketing Contracts

Pinhas Zusman

1. Introduction

Agricultural production is geographically dispersed, and individual producers often enjoy only limited direct access to central auction markets. This is particularly true in rural economies in which the communication and transportation systems are underdeveloped. Furthermore, in most economic systems marketing constitutes a specialized activity, which is carried out by specialized marketing intermediaries. The marketing system through which farm products flow from the original producers to the final consumers consists of the various intermediaries and market facilities as well as the contractual arrangements that mediate exchange between producers, marketing intermediaries and final consumers. These components of the marketing system constitute agrarian institutions of crucial importance.

There exists, at present, a fairly extensive literature dealing with marketing systems, including agrarian ones. Interested readers are referred to the comprehensive review by Wood and Vitell (1986). The main objective of this chapter is to offer a rigorous theory of a particular marketing system which, hopefully, may be extended to a wide variety of rural economic institutions.

The present study is concerned with marketing at the village level. At this level the number of marketing intermediaries and producers is of necessity small. Consequently market imperfections arise; exchange tends to become personalized, and competitive ('auction') markets are supplanted by various forms of bilateral contractual arrangements between producers and marketing intermediaries.

Marketing contracts are often simple transactions in which the title to the good is transferred at a given fixed price at a particular moment in time. In other cases, however, contracts may involve more complex arrangements in which the parties' payoffs depend on their actions and on the realized state of the world. In view of the parties aversion to risk and the prevailing informational asymmetries between agents, marketing contracts are likely to include risk-sharing and incentive provisions in addition to exchange price-like parameters.

In the following sections I shall advance a static theory of marketing contracts which is designed to explain the determination of contractual terms in marketing contracts and the allocation of product to the various distribution channels under equilibrium conditions. The theory portrays the marketing system as a nexus of bilateral contracts among individual actors. The contracts involve agency relations;[1] each agent may deal with several principals and each principal with several agents. As actors are diverse, contracts are idiosyncratic and are reached through bilateral bargaining. The theory draws upon the bargaining theory due to Nash (1953). As contracts are interdependent in many respects, we are interested in the equilibrium set of all contracts in the market — an equilibrium characterized by Zusman and Bell (1989). An earlier application of the contract-theoretic approach to the theory of marketing channels was attempted by Zusman and Etgar (1981).

Although the theory is rather general, it is best illustrated with reference to a concrete example. In particular, we shall consider a simplified agricultural marketing system not unlike those found in developing agrarian economies. Accordingly, I first present a model of a village-level marketing system; second, I characterize the equilibrium set of marketing contracts that make up the system and derive the equilibrium conditions; third, the equilibrium values of the contractual terms are studied analytically and numerically; and finally, the economic efficiency of the contractual system is considered.

2. The Marketing System

The market for paddy at the village level in India will provide the model used in presenting the present theory. Several types of marketing intermediaries may be found at the village level. Thus, according to K. Subbarao, who studied rice marketing in Andhra Pradesh in India, 'The three principal agents who procure paddy stocks for delivery at the mill site are: (a) local commission agents ('brokers'); (b) rice millers' agents, and (c) cooperative processing societies' (Subbarao 1978; 15). I shall adopt this description as my model, but in order to simplify the analysis shall consider only the first two marketing agencies.[2] Furthermore, I shall assume the marketing system to consist of a single miller's agent, a single broker, and n producers whose output consists of a single homogeneous product. The functional characteristics of the various transactors are as follows.

2.1. The miller's agent (the miller)

The miller purchases the product from the ith producer at the fixed price P_i.

The value of the product at the mill site is Z, and the handling cost is $C_M(Q^M)$, where Q^M is the total amount of the product procured by the miller. $C_M(Q^M)$ is assumed to involve increasing marginal cost. Let Q_i be the total amount of product marketed by the ith producer and q_i the amount marketed by him through the broker, so that $Q_i - q_i$ units of product are sold to the miller; then

$$Q^M = \sum_{i=1}^{n} (Q_i - q_i) \tag{1}$$

and the miller's net income at the procurement stage is

$$Y^M = \sum_{i=1}^{n} (Q_i - q_i)(Z - P_i) - C_M(Q^M). \tag{2}$$

The miller is assumed to be risk-neutral. Notice that the miller, in effect, represents any merchant who buys at a fixed price.

The contract between the ith producer and the miller consists of two contractual parameters, P_i and $Q_i - q_i$.

2.2. The commission agent ('broker')

The broker performs two functions: he seeks high-paying buyers, and he handles certain phases of the market logistics for the producer. The search for buyers consists of sampling s potential buyers and entering into a transaction with the one offering the highest price, P_s. The search cost is assumed to be proportional to the number of buyers sampled. The broker's handling cost $C_B(Q^B)$ also involves increasing marginal cost. The total amount of product marketed by the broker is

$$Q^B = \sum_{i=1}^{n} q_i \tag{3}$$

and his net income is

$$Y^B = P_s \sum_{i=1}^{n} v_i q_i - \xi s - C_B(Q^B) \tag{4}$$

where v_i is the percentage commission fee that the broker charges the ith producer and ξ is the search cost per sampled buyer. We shall assume that the broker too is risk-neutral. Notice that P_s is a random variable whose probability density function, g_s, depends on the original distribution of price offers across buyers and the sample size s. It is assumed that the broker and all producers share the same subjective probability distribution of prices.

The contract between the broker and the ith producer includes two contractual parameters, q_i and v_i. Since individual producers are ordinarily not in a position to monitor the search behaviour of the broker, the choice of the sample size s is the broker's discretionary action, and is not spelled out in the contract. Given his contracts with all producers, the risk-neutral broker chooses s so as to maximize his expected income. The first-order condition for maximum $E(Y^B)$ is, therefore,

$$\frac{\partial E(Y^B)}{\partial s} = \left(\sum_{i=1}^{n} v_i q_i \right) \frac{\partial \bar{P}_s}{\partial s} - \xi = 0 \tag{5}$$

where $\bar{P}_s = E(P_s)$, E being the expectation operator.

The second-order condition for maximum requires that $\partial \bar{P}_s / \partial s$ be decreasing in s (i.e., $\partial^2 \bar{P}_s / \partial s^2 < 0$), and, since $\bar{P}_s$ *increases in s*,

$$\frac{\partial s}{\partial q_i} = -v_i \frac{\partial \bar{P}_s}{\partial s} \Big/ \left\{ \left(\sum_i v_i q_i \right) \frac{\partial^2 \bar{P}_s}{\partial s^2} \right\} > 0 \text{ if } v_i > 0 \tag{6}$$

and

$$\frac{\partial s}{\partial v_i} = -q_i \frac{\partial^2 \bar{P}_s}{\partial s} \Big/ \left\{ \left(\sum_i v_i q_i \right) \frac{\partial^2 \bar{P}_s}{\partial s^2} \right\} > 0 \text{ if } q_i > 0. \tag{7}$$

That is, an increase in the quantity marketed by any producer through the broker, or an increase in the broker's commission fee, will encourage him to intensify his search effort — the incentive effect of the commission fee. This will benefit all producers availing themselves of the broker's services. The broker's discretionary decisions concerning information-gathering, therefore, involve certain externalities. The effects of q_i *and* v_i on the search effort, and thereby on the broker's and producer i's expected utilities, are taken into account in the contract between them. However, the associated effect on the other producers is ignored.

2.3. The producer

Producer i has Q_i units of product, of which q_i units $(0 \leq q_i \leq Q_i)$ are marketed through the broker and $Q_i - q_i$ units are sold to the miller. His income is, therefore,

$$Y_i = (Q_i - q_i)P_i + q_i(1 - v_i)P_s. \tag{8}$$

Notice that since P_s is a random variable, so is the producer's income.

The producer preferences are given by his expected utility, $E\{U_i(Y_i)\}$, where U_i is a von Neumann concave utility function. That is, the producer is assumed to be risk-averse.

3. The Equilibrium Set of Contracts

As indicated earlier, each producer may enter two marketing contracts: one with the miller involving the contractual parameters $Q_i - q_i$ and P_i, and one with the broker involving the contractual parameters q_i and v_i. How are these contracts determined?

In the present model contracts are determined through simultaneous bilateral bargaining between transactors, and the resulting equilibrium set of contracts represents the parties' market power.

The solution concept employed in this analysis adopts Nash theory of a two-person bargaining game (Nash 1953) in deriving the contractual values of P_i and v_i in the corresponding contracts, given the product allocation among intermediaries and the terms of all other contracts.[3] Notice that, while q_i and $Q_i - q_i$ are both contractual parameters, it is impossible to determine their values by solving either the producer–miller contract or the producer–broker contract separately. This is because, being allocational contractual parameters, they have to satisfy the product availability constraints and must, therefore, be handled simultaneously. Hence, the allocation of product among marketing intermediaries is obtained by solving for the entire equilibrium set of contracts. However, an additional definition has to be introduced before undertaking a full characterization of the equilibrium set of contracts.

A reallocation of product between marketing intermediaries will be called an acceptable reallocation if it is associated with compensatory changes in the contractual parameters, P_i or v_i, so as to leave the expected utility of the relevant intermediaries unaltered. The equilibrium set of contracts will now be characterized by the following three conditions:

1. Given all other contracts and the product allocation, the agreed price P_i in the contract between the miller and producer i is a solution to a Nash bargaining game.
2. Given all other contracts and the product allocation, the agreed commission fee v_i in the contract between the broker and producer i is a solution to a Nash bargaining game.
3. No acceptable reallocation of product which may raise the expected utility of any producer exists.

Conditions 1 and 2 in effect imply that, given the product allocation, all contracts must be mutually consistent solutions to the corresponding bilateral bargaining games. In particular, if producer i and the broker disagree, the producer's conflict strategy is to sell his entire crop Q_i to the miller at the agreed price P_i. Similarly, if the miller and producer i fail to reach a contract, the producer will sell his entire crop through the broker at the agreed fee v_i.[4] Hence, the other given contracts determine the disagreement payoffs of the parties, and thereby their bargaining power. In other words, if any contract in the equilibrium set of contracts expires, then, given the remaining contracts in the set, the renegotiated contract will be identical to the one just expired.

Condition 3 also implies that in equilibrium no producer can renegotiate a new set of contracts (including a reallocation of his product) more advantageous to him which is acceptable to both marketing intermediaries.

Now, it has been shown by Zusman and Bell (forthcoming) that the equilibrium set of contracts corresponds to a solution of a non-cooperative Nash–Cournot game, where for each i the 'objective function',

$$W_i = \lambda_{Bi} E(Y^B) + \lambda_{Mi} Y^M + E(U_i), \tag{9}$$

is maximized with respect to the contractual parameters P_i, v_i, and q_i, given all other contracts and subject to the broker's discretionary behaviour (equation (5)), the product availability constraint $0 \leq q_i \leq Q_i$, and the individual rationality conditions:

$$E(Y^B) - t_{Bi}^B \geq 0 \tag{10a}$$

$$Y^M - t_{Mi}^M \geq 0 \tag{10b}$$

$$E(U_i) - t_{B_i} \geq 0 \tag{10c}$$

$$E(U_i) - t_{Mi} \geq 0 \tag{10d}$$

where t_{Bi}^B is the broker's guaranteed payoff should he disagree with the ith producer, t_{Mi}^M is the miller's disagreement payoff, and t_{Bi} and t_{M_i} are the corresponding disagreement payoffs of the ith producer. In the maximization of W_i, the coefficients λ_{Bi} and λ_{Mi}, which will henceforth be referred to as the power coefficients, are held constant. However, the values of λ_{Bi} and λ_{Mi} are endogenous to the system, and must be calculated from the final solution values as follows:

$$\lambda_{Bi} = \{E(U_i) - t_{Bi}\}/\{E(Y^B) - t_{Bi}^B\} \tag{11}$$

and

$$\lambda_{Mi} = \{E(U_i) - t_{Mi}\}/(Y^M - t_{Mi}^M). \tag{12}$$

Given the disagreement strategies open to the parties in the present marketing system, the disagreement payoffs are:

$$t_{Mi}^M = \sum_{k \neq i} (Q_k - q_k)(Z - P_k) - C_M \left\{ \sum_{k \neq i} (Q_k - q_k) \right\} \tag{13}$$

$$t_{Bi}^B = \bar{P}_{\bar{s},i} \sum_{k \neq i} v_k q_k - \xi \bar{s}_i - C_B \left(\sum_{k \neq i} q_k \right) \tag{14}$$

where $\tilde{s}_i$ is a solution to

$$\left(\sum_{k \neq i} v_k q_k\right) \frac{\partial P_{\tilde{s},i}}{\partial \tilde{s}_i} - \xi = 0$$

and

$$t_{Mi} = E[U_i\{Q_i(1 - v_i)P_{s^*,i}\}] \tag{15}$$

where s_i^* is a solution to

$$\left(\sum_{k \neq i} v_k q_k + v_i Q_i\right) \frac{\partial P_{s^*,i}}{\partial s_i^*} - \xi = 0,$$

and

$$t_{B_i} = U_i(Q_i P_i). \tag{16}$$

4. Determination of the Contractual Parameters

The contractual parameters may now be determined by maximizing W_i in (9) with respect to P_i, v_i, and q_i subject to the broker's behaviour (5), the product availability constraint, $Q_i - q_i \geq 0$, and the non-negativity requirements $P_i \geq 0$, $v_i \geq 0$, and $q_i \geq 0$. The W_i are maximized for all producers. Forming the Lagrangean expression

$$\Psi_i = W_i + \mu_i(Q_i - q_i), \tag{17}$$

where $\mu_i \geq 0$ is a Lagrangean multiplier, and employing the envelope theorem for s in Y^B, we obtain the following Kuhn–Tucker conditions for maximum W_i:

$$\frac{\partial \Psi_i}{\partial P_i} = -\lambda_{Mi}(Q_i - q_i) + (Q_i - q_i)E(U_i') \leq 0 \tag{18a}$$

$$\frac{\partial \Psi_i}{\partial P_i} P_i = 0 \tag{18b}$$

$$\frac{\partial \Psi_i}{\partial v_i} = \lambda_{Bi} q_i \bar{P}_s - q_i E(U_i' P_s) + \frac{\partial E(U_i)}{\partial s} \frac{\partial s}{\partial v_i} \leq 0 \tag{19a}$$

where

$$\frac{\partial E(U_i)}{\partial s} = \int_0^\infty U_i \frac{\partial g_s}{\partial s} \, dP_s,$$

and g_s is the density function of P_s.

$$\frac{\partial \Psi_i}{\partial v_i} v_i = 0 \tag{19b}$$

$$\frac{\partial \Psi_i}{\partial q_i} = \lambda_{Bi}(v_i \bar{P}_s - C'_B) - \lambda_{Mi}(Z - P_i - C'_M)$$

$$- P_i E(U'_i) + (1 - v_i)E(U'_i P_s) + \frac{\partial E(U_i)}{\partial s}\frac{\partial s}{\partial q_i} - \mu_i \leqq 0 \tag{20a}$$

$$\frac{\partial \Psi_i}{\partial q_i} q_i = 0 \tag{20b}$$

$$\frac{\partial \Psi_i}{\partial \mu_i} = Q_i - q_i \geqq 0 \tag{21a}$$

$$\frac{\partial \psi_i}{\partial \mu_i} \mu_i = 0, \tag{21b}$$

where a prime denotes a first derivative.

Here, μ_i may be interpreted as the shadow price associated with the product availability constraint of the ith producer. Adopting the utility normalization rule that at the solution point $E(U'_i) = 1$, we obtain from (18a) and (18b) that for $P_i > 0$ we must have $\lambda_{Mi} = 1$, so that from (12), (13), and (15) we have

$$E(U_i) - E[U_i\{Q_i(1 - v_i)P_{s^*,i}\}]$$

$$= (Q_i - q_i)(Z - P_i) - \left[C_M(Q^M) - C_M\left\{\sum_{k \neq i}(Q_k - q_k)\right\}\right]. \tag{22}$$

A closed-form solution of P_i may be obtained from (22) by using the approximations

$$E(U_i) \approx (Q_i - q_i)P_i + q_i(1 - v_i)\bar{P}_s - \tfrac{1}{2}R_i q_i^2(1 - v_i)^2\sigma_s^2 \tag{23}$$

and

$$E[U_i\{Q_i(1 - v_i)P_{s^*,i}\}] \approx Q_i(1 - v_i)\bar{P}_{s^*,i} - \tfrac{1}{2}R_i Q_i^2(1 - v_i)^2\sigma_{s^*,i}^2 \tag{24}$$

where R_i is producer i's absolute risk aversion coefficient and σ_s^2 and $\sigma_{s^*,i}^2$ are the variances of P_s and $P_{s^*_i}$, respectively.[5] Substituting (23) and (24) into (22), and setting

$$C_M(Q^M) - C_M\left\{\sum_{k \neq i}(Q_k - q_k)\right\} \approx C'_M(Q_i - q_i),$$

one gets the following solution for P_i:

$$P_i \approx \tfrac{1}{2}\langle Z - C'_M + (1 - v_i)[\bar{P}_{s^*,i} + \{q_i/(Q_i - q_i)\}(\tilde{P}_{s^*,i} - \bar{P}_s)] \tag{25}$$
$$- \tfrac{1}{2}R_i(1 - v_i)^2\{(Q_i^2\sigma_{s^*,i}^2 - q_i^2\sigma_s^2)/(Q_i - q_i)\}\rangle$$

for $Q_i - q_i > 0$. If $Q_i - q_i = 0$, there is no contract between producer i and the miller, and the value of P_i is of no interest.[6] The price, P_i, paid by the miller is thus roughly equal to the simple average of the net marginal value of a unit output to the miller $(Z - C'_M)$ and the expected price received from the broker net of a certain risk premium. General solutions to the other contractual parameters are difficult to derive in closed forms, but they may be obtained numerically. (The numerical calculations are explained and illustrated in Section 6.) It will prove instructive, however, to investigate some special cases, and in particular, the conditions under which a producer will end up marketing his entire product through one of the intermediaries exclusively (i.e., $q_i = 0$ or $q_i = Q_i$). However, before undertaking this exploration, let us note some relevant relations. First, by equations (4), (10), and (14), we have

$$
E(Y^B) - t^B_{Bi} = (\tilde{P}_s - \tilde{P}_{\tilde{s},i}) \sum_{k \neq i} q_k v_k + \tilde{P}_s q_i v_i - \xi(s - \tilde{s}_i)
$$

$$
- \left\{ C_B(Q^B) - C_B\left(\sum_{k \neq i} q_k\right)\right\}. \tag{26}
$$

By (5) and the definition of $\tilde{s}_i$, if $v_i = 0$, then $\tilde{s} = s_i$, and (26) becomes

$$
E(Y^B) - t^B_{Bi} = - \left\{ C_B(Q^B) - C_B\left(\sum_{k \neq i} q_k\right)\right\} < 0 \tag{26'}
$$

which contradicts (10). Hence, if $q_i > 0$, then $v_i > 0$. Hence by (19a), (19b), and (7) we have

$$
\frac{\partial \Psi_i}{\partial v_i} = q_i\{\lambda_{Bi}\bar{P}_s - E(U'_i P_s) - \eta_i\} = 0 \tag{27}
$$

where

$$
\eta_i = \frac{\partial E(U_i)}{\partial s} \frac{\partial P_s}{\partial s} \bigg/ \left[\left(\sum_i v_i q_i\right)\frac{\partial^2 \bar{P}_s}{\partial s^2}\right] < 0.
$$

Next, recalling that $E(U'_i) = 1$ at the solution point, a linear approximation of $E(U'_i P_s)$ in P_s about $\bar{P}_s$ yields

$$
E(U'_i P_s) = \bar{P}_s - R_i(1 - v_i)q_i\sigma^2_s. \tag{28}
$$

Recalling that $\lambda_{Mi} = 1$ and $E(U'_i) = 1$, and using (6), (27), and (28), we get from (20a)

$$
\frac{\partial \Psi_i}{\partial q_i} = v_i\{\lambda_{Bi}\bar{P}_s - E(U'_i P_s) - \eta_i\} - (Z - C'_M)
$$

$$
+ \bar{P}_s - R_i(1 - v_i)q_i\sigma^2_s - \lambda_{Bi}C'_B - \mu_i \tag{29}
$$

$$
= \bar{P}_s - R_i(1 - v_i)q_i\sigma^2_s - \lambda_{Bi}C'_B - (Z - C'_M) - \mu_i \lessgtr 0.
$$

We shall now state two propositions concerning the allocation of product among the marketing intermediaries.

PROPOSITION 1.   If

$$\bar{P}_{\bar{s},i} - C_B'\left(\sum_{k \neq i} q_i\right) < Z - C_M'\left\{\sum_{k \neq i}(Q_k - q_k) + Q_i\right\}, \qquad (30)$$

then $q_i = 0$.

Proof.   By (23),

$$\frac{\partial E(U_i)}{\partial s} = q_i(1 - v_i)\frac{\partial \bar{P}_s}{\partial s} - \tfrac{1}{2}R_i q_i^2(1 - v_i)^2\frac{\partial \sigma_s^2}{\partial s} \to 0, \qquad (31)$$

and, therefore, $\eta_i \to 0$ as $q_i \to 0$. Also, by (28),

$$E(U_i'P_s) \to \bar{P}_s \text{ as } q_i \to 0. \qquad (32)$$

Suppose, now that $q_i > 0$ but very small; then by (31) and (32) we get, from (27), $\lambda_{Bi} \to 1$. Also, by (21a) and (21b), $\mu_i = 0$. For that value of q_i, equation (29) then becomes

$$\frac{\partial \Psi_i}{\partial q_i} = \bar{P}_s - C_B' - (Z - C_M') < 0 \qquad (29')$$

by (30) and the continuity of $\partial \Psi_i/\partial q_i$ in q_i. But then, by (20b), we must have $q_i = 0$, which contradicts the assumption that $q_i > 0$, and we must have $q_i = 0$. If $\partial \Psi_i/\partial q_i < 0$ for a sufficiently small q_i, it must also hold for greater $q_i(q_i < Q_i)$, since the concavity of Ψ_i in q_i, which is required for maximum Ψ_i, implies that $\partial^2 \Psi_i/\partial q_i^2 < 0$. Q.E.D.

PROPOSITION 2.   If

$$\bar{P}_{s^*,i} - R_i(1 - v_i^*)Q_i\sigma_{s^*,i}^2 - C_B'\left(\sum_{k \neq i} q_k + Q_i\right) > Z - C_M'\left\{\sum_{k \neq i}(Q_k - q_k)\right\}, \qquad (33)$$

where v_i^* is the solution value of v_i at $q_i = Q_i$, then $q_i = Q_i$.

Proof.   We shall show that, under (33) and $q_i = Q_i$, conditions (18a)–(21b) are met. Since $q_i = Q_i$, (18a), (18b), (21a), and (21b) are clearly satisfied, while (19a) and (19b) are satisfied by the choice of v_i^*. By (27) and (28), we have

$$(\lambda_{Bi} - 1)\bar{P}_{s^*,i} = -R_i(1 - v_i^*)Q_i\sigma_{s^*,i}^2 + \eta_i \leq 0 \qquad (34)$$

so that by (11) $0 \leq \lambda_{Bi} \leq 1$. Hence, from (29),

$$\begin{aligned}\frac{\partial \Psi_i}{\partial q_i} + \mu_i &= \bar{P}_{s^*,i} - R_i(1 - v_i^*)Q_i\sigma_{s^*,i}^2 - \lambda_{Bi}C_B' - (Z - C_M') \\ &\geq \bar{P}_{s^*,i} - R_i(1 - v_i^*)Q_i\sigma_{s^*,i}^2 - C_B' - (Z - C_M') \qquad (35) \\ &> 0\end{aligned}$$

by (33). Condition (20a) and (20b) are, therefore, satisfied by choosing

$$\mu_i = \bar{P}_{s^*,i} - R_i(1 - v_i^*)Q_i\sigma_{s^*,i}^2 - \lambda_{Bi}C_B' - (Z - C_M') > 0,$$

which is feasible without violating any other condition. Q.E.D.

According to Proposition 1, a producer will sell his entire output to the miller if the expected highest price net of marginal costs that the broker can fetch in the market (given that this producer declines to use the broker's services) is smaller than the marginal net value of the product to the miller. According to Proposition 2, a producer will market his entire product through the broker if the net expected highest price that the broker can fetch (given that the producer markets his entire output through the broker) exceeds the net value of the output to the miller. Notice that the net broker's price is obtained by subtracting the marginal handling costs, C_B', and the 'marginal risk premium', $R_i(1 - v_i^*)Q_i\sigma_{s^*,i}^2$, from $\bar{P}_{s^*,i}$. Hence the more risk-averse is the producer, the less likely he is to market his entire crop through the broker. It also follows from Proposition 2 that, if any risk-averse producer (producer i, say) markets his entire output through the broker, then so do all risk-neutral producers ($R_i = 0$) whose outputs, Q_i, are not greater than Q_i.

Propositions 1 and 2 leave a certain range for mixed choices of marketing intermediaries. In general, one expects risk-neutral producers to prefer the broker, low and medium risk-averse producers to allocate output among both channels, and high risk-averse producers to prefer the miller.

Finally, it is worth noting that the increasing marginal cost assumption enhances the likelihood of intermediaries' coexistence.

5. The Case of Numerous Producers

How are the contractual parameters, and the associated distribution of gains, influenced by the number of producers, n? Evidently, changes in n are bound to affect the structure of bargaining power and thereby the contracts' terms. In order to facilitate the analysis, we shall adopt the simplifying assumption that all producers are identical in all respects; namely, they are all endowed with equal amounts of marketable product, and share the same attitude towards risk. Furthermore, since we are interested in the effects of variation in n, and not in output, we shall also assume that the total amount of output in the village economy is constant independently of n. Finally, it is assumed that both distribution channels are used by producers. In view of our increasing-costs assumption, this is rather natural. Symmetry considerations then suggest that, for all i, the following hold:

$$Q_i = Q; \quad q_i = Q^B/n; \quad Q_i - q_i = Q^M/n; \quad v_i = v; \quad P_i = P;$$

$$\sum_{k \neq i} q_k = Q^B\left(1 - \frac{1}{n}\right); \quad R_i = R; \quad \tilde{s}_i = \tilde{s}; \quad s_i^* = s^*;$$

and nQ = constant.

From equations (11), (23), and (26), we then get, for all i,

$$\lambda_{Bi} = \frac{(Q^B/n)\{(1 - v)\bar{P}_s - P\} - \frac{1}{2}R(Q^B/n)^2(1 - v)^2\sigma_s^2}{v(\bar{P}_s - \bar{P}_{\bar{s}})Q^B\left(\dfrac{n-1}{n}\right) + \bar{P}_s v(Q^B/n) - \xi(s - \bar{s}) - C_B'(Q^B/n)}$$

$$= \frac{(1 - v)\bar{P}_s - P - \frac{1}{2}R(Q^B/n)(1 - v)^2\sigma_s^2}{vQ^B\dfrac{\bar{P}_s - \bar{P}_{\bar{s}}}{Q^B/(n-1)} + v\bar{P}_s - \xi\dfrac{s - \bar{s}}{Q^B/n} - C_B'} \tag{36}$$

$$\rightarrow \frac{(1 - v)\bar{P}_s - P}{\left(vQ^B\dfrac{d\bar{P}_s}{ds} - \xi\right)\dfrac{ds}{dq} + v\bar{P}_s - C_B'}$$

as $n \rightarrow \infty$, since

$$\lim_{n \to \infty} \frac{\bar{P}_s - \bar{P}_{\bar{s}}}{Q^B/(n-1)} = \frac{d\bar{P}_s}{dq} = \frac{d\bar{P}_s}{ds}\frac{ds}{dq}.$$

By (5) we get from (36)

$$\lambda_{Bi} = \{(1 - v)\bar{P}_s - P)\}/(v\bar{P}_s - C_B'). \tag{37}$$

Since $Q^B/n \rightarrow 0$ as $n \rightarrow \infty$, we get, by the argument in the proof of Proposition 1, that $\lambda_{Bi} \rightarrow 1$ when $n \rightarrow \infty$. Also, from (25) it follows that

$$P = \frac{1}{2}\{Z - C_M' + (1 - v)\bar{P}_s\}. \tag{38}$$

Now, since $Q^M > $ and $Q^B > 0$, $\mu_i = 0$ by (21a) and (21b), and by (29) and (20b), therefore, we have

$$\frac{\partial \Psi_i}{\partial q} = \bar{P}_s - C_B' - Z + C_M' = 0 \tag{39}$$

as $n \rightarrow \infty$. Setting $\lambda_{Bi} = 1$ in (37) and using (38) and (39), we get

$$v = C_B'/\bar{P}_s \tag{40}$$

and

$$P = Z - C_M'. \tag{41}$$

The findings of this section are summarized in Proposition 3.

PROPOSITION 3. In the equilibrium set of marketing contracts with numerous identical producers, the expected absolute value of the broker's fee per unit product, $v\bar{P}_s$, is equal to his marginal handling cost, C_B'; and the price, P, paid to producers by the miller is equal to the value of the product at the mill site, Z, net of the miller's marginal handling cost, C_M'.

The marketing intermediaries' price–cost relationships when producers are identical and numerous are depicted in Figures 15.1 and 15.2. The curves

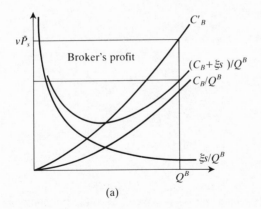

(a)

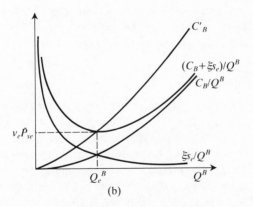

(b)

FIG. 15.1 The broker's fee–cost–profit relationship (numerous producers): (a) single broker; (b) free entry

$\xi s/Q^{B}$ and $\xi s_{e}/Q^{B}$ in Figure 15.1 were drawn using the equilibrium values of s and s_{e}, and the curves are therefore geometric hyperboles. Notice that, with numerous producers and restricted entry (Figures 15.1(a) and 15.2), the marketing intermediaries are able to appropriate the entire difference between the marginal and average cost of marketing as profits. However, under free intermediaries' entry their number will increase to the point where all profits vanish. Owing to the assumed cost structure, the number of miller's agents will tend to be indeterminately large. The number of brokers, on the other hand, will be finite. This is because brokers are engaged in an information-gathering activity, and consequently their cost function comprises a diminishing cost element (Figure 15.1(b)). Notice that under free

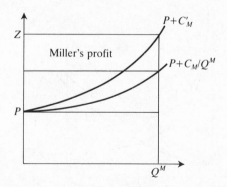

F$_{IG}$. 15.2   The miller's price–cost–profit relationship (numerous producers)

entry the amount sold by each broker, Q_e^B, and the brokerage fee per unit output, $v_e \bar{P}_{se}$, are smaller than under restricted entry. Consequently, the search effort of the individual broker, s_e, and thereby the expected price $\bar{P}_{se}$, are also smaller. It is, therefore, possible that producers will be better off with a single broker than under free entry of brokers.

6. A Numerical Illustration

In order to gain further insight into the determination of the equilibrium set of contracts and its response to environmental and structural changes, a numerical analysis of a particular marketing system was undertaken. The algorithm employed in deriving the equilibrium solutions was based on the Nash uncooperative game representation of the equilibrium set of contracts as derived by Zusman and Bell (1989: Theorem 1) and referred to in Section 3 above. The main steps in the algorithm are as follows. (a) Start with initial values of $\{\lambda_{Bi}\}$, $\{P_i\}$, $\{q_i\}$, and $\{v_i\}$. (b) For producer i, find the value of v_i by maximizing the Nash product $\Gamma_{Bi} = \{E(U_i) - t_{Bi}\}\{E(Y^B) - t_{Bi}^B\}$, given all other contracts, $\{\lambda_{Bi}\}$, q_i, the broker's discretionary behaviour, and the individual rationality constraints (10a)–(10d). Then maximize W_i with respect to q_i given the new value of v_i. (Recall that $\lambda_{Mi} = 1$.) All maximization procedures utilized the grid method. (c) Repeat the process for all producers until $\{q_i\}$ and $\{v_i\}$ converge (to $\{q_i^\alpha\}$ and $\{v_i^\alpha\}$, say). (d) Calculate a new set of $\{\lambda_{Bi}\}$ and $\{P_i\}$, using $\{q_i^\alpha\}$ and $\{v_i^\alpha\}$, and repeat steps (b), (c), and (d) until $\{\lambda_{Bi}\}$, $\{P_i\}$, $\{v_i^\alpha\}$, and $\{q_i^\alpha\}$ all converge to the desired equilibrium values. While no general convergence proof is provided, the algorithm actually converged when applied to the present model.

   The model employed in the analysis was the one developed in this chapter. The probability distribution function of market prices was assumed to be uniform on the interval $[a,b]$, so that P_s, the highest offered price in a sample of s prices observed by the broker, has the following density function:

$$g_s(P_s) = s\left(\frac{P_s - a}{b - a}\right)^{s-1} \Bigg/ (b - a),$$

which has the following mean and variance:

$$\bar{P}_s = (a + sb)/(s + 1) \tag{42}$$

$$\sigma_s^2 = s(b - a)^2/\{(s + 2)(s + 1)^2\}. \tag{43}$$

The broker's choice of s is then given by

$$s = \sqrt{\{(\Sigma q_i v_i)(b - a)/\xi\}} - 1. \tag{44}$$

The handling cost functions of the broker and miller, respectively, were $C_B = \alpha_1(Q^B)^{\alpha_2}$ and $C_M = \beta_1(Q^M)^{\beta_2}$. The producers' expected utility functions were those given in (23) and (24) above. The values of the environmental and structural parameters (a, b, ξ, Z, α_1, α_2, β_1, β_2, R_i, and Q_i) are given in Table 15.1, along with the assumed numbers of producers. The base case values of the parameters were selected so as to be consistent with data provided by Subbarao (1978). They do, however, involve a high degree of arbitrariness, and the results presented in the table should therefore be regarded as essentially illustrative.

Table 15.1 contains the equilibrium values of the contractual parameters (v_i, q_i, P_i), the broker's power coefficients (λ_{Bi}), and the parties' expected utilities. These values are calculated for varying numbers of producers and environmental and structural parameters ('experiments'). Unless otherwise indicated in the first column of the table, all 'experiments' are based on the base-case parameters.

In the first experiment the number of producers is varied, keeping total marketed output fixed. It is evident from the table that, as the number of producers increases, the broker's power, as reflected by λ_{Bi}, increases; the brokerage fee (v_i) increases; and the price paid by the miller to producers declines.[7] The expected income of the marketing intermediaries is accordingly increased. Notice that the sum of all parties' expected utilities also rises (last column of table) with the number of producers. This is due to the increased brokerage fee, which provides an incentive for a more intense search effort by the broker.

In the second experiment, output distribution among producers is unequal. It turns out that the big producers have a stronger market position and consequently enjoy a somewhat lower brokerage fee and a slightly higher miller's price (P_i).

In the third experiment, there exist two groups of producers with different attitudes toward risk. It is then found that in equilibrium the low-risk-averse producers ($R_i = 0.001$) pay a lower brokerage fee and receive a higher miller's price. They also market a larger portion of their output through the broker. The converse is found for the high-risk-averse producers.

In the fourth experiment the range of price variation is broadened from

TABLE 15.1 The effect of variation in environmental and structural parameters on the contractual parameters, broker's power coefficient, and agents' utility*

Environmental/structural parameter	v_i	q_i	P_i	λ_i	$E(U_i)$	$E(Y^B)$	Y^M	$\Sigma E(U_i) + E(Y^B) + Y^M$
1. Number of producers								
4	0.063	221.56	56.28	0.890	28 160	1248	2213	116 101
10	0.069	94.40	56,43	0.936	11 287	1552	2060	116 482
20	0.077	48.97	55.87	0.985	5 602	2015	2626	116 681
2. Distribution of output								
5 producers: $Q_i = 100$	0.072	92.91	56.12	0.968	5 629 ⎱	1675	2141	116 571
5 producers: $Q_i = 300$	0.070	96.85	56.39	0.959	16 922 ⎰			
3. Unequal risk aversion								
5 producers: $R_i = 0.001$	0.071	137.89	56.07	0.961	11 247 ⎱	1732	2647	116 484
5 producers: $R_i = 0.002$	0.075	50.14	55.79	0.959	11 174 ⎰			
4. Limits on the distribution of product price								
$44 \leq P \leq 66$	0.095	140.56	57.57	0.974	11 566	3689	1056	120 405
5. Unequal risk aversion and available output								
5 producers: $R_i = 0.001$, $Q_i = 100$	0.071	100.00	—	0.963	5 630 ⎱	2520	1665	116 425
5 producers: $R_i = 0.002$, $Q_i = 300$	0.071	81.95	56.00	0.964	16 818 ⎰			

*Base-case parameters: no. of producers = 10, $a = 47$, $b = 63$, $\xi = 20$, $Z = 61$, $\alpha_1 = \beta_1 = 0.01$, $\alpha_2 = \beta_2 = 1.8$, $R_i = 0.01$, v_i, $\Sigma Q_i = 2000$. Unless otherwise indicated, $Q_i = \Sigma Q_i / n$ v_i.

[47, 63] to [44, 66]. The mean of the price distribution remains unchanged. This leads to a significantly higher brokerage fee, and a much larger share of the output is marketed through the broker. Consequently, his expected income is more than doubled compared with the base case. A wider range of price variation thus enhances the role of the broker in the marketing system. It also increases the producers' expected utility, since the higher fee and increased marketing through the broker, along with the incentive provided by the increased range (see (44)), leads to an increased search effort on his part and to a higher expected price, $\bar{P}_s$. Notice that the increased range in itself contributes to higher $\bar{P}_s$ (see (42)). The miller's role and his expected income are accordingly diminished.

In the fifth experiment two groups of producers are again distinguished. The first group consists of low-risk-averse–small-output producers, while the second is made up of high-risk-averse–large-output producers. It is then found that the first group markets all its output through the broker, while the second group diversifies its marketing channels, as predicted by our theory.

While the results presented in Table 15.1 by no means constitutes a test of this theory, they nevertheless suggest that it might have captured the essential features of the equilibrium set of marketing contracts.

7. Efficiency Considerations

Is the equilibrium set of contracts Pareto-efficient? This problem in effect consists of two sub-problems, the first related to the efficiency of the individual contract, the second to the inter-contract relationship, that is to the effects of market organization on economic efficiency.

Let us begin with the individual contract. Notice first that, in itself, the contract between a producer and the miller is devoid of any efficiency effect, since its contractual parameters $(P_i, Q_i - q_i)$ do not affect behaviour and are, thus, pure income transfer instruments. The case of the producer–broker contract is, however, different since the contractual parameters (v_i, q_i) do influence the broker's search effort. Yet, being a Nash solution, this contract is Pareto-efficient subject to the constraints imposed by the admissable set of contracts. Accordingly, the search effort, s, is left at the broker's discretion, and brokerage fees are proportional to value of sale. However, if the cost of monitoring and enforcing s is sufficiently low, then a more efficient contract, in which s serves as a contractual parameters, could be devised. Under such circumstances, the present contract is only second-best, as the broker's search effort is suboptimal since he ignores its contribution to the producer's expected utility. Presumably, monitoring and enforcement costs are sufficiently high to justify the elimination of the search effort as a contractual parameter in real-world contracts. Also, given that s is not a contractual parameter, restricting brokerage fees to be proportional to sales links the risk-sharing effect, the incentive effect, and the income distribution effect of the contractual arrangements, thereby constraining severely the efficiency of the individual contract. Thus, contract simplicity induced by bounded rationality entails efficiency losses.

Considering, next, the inter-contractual efficiency effects, we notice that the broker's search resembles a public good, for all producers benefit from a greater s. However, only the marginal effects of v_i and q_i on $E(Y^B)$ and $E(U_i)$ alone are considered in any particular contract negotiations. The broker's search effort and the amount of output marketed through this distribution channel are therefore suboptimal. Under co-operative marketing such externalities are, presumably, internalized, and the associated inefficiencies removed.

8. Concluding Remarks

Marketing contracts emerge under the fairly common conditions of great uncertainty and information asymmetry. (For example, only intermediaries obtain first-hand information on buyers' offers.) Consequently, such contracts often feature risk-sharing and incentive provisions in addition to price-like terms of exchange. Various specialized marketing intermediaries offer different contractual arrangements, and, given producers' diversity, attract different producers' groups. Thin markets along with transactors' diversity tend to create market imperfections and idiosyncratic contracts, thus giving rise to bargaining relations, and the resulting equilibrium sets of contracts reflect the parties' market power. When the number of transactors increases, the cores of these games shrink, and the scope for bargaining diminishes. The theory illustrated in the present analysis views each contract as a bilateral bargaining game. It characterizes the equilibrium set of contracts and allows one to explore its properties: the contractual terms, the choice of distribution channels, the division of gains among transactors, and the economic efficiency of the marketing system.

The theory is applicable to a broad spectrum of market structures, and while analytic results may be difficult to derive in more complex instances, a numerical analysis based on the algorithmic approach demonstrated in this paper should, in general, be possible.

NOTES

1. See, e.g., Arrow (1986), Harris and Raviv (1979), and Shavell (1979).
2. According to Subbarao, village commission agents and millers' agents handled 92 per cent of the marketing at the village level (Subbarao 1978; 17).

3. Nash solution of a two-person (i and j) bargaining game is obtained by maximizing the product $\Gamma_{ij} = \{E(U^i) - t^i_{ij}\}\{E(U^j) - t^j_{ij}\}$ with respect to the contractual parameters taking into account the discretionary behaviour of the players. The expressions t^i_{ij} and t^j_{ij} are the highest payoffs that the players can guarantee themselves in the event that they fail to agree. Nash solutions satisfy certain highly plausible requirements, and represent constrained Pareto optima. See Nash (1953) and Harsanyi (1977).

4. Both marketing intermediaries will agree to market additional output at the current contractual terms; at least up to a point. This is because, for each intermediary, the marginal change in expected income from an incremental increase in the output marketed by him is non-negative. For if it were negative for some intermediary, the producer might offer him an acceptable reduction in the quantity marketed, which could benefit the producer. This is so even if the producer would have to dispose of this quantity at a zero price. Conditions 3 would then be violated. Hence, in equilibrium the marginal gain to each intermediary must be non-negative, and will usually be positive. However, the additional output that the intermediary is willing to market at the given contractual terms may be limited owing to the increasing marginal handling cost. In the following it is assumed that this limit is never reached, either because the 'measure' of each producer is small and/or because the cost function is not too convex. Since, according to Nash bargaining theory, the threats represented by the disagreement point are never executed, an alternative interpretation is that current contractual terms determine the parties' perceptions of the relevant disagreement point.

5. If $q_i^2 \sigma_s^2$ and $Q_i^2 \sigma_{s*,i}^2$ are sufficiently small, then for any $U_i(\cdot)$, (23) and (24) provide good approximations to $E(U_i)$ and $E[U_i\{Q_i(1 - v_i)P_{s*,i}\}]$, respectively. The second terms on the right of (23) and (24) are then the corresponding producer's risk premia, expressed in terms of a certain income (see Arrow 1971; 96).

6. It can be shown that, with suitable probability distribution functions of prices, P_i converges to a finite value as $q_i \to Q_i$.

7. The results in the second row are not exactly in line with the general trend — apparently owing to incomplete convergence of the algorithm.

PART V
Co-operatives, Technology, and the State

Chapter 16 addresses the issues of work incentives under agricultural producer co-operatives, decision on the membership size, and the process of voluntary choice of this institutional form by potential co-operators. In Chapter 17 the authors present an analysis of the motivation, formation, and design of credit co-operatives and show how their degree of success is likely to depend crucially on the particular incentive schemes, extent of control over resources, quality monitoring, and enforcement of punishment rules. In Chapter 18 the authors dwell upon the influence of the structure of asset ownership and of political lobbying for the nature of the public research budget on the rate and bias of technological change in agriculture.

16.

Agricultural Producer Co-operatives

Louis Putterman

1. Introduction

Agricultural producer co-operatives (APCs) are farm enterprises in which the labour of a group of farm households is pooled under an output or net-revenue-sharing arrangement. Land and other non-labour means of production may be held in common, or may be privately owned by the members who contribute it to the group enterprise in return for a share of output or revenue. In the co-operative proper, production has the characteristic of team production in the sense that the fraction of output attributable to the labour of any particular team member is undefined because output is a joint product of many hands. No employment relationship exists among the co-operators, and decision-making is in principle participatory or democratic, as opposed to hierarchical or authority-based. Aside from the co-operative farm itself, co-operative farm communities may have some lands allocated to production on a household or individual basis. The same communities may also support non-farm enterprises, typically also within a co-operative framework.

The most important institutions commonly analysed under the APC rubric are the collective farms of the Soviet Union and Eastern Europe, and similar institutions in Vietnam, North Korea, and the People's Republic of China. Whether these are producer co-operatives in the full sense of the term can be called into question on the grounds that they have been created and controlled by state and party machineries which left little latitude for internal decision-making, and which sometimes have employed coercion as an internal control device. None the less, it is largely with reference to these cases that economists have developed the theory of APCs. Examples of APCs established on a voluntary basis or as the result of agrarian reforms in non-centrally planned economies are numerous but usually are of minor

Support from National Science Foundation Grant no. SES–8520380 is gratefully acknowledged. The author wishes to thank Hans Binswanger for comments on an earlier draft, and John Bonin and Justin Lin for helpful comments on related material.

importance in the overall rural economies of the countries in question. The theory of APCs may be viewed as a tool for understanding the economic behaviour of collective farms and other co-operative and group farms and the problems facing the establishment of co-operative farms in the context of less controlled peasant agricultures. It will be noted, however, that this body of theory has no direct relevance to marketing and input supply co-operatives whose members do not engage in agricultural production as such on a joint basis.

Theoretical analysis of agricultural producer co-operatives has been developed largely as a branch of the theory of labour-managed firms (LMFs) initiated by Benjamin Ward (1958). However, whereas LMF theory has been especially concerned with questions of inter-firm and inter-industry resource allocation and responsiveness to price signals, assuming a mobile labour force and decentralized price formation, APC theory has focused more on the internal effectiveness of group farms in eliciting effort from a given labour force, and in the effects of state pricing policies. Assumption of a fixed labour force and of administered prices follows institutional realities in the Soviet-type economies. The focus on incentives is of quite general applicability to the performance problems of APCs and to the reasons for the relative rarity of the form in countries in which its adopton is not officially mandated.

2. Labour Incentives with Given Price, Membership, and Resources

Assume a technology which maps inputs of homogeneous labour and of non-labour inputs into units of a homogeneous farm product,

$$g = g(L, A, V, K, \theta) \tag{1}$$

where g is output in physical units; L is the sum of labour units ℓ^i contributed by various workers indexed by i; A, V, and K are land, variable inputs, and capital; and θ represents the state of nature. Now, suppressing the non-labour inputs and ignoring state uncertainty, write net value product

$$Q = p\{g(L)\} - C = Q(L) \tag{2}$$

where p is product price and C is the sum of non-labour costs, both of which are fixed in the short run.[1] Note that, if some of the non-labour inputs are contributed by the members in return for compensation, the latter is subsumed within C. The remainder Q is distributed to the members $i = 1, 2, \ldots,$ n who receive shares s^i such that

$$\sum_{i=1}^{n} s^i Q = Q. \tag{3}$$

$s^i Q$, which we shall hereafter denote by y^i, will be thought of as i's income from co-operative labour since, although it may not be tied specifically to the level of i's labour contribution, its payment depends on i's status as a working member of the co-operative.

Beginning with Sen (1966), shares s^i have been assumed in most formal analyses either to be equal,

$$s^i = \frac{1}{N}, \tag{4a}$$

to be proportionate to labour input,

$$s^i = \frac{\ell^i}{L}, \tag{4b}$$

or to be an average of (4a) and (4b) with weight $\alpha \in (0,1)$; that is

$$s^i = \frac{\alpha}{N} + (1 - \alpha)\frac{\ell^i}{L} = A^i. \tag{4c}$$

Shares (4a) correspond to the principle, 'to each according to his needs' assuming equal 'needs'; shares (4b) to the principle, 'to each according to his work'; and (4c) may be dubbed a mixed distribution system. In (4b) and (4c), ℓ^i are assumed to be known or measured perfectly.

The incentive implications of the choice of (4a) or (4b), or, more generally, of the weight α in (4c), are found to depend upon the nature of interactions between labour inputs ℓ^i, ℓ^j, etc., or of the members' conjectures regarding these, and on where resources, technology, and members' preferences place the co-operative on the curves relating marginal and net average products of labour. In particular, assume that, with given inputs of the non-labour factors, the marginal product of labour is first increasing, then declining, passing through the average net product curve Q/L at its maximum, as illustrated by Figure 16.1. Now, differentiating member i's return $y^i = s^i Q$ with respect to ℓ^i, assuming the general form (4c), we have

$$\frac{\partial}{\partial \ell^i}\left[\left\{\frac{\alpha}{N} + (1 - \alpha)\frac{\ell^i}{L^i}\right\}Q\right] = A^i Q_L \frac{\partial L}{\partial \ell^i} + (1 - \alpha)\left(1 - \frac{\ell^i}{L}\frac{\partial L}{\partial \ell^i}\right)\frac{Q}{L} \tag{5}$$

as the marginal return to labour (where A^i stands for s^i of (4c)). (5) appears in Figure 16.1 as a family of dashed lines labelled $\partial y^i/\partial \ell^i$, which, assuming $0 < \partial L/\partial \ell^i < L/\ell^i$,[2] are a weighted average of the curves Q_L and Q/L when $\alpha = 0$, a scalar multiple of the Q_L curve, with the latter curve deflated by $N/(\partial L/\partial \ell^i)$, when $\alpha = 1$, and a weighted average of the first two curves when $0 < \alpha < 1$.

Consider, first, the case of strict distribution according to work ($\alpha = 0$). In this case, (5) may be rewritten as

$$\frac{\partial y^i}{\partial \ell^i} = \eta^i Q_L + (1 - \eta^i)\frac{Q}{L} \tag{5a}$$

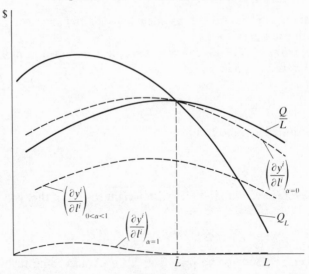

FIG. 16.1   Marginal product, average net product, and marginal return to labour for varying values of aggregate labour input and of the degree of 'distribution according to needs'

where $\eta^i = (\ell^i/L)(\partial L/\partial \ell^i)$ is the elasticity of aggregate labour supply with respect to the supply of labour to the co-operative by member i. For all $0 < \eta^i < 1$, (5a) is a weighted average of the marginal product of labour, Q_L, and the average (net) product, Q/L, and thus lies above the latter curve to the left of $\tilde{L}$ where $Q_L = Q/L$ and below it to the right of $\tilde{L}$, as illustrated by the dashed curve labelled $(\partial y^i/\partial \ell^i)_{\alpha=0}$ in the figure. The rational utility-maximizing member will set his marginal rate of substitution (MRS) between leisure and income equal to $\partial y^i/\partial \ell^i$, but Pareto optimality requires that he choose ℓ^i at which his MRS equals the marginal product of labour, Q_L. Therefore, work incentives are excessive if perceived aggregated labour input exceeds $\tilde{L}$ and inadequate if perceived aggregated labour input is less than $\tilde{L}$. Unless the perceived aggregate labour input is $\tilde{L}$ itself, the individual's private marginal return to labour fully coincides with his marginal labour product $(\partial y^i/\partial \ell^i = Q_L)$ only if the marginal effect of his labour supply on aggregate labour is equal to the inverse of his labour share $(\partial L/\partial \ell^i = L/\ell^i)$.[3]

At the opposite extreme, let distribution be strictly according to needs ($\alpha = 1$). Then (5) can be written as

$$\frac{\partial y^i}{\partial \ell^i} = \frac{1}{N} Q_L \frac{\partial L}{\partial \ell^i}, \tag{5b}$$

and, assuming that the reaction $\partial L/\partial \ell^i$ is less than N but greater than zero, $\partial y^i/\partial \ell^i$ appears as a scalar multiple of the marginal product curve, as illustrated by the dashed curve labelled $(\partial y^i/\partial \ell^i)_{\alpha-1}$ in the figure (which is drawn assuming that $\partial L/\partial \ell^i$ is in the neighbourhood of 1, its Cournot–Nash value). In this case, setting MRS equal to the marginal private return to labour produces a suboptimal labour input regardless of perceived L unless $\partial L/\partial \ell^i \geqslant N$, since the right-hand side of (5b) is less than Q_L for all $0 < \partial L/\partial \ell^i < N$.

Since the value of L relative to $\tilde{L}$ will depend on the relationship between the co-operative's resources and its labour force, absent information on this relationship, it may be said that distributing all of the co-operative's net revenue according to labour contributions could as easily generate excessive as suboptimal work incentives. For example, if the correctly anticipated L lies substantially to the right of $\tilde{L}$, $\partial y^i/\partial \ell^i > Q_L$ when $\alpha = 0$. However, it is clear that for identical members, whose equilibrium ℓ must be equal, there will exist an α such that $\partial y^i/\partial \ell^i = Q_L$ for all i; labelling that value α^*, it can be defined by

$$\alpha^* = 1 - \frac{Q_L}{Q/L} \tag{6}$$

(Sen 1966). α^* is the proportion of distribution according to needs, or simple sharing, that would be selected by a planner or co-operative leader whose objective is to maximize the utility of the members, or by the members themselves through majority voting (see below). If members differ in their preferences regarding leisure and income, equilibrium values ℓ^i and ℓ^j may differ. The value α^* given by (6) will then make $\partial y^i/\partial \ell^i = Q_L$ for the member contributing the average labour input $\ell^{av} = L/N$, and will leave $\partial y^i/\partial \ell^i \gtreqless Q_L$ for others, although the magnitude of the divergences may be small. Browning (1982) shows that it may be impossible to find a set of individualized 'needs' payments capable of making $\partial y^i/\partial \ell^i = Q_L$ for all i while also assuring a balanced budget.[4]

If perceived $L < \tilde{L}$, (6) implies that $\alpha^* < 0$, which means that incentive optimality can be achieved by assessing taxes unrelated to labour input so that more than the value of the average net product can be paid out per contributed labour unit.[5] The intuitive interpretation of both the $L > \tilde{L}$ and $L < \tilde{L}$ results is that, under Cournot–Nash and similar values of conjectures $\partial L/\partial \ell^i$, marginal payout is approximately equal to average net product, which is the value of the labour-day or other labour unit. Since this labour unit value can either exceed or fall short of labour's value of marginal product (VMP), it is necessary to depart from pure 'distribution according to work' by distributing some of the revenue without regard to labour input when L is large or by assessing taxes unrelated to labour input when L is small.

Co-operative managers or leaders aiming to maximize returns per labour unit would try to find a membership size N at which equilibrium $L = \tilde{L}$, as a by-product of which this problem would not arise. But N is not even a medium-term choice variable in collectivized agricultures, wherein each rural dweller is attached to a local co-operative. Where population is large relative to resources, as for example in most parts of China, unless alternative employments are found, it will be impossible to move APCs back towards $\bar{L}$ without causing unemployment in the economy as a whole. The 'super-optimal' incentives under 'distribution according to work' are a 'tragedy of the commons', wherein members seek to earn additional work-points bearing average net product returns although their incremental contributions to output are low. By distributing some revenue 'according to needs', the co-operative can simultaneously increase equality of income distribution, achieve optimal work incentives, and permit full employment in a rural sector that may be overpopulated in the sense (Georgescu-Roegen 1960) that marginal product is below subsistence wages (under which circumstances commercial farms facing a subsistence minimum wage would not offer employment to the full available labour force). On the other hand, political leaders who are concerned more with farm deliveries than with farmers' welfare, or who do not view the peasants' leisure as a good, could in principle use the excessive incentives of the system of strict distribution according to work to extract maximum labour from co-operative members (Israelsen 1980).

The theoretical conclusion of excess incentives in APCs under plausible resource and technological conditions is difficult to reconcile with the conventional wisdom that co-operatives suffer from a problem of *weak* work incentives. Since the most promising approach to solving this dilemma — the introduction of imperfect information — lies beyond the rubric of all but the most recent literature, we will turn before further discussion to a brief examination of responses to price and tax changes analysed within the framework already developed.

3. Responses to Price and Tax Changes

In the model of the LMF with short-run variable labour and a profit-per-worker maximand, an increase in product price ordinarily induces a reduction in labour force and, in the one-product firm, in output offered to the market. An increase in the fixed charge for capital, or in a lump-sum tax on the LMF, produces an increase in labour force and output. The same would apply to a one-product APC maximizing net revenue per worker and able to obtain the desired number of members in a labour market. However, the analyses of Domar (1966) and of Oi and Clayton (1968), which maintain the basic Ward framework, diverge from the perverse price response result: Domar shows that such an APC constrained by an upward-sloping labour supply curve intersecting its Q/L curve to the left of its maximum (at $\bar{L}$) would increase output and membership as p rose, allowing it to attract more workers or labour-hours; and Oi and Clayton show that a similarly modelled APC with a private plot sector would reduce membership but simultaneously transfer labour from the private to the collective sector as the price on that sector's output rose, so that collective output might either rise or fall.

If, as in the discussion of the previous section, membership is taken as given and labour supply is freely chosen by these members, the impact of a change in product price depends on those characteristics of the utility function that govern the slope of the individual labour supply curve in conventional analysis. By inspection, (5) is strictly increasing in p (recalling (2)), so ℓ^{i*} will rise for a small increase in p when the conventional individual labour supply curve is upward-sloping in hourly wages. For example, when income and leisure are separable arguments and utility is linear in income, an increase in p raises (5) without affecting MRS, so increasing ℓ^i is necessary to restore equilibrium, meaning that $\partial \ell^{i*}/\partial p$ and $\partial g/\partial p$ are positive (Putterman 1980). On the other hand, assuming that $U^i(y^i, \ell^i)$ has $U^i_{yy} < 0$, $U^i_{\ell y} \geqslant 0$, and relative risk aversion $- U^i_{yy} y^i / U^i_y = 1$, Israelsen (1980) finds that $\partial \ell^{i*}/\partial p$ and $\partial g/\partial p$ are negative or zero in the range of declining average net product. This shows that income effects can in principle offset the direct incentive impact of a price increase.

Suppose, next, that the co-operative pays a fixed tax based on its cultivable acreage or some other non-variable parameter. As a fixed cost, a change in the level of such a tax would not affect the short-run production decision of a conventional firm, but it affects (5) through its influence on Q (provided that $\alpha < 1$ and $\partial L/\partial \ell^i < L/\ell^i$). While the *existence* of this influence parallels that of the influence of fixed costs in the LMF, the direction of its effect is reversed in the present case if conventional individual labour supply curves are upward-sloping. By reducing (5), a rise in the fixed cost reduces ℓ^{i*} and g unless countervailing income effects dominate (compare, again, Putterman 1980, and Israelsen 1980).

A final topic to be treated under price responses is the effect of output quotas and of two-tier pricing. APCs in socialist countries have often faced quotas of crops that must be delivered to state channels at one price, with options to sell additional amounts (also to the state, in many cases) at higher prices. The essential result here was obtained by Oi and Clayton (1968), who in their variable membership model showed that the incentive effects of the quota and price differential are equivalent to those of the lump-sum tax equal to the added revenue that would have been obtained had all output been sold at the above-quota price. In the Oi–Clayton model, membership is varied to maximize income per member, and each member automatically receives a private plot of given size, so that adding members reduces the size of the collective plot when the co-operative has a fixed total amount of land. If incentives are sufficient to generate over-fulfilment of the quota, then the state can draw more work and output from the collective labour force for less remuneration by implementing a high price differential. The reason is that higher rents or lump-sum taxes lead to a larger optimal membership, since members benefit from sharing the burden more broadly, while, with the above-quota price for collective crops determining the income-maximizing mix of collective and private labour and output, higher above-quota prices will lead the now larger work-force to be allocated more intensively towards collective production. The countervailing decline in the amount of land used in collective production could reverse the final outcome, however.

In the fixed-membership, individual utility-maximizing models, we have seen that higher rents *per se* will increase labour supply only when there are strong income effects, while higher marginal prices for collective output increase the supply of collective labour when substitution effects prevail. However, it is possible to engineer a simultaneous increase in above-quota price and reduction in quota price of such a magnitude that at the original ℓ^{i*} the marginal return to labour, (5), is increased even though income declines, which reduces the MRS if $U^i_{yy} < 0$. To restore equality between the MRS and (5), an upward adjustment of collective labour is required. The combined effect of more work for less income thus remains possible in the model with fixed membership and individual labour supply decisions.

The analysis is further complicated if forthcoming labour would not allow the output quota, which could have the force of law, to be met without an additional quota on labour itself. A binding labour quota would eliminate labour supply choice in a one-sector APC while it would change the allocation problem in a two-sector APC to one in which the leisure–private labour balance is optimized subject to meeting the required collective labour input. It must be noted, however, that with above-quota prices higher than those for below-quota output, and with a resulting discontinuity in the schedule of marginal returns to collective labour, it is conceivable that, once quota output is reached by means of a required labour minimum, marginal incentives will suffice to induce voluntary above-quota labour, producing a distinct above-quota equilibrium with optimization of all elements of time allocation.[6] That is, while there may be an unconstrained equilibrium at which the quota would not be met, once the quota is assumed to have been met by legal requirement there can exist a 'second-best' equilibrium (from the workers' standpoint) in which the quota is exceeded by additional labour flowing into the sector to meet the conditions of utility maximization with respect to the higher above-quota price.

4. Imperfect Monitoring and Uncertainty

The analysis of work incentives in Section 2 provided the result that, since marginal returns to labour would tend to reflect net average more than marginal product of labour, incentives would be excessive when aggregate labour supply was expected to lead to marginal below-net-average product. This result is perplexing in view of the frequent observation that APCs suffer from weak work incentives.

One possible explanation lies in the fact that the models assume that the co-operative member, in selecting his labour input, knows with certainty the production function, the labour inputs of others, and the distribution rule; that there are no exogenous, stochastic factors affecting output; and that the member's labour input is accurately measured in homogeneous efficiency units. If any of these assumptions do not hold, effort must be rendered under conditions of uncertainty regarding its returns. Uncertainty regarding other members' labour and the distribution rule, added to production uncertainty which affects both group and household-level farm labour, would make co-operative production relatively less attractive to risk-averse farmers. However, in planned economies, where co-operative output is sold to the state at fixed prices while private output is sold in free markets at variable prices, price uncertainty could have an offsetting effect in favour of co-operative production (Bonin 1977).

Imperfect information by the co-operative regarding individual members' labour contributions merits special consideration as a source of incentive failure. In the worst case, L can be inferred from output but the individual ℓ^i cannot, forcing the co-operative to pay all workers equally or to otherwise arbitrarily divide net income without respect to actual labour contributions. This case is equivalent to pure 'needs' distribution (4a), and also to what Holmström (1982), who proves that it will not support a first-best effort equilibrium, labels 'simple sharing'. ('Needs' distribution with observability and mutual supervision of labour may be viable but is left to the next section.) An analysis of Nash equilibrium effort allocation in an APC under this depiction of imperfect information, giving explicit consideration of the interdependence of individual workers' decisions through the effect of aggregate L, is provided by Carter (1987).

Somewhat more ambiguity attaches to the modelling of intermediate situations in which information on ℓ^i is potentially obtainable, but at positive cost. One possible approach, paralleling the literature on supervision in conventional firms (Calvo and Wellisz 1978; Shapiro and Stiglitz 1984; Bowles 1985), is to assume that the worker is observed in a given period with probability $0 < \rho < 1$, where ρ increases with supervision or monitoring. When observed, the co-operative knows ℓ^i and can pay the worker by (4b);[7] when not observed, the worker is paid his per capita share of the remaining net output.[8] His expected income is

$$E(y^i) = \rho \frac{\ell^i}{L} Q + (1 - \rho) \frac{1}{N} Q \qquad (7)$$

if the probability of being monitored is uncorrelated with ℓ^i. Clearly, ρ in (7) functions precisely like $(1 - \alpha)$ in (4c). As a result, a worker's effort will in general decline as monitoring and ρ decline, with the limiting case of $\rho = 0$ being the no-information case already discussed. In view of the problems discussed earlier, if monitoring were obtainable in continuously variable quantities at low but positive cost, the efficient co-operative might want to use enough units of monitoring to cause $(1 - \rho)$ to assume the value of α^* in (6), but never more than this; in other words, imperfect monitoring could be a functional substitute for 'needs distribution'. If monitoring is quite costly, however, values of ρ lower than $(1 - \alpha^*)$ might be optimal, adversely affecting the viability of the APC compared with independent peasant production (see Section 6).

That imperfect knowledge of effective labour input is not alone sufficient to render incentives inadequate is demonstrated by Putterman (1986a), Bonin and Putterman (1987a), and Putterman and Skillman (1988). Suppose that

$$\hat{\ell}^i = \ell^i + k\epsilon \tag{8}$$

where ϵ is a stochastic term, $\mu(\epsilon) = 0$, $\sigma_\epsilon^2 > 0$, and k is a shift factor varying inversely with the level of monitoring. If we substitute $\hat{\ell}^i$ for ℓ^i in (4c), it is clear that the risk-neutral worker is indifferent to, and will not adjust his effort in response to, changes in the level of monitoring. Risk-averse workers will be influenced by changes in k, which change the variance of $\hat{\ell}^i$, but the conjecture that their equilibrium effort will increase as the accuracy of measurement rises ($k\downarrow$) is not in general correct; for example, for the entire class of utility functions characterized by non-increasing absolute risk aversion, as well as for the increasing absolute risk aversion case of utility-quadratic in income ($U^i = ay^i - b(y^i)^2 - u(\ell^i), a > 0, b > 0, a - 2by^i > 0$), workers may work more the more accurate $\hat{\ell}^i$ is measured if $L < \tilde{L}$, but will work less the more accurate $\hat{\ell}^i$ is if $L > \tilde{L}$. On the other hand, reasonable conditions support positive effort responses to monitoring when $\hat{\ell}^i$ is multiplicative rather than additive in the error term (Putterman and Skillman 1988) for values of L on both sides of $\tilde{L}$.

A final possibility which has been explored is to assume that the worker-member is paid according to a proxy for effort, call it work-points, and to characterize the functional relationship between that proxy, true effort, and the level of monitoring in a manner than is both intuitively plausible and potentially consistent with the idea that poor monitoring is associated with low work effort. An example is provided by Lin (1986), who posits that

$$\frac{\partial \hat{\ell}^i}{\partial \ell^i} \geqslant 0 \tag{9a}$$

$$\frac{\partial \hat{\ell}^i}{\partial \theta} \leqslant 0 \tag{9b}$$

$$\frac{\partial^2 \hat{\ell}^i}{\partial \theta \partial \ell^i} > 0 \tag{9c}$$

where $\hat{\ell}^i$ is the effort proxy and θ is the level of monitoring, and where (9a) holds with equality for $\theta = 0$. These assumptions suffice to guarantee that $\partial \ell^{i*}/\partial \theta > 0$ provided that workers share a common utility function so that $\ell^i = \ell = L/N$, all i. When the latter assumption is abandoned, $\partial \ell^{i*}/\partial \theta$ cannot be signed in the absence of further restrictions. Moreover, the signing of $\partial \ell^{i*}/\partial \theta$ in the identical-workers case also depends on the assumed non-stochastic nature of the $\hat{\ell}$ function ($\hat{\ell}^i = \hat{\ell}^j$ whenever $\ell^i = \ell^j$); but if each $\hat{\ell}$ is a non-stochastic function of an unobserved ℓ and a collective choice variable, θ, it may be wondered why the co-operative is unable to invert the function to discover ℓ.

5. Incentives in Pure Communes

An APC practising pure 'needs' distribution (4a) has been referred to by Israelsen (1980) and elsewhere as a 'pure commune'. One of the difficulties confronting the theory thus far presented is that, whereas the theory suggests that work incentives should be grossly suboptimal in the commune but potentially optimal in the APC using some distribution according to work, reality is stubbornly resistant to these predictions, if most observers' views of Soviet and Chinese collective farms on the one hand, and of Israeli *kibbutzim* and Hutterite communes on the other, are accurate.[9] While the former practise(d) either all work or mixed work and 'needs' distribution, the latter practise 'needs' distribution only, yet are widely perceived to elicit high levels of effort from their members. Of course, under certain conditions poor monitoring may go some way towards effectively converting the collective farms into communes, in our sense, as suggested in the last section. Such factors as the voluntary nature of the communal APCs and forced character of the collective farms, as well as the external environment of administered crop planning and confiscatory procurement pricing that the latter faced, may also be relevant to explaining collective farm difficulties. On the side of the communal APCs, the efficacy of 'non-material' motivations in a self-selected population are also often suggested. Still, we need not abandon altogether the attempt to relate communal work incentives to some variant of the conventional utility calculus.

Amartya Sen has proposed three modifications of conventional preference structure that could explain sufficiency of work incentives in pure communes. First, Sen (1966) shows that, if commune members place as much weight on others' utility as on their own, on average, then 'distribution according to needs' has incentive effects equivalent to those resulting from distribution to each worker of his or her marginal product. Second, Sen (1977) argues that people as moral beings may have preferences (or 'meta-preferences') over possible preference structures, including those based upon strict self-interest and those involving a high degree of social consciousness. Choice of the latter as a preferred preference may imply co-operative behaviour in spite of self-interest. Third, Sen (1967) shows that, with a somewhat less drastic modification of the utility function, situations that present themselves to the egoist as prisoners' dilemmas may be transformed into 'assurance games'. While agents in the latter may wish to avoid being 'suckered' by co-operating while others cheat, they prefer not to cheat when others are co-operating. Such agents need only be assured that others are doing their part before settling on co-operative behaviour for themselves. In the commune as assurance game, expectations of co-operative behaviour are thus self-fulfilling, and an equilibrium of 'from each according to his ability' becomes possible.

Even these modifications may be unnecessary, according to an argument by Putterman (1983). As has been seen earlier, inadequacy of incentives in communes is based partly on the assumption that members view their work inputs as independent of one another. This is an unrealistic supposition in so far as the work behaviour (effort supply) of each individual has some influence on the effort equilibrium or 'convention' that prevails. If one's effort choices are made in strategic consideration of their impact on others' choices, and if individuals can bind themselves to reacting in predictable ways to changes in the behaviours of other agents, then pure self-interest may sustain an equilibrium of high incentives in the commune, because it is rational to commit oneself to a positive 'matching' or tit-for-tat strategy. An alternative formal approach having the same practical import is to show that the prisoners' dilemma of the pure commune can be solved by precommitment to strategies of withdrawal from Pareto-optimal effort levels in future periods if any member fails to provide such effort in the present. The result is formally identical to the oligopoly solution of Friedman (1977).[10]

An approach based on strategically selected, precommitted reactions to fellow-workers' effort levels, developed by Guttman (1978b), has the distinction of correctly predicting the '*kibbutz–kolkhoz* paradox' without varying the behavioural assumptions or utility functions across institutions. In this model, contributors to a public good (in this case, communal work) first reach Nash equilibrium in reaction rates, then make 'flat' contributions, and finally 'match' one another's contributions at the preselected rates. That the model predicts an optimal effort equilibrium in a commune when effort is observable comes as no surprise, since the same result holds for pure public goods (for example, in Guttman 1987). What is remarkable is that the same model shows 'matching behaviour' to turn the excessive effort equilibrium of the hypothetical collective in which $L > \tilde{L}$ into a suboptimal effort equilibrium, because workers' competition to increase their shares ℓ^i/L by 'matching' turns out to discourage one another's 'flat' contributions (Guttman and Schnytzer 1987).

Unfortunately, the Guttman–Schnytzer result for the *kolkhoz* suffers from the same implausibility as does the standard perfect-information model of the collective farm, namely, that in both frameworks the effort equilibrium of the *kolkhoz* could be rendered optimal by raising the amount of non-work-based (i.e. 'needs') distribution to satisfy (6). It would certainly strike most observers as odd to suggest that the problem of the *kolkhoz* is too much, rather than too little, individual material incentive. This observation tends to return us to imperfect information considerations, whereas it will be noted that the informational requirements of 'matching behaviour' appear if anything more stringent than those of the standard model. However, if strategic interaction is rejected for the *kolkhoz*, how can its use be maintained with regard to the *kibbutz*? A satisfactory answer awaits further work on imperfect information versions of both standard and strategic reaction models.

One may note, at least on intuitive grounds, that purely communal incentives are unlikely to be effective unless the income-sharing groups are small enough to have face-to-face contact and to establish trust relations, and unless they have the commitment to make the incentive system work either for ideological reasons or for a systemically or authoritatively imposed lack of alternatives. Thus, the 'free supply' system of the huge Chinese people's communes of 1959 was ineffective, and widespread distribution of large fractions of team incomes on a physical ration basis between the mid-1960s and the late 1970s in that country can be assumed to have had a strong incentive-dampening effect. On the other hand, 'distribution according to work' itself can be effective only when the co-operative has the monitoring abilities — and the trust in those charged with the task — to implement a discriminating reward system that will not be perceived as arbitrary. This last point suggests the possibility of situations in which adoption of an equal sharing system by mutual agreement, supported by group policing of work obligations, is superior to work rewards that would generate dissension and the breakdown of mutual monitoring and co-operation.

6. Institutional Choice

An important question arising in connection with the study of the APC organizational form is, Under what circumstances will the form be observed, and when, if ever, will it be chosen voluntarily by potential co-operators? Socialist theoreticians Freidrich Engels and V.I. Lenin both asserted that knowledge of the benefits of co-operation would be sufficient to persuade peasant cultivators to join co-operatives; but while official pronouncements held that the vast majority of peasants joined the Soviet and, later, the Chinese APCs voluntarily, few outside observers accept this claim. Moreover, the APC form, while found in many countries, is a marginal phenomenon where not mandated by state and party authority.[11] The Tanzanian leadership, which promoted APCs beginning in 1967, achieved little progress in fostering joint production without coercion (Putterman 1986b). In Peru, where APCs were created from ex-haciendas by a reformist government in 1969, widespread parcellation had occurred by the mid-1980s (Carter 1987).

A simple attempt to examine the question of institutional choice of the APC form was made by Putterman (1980, 1981) and was further analysed by use of numerical examples in Putterman and DiGiorgio (1985) and

Putterman (1987). The authors assume a village entity that holds cultivable land in common and determines by majority rule what fraction of this land should be farmed jointly, with the remainder being equally divided among the households (assumed to have identical labour forces but varying preferences over income and leisure). If any production takes place at the village level, distribution of net revenue follows (4c), with the proportion of 'needs' distribution (α) also determined by voting.[12] For given voting choice over land allocation and distribution rule, households individually decide on time allocation between collective work, household plot work, and leisure, with labour time assumed identical to efficiency labour, labour perfectly measurable, and the standard optimization methods applying.

When land is allocated to both sectors, interior time allocation equilibria require that (5) equals both the marginal product of labour in the household plot and the marginal rate of substitution between leisure and income. Voting over the distribution rule leads to choice of α^* as given by (6) with some divergence if the median labour input, corresponding to the median voter, differs from L/N.[13] Optimal α^* tends to be chosen because members consider the effect of a change in the distribution rule on aggregate labour input. When α is too high, lowering it can attract additional labour units that still receive less than their marginal value product, meaning a gain to the other members; when α is too low, raising it helps to deter incremental labour units that earn more than their marginal product and thereby reduce the earnings of other members. Divergence of the median voter's ℓ^i from L/N creates a disturbing interest in the more direct effect of α on that voter's income, since raising (lowering) α raises the income of a member who works less (more) than the average in the joint production sector.

As for choice of land allocation, the $\ell^{\mathrm{median}} = L/N$ condition generating $\alpha = \alpha^*$ also leads land to be divided between sectors in such a manner that the marginal product of land in the household plot of the household of median industriousness equals the marginal product of land in joint production. If one of these marginal products exceeds the other for any possible intersectoral allocation, land would be allocated either wholly to joint or entirely to household-level production. Divergence of α from optimality is associated with a similar divergence of land allocation from such quasi- or 'median' optimality because it is then desirable to use land allocation on the margin to discourage or encourage joint labour, which either increases or decreases the voter's earnings from the co-operative sector. Under the institutional structure posited, which was modelled after the Tanzanian villages of the 1970s, the analysis suggests that a collective production sector would exist if it enjoyed a scale economy advantage over some size range, and that the adopted rule for distributing co-operatively generated income would create relatively efficient incentives.[14] The allocation of land would also be efficient except for the inequality of marginal products across household plots owing to the combination of the equal plot size rule and heterogeneous labour time

decisions (from assumed variation of 'industriousness'). The latter inefficiency could presumably be corrected by charging the members a market-
clearing land rental and permitting choice of plot size for given intersectoral
land allocation, or even allowing the APC to compete for land with the
household sector in the same internal land market.

A number of adaptations are necessary to apply this model more generally.
Putterman (1986b) considers collective choice of APC labour requirements
and penalties for non-fulfilment, as well as the consequences for land allocation of initially unequal land endowments and of voting choice over the pro-
gressivity of land levies for the APC sector. Bonin and Putterman (1987a)
show that voting over the level of costly monitoring in the probabilistic
information setting of equation (7) produces an outcome identical to centralized, welfare-maximizing choice of the monitoring level provided that
median $\ell^i = L/N$. Suppose, now, that land is initially the private property of
the potential APC members. Then something like the model just described
could still hold if the APC, which would be viable if it had some scale advantages, paid the contributing members rents equal to the land's opportunity
cost. Something like this occurred in the 'elementary producers' co-
operatives' of rural China circa 1954–5, which were joined voluntarily by
about 14 per cent of China's peasants (see Shue 1980; Selden 1982). It is clear,
however, that land would not be voluntarily pooled *without* compensation or
rent payments, absent a withering of self-interest; hence it comes as no
surprise that the transition to 'advanced producers' co-operatives' in China,
which distributed returns to labour only, required some coercion.

The model discussed in this section applies without modification to cases
of *de-collectivization*, in which former APCs are converted to household
farms. This could occur either because of a change in the returns to joint
versus household production owing to technology or price shifts, or because
administratively created APCs, which lack an economic rationale from their
members' standpoints, are given the choice of disbanding. Carter (1987),
writing with reference to parcellation of Peruvian reform-sector APCs in the
1980s, but considering also the contemporaneous Chinese shift to the household production responsibility system, analyses incentive failure in an APC
assuming complete unobservability of individual effort provision. He shows
that, even under individualized production, partial income-sharing may give
higher expected utility to former co-operators assuming productive uncertainty and risk aversion. Since production in the envisioned income-sharing
arrangement takes place at household level, the solution does not involve an
APC in the sense of this paper.

7. Organizational Form and Factor Proportions in the Large-scale Farm

The question of the comparative performance of capitalist versus co-
operative large farms is a difficult one to address on a theoretical level, as it

involves comparative questions of management and supervision for which little formal analysis has been developed. If technological economies of scale can be captured by APCs, they can presumably also be captured by large-scale capitalist farms, and the more efficient of the two could perhaps bid successfully for both land and labour. If APCs performed with even the approximate efficiency of the model discussed in Sections 2 and 6, they might compete well, especially if farmworkers prefer co-operation, or if there exist (thus far unmodelled) incentive effects providing an edge of advantage. An added dimension of the problem enters when we consider that both APCs and capitalist farms are likely to suffer from problems of measurement of labour input which were addressed for the APC in Section 4. An implication of monitoring problems is that, for both forms of large-scale production, imperfect monitoring might reduce work incentives in such a manner that the real effort provided by given workers would be lower than when they were employed in their own household farms.[15] This means that technological economies of scale that may exist potentially for homogeneous inputs defined in efficiency units may be offset partly or entirely by a reduction in real labour (and, perhaps, in the allocative services of labour that influence the productivities of other inputs) in the face of the team incentive problem.

Another implication of introducing the monitoring question is that, if the ability to monitor labour and meter rewards (in the terminology of Alchian and Demsetz 1972) differs across organizational forms, it may be decisive in the competition between APCs and capitalist farms, assuming that one or the other is viable. Some APCs appear to face problems of discipline and differential reward because, in their relatively level organizational milieu, work evaluation and reward differentiation create dissension and are accordingly downplayed. If APCs lack the ability to expel shirking members, this may be a fatal disadvantage in view of the role played by firing in some models of discipline in capitalist firms (see e.g. Shapiro and Stiglitz 1984; Bowles 1985). Another question that arises is how persons assigned to the monitoring task can be motivated to perform it well. If monitoring is itself difficult to monitor, it could conceivably be best called forth by a concentrated claim on an enterprise's residual earnings, as hypothesized by Alchian and Demsetz. On the other hand, members of APCs in a good position to monitor one another may be sufficiently motivated to do so by shared residual claims. It might well be that APCs and other workers' co-operatives are capable of solving the monitoring aspects of the work incentive problem, as the successful cases like the *kibbutzim*, the Mondragon industrial co-operatives, and others show, but that an effective internal organizational equilibrium requires meeting social and attitudinal conditions that are less easily generated or less frequently found than are the conditions for effective hierarchical control.

We might also note that socially optimal and socially preferred institutions may or may not coincide with those that emerge from individuals' choices and competition of organizational forms. One reason for this in the context of the underdeveloped rural economies is that, with the marginal product of farm labour below subsistence requirements, the institutional arrangements that maximize employment and output may not be those that maximize labour productivity or farmowners' profits. If profit-maximizing farms determine employment levels by a standard profit maximization criterion in such an 'overpopulated' economy, then a Georgescu-Roegen (1960) pointed out, either wages would have to fall below subsistence, leading to starvation and loss of human resources, or wages artificially maintained at subsistence would not sustain full employment. Peasant households using the same land resource would employ more labour, since the living expenses of their members would appear as a fixed cost and labour would simply be applied to the point at which its marginal product equalled its opportunity cost in leisure or alternative employment. This may partially explain widespread observations of higher land productivity in smaller rather than larger farms, a finding that has been cited by proponents of land reform. The relevant question for present purposes is whether APCs share the relatively labour-saving propensities of large capitalist farm counterparts facing a subsistence-linked minimum wage. The answer of theory is that APCs will be even more labour-saving than capitalist farms under conditions in which both can earn a profit — which in APCs means a return to labour above opportunity wages — provided that APCs freely vary the number of worker-members to maximize per-worker income (Ward 1958: Ward's paper and related models are further discussed in the next and final section). However, where APC membership is defined, say, by residence, or is otherwise open to rural residents universally, there is no systematic difference between the labour-using propensities of peasant versus co-operative farms. That APCs are in principle similar to the traditional agrarian institutions discussed by Georgescu-Roegen (1960), Lewis (1954), and others, in this respect is intuitively clear when it is remembered that their basis of remuneration is the sharing of average product.

Another social welfare issue concerns land tenure systems and land access. In recent decades development economists have frequently espoused land redistribution not only to maximize rural labour absorption but also as a means of broadening the asset base so as to foster growth with equity. However, where private rights in land are created (or retained) after land reform, a reconcentration process may take place, raising the question of whether restrictions on land concentration should be imposed as a means of assuring continued land access by small farmers. Institutions that give village communities a measure of control over land use, as in the model sketched earlier in this section, may present one means of assuring such access, while the potential to grasp economies of scale through joint production, when such economies are present, may be invoked as an additional advantage.

When and where economies of scale are potentially present in developing country agricultures is itself a question of obvious and crucial relevance to the incidence of the APC form. The much discussed evidence of a negative relationship between farm size and productivity suggests one reason why voluntary formation of APCs might be relatively rare. This evidence is not inconsistent with the hypothesis that, in the absence of incentive and co-ordination problems, group production will permit productivity-increasing forms of farm management rationalization, but adequate solutions of the problems mentioned may be difficult to achieve. Binswanger and Rosenz-weigh (1986) consider that economies of scale in agriculture may arise from superior management skills, lumpy inputs, and the combination of economies of scale in processing and farm-processing plant co-ordination problems. In so far as managerial and co-ordination skills feature promi-nently on this list, co-operatives may operate at some disadvantage relative to plantations, owing to the hierarchical management structures of the latter form of organization. In so far as costly inputs and processing facilities are emphasized, the question of access to capital, which is ignored in the litera-ture that we have surveyed, may be the crucial determinant of which large-scale form arises. While collective structures such as the Chinese communes have proven to be effective instruments of capital accumulation, APCs in competitive market environments could well be at a disadvantage with respect to financing the acquisition of large, costly inputs.[16]

8. Growth and Degeneration of APCs under Free Determination of Membership

So far, we have treated APCs whose labour forces are determined exogenously, using models that assume free selection of labour input by these members. This framework suits well those countries in which the entire agri-cultural population is divided among APCs by residence, and also, as a first approximation, co-operative communities such as the *kibbutz* which are committed to welcoming more or less any new member willing to abide by the rules of the community. Rather different behaviour can be expected, however, of APCs in which the current members or a manager acting on their behalf take membership size as a choice variable in pursuing the objective of maximum returns to their labour. When such a co-operative has the option of hiring non-member workers, its behaviour will depart still further from the initial model. In this last section, the relevant results from LMF theory are summarized and their applicability to APCs is illustrated.

The labour-restricting tendency of membership-varying APCs was already mentioned in the last section. The prediction of such a tendency is based on the observation that a membership-determining APC, being a species of LMF, should be expected to exhibit the same behaviour first predicted by Ward (1958) for the 'Illyrian' firm: that a firm operating the same technology and bearing the same fixed costs for capital as a conventional profit-maximizing firm (PMF) would choose to have fewer workers and to produce a smaller amount of output when the PMF earns positive profits and the LMF workers earn rents above opportunity wages. This result holds because maximum net revenue per LMF worker occurs where net income per worker equals labour's value of marginal product. If the 'twin' PMF earns positive profits, the value of marginal product in the LMF must be above the market wage, implying a smaller level of labour input. The same basic result holds even when members of the LMF can vary their labour hours or work effort, as shown by Ireland and Law (1981).

With the opportunity wage below the value of marginal product at the co-operative's optimal membership level, a profitable LMF would have applicants for membership that it is unwilling to take: workers whose admission to the enterprise work-force would reduce average net revenue, though leaving it above the opportunity wage. As pointed out by Domar (1966) and Meade (1972), a mutually beneficial deal could be struck if it were institutionally permissible for the LMF to reward the same kind of labour with different earnings: the outsiders could be allowed to work for payments above the opportunity wage but below their marginal product, with benefit to both sides. In the limit, the outsiders could be employed at the opportunity wage itself, in which case total labour use would be the same as in the PMF twin, with maximum advantage to the original members and neither gain nor loss for the new workers.

But the idea of a producers' co-operative, which first determines optimal membership so as to maximize average earnings, assuming that all workers will be members, then hires additional labour as employees, is arbitrary and intrinsically unstable. The reason is that the existing worker-members, save one, could benefit further if one of their number were dismissed and replaced by a non-member employee, who would be paid the market wage. If a majority of members had, and were willing to exercise, the right to expel a minority, the process would continue, step by step, until the profitable 'co-operative' consisted of only two members,[17] neither of whom would be replaced if he chose to retire. By such a process, the co-operative would 'degenerate' into a conventional firm (Ben-Ner 1984).

The assumption that producers' co-operatives would dismiss current members in order to raise the earnings of those who remain has been repeatedly criticized by contributors to the LMF literature.[18] Aside from neglecting the realistic element of solidarity that exists among the workers in most enterprises, it ignores the fact that, if worker-members vote on dismissals with positive probabilities of themselves drawing a dismissal notice, they might prefer to receive, with certainty, earnings above opportunity wage although below their potential maximum, rather than accept a lottery the outcomes of which are maximum earnings on the one side, but the opportunity wage on the other. However, the latter problem is offset if there exist hierarchies of seniority or ability, or other groupings within the work-force, which allow a majority to vote for dismissals with confidence that they will not themselves be targeted. Moreover, even if constitutional membership rights or feelings of solidarity retard the contraction of the membership predicted by such simple earnings-maximization models, natural attrition arising from retirements, deaths, and voluntary job mobility will bring about the same results over time, since departing workers will not be replaced under conditions in which doing so reduces the earnings of those who remain.

Agricultural producers' co-operatives having membership-determining powers appear to behave much as the models predict. Unless they are part of a movement that takes membership expansion or job creation as a goal in its own right, or acts under the direction of or in identification with an organization representing workers or farmers as a class (and not only their own immediate members), such APCs tend to expand, if at all, by hiring non-member employees, with new membership largely limited to children and other family members of existing members. The classic cases are the agricultural producers' co-operatives of Peru and Chile, which were created on former haciendas through the agrarian reforms of the 1960s and early 1970s with membership limited to the ex-hacienda workers. The failure of these farms to extend the benefits of the reform by admitting more members threatened to weaken their self-determination powers by prompting governmental oversight and intervention (Kay 1982).[19] On the other hand, the creation of temporary employment by APCs in Peru was reversed by the 1980s parcellation process, which led to the substitution of more intensive exploitation of family labour and the elimination of much outside hiring.

NOTES

1. For greater generality, p itself may be viewed as a random variable from the standpoint of the collective. This possibility is in general suppressed in what follows.
2. Bradley (1971), Bonin (1977), and (in the related LMF literature) Berman (1977), argued that $\partial L/\partial \ell^i = L/\ell^i$ on grounds either that identical members must respond identically to the same environment (Bradley, Bonin) or that effort variations could be co-ordinated to achieve incentive optimality (Berman). However, responses $\partial \ell^j/\partial \ell^i$ must be evaluated at given settings of the exogenous variables (such as prices and rents), and the co-ordinated solution is conceptually inconsistent with individual choice of the ℓ. The comparative static terms $\partial \ell^j/\partial \ell^i$ cannot be signed without restrictions. For further discussion, see Putterman (1985).
3. Here, we are of course assuming that $N \geqslant 2$. A 'one-man APC' is equivalent to a self-employed farmer, and will have $\partial y^i/\partial \ell^i = Q_L$ for any notional value of α in (5).

4. See, however, the two-stage model of Cremer (1982), who shows that efficiency can be achieved in an APC of heterogeneous members by means of work-points and transfers, provided that an efficient wage-and-transfer equilibrium also exists.

5. It is possible that some members could not pay these taxes out of the income due them for labour, in which case absent alternative methods of financing, the scheme might not be possible to implement.

6. A similar result is illustrated in the Oi–Clayton (1968) model: compare Figures 3-A and 3-B on pp. 46–7 there.

7. Aggregate L is presumably known from Q.

8. Note that this scheme guarantees an expected but not an *ex post* balanced budget for the co-operative.

9. The fact that the Chinese agricultural production teams belonged to larger entities known as people's communes introduces some terminological confusion, for they were not communes from the standpoint of income distribution rules. Although they did practise an admixture of 'needs' and work distribution, the latter was at least formally the dominant aspect; see Putterman (1987).

10. Moreover, even if individual effort is unobservable, the same penalty vector can in principle enforce first-best effort provision because shirking by anyone would generate observably reduced output. For the LMF case, see MacLeod (1984) and the earlier discussion by Tyson (1979).

11. The Israeli *kibbutzim*, which contain 25% of Israel's farmers and produce 40% of its farm product, come closest to constituting an exception. The *moshav* co-operatives, which do not produce as a joint enterprise, contain the lion's share of Israel's remaining Jewish agriculturalists, while Arab farmers generally farm on a family basis.

12. Voting on the two institutional parameters is assumed independent, to avoid voting cycles.

13. Since voting choice of the institutional parameters is assumed prior to time allocation, the labour inputs in question here are strictly speaking only notional. In voting, households have in mind the complete consequences of each institutional regime, including how they would allocate their time if it were to be selected. This permits households to rank institutional settings according to their maximum utility levels should any given set of parameters be chosen.

14. Inefficiency remains when $\ell^{med} \neq L/N$ and in any case because, with a single parameter α in (4c) and varying preferences generating unequal ℓ^i, no single value of α can cause (5) to equal $p(g_L)$ precisely for all members. On the latter, see again Cremer (1982).

15. See, e.g. the discussion by Binswanger and Rosenzweig (1986).

16. For a review of the finance problem as discussed in the LMF literature, see Bonin and Putterman (1987b: 61–79).

17. The theorem is usually stated in terms of shrinking to a membership of one, but if the decision-making mechanism is a voting process, there could be no majority for expulsion once membership reaches two.

18. A survey of the relevant literature is provided by Bonin and Putterman (1987: esp. 13–36).

19. For other discussions of the Peruvian and Chilean APCs, see Carter (1985) and McClintock, Podesta, and Scurrah (1984).

17.

Institutional Analysis of Credit Co-operatives

Avishay Braverman and J. Luis Guasch

1. Introduction

Perhaps the most common form of government intervention in the rural sector has been massive lending at subsidized interest rates. The standard justification has been that credit programmes are easier to implement than other policies, such as land reform or infrastructure development, and are beneficial to agriculture. Without subsidized interest rates, goes the reasoning, adoption of technical innovation would be delayed and there would be underusage of costly inputs such as fertilizer. Both effects slow the growth of output and the development of the agricultural sector. It has also been argued that since rural credit markets are notoriously imperfect, access to credit is severely limited for farmers, particularly small farmers; without government intervention a high price of capital would prevail, further screening out the small farmers from the credit markets. Furthermore, because of distorted exchange rates, food price controls, imports of cheap food, and inefficient markets, farmers receive low prices for their products, which hampers their borrowing abilities.

Credit programmes generally aim to reach small farmers. However, despite the remarkable expansion of credit throughout the rural areas of developing countries over the last three decades, few farmers in low-income countries seem to have received or benefited from such credit. An estimated 5 per cent of farms in Africa and about 15 per cent in Asia and Latin America have had access to formal credit. Moreover, there seems to be a high correlation between credit recipients and size of land-holdings (see Lipton 1981, and Braverman and Guasch 1986). The imposition of government interest rate restrictions (credit subsidies) has induced banks to ration credit in a manner that excludes the small farmers from formal credit markets. This is what Gonzalez-Vega (1977) has called 'the iron law of interest rate restric-

The findings, interpretations, and conclusions expressed in this paper are entirely those of the authors and should not be attributed in any manner to the institutions to which they are affiliated. The authors would like to thank J. D. von Pischke and Jacob Yaron for helpful conversations and Colleen Roberts for editorial assistance.

tions'. Rather than equalizing income inequality, low interest rate credit programmes have increased it: on average, 5 per cent of borrowers have received 80 per cent of the credit.

It has thus been common for farmers, particularly the small-scale ones, to resort to the formation of organized credit groups or co-operatives. Although those institutions have many advantages, they have been prone to encourage the wrong economic behaviour. In terms of participation, productivity, volume of credit, and repayment rates, failures have outnumbered successes. Given the level of resources involved and the significance of economic development in rural areas, a better understanding of these institutions is needed. What follows is a normative analysis of co-operatives viewed as institutions organized to improve the plight of small-scale farmers. This analysis is motivated by the theory of incentives in organizations. The purpose is to analyse which structures are most successful. Then a policy to promote credit co-operatives and optimal incentive design could be much more effective than the subsidized credit policies of the past. After a brief description of how credit tends to be allocated in rural markets, we proceed to analyse the issues of formation and design of credit groups, in both static and dynamic settings.

2. Analysis of Rural Credit Allocation

Consider an institution or financial intermediary which aims to allocate a given budget among a number of loan applicants. For simplicity, assume that the demand for loans comes from two types of rural agents or farmers, small-scale and large-scale. The standard differences between the two types seem to be: (1) that loans requested by the small agents are usually smaller than those requested by the large ones; (2) that the collateral small agents can provide is smaller than that provided by the large ones; (3) that the land-holdings of small agents are smaller (if not absent) than those of large ones; (4) that information on past behaviour is more extensive or less costly to collect on large agents than on small ones; and (5) that the output of the small agents is perceived to be subject to greater variation, reflecting perhaps the smaller and less diversified resource base of small farms.

Loan processing has strong positive scale economies. Estimates show that for small loans processing costs can range from 15 to 40 per cent of the loan value (see Braverman and Guasch 1986). These cost differentials, plus the typical lack of collateral and the higher perceived riskiness of the small agents, induce a bias against them in credit allocation. Interest ceilings and limited budgets further strengthen the bias. Interest restrictions stop financial institutions from charging higher interest rates and induce higher demand for credit from the large agents. Thus small agents face significant rationing or exclusion from credit. Their alternative is to use the informal credit market, which usually lends at much higher interest rates, and which also subjects the small agents to rationing. In addition, arbitrariness, patronage, and corrupt practices, frequently undertaken by the financial intermediaries, further limit the access to credit of the small farmers (see e.g. Landman and Tinnermeier 1981; Robert 1979; and Adams and Vogel 1986).

The conventional wisdom has been that providing subsidized credit would remove this bias and increase small farmers' share of institutional credit. Elsewhere (Braverman and Guasch 1987) we have argued against that view and have shown how subsidized credit will reduce small farmers' share, and likely increase the informal credit market interest rate. The natural conclusion is that subsidized credit should be abolished.[1] That would ensure that small farmers' share of credit at the new higher formal market rate would be increased. In addition, the informal market rates they face might decrease.[2] Small farmers will still face rationing, since the arguments outlined above still apply albeit with somewhat less force (see Bell and Srinivasan 1985). We should still expect to observe interest rate differentials according to loan size, because of the higher processing cost for small loans and the higher risks in lending to small farmers.

It is not our purpose here to dwell on the effectiveness of credit policies, but rather to elaborate on actions that small farmers can take to improve their access to credit and thus ultimately their welfare. In particular, we will focus on how credit groups can help.

3. Co-operatives and Credit Groups

The three main obstacles to obtaining credit for the small-scale agents are: (1) much higher transaction costs per dollar lent for small loans; (2) the belief, real or perceived, that small agents are riskier to lend to than larger ones; and (3) the fact that the patronage, corruption, and arbitrary decisions of some lending agents reduce the share of credit funds to small agents. Small-scale agents might form co-operatives or credit groups to overcome these obstacles.

There are many types of credit groups, ranging from purely nominal or umbrella organizations without much member interaction to those fully co-ordinated in all aspects of their operations including production decisions among members. Motivation behind their inception, organizational structure, incentive schemes, enforcement procedures, tradition and cultural legacy, technological structure, and availability of information are important factors in determining their effectiveness.

The advantages of credit groups are multiple. They reduce the credit transaction costs of both lenders and borrowers, enabling the group to offer strong economic incentives to their members such as lower interest rates, price discount on inputs, and relief from individual processing of loans. They might promote scale economies in technical assistance. They might help to circumvent the effects of risk, and also give leverage for dealing with the financial intermediaries. From the lenders' perspective, they may reduce the risk of loan default because of the common practice of joint liability among group members.

That these advantages are clearly perceived is evident in the large number of co-operatives that have been established in the agricultural sector in practically all countries since their inception in Germany in 1847. However, results have been mixed, with failures outnumbering successes.

Why were there so many failures? Although largely an empirical question, to answer it properly one must first know what is the optimally designed credit group. We focus below on the characterization of such a benchmark organization, and on the role and design of incentives in credit groups.

4. The Institutional Design of Credit Groups

Consider a collection of agents, each one involved in his own productive activity, say, agriculture, which is subject to uncertain factors and where the inputs needed are capital and the farmer's own effort. In a general formulation, we could think of those agents as facing two distinct types of risk. The first is an individual or specific risk which is uncorrelated across agents and with the other type of risk; the second is common to all agents or perfectly correlated across agents. The most obvious example of the latter risk in agriculture is the variation in output or yield caused by weather's uncertainty, while those caused by incidence of pests and other diseases would be an example of the first type. We could think, then, of the random element z_i, affecting i's output, as composed of two terms; $z_i = (v, h_i)$ where v is a common (to all agents) uncertainty parameter, while h_i are independent idiosyncratic (specific to agent i) risks. Let $Q_i(v, h_i, a_i, K_i)$ be the output for agent i, which is a function of the effort taken by the agent, a_i, of the amount of capital utilized for production, K_i, and of the two random factors, v and h_i.

The agent's utility is a function of income and of the level of effort undertaken. Disposable income can be decomposed into two terms. One is that obtained from the sale of the output net of repayment of the loan. The other is given by the proportion of the loan the agent uses for consumption or other purposes, not directly linked with the productive activity under study. Let us denote that proportion by α. Also, let Y be the income obtained from the sale of output net of repayment costs. Then, we can express the utility as $U(\alpha K, Y, a)$. Since the availability of those two incomes is not concurrent, they are treated differently in the agent's utility function. We assume preferences represented by a utility function separable in those variables, $U_1(\alpha K) + U_2(Y) - V(a)$, where U_1 and U_2 are concave functions, and V is convex. That reflects diminishing marginal utility of income and increasing marginal disutility of effort. Y can be written as $Y = pQ_i - (1 + r_m)K_i$, where Q is output, p is its market price, and r_m is the interest rate. Let $\bar{K}$ be the credit limit the agents are subject to. Now we can state the optimization problem solved by the agent operating on his own as

$$\max_{a_i,\, \alpha_i,\, K_i} U_1(\alpha_i K_i) + EU_2(Y) - V(a_i) \tag{1}$$

$$\text{s.t. } Y = pQ_i - (1 + r_m)K_i$$
$$Q = Q\{v, h_i, a_i, (1 - \alpha_i)K_i\}$$
$$0 \le \alpha_i \le 1$$
$$0 \le K_i \le \bar{K}.$$

The first-order conditions of I, for an interior maximum, are

$$EU_2'(pQ_a') - V' = 0 \tag{2a}$$

$$U_1'K + EU_2'\{pQ_k'(-K)\} = 0 \tag{2b}$$

$$U_1'\alpha + EU_2'\{pQ_k'(1 - \alpha) - (1 + r_m)\} = 0. \tag{2c}$$

Let the optimal actions taken by an agent not joining a credit group, the solutions to (2), be denoted by K^m, α^m, and a^m. Let the expected utility of that action be $\bar{U}^m$. The higher α^m is, the higher the probability of insolvency. The choice of higher α by agents has been a common argument used to explain the failure of credit to achieve its goal.

Consider now the possibility of agents joining or forming a credit group. The key characteristic of the arrangement is that the group assumes liability for any loans made to any of its members or that it serves as the recipient of all credit, which is then distributed among the members. The security for credit repayment is usually provided by the joint liability of group members, diffusing the risk bias argument held against small agents. Credit to the whole group is stopped until the default is corrected. This provides diversification of risk and induces strong peer pressure for the proper use of credit and its repayment.

The direct benefits to agents in joining a credit group are lower interest rates and presumably higher credit lines. They are a consequence of two essential features of credit groups: joint liability, and a centralized or block request of credit by the group as opposed to a number of individual applications, thereby reducing transaction costs.

Aside from the lower costs of inputs, another benefit the agents can derive from joining a credit group is risk-pooling. The argument is straightforward, particularly when there is no moral hazard problem. Each agent's income is a random variable y_i, with a given distribution, induced by v and h_i. For any realization of v, the distribution of income of each agent is independent and identically distributed across agents, with variance var(y). Suppose the structure of the group is such that the agents' income is pooled together, and that the aggregate proceeds are divided equally among the identical agents. If there are n of them, the variance of the aggregate income is var $(y_1 + y_2 + \ldots + y_n) = n$ var(y). Each agent receives $(1/n)(y_1 + y_2 + \ldots + y_n)$, but the variance of that income is $n \operatorname{var}(y/n) = \operatorname{var}(y)/n$. Thus, the expected income has not changed but its variance has been greatly reduced. With risk-averse agents, their expected utility is now higher.

The argument is not so simple when the agent can take unobservable actions affecting the distribution of his contributed income (output), since then expected income from productive activities in the group regime will in general be different. The trade-off is lower expected income but also lower variance. Of course, the non-productive income might be larger. Let α, a, and K be the agent's optimal choices in the credit group regime. The solution concept we use to determine those values is the Nash equilibrium. An equilibrium allocation under a credit group regime can be thought of as a Nash equilibrium of the game where each agent computes his optimal borrowing, consumption, and production plan, given the actions of the other agents and knowing what the resulting expected distribution of income would be. That allocation has the property that no one can do better by deviating in his choice of actions given what the others are doing. Then the resulting aggregate income is $y_1 + y_2 + \ldots + y_n - (1 + r)nK$, with of course y and K being different from the choices made under an individualistic regime of production, since there, agents were not acting strategically with respect to each other, of course there were no moral hazard problems. Here again the agent's variance of income is reduced to $\operatorname{var}\{y - (1 + r)K\}/n$. Of course, y_i are a function of α, a, K, and r. The chosen values of y will depend on the institutional organization of the group, particularly the incentive structure implemented by the group.

Assuming equal and exhaustive distribution of the proceeds by the group, the problem solved by agent i, under the credit group regime, that gives rise to y is:

$$\max_{a_i, \alpha_i, K_i} \ U_1(\alpha_i K_i) + EU_2(Y) - V(a_i) \tag{3}$$

$$\text{s.t. } Y = [\Sigma_{i=1,\ldots,n}\{pQ_i - (1 + r_c)K_i\}]/n$$
$$Q_i = Q_i\{v, h_i, a_i, (1 - \alpha_i)K_i\}$$
$$0 \le \alpha_i \le 1$$

where r_c is the interest rate charged to the group. Note that this formulation captures the joint liability characteristic of the arrangement. All the proceeds are pooled by the group and all loans are paid out prior to any distribution of income to the members. Then, because of symmetry, all of them receive the same share, independent of their own realization of output Q_i. This formulation is not equivalent to the one (also capturing joint liability) where each agent is allocated his net income less a share of the debt from bankrupt members (when applicable). The latter formulation induces lower expected utility, because of a higher variance on the realized income. The dominance of the former formulation reflects the benefits of risk-pooling.

The first-order conditions for a maximum of problem (3) are:

$$EU_2'(pQ_a')/n - V' = 0 \tag{4a}$$

$$U_1'K + EU_2' \{pQ_K'(- K_i)\}/n = 0 \qquad (4b)$$

$$U_1'\alpha_i + EU_2' \{pQ_K'(1 - \alpha_i) - (1 + r_c)\}/n = 0. \qquad (4c)$$

Every agent solves a similar problem. The Nash equilibrium allocation is the simultaneous solution to the set of n first-order conditions, one for each agent.

There is now a moral hazard problem, since α_i and a_i are not observable by the group, and thus cannot be contracted for. The group only observes K_i and aggregate output. As of now, we assume that Q_i are not observable by the group. Later we will relax this assumption.

To make the claim that a credit group regime dominates individualistic production from the agent's standpoint, we have to compare the expected utility levels under both regimes, namely, the solutions to problems (1) and (3). The trade-offs are clear. Under regime (1), the agent acts unilaterally, keeping all the proceeds induced by his actions, but has to incur higher input costs, and a higher variance of income, *ceteris paribus*, and perhaps credit ceilings; while under regime (3), he benefits from lower costs and lower variance, but receives only one-nth of his contribution. His strategic behaviour *vis-à-vis* the other agents (Nash non-cooperative) will tend to induce a lower contribution towards the general pool. If we evaluate the first-order conditions (4) at the optimal values given by the solution to (2), we obtain that: (a) the sign of (4a) is negative, implying a lower effort contribution; (b) the sign of (4b) is positive, implying that a higher proportion of credit will be allocated to non-productive activities; and (c) the sign of (4c) is positive, meaning that a larger amount of credit will be requested.

The allocation induced by (3) is clearly suboptimal, even relative to the second-best or constrained-efficient one. The credit group regime problem shares many features with the standard common ownership and team production problems. As with those, the equilibrium allocation is not Pareto-optimal. Non-cooperative behaviour there usually yields an inefficient outcome if joint output or liability is fully shared among the agents. Everyone's welfare can be improved by exercising restraint in present consumption, and by increasing the productive activities. The source of the inefficiency is that each agent imposes a negative externality on the others by the diversion of credit and actions from the productive activity. That behaviour is nevertheless optimal for the agent, given the allocation rule of problem (3), since, while he incurs the full cost of the actions taken in the productive activity, he receives only one-nth of the output; a similar argument applies for his use of credit on productive and non-productive activities. That arrangement fosters moral hazard and free-rider problems, since agents cannot be induced to supply proper amounts of productive inputs when their actions cannot be observed and contracted for directly. Moreover, a severe problem that can appear is that the agents might increase their credit demands and the proportion of credit for other non-productive purposes (like current consumption), and decrease their effort contribution, reducing the expected production levels so much that credit group will be unable to repay the loans. Bankruptcy and failure of the credit group as a viable institution would be the end results. Therefore it should be clear that the internal dynamics of the set of actions taken by the members cannot be ignored, and a system of incentives based on the acquired information ought to be implemented to induce the desired or optimal actions. The critical elements in the design of incentive schemes are the nature of the information available, the nature of the uncertainty affecting the agents' output, and the structure of production.

The important question then is whether there are alternative institutional arrangements and incentive mechanisms that can elicit an efficient or at least a better allocation than the one described above for a credit group regime. Presumably, the larger the difference between the allocation induced by (1) and the one induced by the credit group regime, the more attractive and stable the group will be. To resolve the question, we turn to the theory of incentives under imperfect information and moral hazard. We know that in these situations the assignment of an individual or entity to serve the role of a principal can reduce problems significantly, since implementing other allocation rules can induce more efficient outcomes (see Alchian and Demsetz 1972; Mirrlees 1976; and Holmström 1982). We can assign that role to the credit group. The group is empowered to monitor, allocate, and implement incentive schemes. Given transaction costs and risk factors, delegating the monitoring to one or all members will enhance total output relative to what could be achieved on an individual basis. Thus, even though production will take place on an individual basis, the group aspect of the arrangement will require setting up incentive schemes and sharing rules that are usually associated with teams and structures under observability and moral hazard problems. Moreover, in its role as principal, the group can account for any surplus or deficit incurred. This is essential since it is often the case that 'optimal' incentive schemes do not balance the budget. Without that capacity, those schemes might not be implementable.

Under certainty, and where only in aggregate is the outcome observable, one can construct a set of sharing (the output–income) rules, $s_i(y) \geq 0, i = 1,$ ..., n, inducing a Nash equilibrium in actions, which satisfies the conditions for Pareto optimality. Generally, they take the following form: $s_i(y) = c_i$ if $y \geq y(a^*, \alpha^*, K^*)$, and $s_i(y) = 0$ otherwise, where the arguments of y are the Nash equilibrium and Pareto-optimal actions. If all the agents are identical *ex ante*, the sharing rules will also be identical for all agents. The optimal sharing rules are, in general, discontinuous in income, and need not be budget-balancing. This latter feature is essential to solve the free-rider problem, and to neutralize externalities. It reflects the ability to sufficiently penalize deviations from the optimum. The enforcement problem is then overcome by bringing in a principal, in our case the credit group, which will assume the residual of the non-budget-balancing sharing rules (when applicable).

Group incentives can also work quite well under uncertainty, particularly if the agents are risk-neutral. Mirrlees (1976) and Holmström (1982) have shown that a first-best solution can be approximated arbitrarily closely by using group penalties. In that situation, the sharing rules, in general, take the following form: $s_i(y) = s_i y$ if $y \geq \bar{y}$ and $s_i y - k_i$ otherwise, where $\Sigma\, s_i = 1$, and $k_i > 0$. The term k_i describes the penalty to agent i if a critical output $\bar{y}$ is not reached. The effectiveness of these rules, however, is greatly reduced if there are many agents and if they are risk-averse. Of course, the group has the option to subdivide itself into several cells to keep the size reduced when desirable. Under risk aversion and uncertainty in production, the first-best is usually not attainable. Then monitoring becomes quite important since it can help improve welfare and achieve an allocation that approximates the first-best. (See Holmström 1982 for a general statement of the problem.) In our formulation, monitoring should be a viable and quite natural option, since observations by the group of each agent's output can be obtained, generically at fairly low cost.[3]

Let us consider now those situations where the information system is so rich, or monitoring so easy, that total output can be itemized according to the contribution of each agent; this is the case when Q_i are separately observed; then,

$$Q(\S, z) = \Sigma_i Q_i(\S_i, z_i),$$

where $z = (z_1, \ldots, z_n)$, $\S = (\S_1, \ldots, \S_n)$, and $\S_i = (a_i, \alpha_i, K_i)$. If $\bar{z}_i$ are not random or observable by everybody, then efficiency can be achieved by holding each agent responsible for his own output. However, the most frequent case is where the z_i are random and not observable. Then the sharing rules are functions of the output and should describe the proportion of insolvent loan claims to be assessed against agent i. In general, the optimal sharing rule of agent i will depend on something other than i's output. It will depend on i's output alone only if the outputs of all agents are independent.

Generally, the optimal set of sharing rules $\{s_i(y)\ i = 1, \ldots, n\}$ will have s_i depend on some relative or average measure like $\bar{y}$ and y_i alone where $\bar{y}$ is a weighted average of the agents' outcomes. The only assumptions needed to generate these results are that $v, h_1, \ldots, h_n$ are independent and normally distributed. The intuition is that the aggregate measure of peer performance $\bar{y}$ captures all the relevant information about the common uncertainty. In other words, the aggregate measure, $\bar{y}$, is then a sufficient statistic. Clearly, this rationalizes the common practice of comparing performance against peer aggregates, and basing compensations (pecuniary or non-pecuniary) on that differential.

In those contexts, incentive schemes based on relative output performance, or rank-order tournaments, can do quite well, as has been shown in Nalebuff and Stiglitz (1983) and Bhattacharya and Guasch (1988).[4] They can be utilized not only to elicit the desired actions, but also to allocate among the members the excess balance of the credit group, induced by interest rate differentials or non-budget-balancing rules. A rank-order tournament awards agents merely on their performance rank, not on the value of the output itself; thus, it is based on ordinality as opposed to cardinality. An advantage of this compensation scheme compared with others based on cardinality is that it requires less information, since only the ranking of the agents needs to be determined. In particular, when all agents' output (the monitored variable) is subject to a common (correlated) risk or random variable, these reward (or penalty) schemes automatically neutralize that risk or adjust for its effects.

A rank-order tournament generally consists of a set of n prizes $q_1 \geq q_2 \geq \ldots \geq \ldots q_n$, one for each agent, and an observable variable(s) upon which the ranking of the agents is established. If that variable is, say, the output, then the agent with the highest output receives q_1, and so on. Of course, some of the prizes can be penalties.

If the agents are risk-neutral, a properly designed contest can elicit the efficient allocation (see Lazear and Rosen 1981, and Bhattacharya and Guasch 1988) with either homogeneous or heterogeneous agents. Moreover, under risk aversion, such contests may be preferred to individualistic reward schemes, particularly when the risk associated with the common environmental variable, v, is large. Again, the role of a principal is essential for the implementation of these schemes. Among the various forms a contest can take, that with a penalty to the lowest ranked individual will be superior to one with a prize to the highest ranked individual. (See Nalebuff and Stiglitz (1983) for an analysis of relative effectiveness of different types of tournaments.[5])

5. Dynamic Considerations

The analysis developed above has been largely static. It begs the question of why agents do not 'take the money and run', and limits enforcement considerably. In a static framework, threats to agents for departing from the expected or established course of action are not credible, since they cannot be implemented. By the time inferences or observations can be made about deviant agents, the game is over, so retaliation cannot take place. It is only in a dynamic (infinite- or uncertain-horizon) framework that stated punishments can be carried out. Future periods provide the place for disciplining agents who deviated and the agents can take into account the future consequences of any deviations.

A dynamic analysis increases the viability of credit groups. Given the moral hazard and team problems, the success of the credit group in supporting a co-operative scheme that is superior to an individualistic one lies in its ability to punish any defector from the scheme. In this section, we extend the previous analysis to an environment where each agent, within a credit group regime, repeatedly sets his choice variables. The group responds to such choices. This becomes a repeated game, and since we are considering an infinite number of repetitions, it is a supergame. The environment does not change, and decisions can be made contingent on past outcomes of the game.

In our structure, the credit group cannot perfectly observe or infer the actions a_i and α_i taken by the agents. Then the natural strategies for the credit group to consider are trigger output or review. Mentioned by Stigler (1964), their general formulation has been developed by Green and Porter (1984) in collusive market games and by Radner (1985) in repeated games with imperfect monitoring and moral hazard, and are most appropriate in formulations with informational imperfections. Our formulation is a hybrid of those two types of problems. While each agent's problem is more like a repeated moral hazard problem, the fact that it has consequences for group welfare brings in the market element.

Under trigger output strategies, each agent selects his level, agreed by the group, of unobservable actions, until his output (if observable by the group) or the aggregate output falls below a certain specified trigger output Q^*, during some period. Then, in the former case, the agent(s) whose output falls below that selected trigger benchmark is forced out of the credit group for $T - 1$ periods. After T periods, the agent is allowed to return to the credit group to resume co-operation, and so on. If aggregate output is the only observable variable, when output falls below its trigger value the credit group is dismantled for the $T - 1$ periods. After T periods, the credit group resumes operations. The analysis below deals with this latter case, but it also fits the former when the expected utility for any agent in the group does not depend on the number of members. This would be the case if the group is quite large. Then, at the margin or infra-margin, the variation is negligible, since all the scale effects are exhausted at a relatively smaller size. Otherwise, we need to keep account of the size of the group and corresponding probabilities. Our choice is based on ease of exposition.

A trigger output scheme is characterized by four parameters, assuming identical agents, a^*, α^*, Q^*, and T. Note that the capital or loan principal, K, need not be part of it since it is observable, and can be forced on the agent at the onset of each period. The problem for the credit group, then, is to select values of those parameters in order to induce the highest possible expected utility for each agent. Deviations from agreed actions are undesirable to the group because they might lead to insolvency of the agent. Then, because of the joint liability, the group has to cover the losses.

Let $\bar{U}^c$ be the agent's expected payoff per period under co-operative behaviour in the credit group regime. Let $\bar{U}^m$ be the expected payoff per period when operating on his own. Let σ be the discount rate and β the induced probability of having a realization of output below the trigger level. The distribution of that probability depends on a, α, K, the trigger output Q^*, and the random variables v and h.

The overall expected lifetime utility $\bar{U}$ to each agent is given implicitly by

$$\bar{U} = \bar{U}^c + (1 - \beta)\sigma\bar{U} + \beta\{\bar{U}^m(\sigma + \ldots + \sigma^{T-1}) + \sigma^T\bar{U}\}.$$

It contains three elements: (1) the current expected payoff from agreed or co-operative behaviour; (2) the expected utility starting next period when the credit group is still operating, discounted by the probability of that event, namely, that the output is above the specified level; and (3) the expected utility upon the credit group being dissolved for $T - 1$ periods, and resuming operations thereafter affected by the probability of that event. Solving for $\bar{U}$, we obtain

$$\bar{U} = \{1/(1 - \sigma)\}\{\bar{U}^c(1 - \sigma) + \bar{U}^m\beta(\sigma - \sigma^T)\}/\{(1 - \sigma) + \beta(\sigma - \sigma^T)\}.$$

Further manipulations yield

$$\bar{U} = \{\bar{U}^m/(1 - \sigma)\} + (\bar{U}^c - \bar{U}^m)/\{(1 - \sigma) + \beta(\sigma - \sigma^T)\},$$

with the two terms being, first, the expected utility from the individualistic regime from now on, and second, the single-period gains accruing each period from now on from the co-operative behaviour, properly discounted.

Then the credit group is

$$\max \bar{U} = \max [\{\bar{U}^m/(1 - \sigma)\} + (\bar{U}^c - \bar{U}^m)/\{(1 - \sigma) + \beta(\sigma - \sigma^T)\}]$$

$$\text{s.t. } (\partial\bar{U}_i/\partial\alpha_i)|_{a^*} \leq \sigma(\partial\beta/\partial\alpha_i)\{(\bar{U}^c - \bar{U}^m)/(1 - \sigma + \beta\sigma)\}, \text{ and}$$

$$(\partial\bar{U}_i/\partial a_i)|_{a^*} \leq \sigma(\partial\beta/\partial a_i)\{(\bar{U}^c - \bar{U}^m)/(1 - \sigma + \beta\sigma)\}$$

where the first constraint guarantees that it will not be possible to increase the agent's expected utility by increasing the share of capital for non-productive purposes beyond α^*; and the second constraint states that the agent cannot increase his expected utility by decreasing his effort below a^*. The solution of this problem will determine a^*, α^*, Q^*, and T^*, which provides for the maximum expected utility and makes the credit group sustainable.

It could well be that the optimal solution is to set T equal to infinity. Then, if the output level falls below a certain specified trigger level Q^*, the credit group is dissolved forever. However, that policy might not always be optimal, since it might induce agents to make excessive efforts, when on average they all can be made better off by selecting a finite T. It depends on the discount rate and the difference between $\bar{U}^m$ and $\bar{U}^c$. The characteristics of the solution to problem V are as follows. For risk-averse agents, the resulting allocation generates higher levels of utility than those induced in the static framework. In equilibrium, agents do not deviate from agreed actions, but excluding agents or dissolving the group takes place every now and then, during periods of 'bad' realizations of the random variable affecting production. It is optimal for agents to supply less effort or less expected output than the levels they would choose if operating alone but under the same terms (interest rate) of the credit group. Agents go through alternative phases of being in the credit group and operating outside the group. While the latter phase is deterministic, lasting $T - 1$ periods, the former phase has random length. The optimal length of exclusion or dissolution might be infinite.[6] Another advantage of the dynamic formulation of the problem is that, to implement the allocation stated above, the credit group need not have as large a degree of control as is required to implement the sharing rules or contest-induced allocations in the static formulation.

6. Empirical Evidence

The empirical evidence on credit co-operatives is quite extensive and rather a mixed bag. Examples of successful co-operatives and credit groups with failures greatly outnumbering successes are found in East Asia. A large number of credit programmes in that region have achieved most of their objectives, particularly in reaching a large number of small agents, having high repayment rates, and increasing output in a cost-effective manner. Besides early land reform, the success of rural credit programmes in Korea, Taiwan, and Japan has been frequently attributed to strong village co-operative systems which have provided significant incentives to participate and comply, as well as credible enforcement procedures. Peer esteem and social norms served the role of an effective incentive scheme. Other successful examples are scattered throughout different countries, including Kenya, Malawi, and Nicaragua. The success there can be attributed to much better incentive, control, and monitoring systems (see von Pischke, Adams, and Donalds 1983).

Unfortunately, however, the empirical evidence also indicates that the number of failed co-operatives is extraordinarily large. Thailand is a typical example. Despite the extensive co-operative network in Thailand and the government's significant involvement in their development, the success rate has ranged from mediocre to poor. The reasons are as follows. First, there is a lack of sense of belonging and joint responsibility in most members; co-operatives are perceived as merely nominal organizations. Second, co-operatives lack efficient administration and are short on incentive schemes; dishonesty is quite common among officials. Third, there is not much co-ordination with the financial intermediary. Fourth, there does not seem to be much co-ordination between the credit, marketing, and production activities within the co-operative. Last, their large size and lack of proper monitoring activities, coupled with the perception by members that credit funds are more like grants or aid given by the state, induces detachment, high delinquency rates, and the improper use of funds. Poor performance such as Thailand exhibits — even relative to individual farmers — is quite disturbing, since we tend to think of co-operatives as an effective tool for rural development and for improving the plight of small farmers. Delinquency rates through the last decade have ranged from 35 per cent for individual farmers to 60 per cent for farmers' co-operatives and associations on average.

The viability of any credit organization is strongly linked to its success in recovering loans. Strong punitive measures and a proper set of incentives ought to be implemented to induce high repayment rates; those elements seem to be lacking in most credit co-operatives, hence the high failure rates. Most empirical studies of credit group programmes in rural areas in developing countries report low recovery rates. Defining default or non-performing loans as those loans that are still on the books but are past due by 90 days or more, are non-accruing, or have been renegotiated, those studies have indicated default rates ranging from 20 to 95 per cent for credit programmes in Africa, the Middle East, and Latin America. Similar results have been reported in South and South-east Asia (see Braverman and Guasch 1986). To some extent, the reasons for those high levels of default can be attributed to a lack of properly designed incentive schemes, a lack of enforcement procedures, and quite often a self-serving confusion on the farmer's part regarding the nature of credit. It is not unusual for farmers to perceive the loans as grants or welfare. In fact, in some South Asian languages the word used for loans from government institutions (*tagai*, *taccari*) means 'assistance, grant'. Thus the reluctance to repay those loans should not be surprising.

7. Conclusions

We have presented an analysis of the motivation, formation, and design of credit co-operatives. We have shown that they can provide significant advantages to their members, in so far as their intrinsic informational and moral hazard problems are properly accounted for. Particular care to the design of incentive mechanisms is warranted if credit co-operatives are to prove successful. The incentive schemes, degree of control, enforcement, and information-gathering by the credit co-operatives are most important to predict the likelihood of success. Long-term arrangements, rather than one-shot liaisons, can provide higher benefits to the members and financial viability to the organization.

We have also mentioned the empirical relevance of those forms of organizations, describing some of both successful and unsuccessful ventures. By and large, the elements that we have been able to identify as present in the successful incentive schemes are a control of resources, quality monitoring, and enforcement of punishing rules. We believe that a policy of providing assistance to existing and potential credit groups on how to set incentives, implement monitoring schemes, and develop centralized control of resources is most desirable and should receive highest priority. Moreover, it is better and much more cost-effective than the old-fashioned and largely regressive subsidized credit policies. It is just as important to address the political rigidities that so often hamper genuine co-operative promotion.

NOTES

1. The arguments are as follows. The lower the r is, the larger the demands from both types of agents for institutional funds. As stated above, on purely efficiency grounds, if there is need for rationing, the small agents will be the affected ones. Moreover, the larger the difference between r and the 'free' market, the more attractive the subsidized loans (the larger the income transfer) are and the stronger the pressures put upon the lending institution by the larger agents. As a result, the share of the institutional funds going to small agents will decrease as the rate r decreases, and in consequence, the demand for credit by the small agents in the informal market will increase.

2. If, indeed, reaching a large number of small agents is one of the main objectives of credit policies, another option is to intervene directly in the credit market by setting targets or quotas in the composition of the institution's loan portfolio. Then a proportion of the funds allocated by the institution is earmarked for the small agents. A more detailed intervention might entail a description of the number of agents to be reached as well as the size of the individual loans to be allocated. Incentives to induce compliance will need to be developed. They can take the form of tying future availability of public funds to the institution's portfolio composition and performance. Another option would be to offer interest rate rebates on loans granted to the targeted groups of agents up to a certain proportion or volume of funds; this is equivalent to subsidizing targeted loans *ex post* to neutralize the higher transaction cost and risk.

3. Alternative budget-balancing sharing rules that might prove effective if the agents are sufficiently risk-averse are those where all the agents but one (randomly chosen) are penalized — a massacre contract — or those where one agent (randomly chosen) is severely penalized — a scapegoat contract — whenever the output falls below the desired level. Their effectiveness has been shown by Rasmussen (1987) in the absence of production uncertainties. A problem with those rules is that they might require the agents to have significant wealth endowments.

4. Following upon the early work of Lazear and Rosen (1981), and Bhattacharya (1982), the optimality of tournament contracts in that context has been shown for heterogeneous agents by Bhattacharya and Guasch (1988) and for a restricted scenario in which marginal productivity of effort is not affected by common shocks, in Green and Stokey (1983), whereas Lazear and Rosen (1981) and Nalebuff and Stiglitz (1983) have compared tournaments with linear piece-rate contracts.

5. For a game-theoretic analysis of individual incentives to form co-operatives, see Sexton (1986), and Staatz (1983). These studies depart from the traditional organization-oriented approach to co-operative analysis and emphasize the core of the game as the viable solution or allocation. The idea is that, since there are gains to be realized by forming a co-operative, relative to each one acting independently, one has to consider how the gains ought to be allocated among the members, particularly when they are not identical. In addition, for a view of the

traditional analysis of co-operatives and of its motivations see, e.g., Helmberger and Hoos (1962), and Vitaliano (1983).

6. A generalization of the trigger-price strategy models has been developed by Abreu, Pearce, and Stacchetti (1986), where they characterize the optimal strategies. They take a fairly simple form. The punishment phase lasts only one period and carries a more severe punishment than unilateral production. Its usefulness in our framework is questionable, since punishments more severe than exclusion from the group might not be implementable. A policy to force the defector(s) to work as bonded labour for a period might not be sustainable.

18.

Agrarian Structure, Technological Innovations, and the State

Alain de Janvry, Elisabeth Sadoulet, and Marcel Fafchamps

1. Introduction

Following Solow's pioneering study on the role of technological change in explaining economic growth, a number of similar studies applied to agriculture revealed that technology could be at least as important a source of growth in that sector as it had been shown to be for the whole economy. Thus, Lave (1962) found that, in the United States between 1850 and 1958, technological change in agriculture had been twice as rapid as in manufacturing. Much lower rates of technological change were, however, observed in the less developed countries (LDCs). Hayami and Ruttan (1985) estimated that half of the difference in labour productivity between more developed countries (MDCs) and LDCs was explained by the use of modern technical inputs from the industrial sector and by human capital.

Technological change generally substitutes for factors unequally. The bias of technological change thus describes which factor is being saved most by technology. According to the Hicksian definition of bias, for instance, technological change is labour-saving when, at constant factor prices, the labour–capital ratio falls. Alternatively, it is labour-saving when, at constant factor ratio, the marginal product of labour falls relative to that of capital.

While a number of measurements of both the rate and the bias of technological change are available, attempts at identifying their economic and social determinants are recent and few. A major advance was made with the theory in induced technological innovations, which uses price signals to explain rate and bias. We start by reviewing the achievements of this theory to conclude that price signals are indeed a necessary but far from sufficient explanation. Using a transaction cost approach in a context of incomplete markets, we show that the structure of asset ownership is also an important determinant of the rate and bias of technological change. Finally, when technology is a public good generated in public research institutions, collective action can be used to affect the allocation of resources to alternative technological innovations. The structure of political power can thus further distort the rate and bias of technological change. We use a formal model of optimum technological choice to show in what direction structural characteristics of agriculture and collective action affect the bias of technological change. We also use cross-country data to show that structural characteristics and the size of public research budgets do indeed affect the nature of technological change beyond the effect of price signals.

2. Theoretical Framework and Unresolved Puzzles

2.1. The theory of induced technological innovations [1]

The objective of the pure neoclassical theory of induced technological innovations is to explain the rate and bias of technological change as an economic response to market forces by profit-maximizing entrepreneurs and by the state. This theory was cast in its modern form by introduction of the concept of a 'metaproduction function' (Hayami and Ruttan 1985) and of its isoquants, the 'innovation possibility curves' (IPCs) (Ahmad 1966). The IPC is the envelope of all the isoquants (technologies) that an entrepreneur or the state can develop with a given research budget for a given state of scientific knowledge. When relative factor prices change, factor substitution can occur in the short run within a given production function and in the longer run within the IPC by switching to other attainable technologies. The role of technology is thus to allow an increase in factor substitution away from the factors that have become relatively more expensive and towards those that have become relatively cheaper.

Even without changes in relative factor price, technology can also change factor ratios if higher research budgets or advances in scientific knowledge shift the IPC towards the origin in a non-Hicks-neutral fashion. In this case, the factor-saving bias of technological change is determined by the ability of a given research expenditure to improve the relative efficiencies of specific factors of production.

Over time, observed changes in factor ratios will result from the cumulative effects of the following three changes: (1) factor substitution within the production function currently used, (2) factor saving arising from technological change within IPC_t, and (3) factor saving arising from higher research budgets and advances in scientific knowledge that shift IPC_t to an IPC_{t+1} closer to the origin. If the change in IPC is Hicks-neutral, the factor ratio that results from these three changes is undoubtedly towards saving that factor which has become relatively more expensive. If, however, the change in IPC is not Hicks-neutral, it is not impossible that a strong bias in IPC more than compensates for the shift in factor ratios within a given IPC. This would, for instance, be the case if a strong bias in scientific advances towards labour-saving technology occurred at the same time as wages fell relative to the price of labour-saving capital goods.

With land and labour as the two primary factors of production in agriculture, it is useful to decompose capital goods between those that substitute for land and those that substitute for labour (Sen 1968; Hayami and Ruttan 1985). Land-saving capital is usually identified with biological, chemical, and water control investments, reflecting in particular the inputs of the Green Revolution (improved seeds, fertilizers, insecticides, and irrigation). This capital is land-saving because it increases yields. Labour-saving capital is usually identified with machinery and equipment, most particularly tractors. This capital is labour-saving as it increases the land area per worker and the productivity of labour. Correspondingly, technological advances in capital goods can be classified as land-saving or labour-saving changes according to whether they increase the productivity of land-saving or labour-saving capital goods.

Based on this contrast, the production function in agriculture can be usefully represented as a separable, two-level production function such as

$$Q = F\{X_A(E_A A, E_F F), X_L(E_L L, E_M M)\}$$

where

Q = agricultural output
$X_A(\cdot)$ = 'land' input index
$X_L(\cdot)$ = 'labour' input index
A = land
L = labour
F = land-saving capital (fertilizer)
M = labour-saving capital (machinery)
$E_i = E_i(a_i t + b_i \theta_i B)$, $i = A, F, L, M$, efficiency parameters
t = exogenous technological change (scientific knowledge)
B = research budget
θ_i = share of research budget allocated to factor i
a_i, b_i = exogenous parameters.

The usefulness of this classification is that it allows us to expect a high elasticity of substitution within subfunctions (i.e. between land and land-saving capital and between labour and labour-saving capital and technology) and a low or negative elasticity of substitution between the 'land' and 'labour' indexes, which are largely complementary in production. In practice, the classification is not necessarily successful since many types of biological advances are also labour-saving (e.g. herbicides) and many mechanical advances are yield-increasing (e.g. tractors that speed up tasks and allow for one additional crop in the year). Yet, when verified, it is a very convenient dichotomy for policy analysis.

Empirical evidence on the Allen partial elasticities of substitution between inputs in the same subfunction (σ_{AF} and σ_{LM}) and between inputs in different subfunctions (σ_{AL}, σ_{FL}, σ_{FM}, and σ_{AM}) generally supports the proposition that elasticities within subfunctions are higher than elasticities across subfunctions and that they are all systematically less than one.[2] We will use this result in the simulation exercises that follow in this chapter.

Separability of the production function implies that the ratio of the marginal productivities of two inputs within the same subfunction (e.g. L and M) is not affected by the level of use of a factor in the other subfunction (Kaneda 1982). Even if technological change created by shifts in IPC is Hicks-neutral within subfunctions and relative factor prices do not change, technological change may be biased between land and labour if the rate of technological change in land-saving capital differs from that in labour-saving capital (Thirtle 1985a).

Which area of the IPC is explored by technological innovators in response to changes in relative factor prices can be made endogenous by specifying a research production function (a given state of scientific knowledge) and a given research budget, B. Kamien and Schwartz (1968) thus specify a research production function of the type

$$f \left(\frac{\partial E_i}{\partial t} \right) = B.$$

The optimal bias of technological change can then be derived by simultaneously allocating B and the other factors of production in order to maximize the present value of the future stream of net profits. The optimal technological bias is a function of the initial technology, relative factor prices, and the relative costs of acquiring the different types of technological changes.

The research budget, and thus the IPC, can in turn be endogenized by specifying decreasing returns to research expenditures and making resource allocation to research compete with resource allocation to production (Binswanger 1974a, 1974b). This allows determination of both the optimum bias and the rate of technical change and brings out the role of not only factor price ratios but also product price levels and the relative value of output of different activities. In this case, the rate and bias of technical change are found to depend on the relative expected present value of the total cost of factors, the relative productivity of research in acquiring the different types of technology, and the value of output of the activity, which depends on price level and quantity of output.

There exists a large number of studies that have measured the internal rate of return from investment in agricultural research. While there are many conceptual and empirical difficulties with these measurements, they tend systematically to indicate that there has been underinvestment in agricultural research. The internal rates of return estimated tend to range between 20 and 100 per cent, which is quite evidently above the opportunity cost for most public goods programmes (Hayami and Ruttan 1985: 63–6). If this is the case, the size of research budgets is determined not by equilibrium conditions in resource allocation but by non-economic rules. In the following analysis, we consequently take the research budget as exogenous. The rate of technological change is thus determined by the size of this budget, the productivity of resources in the generation of technological advances, and the rate of diffusion of new technologies.

Empirical support for the theory of induced innovations has generally been positive, but it is fair to say that a rigorous and unambiguous test is still to be performed. Over the long pull of history, the qualitative implications of the theory tend to be verified. Thus, in Japan, with rising land scarcity associated with population pressure, the course of technological change was directed at raising land productivity more than labour productivity. In the United States, by contrast, labour scarcity and abundance of land led to technological advances aimed at raising labour productivity.

More precise empirical tests using econometric analysis to relate the bias of technological change to changes in relative factor prices start by observing that, over the long run, there have been enormous changes in factor proportions that could hardly have occurred as a result of substitution among factors in the absence of technological change. The observed factor substitutions are thus postulated to have occurred along the IPC or across changing IPCs as the levels of research budgets and of scientific knowledge have changed over time. Factor substitution within a given production function, technological change within an IPC, and technological change across IPCs are thus confounded in the observed change in factor ratios. Regression results for the United States over the period 1880–1980 (Hayami and Ruttan 1985) tend to show the following results:

$$\frac{F}{A} = f\left(-\frac{f}{r}, \frac{w}{r}, -\frac{m}{r}\right) \tag{1}$$

$$\frac{M}{L} = f\left(-\frac{m}{w}, -\frac{r}{w}\right) \tag{2}$$

$$\frac{A}{L} = f\left(\frac{r}{w}, -\frac{m}{w}\right) \tag{3}$$

where r, f, w, and m are the prices of A, F, L, and M, respectively. The negative signs for the own-price ratios in the first two equations support the theory of induced innovations but not the positive sign in the third. This latter result is attributed to an 'innate labour-saving bias' in technological change (Hayami and Ruttan 1985: 186), or to a greater ability of research to improve the efficiency of labour-saving technological change relative to that of land-saving technological change, leading to rising land–labour ratios in spite of rising land rent–wage ratios. The same result was found by Thirtle (1985c) using US data for four crops in ten regions during the period 1939–78. As we shall see, this observed puzzle could be explained by structural changes leading to the creation of larger farms and transaction costs in the access to labour that raise effective labour costs on the larger farms.

Another anomaly relative to the two-level specification of the production function is that, while machinery and fertilizers (equation (1)) and machinery and land (equations (2) and (3)) are expectedly shown to be complements by the negative signs observed for the corresponding price ratios, fertilizer and labour (equation (1)) are shown to be substitutes by the positive sign observed.

Beyond the crudeness of empirical support for the theory of induced innovations, there are at least two important aspects in which it is evidently lacking. One is the failure to take into account the existence of transaction costs that differentiate factor prices and, hence, optimum factor biases across farms. The other is the failure to incorporate in the model the practice of collective action that biases the performance of the state in delivering public goods such as technology. In the following two sections, we introduce a number of concepts from the theories of transaction costs and collective action that need to be incorporated into the theory of induced innovations in order to increase its explanatory power.

2.2 The theory of transaction costs

In its pure neoclassical form, the theory of induced innovations postulates that perfect markets exist for all products and factors as well as for risk. Prices thus convey all the relevant information to decision-makers, and all agents face equal prices. In this case, resources are efficiently allocated irrespective of the personal distribution of assets. If there are no economies of scale in production, there is only one optimum technological choice for a given research budget and state of scientific knowledge. If, as Hayami and Ruttan (1985) postulate, the state is equally responsive to market signals in the delivery of public goods as are private agents, the technology induced in public research institutions for one particular product will be uniquely determined by relative factor prices, the size of the research budget, and the state of scientific knowledge. There is, consequently, no room for collective action to influence the allocation of a research budget towards alternative technological innovations.

This is, of course, an idealized vision of the world, which abstracts from the pervasiveness of transaction costs. As the recent contributions of Akerlof (1984), Stiglitz (1986a), and Williamson (1985), among others, have amply shown, introducing transaction costs into rational choice models eventually leads to patterns of resource allocation that are markedly different from those of an idealized first-best world. We show here that this is true for the inducements of technological innovations as well. When transaction costs are taken into account, optimum technology becomes conditional on the distribution of assets and, consequently, there no longer exists a single optimum choice across farms. It is this multiplicity of private optima that, in turn, makes collective action to influence public choices in research so important.

Transaction costs refer to a number of costs not typically considered in the neoclassical concept of production costs with atomistic agents, market prices, and zero cost of market-clearing (Nugent 1986). They include the costs of information and of negotiating, monitoring, supervising, co-ordinating, and enforcing contracts. Existence of these costs is created by the possibility of opportunistic behaviour in social relations. In labour contracts, in particular, there exists the possibility that hired labour paid on a time rate basis will shirk, requiring supervision by the owner-operator or family labour. Supervision costs thus represent a transaction cost in the access to hired labour. As the number of hired workers on a farm increases, the ratio of hired to family labour increases, and the price of a unit of effective labour thus increases as well. Another transaction cost is a fixed cost in land transactions, which implies that the price of land tends to decline with farm size.

As opposed to the pure neoclassical theory of the first-best, which is ahistorical, extending that theory by introducing transaction costs makes it specific to a particular structural context. In the following analysis, we consider a situation where there are no economies of scale in production, where landownership is unequally distributed, where there is a rental market for land but no market for land in ownership, where there exists a credit constraint determined by the ownership of land which serves as collateral, where supervision costs on hired labour imply that the price of effective labour increases with employment, and where the price of land declines with farm size. Clearly, these conditions are not universal, and different farm models with transaction costs must be specified for different structural contexts.

While transaction costs have not been formally introduced in the theory of induced technological innovations, their importance in effecting the adoption of new technologies across farm sizes has been noted by Griffin (1974) for Latin America in particular. In this case the technology of the Green Revolution was observed to benefit more large than small farmers because of a decreasing cost of credit with farm size.

The farm-level model we use to introduce transaction costs into the theory of induced technological innovations is one where the production function is a two-level constant elasticity of substitution (CES):

$$Q = \left\{ \gamma X_A^{-\rho} + (1 - \gamma) X_L^{-\rho} \right\}^{+1/\rho} \tag{4}$$

$$X_A = \left\{ \alpha A^{-\rho_A} + (1 - \alpha) (E_F F)^{-\rho_A} \right\}^{-1/\rho_A} \tag{5}$$

$$X_L = \left\{ \beta L^{-\rho_L} + (1 - \beta) (E_M M)^{-\rho_L} \right\}^{-1/\rho_L}. \tag{6}$$

The efficiency parameters are exogenous at the farm level:

$$E_F = E(\lambda_F \theta B) \tag{7}$$

$$E_M = E\{\lambda_M (1 - \theta) B\} \tag{8}$$

where

$E(\cdot)$ = research function

λ_i = productivity parameter, $i = F, M$

θ = allocation of budget B between E_F and E_M.

With transaction costs in the access to labour and land, the farm-level prices of these inputs vary as follows:

$$w = w(L), \; w' > 0, \; w'' < 0$$
$$r = r(A), \; r' < 0, \; r'' > 0$$

while the prices of output (p), fertilizer (f), and machinery (m) are constant.

The farm operator maximizes profit under a credit constraint, $K(\overline{A})$, determined by the size of ownership unit $\overline{A}$. Credit availability constrains total expenditure on inputs, including the rental of land. With constant returns to scale, the credit constraint determines the level of output. The farmer's problem is thus:

$$\max_{A, L, F, M} \; p \, Q(A, L, F, M; E_F, E_M)$$
$$- (1 + \lambda) \, (rA + wL + fF + mM) + \lambda K \qquad (9)$$
$$\text{s.t. } w = w(L), r = r(A).$$

The optimum levels of factor use are

$$A, L, F, M = f(p, f, m, \overline{A}, E_i, \quad i = F, M).$$

Optimum factor ratios change with farm size. As farm size increases, fertilizer per acre and labour per acre decrease while machinery per acre, machinery per worker, and the machinery–fertilizer ratio all increase.

2.3. The theory of the state and collective action

It is well known that much agricultural technology has the character of public goods because the returns from research cannot easily be appropriated privately. This explains the importance of the public sector in the generation of agricultural research. A theory of induced innovations for agriculture consequently needs to incorporate a theory of the state.

In their theory of induced innovations, Hayami and Ruttan (1985) postulate that the state responds to changes in relative prices in a fashion that is optimal for farmers since the state responds to their organizations. As they explain,

Farmers are induced by shifts in relative prices to search for technical alternatives that save the increasingly scarce factors of production. They press the public research institutions to develop the new technology and demand that agricultural supply firms supply modern technical inputs that substitute for the more scarce factors. Perceptive scientists and science administrators respond by making available new technical possibilities and new inputs that enable farmers profitably to substitute the increasingly abundant factors for increasingly scarce factors, thereby guiding the demand of farmers for unit cost reduction in a socially optimum direction.

The dialectic interaction among farmers and research scientists and administrators is likely to be most effective when farmers are organized into politically effective local and regional farm 'bureaus' or farmers' associations. The response of the public sector research and extension programs to farmers' demand is likely to be greatest when the agricultural research system is highly decentralized, as in the United States. (Hayami and Ruttan 1985: 88)

Because there are no differential transaction costs across farms and no economies of scale, farmers' demands are for a unique technological alternative, whatever their scale of operation in a given activity. Collective action can thus be reduced to its simplest form, the transfer of socially unspecific information (demands) to the public sector. There are two problems with this simplification.

One is that, once the existence of structure-specific transaction costs is recognized, the demand for public goods becomes social-group-specific, and collective action takes on its true meaning of distributional struggles at the level of the state. If collective action by large farmers is more effective than that by small farmers, the dominance of large farmers' demands will distort the optimum technological bias towards the factor–price ratios that correspond to their particular types of farms.

The studies of Olson (1965) and Hardin (1982) have helped identify some of the determinants of success in collective action. The main condition for success is the ability of a group to suppress free-riding, and this is largely a matter of the characteristics of the group. Success in collective action is thus expected to be greater the smaller the group, the more homogeneous its origin, the longer its members have been together or it has been in existence, the more complementary the goals of different members, the closer the social and physical proximity among its members, the greater the difficulty of 'exit' as opposed to 'voice' behaviour, and so on (Hirschman 1970; Nugent 1986). These group characteristics have been used to explain why farmers in LDCs usually have less power over the state than industrialists and urban consumers, resulting in the well-known urban bias (Lipton 1977). The same characteristics can be used to explain why large farmers tend to have more success in lobbying than small farmers.

Another excessive simplification in the Hayami–Ruttan theory of the state and public goods is that is fails to endow the state with any type of autonomy from demands by organized farmers. This is a subject on which there exists a considerable degree of controversy (Hamilton 1982). Yet it is, for instance, possible for the state to use technology as an instrument of an income policy and as a surrogate for asset redistribution.

The role of collective action and of autonomous state initiatives in influencing the allocation of public research budgets, and the consequent technological biases in public sector research, have been observed in several studies (de Janvry 1973; Guttman 1978a). With its highly skewed distribution of landownership and its long tradition of strong state interventionism, nowhere is this more visible than in Latin America. In a recent extensive study of the pattern of technological change in that continent, Pineiro and Trigo (1983) observed that international availability of new technologies, expected profitability of the innovation, and changes in relative factor prices are not sufficient to explain technological change. They found, by contrast, that successful occurrences of technological innovations tend to result from either one of the following two conditions.

The first is when the structural conditions for successful collective action are satisfied. This was observed to happen when the producers of a commodity are few, economically powerful, homogeneous, and regionally concentrated. Their lobbies may then be able to influence the allocation of public budgets to research in their favour. This was the case with large-scale sugar plantations in Colombia and with *hacendado* milk producers in Ecuador. The second is when a commodity is of national significance as either a wage good or a source of foreign exchange earnings. In this case, even though the ultimate beneficiaries of technological change are numerous and disorganized, the state may act on their behalf. This is how successful research programmes were implemented in rice in Colombia and corn in Argentina. Situations where producers are not powerfully organized and the commodity is not of national significance tend to result in technological stagnation. This explains the lack of research on peasant crops and peasant farming systems.

In the following model of induced technological innovations, we show that the bias of technological change can be affected significantly by the existence of both transaction costs and collective action.

3. Micro-foundation of Induced Technological Change: Optimal Bias by Farm Size

The farm-level model introduced previously is used to define the demand for technological change that would emerge from a homogeneous group of farms. Keeping exogenous the decision on the size of the research budget B, there is an optimal allocation $\tilde{\theta}$ of this budget between research on land-saving and on labour-saving technological changes which maximizes farm profit. It is determined by including θ as a decision variable of the farm operator in the maximization problem. Since land and labour costs (and, consequently, factor use) depend on the size of ownership unit $\overline{A}$, $\tilde{\theta}$ will also be found to vary with $\overline{A}$. In the general case, the solution for θ cannot be separated from the solution for the levels of factor use as they are jointly determined. Taking land and labour prices as explicit functions of $\overline{A}$, rather than as functions of the levels of factor use L and A, greatly simplifies the exposition of the problem, since it allows decisions on factor use and on optimal technological change to be taken sequentially. The analysis that follows is based on this simplified model. In that case, the optimal levels of factor use and the corresponding unit cost function (c) associated with the two-level CES production function can be explicitly written as functions of the exogenous factor prices (m and f), landownership ($\overline{A}$), and the efficiency parameters (E_i):

$$c = c\{r(\overline{A}), w(\overline{A}), f, m, E_i\}. \tag{10}$$

Total production and profit are direct functions of the unit cost:

$$Q = K/c,$$

$$\text{Profits} = \left(\frac{p}{c} - 1\right)K,$$

where p is the product price and K the total credit available to the farm.
$\tilde{\theta}$ derives from minimizing the cost c;

$$\min_{\theta} c\{r(\overline{A}), w(\overline{A}), f, m, E_i(\theta, B), \quad i = F, L\}. \tag{11}$$

3.1. Optimal budget allocation

Returning to the farm model with efficiency parameters applying to the capital inputs only, the optimal θ is solution of the cost minimization problem with

$$c = \left\{\gamma^\sigma R^{1-\sigma} + (1 - \gamma)^\sigma W^{1-\sigma}\right\}^{1/(1-\sigma)} \tag{12}$$

where

$$R = \left\{\alpha^{\sigma_A} r^{1-\sigma_A} + (1 - \alpha)^{\sigma_A}\left(\frac{1}{E_F} f\right)^{1-\sigma_A}\right\}^{1/(1-\sigma_A)}$$

and

$$W = \left\{\beta^{\sigma_L} w^{1-\sigma_L} + (1 - \beta)^{\sigma_L}\left(\frac{1}{E_M} m\right)^{1-\sigma_L}\right\}^{1/(1-\sigma_L)}$$

are the unit costs of the land and labour aggregates.

The first-order condition implicitly defines $\tilde{\theta}$ as the solution of the equation:

$$\frac{dc}{d\theta} = \left(\frac{\gamma c}{R}\right)^\sigma \left\{\frac{(1-\alpha)R}{E_F^* f}\right\}^{\sigma_A} f \frac{dE_F^*}{d\theta}$$

$$+ \left\{\frac{(1-\gamma)c}{W}\right\}^\sigma \left\{\frac{(1-\beta)W}{E_M^* m}\right\}^{\sigma_L} \frac{dE_M^*}{m d\theta} = 0 \tag{13}$$

where $E_i^* = 1/E_i$ gives the equivalent price decrease of an efficiency gain on factor use. The second-order condition which ensures that the cost reaches a minimum is written

$$\frac{\mathrm{d}^2 c}{\mathrm{d}\theta^2} = \frac{\partial^2 c}{\partial E_F^{*2}} \left(\frac{\mathrm{d}E_F^*}{\mathrm{d}\theta} \right)^2 + \frac{\partial c}{\partial E_F^*} \left(\frac{\mathrm{d}^2 E_F^*}{\mathrm{d}\theta^2} \right)$$

$$+ \frac{\partial^2 c}{\partial E_M^{*2}} \left(\frac{\mathrm{d}E_M^*}{\mathrm{d}\theta} \right)^2 + \frac{\partial c}{\partial E_M^*} \left(\frac{\mathrm{d}^2 E_M^*}{\mathrm{d}\theta^2} \right). \tag{14}$$

The sign of this expression cannot be unambiguously assessed. The second derivatives of E_F^* and E_M^* with respect to θ are positive if the research has decreasing return to scale in E_i^*, and the second and fourth terms are then positive. But, with positive elasticities of substitution σ, σ_A, and σ_L, the second derivatives of the cost c with respect to E_F^* and E_M^* are both negative. However, if these elasticities of substitution are small, and/or if the research function has decreasing returns to scale with a sufficient curvature, the whole expression is positive, and $\tilde{\theta}$ corresponds to a minimum cost. The intuitive reason is that, in this case, for values of θ beyond the optimal $\tilde{\theta}$, the reduction in the cost of 'efficient fertilizer' has little impact on the overall cost and does not compensate for the corresponding increase in 'efficient machinery' cost. The importance of the curvature of the research functions on $\tilde{\theta}$ will be confirmed numerically later in this section.

Assuming that the second-order condition is satisfied, it is quite clear that $\tilde{\theta}$ depends on the structure of input prices. The signs of these relationships are established by total differentiation of equation (13) at $\theta = \tilde{\theta}$. In particular, $\mathrm{d}\tilde{\theta}/\mathrm{d}w$ has the sign of

$$- c^\sigma \frac{\partial^2 c}{\partial\theta\partial w} = -(\sigma_L - \sigma)(1 - \gamma)^\sigma (1 - \beta)^{\sigma_L} W^{\sigma_L - \sigma - 1} m^{1 - \sigma} \frac{\partial W}{\partial w} E_M^{\sigma_L - 2} \frac{\mathrm{d}E_M}{\mathrm{d}\theta}, \tag{15}$$

which is negative for $\sigma_L > \sigma$. Similarly, $\mathrm{d}\tilde{\theta}/\mathrm{d}r$ can be shown to be positive for $\sigma_A > \sigma$.

The demand for technological change originating in large farms, which face higher transaction costs on labour and lower transaction cost on land, will thus be biased towards improvement of mechanization, which can substitute for labour, while the demand by small farmers will be biased towards factor-augmenting technological change in fertilizers.

The impact of changing the prices of the capital inputs on the demand for research can similarly be assessed. The optimal share of the research budget to be allocated to fertilizer is an increasing function of its price f if

$$\frac{\sigma_A - \sigma}{1 - \sigma_A} \frac{(1 - \alpha)^{\sigma_A} (E_F^* f)^{1 - \sigma_A}}{R^{1 - \sigma_A}} + 1 > 0, \tag{16}$$

which is true for $\sigma < \sigma_A < 1$. Similarly, the budget share allocated to research on machinery is an increasing function of the machinery price m if $\sigma < \sigma_L < 1$. This is logical, since the course of technological innovations is directed at saving on the factor that becomes relatively more expensive.

A convenient way of summarizing this information on signs is as follows:

$$\tilde{\theta} = \theta(+f, +r, -w, -m, B),\tag{17}$$

in which the sign in front of each variable indicates the sign of the partial derivative of the function with respect to that variable.

For use in the empirical analysis that follows, the expression that defines $\tilde{\theta}$ can also be written in terms of relative factor prices as follows:

$$
\left(\frac{r}{w}\right)^{1-\sigma} \gamma^{\sigma}(1-\alpha)^{\sigma_A} \left(\frac{R}{r}\right)^{\sigma_A-\sigma} \left(\frac{f}{r}\right)^{1-\sigma_A} E_F^{\sigma_A-2}\, \frac{dE_F}{d\theta}
$$
$$
+ (1-\gamma)^{\sigma}(1-\beta)^{\sigma_L} \left(\frac{W}{w}\right)^{\sigma_L-\sigma} \left(\frac{m}{w}\right)^{1-\sigma_L} E_M^{\sigma_L-2}\, \frac{dE_M}{d\theta} = 0,\tag{18}
$$

which shows that $\tilde{\theta}$ can be expressed as a function of the three relative prices, f/r, m/w, and r/w, and the budget B, with signs that are

$$\tilde{\theta} = \theta(+f/r, -m/w, ++r/w, B),\tag{19}$$

where $+ +$ indicates that the impact of an increasing r/w dominates that of a decreasing f/r if coming from a change in r only.

Allocation of the research budget, therefore, responds to increasing prices of land and fertilizers by increasing the share devoted to fertilizer research, if the elasticities of substitution are all lower than one and the elasticities of substitution within each of the two aggregates are higher than that between these aggregates.

The relationship between factor prices and the optimal allocation of the research budget can be further analysed by numerical simulations in the farm model. To do this, specific values are given to the parameters and variables of the cost and research functions, and transaction cost functions are analytically defined. The initial setup is a symmetrical case between labour and land inputs with

$$
\begin{aligned}
\alpha &= \beta = \gamma = 0.5 \\
m &= f = 1 \\
w &= r = 1 \\
\sigma_A &= \sigma_L = 0.7 \\
\sigma &= 0.2.
\end{aligned}
$$

The research functions are specified as the following relations between θ and the inverse of the efficiency parameters:

$$\frac{1}{E_F} = \frac{1}{2} + \{(1-\theta)B\}^e\tag{20}$$

$$\frac{1}{E_M} = \frac{1}{2} + (\theta B)^e,\tag{21}$$

TABLE 18.1. Simulation results: variation of the optimal θ with factor substitutability, research efficiency, and factor prices

		$\sigma = 0.2$	$\sigma = 0.4$	$\sigma = 0.5$
(a) $w = r = 1$	$\sigma_A = \sigma_L = 0.7$	0.50	0.50	0.50
(b) $w = r = 1$	$\sigma_A = 0.8; \sigma_L = 0.6$			
	$e = 2$	0.86	0.82	0.79
	$e = 4$	0.63	0.60	0.59
(c) $w = 10; r = 1$	$\sigma_A = \sigma_L = 0.7$			
	$e = 2$	0.27	0.34	0.39
	$e = 4$	0.43	0.46	0.47
(d) $w = 10; r = 1$	$\sigma_A = 0.8; \sigma_L = 0.6$			
	$e = 2$	0.76	0.76	0.76
	$e = 4$	0.58	0.57	0.57

with the same e parameters to eliminate any possible innate bias arising from different efficiencies of the two research activities, and with B set to 1.

Simulation results confirm that the curvature of the research function, e, has a paramount impact on the shape of the relationship between total output and θ. For linear research functions (i.e. for $e = 1$), the relation between output and θ is convex, and the optimal θ is then either 0 or 1, implying complete specialization in research. In the following simulations, sufficiently large values of e were consequently chosen to avoid this occurrence.

Table 18.1 gives the optimal θ for different values of the parameters σ_A, σ_L, σ, and e and of the variables w and r.

In the perfectly symmetrical case chosen above, $\tilde{\theta}$ is 0.5 (experiment (a) in the table). Keeping $w = r$ but setting σ_A different from σ_L (experiment (b) in the table), $\tilde{\theta}$ is no longer 0.5. If $\sigma_A > \sigma_L$, $\tilde{\theta} > 0.5$ and vice versa. This rather intuitive result simply says that, when substitution possibilities are better for, say, land, the optimum research strategy will emphasize land-displacing innovations. Also, the departure of $\tilde{\theta}$ from 0.5 gets larger as σ and/or e get smaller. This means that, when the substitution possibilities between land and labour are narrower, or when marginal returns to research are decreasing, an optimum research strategy will emphasize even more innovation on the factor that is easier to substitute for land or labour, as the case may be.

Going back to the case where $\sigma_A = \sigma_L$, $\tilde{\theta}$ is affected by the relative values of w and r (experiment (c) in the table). When $w > r$, namely, on a large farm where the cost of supervision increases the cost of labour, $\tilde{\theta}$ is now less than 0.5. The optimum research strategy is to promote labour-saving technology. As before, the relation between output and $\tilde{\theta}$ is more 'centred' towards 0.5 when σ and e are large. The bias of technological change away from $\tilde{\theta} = 0.5$ is thus reduced when research specialization is less likely (large e) and when substitution between land and labour aggregates is easier (large σ).

Differences between σ_A and σ_L can lead to interesting results. For instance, when $\sigma_A > \sigma_L$, it is possible that the optimal research strategy puts more emphasis on land-saving technology even when $w > r$ (experiment (d) in the table). This means that the substitution advantage of land over labour may be sufficient to counterbalance higher labour costs. The result is understandably somewhat mitigated when σ is very large. Moreover, $\tilde{\theta}$ increases when e and/or σ decreases.

From the above, it is clear that relative factor prices do not determine unambiguously the sign of the optimum technological bias. Simulation results show that the magnitude of partial elasticities of substitution of the IPC is important. How well new technology can substitute itself to land or labour will also have a very important impact on optimal research strategies.

Introducing into the farm model transaction costs that make effective prices change with farm size $\bar{A}$ leads to $\tilde{\theta}$ that also vary across farm sizes. Labour and land cost functions are specified as

$$w(\bar{A}) = \frac{1}{2} + \left(\frac{\bar{A} - 1}{7} \right)^3 \tag{22}$$

$$r(\bar{A}) = \frac{1}{2} + 50 \left(\frac{10}{10 + \bar{A}} \right)^3. \tag{23}$$

For land varying from 0.25 to 45 acres, these functions induce a relative effective price of labour to land that increases from 0.01 to 310. The variation in optimal research allocation, which corresponds to this range of variation in prices, is represented in Figure 18.1, which clearly shows the differences in demands for technological biases that originate in small versus large farms. With $\tilde{\theta}$ specific to farm size, the different classes of farm sizes will have conflicting demands for technological innovations.

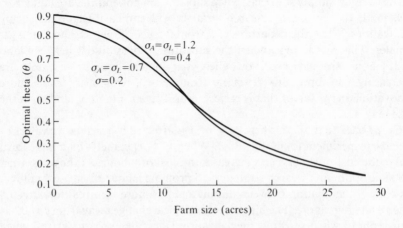

FIG. 18.1   Variation in optimal research bias with farm size

3.2. Factor use and technological bias

How do factors substitute for each other in this model of induced technological change, and how does the mere introduction of technological change bring about a bias in factor use even at constant factor prices? These questions can be partially answered analytically and will be further explored with numerical simulations.

The structural model that determines the optimum levels of factor use is

$$\frac{F}{A} = \left(\frac{1}{E_F}\right)^{1-\sigma_A} \left(\frac{1-\alpha}{\alpha}\right)^{\sigma_A} \left(\frac{r}{f}\right)^{\sigma_A} \tag{24}$$

$$\frac{M}{L} = \left(\frac{1}{E_M}\right)^{1-\sigma_L} \left(\frac{1-\beta}{\beta}\right)^{\sigma_L} \left(\frac{w}{m}\right)^{\sigma_L} \tag{25}$$

$$\frac{A}{L} = \left(\frac{\gamma}{1-\gamma}\right)^{\sigma} \frac{\alpha^{\sigma_A}}{\beta^{\sigma_L}} \left(\frac{w}{r}\right)^{\sigma}$$

$$\frac{\left\{\alpha^{\sigma_A} + (1-\alpha)^{\sigma_A} \left(\frac{1}{E_F}\frac{f}{r}\right)^{1-\sigma_A}\right\}^{(\sigma_A-\sigma)/(1-\sigma_A)}}{\left\{\beta^{\sigma_L} + (1-\beta)^{\sigma_L} \left(\frac{1}{E_M}\frac{m}{w}\right)^{1-\sigma_L}\right\}^{(\sigma_L-\sigma)/(1-\sigma_L)}}, \tag{26}$$

together with the research functions

$$E_F = E(\lambda_F \tilde{\theta} B) \text{ and } E_M = E\{\lambda_M(1-\tilde{\theta})B\}$$

and equation (13), which defines $\tilde{\theta}$.

The explicit dependence on factor prices represents the direct substitution among factors implemented in response to price changes. Within each aggregate, the elasticities of substitution are σ_A and σ_L, respectively. Across groups, the elasticity of substitution between land and labour, for example, is not constant but can be seen to be greater than σ, with the substitutability between both factors in each aggregate contributing to increase the impact of the change of one price w or r on the land–labour ratio.

Introduction of a positive research budget increases the change in the factor ratios. Except for a budget completely specialized in one type of research ($\tilde{\theta} = 0$ or 1), the research activities will raise the efficiency of both fertilizer and machinery and correspondingly will lower their use relative to land and labour. However, the impact of technological change can either increase or decrease the land–labour ratio depending on whether or not the effect of increasing fertilizer efficiency, which reduces the share of the land aggregate, dominates the effect of increasing machinery efficiency.

The following relationships summarize the overall dependency of factor ratios on relative factor prices:

$$F/A = f(-f/r, -\tilde{\theta}, -B)$$
$$M/L = f(-m/w, +\tilde{\theta}, -B)$$

$$A/L = f(-r/w, +f/r, -m/w, -\tilde{\theta}, B)$$
$$\tilde{\theta} = \theta(+f/r, -m/w, ++r/w, B).$$

Identification of the role of induced technological change on factor ratios derives from the following expressions.

1. While direct substitution between fertilizer and land responds only to the relative price of these two inputs, technological change introduces an increase in relative fertilizer use when the price of machinery or the level of wages increases since less research is then devoted to increasing fertilizer efficiency.
2. In the land–labour ratio, direct substitution and the impact of technological change counteract each other. From simple substitutability, an increase in the fertilizer price generates direct substitution of land for fertilizer and thus a higher land use per worker. Technological change response, by contrast, increases research in fertilizer efficiency leading to lower use of both factors, land and fertilizer, and of the land aggregate.

The impact of the size of the research budget on the optimum factor bias is analytically ambiguous. Numerical simulations reported in Table 18.2 permit us to see, however, that a rising research budget always makes $\tilde{\theta}$ converge towards 0.5 if there is no 'innate bias' in research, that is, if the efficiency of research is equal in generating land-saving or labour-saving innovations. The greater the research budget, the more neutrality there is in technological change whatever the elasticities of substitution and relative factor prices. This is due to the fact that there are decreasing marginal productivities in research and that, while the path towards capturing the gains from research is affected by the elasticities of substitution and relative factor prices, at the limit, all potential gains from research become exhausted and there is convergence towards neutrality. Permanence of technological bias with infinitely high research budgets would result only from innate biases in research.

TABLE 18.2. Simulation results: variation of optimal θ with factor substitutability factor prices, and size of the research budget

		$B = 0.8$	$B = 1$	$B = 3$	$B = 10$
$w = r = 1$	$\sigma_A = \sigma_L = 0.7$	0.5	0.5	0.5	0.5
$w = r = 1$	$\sigma_A = 0.8; \sigma_L = 0.6$	0.96	0.86	0.58	0.53
$w = 10;$					
$r = 1$	$\sigma_A = \sigma_L = 0.7$	0.14	0.27	0.46	0.48
$w = 10;$					
$r = 1$	$\sigma_A = 0.8; \sigma_L = 0.6$	0.89	0.76	0.54	0.52

Note: In these runs, $e = 2$ and $\sigma = 0.2$.

4. Macroeconomic Determination of Induced Technological Change

So far, we have derived analytically and numerically the optimum bias of technical change in a farm model with a given farm size. We will now explore the impact that land distribution has on the choice by the state of an optimal research budget allocation for the farm sector as a whole.

With constant returns to scale in production and no transaction costs, relative factor use would be the same for all farms, even if the credit constraint induces some differentiation in the size of operations. In such circumstances, the optimal research strategy would also be the same irrespective of farm size.

Differences in relative factor use are brought about if relative factor costs vary from farm to farm owing to transaction costs. In this case, the size of operation determined by the credit constraint will also affect the relative factor costs and, therefore, the research budget allocation preferred by individual farmers. Global output response to various levels of θ will now be the aggregation over all farms of differentiated impacts. In that sense, the way access to credit is distributed across farms will matter for choice by the state of an optimal θ.

4.1. The state's problem

While each farm's demand for a specific bias of technological change is dictated by its own profit motive, the state, which provides technological change as a public good, has its own objective in the choice of bias. Minimizing food cost through a maximum sectoral output, insuring a minimum level of profit for small farmers, and underwriting the technological demands of the large farmers are alternative possible objectives for the state. To each corresponds a different optimal allocation $\tilde{\theta}$ of the research budget.

We consider first the case where the state maximizes sectoral output. With credit a function of landownership $K(\overline{A})$ and labour and land costs also a function of $\overline{A}$, the sectoral output is

$$Q(\theta) = \int_{\overline{A}} \frac{K(\overline{A})}{c\{\theta, w(\overline{A}), r(\overline{A})\}} f(\overline{A}) \, d\overline{A} \tag{27}$$

where $f(\overline{A})$ is the frequency distribution of farms by size of ownership unit. Assuming that the second-order condition is satisfied, the optimal θ is determined by

$$\frac{dQ(\theta)}{d\theta} = \int_{\overline{A}} \frac{-K(\overline{A})}{c^2\{\theta, w(\overline{A}), r(\overline{A})\}} \frac{dc\{\theta, w(\overline{A}), r(\overline{A})\}}{d\theta} f(\overline{A}) \, d\overline{A} = 0. \tag{28}$$

To separate the role of transaction costs, which vary with farm size, from that of market factor prices (w_0 and r_0), which are observed, farm-level labour and land costs can be written as

$$w(\overline{A}) = w_0 + w^*(\overline{A}) \quad \text{and} \quad r(\overline{A}) = r_0 - r^*(\overline{A}). \tag{29}$$

In a first approximation in taking account of transaction costs, the sector can be treated as homogeneous in the sense that all farms are of equal size. The analysis of a homogeneous sector is a direct application of the farm-level model in which the average farm size $\overline{\overline{A}}$ influences both the direct substitution among factors and the research decisions which combine in defining the factor use ratios.

With increasing transaction costs on labour and decreasing transaction costs on land, there will be an increasing bias in research towards raising the efficiency of labour relative to that of land as average farm size increases (negative sign of the coefficient of $\overline{\overline{A}}$ in the $\hat{\theta}$ function in Table 18.3). At the same time, direct substitution of fertilizer for land decreases while direct substitution of machinery for workers and of land for workers increases (sign of $\overline{\overline{A}}$ in the factor ratio equations of the structural model). Integration of these effects in the reduced model shows that technological change counteracts the direct factor substitution effect arising from varying transaction costs in the determination of fertilizer use per acre and machinery use per worker. Observation of decreasing fertilizer use and increasing machinery use would, however, suggest that the direct substitution effects dominate over the technological change effects. On the land–labour ratio, substitution induced by differential transaction costs and technological change reinforce each other.

A model of induced technological innovations with transaction costs thus suggests that, across regions or countries, technological change will be

TABLE 18.3. *Determinants of the optimum technological bias and factor ratios*

Structural model:

$$\tilde{\theta} = \tilde{\theta}(\,+f/r_0,\ -m/w_0,\ +\ +r_0/w_0,\ -\overline{\overline{A}},\ B)$$
$$F/A = f(\,-f/r_0,\ -\tilde{\theta},\ -\overline{\overline{A}},\ -B)$$
$$M/L = (\,-m/w_0,\ +\tilde{\theta},\ +\overline{\overline{A}},\ -B)$$
$$A/L = (\,+f/r_0,\ -m/w_0,\ -r_0/w_0,\ -\tilde{\theta},\ +\overline{\overline{A}},\ B)$$

Reduced model of factor use:*

$$F/A = (\,-f/r_0,\ +m/w_0,\ -r_0/w_0,\ \mp\overline{\overline{A}},\ B)$$
$$M/L = (\,+f/r_0,\ -m/w_0,\ +r_0/w_0,\ \pm\overline{\overline{A}},\ B)$$
$$A/L = (\,\pm f/r_0,\ \pm m/w_0,\ -r_0/w_0,\ +\overline{A},\ B)$$

---

*When two signs are given, the top one is that which holds if the factor substitution effect for a given technology dominates, while the lower one is that which holds if the induced innovations effect for a given budget size dominates.

sensibly different from what would have been expected on the basis of direct factor prices alone, w_0 and r_0, with a greater bias towards mechanical innovations where average farm size is larger. It also indicates the need for a change in the orientation of research if any transformation in the pattern of land-ownership is happening or is envisaged.

While the effect of average farm size on the technological bias can be derived analytically, the effect of inequality in the distribution of farm sizes requires numerical simulation. This is what we do in the following section.

4.2. The simulation setup

The distribution of access to credit (K) across farms was parameterized using a simple functional form of the Lorenz curve, $y = x^\beta$, where x is the cumulative share of the farming population and y is the cumulative share of K. β is a distribution parameter equal to or greater than one: $\beta = 1$ means perfect equality, while $\beta = $ infinity means perfect inequality. The Gini coefficient can easily be computed on the basis of β: Gini $= (\beta - 1)/(\beta + 1)$. For comparative purposes, note that the Gini coefficient for landownership or usufruct is typically between 0.3 and 0.6 in Africa and between 0.5 and 0.8 in Latin America. Gini $= 0$ for $\beta = 1$ and Gini $= 1$ for $\beta = $ infinity. For $\beta = 3$, Gini $= 0.5$.

From the Lorenz curve, the share of total K by quantile can be derived. Let v be the number of quantiles; then, the average K within the nth quantile is given by the product of $(1/v)^{\beta-1}\{n^\beta - (n - 1)^\beta\}$ by the average access to credit K/N, where N is the total number of farms in the sector.

The average K for each quantile is used to derive, first, the wage rate and the land rental rate and, consequently, the average output per farm for each quantile using the previously derived result that $Q = K/c$. Note that in so doing we have again assumed that access to credit is the parameterized variable that differentiates farmers.

Once average output per quantile is obtained from the above, aggregate output is directly derived by summing over the n quantiles. Total output is a function of θ, and it is possible to derive numerically the optimal θ that maximizes total output by iteration or, more quickly, by second-order Taylor approximation around the optimum. For the subsequent analysis, the population was divided into 20 quantiles.

4.3. Some results

Simulation results show that taking distribution effects into account does not contradict the hypothesis that a larger average farm size is associated with the choice of a more labour-saving technology.

The Lorenz curve specification we used allows us to dissociate the impact on $\tilde{\theta}$ of the distribution of farm sizes from the effect of the average farm size.

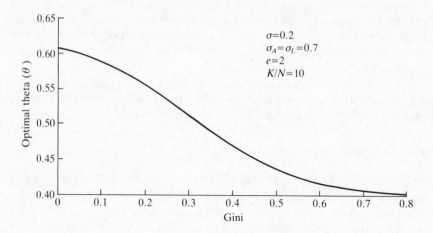

FIG. 18.2   Technology and inequality

Figure 18.2 shows that, keeping the average farm size constant, an increase in inequality reflected by a higher Gini coefficient leads to a $\tilde{\theta}$ that is smaller than the $\tilde{\theta}_0$ computed on the basis of the average farm — that is, for Gini = 0.

In other words, the results tell us that trying to estimate the optimum research budget allocation on the basis of the average farm size without paying attention to land distribution leads to a bias. This bias always goes in the same direction: the true $\tilde{\theta}$ is geared towards a more labour-saving or less land-saving technology, that is, closer to the interests of large farmers. In fact, the bias can never be in favour of small farmers. This means that inequality in assets distribution combined with failures in factor markets can account for at least part of the unexplained bias in favour of mechanization observed by Hayami and Ruttan (1985) and Thirtle (1985a). This calls for adding asset distribution as an explanatory variable when testing for induced technological change.

Furthermore, Figure 18.2 shows that the discrepancy between the optimal θ predicted by the simple average farm model and the optimal θ controlling for inequality in the distribution of assets is larger the larger inequality is: for low levels of inequality the gap remains relatively small, but it grows progressively wider as inequality becomes marked.

Simulation results also show that, as is intuitively expected, less flexibility in production (σ smaller) and less decreasing returns of scale in research (e smaller) lead to a larger impact of asset distribution on the choice of the optimal θ. Indeed, we have seen that quickly decreasing returns to research increases the curvature of the relationship between output and θ and tends to concentrate $\tilde{\theta}$ around 0.5. This is because, in that case, excessive specialization of research in one type of technology is not favoured. Similarly, less

TABLE 18.4. Simulation results: variation of the optimal factor ratios with inequality and substitutability

Gini	F/A	M/L	A/L	F/M
$\sigma_A = \sigma_L = 0.9$				
0.3	5.0	3.2	0.6	1.0
0.5	2.7	4.8	1.9	1.1
0.7	1.3	12.5	12.5	1.3
$\sigma_A = \sigma_L = 1.2$				
0.3	8.3	5.0	0.6	1.0
0.7	1.6	16.7	6.9	0.7

Note: In these runs, $\sigma = 0.1$ and $\theta = 0.5$.

flexibility in production increases differences between farms with different factor costs, and therefore reinforces the effects of inequality.

Finally, we can also use the simulation model to establish numerically the signs of the relation between inequality and factor ratios. These signs could not be derived analytically in Section 4.1. The results in Table 18.4 show that, for given θ, as inequality increases, F/A decreases while M/L, A/L, and F/M increase when $\sigma_A = \sigma_L < 1$. If, however, $\sigma_A = \sigma_L > 1$, F/M decreases with inequality.

5. Lobbying for Technological Change

The farm model has shown that, with transaction costs, different groups of farmers have diverging interests concerning technological change. They will be likely, therefore, to try to affect the research effort in favour of their own optimal technological bias.

Without developing a full model of lobbying behaviour with costs to farmers and impact functions of lobbying on the state's utility function (Zusman 1976), the direction of the bias of technological change created by lobbying activities can be assessed with a few assumptions.

The motivation for and intensity of bargaining by a group of farmers with landownership $\overline{A}$ is the loss in profit that they would incur with any allocation θ of the research budget chosen by the state that deviates from $\tilde{\theta}(\overline{A})$, their own optimal θ. As seen in the farm model, profit per unit of credit is directly related to output:

$$\pi(\theta, \overline{A}) = \frac{1}{K(\overline{A})} \left\{ p - c(\theta, \overline{A}) \right\} Q(\theta, \overline{A}) = p \frac{Q(\theta, \overline{A})}{K(\overline{A})} - 1, \quad (30)$$

and potential loss in profit per unit of credit arising from suboptimal research budget allocation is

$$\pi^*(\theta, \overline{A}) = \frac{p}{K(\overline{A})} \left[Q(\theta, \overline{A}) - Q\{\hat{\theta}(\overline{A}), \overline{A}\} \right]. \tag{31}$$

The impact of lobbying activities on the state's objective function depends on this potential loss. It is approximated here by a linear function

$$g(\overline{A}) \{\pi^*(\theta, \overline{A})\}, \tag{32}$$

in which $g(\overline{A})$ represents the efficiency of lobbying.

The state then maximizes its utility, which is a weighted average of its own objective goal of sectoral output and the utility derived from making concessions to the lobbies of the different classes of farmers. This is equivalent to

$$\max_{\theta} \int_{\overline{A}} \frac{1}{c(\theta, \overline{A})} \{aK(\overline{A}) f(\overline{A}) + bg(\overline{A})\} d\overline{A}. \tag{33}$$

In this model, the structure of the negotiating process and the efficiency of lobbying are completely summarized by the bargaining intensity function $g(\overline{A})$ and by the weights a and b in the state's objective function.

A negotiating structure in which the power of a class of farmers is proportional to the size of their operational units or credit is characterized by

$$g(\overline{A}) = K(\overline{A}) f(\overline{A}).$$

The lobbying model then reduces to the state optimal policy of maximizing sectoral output.

A more 'democratic' decision process, which gives equal power to all farmers regardless of their farm sizes, is represented by

$$g(\overline{A}) = f(\overline{A}).$$

Relative to the state's optimum for sectoral output maximization, the outcome will clearly be a bias towards the demand of small farmers for technological change.

By contrast, if lobbying power is determined by the cohesion of a group and its ability to control free-riding, power will be inversely related to the number of farmers in the group (Olson 1965). In this case,

$$g(\overline{A}) = K(\overline{A}) \{f(\overline{A})/(f(\overline{A})\} = K(\overline{A}). \tag{34}$$

This lobbying model will induce a strong bias in the state's decision towards the requests of the large farmers.

Using numerical analysis, we can simulate the impact that various specifications of the bargaining process have on the optimum θ. Using as a functional form

$$g(\overline{A}) = K^{\alpha}(\overline{A}) f(\overline{A}), \tag{35}$$

TABLE 18.5. Technological bias by type of bargaining

α	$\tilde{\theta}$	Type of bargaining
0	0.63	Democracy
0.5	0.52	
1	0.44	State optimum
1.5	0.38	
2	0.33	
$\alpha = 1$ and $f(\overline{A}) = 1$	0.27	Lobbying

with $\sigma = 0.2$, $\sigma_L = \sigma_A = 0.7$, $e = 2$, Gini $= 0.5$, $K(\overline{A}) = 10$, for the bargaining function, and leaving aside the state's own objective ($a = 0$, $b = 1$), we obtain the results given in Table 18.5. While the state's optimum biases technology away from $\tilde{\theta} = 0.5$ towards the technological interests of the large farmers ($\tilde{\theta} = 0.44$), a democratic bargaining structure can lead to optimal research budget allocations that are favourable to small farmers ($\tilde{\theta} = 0.63$). By contrast, collective action when the effectiveness of lobbies is inversely proportional to the size of class membership will further distort technological biases towards the interests of the large farmers ($\tilde{\theta} = 0.27$).

We thus conclude that, once transactions costs are taken into account to make technological demands farm-class-specific, the mechanisms of decision-making at the level of the state become important determinants of the bias of technological change. The efficacy of collective action and the degree of autonomy of the state are thus essential components of a theory of induced technological innovations.

6. Empirical Tests of Induced Innovations

The induced innovations model that we have developed in this chapter provides us with a set of testable propositions concerning the determinants of change in factor ratios. The expected signs in the relationship between factor ratios, relative factor prices, and structural variables (average farm size, inequality in the distribution of farm sizes, and size of the research budget) are summarized in the top third of Table 18.6.

To estimate these relationships, we use international data for the year 1970 starting from a sample of 45 more and less developed countries for which data on factor use are given by Hayami and Ruttan (1985). This data set is complemented by data on wages (International Labor Organization 1975), tractor prices (Kravis, Heston, and Summers 1982), and fertilizer prices (United Nations FAO, various years). Land rents are calculated as a residual from

$$r = \frac{1}{A}(pQ - wL - fF - mM). \tag{36}$$

TABLE 18.6. Determinants of factor ratios: international comparison

	$\log \dfrac{f}{r}$	$\log \dfrac{m}{w}$	$\log \dfrac{r}{w}$	$\bar{A}$	$d\bar{A}$	$\dfrac{B}{A}$	R^2
Signs expected from theory							
log F/A Substitution only[a]	−	0	0	−	−	−	
log F/A Induced innovation[b]	−	+	−	∓[c]	∓	?[d]	
log M/L Substitution only[a]	0	−	0	+	+	−	
log M/L Induced innovation[b]	+	−	+	±	±	?	
log A/L Substitution only[a]	+	−	−	+	+	?	
log A/L Induced innovation[b]	±	±	−	+	+	?	
log F/M Substitution only[a]	−	0	−	−	?	?	
log F/M Induced innovation[b]	±	±	−	−	?	?	
Observed prices, n = 18							
log F/A Farmland	−2.84	0.59	−0.99 [f]		−0.06	140	0.79
	(2.93)[e]	(0.62)	(1.02)		(1.97)	(2.48)	
log F/A Arable land	−1.35	−0.38	−0.39	−0.02		69	0.89
	(2.36)	(0.67)	(0.67)	(1.94)		(2.26)	
log M/L Farmland	−1.11	1.13	−0.57				0.88
	(1.24)	(1.29)	(0.66)				
log M/L Arable land	−1.10	−1.12	−0.60				0.89
	(1.31)	(1.34)	(0.73)				
log A/L Farmland	0.41	−0.32	−0.23	0.02		+80	0.92
	(0.87)	(0.74)	(0.50)	(5.49)		(−2.55)	
log A/L Arable land	−0.21	−0.10	−0.28	−0.04		−35	0.91
	(0.63)	(0.32)	(0.82)	(5.88)		(2.00)	
log F/M Farmland	−0.78	1.47	−0.97		−0.05		0.79
	(1.53)	(2.71)	(1.87)		(2.33)		
log F/M Arable land	−0.79	1.44	−0.94		+0.05		0.71
	(1.59)	(2.75)	(1.87)		(2.33)		
Price machinery = 1, n = 27							
log F/A Farmland	−0.30	0.55	−0.83	−0.01			0.86
	(0.85)	(0.21)	(2.96)	(1.74)			
log F/A Arable land	−1.05	0.48	−1.25		−0.03	20	0.89
	(2.81)	(1.49)	(4.23)		(1.58)	(1.64)	
log M/L Farmland	−0.20	−1.58	−0.12	0.01			0.90
	(0.52)	(5.45)	(0.38)	(2.35)			
log M/L Arable land	0.37	−1.45	−0.27	0.01			0.89
	(0.94)	(4.70)	(0.85)	(1.56)			
log A/L Farmland	−0.32	−0.19	−0.33	0.01		−54	0.88
	(1.40)	(1.08)	(1.79)	(6.74)		(4.15)	
log A/L Arable land	−0.14	−0.54	−0.05	0.02		−45	0.90
	(0.81)	(3.76)	(0.36)	(6.09)		(6.36)	
log F/M Farmland	0.58	0.45	−0.14		−0.02		0.81
	(1.91)	(1.81)	(0.06)		(1.72)		
log F/M Arable land	0.48	0.54	−0.09		−0.03		0.78
	(1.50)	(2.08)	(0.35)		(1.89)		

[a]Substitution effects are measured as $X_i/X_j = f(f/r, m/w, r/w, \theta; \bar{A}, d\bar{A}, B)$.
[b]Induced innovation effects are measured as $X_i/X_j = f(f/r, m/w, r/w; \bar{A}, d\bar{A}, B)$.
[c]When two signs are given, the top one is that which holds if the factor substitution effect for a given technology dominates, while the lower one is that which holds if the induced innovations effect for a given budget size dominates.
[d]Question mark indicates that the sign is analytically ambiguous.
[e]Figures in parentheses are t-ratios.
[f]Blanks indicate that the coefficient of the corresponding structural variable ($\bar{A}$, $d\bar{A}$, B/A) is not significantly different from zero at a 95 per cent confidence level.

Data on public sector research budgets are taken from Boyce and Evenson (1975). To eliminate the country size effect, the research budget is measured per acre of arable land. Data on average farm size and land distribution are obtained from the World Census of Agriculture (United Nations FAO, 1981). Inequality ($d\overline{A}$) in the distribution of farm sizes is measured as the negative of the percentage number of the largest farms controlling 50 per cent of the land. Two alternative regressions are run where A is either total farmland or arable land. The most limiting data source is that for tractor prices, which reduces the sample of countries to 18. Since there is relatively little international variation in tractor prices, we run an alternative set of regressions where we set the price of tractors equal to 1 to gain degrees of freedom, thus extending the sample of countries to 27.

The results obtained are strikingly consistent with theory, in both the price and the structural determinants of differences in factor ratios across countries. They show that structural variables are indeed important in explaining factor biases in induced technological innovations. In particular, larger farms and/or greater inequality in the distribution of farm sizes decreases the bias towards land-saving technological change (F/A and F/M) while enhancing the bias towards labour-saving technological change (M/L) and the land–labour ratio. The direction of the impact of the size of the research budget on the bias of induced innovations could not be predicted by theory.

A surprising result is that the size of the research budget per acre of arable land tends to increase the technological bias towards land-saving technological change and away from labour-saving technological change. This has three possible explanations. One is that, as the simulation results of Table 18.2 have shown, allocation of the research budget is biased towards labour-saving technological change ($\tilde{\theta} < 0.5$). Both the state's optimum choice and successful lobbying by large farmers have, indeed, been shown to be biased towards labour-saving. A rising research budget may, however, relax this bias, as it allows the demands of all farmers to be accommodated without exclusion. Another explanation is that there exists an innate bias in research towards labour-saving technological change which also implies a labour-saving bias that only decreases with rising research budgets. Finally, it may well be that research on mechanical innovations is principally funded by the private sector, since it is easily patentable, while research on biological innovations, which is more of a public good, is funded by the public sector. Since the research budget measured by Boyce and Evenson (1975) is for public sector research, the observed association between budget size and land-saving bias is not surprising.

7. Conclusion

We have shown in this chapter that introducing transaction costs and collective action into a formal model of induced technological innovations significantly alters the predictions of the pure neoclassical model. It explains, in particular, why different classes of farmers and the state all have different definitions of an optimum technological bias. If the state allocates resources to research so as to maximize sectoral output or value added, technology will be biased towards more labour-saving technological change than the optimum technology for the average farm. This bias will be reinforced by effective collective action by large farmers. Empirically, average farm size, inequality in the distribution of landownership, and the size of the research budget are seen to be important determinants of the observed technological bias. While a larger average farm size and a more unequal land tenure system increase the bias towards labour-saving technology, larger research budgets favour instead allocating a greater share of research expenditures towards land-saving technological innovations. A larger public sector research budget is thus less regressive on the distribution of welfare gains from technological change across farm sizes than is a smaller budget. Progressive effects of technological change, however, will not come about without effective lobbying by small farmers to affect the definition of public sector research priorities.

NOTES

1. For an excellent recent review of this subject, see Thirtle and Ruttan (1986).
2. The main sources of empirical information on these elasticities are Kako (1978), Hayami and Ruttan (1985), Thirtle (1985a, 1985b, 1985c), and Lopez (1980). Average values derived from these studies are: within-group elasticities, $\sigma_{AF} = 0.45$, $\sigma_{LM} = 0.38$; between-group elasticities, $\sigma_{AL} = 0.27$, $\sigma_{FL} = 0.03$, $\sigma_{FM} = 0.13$, $\sigma_{AM} = 0.13$.

Bibliography

Abreu, D. (1984) 'Infinitely Repeated Games with Discounting: A General Theory'. Unpublished paper, Harvard University.

—— Pearce, D., and Stacchetti, E. (1986). 'Optimal Cartel Equilibria with Imperfect Monitoring'. *Journal of Economic Theory*, 39, 251–69.

Abubakar, S. (1977). *The Lamibe of Fombina: A Political History of Adamawa*. Ahmadu Bello University thesis, Zaria, Nigeria.

Adams, D.W. and Rask, N. (1968). 'Economics of Cost-sharing in Less Developed Countries'. *American Journal of Agricultural Economics*, 50, 935–45.

Adams, D.W. and Vogel, R.C. (1986). 'Rural Financial Markets in Low Income Countries: Recent Controversies and Lessons'. *World Development*, 14, 477–87.

Adams, W. and Yellen, J. (1976). 'Commodity Bundling and the Burden of Monopoly'. *Quarterly Journal of Economics*, 90, 475–98.

Ahmad, S. (1966). 'On the Theory of Induced Innovations'. *Economic Journal*, 76, 344–57.

Ahmed, I. (1981). 'Farm Size and Labour Use: Some Alternative Explanations'. *Oxford Bulletin of Economics and Statistics*, 43, 73–88.

Ahmed, M. (1974). 'Farm Efficiency under Owner Cultivation and Share Tenancy'. *Pakistan Economic and Social Review*, 12, 132–143.

Akerlof, G. (1980). 'A Theory of Social Custom, of which Unemployment May Be One Consequence'. *Quarterly Journal of Economics*, 94, 749–75.

——(1984). *An Economic Theorist's Book of Tales*. Cambridge: University Press.

—— and Yellen, J. (1986). *Efficiency Wage Models of the Labor Market*. Cambridge: University Press.

Alchian, A. and Demsetz, H. (1972). 'Production, Information Costs, and Economic Organization'. *American Economic Review*, 62, 777–95.

——(1973). 'The Property Rights Paradigm'. *Journal of Economic History*, 33, 16–27.

Allen, F. (1982). 'On Share Contracts and Screening'. *Bell Journal of Economics*, 13, 541–7.

——(1984). 'Mixed Wage and Rent Contracts as Reinterpretations of Share Contracts'. *Journal of Development Economics*, 16, 313–17.

——(1985a). 'On the Fixed Nature of Sharecropping Contracts'. *Economic Journal*, 95, 30–48.

——(1985b). 'Repeated Principal–Agent Relationships with Lending and Borrowing'. *Economic Letters*, 17, 27–31.

Alston, L. (1981). 'Tenure Choice in Southern Agriculture, 1930–1960'. *Explorations in Economic History*, 18, 211–32.

—— Datta, S. and Nugent, J. (1984). 'Tenancy Choice in a Competitive Framework with Transaction Costs'. *Journal of Political Economy*, 92, 1121–33.

—— and Higgs, R. (1982). 'Contractual Mix in Southern Agriculture Since the Civil War: Facts, Hypotheses, and Tests'. *Journal of Economic History*, 42, 327–53.

Anderson, P. (1974). *Lineages of the Absolutist State*. London: New Left Books.

Arnott, R. J. and Stiglitz, J. E. (1984). 'Equilibrium in Competitive Insurance Markets: The Welfare Economics of Moral Hazard'. Mimeo, Princeton University.

——(1985). 'Labor Turnover, Wage Structures, and Moral Hazard: The Inefficiency of Competitive Markets'. *Journal of Labour Economics*, 3, 434–62.

——(1986). 'Moral Hazard and Optimal Commodity Taxation'. *Journal of Public Economics*, 29, 1–24.

——(1988). 'Randomization With Asymmetric Information: A Simplified Exposition'. *Rand Journal*, 18, forthcoming.

Arrow, J. (1953). 'Le Rôle des valeurs boursières pour la répartition la meilleure des risques', *Econometric*, Colloques Internationaux du CNRS 11, 41–7: translated as 'The Role of Securities in the Optimal Allocation of Risk-bearing', *Review of Economic Studies*, 31 (1964), 91–6.

——(1965). *Aspects of the Theory of Risk Bearing*. Helsinki: Academic Bookstore; reprinted in Arrow (1971).

——(1971). *Essays in the Theory of Risk-bearing*. Amsterdam: North-Holland (first published 1965).

——(1985). 'The Economics of Agency'. In J. Pratt and R. Zeckhauser (eds.), *Principals and Agents: The Structure of Business*, pp. 37–51. Boston: Harvard Business School Press.

——(1986). 'Agency and Market'. In J. K. Arrow and M. D. Intriligator (eds.), *Handbook of Mathematical Economics*, Amsterdam: North-Holland, pp. 1183–95.

Arthur, B. (1985). 'Competing Technologies and Lock-in by Historical Small Events'. CEPR Publications no. 43, Stanford, Cal.

——(1988). 'Self-reinforcing Mechanisms in Economics'. In P. W. Anderson and K. J. Arrow (eds.), *The Economy as an Evolving Complex System* forthcoming.

Ashton, T. H. and Philpin, C. H. E. (eds.). (1985). *The Brenner Debate: Agrarian Class Structure and Economic Development in Preindustrial Europe*. Cambridge: University Press.

Atkinson, A. and Stiglitz, J. E. (1969). 'A New View of Technological Change'. *Economic Journal*, 59, 46–9.

Axelrod, R. (1984). *The Evolution of Cooperation*. New York: Basic Books.

Baier, S. (1980). *An Economic History of Central Niger*. Oxford: Clarendon Press.

Bailey, F. G. (1971). 'The Peasant View of the Bad Life'. In T. Shanin (ed.), *Peasants and Peasant Societies*, Harmondsworth: Penguin Books.

Balde, M. (1975). 'L'Esclavage et la guerre sainte au Fauta-Jolon'. In C. Meillassoux (ed.), *L'Esclavage en Afrique Precoloniale*. Oxford: University Press.

Bandyopadhyay, A. (1984). *Economics of Agricultural Credit*. New Delhi: Agricole Publishing Academy.

Bardhan, P. K. (1977). 'Variations in Forms of Tenancy in a Peasant Economy'. *Journal of Development Economics*, 4, 105–18.

——(1980). 'Interlocking Factor Markets and Agrarian Development: A Review of the Issues'. *Oxford Economic Papers*, 32, 82–98.

——(1982). 'Agrarian Class Formation in India'. *Journal of Peasant Studies*, 10, 73–94.

——(1984). *Land, Labor, and Rural Proverty: Essays in Development Economics*. Delhi: Oxford University Press/New York: Columbia University Press.

—— and Rudra, A. (1978). 'Interlinkage of Land, Labor, and Credit Relations: An Analysis of Village Survey Data in East India'. *Economic and Political Weekly*, 13, 367–84.

—— and Rudra, A. (1981). 'Terms and Conditions of Labour Contracts in Agriculture: Results of a Survey in West Bengal, 1979'. *Oxford Bulletin of Economics and Statistics*, 43, 89–111.

—— and Singh, N. (1982). 'A Note on Cost Sharing and Incentives in Sharecropping'. Mimeo, University of California at Berkeley.

—— and Singh, N. (1987). 'A Note on Moral Hazard and Cost Sharing in Sharecropping'. *American Journal of Agricultural Economics*, 69, 382–3.

—— and Srinivasan, T. N. (1971). 'Cropsharing Tenancy in Agriculture: A Theoretical and Empirical Analysis'. *American Economic Review*, 61, 48–64.

Barnett, T. (1975). 'The Gezira Scheme: Production of Cotton and the Production of Underdevelopment'. In I. Oxaal, T. Barnett, and D. Booth (eds.), *Beyond the Sociology of Development*. Boston: Routledge, Kegan & Paul.

Basu, K. (1982). 'On the Existence of Share Tenancy in a Screening Model'. Mimeo, CORE, Louvain-la-Neuve.

——(1983). 'The Emergence of Isolation and Interlinkage in Rural Markets'. *Oxford Economic Papers*, 35, 262–80.

——(1984a). *The Less Developed Economy: A Critique of Contemporary Theory*. Oxford: Basil Blackwell.

——(1984b). 'Implicit Interest Rates, Usury, and Isolation in Backward Agriculture'. *Cambridge Journal of Economics*, 8, 145–59.

——(1986). 'One Kind of Power'. *Oxford Economic Papers*, 38, 259–82.

——(1987). 'Disneyland Monopoly, Interlinkage, and Usurious Interest Rates'. *Journal of Public Economics*, 34, 1–17.

—— Jones, E. and Schlicht, E. (1987). 'The Growth and Decay of Custom: The Role of the New Institutional Economics in Economic History'. *Explorations in Economic History*, 24, 1–21.

Bell, C. (1977). 'Alternative Theories of Sharecropping: Some Tests Using Evidence from North-East India'. *Journal of Development Studies*, 13, 317–46.

——(1986). 'The Choice of Tenancy Contract'. Mimeo, Vanderbilt University.

——(1988). 'Credit Markets and Interlinked Transactions'. In H. B. Chenery and T. N. Srinivasan (eds.), *Handbook of Development Economics*. Amsterdam: North-Holland.

—— and Braverman, A. (1981). 'On the Nonexistence of "Marshallian" Sharecropping Contracts'. *Indian Economic Review*, 15, 201–3.

—— and Srinivasan, T. N. (1985). 'Transactions in Rural Credit Markets in Bihar and Punjab: An Anatomy'. Mimeo.

—— and Zusman, P. (1976). 'A Bargaining Theoretic Approach to Cropsharing Contracts'. *American Economic Review*, 66, 578–88.

——(1977). 'Sharecropping Equilibria with Diverse Tenants'. *Economie Appliquée*, 30, 391–411.

Ben-Ner, A. (1984). 'On the Stability of the Cooperative Type of Organization'. *Journal of Comparative Economics* 8, 247–60.

Berman, M. D. (1977). 'Short-run Efficiency in the Labor-managed Firm'. *Journal of Comparative Economics*, 1, 309–14.

Bhaduri, A. (1973). 'A Study in Agricultural Backwardness under Semi-feudalism'.

Economic Journal, 83, 120–137; 'Reply', 89, 420–1.

——(1977). 'On the Formation of Usurious Interest Rates in Backward Agriculture'. *Cambridge Journal of Economics*, 1, 341–52.

——(1980). 'Agricultural Backwardness under Semi-feudalism: A Rejoinder'. *Economic Journal*, 89, 420–1.

——(1986). 'Economic Power, Organizational Form, and the Commercialization of Backward Agriculture'. Mimeo, Delhi.

Bhalla, S. (1976). 'New Relations of Production in Haryana Agriculture'. *Economic and Political Weekly*, 27 March, A23–A30.

Bharadwaj, K. (1974). *Production Conditions in Indian Agriculture*. Cambridge: University Press.

——(1985). 'A Note on Commercialisation in Agriculture'. In Raj *et al.* (1985).

Bhattacharya, S. (1982). 'Aspects of Monetary and Banking Theory and Moral Hazard'. *Journal of Finance*, 37, 371–84.

—— and Guasch, J. L. (1988). 'Heterogeneity, Tournaments, and Limited Liability Constraints'. *Journal of Political Economy*, 96, 867–81.

Binswanger, H. (1974a). 'A Microeconomic Approach to Induced Innovation'. *Economic Journal*, 84, 940–58.

——(1974b). 'The Measurement of Technical Change Biases with Many Factors of Production'. *American Economic Review*, 64, 964–76.

——(1980). 'Attitudes towards Risk: Experimental Evidence from Rural India'. *American Journal of Agricultural Economics*. 62, 395–407.

——(1981). 'Attitudes towards Risk: Theoretical Implications of an Experiment in Rural India'. *Economic Journal*, 91, 867–90.

—— and McIntire, J. (1987). 'Behavioural and Material Determinants of Production Relations in Land-abundant Tropical Agriculture'. *Economic Development and Cultural Change*, 36, 73–99.

—— and Rosenzweig, M. R. (eds.) (1984). *Contractual Arrangements, Employment, and Wages in Rural Labor Markets in Asia*. New Haven, Conn: Yale University Press.

—— and Rosenzweig, M. R. (1986). 'Behavioral and Material Determinants of Production Relations in Agriculture'. *Journal of Development Studies*, 22, 503–39.

—— and Sillers, D. (1983). 'Risk-aversion and Credit Constraints in Farmers' Decision-making: A Reinterpretation'. *Journal of Development Studies*, 20, 5–21.

Bliss, C., and Stern, N. H. (1978). 'Productivity, Wages, and Nutrition'. *Journal of Development Economics*, 5, 331–62, 363–98.

——(1982). *Palanpur: The Economy of an Indian Village*. Oxford: Clarendon Press.

Bonin, J. P. (1977). 'Work Incentives and Uncertainty on a Collective Farm'. *Journal of Comparative Economics*, 1, 77–97.

—— and Putterman, L. (1987a). 'Incentives and Monitoring in Cooperatives Under Labor-proportionate Sharing Schemes'. Department of Economics Working Paper no. 87–18, Brown University.

——(1987b). *Economics of Cooperation and the Labor-managed Economy*. Fundamentals of Pure and Applied Economics, no. 14. London: Harwood Academic Publishers.

Boserup, E. (1965). *The Conditions of Agricultural Growth: The Economics of Agrarian Change under Population Pressure.*. London: George Allen and Unwin.

——(1981). *Population and Technological Change: A Study of Long-term Trends.* Chicago: University Press.

Bottomley, A. (1975). 'Interest Rate Determination in Underdeveloped Rural Areas'. *American Journal of Agricultural Economics*, 57, 279–91.

Bowles, S. (1985). 'The Production Process in a Competitive Economy: Walrasian, Neo-Hobbesian, and Marxian Models'. *American Economic Review*, 75, 16–36.

——(1987). 'Contested Exchange: A Microeconomic Analysis of the Political Structure of the Capitalist Economy', unpublished.

Boyce, J., and Evenson, R. (1975). *Agricultural Research and Extension Programs.* New York: Agricultural Development Council.

Bradley, M. E. (1971). 'Incentives and Labour Supply on Soviet Collective Farms'. *Canadian Journal of Economics*, 4, 342–52.

Braverman, A. and Gausch, J. L. (1984). 'Capital Requirements, Screening, and Interlinked Sharecropping and Credit Contracts'. *Journal of Development Economics*, 14, 359–74.

——(1986). 'Rural Credit Markets and Institutions in Developing Countries: Lessons for Policy Analysis from Practice and Modern Theory'. *World Development*, 14, 1253–67.

——(1987). 'Rural Credit Reforms: Evidence of Past Failures and Methodology for Analyzing Institutional Reforms'. Mimeo, World Bank.

Braverman, A. and Stiglitz, J. E. (1982). 'Sharecropping and the Interlinking of Agrarian Markets'. *American Economic Review*, 72, 695–715.

——(1986a). 'Cost-sharing Arrangements under Sharecropping: Moral Hazard, Incentive Flexibility, and Risk'. *American Journal of Agricultural Economics*, 68, 642–52.

——(1986b). 'Landlords, Tenants, and Technological Innovations'. *Journal of Development Economics*, 23, 313–32.

Braverman, A. and Srinivasan, T. N. (1981). 'Credit and Sharecropping in Agrarian Societies'. *Journal of Development Economics*, 9, 289–312.

——(1984). 'Agrarian Reform in Developing Rural Economies Characterized by Interlinked Credit and Tenancy Markets'. In Binswanger and Rosenzweig (1984).

Breman, J. (1974). *Patronage and Exploitation.* Berkeley: University of California Press.

Brenner, R. (1976). 'Agrarian Class Structure and Economic Development in Preindustrial Europe'. *Past and Present*, 70, 30–70.

Brown, D. and Atkinson, J. (1981). 'Cash and Share Renting: An Empirical Test of the Link Between Entrepreneurial Ability and Contractual Choice'. *Bell Journal of Economics*, 12, 296–9.

Browning, M. J. (1982). 'Cooperation in a Fixed-membership Labor-managed Enterprise'. *Journal of Comparative Economics*, 6, 235–47.

Buchanan, J. (1975). *The Limits of Liberty.* Chicago: University Press.

Byres, T. J. (ed.) (1983). *Sharecropping and Sharecroppers.* London: Frank Cass.

Calvo, G. A. (1977). 'Supervision and Utility and Wage Differentials across Firms'. Mimeo, Columbia University, Economics Workshops.

——(1985). 'The Inefficiency of Unemployment: The Supervision Perspective'. *Quarterly Journal of Economics*, 100, 373–87.

—— and Wellisz, S. (1978). 'Supervision, Loss of Control, and the Optimum Size of the Firm'. *Journal of Political Economy*, 86, 945–52.

Carmichael, L. (1985). 'Can Unemployment be Involuntary? Comment'. *American Economic Review*, 75, 1213–14.

Carter, M. R. (1985). 'Revisionist Lessons from the Peruvian Experience with Cooperative Agricultural Production'. In D. Jones and J. Svejnar (eds.), *Advances in the Economic Analysis of Labor-managed and Participatory Firms*, Vol. I, pp. 179–94. Greenwich, Conn.: JAI Press.

——(1987). 'Risk Sharing and Incentives in the Decollectivization of Agriculture'. *Oxford Economic Papers*, 39, 577–95.

——(1988). 'Equilibrium Credit Rationing of Small Farm Agriculture'. *Journal of Development Economics*, 28, 83–103.

Cheung, S. N. S. (1968). 'Private Property Rights and Sharecropping'. *Journal of Political Economy*, 76, 107–22.

——(1969a). *The Theory of Share Tenancy*. Chicago: University Press.

——(1969b). 'Transaction Costs, Risk Aversion, and the Choice of Contractual Arrangements'. *Journal of Law and Economics*, 12, 23–43.

Cleave, J. (1974). *African Farmers: Labor Use in the Development of Small-holder Agriculture*. New York: Praeger.

Cline, W. (1970). *Economic Consequences of a Land Reform in Brazil*. Amsterdam: North-Holland.

Coase, R. H. (1937). 'The Nature of the Firm'. *Economica*, n.s. 4, 386–405; reprinted in *Readings in Price Theory*, selected by G. J. Stigler and K. E. Boulding, American Economic Association Series, Allen and Unwin, London, 1953.

——(1960). 'The Problem of Social Cost'. *Journal of Law and Economics*, 3, 1–44.

Cohen, G.A. (1978). *Karl Marx's Theory of History: A Defence*. Princeton: University Press.

Cooper, R. (1984). 'On Allocative Distortions in Problems of Self-selection'. *Rand Journal of Economics*, 15, 568–77.

Cox, L. S. (1944). 'Tenancy in the United States, 1865–1900: A Consideration of the Validity of the Agricultural Ladder Hypothesis'. *Agricultural History*, 18, 97–105.

Cremer, J. (1982). 'On the Efficiency of a Chinese-type Work-point System'. *Journal of Comparative Economics*, 6, 343–52.

Crott, H. W. (1971). 'Experimentelle Untersuchung zum Verhandlungs verhalten in Kooperativen Spielen'. *Zeitschrift für Sozialpsychologie*, 2, 61–74.

Curtin, P. (1984). *Cross-cultural Trade in World History*. Cambridge: University Press.

Dahl, G. and Hjort, A. (1976). *Having Herds*. Department of Social Anthropology, University of Stockholm.

Das, P. and Gangopadhyay, S. (1987). 'Competition among Lenders with Different Characteristics'. Mimeo, Indian Statistical Institute.

Dasgupta, P. and Ray, D. (1986). 'Inequality as a Determinant of Malnutrition and Unemployment: Theory'. *Economic Journal*, 96, 1011–34.

——(1987). 'Inequality as a Determinant of Malnutrition and Unemployment: Policy'. *Economic Journal*, 97, 177–88.

——(1988). 'Adapting to Undernourishment: The Clinical Evidence and its Implications'. In J. Dreze and A. Sen (eds.), *Food and Hunger: The Poorest Billion*.

David, P. (1987). 'Some New Standards for the Economics of Standardization in the Information Age'. In P. Dasgupta and P. Stoneman (eds.), *Economic Policy and*

Technological Performance, pp. 206–39. Cambridge: University Press.

Deb, R. and Ramachandran, R. V. (1986). 'Efficiency, Non-distortion, and Non-linear Income Taxes in a Finite Economy'. Mimeo, Southern Methodist University, Dallas.

DeBraal, J. P. and Wunderlich, G. (1983). *Rents and Rental Practices in US Agriculture*. Washington, DC: Farm Foundation and Economic Research Service, US Department of Agriculture.

De Janvry, A. (1973). 'A Socioeconomic Model of Induced Innovation for Argentine Agricultural Development'. *Quarterly Journal of Economics*, 87, 410–25.

Demsetz, H. (1967). 'Toward a Theory of Property Rights'. *American Economic Review*, 57, 347–59.

Derman, W. (1973). *Serfs, Peasants, and Socialists: A Former Serf Village in the Republic of Guinea*. Berkeley: University of California Press.

Domar, E. D. (1966). 'The Soviet Collective Farm as a Producers' Cooperative'. *American Economic Review*, 56, 734–57.

Doornbos, R. (1977). *Not All the King's Men: Inequality as a Political Instrument in Ankole, Uganda*. The Hague: Mouton.

Dreze, J. and Mukherjee, A. (1987). 'Labour Contracts in Rural India: Theories and Evidence'. DEP/7, London School of Economics.

Eaton, B. C. and White, W. W. (1982). 'Agent Compensation and the Limits of Bonding'. *Economic Inquiry*, 20, 330–43.

Edelman, J. M. (1964). *The Symbolic Uses of Politics*. Urbana: University of Illinois Press.

Eicher, C. and Baker, D. (1982). 'Research on Agricultural Development in Sub-Saharan Africa: A Critical Survey'. Michigan State University, International Development Paper no. 1.

Elster, J. (1983). *Explaining Technical Change*. Cambridge: University Press.

——(1985). *Making Sense of Marx*. Cambridge: University Press.

Eswaran, M. and Kotwal, A. (1984). 'Access to Capital as a Determinant of the Organization of Production and Resource Allocation in an Agrarian Economy'. University of British Columbia, Discussion Paper no. 84-06.

——(1985a). 'A Theory of Two-tiered Labour Markets in Agrarian Economies'. *American Economic Review*, 75, 162–77.

——(1985b). 'Why are Capitalists the Bosses?' University of British Columbia, Discussion Paper no. 85-06.

——(1985c). 'A Theory of Contractual Structure in Agriculture'. *American Economic Review*, 75, 352–67.

——(1986). 'Access to Capital and Agrarian Production Organisation'. *Economic Journal*, 96, 482–98.

——(1987a). 'Consumption Credit in Risk-behaviour'. Mimeo, University of British Columbia.

——(1987b). 'Credit as Insurance in Agrarian Economies'. Mimeo, University of British Columbia.

Etuk, E. (1986). 'Optimum Farm Plans with Traditional and New Technologies in Zaria'. Samaru Miscellaneous Papers 109, Ahmadu Bello University.

Farrell, J. (1987). 'Information and the Coase Theorem'. *Journal of Economic Perspectives*, 1, 113–29.

Feder, G. (1983). 'The Relation between Farm Size and Farm Productivity: The Role of Family Labour, Supervision, and Credit Constraints'. Mimeo, World Bank.

Feeny, D. (1982). *The Political Economy of Productivity: Thai Agricultural Development 1880–1975*. Vancouver: University of British Columbia Press.

Field, A. J. (1981). 'The Problem with Neoclassical Institutional Economics'. *Explorations in Economic History*, 18, 174–98.

Floro, S. (1987). 'Credit Interlinkage in Philippine Agriculture'. Ph.D. dissertation, Stanford University.

Frantz, C. (1975). 'Contraction and Expansion in Nigerian Bovine Pastoralism'. In T. Monod (ed.), *Pastoralism in Tropical Africa*. Oxford: University Press.

Friedman, J. (1971). 'A Non-cooperative Equilibrium for Supergames'. *Review of Economic Studies*, 38, 1–12.

——(1977). *Oligopoly and the Theory of Games*. Amsterdam: North-Holland.

Froelich, J. (1954). 'Le Commandement et l'organisation sociale chez les Foulbe de l'Adamawa'. *Etudes Camerounaises*, 45, 1–91.

Furet, F. (1978). *Penser la Revolution Francaise*. Paris: Gallimard.

Gangopadhyay, S. and Sengupta, K. (1987). 'Usury and Collateral Pricing: Towards an Alternative Explanation'. *Cambridge Journal of Economics*, 11, 47–56.

——(1987). 'Small Farmers, Moneylenders, and Trading Activity'. *Oxford Economic Papers*, 39, 333–42.

Georgescu-Roegen, N. (1960). 'Economic Theory and Agrarian Economics'. *Oxford Economic Papers*, 12, 1–40.

Ghose, A. (1979). 'Farm Size and Land Productivity in Indian Agriculture: A Reappraisal'. *Journal of Development Studies*, 16, 27–49.

Gonzalez-Vega, C. (1983). 'Arguments for Interest Rate Reform'. In von Pischke, Adams and Donald (1983), pp. 365–72.

Gould, S.J. (1980). *The Panda's Thumb*. New York: W.W. Norton.

Green, E. and Porter, R. (1984). 'Noncooperative Collusion under Imperfect Price Information'. *Econometrica*, 52, 87–100.

Green, J. and Stokey, N. (1983). 'A Comparison of Tournaments and Contracts'. *Journal of Political Economy*, 91, 349–64.

Greenwald, B. and Stiglitz, J. E. (1986). 'Externalities in Economies with Imperfect Information and Incomplete Markets'. *Quarterly Journal of Economics*, 101, 229–64.

Griffin, K. (1974). *The Political Economy of Agrarian Change*. London: Macmillan (2nd edn. 1979).

Guesnerie, R. and Seade, J. (1982). 'Nonlinear Pricing in a Finite Economy'. *Journal of Public Economics*, 17, 157–79.

Guha, A. (1986). 'The Less Developed Economy in Fantasy and Myth: A Review Article'. *Indian Economic Review*, 21, 61–9.

——(1987). 'Consumption, Efficiency, and Surplus Labour'. Mimeo, Jawaharlal Nehru University.

Gupta, M. R. (1987). 'A Nutrition-based Theory of Interlinkage'. *Journal of Quantitative Economics*, 3, 189–202.

Guttman, J. (1978a). 'Interest Group and the Demand for Agricultural Research'. *Journal of Political Economy*, 86, 467–84.

——(1978). 'Understanding Collective Action: Matching Behaviour'. *American Economic Review*, Papers and Proceedings, 68, 251–5.

——(1987). 'A Non-Cournot Model of Voluntary Collective Action'. *Economica*, 54, 1–19.

—— and Schnytzer, A. (1987). 'Strategic Work Interactions, Incentives, and the Kibbutz–Kolkhoz Paradox'. Discussion Paper no. 8709, Department of Economics, Bar-Ilan University.

Haaland, G. (1969). 'Economic Determinants in the Ethnic Process'. In F. Barth (ed.), *Ethnic Groups and Boundaries*. London: George Allen and Unwin.

Hallagan, W. (1978). 'Self-selection by Contractual Choice and the Theory of Share-cropping'. *Bell Journal of Economics*, 9, 344–54.

Hamilton, N. (1982). *The Limits of State Autonomy: Post-revolutionary Mexico*. Princeton: University Press.

Hardin, R. (1982). *Collective Action*. Washington, DC: Resources for the Future.

Harris, M. and Raviv, A. (1979). 'Optimal Incentive Contracts with Imperfect Information'. *Journal of Economic Theory*, 20, 231–59.

Harsanyi, J. (1962). 'Measurement of Social Power, Opportunity Costs, and the Theory of Two-person Bargaining Games'. *Behavioral Science*, 7, 67–80.

——(1976). *Essays on Ethics, Social Behaviour and Scientific Explanation*. Dordrecht and Boston: D. Reidel.

——(1977). *Rational Behavior and Bargaining Equilibrium in Games and Social Situations*. Cambridge: University Press.

Hart, G. (1986a). *Power, Labour and Livelihood: Processes of Change in Rural Java*. Berkeley: University of California Press.

——(1986b). 'Interlocking Transactions: Obstacles, Precursors or Instruments of Agrarian Capitalism'. *Journal of Development Economics*, 23, 177–203.

Hart, O. and Holmstrom, B. (1987). 'The Theory of Contracts'. In T. Bewley (ed.), *Advances in Economic Theory*. Cambridge: University Press.

Hayami, Y. and Kikuchi, M. (1982). *Asian Village Economy at the Crossroads: An Economic Approach to Institutional Change*. Baltimore: Johns Hopkins University Press.

Hayami, Y. and Ruttan, V. W. (1985). *Agricultural Development: An International Perspective*. Baltimore: Johns Hopkins University Press.

Heady, E. (1947). 'Economics of Farm Leasing Systems'. *Journal of Farm Economics*, 29, 659–78.

Helleiner, G. K. (1964). 'The Fiscal Role of Marketing Boards in Nigerian Economic Development'. *Economic Journal*, 74, 582–610.

Helmberger, P. and Hoose, S. (1962). 'Cooperative Enterprise and Organizational Theory'. *Journal of Farm Economy*, 44, 275–90.

Hendry, J. B. (1960). 'Land Tenure in South Vietnam'. *Economic Development and Cultural Change*, 9, 27–44.

Hicks, J. R. (1963). *Theory of Wages*. London: Macmillan.

Higgs, H. (1894). 'Metayage in Western France'. *Economic Journal*, 4, 1–13.

Higgs, R. (1974). 'Patterns of Farm Rental in the Georgia Cotton Belt, 1880–1900'. *Journal of Economic History*, 34, 468–82.

Hill, P. (1972). *Rural Hausa*. Cambridge: University Press.

Hirshleifer, D. (1986). 'A Multiperiod Model of Storage and Futures Trading'. Mimeo, Graduate School of Management, UCLA.

Hirschman, A. (1970). *Exit, Voice, and Loyalty: Responses to Decline in Firms, Organizations, and States*. Cambridge: University Press.

Hogendorn, J. (1977). 'The Economics of Slave Use on Two "Plantations" in the Zaria Emirate'. *International Journal of African History*, 10, 369–83.

Holmström, B. (1979). 'Moral Hazard and Observability'. *Bell Journal of Economics*, 10, 74–91.

——(1982). 'Moral Hazard in Teams'. *Bell Journal of Economics*, 13, 324–40.

—— and Milgrom, P. (1987). 'Aggregation and Linearity in the Provision of Intertemporal Incentives'. *Econometrica*, 55, 303–28.

Hossain, M. (1986). 'Credit for Alleviation of Rural Poverty: The Experience of Graemeen Bank in Bangladesh'. Washington, DC: International Food Policy Research Institute.

Hsiao, J. C. (1975). 'The Theory of Share Tenancy Revisited'. *Journal of Political Economy*, 83, 1023–32.

Huang, Y. (1971). 'Allocative Efficiency in a Developing Agricultural Economy in Malaya'. *American Journal of Agricultural Economics*, 53, 514–16.

——(1975). 'Tenancy Patterns, Productivity, and Rentals in Malaysia'. *Economic Development and Cultural Change*, 23, 703–18.

Hurwicz, L. and Shapiro, L. (1978). 'Incentive Structures Maximizing Residual Gain Under Incomplete Information'. *Bell Journal of Economics*, 9, 180–192.

International Labour Organization (1975). *Yearbook of Labour Statistics, 1975*. Geneva: ILO.

Ireland, N. J. and Law, P. J. (1981). 'Efficiency, Incentives, and Individual Labor Supply in the Labor-managed Firm'. *Journal of Comparative Economics*, 5, 1–23.

Israelsen, L. D. (1980). 'Collectives, Communes, and Incentives'. *Journal of Comparative Economics*, 4, 99–124.

Issawi, C. (1957). 'Farm Output under Fixed Rents and Share Tenancy'. *Land Economics*, 38, 74–7.

Jaffe, D. and Russell, T. (1976). 'Imperfect Information, Uncertainty, and Credit Rationing'. *Quarterly Journal of Economics*, 90, 651–66.

Janakarajan, S. (1986). 'Aspects of Market Inter-relationships in a Changing Agrarian Economy: A Case Study from Tamil Nadu'. Ph.D. dissertation, University of Madras.

Jaynes, D. G. (1982). 'Production and Distribution in Agrarian Economies'. *Oxford Economic Papers*, 34, 346–67.

——(1984). 'Economic Theory and Land Tenure'. In Binswanger and Rosenzweig (1984).

Jodha, N. (1978). 'Effectiveness of Farmers' Adjustment to Risk'. *Economic and Political Weekly*, 18, A38–A48.

——(1984). 'Agricultural Tenancy in Semi-arid Tropical India.' In Binswanger and Rosenzweig (1984).

Johnson, A. W. (1971). *Sharecroppers of the Sertao*. Stanford: University Press.

Johnson, D. G. (1950). 'Resource Allocation under Share Contracts'. *Journal of Political Economy*, 58, 111–23.

Johnson, M. (1976). 'The Economic Foundations of an Islamic Theocracy.' *Journal of African History*, 17, 481–95.

Jones, R. (1831). *An Essay on the Distribution of Wealth on the Sources of Taxation*. Part 1: *Rent*. London: John Murray.

Kako, T. (1978). 'Decomposition Analysis of Derived Demand for Factor Inputs: The

Case of Rice Production in Japan'. *American Journal of Agricultural Economics*, 60, 628–35.

Kalai, E. and Smorodinsky, M. (1975). 'Other Solutions to Nash's Bargaining Problem'. *Econometrica*, 43, 513–18.

Kamien, M., and Schwartz, N. (1968). 'Optimal Induced Technical Change'. *Econometrica*, 36, 1–17.

Kaneda, M. (1982). 'Specification of Production Functions for Analyzing Technical Change and Factor Inputs in Agricultural Development'. *Journal of Development Economics*, 11, 97–108.

Karugire, S. (1971). *A History of the Kingdom of Ankole in Western Uganda to 1896*. Oxford: Clarendon Press.

Kay, C. (1982). 'Achievements and Contradictions of the Peruvian Agrarian Reform'. *Journal of Development Studies*, 18, 141–70.

Koo, A. Y. (1973). 'Towards a More General Model of Land Tenancy and Reform'. *Quarterly Journal of Economics*, 87, 567–80.

Kottak, C. (1972). 'Ecological Variables in the Origin and Evolution of African States: The Buganda Example'. *Comparative Studies in Society and History*, 14, 351–80.

Kotwal, A. (1985). 'The Role of Consumption Credit in Agricultural Tenancy'. *Journal of Development Economics*, 18, 273–95.

Kravis, I., Heston, A., and Summers, R. (1982). *World Product and Income: International Comparisons of Real Gross Product*. Baltimore: Johns Hopkins University Press.

Kreps, D. and Wilson, R. (1982). 'Sequential Equilibria'. *Econometrica*, 50, 863–94.

Kuran, T. (1987). 'Preference Falsification, Policy Continuity, and Collective Conservatism'. *Economic Journal*, 97, 642–65.

Kurup, T. V. N. (1976). 'Price of Rural Credit: An Empirical Analysis of Kerala'. *Economic and Political Weekly*, 11, 3 July 1976.

Kutcher, G. and Scandizzo, P. (1982). *The Agricultural Economy of Northwest Brazil*. Baltimore: Johns Hopkins University Press.

Ladejinsky, W. (1977). 'Agrarian Reform in India'. In L. Y. Walinsky (ed.), *The Selected Papers of Wolf Ladejinsky: Agrarian Reform as Unfinished Business*. New York: Oxford University Press.

Landman, J. R. and Tinnermeier, R. L. (1981). 'The Political Economy of Agricultural Credit: The Case of Bolivia'. *American Journal of Agricultural Economics*, 63, 66–72.

Langlois, R. N. (1986). *Economics as a Process: Essays in the New Institutional Economics*. Cambridge: University Press.

Lave, L. (1962). 'Empirical Estimates of Technological Change in United States Agriculture, 1850–1958'. *Journal of Farm Economics*, 44, 941–52.

Lazear, E., and Rosen, S. (1981). 'Rank-order Tournaments as Optimal Labour Contracts'. *Journal of Political Economy*, 89, 841–64.

Leibenstein, H. (1957). *Economic Backwardness and Economic Growth*. New York: John Wiley.

Leontief, W. (1963). 'When Should History Be Written Backwards?' *Economic History Review*, 16, 1–8.

Lewis, J. (1978). 'Small Farmer Credit and the Village Production Unit in Rural Mali'. In P. Stevens (ed.), *The Social Sciences and African Development Planning*.

Waltham, Mass.: Crossroads Press.

Lewis, W. A. (1954). 'Economic Development with Unlimited Supplies of Labor'. *Manchester School of Economic and Social Studies*, 2a, 139–91.

Lin, J. Y. (1986). 'Supervision, Incentive, and the Optimal Scale of a Farm in a Collective Economy'. Unpublished paper, Department of Economics, University of Chicago.

Lipton, M. (1977). *Why Poor People Stay Poor: Urban Bias in World Development*. Cambridge: University Press.

——(1981). 'Agricultural Finance and Rural Credit in Poor Countries'. In Paul Streeten and Richard Jolly (eds.), *Recent Issues in World Development: A Collection of Survey Articles*. Oxford: Pergamon Press.

Longhurst, R. (1985). 'Farm-level Decision-making in a Northern Nigerian Village'. Samaru Miscellaneous Papers no. 106, Ahmadu Bello University.

Lopez, R. (1980). 'The Structure of Production and the Derived Demand for Inputs in Canadian Agriculture'. *American Journal of Agricultural Economics*, 62, 38–45.

Lovejoy, P. (1978). 'Pastoralism in Africa'. *Peasant Studies*, 8, 73–85.

——(1979). 'The Characteristics of Plantations in the 19th Century Sokoto Caliphate'. *American Historical Review*, 84, 1267–92.

——(1983). *Transformations in Slavery*. Cambridge: University Press.

Lucas, R. E. B. (1979). 'Sharing, Monitoring, and Incentives: Marshallian Misallocation Reassessed'. *Journal of Political Economy*, 87, 501–20.

Luce, R. D. and Raiffa, H. (1957). *Games and Decisions*. New York: John Wiley.

MacLeod, W. B. (1984). 'A Theory of Cooperative Teams'. CORE Discussion Paper no. 8441, Université Catholique de Louvain.

Marshall, A. (1920). *Principles of Economics*. London: Macmillan.

Matlon, P. (1977). 'The Size Distribution, Structure, and Determinants of Personal Income among Farmers in the North of Nigeria'. Ph.D. dissertation, Cornell University.

Mazumder, D. (1975). 'The Theory of Sharecropping and Labor Market Dualism'. *Economica*, 32, 161–73.

McClintock, C., Podesta, B., and Scurrah, J. (1984). 'Latin American Promises and Failures: Peru and Chile'. In B. Wilpert and A. Sorge (eds.), *International Yearbook of Organizational Democracy*, Vol. II, pp. 443–71. New York: John Wiley.

McCown, R., Haaland, G., and DeHaan, C. (1979). 'The Interaction between Cultivation and Livestock Production in Semi-arid Africa'. In A. Hall, G. Cannel, and H. Lawton (eds)., *Agriculture in Semi-arid Environments*. New York: Springer-Verlag.

Meade, J. E. (1972). 'The Theory of Labour-managed Firms and of Profit-sharing'. *Economic Journal*, 82, 402–28.

Meillassoux, C. (1981). *Maidens, Meal, and Money: Capitalism and the Domestic Community*. Cambridge: University Press.

Menger, C. (1883). *Problems of Economics and Sociology*, trans. F. J. Nock. Urbana: University of Illinois Press, 1963.

Miliband, R. (1983). 'State Power and Class Interests'. *New Left Review*, no. 138, 57–68.

Mill, J. S. (1848). *Principles of Political Economy*. London: W. Parker.

Mirrlees, J. A. (1974). 'Notes on Welfare Economics, Information, and

Uncertainty'. In M. Balch, D. McFadden, and S. Wu (eds.), *Essays in Economic Behaviour under Uncertainty*, pp. 243–58. Amsterdam: North-Holland.

——(1975). 'Moral Hazard and Unobservable Behaviour'. Mimeo, Nuffield College, Oxford.

——(1976). 'The Optimal Structure of Incentives and Authority within an Organization'. *Bell Journal of Economics*, 7, 105–31.

Mitra, P. K. (1983). 'A Theory of Interlinked Rural Transactions'. *Journal of Public Economics*, 20, 167–92.

Mookherjee, D. (1986). 'Involuntary Unemployment and Worker Moral Hazard' *Review of Economic Studies*, 53, 789–94.

Mukherji, B. (1982). 'Usurious Interest Rates and Price of Collateral: A Note'. *Indian Economic Review*, 17, 49–61.

Muth, J. (1961). 'Rational Expectations and the Theory of Price Movements'. *Econometrica*, 29, 315–35.

Myerson, R. B. (1985). 'An Introduction to Game Theory'. Discussion paper no. 623, Centre for Mathematical Studies in Economics and Management Science, Northwestern University.

Nagaraj, K. (1981). 'Structure and Inter-relations of the Land, Labour, Credit and Product Markets of South Kanara. Ph.D. dissertation, Indian Statistical Institute, Calcutta.

——(1985). 'Marketing Structures for Paddy and Arecanut in South Kanara: A Comparison of Markets in a Backward Agricultural District'. In Raj *et al.* (1985).

Nalebuff, B., and Stiglitz, J. E. (1983). 'Prizes and Incentives: Towards a General Theory of Compensation and Competition'. *Bell Journal of Economics*, 14, 21–43.

Nash, J. R. (1950). 'The Bargaining Problem'. *Econometrica*, 18, 155–62.

——(1953). 'Two-person Cooperative Game'. *Econometrica*, 21, 128–40.

Newbery, D. M. G. (1974). 'Cropsharing Tenancy in Agriculture: Comment'. *American Economic Review*, 64, 1060–6.

——(1975). 'The Choice of Rental Contract in Peasant Agriculture'. In L. Reynolds (ed.), *Agriculture in Development Theory*, Ch. 5. New Haven: Yale University Press.

——(1977). 'Risk-sharing, Sharecropping, and Uncertain Labour Markets'. *Review of Economic Studies*, 44, 585–94.

——(1983a). 'Futures Trading, Risk Reduction and Price Stabilization'. In Manfred E. Streit (ed.), *Futures Markets*, Ch. 9. Oxford: Basil Blackwell.

——(1983b). 'Commodity Price Stabilization in Imperfectly Competitive Markets'. In G. G. Storey, A. Schmitz, and A. H. Sarris (eds.), *International Agricultural Trade*, Ch. 11. Boulder, Colo: Westview Press.

——(1984). 'Commodity Price Stabilization in Imperfect or Cartelized Markets'. *Econometrica*, 52, 563–78.

——(1988). 'Missing Markets, Consequences and Remedies'. In F. H. Hahn (ed.), *Essays in Non-Walrasian Economics*. Oxford: University Press.

—— and Stiglitz, J. E. (1979). 'Sharecropping, Risk-sharing, and the Importance of Imperfect Information'. In J. A. Roumasset, J. M. Boussard, and I. Singh (eds.), *Risk, Uncertainty, and Agricultural Development*, Ch. 17. New York: Agricultural Development Council.

——(1981). *The Theory of Commodity Price Stabilization*. Oxford: University Press.

——(1982). 'Optimal Commodity Stock-piling Rules'. *Oxford Economic Papers*, 34, 403–27.

——(1984). 'Pareto-inferior Trade'. *Review of Economic Studies*, 51, 1–12.

Norman, D. (1972). 'An Economic Survey of Three Villages in Zaria Province. 2: Input–Output Study, Vols. 1 (text) and II (basic data and survey forms)'. Zaria: Samaru Miscellaneous Papers no. 37, Ahmadu Bello University.

Norohna, R. (1985). *A Review of the Literature on Land Tenure Systems in Sub-Saharan Africa*. World Bank Agricultural Research Unit Paper no. 43.

North, D. C. (1981). *Structure and Change in Economic History*. New York: W. W. Norton.

——(1986). 'Institutions and Economic Growth: An Historical Introduction'. Paper presented at the conference on the Role of Institutions in Economic Development, Cornell University, November 1986.

—— and Thomas, R. (1973). *The Rise of the Western World*. Cambridge: University Press.

Nozick, R. (1974). *Anarchy, State, and Utopia*. New York: Basic Books.

Nugent, J. (1986). 'Applications of the Theory of Transactions Costs and Collective Action to Development Problems and Policy'. Paper presented at the conference on The Role of Institutions in Economic Development, Cornell University, November 1986.

O'Fahey, R. (1973). 'Slavery and the Slave Trade in Dar Fur'. *Journal of African History*, 14, 29–43.

——(1985). 'Slavery and Society in Dar Fur'. In J. Willis (ed.), *Slaves and Slavery in Muslim Africa*. London: Frank Cass.

Oi, W. Y. and Clayton, E. (1968). 'A Peasant's View of a Soviet Collective Farm'. *American Economic Review*, 58, 37–59.

Okun, A. M. (1981). *Prices and Quantities: A Macroeconomic Analysis*. Washington, DC: Brookings Institution.

Olivier de Sardan, J. (1983). 'The Songhoy–Zarma Female Slave: Relations of Production and Ideological Status'. In C. Robertson and M. Klein (eds.), *Women and Slavery in Africa*. Madison: University of Wisconsin Press.

Olson, M. (1965). *The Logic of Collective Action: Public Goods and the Theory of Groups*. New York: Schocken/Cambridge: University Press.

Panikar, P. G. K. (1987). 'Recent Trends in India's Rural Credit Market'. Mimeo, Centre for Development Studies, Trivandrum.

Pant, C. (1983). 'Tenancy and Family Resources: A Model and Some Empirical Analysis'. *Journal of Development Economics*, 12, 27–39.

Patnaik, U. (1976). 'Class Differentiation within the Peasantry'. *Economic and Political Weekly*, 11, A82–A101.

Phelps, E. and Pollack, R. (1968). 'On Second-best National Saving and Game Equilibrium'. *Review of Economic Studies*, 35, 185–99.

Pineiro, M., and Trigo, E. (eds.) (1983). *Technical Change and Social Conflict in Agriculture: Latin American Perspectives*. Boulder, Colo.: Westview Press.

Pingali, P., Bigot, Y., and Binswanger, H. (1987). *Agricultural Mechanization and the Evolution of Farming Systems in Sub-Saharan Africa*. Baltimore: Johns Hopkins University Press.

Platteau, J.-P. and Abraham, A. (1987). 'An Inquiry into Quasi-credit Contracts: The Role of Reciprocal Credit and Interlinked Deals in Small-scale Fishing Communities'. *Journal of Development Studies*, 23, 461–90.

Platteau, J.-P., Murikan, J., and Delbar, E. (1985). *Technology, Credit, and Indebtedness in Marine Fishing: A Case Study of Three Villages in South Kerala.* Delhi: Hindustan Publishing Corporation.

Porter, R. H. (1983). 'Optimal Cartel Trigger-price Strategies'. *Journal of Economic Theory*, 29, 313–38.

Prasad, P. (1974). 'Reactionary Role of Usurers' Capital in Rural India'. *Economic and Political Weekly*, 9, 1305–8.

Pratt, J. W. (1964). 'Risk Aversion in the Small and in the Large'. *Econometrica*, 32 122–36.

Putterman, L. (1980). 'Voluntary Collectivization: A Model of Producers' Institutional Choice'. *Journal of Comparative Economics*, 4, 125–57.

——(1981). 'On Optimality in Collective Institutional Choice'. *Journal of Comparative Economics*, 5, 392–402.

——(1983). 'Incentives and the Kibbutz: Toward an Economics of Communal Work Motivation'. *Zeitschrift fur Nationalokonomie*, 43, 157–88.

——(1985). 'On the Interdependence of Labor Supplies in Producers' Cooperatives of Given Membership'. In D. Jones and J. Svejnar (eds.), *Advances in the Economic Analysis of Labor-Managed and Participatory Firms*, Vol. I, pp. 87–105. Greenwich, Conn.: JAI Press.

——(1986a). 'Work Motivation and Monitoring in a Collective Farm'. Brown University, Department of Economics, Working Paper no. 84–28.

——(1986b). *Peasants, Collectives and Choice: Economic Theory and Tanzania's Villages.* Greenwich, Conn.: JAI Press.

——(1987). 'The Incentive Problem and the Demise of Team Farming in China'. *Journal of Development Economics*, 26, 103–27.

—— and DiGiorgio, M. (1985). 'Choice and Efficiency in a Model of Democratic Semi-collective Agriculture'. *Oxford Economic Papers*, 37, 1–22.

—— and Skillman, G. Jr. (1988). 'The Incentive Effects of Monitoring Under Alternative Compensation Schemes'. *International Journal of Industrial Organization*, 6, forthcoming.

Quibria, M. G. (1982). 'A "Layman's" Geometric Proof why "Marshallian" Sharecropping Contracts Should Not Exist'. *Bangladesh Development Studies*, 9, 97–99.

—— and Rashid, S. (1984). 'The Puzzle of Sharecropping: A Survey of Theories'. *World Development Report*, 12, 103–14.

Quizon, B., Binswanger, H. P., and Machina, M. J. (1984). 'Attitudes toward Risk: Further Remarks'. *Economic Journal*, 94, 144–8.

Radner, R. (1981). 'Monitoring Cooperative Agreements in a Repeated Principal–Agent Relationship'. *Econometrica*, 49, 1127–48.

——(1985). 'Repeated Principal–Agent Games with Discounting'. *Econometrica*, 53, 1173–98.

Raiffeisen, F. W. (1966). *The Credit Unions as Means to Remedy the Distress of the Rural Population as well as of the Urban Craftsman and Workers.* The Rhine: Raiffeisen.

Raj, K. N. (1979). 'Keynesian Economics and Agrarian Economies'. In C. H. H. Rao and P. C. Joshi (eds.), *Reflections on Economic Development and Social Change.* Delhi: Allied Publishers.

——, Bhattacharya, N., Guha, S., and Padhi, S. (1985). *Essays on the Commercialization of Indian Agriculture.* Oxford: University Press.

Ransom, R.L. and Sutch, R. (1977). *One Kind of Freedom: The Economic Consequences of Emancipation*. New York: Cambridge University Press.

Rao, C. H. H. (1971). 'Uncertainty, Entrepreneurship, and Sharecropping in India'. *Journal of Political Economy*, 79, 578–95.

——(1975). *Technological Change and Distribution of Gains in Indian Agriculture*. New Delhi: Macmillan.

Rao, J. Mohan (1986). 'Agriculture in Recent Development Theory'. *Journal of Development Economics*, 22, 41–86.

Rasmussen, E. (1987). 'Moral Hazard in Risk-averse Teams'. *Rand Journal of Economics*, 18, 428–35.

Reid, J. D. Jr. (1973). 'Sharecropping as an Understandable Market Response: The Post-Bellum South'. *Journal of Economic History*, 33, 106–30.

——(1975). 'Sharecropping in History and Theory'. *Agricultural History*, 49, 426–40.

——(1976). 'Sharecropping and Agricultural Uncertainty'. *Economic Development and Cultural Change*, 24, 549–76.

——(1977). 'The Theory of Share Tenancy Revisited — Again'. *Journal of Political Economy*, 85, 403–7.

Reserve Bank of India (1986). 'Assets and Liabilities of Households as on 30th June 1981 — Salient Aspects'. *Reserve Bank of India Bulletin*, 40, 437–53.

Richards, A. (1986). *Development and Modes of Production in Marxian Economics: A Critical Evaluation*, Chur, Switzerland: Harwood Academic Publishers.

Robert, B. Jr. (1979). 'Agricultural Credit Cooperatives: Rural Development and Agrarian Politics in Madras, 1893–1937'. *Indian Economic and Social History Review*, 16, 163–89.

Roberts, R. (1981). 'Ideology, Slavery, and Social Formation: The Evolution of Maraka Slavery'. In P. Lovejoy (ed.), *The Ideology of Slavery in Africa*. Beverly Hills: University of California Press.

Robertson, A. F. (1987). *The Dynamics of Productive Relationships: African Share Contracts in Comparative Perspective*. Cambridge: University Press.

Roemer, J. (1982). *A General Theory of Exploitation and Class*. Cambridge, Mass.: Harvard University Press.

Rogerson, William P. (1985). 'Repeated Moral Hazard', *Econometrica*, 53, 69–76.

Rosenzweig, M. and Wolpin, K. (1985). 'Specific Experience, Household Structure, and Intergenerational Transfers: Farm Family Land and Labor Arrangements in Developing Countries'. *Quarterly Journal of Economics*, 100, 961–87.

Ross, S. (1973). 'The Economic Theory of Agency: The Principal's Problem'. *American Economic Review, Proceedings*, 63, 134–9.

Rothschild, M. and Stiglitz, J. E. (1970). 'Increasing Risk I: A Definition'. *Journal of Economic Theory*, 2, 225–43.

——(1971). 'Increasing Risk II: Its Economic Consequences'. *Journal of Economic Theory*, 3, 66–84.

——(1976). 'Equilibrium in Competitive Insurance Markets'. *Quarterly Journal of Economics*, 90, 629–50.

Roumasset, J. (1979). 'Sharecropping, Production Externalities, and the Theory of Contracts'. *American Journal of Agricultural Economics*, 61, 640–7.

——(1984). 'Explaining Patterns in Landowner Shares: Rice, Corn, Coconut, and Abaca in the Philippines'. In Binswanger and Rosenzweig (1984).

—— and James, W. (1979). 'Explaining Variations in Share Contracts: Land Quality, Population Pressures, and Technological Change'. *Australian Journal of Agricul-*

tural Economics, 23, 116–27.

Rubinstein, A. (1979). 'Offenses that May Have Been Committed By Accident: An Optimal Policy of Retribution'. In S. Brahms, A. Shotter, and G. Schrodianer (eds.), *Applied Game Theory*, pp. 406–13. Wurtzburg: Physica-Verlag.

Rudra, A. (1975). 'Sharecropping Arrangements in West Bengal'. *Economic and Political Weekly*, 10, A58–A63.

——(1982). *Indian Agricultural Economics: Myths and Realities*. New Delhi: Allied Publishers.

Ruthenberg, H. (1971). *Farming Systems in the tropics*. Oxford: Clarendon Press.

Ruttan, V. W. (1966). 'Tenure and Productivity of Philippine Rice Producing Farms'. *Philippine Economic Journal*, 5, 42–63.

Sah, R., and Stiglitz, J. E. (1985). 'Perpetuation and Self-reproduction of Organizations: The Selection and Performance of Managers'. Presented at World Congress of Econometric Society, Cambridge, August 1985.

Salop, S. (1976). 'Information and Monopolistic Competition'. *American Economic Review*, 66, 240–5.

Sarap, K. (1986). 'Small Farmers' Demand for Credit with Special Reference to Sambalpur District, Western Orissa. Ph.D. dissertation, Delhi University.

Schotter, A. (1981). *The Economic Theory of Social Institutions*. Cambridge: University Press.

Schumpeter, J. A. (1954). *History of Economic Analysis*. London: George Allen and Unwin.

Scott, J. T. (1970). 'Leasing Arrangements for Less-developed Countries: An Extension of Leasing Theory'. *American Journal of Agricultural Economics*, 52, 610–13.

Scott, J. (1976). *The Moral Economy of the Peasant*, New Haven, Conn.: Yale University Press.

Seabright, P. (1987). 'The Effects of Environmental Risk on Economic and Social Behaviour in Rural India'. Report to the Overseas Development Administration. Mimeo, Churchill College, Cambridge.

Selden, M. (1982). 'Cooperation and Conflict: Cooperative and Collective Formation in China's Countryside'. In M. Selden and V. Lippit (eds.), *The Transition to Socialism in China*. Armonk, NY: M. E. Sharpe.

Selten, R. (1975). 'Re-examination of the Perfectness Concept for Equilibrium Points in Extensive Games'. *International Journal of Game Theory*, 4, 25–55.

Sen, Abhijit (1981). 'Market Failure and Control of Labor Power: Towards an Explanation of "Structure" and Change in Indian Agriculture'. *Cambridge Journal of Economics*, 5, 201–28 and 327–50.

Sen, Amartya K. (1966). 'Labour Allocation in a Cooperative Enterprise'. *Review of Economic Studies*, 33, 361–71.

——(1967). 'Isolation, Assurance and the Social Discount Rate'. *Quarterly Journal of Economics*, 81, 112–24.

——(1968). *Choice of Techniques: An Aspect of the Theory of Planned Economic Development*. Oxford: Basil Blackwell.

——(1977). 'Rational Fools: A Critique of the Behavioural Foundations of Economic Theory'. *Philosophy and Public Affairs*, 6, 317–44.

——(1981). *Poverty and Famine: An Essay on Entitlement and Deprivation*. Oxford: Clarendon Press.

Sexton, R. J. (1986). 'The Formation of Cooperatives: A Game-theoretic Approach with Implications for Cooperative Finance, Decision-making, and Stability'. *American Journal of Agricultural Economics*, 68, 214–25.

Shaban, R., (1987). 'Testing between Competing Models of Sharecropping'. *Journal of Political Economy*, 95, 893–920.

Shapiro, C. and Stiglitz, J. (1984). 'Equilibrium Unemployment as a Worker Discipline Device'. *American Economic Review*, 74, 433–44.

Shavell, S. (1979). 'Risk Sharing and Incentives in the Principal and Agent Relationship'. *Bell Journal of Economics*, 10, 55–73.

Shetty, S. (1988). 'Limited Liability, Wealth Differences, and the Tenancy Ladder in Agrarian Economies'. *Journal of Development Economics*, 29, 1–22.

Shue, V. (1980). *Peasant China in Transition: The Dynamics of Development Toward Socialism, 1949–56.* Berkeley: University of California Press.

Singh, N. (1983). 'The Possibility of Nonrenewal of a Contract as an Incentive Device in Principal–Agent Models'. University of California at Santa Cruz, Working Paper no. 117.

——(1985). 'Monitoring and Hierarchies: The Marginal Value of Information in a Principal–Agent Model'. *Journal of Politcal Economy*, 93, 599–609.

Sismondi, J. L. S. de (1818). *Political Economy*. New York: Augustus Kelly, 1966.

Skinner, E. (1964). *The Mossi of Upper Volta*. Stanford: University Press.

Smith, A. (1776). *The Wealth of Nations*. New York: Modern Library, 1937.

Solow, R. (1957). 'Technical Change and the Aggregate Production Function'. *Review of Economics and Statistics*, 39, 312–20.

Spence, A. M. (1977). 'Nonlinear Prices and Welfare'. *Journal of Public Economics*, 8, 1–18.

Spencer, D. and Byerlee, D. (1976). 'Technical Change, Labor Use, and Small Farmer Development: Evidence from Sierra Leone'. *American Journal of Agricultural Economics*, 58, 874–80.

Spillman, W. J. (1919). 'The Agricultural Ladder'. *American Economic Review*, Papers and Proceedings, 9, 170–9.

Srinivasan, T. N. (1972). 'Farm Size and Productivity: Implications of Choice under Uncertainty'. *Sankhya* (Indian Journal of Statistics, Series B), 34, 409–20.

——(1980). 'Bonded Labour Contracts and Incentives to Adopt Yield-raising Innovations in "Semifeudal" Agriculture'. *Indian Economic Review*, 14, 165–9.

Staatz, J. M. (1983). 'The Cooperative as a Coalition: A Game-theoretic Approach'. *American Journal of Agricultural Economics*, 65, 1084–9.

Stenning, D. (1959). *Savannah Nomads*. Oxford: University Press.

Stigler, G. (1964). 'A Theory of Oligopoly'. *Journal of Political Economy*, 72, 44–61.

Stiglitz, J. E. (1974a). 'Incentives and Risk-sharing in Sharecropping'. *Review of Economic Studies*, 41, 219–55.

——(1974b). 'Alternative Theories of Wage Determination and Unemployment in LDCs: The Labor Turnover Model'. *Quarterly Journal of Economics*, 87, 194–227.

——(1985a). 'Information in Economic Analysis: A Perspective'. *Economic Journal Supplement*, 95, 21–40.

——(1985b). 'Economics of Information and the Theory of Economic Development'. *NBER* Working Paper no. 1566.

——(1986a). 'The New Development Economics'. *World Development*, 14, 257–65.

——(1988). *Economics of the Public Sector* (2nd edn.). New York: W. W. Norton.

——(1987). 'Learning to Learn, Localized Learning, and Technological Progress'. In P. Dasgupta and P. Stoneman (eds.), *Economic Policy and Technological Performance*, pp. 125–53. Cambridge: University Press.

——(forthcoming). *Information and Economic Analysis*, Oxford: University Press.

—— and Weiss, A. (1981). 'Credit Rationing in Markets with Imperfect Information'. *American Economic Review*, 71, 393–419.

——(1983). 'Incentive Effects of Termination: Applications to the Credit and Labour Markets'. *American Economic Review*, 73, 912–27.

Strotz, R. (1956). 'Myopia and Inconsistency in Dynamic Utility Maximization'. *Review of Economic Studies*, 23, 165–80.

Subbarao, K. (1978). *Rice Marketing Systems in Andhra Pradesh*. New Delhi: Allied Publishers/Institute of Economic Growth.

Sugden, R. (1986). *The Economics of Rights, Cooperation and Welfare*. Oxford: Basil Blackwell.

Sundari, T. K. (1981). 'Caste and the Rural Economy'. Working Paper no. 13, Centre for Development Studies, Trivandrum.

Sutinen, J. G. (1975). 'The Rational Choice of Share Leasing and Implications for Efficiency'. *American Journal of Agricultural Economics*, 57, 613–21.

Swain, M., (1986). 'Usurious Interest Rates in Backward Agriculture: Interlinkage. Competition, and Monopoly'. M. Phil. dissertation, Delhi University.

Swanson, R. (1981). *Household Composition, Rainfall, and Household Labor Time Allocation for Planting and Weeding*. Ouagadougou, Burkina Faso, SAFGRAD Farming Systems Unit, Document no. 4.

Swindell, K. (1978). 'Family Farms and Migrant Labor: The Stranger Farmers of the Gambia'. *Canadian Journal of African Studies*, 12, 3–17.

Tapsoba, E. (1981). 'An Economic and Institutional Analysis of Formal and Informal Credit in Eastern Upper Volta'. Ph.D. dissertation, Michigan State University.

Thirtle, C. T. (1985a). 'Induced Innovation in United States Field Crops, 1939–78'. *Journal of Agricultural Economics*, 36, 1–14.

——(1985b). 'Accounting for Increasng Land–Labor Ratios in Developing Country Agriculture'. *Journal of Agricultural Economics*, 36, 161–70.

——(1985c). 'The Microeconomic Approach to Induced Innovation: A Reformulation of the Hayami and Ruttan Model'. *The Manchester School*, 53, 263–79.

—— and Ruttan, W. (1986). 'The Role of Demand and Supply in the Generation and Diffusion of Technical Change'. University of Minnesota, Department of Economics, Bulletin no. 86–5.

Thorner, D. and Thorner, A. (1962). *Land and Labor in India*. New York: Asia Publishing House.

Tilly, C. (1984). 'Warmaking and Statemakings as Organized Crime'. In P. Evans, T. Skocpol, and D. Rueschemeyer (eds.), *Bringing the State Back In*. Cambridge: University Press.

Toulmin, C. (1983). 'Herders and Farmers or Farmer-Herders and Herder-Farmers?' Overseas Development Institute, Pastoral Network Paper 15d.

Townsend, N. (1978). 'Biased Symbiosis on the Tana River'. In W. Weissleder (ed.), *The Nomadic Alternative*. The Hague: Mouton.

Tun Wai, U. (1958). 'Interest Rates Outside the Organised Money Markets of Underdeveloped Countries'. *IMF Staff Papers*, 6, 80–142.

Tyson, L. D'Andrea (1979). 'Incentives, Income Sharing, and Institutional Innovation in the Yugoslav Self-Managed Firm'. *Journal of Comparative Economics*, 3, 285–301.

Udry, C. (1986). 'Herders and Farmers: Material Aspects of Intergroup Production Relations'. Mimeo, World Bank Agricultural Research Unit.

Ullman-Margalit, E. (1977). *The Emergence of Norms*. Oxford: Clarendon Press.

United Nations (various years). *FAO Fertilizer Yearbook*. Rome: UN Food and Agricultural Organization.

——(1981). *1970 World Census of Agriculture: Analysis and International Comparison of the Results*. Rome: UN Food and Agricultural Organization.

Vitaliano, P. (1983). 'Cooperative Enterprise: An Alternative Conceptual Basis for Analyzing a Complex Institution'. *American Journal of Agricultural Economics*, 65, 1078–83.

von Pischke, J. D. (1983). 'A Penny Saved: Kenya's Cooperative Savings Scheme'. In von Pischke, Adams and Donalds (1983).

——, Adams, D. W., and Donalds, G. (1983). *Rural Financial Markets in Developing Countries*. Baltimore: Johns Hopkins University Press.

Walker, T. S. and Jodha, N. J. (1982). 'Efficiency of Risk Management by Small Farmers and Implications for Crop Insurance'. ICRISAT Conference Paper 114, Patancheru, India.

Ward, B. (1958). 'The Firm in Illyria: Market Syndicalism'. *American Economic Review*, 68, 566–89.

Wharton, C. R. (1962). 'Marketing, Merchandising, and Money-lending: A Note on Middle-man Monopsony in Malaya'. *Malayan Economic Review*, 7, 24–44.

Williams, J. C. (1982). 'The Origin of Futures Markets'. *Agricultural History*, 56, 306–16.

Williamson, O. (1985). *The Economic Institutions of Capitalism*. New York: Free Press.

——(1987). 'Corporate Finance and Corporate Governance'. University of California, Berkeley Business School Working Paper no. EAP-26.

Wilson, R. (1968). 'The Theory of Syndicates'. *Econometrica*, 36, 119–32.

Winters, D. L. (1974). 'Tenant Farming in Iowa, 1860–1900: A Study of the Terms of Rental Leases'. *Agricultural History*, 48, 130–50.

Wood, V. R. and Vitell, S. J. (1986). 'Marketing and Economic Development: Review, Synthesis, and Evaluation'. *Journal of Macromarketing*, 6, 28–48.

Working, H. (1962). 'New Concepts Concerning Futures Markets and Prices'. *American Economic Review*, 52, 432–59.

Wright, G. (1978). *The Political Economy of the Cotton South*. New York: W. W. Norton.

——(1987). 'The Economic Revolution in the American South'. *Journal of Economic Perspectives*, 1, 161–78.

Yellen, J. L. (1984). 'Efficiency Wage Models of Unemployment'. *American Economic Review*, Papers and Proceedings, 74, 200–5.

Young, A. (1788). *Travels in France during the Years 1787, 1788, 1778*, Vol 2. Dublin reprint, 1973.

Zusman, P. (1976). 'The Incorporation and Measurement of Social Power in Economic Models'. *International Economic Review*, 17, 447–62.

—— and Bell, C. (1989). 'The Equilibrium Vector of Pairwise-Bargained Agency Contracts with Diverse Actors and Principals Owning a Fixed Resource'. *Journal of Economic Behavior and Organization*.

—— and Etgar, M. (1981). 'The Marketing Channel as an Equilibrium Set of Contracts'. *Management Science*, 27, 284–302, 11, 81–114.

Index

marketing
  boards 289–91, 296
  contracts and intermediaries 296–315
Marx. K. 14, 15*n*
McIntire, J. 141*n*, 287
Meade, J. 337
Meillassoux, C. 131, 287
Menger, C. 10
Milgrom, P. 44, 47, 52, 56
Miliband, R. 15
Mill, J.S. 46
Mirrlees, J. 43, 347, 348
moneylenders 134, 139, 141, 147–54, 156–7,
  164, 171, 222, 226, 236, 243–52, 256,
  258–9, 287
monitoring costs *see* transactions costs
Mookherjee, D. 119*n*
moral hazard and adverse selection 4, 5, 12,
  23, 28, 29, 38, 42, 43, 54, 85, 95, 97, 124,
  128–30, 135, 164, 169, 172, 223, 225,
  231–5, 238–9, 242, 278–9, 283, 284,
  287–8, 294, 295, 344, 346–7, 349–50, 353
Mukherji, B. 153
Murickan, J. 165*n*
Muth, J. 280
Myerson, R.B. 104

Nagaraj, K. 148, 164*n*
Nalebuff, B. 348, 349, 354*n*
Nash, J.R. 75, 298, 315*n*
Newbery, D. 33, 35, 39–41, 44, 46, 56–7, 61,
  62, 70–2*n*, 120*n*, 262*n*, 270, 275, 280, 283,
  289–91, 295*n*
North, D. 6–8, 13, 14, 16*n*
Nozick, R. 16*n*
Nugent, J. 36, 54, 55, 70*n*, 362, 364

Oi, W. 324, 325, 339*n*
Okun, A. 238
Olson, M. 13, 364

Pant, C. 42
Pearce, D. 355*n*
Pineiro, M. 365
Pingali, P. 142*n*
Platteau, J. 165*n*, 235, 236*n*
population change 6, 16
population growth and density 122, 123, 125,
  127, 133–4, 136–7, 140–41, 143
Porter, R.H. 262*n*, 350
Prasad, P. 171
Pratt, J.W. 268
profits 77, 79–80, 132, 136, 154–9, 162,
  223–6, 229, 233–6, 244, 246, 248, 252,
  253, 262, 280, 309, 337, 363
Putterman, L. 325, 328, 330, 331, 333, 339*n*

Quizon, J. 273

Radner, R. 46, 120*n*, 350
Raiffa, H. 87
Ramachandran, R. 164*n*
Ransom, R.L. 242*n*
Rao, J.M. 33
Rashid, S. 33
Rask, N. 72*n*
Rasmussen, E. 354*n*
rate of return 129, 183, 359
Ray, D. 105, 199*n*
Reid, J.D. 39, 43, 72*n*
Richards, A. 33
risk 4, 6, 12, 21, 38, 40–2, 47, 51, 75, 80–1, 84,
  88, 90, 122–31, 133–4, 136, 138–41, 149,
  170, 172, 177–82, 188–9, 200, 211, 222–3,
  226, 228, 230, 239, 272–7, 286–94, 307,
  311, 342–3, 347
  aversion 26, 38, 43–5, 47, 54, 66, 74, 77,
  82–6, 88, 90, 91, 95, 122, 124, 166, 170,
  180–3, 186–9, 214–15, 235, 236, 270, 274,
  298, 300, 307, 310, 327, 328, 333, 344,
  348, 349, 351, 354
  cost of 268–75, 278–9, 287, 293
  neutral 43, 44, 48, 52, 57, 63, 71, 72, 74, 76,
  80, 82, 85, 95, 103, 173, 224, 226, 229,
  235, 250, 299, 307, 328, 348–9
  sharing/pooling 25, 33, 34, 38–42, 48, 52,
  57, 66, 73, 95, 225–31, 235, 239, 270–2,
  275, 279–85, 288, 293–4, 298, 313, 314,
  344–5
Robert, R. Jr 342
Roemer, J. 11–12, 166–8, 182, 288
Rosen, S. 349, 354*n*
Rosenzweig, M. 33, 69*n*, 122, 124, 128–9,
  134–6, 139, 143*n*, 336
Ross, S. 43
Rothschild, M. 268, 278
Rubinstein, A. 46
Rudra, A. 119*n*, 148, 153, 164*n*, 171, 240
Russel, T. 169
Ruttan, V. 8, 11, 356–61, 363, 364, 376, 379

Sarap, K. 147, 162, 164*n*, 165*n*
Scandizzo, P. 177
Schlicht, E. 15*n*
Schnytzer, A. 330
Schotter, A. 9, 10
Schwartz, N. 359
Scot, J. 171
screening 56–66, 262
Seabright, P. 295*n*
Selten, R. 103
Sen, A. 13, 166, 177, 321, 323, 329, 358
Sengupta, K. 222, 247, 248, 262*n*
Sexton, R.J. 354*n*
Shapiro, C. 12, 29*n*, 43, 51–2, 97, 98, 105, 327
sharecropping 7, 21, 24–5, 28, 33–72, 95, 110,